ATLANTIC EMPIRES

ATLANTIC EMPIRES

The Network of Trade and Revolution, 1713–1826

Peggy K. Liss

THE JOHNS HOPKINS UNIVERSITY PRESS • BALTIMORE & LONDON

The Johns Hopkins University Press, Baltimore, Maryland   21218
The Johns Hopkins Press Ltd., London

Liss, Peggy K.
Atlantic empires.

(Johns Hopkins studies in Atlantic history and culture)
Includes bibliographical references and index.
1. America—Commerce—History.   2. Europe—
Commerce—History   3. United States—History—
Revolution, 1775–1783—Influence.   4. Latin America
—Colonial influence.   I. Title.   II. Series.
HF3211.L57   1982   382'.094'08   82–13099
ISBN 0–8018–2742–6

To Rebecca and Anne, who were not here at this book's inception, but on whom I count to carry on, with spirit and in whatever way they may deem best.

CONTENTS

PREFACE

Although this study is linear in time, overall it may seem less a narrative than a plum pudding. That impression in turn must give way to the perception of a network, one linking trade and revolution and, within them, entrepreneurs, intellectuals, and patriots, and one spanning years, miles, and societies. An intricate mathematical model might better present the complex of factors, and their interaction through time and space, with which this history is concerned; but for those of us valuing nuance and devoted to words, to thinking in them and to seeing often in terms of them, to form such a model does not appeal. Instead, this book. Within it, the material and ideational appear and reappear, join and separate, their interplay a central theme of international relations within the Atlantic world from 1713 to 1826, from the Treaty of Utrecht to the conference at Panama.

Even though in the past decade the eighteenth century in Latin America and Iberia has become the Resorts International of graduate students and young scholars, and some not so young, questions raised on my initial encounter with it twenty years ago have remained substantially unanswered; and so this late, large entry into the field (or pot). Those questions were broad ones: What were the interconnections between what went on in Europe and America, domestically and internationally, even multinationally? What were the connections among the various revolutions—the commercial, the Industrial, the American of 1776, the French, and those of Latin America—and among them all and the Enlightenment and nascent liberalism? How similar, or different, were the perceptions and outlooks of people directing nations and societies throughout the Atlantic world? How did the Atlantic trading network fit within the broader historical context and what connection had commerce to other aspects of international affairs? Why did not historians of international relations go much beyond politics and diplomacy?

Some do, now. Yet, world-embracing models of capitalism, dependency, imperialism, and underlying structures, although useful, are too theoretical and general to satisfy a historian who relishes, within the large scene, that wealth of individual variation signifying vitality. History, the story through time of human beings, in the last analysis is sloppy, not neat. "What is the value," as James

Henretta has asked, of a history "that primarily demonstrates the conceptual skills of the author and eliminates the contradictions inherent in the lives of the actors"?[1] Paul Dietl has addressed a related point in arguing that what sets history apart from science is that the whys of history cannot be deduced with accuracy because, among other reasons, "there are many features of ordinary language, jurisprudence, and historical narration which seem to presuppose that one could have acted differently in . . . similar circumstances."[2] Or, as Georges Lefebvre phrased it a while ago, "events have their immediate roots not in their antecedents but in men who intervene by interpreting those events."[3] Similarly, Perry Miller imposed a caveat, restoring scope: "What constitutes the present being is a series of past decisions; in that sense, no act is spontaneous, no decision unposed."[4]

I have felt yet another compelling reason to pay attention to individuals, even while dedicated to presenting the broadest manageable picture. It is that emphasis on the individual parallels what occurred within the period under discussion when, at the end of the eighteenth century, in conjunction with romanticism and the development of historicism, more and more people expressed an acute awareness of themselves as historical beings and as makers of history, as well as the other way around. And, to go a step further, these same people often saw themselves as entrepreneurs, intellectuals, or patriots—and frequently as more than one, and sometimes as all three. Such people were principal participants in the international relations of the Western world from 1713 to 1826, relations largely predicated on the pursuit of knowledge, wealth, and power. The majority of individuals in this book, therefore, are people of property and talent—ambitious and energetic beings who desired fame and, usually but not always, fortune.

Beginning as a Latin Americanist venturing into foreign territory, I have enjoyed acquiring a great deal of new information and indulging in some iconoclasm along the way, abetted by a relatively unusual vantage point. My views on a number of open historical questions appear in telling the story. My luxuriant, indeed near-interminable, notes serve where necessary to explain the history of the debate and to list participants. The number and length of these notes I feel are proper in order to do this fairly, as well as to pay my debts and to make clearer some vital esoterica (the last certainly a rare species).

A certain present-mindedness I do not think can ever be avoided. I do sense within the United States the rekindling of interest in searching out the history of what, after all, is the only system (or near system) we have, one based on capitalism as a major organizing principle, one whose makers and leaders have been entrepreneurs, intellectuals, and patriots, and one that was forged in the eighteenth century, within an international context where trade and revolutions loomed large. So it is, or anyway has been; for, as most celebrants of the bicentennial of the American Revolution concluded, and as the energy crises have driven home, the era of material progress may be winding down. In 1967, Fernand Braudel could say that "the men of the eighteenth century were contemporaries on the level of ideas. Their minds and passions were the same as ours."[5] Today, fifteen years later, I am not so certain—in fact, not certain at all. My own attitudes and biases concerning the period and people I write about here form, like the history itself, an intricate web, and it houses a large number of paradoxes. There is admiration and dismay, enthusiasm and repulsion, approval and moral outrage; all in all, a mixture of emotional and moral reactions to the human past not unusual among civilized people, including most historians.

There was a time I would shop first and then check the larder, so that I would end up with three bottles of vinegar and no oil. By the time I came to writing history, I was looking into stock on hand before going further, whether in buying groceries or evaluating the past. The form and content of this book, too, is a stocktaking (and in a very disorganized pantry), to a great extent predicated on the current state of informed knowledge of the various areas discussed. It is also meant to serve as a first step toward planning the direction of future forays into the history of the period. And since there exists a vast difference between the current state of research and understanding concerning England and its America and concerning the Iberian nations and their colonies, I have had to reconstruct and to provide more background on Latin America in these years, and thus to devote more space to that region than is strictly equitable for a balanced account. Related, the large amount of detail I present stems from the reluctance of most scholars to tie together the political, economic, social, and intellectual strands of the era, unless those strands are gathered into a theoretical framework where detail is usually used only as a case in point and within an inductive and often very subjective context, with little respect shown for what the data may reveal. I have, however, presented more detail on Spain and its America than on the Portuguese empire, and I have skimped on France and its people, but have touched on its presence and impact where germane. I justify this decision on grounds of the limitations of space and the thrust of this study; greater attention to either empire would not have significantly affected interpretations made within the scope of this work.

My appreciation to Nettie Lee Benson, who read the manuscript in an earlier draft, and to Sacvan Bercovitch, Mark Burkholder, Joseph Ernst, John Hébert, Lawrence Kaplan, J. R. Pole, Lee Shneidman, and Carl Ubbelohde, who have read and commented on chapters of it. Valuable suggestions came from the late Arthur Whitaker and from Marvin Bernstein, on the paper from which this book grew. A conversation with Robert Gilmore helped; and Jacques Barbier, León Helguera, Jerome Mushkat, and Robert F. Smith have provided welcome information. Finally, Georgette Dorn and Everette Larson of the Library of Congress have answered numerous questions, wise and otherwise.

ATLANTIC EMPIRES

1

"ENGLAND IS A
TRADING NATION"

The war to decide the Spanish succession—sometimes referred to as the first world war—and its outcome, a peace with global implications, were important to the Americas, to their relations with Europe, to internal relations within each subregion, and to their dealings with one another. The first of an eighteenth-century series of conflicts in which England, dominating its allies, fought France, the war opened an era of British preeminence lasting for two centuries. The principle of balance of power, which emerged as a military fact, would henceforth be of primary importance in European international relations. That principle largely supplanted the European tendency to make alliances and to fight wars along religious lines. Thereafter, religion was relatively unimportant, but balance of power, commerce, and sea power were paramount; and closely related was the new value put on colonies.

In many ways, the Treaty of Utrecht in 1713 marked a watershed in European relations, one with consequences for America. Utrecht, first of all, formally established realms—that is, territories, their peoples and rules—as sovereign and as within international law. From then on, the international order was assumed to be made up of sovereign states, necessarily represented by their rulers. Second, when, with Utrecht, Philip V, the grandson of Louis XIV of France, in becoming monarch of Spain renounced his claim to French rule and swore not to unite France and Spain, state interest emerged as dominant over dynastic. Individual sovereigns were afterwards more important both in theory and in fact than were family connections. Third, Utrecht not only established a balance of power but connected it to an English Atlantic hegemony. The English, as architects of the peace, arranged this balance. They reduced the Dutch to the status of British clients, ensured their own naval security, and effectively checked their continental rivals. Finally, as victors, they chose for themselves not European spoils but acquisition of trading rights and of strategically and commercially important colonies. England gained Gibraltar and Minorca from Spain, Nova Scotia from France (which also give up claims to Newfoundland and the Hudson Bay area), and, again from Spain, the right of *asiento*, of supplying Spanish America yearly with a stipulated number of blacks as slaves. This right provided direct legitimate entry to

1

trade with the Spanish colonies. Utrecht also granted England's client state, Portugal, title to the region that was the colonial smuggling center for goods to Spanish South America—Colônia do Sacramento on the Río de la Plata. Much of the contraband was in British manufactures coming through Lisbon and Brazil.

A system of competitive states resulted from Utrecht. They had in common administrations bent upon centralizing policies and power and upon mobilizing available resources, among them the recently recognized one of population; and of great and enduring interest was sea trade. In England it was considered the key to economic development, and in France in 1709 Louis XIV himself commented, "The main object of the present war is the Indies trade and the wealth it produces."[1]

Control of the Spanish throne had signified to all contenders a way to the bullion and the legitimate trade of Spanish America. From the seventeenth century on, Holland, England, and France, taking advantage of declining Spanish sea power, had engaged in shipping contraband to the Spanish colonies. Although French ships and goods had greater legitimate contact with the Spanish Indies (as Spain referred to its American dependencies), quantities of English goods and re-exports went to Spanish America, both legally and illegally, through Spain. The British also continually smuggled to Spain's America directly from England, or through British America, or via Portugal and Brazil. During the war this trade continued. Afterwards England gained direct legal access to Spanish America, and an outlet for contraband as well, through the asiento, previously a French monopoly.[2] French policy from Louis XIV on seesawed from interest in overseas trade to internal commercial priorities. Dutch supremacy in the carrying trade to America gave ground to English. Although both English and French trade with Spanish America increased through the eighteenth century, it was England that came to dominate, legally and otherwise. Moreover, at British insistence the Treaty of Utrecht included a promise by Spain never to transfer its American territories to any other nation, and a promise by England to protect them from such alienation. One historian has astutely interpreted these clauses as an English antecedent to the Monroe Doctrine.[3] Trade and balance of power, and territory as it related to them, were the desiderata of eighteenth-century European states in America.

Modern state-building, the goal of the eighteenth-century governments under discussion, required the development of an internal balance between a strong crown and an independent landed aristocracy, a balance that was achieved in England. It required commercialization of agriculture, solely an English phenomenon, and a weakening of the traditional landed aristocracy, which also had happened only in England, where the aristocrats were "a postrevolutionary elite, heirs of Roundheads."[4] It also depended, as Charles Tilly put it, upon preventing a coalition between the middle and upper classes against the peasantry and working class. Again, this was the case solely in England, and even there perhaps a difference largely in degree and of perception of social relations.[5]

In England, the king in Parliament—or a Parliament including the king, depending on emphasis—had become sovereign. A number of trading and trade-related men sat in the House of Commons. The dominant landed interest had investments in commerce and industry. Government and oligarchy were little interested in the domestic market; they were generally agreed on the desirability of an expanding commerce overseas, and showed increasing interest in trade with the non-English Americas. Between Utrecht and the War of Jenkins' Ear, which began in 1739 and merged with the War of Austrian Succession (1740–48), strong interest groups emerged and formed organized lobbies. Manufacturers (their product stemming from workshops and cottage industry) and the great merchants could determine government policy. Moreover, in choices between the interests of commerce and those of industry, the manufacturing interests, who were able to count on large stretches of the countryside and often on aristocratic landlords, frequently prevailed over those international merchants who could mobilize only London and a few ports. Policies of protection and of capturing the export market for British goods predominated.[6]

Trade, as Lewis Namier observed, was the watchword in politics.[7] Englishmen in the main still thought, as had Walter Raleigh, that "whoever commands the trade commands the riches of the world, and consequently the world itself."[8] In addition, the word *trade*, traditionally referring both to occupations and to the buying and selling of goods, was itself undergoing an expansion of meaning in keeping with England's economic growth.[9] Economic policy was becoming more thorough, more closely reasoned, and more singlemindedly addressed to English prosperity, which was considered identical with English security. In administration, profit and power received joint consideration, and expert civil servants, succeeding the old Elizabethan export-import agencies, strove to maintain truly national commercial control.[10]

Certain principles were both common opinion and part of governmental policies and goals. They included a cluster of ideas about the empire and the colonies and some economic ideas today termed neomercantilistic; in turn, each of these various ideas, opinions, and policies was predicated on certain shared British assumptions concerning the individual, society, and the universe. As one recent commentator summed it up, "in the eighteenth century England stood for Protestantism, parliamentary government, and progress, for nationalism at home and imperialism abroad."[11]

In the literature, the press, and the political rhetoric of the seventeenth century, assertions of British nationhood associated with religion and with the notion of the English as a chosen people had accompanied commercial and colonial expansion. Oliver Cromwell in particular had expanded national allegiance into a form of imperial sentiment and joined it to republican principles.[12] The term *empire* had appeared in seventeenth-century American petitions, and in 1688, England was generally assumed to possess an "empire of the sea."[13] The union in 1707 of England and Scotland into Great Britain, along with maritime and mercantile achievement and expansion, had, by the early eighteenth century, coupled Britain in the popular mind with imperial grandeur.[14] Moreover, in the seventeenth century virulently anti-Spanish and anti-Catholic polemics and tracts contributed to formulating what had become an anti-Spanish prejudice by 1660.[15] This prejudice added vehemence to assertion of British empire when the enemy was Spain. A Spanish attempt to regain Gibraltar in 1727 called forth an epic poem on the British "Empire O'er the conquered seas," an empire of naval power "unencumbered with the bulk immense of conquest."[16] During the War of Jenkins' Ear a decade later, not only did *Rule Britannia* appear and some lines by Richard Glover invoke the goddess Commerce, but it was the capture of Spanish Porto Bello in November 1739 that occasioned some verses that responded to the public mood in prophesying:

> I see thy commerce Britain, grasp the world:
> All nations serve thee . . .
> Shores yet unfound, arise! in youthful prime,
> With towering forest, mighty rivers crowned:
> These stoop to Britain's thunder. This new world,
> Shook to its centre, trembles at her name:
> And there her sons, with aim exalted sow
> The seeds of rising empire, arts and arms.
> Britons, proceed, the subject deep command,
> Awe with your navies every hostile land.[17]

This literary, imperial vision, celebrating Great Britain as the hub of a "Grand Marine dominion," assumed colonies were adjuncts of empire rather than integral parts of it. Although the plantations in British North America—that is, the colonies—had begun as commercial enterprises, without crown initiative or support, they had grown from trading posts to communities of Englishmen overseas who enjoyed a measure of self-government and controlled their own assemblies. Still, they existed, it was then generally believed, for the prosperity of the mother country. In England only Dissenters viewed colonists as "brethren across the sea."[18] A common attitude toward American colonies, a competitive one reflecting a distaste for Spain, was expressed in one instance thusly:

> When we do but cast an Eye on the vast Tract of Land, and immense Riches which the *Spanish* Nation have in little more than one Century very odly acquired in *America*; insomuch, that the simple Privilege of trading with them, on very high Terms, is become a Prize worth contending for among the greatest Powers in *Europe*, surely we must on due Reflection acknowledge that the Preservation and Enlargement of the *English* Settlements in those Parts is of the last Consequence to the Trade, Interest, and Strength of *Great Britain*. And moreover . . . the Brightening of this Jewel in the Crown, may not perhaps be thought unworthy the Care of the present happy Reign, to which the Improvement, and future Security of so large a Part of the *British* Dominions, the Advancement of Trade, and universally supporting the glorious Cause of Liberty, seem to be reserved by the peculiar Hand of Providence.[19]

During the War of Spanish Succession, in 1707, Daniel Defoe had written in his *Review* concerning Spain's "vast Tract of Land" and its wealth in America:

> If we were to possess the silver and gold of Peru, and the wealth of Mexico, the scattering of our people and the bringing our manufactures to be wrought in those populous

countries would make the gain of them be less to us than they are now—that is, in an open trade to Spain.

We want not the dominion of more countries than we have; we sufficiently possess a nation when we have an open and free trade to it . . . our trading to Old Spain has been a full trade to New Spain, a trade by which England has always drawn as much money from America as Old Spain itself.[20]

After Utrecht, Britons would increasingly seek more, and more direct, trade with Spanish America. Commerce, rather than territorial expansion, would become the official desideratum, in regard to Spain's colonies in America and to Britain's own as well. Empire did not solely, or even primarily, mean territory. The basic tenets of relations with Anglo-America were embodied in the Navigation Acts of 1660 and those immediately following, and rested upon the assumptions that colonies existed to protect and stimulate British trade, to keep foreigners out of certain branches of it, and to maintain England's naval strength. These acts, which resulted from the Cromwellian struggle with the Dutch for control of the seas and the carrying trade, also established the principles that colonies should be subordinate to Parliament and that the shipping of the mother country should monopolize colonial commerce.[21] In governing circles in early eighteenth-century Britain its colonies were valued, therefore, specifically for strategic considerations and as a nursery for seamen. Strategic considerations included a desire for balance of power in colony-holding itself and for expansion to safeguard present possessions. Good policy was thought to dictate curtailing rival colonial expansion and reducing competing trade, in line with the general belief in a static theory of economics that assumed limited resources. As Adam Smith later summed up these sentiments: "Nations have been taught that their interest consisted in beggaring all their neighbors."[22]

Yet, certain eminent commentators were questioning imperial arrangements involving colonial holdings. In Scotland in 1740 Francis Hutcheson, in positing a system of moral philosphy, approached the topic by reflecting upon "colonial liberty and happiness" and concluded that "the insisting on old claims and tacit conventions to extend civil power over distant nations and to form grand unwieldy empires, without regard to the obvious maxims of humanity, has been one great source of human misery." At the same time there flourished a strong popular interest in colonial expansion simply for the sake of England's greater glory, and this jingoistic attitude was catered to and sometimes encouraged by politicians.[23] Moreover, colonies existing for exploitation were and continued to be more favored by the government than those devoted to settlement. The West Indies, that is, were esteemed more than North America, and especially more than the provinces from Maryland up. Trade with foreign colonies was of course considered fair game. However, before 1750 there was not a clear distinction between varieties of commerce, between the prevailing carrying trade in re-exported goods and the rising business in export of British manufactures.

Mercantilism, concluded its leading expositor, Eli Heckscher, "is simply a convenient term for summarizing a phase of economic policy and economic ideas."[24] The term has frequently been used to describe the European economic system between 1600 and 1750, and its principles intermeshed with imperialism and colonialism in their major economic aspects. What Adam Smith referred to as "the mercantile system," as another scholar has observed, in its time "represented an ordered balance between the claims of fiscal need and economic interest," between government and private enterprise.[25] Mercantilist principles evolved in England as a working system and were absorbed into governmental policy in the early seventeenth century. They supported a system of restrictive control and marked a shift of older local controls to the state and a new emphasis on a national economy. Their basic assumption was that wealth and power were the proper ends of national policy and were bound up with trade.[26] After 1660 these principles were manifest in government planning. They had weight in shipbuilding, in concern with production and manufacturing, and in great attention to international, largely commercial, rivalries. Mercantilism then meant concentration on national wealth, which was equated chiefly with a favorable balance of trade, and securing it through encouraging population growth in order to gain a plentiful supply of labor at low wages and (less emphasized) thus necessarily to increase production and consumption.[27] Mercantilism in the early eighteenth century embraced principles that were both protectionistic and competitive. It sanctioned government regulation of foreign trade and colonial development, including encouraging exports. It supported placing high duties on competing imports, retaining bullion and skilled artisans, negotiating favorable commercial treaties, and tenaciously supporting the carrying trade, most of it then in the hands of chartered companies. The concern was for the producer and especially the distributor, including of re-exports; the consumer, the laborer, and the domestic economy were largely on their own.[28]

After Utrecht, some aspects of mercantilist thinking lost credence, particularly the idea that specie should not leave the kingdom (thus, in 1725 Erasmus Philipps commented that without trade, money "is stagnated water"[29]), and others underwent development and exposition, so that eighteenth-century English economic theory and practice are often referred to as neo-mercantilistic. Suffice it to repeat that the mercantilist of the eighteenth century saw "the world as an oyster and . . . set to work to build a foundry for making the tools best fitted to open it up."[30]

Eighteenth-century economic ideas, however referred to, were in turn predicated on some widely shared, more general assumptions encompassing the individual, society, and the universe. They in fact "contained the seeds of the sciences of human behavior."[31] Isaac Newton, Thomas Hobbes, and John Locke, writing in the seventeenth century, had strengthened the emerging idea of a more secular world. By the eighteenth century, as Lewis Namier remarked, "the dominant terms of . . . England were property, contract, trade and profits."[32] Then prevalent there as on the continent, indeed in great part sired by some of England's better seventeenth-century minds, were certain key aspects of the Enlightenment.

The designation "the Enlightenment" now refers to both the age and the cultural movement which by midcentury pervaded it. Enlightened ways of looking at the world, on both sides of the channel, were characterized by an expressed interest in natural science and natural law, and in the rational order of nature. They included a questioning of the principle of authority, enthusiasm and espousal of greater simplicity, a desire for intellectual and moral progress, and faith in reason and in science and its offspring, applied technology. Within the enlightened view of the universe, general belief prevailed that assimilating useful knowledge would uncover universal laws, harness nature, and enable a more just and reasonable social existence.[33] On the continent the enlightened spirit, prominent among individuals engaged in seeking means to reform political structures and policies, was a more fervent, housecleaning one, bent upon an orgy of straightening up, of hunting out abuses and useless accretions of tradition and, through rational reform, letting in a cleansing and corrective light. It was an optimistic state of mind, one oriented toward the future and toward evolutionary reform within current political and social systems. In contrast, eighteenth-century Englishmen believed their seventeenth-century revolutions had brought reforms setting Britain on the road to progress, and they had only to continue diligently in the same direction in order to remain front-runners in the quest for national progress and individual happiness.[34]

In an outstanding essay, Alfred North Whitehead spoke of "the inherent confusion introduced by the ascription of misplaced concreteness to the scientific scheme of the seventeenth century."[35] This sort of "misplaced concreteness" came to pervade not only much scientific speculation but also public and private beliefs and attitudes in eighteenth-century Britain, while on the continent it often cropped up as a radical alternative to discredited religious concepts. The faith in mathematics and an orderly universe—major premises of Newtonian physics— had been translated by Locke into philosphical terms. Assimilated into the common fund of belief, in the eighteenth-century they underlay the growing faith in the ability of human beings to understand and control that universe. This outlook invigorated enlightened rationalism, science, notions of morality, and the concepts of political economy. It put greater value on the material world and supported the progressive spirit propelling England toward expanded commerce, industrial and technological growth, and greater governmental efficiency. Intimately related was the widely held belief that according to natural law, happiness was attainable on earth and through human effort; as Namier has perceptively remarked, there was a connection between the discovery of the theory of the atom and the new quantitative theory of happiness. By the latter part of the century, happiness was based on utility.[36] The concept of an ordered, harmonious universe in eighteenth-century Great Britain became associated with the related and relatively new idea that individual private interests and general public interest could naturally blend within a society to yield greater general happiness. This convergence marked a juncture of the Enlightenment and nascent classical liberalism.

To formally educated people of the eighteenth century, the universe appeared more secular, more orderly, and more possible to understand and master than heretofore. It therefore seemed more worthwhile to pay increased attention to the material world and its resources. Englishmen then demonstrated an intensified global interest related both to desire for economic expansion and to a greater scientific curiosity. They also tended to view European societies as properly organized into an international system of nation-states governed by laws and kings; among them, the English assumed their own parliamentary system to be the best and most free. Under it individuals might rise in society through talent and hard work to become people of property. The poor were a mixed lot, but (whether poor through laziness or misfortune) workhouses were the thing to sustain the idle and keep them busy. The propertied were England's best, and England the world's best. What would later be termed English liberalism, formed in and from this milieu, was, as one historian has expressed it "a convenient ideology for the national economic top-dog."[37] It was also a convenient outlook for top-dogs within Britain, and for aspiring and energetic hounds of less august pedigree.

The century from 1660 to 1760 has been well termed the English Commercial Revolution.[38] Foreign trade rose rapidly after the Navigation Laws, a rise abetted by the system of international finance that came into being in the late seventeenth century,[39] by the founding of the Bank of England in 1694 and of the Board of Trade and Plantations in 1696 (signaling a new, comprehensive administrative structure), and by the courts of admiralty in the colonies. Administration was strict until Walpole, then lax until the Seven Years' War. In the carrying trade until the mid-eighteenth century, in British exports woolens predominated, going mostly to Spain and Portugal and often thence to their Americas. Other major trade was in Africans and re-exports, especially of Asian cottons to Africa and America, and of American and other East Indian products. Re-exporting was thought advantageous, since it furthered the national carrying trade. The value of the British carrying trade more than doubled during the first half century; at the same time, its major destinations shifted from Europe to America.[40]

By 1713, England controlled the seas, her foreign trade dominated by chartered companies. Their directors, great merchants, often were also directors of the Bank of England, and sometimes were members of Parliament. In the early part of the century, domestic trade and industry progressed more slowly. Robert Walpole, who dominated the government from 1722 to 1744, encouraged industry in order to encourage commerce. Walpole removed all restrictions on the export of English manufactured goods and admitted in duty-free the raw materials industry needed, while at the same time protecting English manufactures. This, the heyday of the mercantile system, forwarded economic expansion. The attendant accumulation of commercial and agricultural capital marked the beginning of the long period of moderate growth that culminated in the industrial revolution.[41]

England, finding in Spain and Portugal, and indirectly in their colonies, as Defoe reported, a major market for woolens and a large one for other goods, also found in that trade a splendid source of bullion. The bullion orginated in America. Well before 1700, the British had established factories (that is, commercial houses) in the Iberian peninsula. England had become a major carrier for the Iberian nations and virtually held Portugal as an economic colony.[42] Goods shipped from Britain to Spain and Portugal in the first half of the eighteenth century were to a considerable extent destined for re-export to Latin America. This trade and British commerce directly with Latin America expanded after 1713; for although Spain forbade foreigners to traffic with its America, the granting of the asiento provided an opening wedge. As we have seen, Englishmen had long felt, and continued to feel, as did the "anonymous British sailor" who subtitled his tract, rather cumbersomely: "the sovereign sole Dominion claimed by the crown of Spain to the West Indies is founded upon an unjustifiable possession (. . . especially when she takes upon herself to question the *Lawful* Rights and Possessions of the *British* Nation in that Part of the World.)"[43]

From the sixteenth century, English traders and privateers had broken the Spanish monopoly through contraband activities. In the seventeenth century, smuggling to Spanish America increased and Britons put to use newly acquired West Indian islands (notably Jamaica, taken from Spain by Thomas Penn in 1655) as bases for illegal but lucrative commerce. By then, Spanish American trade had become a prime objective for some English merchants. At the same time, English economic writers were pointing out the lessons of Spanish failure and Dutch success and that the nation with a developed trade and industry ends up with power and bullion as well. It was then that Spain was viewed as *the* horrible economic example by such writers.[44] The carrying trade flourished and, after Utrecht and the granting of the asiento, a new, direct, legitimate commerce began with Spanish America and the old contraband trade soared.

The English crown assigned the monopoly of the Spanish American slave trade to the South Seas Company, which, it was understood, would take upon itself part of the national debt. The company, floated by English bankers and financiers, thus received sole right to supply 144,000 *piezas* (a *pieza* was an able-bodied male or his labor equivalent) for twenty-five years. Certain aspects of the asiento are important here. First, it established the English in distribution centers in Spanish America—in Buenos Aires, Arequipa, Panama, Porto Bello, Cartagena, Santiago de Cuba, Vera Cruz, Campeche, the city of Mexico, Lima, Potosí, and Santiago de Chile. From these locations, agents reported on local markets and conditions. They also made commercial contacts in the cities and their hinterlands. Second, Jamaica, Barbados, and Buenos Aires became company entrepôts for Spanish America, and the company's activities helped to pattern Jamaican trade with the Spanish colonies from Florida to Chile, and that of Barbados with Caracas and its vicinity. From Buenos Aires, company convoys went out overland to Paraguay, Chile, and Peru.[45] Third, England was also permitted to send each year one ship to carry 500 tons of goods to Porto Bello. While the so-called annual ship sailed infrequently, when it did its wares undersold and outsold the cargo of the convoyed Spanish merchant fleet. The English, of course, brought in both exports and re-exports; so did the Spanish, who in fact often carried goods purchased from the English, their cost vastly increased because they came by way of Spain. Other, smaller ships replenished the merchandise of the annual ship as it was unloaded, and British men-of-war convoyed and protected it, even traded, resulting in a free-flowing supply of contraband.

Yet, the major share of South Sea Company smuggling occurred not through these subterfuges, but in vessels ostensibly importing only blacks. An inner ring of company directors profited most, running vast amounts of contraband through the ships, depots, and convoys meant for the slave trade. Interestingly, the Spanish government's representative on the South Sea board of directors from 1732 to 1737, who strove to eradicate bribery of Spanish officials by smugglers, was a member of a merchant family centered in London. He was Sir Thomas FitzGerald, or Don Tomás Geraldino, who went on to become Spanish minister to London from 1737 to 1739. The FitzGeralds, one scholar concludes, were "part of a vast family network stretching over Ireland, England, France, and Spain."[46] They represent both carryovers from older family-centered trade networks and har-bingers of more modern multinational trading syndicates. Finally, also busy in smuggling to Spanish America were private English (and Dutch) ships. These, referred to as interlopers, included some owned by North Americans, and they respected neither the Spanish nor British monopoly trades; that is, these smaller traders were among early exponents of what was then referred to as free trade. They opposed exclusion by foreign governments and by their own nation's chartered companies.[47]

Free trade doctrines had appeared in late seventeenth-century economic tracts and been discussed in Parliament. The concept of free trade then emerged as a relative and limited one; it meant more free than the norm, and was a request for unrestricted competition among national carriers within the empire and for open season on foreign markets. Directed largely against company monopolies, it also served to advance the broader principle of removing restraints on trade. Farmers, middlemen, new industrialists, interlopers, and colonials then pressured for a positive free trade policy.[48] In addition, by the early eighteenth century free trade was also a synonym for smuggling and interloping commerce. For the British, this traffic with Latin America centered on the entrepôts of Jamaica, Nova Colônia do Sacramento (a town on the north bank of the Río de la Plata above Montevideo and opposite Buenos Aires) and, later, the Juan Fernández islands off Chile. Among British participants were North Americans, who were trading salted fish, Afri-cans, their own products, and British goods, directly and through intermediate ports to the Spanish Indies.[49]

The English in Asia, from factories in Surat, Bantam, and Madras, especially, and later, Calcutta, also traded with the Spanish, those in Manila, receiving for Indian cotton and English merchandise Mexican and Peruvian silver. Thus, the Atlantic trading networks fit into a global system. Spain sent its Manila galleon from Acapulco to the Philippines. It took out silver and returned with Chinese silks for the wealthy and those cottons—some, at least, bought from the British in India—worn by all classes in Spain's America. Smuggling from Manila pros-pered, too, with much contraband (including the silks and tea of the Far East) coming into Spanish America, then going through the Antilles to England, often with an assist from British North Americans.[50]

The War of Jenkins' Ear was one in a chain of eighteenth-century European conflicts stemming from international rivalries and particularly from that between England and France. These were wars fought for the first time on a global scale, with much combat in and concerning America. Spain and England had reached open hostilities before, in 1718 and 1727. In 1739 the war, stoked by British smuggling into Spanish America, begun by England, and justified as an answer to Spanish *guarda costa* attacks on English shipping, was favored, indeed urged, by voluble public opinion. Expressions of popular sentiment echoed the spirit of *Rule Britannia* and called for revenge for Jenkins upon the barbarous Spaniards; manufacturing and some merchant interests also endorsed the war.[51]

The party of peace included those with interests in the chartered companies, especially the merchant princes with "magnificent and secure profits."[52] Among those in opposition, and thus in the minority, was Walpole. His equation of trade and peace, although unpopular at the time, would become prominent in British foreign policy when, by the 1780s, England did control the Atlantic carrying trade, by then a commerce free of chartered companies and usually in British manufactures. In 1739, although Walpole's exclamation, during a public debate on the war in Commons, "This is a trading nation and the prosperity of her traders is what ought to be primarily in the eye of every gentleman in the house,"[53] expressed a general sentiment, many Britons differed with him on how many and just which traders should prosper, and on where that prosperity lay. His equation of trade solely with distribution, too, was becoming obsolete. Daniel Defoe had expressed the feelings of the war party: England may gain by a war with France, but never loses by a war with Spain.[54] A parliamentary majority believed, as Richard Pares put it, that "a vigorous and intelligently-managed naval war" was just the thing to stimulate English trade, slow since 1713. And so it was, for demand rose in 1739.

The effects of war on the English economy during the eighteenth century is an issue of ongoing debate among economic historians. Did war deflect British energies from more rapid economic progress, or did it spur industry and the economy in general? What may have been is conjectural. What happened was that the copper industry throve in the 1740s, and iron during the Seven Years' War (1756-63). Shipbuilding in England and in British North America rose so that the navy doubled between 1714 and 1763. Employment, consumption, and the output of consumer goods were higher in wartime, and government needs spurred the development of the London money market. Shepherded by the British navy, English shipping continued its traffic with friend and enemy and increased its volume of trade.[55] All of this helps to explain why Captain Jenkins and England's eighteenth-century military and naval heroes were taken not only to the bosoms of most Britons but also to those of its manufacturing and allied merchant interests.

In 1739, England went into war largely in response to a widespread desire for a broader, more open, and more direct entrée to the American carrying trade and to French and Spanish American markets. Parliamentary petitions and speeches, complaining of Spanish interference with English trade, termed it an assault on "British liberties."[56] Smuggling throve throughout the war. The asiento was suspended, and when England surrendered it in 1750, in exchange for £100,000 and a most-favored-nation treaty with Spain, its demise was a victory for British interlopers.[57]

From 1739, rumor sped in England of creole and Indian unrest in Latin

America. In 1721 Defoe, assuming discontent among Spanish American inhabitants, had asked, "How are the Spaniards sure, that if the Inhabitants of *America* shall at any time come into a free Trade with *Europe*, by Means of a War, they will ever be brought to quit that Commerce again?"[58] Some British pamphleteers, both reflecting and molding opinion in this period, proposed the liberation of Mexico and its port, Vera Cruz, and giving to Mexicans guarantees of religious toleration, liberty, and property. Some urged annexing Spanish colonies—with the consent of their inhabitants, if possible. Others wanted to see Spanish Americans free, with their own governments, but bound to England by a defensive alliance and protected by the English army and fleet. Some of these writers also anticipated later free trade sentiments in stating that since other powers would not permit an English monopoly on Spanish American trade, free trade for all would be to England's best advantage, for Britain had cheap manufactures and colonies fit for trading bases. Still other pamphleteers simply opted for treaties of commerce.[59] The range of these opinions was echoed in instructions to British expeditionary leaders in America.

Government officials, too, favored exporting liberty of trade—that is, direct British trade with foreign colonies in America—and fomenting revolution to obtain it. Edward Trelawney, Governor of Jamaica, in 1740 suggested promoting Indian revolts in Spain's colonies and destroying Spain's empire in order to "lay a foundation for a most extensive and beneficial trade with the inhabitants."[60] He wanted independent Spanish American governments and open trade, but he also wanted to occupy Panama and certain other commercially advantageous ports and places. The following year, a council of war he and Admiral Edward Vernon attended produced a document endorsed in Vernon's hand opposing an English expedition against Cuba because, it read, "I cannot think Santiago de Cuba of consequence while we are masters at Sea. . . . Possessions in the West Indies will be a Detriment instead of a Benefit to Great Britain, and no possessions but such as may be useful in commerce are for our Benefit. Panama is of that nature."[61]

Panama, it went on, could be taken, with the help of "Mosquito Indians [those of the Honduran coast] and Jamaica Negroes." Conquest, however, would stir the envy of neighbors. "We are masters of the American seas" and should open free trade for all nations to all ports of the Spanish dominions, for Great Britain "will never be out-traded to Spanish America, if we can have the common discernment not to obstruct our own trade." Spanish Americans lived "under the tyranny of Old Spain, a tyranny they have long groaned under, and which they are ready to shake off, whenever they shall have a proper opportunity." And, the unsigned statement went on, "if we enter into an alliance with them, as with a free people," England will have a just title to defend them as allies. There followed a classic statement of eighteenth-century British interests in the emancipation of peoples: "It well becomes a free people to place others in the same condition with themselves. To deliver so many nations from tyranny will be truer glory than Alexander gained with all his victories. Let me add to this, that we shall thereby greatly increase our own Riches, which is the end of all conquests."

The document summed up the English interest in trade and territory. Trade was the major interest, territory was valued primarily for commercial and related strategic purposes. In much the same vein, Sir George Anson then suggested use of the Falkland islands (called by the Spanish the Malvinas) as a British way station to the Pacific.[62] All these suggestions mirrored a then-potent view of British empire. It was a view that adumbrated sentiments later to be embodied in Anglo-American attitudes and policies, owing much to such antecedents and contributing to shaping Latin American policies in the new United States of America.

The British ministry instructed its military and naval leaders in the West Indies to have proclamations distributed to inhabitants of the Spanish dependencies informing them that their rights and privileges included direct commerce with Britain and urging them to separate from Spain. Spanish Americans were to be promised tax and tribute relief, respect for property, and treatment as British subjects if they did so. In short, the war was to include a campaign for annexation by consent and for purposes of trade.

When Vernon took Porto Bello in 1740, he not only disorganized the Spanish trading system, but published a proclamation offering the populace English protection and inviting it to trade freely with all British subjects.[63] Similarly, Anson was instructed to seek Indian cooperation when his naval expedition should reach the Pacific coast of South America, and was inaccurately informed that Spaniards in Peru had long been inclined to revolt. If they did, and formed their own government, he was ordered, "You are to insist on the most advantageous conditions for the commerce of our subjects."[64] He carried with him a proclamation to that effect, which also said the King of Spain could not protect Spanish Americans. It offered them political alliance with England, free practice of their religion, a naval force, and a garrison; and it promised that a variety of merchandise would come into nearby ports. Similarly, Admiral Charles Knowles carried instructions, adapted to suit local conditions, in his attempt on the Venezuelan port of La Guaira in 1743. He was to publicize the tyranny and oppression of the Basque Guipúzcoa, or Caracas Company, recently chartered by Spain and granted a monopoly on the trade of Venezuela. All expeditionary leaders were also ordered to conclude provisional commercial agreements with inhabitants if they could.[65]

Vernon and the others strove to hamper Spain's commerce with its colonies while abetting British trade with them, including that of British merchants and smugglers, most of them based on Jamaica, and of British North Americans.[66] During the war, the Board of Trade gave Jamaican merchants market information on Spanish America. Under government orders, Vernon and the navy convoyed and defended English ships trading with enemy colonies. Trelawney expressed interest in the Mosquito Shore as a smuggling route to the Spaniards and their indigo in Guatemala and Mexico. He foresaw that if a canal were built, the area might also become a route to the Pacific. As Richard Pares concluded, "the war of 1739 was unmistakably a war of trade."[67]

In 1748, in the Treaty of Aix-la-Chapelle, Britain once again demonstrated

preference for trade and strategic advantages over territory per se. The war years
had increased the earlier English impetus toward diversity in manufacturing and
toward expanded trade (legal and otherwise) with North and South America so that
during the conflict and afterwards more British goods went by British ships to
America. This in turn further encouraged English industry. A remarkable expansion, beginning in the 1740s, accelerated after mid-century. England in 1750 had
the fastest population growth in Europe, the highest standard of living per capita,
the cheapest food, the lowest barriers to social mobility, and the most advanced
financial structure. Unlike European rivals, notably France, its energies did not
flow into territorial aggrandizement or into supporting an army.[68] England also had
the largest merchant fleet in Europe, one accounting for a third of all Europe's
tonnage and the greatest proportion of European trade with America.[69] By 1750,
too, "the public had learned the habit of investing in stocks," and even foreigners
were putting money in the Bank, in British government funds, and in the East
Indian and South Sea Companies, and they felt secure with English cash and letters
of credit.[70]

War had also left a backlog of demand, which resulted in a surge of trade,
domestic and foreign, at mid-century.[71] And William Pitt, who came of a merchant
family, had entered the government in 1746 and soon dominated it. Pitt energetically pushed an aggressive overseas trading policy, one supported by public
opinion. As European nations worked harder for self-sufficiency, England went
beyond that goal to contend for all colonial trade. Although trade with Spain and
Portugal was at its height in the second third of the century and Latin American
gold and silver flowing into Europe, it was clear those nations were bent on
minimizing their British imports.[72] The period of peace between 1748 and 1756
divided preindustrial from emerging industrial England. During the 1750s there
appeared elements of acceleration—especially a sustained rise in the rate of
growth in total output—that would culminate in the era of the great surge in the
British economy between 1780 and 1800.[73] Wartime needs and growth in industry
had allowed more diversity in English exports. Although Britain's was still largely
a cottage industry, the production of inexpensive cotton cloth and of a variety of
other goods expanded and increasingly supplied the colonial markets, including
Latin America.[74] Cheap cotton goods still figured prominently in a triangular
exchange; and a growing commerce with Africa, and in Africans, gave added
impetus to developing a domestic cotton industry. Profits, reported and otherwise,
from the expansion of the slave trade and the related demand for these textiles
before 1760 certainly influenced the pace and direction of England's output and
carrying trade.[75] In this process, too, England's aggressive use of its naval and
commercial sea power (so evident in Latin American relations as well as in others)
came to be important in developing the structures, experience, attitudes, and
momentum enabling the surge of the British economy in the late eighteenth
century. The British carrying trade in general—in exports, re-exports and
imports—, including that directly and indirectly with Latin America and the
activities of mainland North American colonists, contributed greatly to bringing

about and maintaining the era of sustained economic growth that would begin mid-century and culminate in the industrial revolution.[76]

Technology developed in interaction with industry. By the 1750s, an invigorated interest in applied science was reflected in university curricula and in the founding of the Royal Society of Arts in 1754, explicitly to stimulate industrial and agricultural techniques. Attitudes toward colonies and theories of political economy also underwent some alteration in the middle of the century. Before 1748, the policy toward the thirteen North American mainland colonies had been one of accommodation for a quarter of a century. However, British North American interests had prevailed only when they coalesced with English; and even then those of the West Indies had received preference. One example of such favoritism was in the passage of the Molasses Act in 1733 over the protests of the northern colonies. Even so, Walpole's initial interest in internal problems of trade and finance had shifted to a belief in what we would term capitalistic development as the means to increase national wealth and international power and to remedy all economic ills. Assuming the state should stimulate that wealth, he had encouraged industries and made every effort to develop commerce and to secure a favorable balance of trade—his greatest aim. He worked toward a self-sufficient empire, with colonies complementing and subordinate to the metropolis. He opposed colonial manufactures, but in general was lax in enforcing restrictive legislation, notably the Navigation Acts and the Molasses Act of 1733. This "policy of drift," as one historian characterized it, "was not the presence of oppression, but the absence of foresight."[77]

With peace (and Walpole gone), some reform of the mainland colonies seemed necessary to Lord Halifax, chairman of the Board of Trade, in view of the colonists' wartime assertiveness, and particularly their flouting of the Navigation Acts. Reform meant restriction and included the Iron Act of 1750, which discouraged colonial manufacture of finished iron. Two more disciplinary measures followed in 1752: the Currency Act designed to prevent Americans from paying sterling debts to British merchants in inflated colonial paper money, and the extending of the Board's original jurisdiction so that royal governors in America were now directly responsible to it. In this period, too, the Board of Trade tried and largely failed to reduce the rising power of the colonial houses of assembly. And to strengthen preparedness in the ongoing rivalry with France and Spain, in 1751 it suggested a military union of colonies. The mid-century ordinances, their effective imposition delayed by the Seven Years' War, were early steps toward what was to become in the 1760s a program for reorganization of empire. They were based upon the beliefs that colonists should be properly subordinated to the mother country and should help finance and mount their own defenses; and they raised discussions of the broader issues of the nature of the empire and the relation of colonies to metropolis.[78]

By the 1750s, economics was advancing from a skill or applied science concerned with practical problems to a more speculative and theoretical study that sought out and laid down rules concerning general problems. It was becoming

either French or neutral. With this treaty and subsequent commercial ones, England also gained logwood rights in Honduras and tax preferences, and permission to export gold and silver from Spain and Portugal with no search of British ships. The peace in 1763 was a victory of landed, industrial, and West Indian interests over the great international merchants. At that time, domestic manufactures and distributors were growing in power and influence. Overseas commerce, earlier "a foundation and purpose of Empire," then became more centered on national manufactures.[88]

English trade, little challenged during the war, afterwards met increased resistance and policies of competition from France, Spain, and Portugal. Yet, spurred by wartime demand, British goods had become cheaper and more varied; capital, men, and ships more plentiful. War had once more brought increased demands on heavy metal production, on shipbuilding, and on other capital goods industries. This in turn generated more consumer goods and produced higher levels of employment, earnings, and overseas trade,[89] so that after 1763 other nations, their policies notwithstanding, could offer relatively little contest. Yet, for Britain the problem remained of attracting more trade, including with the Iberian empires.

After 1763 Britain, France, Spain, and Portugal all sought to strengthen colonial defenses and to remedy administrative laxity spotlighted by the war. They took steps to increase control over their colonies, make colonies more profitable to home governments and investors, and make certain those colonies did not compete economically with the metropoli. They also worked harder to expand trade with their own dependencies. All remained devoted to national protection and to advancing national power and wealth. More than ever, they were concerned with the international balance of power and with pursuing policies based upon modi- fied, but still mercantilist, assumptions.

From 1763 to 1776, Britain, although its enactments and administrative reor- ganization were more piecemeal and haphazard, like Spain and Portugal strove to bolster its national economy and commerce through intensified and expanded governmental activity, including through closer regulation and more effective administration of its colonies and their trade. This effort corresponded not only to a now more developed view of colonies as adjuncts to the metropolitan economy, but also to England's sizable and worrisome public debt.[90] The war with Spain and France had both caused acute fiscal pressures and exposed the need for tighter imperial control. Two offshoots of the newly rigorous and assertive British approach to America are important here. First, for British North America there were attempts to ensure commercial dependence upon England and to impose a policy of common defense, which included protection of the vast, newly acquired western lands. That defense was to be partially funded through taxes levied in the thirteen colonies. Second, regarding Latin America, there was what can be summarized as a resurgence of a private and public over-optimism concerning the potential there for trade.[91] Let us look more closely at the second ramification first.

Wartime commerce with Latin America, which was said to have reached in the later 1750s an "amazing and unnatural height," had been curtailed by stringent government measures from 1759 to the war's end. Afterwards, its glowing possibilities of markets and bullion advertised in pamphlet literature, it attracted renewed British attention.[92] Moreover, several other factors heightened the attraction of direct trade with Latin America. Between 1764 and 1766, British trade in general dropped and industry, especially cotton, suffered. Board of Trade surveys then found a distaste for preferential trade treaties and a growing sentiment for freer trade, based on the belief in the competitive advantages of superior skills, resources, credit, and business practices. Throughout the sixties, too, the climate of trust between England and Spain and Portugal worsened, and English exports to them decreased. With the war, British merchants had left both countries, although their clerks and associates had stayed and done business and, with Spanish defeat, Britain gained a new preferential trade treaty. Yet, after 1763 British pamphleteers echoed informed opinion, which mixed fear of the resurrected Family Compact between Spain and France with expectations of belligerency and with alarm at the new commercial spirit visible in the Iberian nations. British trade with Portugal also diminished in the 1760s, and when Portugal entered the war in 1762 Brazilian demand was down, for Brazilian gold output and trade in sugar had declined. Most English merchants trading with Iberia then felt that in the face of governmental disapproval there and of an increased push by Britons for direct commerce with Latin America, their peninsular business was doomed.[93] A new generation of English businessmen did want more direct trade with the Spanish Indies and Brazil, smaller credit outlays, and quicker returns than through the legitimate routes via Lisbon and Cádiz. They knew that a greater markup and higher profits were to be had in America through independent trading in manufactures and blacks.[94]

The British government, favoring this direct commerce and worried by the new Iberian assertiveness and Spain's realliance with France, not only had opted for possession of Florida but, from 1763, authorized several expeditions to occupy the Falklands. In doing so, it echoed Anson's earlier conclusions (and in 1770 narrowly averted war with Spain over those islands). It also took other measures designed to augment approved British and British West Indian trade with Latin America.

A British Free Port Act of 1766 (and its 1772 extension) was intended to restore the Spanish trade of Jamaica's merchants, which had fallen off following the British campaign against smuggling that had started in 1759. The Act was also designed to legalize, on Britain's part, the commerce in the produce of the mainland colonies with the French—and indirectly with the Spanish—West Indies; to stimulate the British slave trade with Jamaica, Barbados, and Buenos Aires; and to encourage trade in English manufactures, especially cottons. The act sanctioned only some of what was being smuggled. It signified freer trade and revision of the Navigation Acts, and it allowed only imports not competing with those of Britain and her colonies, and exports only in British manufactures, blacks, and North American provisions.[95] It signaled a British drive for a preeminent position in America through out-trading rivals, as had been done initially in the late war, and it represented an early variety of cold and aqueous warfare. Spain may have led the way by decreeing its own free port act the previous year, opening specific Caribbean ports to foreign ships which were to exchange enumerated legal goods and gold and silver for other cargoes on payment of nominal duties. That measure, incidentally, as Lord Rochford, the British Ambassador to Madrid, then accurately predicted, would be of advantage to Britain and mean a greater call for its goods by merchants in Spain.[96]

Although the asiento had ended at mid-century, the slave trade from Africa to the Caribbean, which continued to be both a market in itself and an emporium for Latin America, had greatly expanded and was increasingly monopolized by Britons and British Americans, with and without Spanish licenses. They supplied the Spanish Havana Company's depots and they also employed small Spanish ships and merchants as outlets for contraband blacks and manufactures. The increased number of slaves was a source of the greater demand for cotton cloth and continuing imports of North American provisions. And since the Free Port Acts were cumbersome and the duty on slaves in Jamaica high until 1773, smuggling of blacks, manufactures, and foodstuffs persisted and was profitable.[97] As Lord Grantham, English Ambassador to Spain, wrote reassuringly in 1772: notwithstanding French treaties with Spain, British manufactures "would not want a vent as they clandestinely find their way to the coasts of America."[98]

On the coasts of Panama and Venezuela, British survey parties were reported captured in 1768, and there is evidence that Lord Shelburne, as Secretary of State, agreed to support a revolution, proposed by Mexicans, to establish British control of Vera Cruz and San Juan de Ulúa, its fortress island, and also to encourage revolts in Chile and Peru.[99] The French minister to Spain correctly concluded from all this that England wanted mainland bases to intercept and appropriate the trade among Spanish possessions.[100] Moreover, as Louisiana (now Spanish) was replacing Florida (now British) as a major center of smuggling to Spanish America, the first English governor in Florida declared that New Orleans "must serve as a means to introduce our commodities to the Spanish dominions without a rival and so in a manner deliver to us the key to the wealth of Mexico."[101] Britons and British Americans did trade in New Orleans and on the Mississippi until the new governor, Alexander O'Reilly, ousted them, reporting in exasperation, "I found the English entirely in possession of the commerce of this colony." They undersold the French, he added, and "got all the silver."[102] They also quickly regained control of that commerce until 1776, when the English were expelled and Anglo-Americans enjoyed greater opportunity. As a parliamentary petition explained in 1767, the Spanish American trade was important to the slave business and to British textile manufacturers. Moreover, British trade with the Spanish Indies was an integral part of a very complex and delicate commercial system, and any change in that system would affect the empire, for with change the West Indies and the mainland colonies could not pay for purchases in England.[103]

Let us return to the first ramification of British policy, that affecting British

North America. "If the 'new colonial policy' was composed of such ideas as centralization and uniformity of orderly development," hypothesized one historian a long while ago of a recently rediscovered truth, "it was for the most part an effort to realize old aspirations"—that is, those aspirations that were patent in colonial measures proposed or taken at midcentury and during the Seven Years' War.[104] By 1761, British frontier policy was plainly conflicting with colonists' seeking land and trade, for the British government saw a need to reconcile westward expansion with Indian protection and good will and did so by closing the country beyond the Appalachians to settlement. From 1759, the navy, which had earlier protected such commerce, attempted with only partial success to suppress the indirect Anglo-American trade with Spain and France and their colonies, most of which went through the entrepôt of Monte Christi off Santo Domingo. In 1760, Britain began to enforce the Molasses Act of 1733, in the process issuing writs of assistance—search warrants—to customs officers in order to curtail trade with the enemy.

The war had confirmed the need, felt for some time, of a tighter and more coherent organization of empire. In 1764 and under George III, the government, beset by fiscal pressures, desiring to tax the colonists for American defense, and pursuing more vigorously policies protecting home industry and merchants, put additional duties on foreign sugar and on luxuries from Europe, and it enumerated certain colonial products that could be exported only to England. It also cracked down on customs evasion, prohibited printing paper money in all the thirteen colonies, and passed a quartering act. Then, in March 1765 Parliament approved the Stamp Act, the first direct, internal colonial tax. A business tax was also levied in order to pay customs authorities. An explosion of adverse colonial reactions caused the repeal of the Stamp Act in 1766, but the following year the Townshend duties taxed certain English manufactures and East India tea entering America, while the customs service was reorganized and vice-admiralty courts given additional powers. These measures as a whole demonstrated newly stiffened attitudes toward the colonies and an attempt to buttress parliamentary sovereignty over them. Pitt was in the minority in being aware, as Ian Christie put it, that "colonists must be grasped in the arms of affection," and even he proposed Parliament's general legislative power be asserted over the colonies—although he astutely sidestepped the issue of its right to levy internal taxes.[105]

In response to colonial outcry and to nonimportation and nonconsumption agreements, and with the support of British merchants seeking to collect on overdue colonial accounts, in 1770 all duties, except those on tea, were repealed. Yet, a general credit crisis intensified fears in government circles of economic and political ruin of what Christie termed "the protectionist imperial commercial system. . .without which, they believed, Great Britain could not sustain the wealth and power of an independent Great Power."[106] The government and British public did not understand the essential unity of the Anglo-American commercial system.[106] Incensed at the spirit of colonial resistance and underestimating its depth, the government again asserted the supreme power of Parliament and in

1774 levied what colonists called the Coercive or Intolerable Acts. An English newspaper correspondent expressed a prevalent point of view: "I have always considered the colonies as the great farms of the public and the colonists as their tenants. . . . It is time to look about us, and keep them to the terms of their leases."[107]

Within the government, Lord Shelburne, in his emphasis on utilitarian considerations, was nearly alone in seeing there was more than one way to secure colonial dependence and to further empire. Most of his fellows exhibited very little understanding of colonial economic arrangements and how they worked to England's benefit. The others did not give sufficient weight to evidence that colonial trade yielded large returns to Britain, and that the American market had changed and expanded into a more important and more lucrative one for Britain. They were unduly influenced by merchants who, shortsightedly, were seeking remittances. In general terms, they held to economic views even then obsolescent, to older protectionist concepts based upon concern with exchange. But even then these views were giving way—as the push for Latin American trade indicated—to economic liberalism's emphasis on production and looser protectionism.

On the eve of revolution in America, two fallacies in prevailing mercantile ideas, related to retention of colonies and to imperial and international arrangements, were being pointed out, most notably by Adam Smith in *The Wealth of Nations,* published in the busy year of 1776. The first, earlier described by his friend, David Hume, was what economists now refer to as the "price-specie-flow mechanism" whereby specie inflow in time would raise the price level at home and make national products uncompetitive abroad. The second was that commerce is useful not because of differences in natural resources, but in relation to comparative production costs. These criticisms helped to shift emphasis from functions of exchange to those of production, and to put a premium on cheap and plentiful labor and access to raw materials, on technology, and on more open commerce.[108]

Yet, in counseling free trade, Adam Smith and other economists of the period did not mean absolute liberty of commerce. Smith did not completely abandon what he called "the mercantile system." He argued for protection of internal industry, thought the carrying trade not a very preferable investment, and believed free-flowing commerce a more intelligent policy and more to England's advantage. He did more. Uniting and expanding upon existing theories of political economy, he scored outmoded usages and set down broad new philosophical propositions intimately associated with the idea of liberty. He applied political economy—indeed, saw it as central to all human activity—and he advocated free individual and state competition, discerning greater cooperation in its sum. Economic growth—the production of wealth—he proposed as a possible social benefit, one leading to civilization, which he interpreted as a benign situation promising justice. Enabling this optimistic proffering of general principles was his belief, which owed much to Newton, in a divine plan ordaining a harmonious universe and allowing the possibility of happy endings achieved through free play of natural forces. Freedom, or liberty, stood at the intersection of his economics and moral philosophy. This nexus owed a good deal to his mentor, Hutcheson, and was common to what J.G.A. Pocock referred to as "the Scottish school of sociological historians," whose great achievement Pocock found to be "the recognition that a commercial organization of society had rendered obsolete much that had been believed about society before it."[109] Smith himself saw this reorganization as a revolution, by which he meant, borrowing a term from astronomy, a complete turn of affairs, specifically remarking that towns and industry had come to determine the policy of Europe and, in doing so, had "brought about a revolution of public order, a revolution of the greatest importance to human happiness," and he went on to look forward to "a revolution of human wisdom."[110] Clearsighted or not, his economic theory served to buttress belief that economic growth could offer a universal panacea for social, economic, and political ills.

Smith, in accord with these views, and Josiah Tucker, who had been consulted and heeded by Shelburne, opposed the then dominant opinion: they saw colonies as expensive to maintain and defend, and thought holding them not in the best interests of the nation. Their reasoning was similar to that of the pamphleteers who had noted earlier in relation to British expansion in Spanish America that colonial raw materials and markets could remain available without expensive political ties. In addition, Smith contended that colonial trade had been overdeveloped to the detriment of foreign. Hume, too, believed that American independence would be to Britain's eventual advantage, that whatever small adverse reaction there might be would hurt navigation and general commerce more than manufactures.[111] What in effect was working in English relations with foreign colonies—commercial advantage without political control—these commentators felt could work in relation to one's own. It was a hypothesis still based on adherence to national advantage, and one soon to be tested.

Before 1776, public opinion supported the government's stand on America, one predicated upon a range of embedded assumptions that had not only come to include a more developed view of colonies as rightfully subordinate to the metropolis, but also that that condition was in accord with the British constitution. Earlier Walpole's critics in the Old Whig, or Country, faction, in reaction to the shift of the dominant political concern from land to money and commerce, had justified their arguments by putting forth certain ideas regarding the constitution— ideas based on principles enunciated by adherents to the violent changes of government during the seventeenth century. These oppositional views were taken up by American dissidents of the 1760s and 1770s who, in choosing to argue on constitutional grounds, escalated concern on both sides of the Atlantic with the nature of the constitution.[112]

In all views of the constitution, the sacred and secular coalesced in the idea of an elect nation and of a law rooted in the history of Britain and emanating from divine law, a law of nature perceived by reason and guaranteeing natural rights. In England, these notions served to confirm a pervasive belief that since the king in Parliament was sovereign in Great Britain, therefore Parliament had exercised, and should continue to exercise, supreme authority over the colonies. Yet, over the years, the working *imperial* constitution, as we have seen, was not the same as the British constitution. The specifics of colonial attachment had never been made explicit. The position of the colonies within the empire had never been legally formulated—if they were within the empire. The closest the government had come to specifying the place of the thirteen colonies within the imperial system, and in relation to the constitution, was in the seventeenth-century Navigation Acts. Until 1759, however, Britain had not strictly imposed those acts and British statesmen had in somewhat offhand fashion simply tailored colonial policies to expedience. Thus, Walpole's conciliatory stance itself became part of the precedent Americans thought made up the imperial constitution.

In the 1760s, then, the British government strove to extend an expanded and radicalized domestic constitutional theory to the American colonies, and to base new restrictive measures on it. The government tried, that is, to stretch the idea of the national constitution in order to tighten colonial dependence and a de facto imperial system. It did so by reaffirming the British right to oversee Anglo-America, thereby more sharply defining the colonies as adjuncts to the mother country and putting forth a more developed view of the nature of the constitution. The colonists would not be belatedly fitted into either a comprehensive scheme of administration or the English interpretation of colonial ties. For since the seventeenth century, the colonists themselves had evolved political structures and a constitution of sorts, made up of American custom and of British precedent as they viewed it. They had increasingly managed their own expanding society and economy and their own political arrangements, and would submit to no greater political and economic subservience. In addition, freed from the threat of French encroachment, they no longer felt the need of British might and they now chafed under what for over a century had been the strongest working tie Britain had to North America, the navigation system. On their parts, Britons had come to fear Anglo-American competition in certain exports and in the carrying trade with Europe and the other Americas. In the 1760s and 1770s, differences were aired in debate over the nature of the binding tie and the imperial constitution. Variations in ideology surfaced, intensifying conflict and bringing on revolution. But bound up with these differences, interacting with them, and sometimes undergirding them, were economic, especially fiscal and commercial, issues grown out of alterations in theory and fact in both Europe and America.

Three relatively recent revisions of English history need to be mentioned here: situating the beginning of the industrial revolution in the 1740s, denying that the American Revolution marked a watershed in the British imperial system, and finding that England's was a predominantly commercial empire before 1776 and remained one. All allow a clearer view of the confluence of what have been termed three eighteenth-century revolutions: the financial, the industrial, and the American. They also allow us to see them as concomitant with a transition in attitudes under way in Britain and Anglo-America. In both places, new concepts were beginning to spread and to modify older assumptions concerning many aspects of daily life. Affected were faith, morality, economic theory and practices, the sciences, the functions and functioning of government, concepts of colonies and empire, and English relations with the Americas. In regard to Latin America, these changes bore upon assumptions concerning relations between England and Spain. These assumptions had been in formation in Britain for several centuries, but only during the eighteenth did they converge with ideational shifts and domestic growth, nascent industrialization, and a vigorous search for markets to lead, in the 1760s, to a public campaign for freer and more direct trade with the Spanish colonies.

The same year, 1776, marked the appearance of *The Wealth of Nations,* the outbreak of the American Revolution, and also, appropriately, Edward Gibbon's monumental account of the decline and fall of a great empire. By then, everywhere in the West political economy had come to mean the conscious and inseparable linking on all levels of politics and economics, and the interaction of theory and practice. Old Whigs, a minority, deploring a fall from virtue, saw commerce and corruption as identical. Men in power favored the former; their use of political influence to further self-interest had given rise to the charges of the latter. Although, like contemporaries in America, Adam Smith cautioned prudence in pursuing self-interest and warned against the extremes of material accumulation and against merchants and entrepreneurs bent on monopoly, he then fed the dominant opinion in investing material existence with great moral worth. With this sanction, as a recent writer concludes, "Men came in the end to feel that free trade was an almost religious cause because it could promote—or its absence could hinder—the coming of a better moral order."[113] The announced marriage of politics and economics intensified recognition in Europe and America of the value of gaining political control of the economy by those involved in it and sped the demise of the old Atlantic empires.

British relations with all America in the eighteenth century rested on trade; at first in both exports and re-exports and then, from mid-century, predominantly on export of British manufactures. This changeover paralleled a shift in emphasis in advanced theories of political economy from the functions of exchange to those of production in creating wealth, and it paralleled, too, an entrepreneurial thrust, the onset of the industrial revolution, and the beginnings of a more rigorous governmental policy toward the thirteen North American colonies, one that included favoring, at colonial expense, England's direct trade with Latin America. It was a goal that required and exacted both increasing vigilance against colonial smugglers and assertion of the right to tax Anglo-American commerce including that with Latin America. When political economists, enlightened forerunners of liberalism, put forth neomercantilistic views emphasizing foreign trade in national manufactures and espousing freedom for individual British European exporters and ships to out-trade all comers to the Americas, Anglo-Americans tended to be thought of as outsiders. Ultimately, policies concomitant with this shortsighted exclusion contributed to bringing on the American Revolution. Another complex of eighteenth-century revolutions—political, economic, and intellectual—had, by then, altered Britain's relations with other European powers, with its own colonies, and with all the Americas.

2

THE THIRTEEN COLONIES:
TRADE, BRITISH LIBERTY,
AND IBERO-AMERICA

Most colonial British North American contact with Latin America occurred through commerce and war. From the seventeenth century on, Anglo-American merchants, ships, and produce figured in direct and indirect trade with Spain and Portugal and their American dependencies. Moreover, from 1662 New Englanders were cutting and carrying logwood from Campeche and the Yucatan coast; by 1715, 5000 of them had migrated to settlements there and in Honduras. Earlier, in 1655, colonists from the mainland had been among the British who, under Thomas Penn, took Jamaica, which subsequently became the hub of England's West Indian commerce, including some with Latin America and some by the men and ships of the thirteen colonies. Especially after Utrecht, North Americans profited greatly from the contraband trade in logwood and by trade centered on Jamaica. In addition, many New England merchants began as fish dealers to London shippers who then transshipped to the Iberian peninsula, but the yankees soon carried their wares to Spain and Portugal themselves.[1] Thomas Hancock, who left to his nephew John the largest mercantile firm in the colonies, shipped dried fish to Bilbao in 1731 as his first cargo, and sent one annually thereafter. The pattern of this trade is instructive. Hancock's agents in Bilbao, Malaga, or Lisbon sold the fish, bought sterling bills, and remitted them to Hancock's London representative, who purchased and paid for British goods with them.[2]

In the early eighteenth century, roundabout voyages following specialized trade routes were common among New Englanders. In 1713, New England ships got wines from the Azores. Some of them ran a triangle trade between England, Ireland, and Spain. Carrying in reserve Spanish papers and a Spanish flag, they transported Iberian wines and fruit to England and Ireland, and pork, provisions, candles, and small beer—ostensibly for Gibraltar—to Cádiz. One route customarily taken by Hancock's ships was to Newfoundland for fish, to Bilbao, then to Cádiz with freight, and back to Boston by way of Madeira where fish was traded for wine; also brought home were Spanish lemons. Another loop included a return stop at Dutch Surinam to take on rum and illicit continental European wares. Some New England ships ran the roundabout trade to Africa for slaves, put on wine in Madeira, and unloaded blacks in Barbados, taking on sugar, molasses, and specie.

Many smuggled the cheaper sugar and molasses of foreign colonies in the West Indies, particularly of the French, and some engaged in an inter-Caribbean carrying trade calculated to obtain Spanish American gold and silver, so necessary to pay for purchases from Britain. Provisions from New England and Carolina rice went to Brazil by way of Portugal.[3]

As the eighteenth century progressed, British North American privateers were very active against Spanish shipping, and some colonists built fortunes during the War of Spanish Succession. By 1713, Anglo-Americans had entered the inter-loping trade with foreign islands and with the northern coast of South America, thereby trading directly and indirectly with Spanish American colonies. Lax enforcement of the Navigation Acts and connivance of colonial officials of all nationalities enabled this commerce.[4] South Carolina, Georgia, Philadelphia, New York, and New England had a direct coasting trade with the West Indies, Spanish Florida—particularly Saint Augustine and Mobile—and New Orleans.[5] Georgia and South Carolina were also outposts of the Jamaican trading region and were within the commercial network dominated by the South Sea Company in the early 1700s; and Saint Augustine and the other Spanish mainland ports served as entrepôts to Mexico and the Caribbean. Most Anglo-American imports from Latin America were in undutied contraband, gold, and, especially, silver. The smuggling trade was extensive and important, although not quantifiable. As the elder Arthur Schlesinger pointed out, it helped North Americans to use fisheries, forests, and fertile soil; to build towns and cities; to supply cargoes for ships; and to liquidate debts to British merchants and manufacturers. He added that this trade became customary and made of the colonists habitual scofflaws.[6]

A small legal slave trade to North America from Africa began in 1619. It expanded, especially to South Carolina with an increase in exports of rice and indigo from there, including a good deal to Spain and Portugal from the 1680s on. From 1713, blacks were carried from Africa to the Americas by independent traders, including in North American ships. Some of those ships supplied the Jamaican slave market selling to Spanish America. Some instead engaged, as interlopers, in more direct Spanish American commerce. British American slavers went to Africa, the West Indies, and the Spanish colonies. Some vessels made direct voyages; others traded from the West Indies to Africa and back to the West Indies. While Boston and Salem were leading slaving ports until 1750, their more eminent merchants did not get involved in that trade, but those of Rhode Island did. There is also evidence that between 1684 and 1756, North American vessels brought home with them as "negro" slaves some free inhabitants of Spanish America, including Indians from Mexico and Brazil.[7]

By the 1730s, then, many of the interlopers in the American trade with dependencies of other nations were ships from the middle and northern mainland colonies, exchanging food, provisions, blacks, and merchandise, mostly English. British North Americans' preference for cheaper foreign sugar and molasses was often part of an intricate contraband trade handling exchanges of the produce of many nations among various ports in the Americas, and sometimes on deserted coasts, and it was a cause of the Molasses Act of 1733 and of the War of Jenkins'

Ear. During the entire period of the South Sea asiento, an international, indeed multinational, network of smuggling involved English, British American, and French traders, ships, and ports. It included Dutch trade with the Venezuelan coast and the West Indies, and the Portuguese commerce by way of Brazil and Colônia do Sacramento with Spanish South America. The latter was largely in blacks and English goods, and was often carried in English bottoms. In addition, British North American free traders, vying with the South Sea Company, in the 1730s did their part in stirring up the Spanish *guarda costa* and thus contributed to giving immediate cause for the War of Jenkins' Ear. When war was declared on Spain in 1739, New England ships may well have had most of the British interloping trade. In the 1730s, too, North American trade rose with Lisbon and Cádiz. Over one-fifth of the tonnage cleared from Philadelphia went to Iberia, as did some shipping from other ports, and Philadelphia's commerce with southern Europe continued to increase steadily.[8]

Anglo-American trade with the West Indies and Latin America, although not with Spain and Portugal, accelerated during the war—in turn spurring shipbuilding, commercial venture, and economic expansion in the thirteen colonies—for despite an embargo, British command of the seas allowed much greater and more direct English and North American interchange with Latin America.[9] As more, and more independent, vessels took over the business of the South Sea Company, especially after 1739, more of them were also from the northern colonies.[10] In the 1740s and 1750s, this commerce centered on the islands and in Central America from Campeche to Costa Rica.[11] The war also stimulated privateering. North American ships carrying commissions of marque and reprisal not only took a large proportion of all Spanish and French prizes, but also provided armed protection and escort for mercantile vessels, when urged or paid to do so by prominent colonial merchants.[12] In the fall of 1744, the *South Carolina Gazette* estimated there were 113 British colonial privateers, and also many Spanish ones.

Despite hostilities, Anglo-American ships provisioned Saint Augustine and Havana. Moreover, an illicit trade between South Carolina and Saint Augustine, and between many of the thirteen colonies and the French, and thus also, indirectly, with Spanish America, then throve in ships sailing under flags of truce and meant for the exchange of prisoners of war.[13] Between 1743 and 1746, quantities of re-exported British North American goods went through Louisiana to the Spanish colonies.[14] In Boston Thomas Hancock,although he lost much of the Iberian fish market, built his fortune. In spite of the 1741 Massachusetts Staples Act and the 1745 embargo in New England, he smuggled more and more goods and provisions to the West Indies. He supplied the expeditions against Havana with beef and pork and also did well selling wine and cider to volunteers drilling daily on the Commons.[15] During the war years, too, New England, New York, and Pennsylvania carriers especially profited in the expanding logwood trade with Campeche and Honduras bays, and that trade and the settlements facilitating it, a cause of the conflict, remained a continuing source of friction between the British and the Spanish. At the war's end, some North American veterans were sent from

Jamaica to settle the island of Roatan in the Bay of Honduras in order to protect the logwood trade and to encourage British commerce with Mexico. The founding of British Honduras resulted.[16]

So widespread was North American wartime trade that afterwards, at a British Board of Trade meeting, Admiral Knowles, although with some exaggeration, blamed British North American smuggling of provisions to the enemy for the failure of English naval operations in the Caribbean. He also asserted that as many as forty-three British colonial ships under flags of truce were seen anchored at one time off Santo Domingo and, quite rightly, that flags of truce had become a standard pretext for smuggling and their sale a business with some northern colonial officials.[17]

By the interwar period between 1748 and 1756, Anglo-Americans were pursuing a more direct trade with Spanish colonies, where before they had dealt with them largely through Jamaica and other areas of the British West Indies. An increased demand for North American wheat in the prospering West Indies sugar colonies, British and otherwise, where each planter now held on the average eight or ten slaves needing food and clothing, not only profited Hancock but helped to make prominent ports of Philadelphia and New York. Baltimore, too, grew, with the growing ascendency of wheat over tobacco in western Maryland and in neighboring areas of Pennsylvania. Even New England ships carried the grain and flour of the middle states. The coasting and West Indian trades became main haunts of a greater number of British American ships, whose small size and relative closeness to port gave them advantage over the English.[18] Despite a desire to clamp down on it, the Spanish government had to allow or overlook at least some of the Anglo-American shipping to Spanish America, for provisions were needed there beyond Spanish ability to supply them. From two to seven ships each year plied between Charleston and Saint Augustine, which also received cattle driven overland from South Carolina and Georgia. Charleston traded with Havana and with Cádiz and Seville, and Spain permitted Carolina rice to be brought to the northwestern Spanish provinces. In Saint Augustine, Havana, and other Spanish ports, as well as through direct and indirect smuggling operations, much of the exchange was for gold and silver, always important in paying for British merchandise. The Spanish Havana Company, responsible for supplying Cuba and Florida, after 1750 contracted with New York and Charleston merchants in order to provision Florida. It dealt with them and Jamaican traders in order to supply the Spanish islands, and got blacks through Jamaica. The Company, as a Cuban historian has concluded, "was transformed into a simple intermediary of these merchants."[19]

Commerce with the Iberian peninsula also expanded at mid-century. South Carolina sent rice; New England, New York, and Philadelphia exported fish, lumber, wheat, flour, and ships. Perhaps one-third or more of the returns were in gold and silver. Much of the profits of the New England fishery derived from this traffic. By 1755, Americans were doing business with a firm in Bilbao that would come to figure prominently in political as well as commercial relations with

America after 1776—the house of Gardoquí. Also to become involved in politics and to do well in business in the revolutionary era was the Philadelphia merchant, Thomas Willing, the future partner of Robert Morris. Willing, in 1757, wrote of his conviction that without the Southern European trade, his city would have "no vents for half our produce."[20] With no other area did Philadelphia have so favorable a balance of trade, one allowing a good deal of credit on England and cash for British goods.

During the French and Indian, or Seven Years' War, most British exchange with the French and Spanish islands was in contraband carried in North American ships through the neutral West Indies (which included the Spanish until 1761) and Dutch Curacao and Saint Eustatius. A favorite port was Spanish Monte Christi, a scruffy island off Santo Domingo. It was inhabited by a few score Spanish subjects and some British North Americans who were devoted to smuggling. Small Spanish boats carried goods between Monte Christi and the traders of Saint Domingue. Other boats came from Spanish colonies to Monte Christi, Jamaica, Florida, and the free ports to exchange provisions, fruits, mules, cattle, and specie for British manufactures—woolens, some cottons, and hardware—and for North American and French goods and foodstuffs.[21]

With British-French hostilities official in 1757, British colonial privateering again flourished and smuggling increased three to four times over.[22] Since the British navy effectively excluded most French shipping from America, the Anglo-Americans busily filled much of the vacuum, including in trade with Spanish America. Although a British embargo was in effect on neutrals who might trade with France and its colonies (thus holding down interchange with Iberia and its colonies and keeping Spanish ships away), exceptions were made, one of them the ongoing Anglo-American provisioning of Saint Augustine.[23] And when the English conquered the French colonies of Guadaloupe in 1759 and Martinique in 1762, and Spanish Cuba in the latter year, Anglo-Americans had a large share in supplying those islands. By1760, there were reports of North Americans glutting all West Indian markets.[24] When Spain joined the war, the Bay of Mexico was said to swarm with "English" privateers, as well as Spanish ones. Spanish privateers then harassed the Atlantic coast, but few Spanish ships, including the usual ones from Vera Cruz, made it to Saint Augustine with provisions.[25] With the English occupation of Havana, slave imports soared and most blacks probably came in on ships owned by North American colonists. After the war, this commerce continued.[26]

William Pitt, echoing Knowles's valid complaint about North American colonists, declared they were again supplying the enemy "with provisions and other necessaries, whereby they are principally, if not alone, enabled to sustain and protract this long and expensive war." This time the government took effective action. In 1759, the British navy moved against smuggling in the Caribbean; an act of Parliament in 1760 sanctioned this interference as a war measure and put penalties into the Molasses Act. It marked the beginning of more efficient suppression by England of the customary and growing contraband trade in

America, although some still went on.[27] When North Americans found the British navy lowering their illegal commerce after 1760, they changed routes and tactics. They chose to rely heavily on the more indirect trade to Spanish America through Monte Christi, Saint Eustatius, and other free ports. Yet, even the Monte Christi trade dropped in 1761. And although 1762 was a good year in Caribbean commerce, a circumstance undoubtedly related to the capture of Havana, British measures were widely viewed as responsible for the subsequent financial setbacks and the lowered remittances to England.[28]

After the war, British North American trade persisted with Havana. It followed English commercial penetration deeper into the Gulf of Mexico and Central America, and progressed further down the South American Atlantic coast. By the 1770s, some of it had begun to go by way of the English bases in the Falklands and the Juan Fernández islands into the Pacific and up that coast.[29] From 1763 too, England continued to enforce the Molasses Acts; in 1764 seizures of violators mounted. And British acts then making any foreign ship hovering off British American coasts liable to seizure made smuggling more difficult, especially for North Americans dealing with Spaniards through Jamaica and West Florida. Thomas Hancock's firm now shifted to some extent to whaling; it shipped sperm oil to London, where prices were high. Still, Anglo-American merchants in 1764 managed some illegitimate trade. The major item exported to the foreign and British West Indies was flour; and, with British and Spanish harvests bad, trade with the Iberian peninsula rose to boom dimensions in 1769.[30] Carolina rice was exported to Portugal from Philadelphia by Willing and Morris, until restricted by the Revenue Act of 1766.[31] Most North American ships going to southern Europe in the 1760s cleared from Portugal to other European ports.

Philadelphia and New York had outstripped Boston's shipping. New Englanders still carried wheat, corn, fish, and re-exported British goods, but ever more frequently their whaling vessels were venturing into South American waters, and they traded clandestinely where they could.[32] By 1777 New Englanders were whaling down to the Río de la Plata. That year seventeen of them were reported off Brazil. In addition, the years between 1764 and 1777 witnessed an upsurge in the Atlantic slave trade, including that of the British colonists with Latin America.[33] Although until the revolution southern Europe was the predominant legitimate foreign export market of the northern colonies, the West Indies continued to receive most commodity exports.[34] Despite the vicissitudes of the 1760s, British North Americans had profitable dealings with Havana, Puerto Rico, and Santo Domingo. In British Florida, Spanish trade was encouraged. With the French ousted and the Mississippi River opened, "British" smugglers controlled the commerce of Louisiana. New Orleans, a hub of Spanish, English, and French trade, imported flour from New York, Baltimore, Philadelphia, and Illinois; and there Americans traded British manufactures for Campeche wood, Guatemalan indigo, other colonial products, and silver. And Anglo-Americans traded illegally with Spanish West Florida and Texas as well.[35] After 1763 ships from the thirteen colonies engaged in less and less roundabout or triangular trade and in more shuttle and bilateral voyages. They were aided by newly lowered costs—of freight, packaging, stockholding, insurance, and credit—and by improved business organization and the growing security of trade.[36] Seaboard merchants sent to England more and more cargo from non-British American sources, registered as British. Among commodities, only the sale of tobacco produced more earnings than did shipping. The growing stock of British North American capital was probably due to domestic shipping more than to British investment, and undoubtedly was helped by receipt of Latin American gold and silver, including from southern Europe. By the 1770s, British North Americans had established markets and sources of raw materials in other areas of America, notably the Spanish and French dependencies, and in Spain and Portugal. Liberty to the thirteen colonies in 1775 appeared to hold out the promise not only of political independence but of greater commercial freedom.

Throughout the eighteenth century, British Americans not only traded with Latin America, but had other, usually related, sorts of contact with it, and developed attitudes in the course of these complex relations bearing both on Latin America and on their own situations. Some North Americans maintained cultural relations or settled in Latin America, or participated in English campaigns. And usually those who did became involved in more than one of these activities. Thus, as the War of Spanish Succession broke out, in New England Cotton Mather, the eminent Puritan preacher, who also expressed a great interest in natural science, and Samuel Sewall, who had commercial interests in the Spanish Caribbean, dreamed of unifying the Americas through religion. Mather learned Castilian and read the tracts of the sixteenth-century Spanish friar, Bartolomé de Las Casas, condemning the Spanish conquerors and praising the Indians. Mather and Sewall wanted to print ten thousand Protestant Bibles in Spanish to distribute in Spanish American cities; and they anticipated encouraging trade with Britain there.[37]

During the conflict from 1739 to 1748 (the phase from 1744 to 1748 was known in Anglo-America as King George's War), mainland Anglo-Americans felt directly threatened by the French and the Spaniards, on frontiers and from the sea. Spanish privateers from 1739 to 1741 plied the length of the Atlantic coast, seizing, it was said, 316 ships en route to or coming from British American ports.[38] War fever elicited patriotic outpourings and fanned existing antipathies and the desire for expansion. Thus, the popular Virginia governor, Sir William Gooch, who was to lead the Anglo-American contingents, expressed the same sentiments being voiced in England, ones reminiscent of earlier British attitudes, in a rousing speech to the Virginia Assembly endorsing what he construed to be an English holy war against the Spaniards.[39] And the Lieutenant Governor of New York argued for conquest of Spanish America and for enlarging the markets of British North America, and he spoke of "territory in Cuba" as desirable for both purposes.[40] Later, in 1745, the capture of Louisberg was popularly hailed. A poem published in the widely read *New England Almanac* proclaimed it God's victory against "Superstitious Papists false and base."[41] And Jonathan Edwards, outstanding preacher of the Great Awakening, saw heaven's wrath in the devastation of Lima and its port by an earthquake in 1746: "All the ships in harbor were dashed to pieces, as it were in a moment, by the immediate hand of God."[42]

At the beginning of the war, in a wave of enthusiasm some thirty-six hundred mainlanders volunteered to join British military and naval campaigns in the West Indies, and to receive promised shares of Spanish booty. There was a rush for commissions, and recruits of all social strata and ethnic backgrounds were accepted, with the explicit exception of "papists." Some thirty-five hundred colonists, most of them from Massachusetts, joined the English forces at Jamaica, and North American ships shuttled supplies and provisions to them, to all the British expeditionary forces, and to many British West Indian islands.[43]

In Georgia, whose boundaries were a cause of the war, General Oglethorpe kept Indians friendly, and, at the head of an overland expedition, he unsuccessfully laid siege to Saint Augustine. That Spanish outpost was relieved from Havana, whose governor, the Conde de Revillagigedo, tried, also unsuccessfully, to incite a slave revolt in Georgia. Spanish attempts on both Georgia and South Carolina were subsequently repulsed. In the Caribbean, Anglo-Americans took part in the disastrous campaign against Cartagena and in the more successful march on Santiago de Cuba. Under Vernon in Guantánamo were six hundred Anglo-Americans, including Lawrence Washington. North Americans wanted to colonize, the English did not; and so the ephemeral colony of Cumberland and a precedent for seeing Guantánamo as gateway to Cuba. In addition, of the thousands of men from Britain's America who went to war, less than one out of ten survived. Most of those who did went home with a dislike for the British West Indies. They also had become acutely aware of British contempt for, and differentiation of them as, Americans. In the first general use of that designation, *American,* the English had employed it derogatively. North American volunteers had been given much working, rather than fighting, duty, been forced to labor alongside black slaves and to crew on ships, and been refused care in the same hospitals as sick and wounded Englishmen. Moreover, reports of these occurrences had preceded them home through letters and newspapers and continued to spread.[44]

The war had not only exposed and helped to fan widespread feelings among British colonists of antipathy toward the French, the Spanish, and Roman Catholicism, it had also helped to disseminate in the thirteen colonies sentiments favorable to British territorial expansion in the Americas. At the same time, it had revealed to many Anglo-Americans that they were different from Englishmen. Yet, separatist attitudes belonged to the future, and a sense of British identity and admiration for the metropolis and its leaders still remained strong. Thus, Lawrence Washington, whose half-brother George would find other loyalties, returned home to name his Virginia estate for his commander, Admiral Vernon.

From wartime onwards, expansion and ebullience characterized North American society and the economy. Gradual growth from 1720 to 1745 gave way to unprecedented growth from 1745 to 1775.[45] There were more people, more cultivated lands, more commerce, more and larger towns, and greater wealth. As one historian wrote, by mid-century the thirteen colonies had not only much *de facto* autonomy, but also "authoritative ruling groups with great social and economic power, extensive political experience, confidence in their capacity to govern, and broad public support."[46] In a political system increasingly aristocratic and dominated by Americans, the lower houses of assembly gained power at the expense of royal government, and popular dependence on local leaders increased. Yet population and affluence, although greater, were obviously more unevenly distributed than they had been a generation earlier. There was more concentration of wealth and political power and a decline in social equality and opportunity. These imbalances, and frustrations associated with them, contributed in the 1740s and 1750s to widely-manifested resentment, to clashes of haves and have-nots, and to local factional political disputes throughout the thirteen colonies. In Boston, most burdened with poverty and taxes, inhabitants found the imposts levied to pay for the campaigns against Cartagena and Louisberg to be particularly irritating.[47]

Together with social and political instability, and both in response to change and as harbingers of further alterations, some contemporary European currents took on variant, American forms by mid-century. The moderate Enlightenment— grounded in Locke and Newton and emphasizing reason, useful knowledge, balance, order, universalism, and religious compromise—became popular among a small but influential number of "the more prosperous, urban, successful, striving, and up-to-date" planters, businessmen, and professional people, including members of the clergy, lawyers, artisans, and colonial governors.[48] In 1742 in Philadelphia, which was becoming the leading North American port and the second city of the British empire, Benjamin Franklin proposed that an enlightened academy be founded—a philosophical society to promote useful knowledge. Franklin, in his enthusiasms for natural and applied science, for education, farming, and commerce, and in his advocacy of public service, moral virtue, and getting ahead, both personified and did much to disseminate the Anglo-American Enlightenment. Enlightened and protoliberal attitudes, cropping up in almanacs, education, and sermons, were to become widely diffused in combination with other fashionable modes of thinking. They would become part of a particular Anglo-American synthesis, restrained and optimistic, compounded of faith in material progress, moderation, and common sense, one reaching a crest in the revolutionary years.[49]

Much more popular was the giant wave in the century's middle decades of Calvinist-based religious revivalism, the broad movement subsequently known as the Great Awakening. It was shot through with emotion and enthusiasm and it exalted individual experience and conscience, even pietistic individualism and self-righteousness.[50] Both movements, the Enlightenment and the Great Awakening, evidenced the growth of voluntary associations, challenged the validity of prevailing standards and authorities, including those of church and state, and inveighed against submissiveness and passivity. Both were colored by elements of earlier American experience, including Puritan individualism and covenant theology, dissent, and pietism. Both also showed influences of English sources—of those eighteenth-century dissident, radical Whig philosophies legitimated in the seventeenth-century revolutions, philosophies having roots in renaissance Florentine humanism and, further back, in classical antiquity.[51] All of these elements and influences together—and a number of people felt the crosscurrents of them all—contributed sanctions, attitudes, and vocabularies to the current emotional and intellectual ferment. In addition, they contributed to a store of norms, values, and beliefs from which would be drawn many of the ideological and legitimating elements, the justifications for political theories, and a good deal of the spirit, characterizing the American Revolution.[52]

These new religious and intellectual trends not only spread but they converged with still other new notions, adapted from liberal tenets of political economy, as well as with certain American goals and with a heightened American self-awareness, all having significance for future relations with Europe and the other Americas.

At midcentury in British America, most people were involved in the market economy and in commercial life. In America, as in England, economic prosperity was then nearly universally pursued, and was frequently lauded as valuable to self and society. Economic issues and concepts were aired. Pamphlets and newspapers proliferated, and from the twenties and thirties on they frequently mentioned the mutual dependence of agriculture and commerce. Writers publicized the importance of the export trade to city and countryside, and furthered the idea that only by a favorable balance of trade would gold and silver "tarry among us." (Coinage and bullion were always rare; paper money and bills of exchange often substituted for them in commercial transactions.)[53] Moreover, even before the War of Jenkins' Ear and General Gooch's variety of crusading fervor, religion, commerce, and civilization were at least on occasion spoken of as intermeshed, as by Cotton Mather, who said, "'Tis not *Honest*, nor *Christian*, that a *Christian* should have no *Business* to do." A Boston pamphleteer in 1736 asserted that "trade enlarges peoples' hearts to do generous things...Christianity has been greatly served by Trade and Merchandise by Means whereof a great Part of the world has been gospelized." Elsewhere he remarked, "A well developed trade is a sign of civilization"[54]—which indeed it always has been. And J. R. Pole sums it up thusly:

> During the late colonial period it became increasingly common to claim that commercial prosperity sought through personal enterprise made a true contribution to the public interest, and the popularity of this thesis suggests the very real need to alleviate the strains of conscience by introducing a justificatory psychology of economic success.[55]

Yet, a more widespread tension existed in America than in England concerning the moral worth of commerce, a tension fed by Puritan tradition and a more agrarian environment. Fears and cautions surfaced in print, in speeches, and in the pulpit. They echoed cries of earlier religious and political dissidents—Puritans and radical Whigs—and attacked corruption, unbridled self-interest, and the disruption of community and family life. No one better exemplified the climate of ambivalence, of joy in material accumulation and misgivings concerning its effects, than Benjamin Franklin. In 1755, he praised trade and civilization, yet warned that with commerce and arts could come luxury and corruption. Other contemporaries noted the correlation between too much attention to luxury and the depressed state of trade in France; the Spanish were dismissed as lazy and unproductive. English trade, of course, was known to be expanding through the sale of cheap and popular necessaries.

American commentators in the main tended to identify with British interests, to cite British economic writings, and to harbor many of the same ideas as British mercantilists. Still, increasingly they considered themselves belonging to near-independent economic and political entities within the empire, and they manifested self-awareness as members of a separate, American community of interests, in a unity spurred more and more by rising intercolonial commerce and communications, by friendships and relationships among the more powerful and affluent colonists, and by ever more numerous ties forming among towns and cities.[56]

Rapid population growth, in accord with current views of European economists, also heartened American leaders. In 1751, Benjamin Franklin, responding to the Iron Act, looked back with pride on the capture of Louisberg by Americans, then forward to predict Americans would in a hundred years outnumber Englishmen. "What an accession of power for the British Empire by sea as well as by land!" he prophesied. "What an increase of trade and navigation! What numbers of ships and seamen! We have been here but little more than 100 years and yet the force of our Privateers in the late war, united, was greater both in Men and Arms than that of the whole *British* Navy in Queen *Elizabeth's* Time."[57] He repeated the prevalent British idea that population was wealth and that empire was trade, ships, and seamen, but added the un-British notion of a transatlantic empire embracing both Great Britain and the colonies. It was his opinion that "a vast demand is growing for British manufactures, a glorious market," which would soon be too large for England to supply and so "American manufactures should not be restrained."

Unlike the classical Roman idea of empire, or the then-current English one, Franklin and other Americans viewed their own situation not as provincials within an empire belonging to the mother country, but as fellow Britons, if with strong regional attachments to their places of birth. Franklin was concerned with increasing the population and with its sustenance; and, after 1748, when the westward movement gained momentum, with frontier defense and lands—that is, with security and expansion. These interests led to his suggestion in 1754 of a federated empire—and thus, implicitly of constitutional reform—at the conference in Albany called by the government in London to unify colonial defense against the French:

> Now I look on the Colonies as so many countries gained by Great Britain . . . and being separated by the ocean, they increase much more its shipping and seamen; and since they are all included in the British Empire, which has only extended itself by their

means...what imports it to the general state, whether a merchant, a smith, or a hatter, grow rich in *Old* or *New* England?...And if there be any difference, those who have most contributed to enlarge Britain's empire and commerce ...ought rather to expect some preference.[58]

The implication, here and elsewhere, was that Anglo-Americans were mature Britons within the empire and important to it, shouldering a large share of responsibility for the imperial economy, territorial expansion, and protection.[59]

Franklin's interest in American defense, it should be noted, was first expressed in 1747, in reaction to French and Spanish privateers capturing a ship in Delaware bay. A sense of Anglo-American self-importance as defenders, and thus imperial bulwark, against the Spanish and French, also surfaced in the years of undeclared warfare in speeches and sermons by other eminent Anglo-Americans. Thus, in Boston in 1754, Jonathan Mayhew, a leading preacher of the Great Awakening, exhorted the Massachusetts legislature:

Shall the sword rust?...Shall our military garments be moth-eaten for want of use, when such things are doing! It is impossible, Gentlemen, you should be anyways backward, or parsimonious in such a cause as this, a cause wherein the glory of God, the honour of your King, and the good of your country are so deeply concerned; I might add, a cause whereon the liberties of Europe depend. For of so great consequence is the empire of North America...that it must turn the scale of power greatly in favour of the only Monarch, from whom those liberties are in danger; and against the Prince, who is the grand support and bulwark of them....[60]

Here the notion of empire is exclusively American, but concepts of Anglo-American value to Europe and of the American tie to the English monarch are very clear. Mayhew, here and elsewhere, combined—as did other clergy—piety, liberty, and America in radical Calvinist defense of the rights of man, appealing to a social contract and the law of nature. Thus, in 1750, arguing against Anglican commemoration of the death of Charles I, he defended the individual's right to rebel against those injuring the public and found divine sanction in resistance to tyrants. Mayhew's argument was that British government itself rested upon rebellion, that against Charles I.[61]

In much the same militant spirit, but with even greater religious emphasis, another noted preacher, Aaron Burr, the president of Princeton College, whose son would become even better known, spoke on New Year's Day of 1755:

God has in his sovereign Goodness, chosen the *British Nation* to be the *Bulwark* of the Reformation; to hold up a Standard against those *Superstitions* and *Impostures* of Roman Catholicism. . . . On the one Hand, there is *Poverty*, *Slavery*, Persecution and Death; on the other, a fruitful Country, pleasant Habitations, *British* Liberty, and what is dearer than all, undefiled Christianity....I doubt not, by the Smiles of Heaven, we should soon make our Enemies flee before us, and again sit quietly under our Vines and Fig-Trees, and eat the Good of the Land.[62]

Burr was among those divines and secular leaders coupling religion with patriotism and believing Americans a chosen people with a sacred mission. He spoke of a country not England but within an imperial British context. Both preachers harangued audiences in terms expected to reinforce and intensify generally held sentiments concerning British American patriotism and its ingredients. These included a sense of moral right and of superiority to the enemy, a belief in the close relationship of *British* to *liberty* and of British America as liberty's fortress, and, as made explicit by Burr, an identification of liberty's opposite, *slavery*, with Roman Catholicism.

The young John Adams voiced similar feelings of American capabilities that same year, 1755, but went further, to envision a future with America as the hub of an empire based on sea power:

> All that part of Creation that lies within our observation is liable to change. Even mighty States and Kingdoms are not exempted...Soon after the Reformation, a few people came over into this new world for conscience' sake. Perhaps this apparently trivial incident may transfer the great seat of empire into America. It looks likely to me: For if we remove the turbulent Gallicks, our people, according to the exactest computations, will in another century become more numerous than England itself. Should this be the case, since we have, I may say, all the naval stores of the nation in our hands, it will be easy to obtain the mastery of the seas; and then the united force of all Europe will not be able to subdue us.[63]

Although the colonists' insistence on American importance probably owed something to a nagging sense that they were inferior in British eyes, also evident was their belief in a brilliant future, in an American mission as a chosen people within heaven's plan to exemplify virtue to the world. Cotton Mather's attitude in relation to Latin America early exemplified this outlook. Mather was also the first Anglo-American to use *America* in its modern sense and, as Sacvan Bercovitch says, he fixed the terms placing the idea of America within the divine scheme. Mather and later New England clergy associated religion and patriotism. During the Great Awakening, so did revivalists in other regions as well, so that at mid-century the older Puritan sense of mission was broadened and democratized into one embracing all white Protestants in America. In addition, it coalesced with economic and social attitudes in part derived from dissenting Whig theories, in part taken from liberal notions of political economy, and in various combinations voiced in sermons or by rising American leaders such as Franklin and Adams.[64]

Sentiments concerning America's divine mission and its preeminent position within the empire increased from these years, when undeclared warfare broke out, through those of the war's formal tenure, 1757–63. In the Seven Years', or French and Indian War, amid protestations of British patriotism—a major theme in speeches and the press—expressions of American self-assurance and self-awareness became common. Patriotism was spurred by Anglo-American participation in British victories—not only against the French, but also from 1762 over the Spanish. A force of North Americans took neutral Dominica for Britain in 1761. Troops from Connecticut and Rhode Island took part in the capture of rich and strategic Havana in 1762 and, as in England, celebrations attended the news of its fall in the thirteen colonies. That victory, Lord Albemarle reported to the king, was due to the opportune arrival of North American troops, for his own were decimated by disease.[65]

The British campaign against smuggling, as well as depressed economic conditions, undoubtedly contributed to Anglo-American enthusiasm for the capture of both Havana and Puerto Rico and their opening to commerce. Sermons, poems, and broadsides in at least one city, Philadelphia, revealed a great popular expansionist interest in holding Cuba, and Havana's fall was an occasion for religious thanksgiving.[66] There was joy, too, in the South, much of it attributable to being freed from the threat of privateers. The governor of North Carolina, addressing its upper house, proclaimed the victory "a Manifestation of Divine Providence in favor of the Protestant Apostolick Religion and the cause of liberty."[67] Speeches and pamphlets throughout the colonies declared the divinely favored Americans largely responsible for Britain's triumph and ascendant international position.[68] Clearly, territorial expansion was favored by the populace in both England and its North America, and it continued to gain favor with colonial leaders while it was losing it in Britain among men of affairs. Moreover, in North America, among both the public and the prominent, it embraced a commercial mercantile interest in enlarging trade and in acquiring land.[69]

The war's end brought the British North American boundary to the Mississippi River. The inhabitants of British colonies, who now shared the continent only with the Spanish, had increased in number. Most of them were small, self-employed property holders, and by 1776, south of New England an estimated half of the population was non-English. Both commercialization and inequality continued to mount, and a British sense that public issues should be debated still prevailed. The colonists then vented an exuberance compounded of victory, being rid of a feared adversary and neighbor, territorial expansion, general prosperity (despite immediate depression), a sense of their own maturity, and general self-congratulation. Yet, they also felt a letdown in military activity, business, and commerce, and retained feelings of inferiority, intensified by renewed contact with Englishmen during the war who proclaimed American culture provincial and American soldiering abysmal. There had come to exist, that is, an ambivalence—optimism and self-assertion coupled with doubt and a sense of inferiority, the last itself a unifying factor making the English outsiders. In these circumstances, the British government unwisely chose to maintain its newly stern and distant visage, along with closer, stricter, more rigid, and more resented supervision.[70]

The shift in official attitudes was made evident during the war, when the British measures imposing altered imperial policies were perceived by Americans as inimical to their customs, their habits, and their livelihood, as oppressive and as against their interests. The clampdown on smugglers and the measures inhibiting trade from 1757 exemplify this point. In the 1760s, colonists became more aware of the importance of interests per se in Parliament. They saw American lobbyists ignored in London and felt their welfare and wishes sacrificed to those of the British West Indies; and some of them came to feel there existed in England an anti-American conspiracy. The American reaction—rational, ideological, moral, and emotional—to English colonial policies, first perceived as wartime measures, then from 1760 on as a new stance, engendered various sorts of strain, caused examination of the relationship to England, brought on formulation of more exclusively American political views, and moved on to raising the interlocking primary issues of American constitutional rights and the nature of ties to England. The situtation thus elicited the often-quoted verdict of John Adams: "The Revolution was in the minds and hearts of the people, and in the union of the colonies, both of which were accomplished before hostilities commenced. This revolution and union were gradually forming from the year 1760 to 1766."[71]

In 1757, when authorities imposed a ban on shipping and trade through ports north of Virginia (in order to collect ships for an expedition against Louisberg), the Pennsylvania Assembly in a remonstrance raised the issues of liberty and rights: "A People cannot be said to be free, nor in the Possession of their Rights and Properties, when their Rulers shall by their sole Authority, even during the sitting of their Assemblies, stop the Circulation of their Commerce, discourage the Labour and Industry of the People, and reduce the Province to the greatest Distress."[72]

In 1759, the British navy began to harass smugglers; and in 1760, the government ordered the Molasses Act enforced and issued writs of assistance. New England merchants objected, and speaking for them, James Otis declared in 1762 that although "the British constitution of government as now established in his Majesty's person and family is the wisest and best in the world," the new policies were sullying it.[73] He also said that the British system best fulfilled the requirements of natural law. These two points—a constitution vesting authority in the king and the supremacy of natural law—would emerge as dominant American themes in the escalating arguments against England's right to dominate the colonists.

The next year, flushed with victory, Americans saw the government close hard-won Western lands, overhaul trade laws and, in 1764, levy the Sugar and Quartering Acts. On the frontier, "traders and squatters alike defied regulations; and what regulations existed, while they failed to protect the Indians succeeded in irritating the colonists." Moreover, "it was soon apparent that the northern colonies were now to be restricted in fact to those old inadequate markets and sources of supply to which they had previously been confined in theory."[74] In the ports, amid escalating competition, British houses strove to bypass American wholesalers by having their own agents in America sell to retailers and through auction. New young merchants—enterprising and highly competitive—emerged to employ American capital in retailing and overseas trade. Older merchants, never keen on competition, hated this sort particularly. And old and new suffered with customs enforced, coastal trade impeded, and the lack of paper money accentuated by a new emphasis on cash payment.[75]

By 1765, James Otis asked "why trade, commerce, arts, sciences, and manufactures should not be as free for an American as for a European."[76] The Stamp Act then coalesced with overstocks of British dry goods and a slump in wheat and tobacco prices to serve as a further irritant and as a focus of rising discontent and unity. Objected to as an innovative internal tax, it was attacked in resolutions by assemblies, aroused protests centered on no taxation without representation, and in the press brought on discussions of the nature and limits of parliamentary power.[77] In a notable published speech, John Dickinson of Pennsylvania presented arguments steeped in familiarity with germane British economic theory to point out to English merchants mutual benefits to be gained through repeal of the Stamp and Sugar Acts. He cited the English economists, Josiah Child and Malachi Postlethwayt, in stating American markets were immensely beneficial to Britain, then went on to explain that Americans needed remittances for that trade and Britain would be wise to keep open those channels bringing them in. England should, in other words, promote "our trade with Spain, Portugal, and the foreign colonies in the West Indies."[78] In the late war, he added, "with a vast expense of blood and wealth we fought our way. . . up to the doors of the Spanish treasuries, and by the possession of Florida might obtain some recompense for that expence." Americans and Spaniards want mutual trade at Pensacola, but British men-of-war turn back Spaniards bringing cash, Dickinson lamented, leaving Americans less advantage of Florida than before it was British, for then Spanish governors had permitted a profitable trade. In the present situation, Americans are left with two choices: to continue disadvantageous commerce, or to manufacture instead of being supplied by Britain. Here again, he mentioned the Spaniards, who, although "a proud and indolent people," were driving out British cloth imports by making their own textiles. A variant point, indicating a common frame of reference, was made by a New York politician, William Smith, Jr., who wrote: "The Spanish Emigrations drained the old State, chiefly because they sent her *Money* instead of *Merchandise*, Spain was converted into a Castle of Indolence. . . ."[79]

Repeal of the Stamp Act in 1766 appeared a victory for American public sentiment, a defeat for the British government; passage and repeal hardened American discontents and induced American unity. In 1766, too, the Declaratory Act, which did not mention taxation but insisted that Parliament had the right to legislate for America, was well understood by leading colonial dissidents who, then coming into power in politics, were sparking discussions of American rights and of the nature of American ties to Britain.[80] One of them, Richard Bland, a Virginia lawyer, stated that Parliament had the power, but not the right, to subject the colonies, and that colonists retained individual rights to secede and inaugurate a government. And John Adams responded to the Stamp Act with a vision, in tone very similar to James Thomson's *Liberty* (1735): "I always consider the settlement of America with reverence and wonder, as the opening of a grand scene and design in Providence for the illumination of the ignorant, and the emancipation of the slavish part of mankind all over the earth"—except that Adams went on to mention once more the possibility of America becoming the new great seat of empire.[81]

The nonconsumption movement of 1767 and 1768, following the Townshend duties and an economic downturn in 1767, and the nonimportation movement of 1768 to 1770, were bids for greater economic autonomy. They brought together in common cause merchants, artisans, and mechanics, all of them agreed on promoting colonial manufacturing and exports. John Hancock was tried and made an example of because a ship of his, appropriately named the *Liberty*, in 1768 smuggled in Madeira wines without paying customs duties. John Adams, in defending him by contending that according to "constitutional law" all Americans were not but should be represented in Parliament and that Americans should enjoy rights equal to Englishmen, heated discussion of the question of the nature of imperial ties.

New York and Philadelphia merchants were then doing business with Dutch firms. That commerce included exchange through the Dutch West Indies and Portuguese islands, principally for tea. Trade was good only with southern Europe, where poor harvests in Spain and Portugal caused North American wheat and flour sales to attain new heights. Imports and credit improved, but money remained scarce and exchange rates down in the face of ever greater competition and demand for cash, not credit. In this situation, most American merchants favored greater local power, and a few, like Christopher Gadsen of Charleston, went further, advocating breaking away from Britain's trading system and instituting a "free and open trade with all the powers of Europe."[82]

With the nonimportation agreements especially, pamphleteers and the press combined economic with religious, moral, and political strands, attacking England's vices, counseling America's salvation, and frequently saying much about liberty, that potent political, social, and economic catchall. It was in these years that the Sons of Liberty, in the words of one historian, "set an example of intimidation by riot," and Samuel Adams, the "broker between the populace and the Whigs," and his associates urged resistance and attracted followers and emulators.[83] James Wilson, later a signer of the Declaration of Independence, wrote in 1768 (in a pamphlet published in 1774) that the colonies owed obedience only to the king, that government was founded on consent, and that "the happiness of the society is the *first* law of every government."[84] Dissenting clergy exhibited intense defiance of Britain. One anonymous Baptist preacher went so far as to declare that colonists "have as just a right before God and man to oppose the Lords and Commons of England when they violate their rights as Americans as they have to oppose any foreign enemy."[85]

In 1770, although all duties except that on tea were repealed, that tax, its symbolism understood, rankled; sterling bills remained scarce, trade was still off, and the exchange rate rose. Nevertheless, fed by a British credit boom, Anglo-America experienced general economic expansion. Shipments to southern Europe continued and, for the first time since the early 1760s, large cargoes went to the West Indies. Tobacco and wheat prices rose; Virginians, and then merchants and planters in North Carolina and Maryland, sought less dependence on British exporters and more local economic control. Merchants ended nonimportation (thereby splitting with artisans who had enjoyed the protection it offered their manufactures) and once again soon became overstocked. In mid-1772, triggered by financial panic, first in Britain, then internationally, the two-year boom collapsed. The Tea Act followed. In the aftermath of growing demands for greater economic and political autonomy and a spreading feeling of shared concern, this situation brought on a renewed, uneasy alliance of port merchants with radicals, artisans, and mechanics, one that would falter but hold throughout the Revolution. In addition, improved markets in southern Europe and the Caribbean and rising prices (until 1775 and with the exception of the tobacco market) led some merchants to prefer to ship less to England and more to the Spanish and French West Indies, and undoubtedly gave an additional impulse to the desire for greater freedom of trade.[86]

The tea party of December 1773 and the measures to punish Boston, known as the Coercive, or Intolerable, Acts, resulted in the Continental Congress, an alternative preferred by merchants to renewing nonimportation, and also in a combination of complaints—political and economic, scoring all legislation concerning trade and taxation—directed against what was referred to as the ruinous system of colonial administration from 1763. The Congress itself soon passed new agreements against importing and consuming British goods, and it sought redress. Its resolutions of 1774 and 1775, reflecting positions earlier taken by pamphleteers, asserted that the colonies were not subordinate to Parliament but were bound only, by obedience and loyalty, to the king. He, as chief magistrate, was expected to do justice and veto parliamentary acts infringing their rights. Members raised the question of who regulates trade—Parliament or the colonies—and in the Philadelphia proclamations of October 20, 1774, the eighth clause was an economic manifesto: "We will...encourage frugality, economy, and industry, and promote agriculture, arts, and the manufactures of the country, and will discountenance and discourage every species of extravagance or dissipation."[87] Attacks on self-indulgence associated indulgence with imports, extravagance with too much trade, and now held up England as an example of Old World extravagance and corruption.[88]

By 1774, pamphlets and letters combined older religious and secular visions: They repeatedly referred to America as the seat and refuge of liberty, and as possibly the foundation of the world's greatest empire. They envisioned an America established on principles of both civil and religious freedom, the site of God's kingdom on earth—an America that would become a successor to the British empire and constitution, now fallen from virtue into decay. Dissident leaders had found justification for denying parliamentary sovereignty in a prior British constitution, in an American pact with the king, and in appeal to a higher law, the law of nature. Some of them managed to gather older civil and religious traditions of dissent within a single powerful argument for a form of commonwealth arrangement within the British Empire.[89] Thus, John Adams, in the *Novanglus* letters, invoked the British constitution, further defining it as republican, "a government of laws and not of men," the king as its first magistrate, and Massachusetts as linked solely to the monarchy. Its inhabitants, he explained, had taken oaths during the seventeenth-century revolutions to the king only, and not to Parliament; Americans had not consented to the Revolution of 1689 and to Parliamentary supremacy.[90]

Adams then spoke for Massachusetts. Analogous was Jefferson's tendency, as

was common in Virginia, to refer to that colony as his "nation."[91] Another
Virginian, Patrick Henry (representing farmers and speculators in western lands),
exhibited not a change but a shift in emphasis to a broadened scope of patriotic
attachment when he declared, "I am not a Virginian, but an American."[92]
Jefferson went further, however, in his *Summary View of the Rights of British
America*, when he deftly posited an expanded consciousness of Americanism
within the context of the British heritage of the thirteen colonies. Like Adams, but
appealing to still older precedent, he alluded to "our Saxon ancestors" and to
restoring ancient Saxon principles, and he defended the legitimacy of *royal*
sovereignty only, and not that of Parliament in America. The monarchy, he agreed
with Adams, was *the* "central link connecting the several parts of the empire."[93]

George Washington, in a letter of 1774, could draw upon much of what had
become by then an arsenal of revolutionary language when he endorsed law, the
constitution, the rights of mankind, happiness, life, liberty, property, and a free
government.[94] Finally, Alexander Hamilton, a master at expounding political
philosophy, who in that same year bundled the law of nature, the genius of the
British constitution, and American charters as guarantors of American lives and
property, and who also made a telling point for natural rights by insisting virtue
predated society, in 1775 put full rhetorical weight upon natural law and natural
rights. In doing so, he omitted all mention of man-made precedents, including
those in British law: "The sacred rights of mankind are not to be rummaged for
among old parchments or musty records. They are written, as if with a sunbeam, in
the whole *volume* of human nature by the hand of divinity itself and can never be
erased or obscured by mortal power."[95] This sort of prose blossomed in Thomas
Paine's *Common Sense*, published early in 1776, and that tract, the first unqualified argument for American independence, broke the last ideational link to
the British monarchy in declaring that the king of America reigns above, and that
law is king.

A political philosophy with roots in European and American history, developing cumulatively from the early 1760s in interaction with altering political, social,
and economic conditions, in 1776 found inspired expression in the Declaration of
Independence. There it flowered, displaying vital emotional content—an impelling sentiment of colonies now mature and ready for emancipation. And perhaps as
much as anything it signified that "the idea of British injury to self-esteem
overcame a feeling of dependence for self-respect on the British connection." In
July 1776, the rebels expected only a brief scuffle, and then liberty.[96]

While the American Revolution was predominantly political in the sense that it
was above all a movement to be free of English political control, it was also, as
recently rediscovered by eminent scholars, ideological and emotional, in the sense
explained by John Adams—that is, it was brought about and carried through by
alterations in individual and group perceptions.[97] Moreover, it had social causes in
that it encompassed a contest for who would rule at home and, within it, social
turmoil and factional battles which, visible among groups and regions at mid-
century, were vigorously pursued thereafter. Finally it was, in conjunction with all

of these, an economic movement, in part brought on by growing economic competition within the colonies, and with Britain and British merchants, and by rapid change within America. A piece of Tory doggerel, much to the point, succinctly explained the northern patriots as a coalition of John Presbyter, Will Democratick, and Nathan Smuggle.[98]

In addition, alterations in the British economy and attitudes within Britain toward the American economy had an impact, as did competition for the trade of the other Americas and southern Europe. The British attempt to constrict and tax American commerce clashed with the growing Anglo-American desire to expand manufactures, settlement, the money supply, and commerce by freeing trade. The indivisibility of their own, and their compatriots', social wellbeing, political power, and economic freedom and advance was much in the minds of the founding fathers before the Revolution.

The English measures of the 1760s themselves had strong economic components, and many of the perceptions that were a significant part of colonial reaction to them were economic ones, demonstrating what one historian pointed out as "the colonists' understanding of the inseparability of liberty and property."[99] It was economic conditions, too, especially from 1763, that exacerbated longer-standing colonial grievances and, while much of the adverse reaction of colonials to English measures was emotional and ideological, economic elements were significant within—indeed were an integral part of—the emotional and idelogical conflict with England. The old question—was British interference resented primarily because it jeopardized colonial freedoms, or because it jeopardized colonial pocketbooks?—presents a false dichotomy, for the two, as colonists almost always acknowledged, were intermeshed.

By July 1774, in his draft of instructions to the Virginia delegates in the Continental Congress, Jefferson simply assumed "that the exercise of a free trade with all parts of the world was possessed by the American colonists as of natural right," and that it had been "the object of unjust encroachment by Parliament"—that the Navigation Acts were in fact actions of parliamentary tyranny.[100] And in pamphlet and press warfare, writers combined constitutional and commercial arguments, demanding that Britain restore the legitimate imperial arrangement; and, presenting a golden age of commerce as concomitant with independence, they discussed political and commercial liberty as synonymous. In April 1776, on a Resolution introduced by Benjamin Franklin, the Congress issued a "commercial declaration of independence" from England and opened American trade to all comers.[101] The declaration of political independence came three months later.

The recent reemphasis by scholars of continuities from British to British North American tradition should, but seldom does, include continuities in economic—especially commercial—attitudes, interests, and activities; yet such continuities were present throughout the eighteenth century and beyond. They are visible from 1763 on, even in adverse American responses to English policies, and are inseparable from American conceptions of the nature of imperial ties. Clearly,

American interest in commerce paralleled British, particularly interest in a less restricted and more direct trade with the other Americas. Moreover, in the late 1760s Americans began to add to pleasure in re-exporting goods a recognition of the importance of increasing their own manufactures and exports, unconfined by British regulations. From English sources, too, they garnered precedent for preoccupation with combating extravagance and idleness, and for correlating self-interest and individual liberty with communal wellbeing.[102]

In sum, from the 1750s, as North American interests lost ground in Parliament, in the colonies rudimentary mercantile structures and shipping increased and expanded, competing not with British manufactures—most manufacturing was forbidden in America and American vessels often carried English goods—but in the carrying trade and its markets. Increasingly throughout the century, British North Americans took, both legally and otherwise, their own produce and the re-exported goods gotten from England to Spain, Portugal, and Latin America, or to intermediate ports for transshipment to those destinations. Commercial relations, direct and indirect, with Latin America and Iberia were important in the development of British North American shipping and merchandising, and thus were important to the general economy. And the various aspects of Anglo-American contact with Spain and Portugal and their colonies contributed to intensifying rivalries and dissatisfactions with England, and therefore to the onset of the American Revolution.

During hostilities from 1739 to 1748, the British navy protected and gave impetus to the interloping trade involving smuggling—including, indirectly, through British islands—in North American produce as well as in re-exported manufactures and in blacks; the Spanish trade was part of a complex network. British restrictions on currency and banking in the colonies subsequently made the Iberian and Latin American trades, always valuable for specie and letters of credit on London, even more tantalizaing. Those trades, and war against the Spanish and French, helped to stimulate shipping and shipbuilding along the North American seaboard. Official promotion of shipbuilding, moreover, abetted funneling the productive energies and capital of colonists into it. In addition, exports from mid-century on, incuding much wheat and flour, to Latin America and Iberia encouraged the growth of the middle colonies, as did the growing carrying trade. Supplying blacks as slaves to Latin America also gave the colonial economy a boost, and much of the exported British American foodstuffs and textiles was re-exported and went to feed and clothe those slaves. Merchants on the Atlantic seaboard became socially prominent and influential, and some smuggling or extralegal activity involving Iberia or Latin America or both was normal among them. They suffered when England seriously opposed smuggling during the Seven Years' War but the British capture of Havana in 1762 began in earnest a long and expanding Anglo-American involvement in Cuban commerce and investment, and the post-1763 British interest in Latin American markets was shared by North American colonists, who were ready to compete for them with Englishmen.

British North Americans also shared English attitudes toward Spaniards and

Portuguese and their colonies, expressing superiority, anti-Catholicism, xenophobia, traditional enmity, and colonial rivalry. The British campaigns against Latin America intensified those antipathies, although among participants customary trade may have mitigated them. Further, much like the English, a number of educated British North Americans, who were touched by the Enlightenment and by tenets of political economy and nascent liberalism, in public utterances, the press, and the learned gatherings that were the beginnings of learned societies, displayed an exotic curiosity in the Latins and their lands, one mingled with a lively commercial interest and one that was to continue, uninterrupted by the events of 1776—in fact, heightened by them.[103] This interest, shared by Cotton Mather and Benjamin Franklin, both of whom studied Spanish, was usually expressed in terms of natural scientific enquiry, and was to burgeon on both sides of the Atlantic. On their parts, Spain and Portugal saw little exotic in England and its colonies, but found in that empire other attractions—as well as reciprocal antipathies.

3

"RICH IN INTENTIONS AND PROJECTS":

SPAIN AND PORTUGAL

In Iberia, traditional society and economy prevailed throughout the eighteenth century. The Bourbon dynasty brought constitutional unity to Spain, but only superficial, cosmetic reform. It also brought a sense of pressing need to catch up to the rest of Europe in wealth and power, and a desire to do so through activity directed by the state. Philip V (1700–1746) and his son, Ferdinand VI (1749–59), appointed able ministers who began formulating projects that would affect American relations for the next one hundred and fifty years. With the Bourbons, the official concept of monarchy altered from the old, essentially passive idea of existing to preserve justice and lead in war to the more dynamic one of being responsible for stimulating the economy, directing the productive energies of society, and establishing institutions for the process today called modernization. One result was the initial Bourbon reforms: These were largely centered on governmental administration, the navy, and overseas commerce, and were at first extremely piecemeal. Then, under Charles III (1759–88), the state put forth a full-fledged program in Spain and its America to regulate and centralize political authority and to oversee economic activity, avowedly in order to mobilize Spanish society (still understood largely, in the medieval sense, as a corporate entity), for its own greater well-being and its international security, strength, and prestige.

Certain points relating to differences between Iberia and England should be kept in mind. First, Spanish, as well as Portuguese, society retained its traditional divisions of nobles, clergy, and commoners throughout the century. The old order disposed of economically and politically in England in the seventeenth century remained ascendant in eighteenth-century Spain and Portugal. Although after 1713 political offices and political power in Spain passed from the grandees of Castile to the lower nobility, the old regime endured, as did one of its chief bases, landholding. The upper nobility, although excluded from high office, continued to hold over half the land and to hold it under seignorial jurisdiction. In controlling land, the church and the crown followed the aristocracy in a ratio of 3:2:1. An estimated eighty percent or more of the population were peasants, over half of them landless. The small middle class, perhaps at most six percent of the whole, approached being a thriving bourgeoisie only in some ports and in Madrid and Barcelona, and, except for the Catalans, most Spaniards were content to wait, as one historian remarks, for economic ideas and incentives to come from the government.[1]

Second, Spanish agriculture—a shambles in 1713, and manufacturing—almost nonexistent then, while growing more prosperous through the century, improved little in technology and remained far behind their English and even French counterparts. Yet, again especially in Catalonia, both expanded, and, as population increased, were directed to broader markets. But no agricultural or industrial revolution took place. Thus, although much has been written on change in eighteenth-century Spain, progress was limited to benefiting a traditional society. Actual achievements were even more limited, largely to increasing the sort of governmental bureaucracy and economic direction associated with enlightened despotism.

Third, real power continued to reside in the ruler and the wealthy nobility, and reasonable cooperation between them, despite appearances to the contrary, endured throughout the 1700s; the Spanish parliament, or *Cortes,* had no power and seldom met. The church in Spain, too, remained strong. Bourbon policies and reforms never seriously attacked these arrangements, but, rather, fortified them. And as earlier, as an economist comments: "Spain's economic, political, and military position was so much geared to the production and export of bullion that it would be hard to conceive just what its position would have been without it."[2]

Fourth, in Portugal until mid-century an influx of Brazilian gold buoyed up a spendthrift king, John V (1706–50), and some portions of society, and it financed prodigies of ultra-ornate architecture. Thereafter, less specie came in and depression ensued. Most of the country remained poor and little touched by eighteenth-century winds of change. American precious metals had an impact there much like they had had on Spain nearly two hundred years earlier, discouraging domestic industry and making the country a way station for colonial treasure. Portugal's wealth flowed mostly to England, to pay for lightweight woolens, some ironware, and other manufactures for use at home or for re-export to Brazil, often in English ships. It also purchased British wheat, some from the mainland colonies. England had Portugal as an ally in the War of Spanish Succession and, afterwards, continued to dominate Portuguese trade through the factory at Lisbon.[3]

Spanish and Portuguese society in their organization, habits, and outlooks were ill-equipped to overtake Britain. Moreover, with entrenched traditional interests, empires rich in gold and silver, and an antiquated economic outlook that overvalued that wealth for its own sake, it was mid-century before either even seriously tried. Then, of course they failed, for it was England's game, evolved over time by combined public and private interests and thrusts, attitudes and policies, and by happenstance, and England was way ahead. Still, in Iberia new concepts simmered and some alterations took place.[4]

Spanish policy was until the 1760s concerned much more with domestic and

American trade and its revenues than with internal colonial arrangements. Until then, royal ministers, despite some early attempts to reform American *cabildos*, or town councils, and *audiencias*, which functioned as regional magistracies and advisory councils to governors and viceroys, probably paid even less attention to affairs in the American colonies than did other powers in theirs. Spain continued to govern within old structures what Spaniards still referred to as the Indies, and, unlike English practice, to levy internal taxes there. However, in the colonies as at home, from 1713 on chief administrators tended to be new sorts of men—usually of military background, proven administrative ability, and more bureaucratic temperament—loyal minions mirroring the ministers who sent them out. By the eighteenth century, Spanish America—largely self-sufficient in necessities, with most of its imports foreign luxuries and its greatest export specie—was dominated by entrenched American-born Spaniards, or creoles, who owned property, held offices, and had great influence upon royal authorities. And until mid-century, in the quest for funds and especially during wartime, the government reinforced this creole predominance by the selling of offices. Political ties to the peninsula were in the main administrative and bureaucratic.

Much foreign capital was invested in the trades with Iberia and its Americas from the late seventeenth century. French and English manufactures and merchants figured prominently in commerce with Latin America. Spain's was monopolized by Seville and, after 1717, by Cádiz, and was carried in both national and foreign ships. In American ports, such imports were delivered to specific Spanish merchants—members or agents of the powerful *consulados*, or merchants' guilds, of Lima and Mexico City. Since after Utrecht few Spanish merchant ships remained for fleet sailings, *registros*, or licensed individual—usually French—vessels, customary during the war, plied between Cádiz and the permissible American ports of Havana, Vera Cruz, and Porto Bello (Panama). Few Spanish fleets sailed to America, although the fleet system was reestablished in 1720. The British had the asiento. Samuel Pufendorf's remark, made earlier, remained valid: Spain kept the cow and the rest of Europe drank the milk.[5]

While in England at this time a dialogue went on between economic theory and practice, in Spain to a greater extent theory outran effective implementation, even though it was most notably elaborated in the form of specific recommendations by royal ministers. Thus, when a colonial reform program began in earnest in the 1760s, it invoked a sort of official, secular scripture. Moreover, it came both as an attempt to emulate English (and to a lesser extent French and Dutch) successes, and to implement ideas of earlier Spaniards who had also been influenced by the colonial theories and experience of those other nations.

Gerónimo de Uztáriz was among the earliest and most influential of Spanish Bourbon ministers who set down their views. While overseeing war and commerce, Uztáriz in 1724 had his *Teória y práctica del comercio y de la marina* published for private circulation.[6] He sought, within a tradition of national self-examination, to uncover the causes of Spanish decadence and to propose means to restore, augment, and conserve the monarchy. The means he saw as emulating French steps taken in favor of industry and commerce and England's great advantage, its trade with America. He overlooked the strong national agricultural base of both France and England. Avowedly an admirer of Jean Baptiste Colbert, Uztáriz, like that seventeenth-century French statesman, recommended that the state be more active in the economy as protector and participant, and he most urgently advised that it take specific steps toward a systematic organization of the navy and of overseas trade. Colbert's goal had been to make the nation a self-sufficient economic unit and to increase wealth from which came taxes. To this end, he had primarily emphasized expansion of navigation and commerce, accompanied by military and industrial growth and tariff war, with the government creating and administering manufacturing and performing functions of capital investment.

Uztáriz combined these goals with lessons from British and Dutch practice. He proposed expanding the merchant marine so that no money would go to foreign shipping. That Spanish ships would of necessity carry foreign goods concerned him less, although he did suggest higher duties on those manufactures and low or no taxes on national exports. He counseled lower import and export rates in peninsular trade with Spanish America and reduced fees on re-exports from Spain of American raw materials, arguing that these would discourage smuggling and encourage foreigners to buy in Spain its colonial products—cacao, hides, tobacco, and fine woods—and he took some steps in this direction. He also opposed chartered companies as impractical. At bottom, however, he retained the Spanish habit of identifying wealth with treasure; he wanted commercial and industrial growth in order to sell more, buy less, and thus ultimately to retain more specie. Uztáriz incidentally revealed national sensitivity to how the rest of Europe looked at Spain in his remark that the way the Spanish carried on commerce had depopulated and weakened the monarchy, "as is seen and publicized by other nations in their books." To eighteenth-century Spaniards, improving imperial trade was, ever more acutely, a matter of national honor.

Uztáriz strongly influenced his successor, Baltasar Patiño, who was chief royal minister from 1727 to 1736. Although preoccupied with the Italian ambitions and campaigns of the king and his queen, Elizabeth Farnese, Patiño found time and funds to create a navy, and he embarked upon a more rigorous colonial policy based on the principle that the colonies and their trade should ultimately supply Spain regularly with money. To this end, he sought peace with Britain, actively opposed British interlopers in America, and moved to counteract the drain of business and its revenues, including through the customary flouting of royal authority by American Spaniards.[7]

American merchants, members of the consulados of Mexico and Lima, had evolved effective systems of profiting at the expense of *flotistas*—the merchants and their agents involved in the convoyed fleet trade. When Patiño took charge, wealthy Mexican wholesalers were refusing to allow manipulation from Spain of markets they considered theirs and were struggling, successfully, with flotistas who were striving to channel all buying of overseas goods through a single fair and all shipping through themselves. In South America, the existing fair, at Porto Bello, "was simply being laid waste by disloyal subjects and foreign opportunists."[8] That is, smuggling flourished. Abetted by British participation in the fair through the asiento and "annual" ship, and with the collusion of the British navy, it throve in inlets and small ports around Porto Bello and at other coastal spots. Some of this sort of smuggling, as well as legal trade, funneled through the consulado of Lima, which continued, as the viceroy's protests to court attest, to outfox Spanish officials and traders.

There was more at stake in all this than the trade between Spain and America, for America was in turn a conduit for European commerce with Asia, as we have seen, and thus was part of a global network. Patiño now chose to charter privileged companies, including the successful Guipúzcoa, or Caracas Company (founded by Basque businessmen), principally in order to obtain greater advantage for nationals and the state from the profitable trade in Venezuelan cacao. At the same time, the government took other steps that helped to maintain Cádiz in its predominant role in American commerce. A royal order of 1729 approved the new statutes of the consulado of Cádiz, prohibited natives of the Indies from being consignees of cargoes, and stipulated that only Cádiz consulado members were to handle goods in America. Americans could not ship on their own accounts but only through agents sent out in the flotas from Spain. A decree of 1735 again forbade merchants of Peru and New Spain to ship on their accounts, or to send money back to Spain to purchase goods; they were to purchase through registered firms in Cádiz only. As a result of Mexican protests, the onset of war, and greater Spanish American trade with Britain, the order was modified in 1738, when Mexican merchants were permitted to ship to Spain, but to consign solely to Cádiz merchants. Decrees of 1742 and 1743 subsequently allowed American Spaniards to ship to other consignees, and in 1747 merchants of New Spain and Peru could remit funds and goods with "the absolute liberty they had before 1729," but the Cádiz consulado's interpretation, that that permission concerned only private goods, not merchandise, stuck through the 1750s, and in 1769 the crown again ordered no consignments by or to Americans.[9]

Thus, commercial policies inaugurated after Utrecht and translated into specific measures in the 1720s were based on the premise, still held to the 1790s, that it was the nature of colonies to trade exclusively with the metropolis, in accord with the law of nations.[10] And they corroborated another observation, that "the Spanish Bourbons sought to suppress smuggling almost as ardently as the Spanish Hapsburgs had sought to suppress heresy."[11] Moreover, these policies contributed to a conscious struggle between peninsulars and Americans for domination of American trade, and as Rafaél Antuñez y Acevedo pointed out, drew for the first time a legal distinction between Spaniards born in the peninsula and in America.[12] They went further—they assumed limits proper on American ability or capacity to be involved in commerce, and continued to rile merchants born in the Indies.

Patiño also began taking stock within America. He charged a Spanish officer there, Dionisio Alsedo y Herrera, who had been secretary to the viceroy of Peru and who held posts in the treasury and the consulado in Lima, with getting precise information about the English asentistas, their annual ship, and smuggling in general. And in 1735, he sent two very young men, Jorge Juan and Antonio de Ulloa, both trained in the select *Guardia Marina* and in navigation, mathematics, and astronomy, to South America. Their advertised mission was to assist French scientists in measuring an arc of the meridian at the equator; their private instructions were to report to the government on Spanish American defenses, resources, and conditions. They were, in effect, to combine the current vogue for scientific expeditions with the old Spanish institution of the *visita*, or tour of inspection. Juan was twenty-two years old, Ulloa nineteen. They were keen observers, and both their public and confidential reports on their nine years in the viceroyalty of Peru are still read. The *Voyage to South America*, published in five volumes in 1748, provided Europe with its first Spanish, and its most comprehensive, if bland, account of that region since the sixteenth century, while their private report, *Noticias Secretas*, somehow published in London in 1826, damned Spanish colonial administration and social relations. The *Voyage* appeared, soon after its Spanish edition, in German, French, Dutch, and English.[13]

In Peru, Juan and Ulloa, who helped prepare Lima's defenses against the expected arrival of Anson, had no trouble in seeing that other nations wanted the trade of the Indies. They scored the poor state of Pacific Coast defenses and the bad system of supply and exchange, and rightly feared not English territorial designs per se, but English seizing of ports for commerical and strategic enclaves. Foreign nations had been prevented from taking South American ports, the keys to control of the continent, they wrote, only by one another. They also found smuggling to be universal and considered it primarily a crime against the royal treasury. Reflecting attitudes common at court, they were interested in insuring returns from trade, destroying illicit commerce, protecting the royal prerogative, and combating subversion of the populace. And they advised Spain to abolish monopolies and fleets and send cheaper goods.

Juan and Ulloa were the first of a number of Spanish "scientific" envoys sent out by a government that recognized an advantageous interrelationship between an enlightened interest in the physical world, the developing of colonial natural resources, and the wealth and power of the state. Juan, an engineer, and Ulloa, of more humanistic bent and with a greater enthusiasm for the natural sciences, in their interests represented a major aspect of the enlightened component of enlightened despotism—the tendency to gather useful and universal knowledge to employ in state service. The first four of the five volumes of their *Voyage* were written by Ulloa and pervaded by the spirit and vocabulary of *las luces*. He began by proclaiming that "nature is admirable in all its works," that it had in fact "sowed the world with marvels." All culture and civilization, he assumed, rested on reflective knowledge of the workings of nature; the basis of education was "the study of the world and its parts." He respected "*el autor de la Naturaleza*" and scoffed at religiosity.[14]

Ulloa's interest in natural science and his cosmopolitan attitude were reinforced when, after being captured on his homeward voyage in 1746 by New Englanders holding Louisberg, he was sent to London, where he was received kindly by, and elected a fellow of, the British Royal Society. His outlook not only indicates that some well-connected Spaniards by mid-century understood and esteemed the new currents of thought and activity fashionable among enlightened Europeans, but also shows that they tended to combine these trends with traditional attitudes. Thus, Ulloa wrote, much as had the conquistador, Bernal Díaz del Castillo, that his "heart was inclined to try difficult things, animated by opposition."[15] It should be added that this thirst for adventure and novelty had also characterized royal officials in America in the early sixteenth century, men who had taken up the new reforming concepts of the time and vigorously employed them to curb the conquerors and add strength and luster to royal authority. They too were among Ulloa's intellectual and professional progenitors.[16]

Outstanding in his own time—and he had a long life—and thereafter as the prime exponent and disseminator of an eclectic philosophy, particularly Spanish, was Benito Jerónimo Feijoo (1676–1764), a Benedictine monk who avidly studied ideas current in England and France. Through his voluminous writings Feijoo became for Spaniards the adapter of the concepts of seventeenth-century rationalism and of the early eighteenth-century Enlightenment. No single Spanish writer of the century had more impact on his countrymen and on Spanish Americans. Feijoo, as one critic explained, was "part of the renovating anxiety of the period."[17] His avowed purpose was to comment critically, in the light of free reason and science, not only on all errors and superstitions believed in by Spaniards, but on everything—natural science, moral problems, pure speculation, economics, medicine, technics, philosophy, witchcraft, and the current state of Spanish life. At the same time, he remained faithful to Roman Catholicism, as did most enlightened Spaniards, and he said, in the Spanish tradition of espousing renewal rather than innovation, that he wanted to renovate the liberalism of those sixteenth-century scholars, Luis Vives and Melchor Cano, "to transform the spirit without attenuating the soul."[18]

Feijoo opposed mindless patriotism—he was influenced by the cosmopolitanism of the Enlightenment and declared himself a free citizen of the republic of letters—but he belonged within the tradition of commentators who called upon Spaniards to remedy the sad state of their country. He shared the interests of Uztáriz, Patiño, and others in reforming the economy, government, and Spanish cultural life, but Feijoo also stressed the need for agricultural reform and for a larger and more industrious populace. To these ends he advised Spaniards not only to cultivate the natural sciences as did other prosperous countries but to work harder, because—and here he attacked the traditional and predominating Spanish disdain for manual labor—work exalted mankind and produced wealth. Although often presented as disseminating French concepts and culture, Feijoo had reservations regarding the French and was less critically a follower of English thinkers whom, however, he encountered through French translations and commentators. Above all, he brought to the Spanish world the ideas of Francis Bacon and Isaac Newton.[19]

Feijoo was more sanguine concerning America's future than about Spain's. In his *Teatro crítico universal* (1726), he defended creoles and Indians against common Spanish slurs on their intellectual and physical capacities; in admiring Indian skills and military ability, he cited the opinions of earlier Spaniards in America, including Hernando Cortés. He found creole intellectual liveliness greater than peninsular, and decided that it matured earlier and lasted longer. He astutely concluded that Spanish Americans over thirty might appear dull to Europeans because they had come to neglect study, having lost hope of reward through pursuing it. His books, widely read in America through the century, incidentally nourished among creoles both American pride and American grievances.[20]

The war from 1739 to 1748 provided Spaniards with additional, concrete examples of Spain's mercantile and naval shortfallings, of its colonial weaknesses, and of British strength. It corroborated the equation of balance of power with balance of trade. It placed in relief the greater value of exporting national manufactures in national ships and gave further impetus to reform. The British were seen to disrupt sea trade and internal Spanish American commerce during the conflict. Spanish colonial officials were known to connive with British smugglers, many of them colonists. It was British control of the seas and destruction of Porto Bello, the site of the fair held following the arrival of Spanish fleets, which made the registro system not only again the norm but also signaled the demise of the fleets to South America when in 1740 trade resumed from Spain to Chile and Peru. The old Cádiz-affiliated merchants freighting the fleets suffered; new, more venturesome entrepreneurs profited. The sailings of the Caracas Company were halved, and the viceroyalty of New Granada, including the coasts of Colombia and Venezuela, was established in 1739 to facilitate Spanish American commerce and to better defenses and administration.[21]

Coming to high office during the war was Patiño's protégé, José Campillo y Cossío (or Cosío), minister of the treasury in 1741 and subsequently minister of marine, war, and the Indies, who went beyond his mentor and Uztáriz to take a more comprehensive view, to look at "the lamentable constitution" pertaining in the Spanish system of government, "a system equally political and economic," and, in 1743, to propose remedies for the situation in America. He sought, ultimately, "that all may be for the greater authority of our grand Monarch, for more benefit to the public good of his dominions and augment of his royal treasury." Campillo saw one nation's gain as another's loss, and his plan was based upon the conviction that it was necessary to consider commerce "as the fundamental principle of all the other interests of the monarchy, for it is the invigorator of agriculture, the arts and trade, and of manufactures and industry."[22] Commerce he compared to the circulation of the blood (falling back onto an old organic simile, long favored by Spanish political theorists); it sustained the body politic.[23] He proposed freedom of trade to America for all Spaniards, and advised reduced and reformed duties, specifically in order to combat contraband and to stimulate Spanish agriculture and manufactures and cheapen their price. He was certain increase in consumption would result, giving occupation to royal vassals, which would in turn stimulate industry, enrich the crown, and contribute to Spanish prosperity.[24] Under the existing system, he argued, the wealth of Spain's colonies went to foreigners, principally the British. His views, set down in manuscript during one struggle with Britain, would have great weight in determining the nature of the governmental reform program launched in the 1760s, during another.

Assuming the American dependencies to be held primarily for Spanish benefit, he compared the returns England and France received from their sugar islands to Spain's from its America, and concluded that "Spain suffers from the present system of trade with the Indies. . . one need only reflect upon how little is extracted from a possession of such size."[25] The old system he found literally made the worst of both worlds, for Spain got little from the colonies and misery was widespread in America. Instead, he proposed making the inhabitants of America, and particularly the Indians, "useful vassals," beneficial to the monarchy in expanding both American exports to Spain and American consumption of Spanish products. And, using the English example of what one scholar describes as "an agricultural export sector based on a free peasantry,"Campillo opposed the traffic in blacks and proposed economic growth through offering Indians incentives, including land, to move beyond their subsistence economies into broader imperial participation as producers and consumers. This suggestion rested upon his belief that self-interest is a strong goad to work, an idea only then coming into its own in the writings of British political economists. He was probably familiar with Hume's *Treatise on Human Nature,* and certainly saw economic and social benefit as intertwined with the principles of property and freedom. He also spoke of population as national wealth, and he paralleled the new British emphasis on principles of political economy. But at bottom he carried on the Spanish romance with specie: "True wealth consists in the products of the land and in the industry of men. . . . After them there is not in the world treasure equal that of the mines of our Indies."[26]

He suggested that Spain begin by getting rid of abuses within American government. Campillo advised a *visita general* by officials from Spain, and he wanted regional intendants installed to strengthen central control and to introduce reforms at local level. Within his program for freer trade, he advocated that merchants, as in England, be relatively unhampered by restrictions, and he recommended regular sailings from Spain to the Indies, with Havana as Spain's American emporium, and that more, but not all, Spanish ports, rather than just Cádiz, be opened to commerce with America. He explicitly opposed manufacturing in America, especially of textiles, and he warned, prophetically, that demand in the Indies and Spanish production must advance together or Spain's situation would worsen in respect to other powers.

After 1748, the *junta de comercio,* or board of trade, was revived and given real power, and it began to systematize a process of development within Spain, including abolishing local and regional imposts hindering commerce. Military commitments were cut back, funds poured in from the Indies, and in 1751 the very influential minister, the Marqués de Enseñada, called for the appointment of new, innovative men to high posts in government to balance traditionalists. By then, Catalonia had grown in population, agriculture, commerce, and manufacturing, despite the war and with the assistance of the profitable trade in Venezuelan cacao and in Cuban rum, sugar, and tobacco. A small but prosperous Barcelona bourgeoisie, a social class of great merchants and shipowners, had emerged by the 1730s with profits from international commerce. The English trade remained most important, and the commercial treaty of 1667, reinvigorated with Utrecht, was again renewed in 1750. Although Spain at mid-century still lacked many of the financial mechanisms, incorporated companies, joint-stock operations, and credit systems of England, France, and Holland, as well as the French and especially English emphasis on promoting manufactures and their export, mercantile arrangements were shifting and broadening, Jośe de Carvajal y Lancaster, then chief minister, could write in 1748, "Whether Cádiz flourishes or not is not of primary interest to His Catholic Majesty."[27]

Even so, and although the fleets to South America had ceased sailing with the war, those to Mexico went only sporadically, and the crown now looked to chartered companies to revive American commerce, the Cádiz monopolists and their domination of American shipping endured. The Caracas Company, its Basque investors, and their associates, the Five Guilds of Madrid—who were in charge of distributing its cacao—were also successful. The Company enjoyed ministerial favor and investments guaranteed by the government, despite widespread colonial displeasure with its practices. Thus, in 1748 when a large-scale revolt erupted in Venezuela against its expanding monopoly on cacao, the authorities restored order and dealt harshly with rebel leaders. In 1752, however, Americans did gain a concession of sorts in being allowed to hold Company stock.[28]

Occasioned by this revolt, debate in government circles during 1750-51 on whether or not to reinstate the Company in its South American operations shed light on then-current official economic attitudes. Among the opinions presented to the court were some favorable to "free trade" with the Indies—that is, as it was understood also in England, without chartered companies but among nationals only. One held that other European nations were abolishing such companies, that possession of America was rooted not in this sort of restricted commerce but in inhabitants' "love for the king."[29] Another cited with approval the British example of constant concessions to New England as a guide in quieting disturbances. Yet, the realistic issue then was only the nature and extent of Spanish monopolies, and the minister of the Indies, the Marqués de Enseñada, and the king heeded advice to retain the Company, especially arguments that the alternative was loss of royal prestige and probably sedition in America.

Enseñada, Carvajal, and, from 1754, Ricardo Wall were chief ministers during these interwar years. Carvajal, even more devoted than his predecessors to building Spain through developing its active, exclusive trade with the Indies, proposed chartered companies for each American region. "America," he ex-

plained, "is the soul of our greatness";[30] and elsewhere, using the old organic
analogy, "commerce is the blood of a state."[31] He urged, in order to maintain the
empire, that Spain not try to recover what had been lost in America but instead "let
go the old and turn toward *lo moderno*."[32] Proud of his descent from John of
Gaunt, recognizing British power and England as Spain's best market for domestic
produce and so for earnings, Carvajal concluded that alliance with Britain was
preferable, that "one expensive friend was better than three robbers."[33] England,
he argued, did not want more territory in the New World and, too optimistically,
he looked forward to the British navy protecting Spain's colonies during the
coming years of internal reform and development of their resources. Yet he was,
with good cause, wary of the activities of Englishmen and their representatives
domiciled in Spanish America. In 1748 he wrote to his protégé, Wall, that the
asiento had caused great damage by competing with goods carried by registered
vessels and fleets: "As to contraband, there is no limit to it. . . it is a muffled file,
wearing away the trade of Spain."[34]

Carvajal dreamed, rather illogically, of British governmental assistance in
combating British commercial encroachment in Spanish America. Wall, who
succeeded him, also saw advantage in warm relations with England, but they were
cooled by the Spanish dispute with Britons and Anglo-Americans logwooding on
the Yucatán peninsula and in Central America—a continuing irritant, to be a cause
for Spain joining France against England in 1761. Both Carvajal and Wall
deliberately wooed Britain in order, with English help, to build up the armed
forces they foresaw necessary for a future, inevitable maritime war; but in
pursuing this policy they neglected traditional considerations of maintaining
equilibrium in America, taking too little alarm when England and France went to
war, until it was too late.[35]

Portugal in 1750 got a new king, the lackluster José I and, after 1755, a chief
minister, and soon national dictator, Sebastião José de Carvalho e Melo, who in
1770 became the Marqués do Pombal, and was *the* power until 1777. Stanley
Payne has succinctly summed up his regime: "There has been much debate over
the relative 'enlightenment' of Pombal's government, but of its despotism there
was never any doubt. It was more authoritarian than any of its contemporaries in
western and central Europe, not excluding the Prussia of Frederick the Great."[36]

Carvalho e Melo, of country gentry, or petty fidalgo, background, as an aspiring
bureaucrat was envoy to the Court of Saint James from 1740 to 1744. In London,
although he smarted under English deprecation of other, visiting Portuguese, and
although he never learned English, he was greatly impressed by British prosperity,
naval strength, and superiority in trade. To learn their causes he avidly read
English books, especially the early political economists, and state papers and
documents, all in French translation; he knew, too, the writings of Sully and
Colbert. Then, moving on to Vienna, he acquired a wealthy and well-placed wife
and returned home to new status and honors.[37]

As Portuguese prosperity receded with dwindling Brazilian output of gold, and
as the sugar industry suffered from English and French competition, Melo sought a

lessened dependence on Britain—by undercutting the hold of the English factory at Lisbon on the empire's finance, consumption of luxury goods, exports, and carrying trade. But attributing British prosperity too largely to Portugal's Brazilian gold, he oversimplified England's reliance on that commodity and thus both England's need of Portugal and the importance of bullion. He sponsored chartered companies for Portugal and for Brazil, where he wanted to revive production of gold and profit from marketable exports. To these ends, he paid a good deal of attention to increasing the Brazilian population: He wanted more immigration there, including of Africans as slave labor, favored European-Indian marriages, and averred that "the power and wealth of all countries consists principally in the number and multiplication of people."[38] He also counted on Portuguese Americans and the relatively few civil servants in Brazil to expand an economy already geared to export.

In 1755, he chartered the state-run company of Pará-Maranhão, in order to control the trade of the Amazon region, and in 1759 licensed that of Paraíba-Pernambuco, principally in order to manage and increase profit on sugar exports. His program included wresting control of much of the labor and commerce in northern Brazil from the Jesuits. He saw that religious order as depriving the state of huge revenues; clearly it paid no taxes, held vast numbers of Indians in mission villages *(aldeias)*, owned cattle ranches, and engaged in much legal and illegal trade, including with interloping itinerant traders, *comisarios volantes*, in a network with the English. In the south, Jesuits, in the years 1754-56, were prodding the resident Guaranís to armed resistance against a combined force of Spanish and Portuguese sent to impose the terms of the Treaty of Madrid (1750), which ceded Colônia to the Spanish in exchange for Portuguese jurisdiction over the land and peoples of seven missions east of the Uruguay River in Rio Grande do Sul.

In 1756, Melo abolished the Society's temporal control of mission villages in Maranhão, declaring Indians liberated. The following year he launched a program of Indian acculturation and integration into the national economy, appointing directors to oversee trade with Indian communities with the rationale that liberty of trade is the very soul of commerce. The directors cornered Indian commerce and labor, became petty tyrants, and in Pará profited from exports of cacao and drugs in league with itinerant traders, much as had the Jesuits.[39] Interloping Portuguese merchants were ordered out of Brazil, although some managed to stay, and, in 1759, the Society of Jesus was expelled from the Portuguese empire and its property confiscated by the state, Melo having convinced the king that Jesuits were involved in an attempt at regicide.[40] Their commercial successors in Portugal's America, the chartered companies, like the Spanish Caracas Company, did stimulate legitimate colonial exports, decrease contraband, and augment royal revenues. In addition, between 1757 and 1777 over five thousand blacks were carried into Pará and Maranhão, most of them from Portuguese Guinea, and between 1760 and 1775 over thirty thousand of them were brought from West Africa into the sugar area of Pernambuco-Paraíba. It has been estimated that in 1700 Brazil had a population of three hundred thousand, and that by 1800 there were three million people, half of them slaves.[41]

Portugal, forced into the Seven Years' War by Spanish invasion in 1762, did poorly; Melo had neglected the army. Extricated by peace in 1763, it regained Colônia, but Melo retained a dread of British seizure of Portuguese territory in America—in 1761, the Spanish minister to London had written Wall that Melo in conversation mentioned the English conquests in North America and his fears for the Iberian colonies[42]—and at the war's end he briefly talked to the Spanish about making common cause. Yet he realized that the combined French and Spanish threat to Brazil was the more probable one; the British alliance held. But in 1766, the fleets to Río de Janeiro and Bahia were abolished and administration within Brazil received more vigorous attention. For a decade after his arrival in Brazil in 1769, its viceroy, the Marqués de Lavradio, under whom Brazil was unified administratively (from 1772), sponsored development of new products for export and promoted some manufacturing. Brazilian authorities under Melo also worked to reorganize the military and fiscal systems, to unify the provinces, and to involve local leaders in their administration.

By the late 1760s, however, gold and sugar exports had fallen further, and so had imports from Britain. Melo had instituted a *junta do comercio* in Lisbon in 1756 to supersede a private guild in overseeing trade with Brazil. Made up of wealthy, mercantile, national associates, it was enlarged in the mid-1760s and, spurred by depression and the need for import substitutes, it established or expanded a number of Portuguese factories under state supervision. Primarily, and anachronistically, it tried to replicate luxury imports, principally silks. Only a few of the plants did at all well.

By the early 1770s, the greatest benefits from innovations on both sides of the Atlantic adhered to a small coterie of family, clients, and merchants around Melo, who had become the Marqués do Pombal. He then instituted some additional reforms. He changed, after 250 years, the curriculum at the University of Coimbra, putting new emphasis on useful knowledge—on physical and natural sciences, law, mathematics, and medicine. He curbed the Inquisition (directed by the state in the 1760s), prohibited persecution of New Christians (a euphemism for Jewish background), and between 1771 and 1773 he abolished slavery in Portugal, largely in order to divert blacks to Brazil as field hands and miners of gold. Free discussion of enlightened topics and politics was suppressed in Portugal, and a Board of Censors was set up in 1768. Government jails held hundreds of political prisoners. In a contracting economic situation, Pombal was hated and widely opposed for his highhanded and repressive methods, his coterie, and for disruption of customary usages. He fell in 1777 with the death of the king.[43]

Pombal's policies had been instituted a decade before somewhat similar reforms in Spain and Spanish America, but his put far less emphasis on developing a navy and promoting private industries, and less, too, on developing peninsular agriculture for internal consumption. Portugal then relied instead largely on wheat from British North America. There was no group of able young ministers advising the Portuguese crown; Pombal discouraged all potential competitors. In Portugal it was Pombal and the state. Yet, he appears to have emulated the British to a greater extent than did Spain in colonial affairs, and even to have gone beyond England in relying more heavily on colonials to administer, defend, and develop their relatively sparsely settled country. And in Brazil he did not inhibit manufacturing to the extent forbidden in either British or Spanish colonies because it competed with metropolitan production or with the carrying trade profiting the state. There was little afoot in Portugal with which to compete. But he did curb the raising of agricultural products analogous to those exported from Portugal, notably wine and olive oil.

In 1776, his last year in power, Pombal ordered an attack on Spanish La Plata. The Portuguese again did poorly, and this circumstance heartened the victorious Spanish to join France against Britain. In 1776, too, he closed Portugal's ports to the ships of the Anglo-American insurgents in order now to court English support for Brazilian expansion. English response was small; the greatest immediate result was retaliatory attacks by North American privateers.[44]

Like Pombal, Charles III of Spain thought British commercial dominance was due largely to greater monetary wealth and to favorable treaty provisions, rather than, as it was, to superior capital, finance, technology, and resources, and to successful private and public cooperation in developing them. Upon coming to the throne in 1759, Charles found that the powerful merchant guild of Cádiz was closely linked to English interests and engaged largely in re-exporting British wares. He concluded that among Spain's greatest problems were British treaties, smugglers and interlopers, and British logwood settlements; and he saw that the French loss of Quebec to England in that same year left Spanish Florida and Mexico virtually defenseless. In 1760, in order to compete with Britain in markets within the Spanish empire, he gave great attention to stimulating Spanish manufacturing and to revising the revenue systems, trading monopolies, and laws affecting trade with America. The following year, concerned with the equilibrium of power in America that he thought had been established at Utrecht, and believing that going to war would end the Spanish commercial treaties with England, he reversed Spanish policy of the 1750s in signing a (third) family compact with France. He entered the war against England in alliance with France and placed an embargo on British goods; but since English merchants controlled the largest Spanish wholesale houses and the British navy the sea, enforcement of the embargo was weak and British trade continued.[45]

Before the war's end, the government had inaugurated a campaign against contraband and had begun planning to reorganize administration and the economy in America. The British capture of Havana and Manila in 1762 illuminated the weakness of Spanish colonial fortifications and land and sea forces, and demonstrated what Britain's more open system of trade could do for commerce and commercial agriculture. By then, the Spanish, whose American dependencies were certain to neighbor those of England, and who were well aware of the British interest in commercial expansion in America, overestimated the British desire for more territory there (although probably not that of British North Americans). Reports through the 1760s of British spies looking for bases on American coasts from which to free the Spanish colonies, of the English fomenting creole plots for independence, of expanding British logwooding activities, and of expeditions to the Falklands in 1764 and 1765, did nothing to change Spanish minds. The subsequent loss of Florida, which had guarded the Gulf of Mexico, and compensation for it with Louisiana, considered by Spain inadequate since its strategic value was less and its large sprawl a headache, served to heighten the government's making a priority of reform in America.

Defeat—and royal advisors—had pointed out to the king England's strength and its internal structural bases, so that after 1763 royal policy took on a more urgent, systematic quality. It was now based on awareness of Spanish deficiencies— wealth, capital, raw materials, and skills—and of the resistance of vested interests to change. From then on, with an eye on English reactions and by adapting England's own methods, Spain attempted to wage economic warfare against Britain. America figured as importantly in that campaign as in the continuing, and intermeshing, quest for Spanish economic wellbeing.

Before the war ended, a committee had begun, on royal order, to draw up a plan of reform for the Indies. Its members were guided by the proposals of Bernardo Ward, which were written down after his tour of Europe from 1750 to 1754, circulated in manuscript, and subsequently published in 1779 as *Proyecto económico*. The first part concerned the peninsula. The second, Ward's suggestions for America, repeated word for word Campillo's *Nuevo Systema,* and it was this that was put into effect.[46]

Two royal ministers in particular, Joseph Moñino, later Conde de Floridablanca, and Pedro Rodríguez de Campomanes, subsequently Conde de Campomanes, proved outstanding in advancing not only their own careers but also regalism and the royal program. They were among those royal advisors and ministers who were new men, *manteistas,* lesser aristocracy educated not, as was traditional, in the *colegios mayores* of the Jesuits, but instead in the less prestigious universities. They were men brimming over with ambition channelled into devotion to king and state, men who were determined to overcome the now acutely embarrassing and obviously dangerous Spanish decrepitude, and who were certain that to do so they needed primarily to remove the obstacles to progress clamped upon Spain and its America by custom and accretion. They built upon the criticisms and sentiments expressed by Feijoo, earlier *proyectistas,* Campillo, and Ward; and, as all of them had been, were also strongly influenced by economic policies advanced in other European countries and particularly in England. Under these people during the 1760s and 1770s, a high moral and intellectual tone infused a series of proposals, some of them translated into reform measures directed to Spain, some to Spanish relations with America, and some to reform within Spanish America.

Their program for Spain was comprehensive and centered on reforming agriculture, trade, the church, education, and attitudes. As Barbara and Stanley Stein explain, "A hierarchical society was to be made functionally efficient by increasing its productive classes, encouraging entrepreneurial elements, reducing ecclesiastical and aristocratic sectors while incorporating the upper nobility into the true service of the state."[47] And as another historian put it, although the treasury was drained by war, "the state was rich in intentions and projects."[48] Moreover, by 1758 the concept of political economy, to which Campillo had referred a bit obliquely in the previous decade, was being employed in Spain. In the 1760s, its principles were invoked and more systematically invested in plans to expand and better domestic agricultural production and distribution and to break down internal barriers to free commerce. Campomanes's tract of 1764, which advocated abolishing taxes on the domestic trade in grain, was followed by a royal pragmatic to that effect. Pablo de Olavide, a friend of Campomanes and fellow thinker, as intendant of Seville made an ambitious but unsuccessful attempt to found new, model agricultural towns with foreign though Catholic settlers in the Sierras Morenas. Olavide, an enthusiast of enlightened culture, English and French, and of progress, and a playwright given to holding *tertulias,* or salons, in his house, was a Peruvian creole; the nephew of a viceroy, he had been a magistrate in Lima.[49]

Although agricultural reform was impeded by bad weather, poor crops, and the opposition of powerful landed interests—so that an incidental result was the import of large shipments of grain from England's North America—within Spain there was some advance in breaking down regional and local commercial barriers. Some new roads and easing of taxes helped. Manufacturing, notably of cotton textiles, expanded in Catalonia, even though a royal decree in 1760 removed protection from cotton goods (until revoked in 1770); and Catalans pushed for growing cotton in America.[50] The newly assertive crown, its ministers, and some enlightened prelates now dusted off concepts of divine monarchy in order to gain greater state control over the Spanish church. From 1761 on, Charles clashed with the papacy concerning the boundaries of church and state authority. Although opposition within Spain was strong, the crown continued to whittle away at church power and prerogatives, and from 1768 Charles pressed his authority over the Inquisition. The contest had little effect on faith among the Spanish populace, but in America did lead to appointments of ultraregalist high clergy, and had some other results.

As in Portugal and France, regalists found a symbol of ultramontane and traditional papal power, and even of superstition—that quality so abhorred by the Enlightenment—in the Jesuits. Although in practice the Order was far from being simply pro-papacy and anti-crown, to royal ministers it did represent a faction allied with their rivals at court—the older, higher, and mostly Castilian and Andalusian nobility. When, after Spain's losses and British supremacy at sea during 1761-63, a delay in shipping American bullion abetted inflation from 1763 to 1765 and then bad harvests occurred in 1765-66, riots, mostly for cheaper bread, ensued in Madrid and the provinces. The lower classes blamed Charles' Italian minister, Squilache, for the Spanish defeat, for the poor grain supply, and for a decree prohibiting popular Spanish dress; and there is evidence that vested interests opposed to new policies backed the crowd. Prodded by Campomanes and Manuel de Roda, the king blamed the Jesuits, and the Order was expelled from Spain and its America.[51]

It has never been ascertained to what extent the Jesuits' prestige and power in

Spanish higher education contributed to their removal, but Campomanes in particular put great emphasis on ridding Spain of traditional scholastic education and on the importance of implanting a new mentality, one devoted to creating attitudes associated with enlightened and liberal principles. From 1767, the old Jesuit schools in Spain and its America were turned into, or replaced by, centers of new, usually more secular and practical, education. The most prestigious of them in the peninsula was placed under the direction of Jorge Juan, that staunch royal servant and son of the Enlightenment. With the Jesuits gone, the government for the first time took direct charge of Spanish education. "The new evangel," as it has been properly described, proclaimed more secular and useful education and culture as patriotic principles and instruments for the regeneration of Spain.[52] Royal ordinances established procedures for filling university chairs and stipulated texts and new courses of study emphasizing civil and natural law and mathematics; political economy was to be taught within law, the traditional training ground for government position. Olavide, whose plan inspired these educational reforms, envisioned universities as "the workshops forming men who will serve the state by instructing and directing the masses." Teachers should loyally defend regalism and be rich in useful knowledge, not sophisms *(sofistiquerías),* which wasted time and tired the head. And in the same spirit, Campomanes, the apostle of technological and professional education, regretted that, although the invention of the sewing needle was more useful to mankind than the logic of Aristotle, there were more commentaries on Aristotle in Spain than makers of needles.[53]

Instrumental in augmenting the circulation of books in Spain and its America was a royal order of 1762, suppressing the tax on their sale because, it stated, the king was interested in spreading knowledge and because, since "liberty in all commerce [is] the mother of abundance, it should be also in that of books, and it is not just that not having any tax for foreigners it should be only the Spanish who suffer through their own laws."[54] The tax on "necessary"—that is, text—books was to continue. Periodicals, too, became more popular, and some of those published in Madrid from 1763 on apprised Spaniards and Spanish Americans of rebellion developing in Anglo-America. Reported in detail was the interplay between British innovations and colonial resistance, even to faithfully transcribing American arguments against what the colonies perceived as British despotism.[55]

Closely related was state sponsorship of regional societies combining economic and patriotic purpose, following the success of the initial Basque *Amigos del País.* Founded in 1764, it was modeled on the Royal Society of London and attracted "newly-titled heirs to commercial fortunes made in the purchase of colonial staples."[56] These clubs were meant to gain support for the new ideas and programs of the state. They were to foster national patriotism and to bring the aristocracy within the reform movement as allies at the regional level. They were to disseminate useful knowledge chiefly in order to spur regional economies through developing agriculture and skilled labor. The economic societies were expected to alter outlooks as well as to promote material advance, in accord with the enlightened emphasis on the importance of outlook, which was to be inculcated through education and was thought to be synonymous with rational common sense. As "active agents of progress" directed by both ecclesiastical and lay public leaders, real and aspiring, the economic and patriotic societies throughout the Spanish empire represented a new sort of secular, aristocratic voluntary association devoted to immediate civic and state betterment. They were the new missions of the eighteenth century. Their tone was set by the founder of the Basque society, the Conde de Peñaflorida, who exhorted his colleagues in 1765: "My friends, love your native land, love your common glory, love man, and finally show yourselves worthy friends of the Country and worthy friends of Humanity."[57]

That year, too, the crown took two decisive steps to implement new policies in America. Charles, advised by his ministers that Seville and Cádiz could not adequately supply America, that when they did it was with lightly taxed re-exports, that, in fact, the Spanish islands in the Caribbean were largely provisioned by foreigners anyway, and hoping to decrease smuggling and increase royal rents, enacted what is often referred to as the free trade decree of 1765. Nine Spanish ports were permitted in the next few years to trade with Cuba, Santo Domingo, Trinidad, and Margarita, and duties were lowered on ships and imports in order to make that commerce competitive with foreign trade.[58] Earlier, immediately after the war, Spanish army units had been sent to Mexico and a *visitador*, General O'Reilly, to Cuba, where the administration was reformed and in 1764 placed under an intendant, the first in America.[59] Then, in 1765, José de Gálvez, a French protégé and *manteista,* went out as *visitador* to New Spain, or Mexico, to institute reforms designed to better defense, governmental efficiency, Spanish markets, and royal revenues—and to do so in part by making Mexico itself more prosperous.

The program Gálvez was to inaugurate in Mexico would set a precedent for South America; and, from the outset, his paramount interest was Spain. Before his appointment, he had cited Colbert's dictum that "protection and liberty are the two principal bases of commerce," in referring to Spain's trade with its America (although Colbert had used those terms in relation to French domestic exchange), and his focus remained Spanish power and wealth.[60] His formal instructions from the king was concerned at bottom with the *real hacienda* or royal treasury receipts, and ways to stimulate them. He was to give special attention to promoting mining and collecting mine revenues and to impeding all sorts of smuggling. An ambitious civil servant, Gálvez was, during his six years in Mexico, always vigorously supported by Campomanes, Moniño, and, after 1766, the viceroy and the military commander there. He carried out his assignment so well that in 1776 he became Minister of the Indies.[61] During his first three years in New Spain, he was its real ruler, then afterwards closely associated with the new viceroy, the ultraregalist Marqués de Croix. During those years, he reformed the financial administration of the central provinces, particularly by four measures: replacing the farm system for state taxes with direct administration, increasing the efficiency of tax collection from the Indians, raising the caliber of customs officials, and reforming and

increasing internal and external customs houses. To raise revenue, he also
rigorously imposed new state monopolies, the most important on tobacco. He
encouraged raising primary products for export and all production not competing
with Spanish for the domestic market. He campaigned against hostile frontier
Indians and extended boundaries up the California coast in order to forestall British
and Russian claims there; from bases in the old Jesuit missions in Lower California
he sent out eighty-five expeditions. A line of Franciscan missions was strung up
the coast, and San Francisco Bay was settled in 1775.

To the same ends, he consciously changed relationships within Mexican
society, demoting and undercutting old privileged groups—the clergy, the guilds,
including the consulado of Mexico (affiliated with Cádiz), and the creole
aristocracy—and promoting new ones: a state bureaucracy, the army, and more
competitive and energetic entrepreneurs, merchants and mineowners, some of
whom were granted titles. He also implemented the program to replace Americans
with peninsular Spaniards in public office, a process that reached its height
between 1776 and 1777. Gálvez was predisposed to employ and prefer his
countrymen from Málaga and the numerous Basque emigrants as well. These were
men often imbued with an ethic of hard work and getting ahead, with a commercial
bent, a high moral tone, and liberal notions—that is, with a cast of mind
commending them to leading ministers and the king. Much of his reform program
was a putting into force of Campillo's and Ward's suggestions; it included the plan
to increase Indian purchasing power and production and thus Spanish exports,
markets, and tax receipts.[62] The program was accompanied by intensified attempts, begun in the 1750s, to get Indians to speak Spanish and dress in European
style, and to abolish the old policy of segregating Indian communities. That
policy, instituted in the sixteenth century to keep them from contact with Spaniards
of less probity than the friars, was now viewed as an obstacle to making them
useful vassals. In 1767, one accusation against the Jesuits in Spanish America, as
it had been in Brazil, was their maintenance of separate, sequestered Indian
communities.[63] In sum, as the foremost commentator on his visita concluded,
Gálvez's reforms were "simply an enforcement of more rigid adherence to the
paramount interest of the mother country in the productive wealth of New Spain.
The burden of the upkeep of the empire was more firmly yoked upon the neck of
the most prosperous colony."[64]

The crown took other steps to reconquer America in the 1760s. Since the War of
Spanish Succession, Bourbon rulers had continued the wartime practice of
appointing military men to top regional posts in America. Their caliber improved
and their military aspect intensified after 1763. Wrote the British Ambassador:
"They are sending the very ablest officers they have to that part of the world."[65]
These officials were also usually ultraregalist proponents of court attitudes and
advocates of the Spanish blend of enlightenment and political economy. The
viceregal courts emulated that of Madrid. The viceroys held tertulias for eminent
people and they employed like-minded men of lower gentry background. And very
similar to the new royal officials in outlook and ability were the high colonial

clergy appointed in the 1760s, particularly to Mexico, that showcase of reform, Spain's richest source of silver, and, since 1763, an area greatly exposed to Britain and it's America.[66]

As in Spain, American education became more secular after the expulsion of the Jesuits. In 1767, the completely lay and private Mexican *Colegio de las Vizcainas* opened and others followed, with a new emphasis on natural and exact sciences. Although in the university and some of the schools of the religious orders old methods largely held sway, Gálvez and other officials continued to sponsor studies and institutions training Americans for work useful to developing and exploiting natural resources, including population.[67]

At the same time, in their zeal for improvement, these new men, who were from non-Castilian Spain and lacked a traditional aristocratic education, were unaware of the true tensile strength of customary colonial bonds and of their real importance to upholding central authority. Rather, to Gálvez in particular, the ideological ties of subjects, or vassals—as royal decrees and official writings designated them interchangeably—in Spanish America to crown and metropolis seemed nebulous, passive, and not conducive to securing participation in national development. He and other royal ministers believed that passive subjects must be turned into active economic collaborators in making the colonies agents of Spain's resurgence. Indeed, here, if anywhere, was the revolutionary content of the Bourbon reform program.

Campomanes exemplified the new viewpoint in his attitude not only toward the need for a new mentality but also toward Spanish history and tradition. Historical explanations permeated his opinions and projects and superseded older rationales grounded in religion and metaphysics. Like earlier Spanish writers, he justified reform with impressive Spanish precedent. He and other enlightened Spaniards insisted Spain had fallen from the glory and prosperity of the Gothic period—one of northern Spanish domination—into the present, prevailing decadence, a Habsburg legacy. Their argument ran thusly: Loss of territories in the War of Spanish Succession had helped buck the trend and had strengthened Spain, a great nation and one now more powerful for having fewer appendages. Since then, kings had abandoned the chimerical illusion of a universal empire and a policy of conquest, and had concentrated on promoting national enlightenment and the national economy. With the intellectual rebirth inspired by Feijoo, the introduction of an enlightened spirit, new philosophical systems, and new awareness of science, the nation had awakened (a key concept) from its lethargy and was participating in the general progress of humanity through the wise direction of its government. The nobles were newly useful; the populace was augmented; agriculture, industry, commerce, and navigation were benefited; and Spain was marching toward eventual general happiness.[68]

Integral to this point of view was a new, composite imperial—termed national—theory. Spain and its colonies were to be viewed as a single, corporate entity, synonymous with a mystical concept of the nation-state. Its head and *motor* was the monarch, who held authority from God and who was the core and visible symbol of state power. His subjects owed him unconditional obedience. The nation-state was at once a great family and the defender of its members. Campomanes and Moniño explicitly fit the colonies within this version of Spain as a single, tightly unified nation. In their writings, both of them spoke of colonies as natural phenomena, as the extension of peoples, and as of two general types, military and mercantile. The mercantile, including those of England and Holland, were estimable; the military, to which they thought Spanish colonies had been similar, were odious. Yet, religious principles and "suavity of laws" had made Spanish domination acceptable to colonials, and Spaniards had brought to America civilization and religion. Spain had erred in economic policies, however. A new colonial policy should right matters.

When Campomanes and Moniño were called into an extraordinary council meeting in 1768 to discuss colonial unrest following the expulsion of the Jesuits and rumors of a widespread plot to rise against the king (its leaders were reported to be in communication with "a maritime nation" to which they promised exclusive trade), these Spanish ministers first explained that the British colonies, in calling attention to poor treatment by the English government and terming its actions despotic, were providing yet a further bad example and impetus to resistance to Spanish Americans, then declared that the present Spanish program too was failing to "make the colonies want or love the nation."[69] Colonials must see their interests as united to those of the mother country. They should feel a part of "un solo cuerpo de nación," composing with Spain "the same state and monarchy." And this nation, they went on, could best be held together by a love aroused through more commercial interchange. As a major remedy for both Spanish decadence and colonial disaffection they proposed freer trade between Spain and its America.

Rather naively, they found it proper that Spanish Americans, as individuals of the same nation, should satisfy their economic bent, yet with complementary activities and with Spain able to show a favorable balance in trading with them. (Campomanes and Moniño did support direct trade between American ports, in private hands and at lower duties, in order to compete with contraband and to spur internal commerce and exchange with the Indians.)[70]

These opinions, and policy in line with them, both seriously misjudged Americans and, in effect, superimposed a new ideology of empire and nation as coterminous upon the traditional concept of imperial Spain. The old notion, articulated in the sixteenth century (under the Habsburg Charles V) and developed in law, assumed a Spanish America subdivided into kingdoms and incorporated into the royal patrimony or monarchy, as were the peninsular kingdoms. Although the idea of America as composed of kingdoms had dimmed, its inhabitants still considered themselves bound to the monarchy and the faith, but not otherwise politically attached, to the peninsula and its populace. Royal ministers, in taking as their point of departure later Habsburg notions of American dominions as colonies, thereby—perhaps unwittingly—foreswore concepts of imperial attachment long cherished by propertied Spanish Americans, those creoles who claimed to be heirs of the Spanish conquerors, and as such entitled to dominate America and its other peoples. While ministers believed they were offering colonists a greater share in the imperial nation-state, such creoles saw the new official outlook as a rejection of their privileged and relatively autonomous stature, which was sanctioned by custom and law. Thus, as Britain's government altered its attitude toward America so, partly in response, did Spain's. However, the British attempted to define terms of empire explicitly for the first time, while Spaniards put aside the old concept of Spanish empire, embodied in law and hallowed in tradition, and even the idea of empire itself, to propose a rather romantic vision of a nation spanning the Atlantic, a view even more contrary than was England's to colonial usages and beliefs.

Through the 1770s, the Spanish government continued its reform program at home and in Spanish America along general lines established during the 1760s. And among Spaniards of means, the critical spirit and a faith in progress through economic development became more fashionable. To know something of natural law, to read gazettes and foreign books, belong to learned societies, attend tertulias, make the grand tour of Europe, and to have one's children educated abroad, were all the thing to do. French cultural fashions were in vogue; French authors and language chic; yet, at a more substantial level, educated Spaniards were aware of and admired British concepts and, particularly, British economic arrangements. In opposition to all this, however, and remaining predominant, was a potent traditional element in society, its strongholds the clergy, the nobility, and the people. Of broad change there was little. It was, in fact, in the 1770s that the word *cacique,* previously an American term signifying a petty and oppressive chieftain, began to be used in Spain for district leaders and powerful landlords, and that a new elite of landed aristocrats emerged. This group included landholding farmers and middle-class investors in land. Except in Catalonia, most money made in trade went into land and urban property, and little into productive reinvestment. In the last analysis, the reforms of Charles III, including those in America, largely profited the entrenched landed proprietors of Spain.[71]

The decade did see more discussion in print of agricultural and industrial problems, and of the Spanish state of mind, by its two foremost political economists and social commentators, Campomanes and his younger colleague, Gaspar Melchor de Jovellanos. Campomanes published tracts on *industria popular*—that is, on stimulating manual labor, crafts, and the will to work—and on popular education (with much the same goals in mind). Like Hutcheson, Adam Smith, and others, he assumed the existence of a self-regulating natural order and the operating of human instincts implanted by a benign Providence. The problem was to remove the blocks, and especially to develop attitudes conducive to getting Spaniards to value hard work. Accordingly, he and other reformers reinterpreted the old notion of honor, associated with aristocratic values, attaching it to the newer intermeshing of work and public service; and they gave a high priority to public virtue in order to reconcile the idea of nobility held by so many Spaniards, of *hidalguía,* with that of patriotic endeavor. He was the principal promoter of economic societies, imbued with this outlook; in a circular of 1774 he recommended, with a good deal of success, that authorities establish them locally. His colonial policy was manifest in his support of Gálvez and in his being responsible for the publication of Ward's book in 1779.[72]

Jovellanos, who was in his thirties and had been influenced by Olavide and Campomanes, during that decade reflected in his writings the high tide in Spain of enlightened optimism and liberal faith in social progress through material advance. He expressed these ideas through a vocabulary generously laced with *liberty, utility, common good,* and other favorite phrases of the economically oriented—terms that in Anglo-America were taking on a highly political connotation. Political economy he called "the science of the citizen and the patriot." Comfortable with the presuppositions of the Enlightenment, political economy, and nascent liberalism, he attempted to make use of many of them in relation to specific Spanish problems, but always from the point of view of the state—and most often he cited them as general rules to which current problems must for the moment be excepted. Thus, in a *dictamen* of 1774 he advocated commercial liberty as a principle, while specifically urging an embargo on the export of olive oil. He assumed a free market economy normal and in harmony with "the natural justice of prices," but in the 1790s would come to write, more cynically and explicitly, that interference in it was necessary, "when the general good, which is the supreme reason of governments, indicates the need." Jovellanos was greatly influenced by British concepts. He learned English while in Seville; by 1776 he had read Locke, and also the Abbé Raynal and other writers who commented on American history and on the background of the American Revolution. By the 1790s, he proudly claimed to have read Adam Smith three or four times through.[73]

In 1776, Spain escalated La Plata to a viceroyalty to counter Portuguese smuggling and territorial encroachments supported by the British, and to protect the Falklands-Malvinas. Venezuela, Guatemala, Cuba, and Chile soon became separate administrative units, Captaincies General. San Francisco had just been founded in order to preempt British and Russian claims.[74] And there were new audiencias assigned to Buenos Aires, Cuzco, and Caracas. On September 27, 1776, José de Gálvez suggested that Spain should press the British colonists to vigorous resistance in order to divert English forces from trying to stop a Spanish attack planned on Portugal for the next spring. Charles III's top priorities were to curb British power, to dam the flow of contraband, and to halt British commercial expansion—to dislodge England not only from Gibraltar and Minorca but also from the Floridas, and consequently from the Gulf of Mexico, from Campeche and Honduras, and from the Falklands. His first minister, Grimaldi, wrote of war with England as inevitable. When asked by the Count de Vergennes if Spain was ready to join France in such a conflict, Grimaldi replied, on March 14, 1776: "It is certainly desirable for us that the revolt of these people in the 13 colonies keep up and we ought to want the English and them to exhaust themselves reciprocally; the King is ready and offers to join reasonably in all expenses."[75]

A few eminent Spaniards saw in the American Revolution enlightened ideals in practice, much as the Anglo-American rebels saw their cause. Thus, Jovellanos's friend, the Conde de Cabarrús, a leading economic advisor to the king, in his 1778 "Discourse about the Liberty of Commerce" fulsomely lauded

> those colonies that renovate all the civilization and *las luces* of Europe with the simplicity of their old customs, which composed of farmers, of sailors, of merchants, know they must cultivate these useful professions to the point that they may defend their rights valorously with arms and assure them with the best legislation, so that among those colonies which give the other conquered nations of America lessons of humanity and of justice, the happy exiles of our hemisphere appear to have found refuge.[76]

This address was published in 1787 in the *Memorias* of the Madrid Economic Society, which circulated widely in Spanish America among corresponding members and residents influential in government and society.

Cabarrús also, early in 1778, urged the expansion of free trade, mentioning the advantages Spain was obtaining from Cuba, where monopoly had been lifted. The Free Trade Regulation *(reglamento)* of 1778 followed, opening commerce from most Spanish to many Spanish American ports. In that decree, too, consulados were ordered established in all opened ports and were to be aided by economic societies and dedicated to promoting agriculture, industry, and more navigation to Spanish America. Floridablanca later remarked that Ward's ideas on the system of government and commerce in America were one of the motives of war with Britain in 1779. It is not surprising that Ward's manuscript was published that year.

Charles III joined France against England in 1779. Thereby, despite its basically regalist and autocratic complexion, the Spanish government chose to side with the American colonists in their struggle for independence. Although Spain was not directly allied with the British American colonists, from 1776 the Spanish did secretly provide aid and funds to the insurgents. As José de Gálvez explained to the governor of Louisiana, his nephew Bernardo, in 1779, England was doing great damage to Spanish commerce in the Gulf of Mexico and Louisiana. It was planning to detach portions of the Spanish empire and was encouraging Russia against Spain, so that England's loss must be Spain's advantage.[77] Most farsighted was the eminent and enlightened Conde de Aranda, then Ambassador to France, who, although initially favoring Spain's abetting the rebels, called attention to the threat an independent and powerful British America could pose to Spain's hold on the New World. During the war, he and a few other prescient Spaniards, less sanguine than Cabarrús, expressed fears that the independence of the British colonies might be a bad example to their own.[78]

Spain's entry into the conflict brought pressure on its own American colonies for funds and supplies. It also presented problems of outmaneuvering Britain at sea, as well as the rather odd spectacle of an absolutist state fighting more or less in concert with a revolutionary republic. During *this* war, though, Spain was not on the losing side and, as counterweight to British sea power, relied on the French fleet and the ships of the thirteen colonies, now trading vigorously with the Spanish Caribbean, Cuba, Louisiana, and Spanish Florida. From the Spanish point of view, this was a short-term advantage but perhaps a long-run threat, a continuation, or anyway an amoeba like reproduction of English commercial aggressiveness, combined with Anglo-American interest in territory. Yet, the revolution of 1776 offered Spain an opportunity to make the New World balance of power more even. And since, with the *reglamento* of 1778 Spain began to profit from commerce with its colonies much more than at any time in the century, the fact that the British rebels were profiting too was then of less moment.[79]

This résumé of eighteenth-century Spain and Portugal, focusing on aspects of importance to America, has shed light on certain major historical themes. First, it should help to clarify the nature of Spanish Bourbon enlightened despotism and its policies concerning America. Historians writing on Latin America have ranged from seeing the Bourbon reforms as a beneficial revolution to describing them as a "monstrous flowering of regalism . . . a result of that *revolución ofinisca, togada, doctoril, y absolutista* by intelligent men of military brutality, which reached a climax with Alba and Wall, Roda and Aranda, Moniño and Campomanes."[80] It is now generally conceded that "the reign of Charles III was the height of Spanish colonialism in America."[81] Still, the reforms did not, contrary to much historical interpretation, represent the Spanish reconquest of America, but rather only an attempt at it. That attempt was forestalled by war and Spanish weakness, by lack of funds, by too radical a departure from the older, customary, Spanish system in America, by the active commercial presence of other nations, and, as we shall see, by various sorts of Spanish American resistance. In both Spain and Portugal, reforms were at bottom an attempt to compete within the Iberian empires with British manufactures, commerce, and maritime power, and they failed.

This leads to another point. The economic and commercial purposes of the reform programs have been continually understated until very recently, and so has the fact that the reforms stimulated imperial exchange but did not cut out foreign commerce. Both throve from the 1760s, and a growing role was played by British American ships carrying their own exports and re-exports from England and other countries, as well as blacks for slave labor.

The English government understood that national wealth and power could mount through the benefits of private trade with its own colonies and by cornering foreign colonial markets. Spain and Portugal too sought national wealth and power in league with national merchants, but through more stringent state-regulated and sometimes state-operated monopolies. In Iberia, the immediate aim was more wealth and power from trade in national ships and goods within the empire, and the ultimate goal one of competing across the board with England and France. While there was among enlightened ministers a desire to make the American colonies more prosperous (again in the metropolitan interest), they avoided confronting the double-bind problem inherent in trying to increase quickly both trade with the colonies and governmental receipts from them. Instead, they differentiated between the long-term goal of a free, untaxed flow of goods between Iberia and its America and the short-run necessity of limiting shipping and of placing import and export duties and numerous internal taxes on such goods, on both sides of the

Atlantic. And although they thought that ideally most governmental revenues in America should remain there, they repeatedly ordered that large amounts of them be sent to Europe.

The goal of Spanish enlightened ministers, and of Pombal, like that of the French philosophes, was not to turn out the old establishment but to convert and overhaul it. By the 1770s, such men had adapted certain assumptions from England, France, Holland, and from their own national intellectual progenitors. These were ideas and principles associated with political economy and nascent liberalism, especially faith in material progress and a morality of hard work; and their absence was used to explain Spanish backwardness. This backwardness was usually called decadence and viewed much as a secular version of a fall from grace. At bottom, the old Iberian emphasis on bullionism continued to loom large in both economic theory and public and private goals, even while lip service was being given to tenets elsewhere connected to those mercantile concepts systematized by Adam Smith. Spanish liberalism emerged within this schizoid ambience.

The Iberian case brightly illuminates some of the inherent contradictions in official advocacy of such antithetical pairs of concepts as individualism and a corporate state, scientific knowledge and censorship, freedom and absolute obedience to the monarch, free play of supply and demand and strict governmental supervision of the economy, enlightenment and despotism. The more positive member of each of these pairs was often the goal expected to be furthered by the less admirable, more useful and expedient member, which was viewed as a necessary means to a praiseworthy end. Immanuel Kant called his age an Age of Enlightenment but not an enlightened age; in eighteenth-century Iberia, the relatively few adherents of the Enlightenment (who in Spain had a relatively large amount of political influence) and their attitudes bear out his observation. Iberian enlightened despotism, in addition, showed relatively little concern for the welfare of the laborer or the plight of the poor, for ending the subjugation of women and children, for penal or judicial reform, or for individual liberty. And the example made of Pablo de Olavide, who ran afoul of some clergy during his founding of new agricultural villages and who eventually because of his freethinking was condemned by the Spanish Inquisition in the fateful year of 1776 (although he escaped to France), indicates how far government intentions and reality still diverged. Francisco Goya's depictions of the light and dark sides of Spanish lives and minds brilliantly exposed the contradictions and paradoxes of the Iberian peninsula in the late eighteenth century.

Finally, the new enlightened spirit did open to question the holding of old fundamental beliefs as truths, particularly the widespread blind veneration for the authority of the church and those values it endorsed. It undermined the old faith by introducing a newer one in the ultimate authority of the nation-state and its visible expression, the monarch. It presented a new, alternative, more secular outlook on human existence and its social organization, one having much in common with the ideas of the continental Enlightenment and with British liberalism. Yet, at the same time, the traditional religion continued to prevail, and the concept of society remained paramount over that of the individual, and that society was a hierarchical one, if more mobile and complex than before. In promoting the new values, little emphasis was put on self-restraint as a concomitant; rather, the assumption remained that restraint was to be applied by external agencies, especially the state. And although belief in progress and a beneficent universe was voiced by some eminent enlightened people, a basically Hobbesian view of human nature was more usual—thus, Floridablanca's remark, in 1770, which smacked of *realpolitik:* "Greed and interest are the main incentives for all human toil, and they should only be checked in public matters when they are prejudicial to other persons or to the state."[82] There was little in Iberia of the republican humanism evident in England among radical Whigs. Thus, one of its cornerstones, the concept of virtue, in the writings of Spanish liberals, while it was associated with public service, carried instead of the idea of ultimate civic responsibility for public affairs that of state service.[83]

By the 1770s, then, impelled by international considerations and by Spain's lamentable position within the power structure of the Atlantic world, that state was opening to the gentry and the mercantile segment more avenues to advancement and was fostering among them a newly respectable desideratum, material prosperity. It was bestowing new approval on the dictates of self-interest as a guide to action and was implicitly sanctioning greater social mobility. These three inherently revolutionary concepts were inimical to Spain's traditional society and its religiously derived values. In Portugal, while opportunities were more limited, similar sorts of alterations occurred in mentality. Still, in Spain and in Portugal power and ideological predominance remained with the partisans of tradition, and the newer broadly European ideas and the new governmental programs were but two aspects of limited and largely superficial renovation. The reformers were in some senses more successful in Latin America, ultimately to their own undoing.

4

"THESE VAST PROVINCES":

LATIN AMERICA TO 1776

From the beginning of the eighteenth century, Latin America experienced expansion in population, settled areas, mining, agriculture, stockraising, and imports and exports. It also underwent a good deal of readjustment in its internal relationships and in those with Spain and Portugal and with other European states and their American colonies. A dialectic of sorts went on between external events and internal situations. Internally, alterations took place in administration, economies, and societies, in ideas, tastes, and trade routes, and in relationships among regions. Latin America was affected by international rivalries, by the policies and activities of home governments, by those of other nations and their colonies—both through Spain and Portugal and directly—and by factors arising within its own borders. In all this, as the century progressed, relations, largely carried on through trade, with England and its America played an increasingly influential role.

After Utrecht, a number of wartime changes endured and led subsequently to still further alteration of old arrangements. The Spanish fleet system persisted but never recovered, nor did the distribution system dependent upon it. The crown continued to license registros. The Porto Bello fair and the one established for Vera Cruz in the 1720s, as we have seen, never achieved exclusivity and were undermined by the English asentistas. Instead, Spanish Americans were supplied by registros and smugglers. Through subterfuge and smuggling they received British North American flour, Madeira wines, English textiles, and black slaves, largely by way of Jamaica. In the islands and along mainland coasts contraband throve; it was carried not only by English asentistas and foreign interlopers, including New Englanders, and the Dutch from Curacao, but also in numerous small boats, locally owned. Among illegal exports were mules and cattle, hides, wood, tobacco, and occasionally blacks and Indians from the Santa Marta-Cumaná coast, as well as two-thirds of Venezuela's cacao, much Peruvian and Mexican silver, and, from Brazil, gold and other products.[1]

Factories of the English South Seas Company were established in Cuba and in the ports of Vera Cruz, Campeche, Porto Bello, and Caracas; and in Buenos Aires the Company also held a good deal of land. It managed, despite restrictions, from time to time to send its agents and wares—blacks and merchandise, mostly textiles—inland almost everywhere, to do business with local merchants, and to hold authorized and unauthorized fairs of its own. In addition, from the seventeenth century on, fleets from Portugal had carried English, Flemish, and French cloths to Brazil and Colônia do Sacramento, and a good deal of this merchandise then went up the Río de la Plata and overland into Argentina, Paraguay, Chile, Bolivia, and Peru. Spanish merchants in Peru had agents in Brazil, and the Spanish founded Montevideo in 1724 in an effort to compete with this contraband trade.[2]

We have seen that during the War of Spanish Succession, with British hindrance of trade between French Louisiana, Mobile, and Vera Cruz, and with the supply route via the isthmus to South America closed, not only did the Caribbean and Mexico do business with Jamaica, but Porto Bello lost much trade to it and to Buenos Aires, where registros put in before rounding Cape Horn. Chile profited as well, and Cuban prosperity began with the French market for tobacco.[3] After the war, the Cádiz consulado secured decrees confining both fleet and registro goods to its own and allied merchants in America and prohibiting American merchants from acting as agents of Spanish exporting firms. Still, many merchants within Latin America profited, both legitimately and otherwise, from a new abundance of goods, through doing business with asentistas and interlopers, and through internal exchange, although sudden plenty tended to glut the always small markets, and the influx of foreign wares constrained certain established internal industries. There emerged a postwar pattern that included the presence of mercantile arrivistes, especially in fringe areas and ports; yet, while the older great merchants of the consulados of Lima and Mexico were challenged by, and complained bitterly of, these contenders, they themselves came to enjoy a prestige equal to *hacendados*—the owners of haciendas, or large ranches—and became landowners, powerful figures, and some of the wealthiest men in the Americas. A significant factor in all this was their investment in, and control of, the illegal distribution of goods flowing from Manila through the islands and South America. Oriental stuffs predominated in Spanish dress from Panama to Chile. The trade was more profitable than that in imports from Spain. It was still thriving, despite repeated prohibitions, in 1776.[4]

In Venezuela, however, the Basque Guipúzcoa, or Caracas, joint-stock company, in operation in 1730, soon gained a monopoly of legitimate trade and came to dominate the province. It successfully cut into, although it did not stop, the trafficking with English and Dutch smugglers along the northern coast of South America; the company commandant, honoring the asiento right to buy cacao with proceeds from the sale of blacks, initially allowed English ships to lade full cargoes.[5] The Company, however, did hinder smuggling, and it also cut into other, legal trade within Spanish America and with Spain, engendering widespread animosity.

The war from 1739 to 1748, occasioned in the first place by aggressive commercial rivalry and especially by British smuggling, sped innovations begun earlier. With Spanish and allied shipping again hampered and with an increased

need for supplies, not only did the British and their colonists do well by provisioning Spanish America, but Spanish-licensed individual ships again became
the legitimate norm; and among them, too, were many British vessels—although
the English government did not approve since, unlike the contraband trade, Spain
gained bullion and duties in this commerce. Vernon's capture of commercially
strategic Porto Bello in 1739, even though he held that port for only two months,
permanently ended the Spanish South American fleet, the *galeones* (although not
the *flota* to Vera Cruz, which was revived in 1754 at the behest of merchants of
Mexico and Cádiz), and brought a large trade with British colonies and changes
conducive to more business with England. It also contributed to freer trade in
general, to deep and permanent shifts in internal Latin American commercial
arrangements, and to altering other relations as well. Certain measures attributable
to Spain's awareness of the value of heretofore peripheral regions, measures
abetting the growth of South American towns other than Lima, and their hinterlands, date from that year. Santa Fé de Bogotá was made a separate viceroyalty in
1739 and, in 1742, Venezuela became more autonomous, receiving a governor of
its own. By 1751, Panama had lost its audiencia and had been relegated to the
jurisdiction of Bogotá.[6]

With Porto Bello no longer the exclusive conduit to and from Europe, Lima and
its merchants lost business not only to Venezuela, New Granada, and Buenos
Aires, but also to Pacific ports; and attendant internal commercial changes
provided larger markets in the hinterlands to towns on the periphery, also at Lima's
expense. Guayaquil in particular prospered as a shipping and shipbuilding center,
its products in demand to carry goods, food, and war materiél, as Juan and Ulloa
reported, beginning with preparations for defense against Anson's squadron.
Guayaquil, too, was permitted for a time to export cacao to Vera Cruz and
Acapulco in exchange for provisions and in competition with Venezuela.[7] With
hostilities in 1737, the armada of Vera Cruz was transferred to Havana, raising the
military population, shipbuilding, and demand in Cuba, while the Mexican
viceregency underwrote Cuban expenses. Mexico also subsidized Venezuela and
St. Augustine.

In the Caribbean and Mexico, both legal trade and contraband swelled, including in beleaguered Florida, which traded with the enemy, Britain, and its
mainland colonies. When ships of the Caracas Company put in at British West
Indian ports to take on textiles and North American wheat and flour, their crews
indulged in contraband transactions of their own. And in 1741 the Company was
introducing into South America, without duty, blacks ostensibly captured from
British ships.

Juan and Ulloa, in their *Noticias Secretas*, shed light on the interlocking
mechanisms of changing domestic and foreign trade. They observed that even
before 1739 more contraband than licit goods came into Pacific ports, and they
reported that illegal goods reached South America from New Spain (especially
Chinese goods from Manila); that the Porto Bello fair was in the 1730s a front for
contraband, including in blacks, coming from the Panama coasts; and that most

large wholesale merchants dealt in a combination of legal and smuggled merchandise. In both sorts of transactions, those merchants defrauded the royal
treasury.[8] With the approach of war and reliance on registros, Juan and Ulloa
found that cargoes were sold to all comers, which meant that large merchants from
Lima had lost their monopoly on wholesaling. On the eve of Vernon's attack,
merchants from Bogotá, Popoyán, and Quito, discovering they were prohibited
from selling their own goods at Porto Bello or Cartagena while convoyed ships
were there, bought and sold illegally at hidden spots along the Panama and
Guayaquil coasts; and Spanish merchants who had arrived on those ships sold their
original goods, then restocked with contraband. Officials cooperated. They
arranged false bills of lading and got a percentage of illicit sales. Even those Lima
merchants who preferred to buy legitimate goods customarily put their profits into
contraband purchased this way through intermediaries, since they found it the only
means to keep capital invested. Lima merchants traditionally ran two separate
trades, one in European exports and one in domestic textiles. Juan and Ulloa
concluded that limeños thought of smuggling as the customary business it was and
were heard to comment that of course it was also universal in Spain.[9]

A variant situation pertained in New Spain. There the consulado traded with the
East by way of Manila as well as with Europe, and it dominated both the interior
market and agricultural exports through owning local stores and through advances
to local merchants and to officials who dominated peasant communities—either
the *corregidores* or the *alcaldes mayores*. Its members too engaged in illegal trade,
including with the British and, despite prohibitions, did business directly with
Europe, including with countries other than Spain, and shipped their funds not
only to Cádiz but by way of Jamaica to London. And in all of this, they felt
pressure from interlopers.[10]

By the 1750s, then, Buenos Aires, Santiago de Chile, Venezuela, Bogotá, and
Guayaquil, and their hinterlands were prospering at the expense of Lima and the
Andean highlands. In New Granada, settlers from northern Spain opened the rich
farmlands of Antioquia. Venezuela had changed from a province subsidized for
centuries by Mexico to one yielding a surplus in cattle and cacao. Population and
revenues increased in them all (and, especially after 1754, so did small farmers
when the government began to sell off crown lands or to legalize occupation
without compensation). Rural towns grew in number and residents as did rural
estates. Yet, while peripheral areas expanded and became more prosperous,
legitimate commercial opportunities did not keep pace. The Lima consulado
retained its official monopoly on South American overseas commerce, except for
Venezuela, where the governor and Caracas Company factors were in complete
alliance, and where the Company then paid reduced prices for cacao, would export
no hides, and was charging more for imports, including blacks obtained through
the British and the Dutch. There is convincing evidence that Venezuela could have
developed as well or better without the Company, for it restricted not only the old
smuggling activities but also the legitimate markets of many regional planters,
cattlemen, and merchants.[11]

In Cuba, which had prospered during the war as the hub of Spain's trade and the center of its military activity, *habañeros*, economically stimulated, had applied to form a chartered company in 1738. In 1740, the Havana Company was authorized in order to promote the royal tobacco monopoly and trade with Spain. That Company, directed by Cubans and Spaniards, was charged with provisioning Saint Augustine as well and did so with a subsidy from Mexico spent in New York and Charleston, then enemy ports. Lacking capital, it became and remained an intermediary between the merchants of Jamaica and British North America and Spanish dependencies. It kept tobacco prices low and export limited in Cuba, but did mark the inclusion of Americans. Yet, by the 1750s lines were none too clear between privileged, government-endorsed traders and their favored suppliers and nonlegal but powerful contrabandists, all of whom prospered from expansion in tobacco and sugar but felt impeded by lack of slaves, even with the contraband trade in them.[12]

Contraband, carried by small boats, flowed between Florida and Cuba. This network adumbrated some of Cuba's later importance to both the Spanish and the Anglo-Americans. Saint Augustine continued to trade with English mainland colonies after the war; Vera Cruz trade with French Louisiana increased, and its port, New Orleans, was also a center for commerce with the Spanish islands, Gulf ports, and northern South America, mainly in French and regional goods. Even though the Spanish American market was glutted in 1750, in New Orleans Spanish ships from Campeche took on dry goods, and lumber as well, for the Spanish West Indies and Mobile. New Orleans also got Mexican trade through Dauphine Island in the 1750s, was an entrepôt for New Mexico, Texas, and Cuba, and was a port of call for Spanish ships between Vera Cruz and Havana.[13]

With the Seven Years' War, the introduction of foreign goods in foreign ships to Latin America soared despite Spanish edicts against smuggling; so did collaboration in this business by local officials, planters, and merchants. The government, too, promoted certain interregional exchange; thus, it permitted residents of "Florida and Pensacola" to carry pitch, tar, resin, medicinal herbs, and timber to Vera Cruz, Havana, Campeche, and other ports where these goods were free of most duties. Venezuela experienced a silver shortage not accounted for by legal trade, although under royal order one hundred thousand pesos from the Mexican treasury was invested there in 1760 in order to promote commerce. After Spain entered the war, six Caracas Company ships were lost and smuggling mounted. More English contraband than ever before reached South America through Colônia do Sacramento, and it arrived at other Spanish colonies, especially New Spain, through British-occupied Havana, which was inundated with merchandise.[14]

Under the British, over seven hundred ships entered "the Havannah," many of them from British North America (where before perhaps fifteen vessels a year had come), bringing in textiles, foods, timber, animals, ironware, and blacks. Cuba received somewhere between three thousand and ten thousand Africans during the occupation. Sold at one-third the Spanish price, their labor boosted sugar production which, soaring from the 1760s, both challenged the primacy of tobacco and brought repeated calls for still more slaves. Population, domestic textiles, cotton, and food production all expanded too from then on, aided by general inflation. English and mainland North American interest in the colony, particularly in its sugar, was made patent to Cubans. Even though the British seized all Havana Company property and ships—since, was the rationale, the Spanish crown had an interest in it—Cubans did a vastly better business under the British, especially with merchants and ships of the mainland English colonies. Moreover, even before the British appeared, Cuba had once again enjoyed increased prosperity during wartime and after 1763 it continued, abetted by both greater British North American trade and Spanish attention to defense. Especially after 1767, Cuban trade with British colonies to the north swelled, with specified shipments and destinations authorized to procure essential supplies, particularly North American flour. Residents of Havana then owned vessels in association with several merchants at New Orleans involved in the trading network encompassing Vera Cruz, Texas, Campeche, and New Mexico.[15]

After 1763, too, in Spanish America, a larger population, a general and mild inflation, a mounting internal market—resulting from prior and continuing growth in population, mining, and agriculture and from changes in taste—coalesced with a greater English need of raw materials as industrial growth accelerated, and with British desire for carrying trade and markets. Spanish and British reforms made doing business with the ships and merchants of Anglo-America more difficult, but not impossible. A number of Spanish Americans continued to send contraband ingots and coins in small ships to foreign islands and took in return blacks, manufactured articles, or letters of exchange drawn on London banks; the Caracas Company traded through Santo Domingo in the years when Monte Christi and Dutch St. Eustatius were flourishing and Anglo-Americans were frequenting them. In addition, with the chronic Spanish shortage of wheat after 1765 and, especially, an acute Venezuelan scarcity in 1773–74, foreigners were allowed to re-export flour from Cádiz to Spanish America and the Caracas Company to import it from foreign colonies. The governor of Caracas sent ships to Puerto Rico for flour, the Company went to Curacao for it, and still it remained scarce. Much of the flour imported into Spain and its America from the 1760s undoubtedly originated in British North America.[16]

Increasing imports of blacks was another sign of growth and of more open commerce, as well as of governmental encouragement of the slave trade in order to spur Latin American economies. More slaves came through the English and British Americans, and this commerce continued to bring with it other trade as well. Thus, from 1763 the Spanish asentista for Caribbean areas outside Caracas Company boundaries, who was assigned Puerto Rico as an entrepôt, got blacks from the British, and with each one had to purchase flour, other provisions, and textiles, ostensibly because the slaves needed them. Havana became the chief slave emporium after 1773. The Caracas Company itself, contracting to provide two thousand blacks to Caracas and Maracaibo after 1765, got them from English,

French, and Dutch sources. The Company also helped to supply the Puerto Rican depot with slaves from 1765 to 1769. By the 1770s, the British free port act had made restricted Spanish slave trading untenable, and with war in 1779 the Spanish asiento system, long moribund, died.[17]

All this said, by the 1770s the Spanish "free trade" edict of 1765 had resulted in more trade with Spain. It cut into the Cádiz monopoly, ended fixed prices, and enabled less wealthy and established merchants to do more business. It permitted the involvement of more Spaniards and Spanish Americans in transatlantic and domestic trade, and it again spurred investment by displaced merchant princes in agriculture, stockraising, and mining within their regions. In 1764 an observer, commenting on the large volume of smuggling engaged in by Venezuelans, and on both the great contraband and licit trades with Mexico, Bogotá, Curacao, and the Caribbean, had noted the essentially mercantile character of Venezuela's population. Residents of Buenos Aires, the traveler who signed himself Concolorcorvo wrote, thought only of business.[18] In La Plata, every man of substance was then a merchant, as were many throughout the Spanish Indies. Reforms of the 1770s, establishing exemptions from duties for goods sent to Chile and Peru and free trade with the most important ports of Spain, only consolidated and accelerated Buenos Aires's commercial rise.[19]

Some Spanish Americans profited from governmental attempts to stimulate interprovinicial trade not competing with Spanish commerce. Royal decrees of 1769 allowed such trade between Peru and Bogotá, and one of 1774 permitted shipping on the Pacific between them both and New Spain and Guatemala. That decree stated its purpose was "to promote industry and agriculture" and thus give "more utility to the state and [its] people," and to avoid smuggling, and it opened trade to all *naturales*—native-born or naturalized residents.[20] After 1770, when regulations of 1765 for the islands were extended to Louisiana allowing a new system of free commerce "in native products" with Havana and Santo Domingo, "since the old commerce with Florida had ended," much smuggling ensued and British North American wheat through Louisiana again displaced Mexican grain in Havana, as it had during the last war. The growth of Cuban sugar then required imports of copper from New Spain and Peru. Further, viceroys allowed commerce in (prohibited) wines, olives, and brandies, indicating an official response to colonial pressure, and also sanctioning legal routes for transhipping contraband.[21]

While new policies allowed much inter-Spanish American commerce not competing with Spanish exports, they tied the mounting legitimate Spanish American trade more directly to Spain. Thus the 1765 decrees and a 1769 edict, allowing Venezuelan growers to ship with the Caracas Company on their own accounts at just rates, brought large cargoes of private cacao into the peninsula. There they sold exceedingly well, helped by fear of a war with England over the Falklands-Malvinas.[22] Yet, by the 1770s, ongoing internal expansion presented a greater market and more carrying business to both Spanish and foreign trade. Concolorcorvo mentioned that hides then went from Montevideo not only to Spain but also that "vast quantities were sent surreptitiously to Portugal"—and from there many went to England.[23] In La Plata, *estancias* were replacing wild cattle hunting, and more leather was being exported to Europe for both clothing and moving parts of machinery. Buenos Aires salt beef, processed in *saladeros*, or meat-salting plants, mostly run by Spanish immigrants, went to the Caribbean, particularly to Cuba for the enlarged Havana garrison and growing numbers of slaves, and to Spain and to foreign merchants as well. Conversely, the saladeros depended on imported barrel slaves, many of them from North America. Contacts were probable with Anglo-American whalers venturing as far south, in the 1770s, as Patagonia. And the war with Portugal over La Plata boundaries from 1774 to 1777 required both imports of materiél and increased internal purchases, besides contributing to the decision to make Buenos Aires a viceroyalty.[24]

New Spain—responsible for underwriting and providing, not only its own, but also Caribbean expenses and defense—was the American province most prized by Spain in the eighteenth century, and the wealthiest; it was also least open to direct contact with foreign traders. Yet, contact there was. After 1763, the British were much closer and, in exchange for gold and silver, contraband flowed through the British logwooding settlements in Campeche and Tabasco, as well as by way of Pensacola and New Orleans. José de Gálvez was infuriated at finding smuggling rampant and British ships riding at anchor in Vera Cruz in 1767; the Jalapa fair that year was a failure because the market had been saturated beforehand. That by the latter part of the eighteenth century British merchants had founded some of the outstanding commercial houses in Vera Cruz is a phenomenon still to be properly studied, but quite probably traceable to the advent of the asentistas.[25]

We know that growing British, including Anglo-American, commercial and territorial penetration was an important reason for the reforms Gálvez introduced in New Spain. He himself had written on the eve of his appointment as visitador, "Spanish America is more exposed to the insatiable ambition of certain European powers...England especially aspires to dominate the entire commerce of both hemispheres." This problem was therefore at least an indirect cause of significant alterations in Mexico's economy and society, for those reforms contributed to promoting further growth in commerce, population, mining, agriculture, ranching, and internal industries. They resulted, too, in many more state employees, more laborers on salaries, the spread of a new economic mentality, new sorts of entrepreneurs, and sharpening rivalries between creole and Spanish merchants.[26]

By the 1770s, the impact of such Spanish policies was being promoted throughout Spanish America by means of lowered duties and other measures designed to expand agriculture and commerce with the metropolis. Natives of the Windwards could take their products to Spain on equal terms with Spaniards from 1765 on. Cotton was freed of duties in 1766, numerous other products in 1774, and sugar in 1777, and they were also freed of re-export duties from the peninsula. Yet, writing in 1774, Concolorcorvo reflected peninsular concern in stating that "the English... are profiting most from the Spanish conquest through their consumption of goods produced here in the provinces," and that the resale of those goods kept England flourishing; but he went on to add a concern—very American, and not shared with the metropolis—that abundant European products sold cheaply in South America were displacing native manufactures.[27] Rather, the government's interest was in replacing imported, largely British, textiles with Spanish manufactures. It was a divergence that would become more important in the succeeding decades.

From the seventeenth century, British wares predominated in the annual fleets from Lisbon to Brazil until those sailings ended in 1766. The British were active at Colônia do Sacramento, and their goods flowed through southern Brazil and that entrepôt into Spanish America. During wartime, British ships frequented Brazilian ports and by 1714, we have seen, there was a customary trade between Portugal and English colonies in America. Most merchants in major Brazilian ports, although native-born or Portuguese, were simply commission agents for Lisbon and Oporto firms that were, in turn, intermediaries for and financed by Englishmen and, to a lesser extent, other foreigners. However, by the 1750s these people were being challenged by itinerant merchant interlopers, the comisarios volantes, who bought goods in Portugal and peddled them in Brazil, and who were associated with universal British traders of similar stripe in Portugal; some of them also had connections to the Jesuits in Brazil. Thus, expulsion of the Jesuits in 1759 rid the state, and these nobles and their associates who were involved in overseas trade, of one commerical leak, and the government clamped down on the free traders.[28]

Brazil's gold production peaked between 1740 and 1760; it had mounted through the first half of the century, joined by diamonds in the 1730s. Perhaps two-thirds of the bullion eventually went to England, including the large amounts smuggled out of Brazil and Portugal. Still, some Brazilians, notably merchants and officeholders, benefited immensely, as did the Portuguese crown and nobility. Not only did royal revenues mount steeply but taxes, farmed out, tied the colonial oligarchy, as contractors, to the administration. In the early part of the century, Brazilians were powerful in regional governments and in the domestic slave trade; that power endured and was strengthened under Pombal when they gained control of more Indian labor by wresting it from the Jesuits.

Contemporaneously with Gálvez's visita in Mexico, the Pombaline reforms in Brazilian government included some centralizing structural changes, particularly the erecting of regional subtreasury boards responsible for all expenditures and tax collection except the royal fifth, and thus for much local administration. More competent officials were appointed and charged with finances, defense, and developing economic resources. In the north and northeast, the new companies had begun to stimulate sugar, cotton, rice, cacao, and their processing. While in the 1760s the price and market for sugar fell off, the introduction of Carolina rice in 1776 sparked productivity in Maranhâo, and *Maranhense* cotton came to enjoy a steady market and demand, which increased as did that for rice and sugar, with revolution in British America.[29] In southern Brazil contraband throve, particularly with Buenos Aires while Portugal was neutral in the Seven Years' War. Then from

1762, the Spanish blockade of Colônia and the ongoing dispute with Spain over Río Grande do Sul, culminating in the boundary war between 1774 and 1777, cut deeply into gold smuggling and the sale of British goods to Brazil.[30]

Outstanding for his efforts to implement Pombaline reforms, and particularly to diversify production, was the viceroy, the Marqués de Lavradio, who, although as loyal and diligent as Spanish viceroys, had less power. For the Brazilian system, always more disparate than that in Spanish America and geared to a sparser population, had a smaller bureaucracy, provided the least services of all colonial governments, and was greatly reliant upon Portuguese Americans in private and public capacities.Lavradio, like the companies, encouraged the processing of certain commodities for export—wheat, cochineal, and indigo among them, the last two in order to compete with Mexico and Central America—and he spurred the manufacture of canvas, iron, rigging, and leather goods, and the processing of rice. He did, however, discourage that colonial manufacturing competing with the metropolis, the flourishing weaving of textiles in the interior, especially in Minas Gerais. To the same end, although he dealt summarily with the men of one New England whaler sent out by Aaron Lopez of Providence, putting them in prison on suspicion of smuggling in 1773, he subsequently released some of them so they might teach Brazilians their legitimate trade, the deep sea pursuit of the sperm whale. From 1771, he also held in the palace intermittent meetings of a scientific society, most of whose members were Portuguese, but prohibited printing presses.[31] Brazilians, with fewer cultural institutions of their own than creoles had, did enjoy greater entrepreneurial freedom. Lavradio's high-handed treatment of the New Englanders may have owed something to Pombal's altered policy in the 1770s, when he sought British support for Brazilian expansion and British aid in the war with Spain.

In sum, from mid-century in Brazil a more fluid society was emerging, Portuguese and native born, no longer based solely on landed wealth, and much of it was mercantile. Mobility was easier. Social status and power were interlinked with public office. Investment patterns were changing—in Bahia, for example, from sugar and cattle to lending and financial speculation. A large chunk of Río's population was also involved in trade. "A thriving and largely Brazilian-based merchant fleet supported by planter and mining capital" and with Brazilian crews benefited from the "seemingly inexhaustible...demand for slaves." From 1765 on, important landowners and merchants sat on the regional subtreasury boards. Brazilian nabobs also had a substantial part in the military, judicial, and economic management of their areas as militia commanders and officers, as magistrates and fiscal officials, and as entrepreneurs as well. Within this situation, and intensified by economic depression as the century wore on, disputes and antagonisms that customarily had flared among officeholders and between families extended to conflicts with royal officials sent from Portugal. Abuses were endemic. Among Brazilians who held local tax farms (of the sort abolished in Mexico in the 1760s), many owed the treasury huge sums.[32]

Lavradio attributed Brazil's problems and his own too modest successes to insufficient government funds, lack of enough private investment—Río merchants proving recalcitrant—and the indolence of Brazilian planters. That is, he put most of the onus not where it most likely belonged, on the government, the survival of old ways, and a shrinking economy, but on the Brazilian character. He disliked his charges, in his dispatches reporting them to be lazy and careless, and attributed such traits not to social conditions, as did more enlightened spirits, but to innate Brazilian proclivities. (He also distrusted foreigners, especially Spaniards and the English, and displayed a strong antipathy to blacks; he was, however, conscious of European and Brazilian wrongs to Indians.) The change of rulers in 1777, Pombal's fall, and Lavradio's departure altered to some extent but did not ameliorate Brazilian problems. Eminent Brazilians, although they felt metropolitan control less pressingly than did Spanish Americans, in the late 1770s also had less cause to expect good things from the state. Yet, more intimately associated with it politically from the beginning than their creole counterparts, Brazil's oligarchs would continue to exercise much real and formal social, political, and economic power.

In Spanish America at the beginning of the eighteenth century, creoles customarily saw themselves as rightful lords of the land and heirs of the conquistadors whom they viewed as having subdued, civilized, and brought Christianity to the Indians. This pride in heritage, typifying *criollismo*, or creole nativism, was manifest particularly in literature and among landed families. It also perpetuated the original conquerors' rationale for their own continued preeminence, that of defending the country, although in the eighteenth century it dovetailed nicely with arrangements in effect only in certain areas, notably in northern Mexico. There, hacendados had private armies and a patriarchal relationship with the men who made them up (as did many Brazilian planters). Thus, Gálvez attributed success in quelling the rising in San Luis de Potosí in 1767 to a creole landowner, Francisco de Mora, who led such a force against the rebels.[33] A widespread sentiment of criollismo was exhibited by the people then dominating town councils and, until mid-century, also *audiencias*, which functioned both as regional law courts and advisory councils to viceroys and captains-general. Such men were usually landed, most had purchased or inherited their offices, and, as the century wore on, more of them were large merchants. These people usually spoke as inhabitants of a substantial part of the empire and their complaints were in the nature of habitual appeals to the crown for redress of grievances. They tended to resent the growing number of newly arrived Spaniards who were receiving American honors, position, and wealth, and who were successfully competing with them or their sons, including for the hands of creole heiresses.

Thus, Antonio de Ahumada, a minor official, in his *representación* to Philip V in 1725 made a classic Mexican statement of creole attitudes and sense of affront. Speaking of New Spain as "our nation" and of "la imperial México," he assumed that Mexican birth was the sine qua non for office.[34] Specifically, he was reacting to two Bourbon tendencies. The first was a preference for Europeans; Ahumada insisted that creoles had the legitimate right, in accord with the law of nations, to hold all governmental and ecclesiastical postions in the Indies and that in denying them this birthright the crown denied their Spanish blood—that is, their descent from the conquistadors.

The second was the peninsular habit of mind that tended to lump creoles with Indians and to think of them both as inferior by nature. (Juan and Ulloa spoke of this tendency in slightly, but significantly, different terms, reporting that creoles resented Europeans because the latter insinuated that all people born in America were half-breeds.) Ahumada referred to creoles as "Americans" whose ancestors had conquered and populated the land and who, like those forebears, remained responsible for holding it, and for seeing to it that the Indians did not revolt. He suggested that it would be better to govern the empire by bestowing preferments and posts upon Americans than to retain it by Spanish arms. Americans have customs, he added, unknown to Europeans—and here he repeated a comment made by the sixteenth-century Spanish Jesuit and chronicler of America, José de Acosta, a comment that would again surface in arguments made from 1808 on, that there existed a separate American constitution: "America can not be regulated by the laws of Rome and Spain."[35] Still, Spaniards receiving American positions in this period often married into, or became otherwise associated with, the creole aristocracy, so that they were often assimilated into American society. Some fathered creoles, and in general they came to strengthen ties between colonies and metropolis. Ahumada's protest may have been largely one of a disappointed office seeker, or a creole of dwindling fortune, or even of a rejected suitor.

American inhabitants knew of and aired Spain's economic weaknesses and complained to the crown, as would lobbyists, of being discriminated against, and of Spanish attempts to benefit at American expense while mismanaging American wealth and allowing it to seep out of the empire. Recall that at the opening of the century, Lima merchants had written against French ships glutting their markets, and in the city of Mexico, the consulado objected that the royal decree of 1729 was prejudicial to American merchants. Moreover, the year before, with Spain on the brink of war with England, a tract, translatable as *Interests of England not well understood in the present war with Spain*—its author listed as an Englishman, one Charreti, and its translator into Castilian a Jesuit, Juan de Urtássum—was passed by the official Mexican censor. He was Juan Manuel de Oliván Rebolledo, a judge of the audiencia, or *oidor*, who also added an appendix stating Spain must manufacture in order to offset drain of specie. And he concluded that "the small amount of blood running in the body of Spain comes from the Indies," and that foreigners were receiving that wealth from Spanish hands.[36]

In Cuba in the same decade, the new royal monopoly on tobacco caused uprisings in 1717, 1720, and 1723 involving people of all social strata. *Cabildos* (town councils) there then complained of a lack of Spanish shipping and clothing, and a glut of sugar, hides, and tobacco, and explained that islanders, lacking any other recourse, had resorted to contraband. Cuba, however, became unique when in 1740 some of its creoles not only joined Spaniards as directors and stockholders of the Havana Company but also became its managers. As such, they took charge of the tobacco monopoly, built ships for the navy, and supplied forts, warships, the coast guard, and, to repeat, Florida garrisons. They both purchased supplies from Anglo-American merchants and helped the captain-general, the Conde de Re-villagigedo (the elder), to organize and send the expedition against Georgia in 1742.[37]

After Utrecht, then, although only Cubans were permitted so large a share in imperial commerce, throughout Spanish America creole merchants, other busi-nessmen, and landowners, rising and arrived, retained a substantial stake in the establishment. Yet, some of these same entrenched creoles, we have seen, came to feel unjustly treated by the authorities and, more than ever, justified in cir-cumventing them . One concomitant was the protest by more substantial Mexicans than Ahumada against restrictions upon their international trade, and the getting around those restrictions, including in the Manila trade and by doing business through British asentistas. In Venezuela not only did the Caracas cabildo, made up of landed aristocrats and large shippers, continue in its petitions to express resentment of the Guipúzcoa Company and to claim abuse of local custom, but in 1738 these same people, who had long monopolized the sizable trade between Venezuela and Vera Cruz, reported to the crown that the Company was usurping creole political and commercial prerogatives and damaging the region's economy, for cacao sent to Mexico was the sole source of Venezuela's silver. They pointed out that recent changes in trade also adversely affected the clergy, whose finances were bound up with their own. They said, with truth, that the Company had gotten cacao prices lowered and, with the help of the governor, had attempted not only to secure the bulk of Venezuelan cacao for its own shipments to Spain but also to take over the Venezuelan-Mexican trade. Moreover, its ships could not adequately supply regional needs; from 1733, for example, the governor had found it essential to allow purchase of "English" wheat.

That year, in wartime, the Company gained a complete monopoly on Ven-ezuelan trade and creoles were implicated in several local popular revolts. Then, at the war's end in 1749, when the government repeated strictures on creoles in transatlantic trade, members of the Caracas cabildo supported an uprising in-volving people of all classes. The revolt was given impulse by several factors: War had left a residue of scarcities and a rise in the cost of imported necessities, cacao prices had plummeted, and the governor had moved against smuggling in the cacao-growing Yaracuy valley. Numerous propertied creoles concurred or par-ticipated in the rebellion—led by one of them, Juan Francisco de León— essentially to regain control of their country. A wealthy cacao grower of Canarian background, León, the acknowledged regional leader of the Yaracuy, directed a mass rising of mestizos, blacks, mulattoes, and Indians against the Company's attempt to control that area's economy. On several occasions, at the head of a vast following, he occupied Caracas. The procedure was standard: He always arrived in orderly fashion, with little or no bloodshed, treated the governor politely, and called a *cabildo abierto*, or town meeting, of "the more discreet inhabitants." That assembly indicated the nature and extent of rebel goals in invariably shouting, "Long live the king! Death to the Company!" One such session resulted in a plaint requesting a return to "liberty of contract" and "freedom for all importations," and it charged that Venezuela was maintained in slavery to the Company.

León's *representación* of 1750, made in the name of the nobility and *plebe*, or commoners, of Caracas, asked unregulated cacao prices, freedom to carry cacao to any Spanish American port and to sell to the highest bidder, and the traditional right of one third of all shipments for growers to export on their own accounts. It requested too the elimination of intermediaries and of export duties, no exceptions to goods or fruits that might be exported, freedom of navigation to Vera Cruz, and abolition of all restrictions on tobacco and *aguardiente*, or rum. It also stated that more imports would discourage contraband.

This perception of the Company as an external threat brought about a (transient) unity within Venezuelan society, overcoming internal divisions, and this unity and certain expressions elicited by the situation took on a protonational complexion. León's son summarized this sentiment in writing to the crown: "We have the obligation to defend our patria and if we do not we will be everyone's slaves."[38]

Also to the point, the governor reported hatred of the Company was so widespread that León, had he so desired, could have taken over the province. When the governor, who was at first conciliatory, captured the rebel leaders and exiled or executed many of them, a notable exception was made in the case of the elderly creole shipowner, planter, and merchant, the Conde de San Javier. He had controlled much of the trade between Venezuela and Vera Cruz, an exchange still absorbing more cacao than that with Spain, and wanted the Company expelled and duties lowered to meet foreign competition. No charges were formally brought against him because, as the governor explained to Madrid, the whole colonial nobility was related and would hold his punishment against the Basque Company.[39] As another conciliatory gesture, and at the request of a cabildo abierto, limited participation in the Company was then opened to Spanish Americans; among those buying shares, it is worth mentioning, was a wealthy and respected family of Basque extraction, the Bolívars.[40] Such gestures, as well as ongoing factions within creole society and higher cacao prices (until 1758), defused general resistance to the economic policies of the authorities. Nevertheless, old habits persisted. Contraband rose substantially after 1752 and creoles continued to berate the Company, the Caracas cabildo charging it did not buy enough cacao, paid slowly, and introduced insufficient goods, and that especially scarce were calicos worn by the poorer inhabitants.[41]

By mid-century everywhere, a conservative criollismo was intensifying within the regions. Hacendados whose crops and cattle prospered but had little market and that at low prices, who needed more laborers, whose trade had been coopted, or whose contraband activities were cut into by government vigilance or the activities of licensed monopolists, felt themselves circumvented in fortunes and power. Adversely affected by wartime shifts in trade, then by renewed pressure from Cádiz and governmental concurrence, were some of the merchants of the consulados of Lima and Mexico and their correspondents, including planters and smaller traders. The rise and the assertiveness, with official benediction, of fringe areas was a major irritant, as was greater scrutiny by the peninsular government. Peruvians and the consulado of Santiago de Chile, often at odds, did unite in complaining of the government's monopoly on tobacco.[42]

Even so, friction among American regions, and particularly between viceregal centers and peripheries, outran annoyance at Madrid's policies. Thus, in 1750 the consulado of Lima protested to the viceroy, that "the commerce of Buenos Aires has always been pernicious to that of Peru and no less to the royal prerogative," and a spokesman for the Buenos Aires council retaliated by decrying "the tyrannical disorder" caused by *limeño* greed. Lima officials and their consulado viewed Chile in much the same light. On their part, *chilenos,* although doing business with Peru, had profited from direct trade with Europe around Cape Horn during the war, and in Chile great oligarchic clans were emerging. In 1755, the Santiago cabildo vehemently argued Chilean separateness. In complaining of Peruvian merchants cornering Chilean wheat, the cabildo reminded the king that "natural law dictates that each kingdom or province prefers to manage its own provisions, rather than have foreigners do it."[43]

A creole sense of regional belonging incorporating a large element of patriotism was the frequent reaction to pressure from Spain or other American provinces. Thus, in Chile the cabildo then lauded its own "sons of the patria," while a Peruvian, José Eusebio Llano Zapata, in 1760 extolled the wealth and literary and scientific glories of all South America—the viceroyalty including much of it—and defended its conquerors.[44] Earlier, Brazilian poets and historians had praised the size and attributes of their country, one declaring, "Of the New World . . . Brazil comprises the major part . . . Brazil is an earthly paradise."[45] Mexico offers particularly rich evidence of regional patriotism and its evolution. There a strong sentiment of particularism within the empire had been present from immediately after the conquest. It had been appreciated and fostered by authorities because it ultimately abetted attachment to Spain, and had been cherished by people of all situations for varying reasons and in various guises. Yet, early in the century a few periodicals, published sporadically, had signaled the emergence of new elements within expressions of patriotic self-awareness habitual to creoles. One, the *Gaceta de México,* was founded in 1722 in order, its editor announced, to extol *"la nobilísima México"* and to keep Mexicans abreast of news of scientific discoveries and of medical remedies culled from foreign books and journals.[46]

Interest in scientific advance, that is, had joined regional patriotism as an esteemed social value to mark the appearance of a more modern variety of creolism, and at mid-century it found additional components and two influential champions. Both men were clerics, as was their acknowledged mentor, the eclectic, enlightened Spaniard, Feijoo, and both were sons of Basque immigrants. They were Juan José Eguiara y Eguren and Rafael Campoy. Eguiara was educated at elite Jesuit colegios in the capital; he taught philosophy and theology at the University of Mexico and became its chancellor in 1758. By then he had begun publishing a rather indiscriminate list of over two thousand works written by Mexicans, his *Biblioteca Mexicana.* He defined being Mexican as a state of mind common to those who were born or had studied or lived in the viceroyalty. The *Biblioteca* was an impassioned cataloguing (in itself an unusual feat) written to refute a Spaniard, the Dean of Alicante, who, embroidering upon opinions stated by French philosophes, had characterized New Spain as so barbarous and so enveloped in dark clouds of obscurantism that it could even turn enlightened and cultured Europeans into ignoramuses.

Eguiara wrote in Latin in order, he said, to vindicate "our patria" and "our nation" and to speak for those who, like himself, were neither solely Spanish nor Indian, but mestizo and Mexican. He took issue with purely Hispanic creolism in noting that pre-Hispanic peoples had cultivated poetry, arithmetic, astronomy, and other arts and sciences, and that they had produced a great civilization, one destroyed by the Spanish conquest. He explicitly praised the old indigenous "imperial city of Mexico," "its emperors," and its civilization as "our progenitors," then asserted that there existed a creole culture, and that it was heir to and equaled ancient Mexican culture in grandeur. He was within the tradition of earlier creoles who had investigated pre-Columbian civilizations and claimed them as Mexico's own classical antiquity; but Eguiara went even further, in citing Feijoo's defense of Spanish Americans and concluding that Mexicans were more capable and intelligent than Europeans. Eguiara broadened Ahumada's criollismo, expressed more respect for Indian peoples, or anyway for those of the great civilizations of the past, and voiced a consciousness of the dilemma of being Mexican and thereby heir to two cultures while belonging to neither.[47]

In the same period, this special and intensified sense of Mexican uniqueness was epitomized in Mexicans' securing papal sanction, in 1756 and after a long campaign, to refer to the indigenous Virgin of Guadalupe as the patroness of Mexico. She had long symbolized God's special favor to native-born Roman Catholics of every lineage, allowing belief in themselves as being an elect, chosen people. Although from mid-century the clergy in New Spain were divided into *modernistas* and strict traditionalists, *misoneístas,* the Virgin had many adherents in both factions. Her cult had begun as a unifying force among the diverse social and racial groups, and it remained one, abetting in them all the growth of a primary sense of Mexican belonging.[48]

Over the years, members of the Society of Jesus had been among those most devoted to her cult. Rafael Campoy was no exception. At the same time, he was avowedly modern. He admired Bacon and Descartes (probably emulating Feijoo), was interested in the natural sciences and in developing the resources of his homeland—which he and other Mexicans often referred to as *América septentrional,* or North America—and he saw in reform of Mexican education the key to progress. He spoke out against the prevailing scholastic method as decadent, and he advocated instead that a critical approach be taken to learning and that schools get rid of derivative works and return to original classical sources and texts in the humanities.[49] He inspired, we shall see, a small but influential group of younger creole Jesuits.

Spain's brief sally into war against Britain in the early 1760s not only acted as catalyst for a systematic colonial reform program, but it also disclosed to Americans Spain's weakness at sea and, particularly in the capture of Havana, Britain's naval and mercantile strength, as well as some advantages held by British North American colonists. New Spain bore the economic burden of Cuba's supplies and garrisons and much of that for the entire Spanish Caribbean. Mexicans experiencing recession in 1762 not only watched Havana prosper with more open trade under the British, but also saw Puebla wheat, during the war and thereafter, meet great competition in Havana from British North American grain.[50] Within Puebla, one outspoken creole, a priest, was then denounced to the Inquisition for publicly declaring that "we would be better off with the English than the gachupines."[51] (*Gachupín* was the Mexican term for peninsular Spaniard; it meant spur-wearer.)

Afterwards, dissatisfactions with Spanish commercial strictures were more evident. There was an economic upsurge at war's end, then depression from 1764 to 1767 and more evidence during it that creoles had seen a preferable alternative to the closed Spanish commercial system. Inhabitants of Guatemala, Santo Domingo, and "some of the most considerable merchants of Cartagena" then offered to open trade with Britain. In 1764, the French ambassador in Spain reported that a Peruvian merchant had gone to Europe to find trade on his own account and that both Spanish Americans and the British wanted direct interchange through such men—that if allowed, Americans would become increasingly powerful and independent. In Mexico in 1767, a denunciation was made to inquisitors indicating the presence of a tract entitled *Protección de la Nación Inglesa a la América Oprimada*.[52]

Seen in this light, the Puebla plot of 1765 was probably a reaction by a group of creoles with commercial interests who belonged to the old oligarchy. Those conspirators presented themselves, we recall, as members of the nobility and the clergy and made the traditional creole argument that, although their ancestors had conquered the land "at the cost of their blood and fortunes," they themselves were being excluded from high office and prerogatives, and were being treated "like the lowest of the low" in Spain, even by their own family connections, while the merchants among them suffered from high taxes on European goods and from lack of capital.[53] They also clearly lacked political acumen; wanting a change of government, they were uncertain how to achieve it. In the next few decades, such people would gain greater political know-how.

Other members of the old oligarchy were more sanguine, prospering by having gone into ranching, agriculture, and mining during the war. Despite a short-term recession, their sons and some more recent arrivals benefited from a general economic upswing and the dramatic revival of mining. Such men more often chose to sit on town councils and promote civic betterment, as they construed it, through encouraging work projects for the poor and through beautifying one's town with handsome neoclassic art and architecture. It was during the 1760s that quite a few titles of nobility were conferred on creoles, most of them recently wealthy. Even so, their political power was circumscribed, for where in 1750 they had predominated in offices (three-quarters of them purchased) throughout Spanish America, from 1751 to 1777 they suffered from the crown's policies of abolishing sales of audiencia seats (though not of lesser local posts), of appointing on merit, and of preferring Spaniards. By 1776, peninsulars dominated American magistracies. Creoles might purchase titles, but not high political position: In this particular they experienced loss of place and prestige. In the same decade, growing numbers of Spanish immigrants came not only to direct the government and to fill both existing and new administrative posts, but also arrived in America in the army or as budding entrepreneurs bent on gaining wealth and position.[54]

Thus, from 1763—especially in Mexico where Gálvez was introducing the new colonial program, and regional wealth and opportunity were attracting more European Spaniards—talented and ambitious young creoles were taking their cue from the new spirit emanating from the viceregal court, and from the novel ethic centered on work and material progress visible among recent arrivals. In the main, they looked forward eagerly to being part of this new imperial milieu. One indication is the activities and opinions expressed by Campoy's disciples, the small but dynamic coterie of young creole Jesuits who declared themselves fervent partisans of *modernismo*. As teachers in the Mexican capital and the provinces, they introduced educational reforms centered on neoclassicism and directed against what one of them, Francisco Javier Clavijero, termed "that philosophy which tires the minds of the young with no utility."[55] In their writings they advocated educational and material advance as the key to social well-being and prided themselves on striving to be useful to their *patria*, meaning Mexico or one of its regions. Their outlook paralleled that of those enlightened Spaniards who were members of economic and patriotic societies and were among the more innovative officials. They admired "wise moderns"—not only of Spain, but also of France, England, and British America. In 1763, Clavijero in a public address praised Bacon, Descartes, and Benjamin Franklin. Francisco Javier Alegre, another of these moderns, enjoyed the company of foreign merchants, learned English during a stay in Havana, and is known to have been familiar with theories of the origin of society propounded by Locke and Hobbes.[56] Interestingly, several of them were sons of Spanish administrators who had married *criollas* and settled in America. Well documented is the case of Clavijero, whose father, Blas, purchased the lucrative post of alcaldía mayor in Mixteca Baja where he prospered, combining public office and private enterprise. Within the network of peninsular Spaniards monopolizing the import trade and distribution inside New Spain, he pressed goods on his Indian charges. He also held contracts to provision garrisons and ships. He had a store and a hacienda, and engaged in trading cacao. Among his possessions was a large library, where his son the future Jesuit probably first read Feijoo.[57]

While in Mexico, these Jesuits confined their writings largely to new epics on classical models. These men also carefully presented circumspect criticism of traditional usages in education and advocated improving material conditions through inventorying resources and applying useful knowledge to better economy and society. Clavijero, in his *Descripción de la ciudad de la Puebla de los Angeles o Angelopolis,* a tract bearing out the last tendency, incidentally shed light on Puebla's problems, attributing depression there to Michoacán taking the region's wheat market and to loss of trade with Peru.[58] These creoles parted company with enlightened Spaniards principally on one issue, that of their Order. After 1767, in exile in Italy, very homesick and angered by philosophes' slurs on all America, they composed Mexican histories and epic poetry encrusted with a patriotism devoid of imperial attachment and emphasizing the creoles' indigenous heritage and Mexican distinctness. These books, infused with a spirit of nascent nationalism, immediately became well known and esteemed by their compatriots, to whom they were addressed.[59] Other Jesuits from other Spanish American regions followed similar pursuits, with similar effect.

Certain other repercussions from the expulsion of the Jesuits should be mentioned. Although the Order had infuriated enlightened ministers by its relative autonomy and disregard of state policy in doing business domestically (Jesuits in Puebla were traditionally producers and marketers of grain), interregionally (Jesuit haciendas on the Peruvian coast sent sugar to Chile by way of Lima and sold rum in Guayaquil and Lima), and internationally (as in Brazil), Jesuits had also customarily mediated social and political conflict within the traditional imperial linking of state and clergy, crown and faith. Most recently, they had intervened during the uprisings in Quito in 1765 against the new government monopoly on rum and even, ironically enough, as in Pátzcuaro, to quell demonstrations against their own expulsion. The Spanish government, in this context, ousted a valuable ally at a time when change within the divisions of society was accelerating. At lower levels, mobility was increasing and so was racial and ethnic intermixture. Population continued to expand and, in some areas of Mexico and elsewhere, there was more opportunity for salaried work in mines, on farms and ranches, in small workshops and home industries, and in sugar mills, though wages were minimal at best and often soon turned into debt peonage. When the government introduced new policies into this situation, conflict ensued. Riots and uprisings occurred, particularly where changes and governmental attention were most focused. The most prominent rebellions took place in the Bajío, north of the Mexican capital and extending to San Luis de Potosí. Moreover, ruthless suppression of revolts there—hundreds of people were executed and more sentenced to frontier garrison duty—by Gálvez and the army exposed a new Spanish toughness and intransigence and an official decision to maintain a quasi-military rule over what was expected to be a more submissive populace.[60] At the same time that British Americans were protesting the Stamp Act, Mexicans became aware of the new stance their government was taking toward the colonies, but there was no unified sentiment within Spanish America, or New Spain itself, against the new imperial program. And the expulsion of the Jesuits simply added to the complexity of a broad spectrum of attitudes concerning imperial attachment.

Before 1767, Jesuits had a near monopoly on secondary education, and in teaching and preaching they had imparted beliefs and assumptions that generally

ATLANTIC EMPIRES

supported traditional ties of Americans to the Spanish monarchy. They had
assimilated new, potentially disruptive concepts into the prevailing intellectual
framework. They had, that is, maintained those customary terms of imperial
belonging tying American Spaniards to the Spanish crown and church as loyal
vassals and faithful believers who were overseeing one kingdom of empire for
monarch and God, an interpretation agreeing with the principal tenets of criollismo. After 1767, the new official emphasis on secularity in politics and
education undermined this intertwining of temporal and spiritual authority—
indeed, the principle of authority itself—and nowhere was the breakdown of this
alliance made more visible than in the expulsion itself, first of all, and then in
changes in education introduced under government aegis. Thereafter, education
tended to polarize. Many proponents of modernism paid less attention to the old
religious bases of learning and tended instead to emphasize with redirected fervor
utility and the physical sciences, while traditionalists more stubbornly defended
the old ways and the old authorities. John Tate Lanning found that in colonial
education in general there occurred a marked rise in interest in the senses and a new
and "absolute fascination with the body."[61] In Lima, the viceroy, Manuel Amat,
in 1770 created the first American Academy of San Carlos, which emphasized
secular, practical knowledge. Other academies followed in major South American
centers, disseminating the values of utility and innovation and of material progress
as patriotic duty, and not perpetuating as necessary the connection of Spain to
everything civilized. Amat also backed university reform; and though more
traditional factions soon regained control of the older universities everywhere,
other schools and academies carried on in more modern spirit, and an eclecticism
more secular than Feijoo's came into texts, student papers, and talks. In addition,
the mounting number of Spanish Americans who associated with the Basque
economic society attested both to the social cachet attendant upon advocating
reform and the dissemination of enlightened and protoliberal tenets then prevalent
among reformers in Spain.[62]

Finally, in expelling the Jesuits the government showed itself both as changing
traditional terms of attachment and as lessening its trust of Spanish Americans.
Thus, in Mexico the viceroy, the Marqués de Croix, edgy about adverse public
reaction to the expulsion and about rumors of conspiracy in Puebla, sounded a new
note in imperial relations—and, in the course of showing a novel, harsh authoritarianism, by invoking a nonexistent tradition he weakened the pertaining one.
Croix decreed the death penalty for "those subjects of the great monarch of Spain
who do not conform to the thesis that they were born to be silent and obey, and not
to think or talk about high affairs of government."[63] Silence, however, was no part
of traditional ties to the empire. Since the sixteenth century, Spaniards in America,
including creoles, had respectfully spoken their minds, in petitions to the crown.
And Croix's parallel official in the church, the ultraregalist Archbishop of Mexico,
Francisco Antonio Lorenzana, manifested similar tendencies.

There was good reason for their edginess. Leading creoles were among Jesuit
partisans, even relatives, and these people both regretted the loss of the order per se

and saw the expulsion as symbolic of the new tougher governmental stance and of their own loss of customary authority. Moreover, not only was there rumor of conspiracy in Puebla, but with England as a next-door neighbor there was greater threat of subversion. There was too the huge territory of Louisiana to administer. When Antonio de Ulloa arrived in New Orleans in 1766 as its first Spanish governor, he reported being warned by his French predecessor in office that the inhabitants were incorrigibles "infected with the rebellious spirit of republicanism."[64] That spirit took form in the new Spanish colony in 1768 in an uprising against Ulloa. It was led by debtors and smugglers, among them some of Louisiana's most prominent men. The revolt was accompanied by cries for liberty and against despotism and slavery; its leaders sought return to French control or transfer to British. Some of them secretly corresponded with the British in Pensacola (who showed little interest) and were planning a republic when General O'Reilly and his forces from Cuba effectively took over.[65] The year before, Lorenzana had informed Madrid of plans for a "universal rising" against the monarchy. He had reported the conspirators to be aristocratic and in communication with "a maritime power" with whom they would trade exclusively, and that among the prominent instigators were Jesuit partisans. Gálvez subsequently exiled nine leading creoles who were known to have criticized governmental policies and to be Jesuit supporters, among them the jurist Francisco Javier de Gamboa, who returned in the 1770s and rose to political power in the 1780s.[66] Such men correctly interpreted the expulsion as a shift in reliance for maintaining internal order away from the clergy, often native-born and socially well-connected, to the military, whose top officers came from Spain. Lorenzana then, even in church offices, exhibited a marked preference for peninsulars. Reacting to all this, Moniño and Campomanes, we recall, urged that creoles be induced to love the nation. Thus those royal ministers inadvertently made matters worse by implicitly rejecting the creole notion of terms of imperial attachment in construing the old ramshackle empire as *"un solo cuerpo de nación"* (a single, national body).

Related is the *representación* of 1771 made, as had been Ahumada's appeal half a century earlier, in the name of the city council of the Mexican capital. That cabildo was now composed of rather traditionally minded upper class creoles who were reacting to new policies and in particular to slights to creoles offered by Lorenzana during the recent fourth Mexican church council. They had smarted under the new regime from at least 1765 when, angered by the recent imposition of the tobacco monopoly, they had protested that that measure both usurped a function of the city and had been instituted improperly—that is, without consulting them. Six years later, the same cabildo defensively countered continued slights by asserting a heightened sense of Mexican capability and of both Mexican and broadly American particularism. Members said that as Americans of Spanish background they resented being lumped with Indians by libelous Europeans, and they declared new Spanish immigrants to be foreigners with no interest in America; it is, was their argument, natural to love best one's native soil. American

Spaniards did, and they were familiar with local conditions, so different (they implied) from those of Spain. "We have always considered ourselves sons of Your Majesty," just like the natives of old Spain, for old Spain and New Spain "are two wives of Your Majesty."[67] These creoles insisted, touchily and wrongly, that ethnic mixture was uncommon—indeed, some of them came of aristocratic mestizo families, and they denigrated *castas* (people of racially-mixed lineage) and blacks. They also expressed sentiments of Americanism and great concern for world opinion: "What will the rest of the world say of America?" And combining two metaphors that would become increasingly popular, they asked to be permitted to "show the world our qualities . . . Thus will Your Majesty be more glorious, for the honor of children is the glory of their parents."

Though claiming the old patrimonial relationship with the monarch endured, they wrote as newly rambunctious minors (apparently a more congenial role than that of slighted wife), not so differently than did British colonists during the Seven Years' War. Mirroring the recent tendency to value population, they concluded that the great number of people in Spanish America made their subordination to Europeans inhumane and against the law of nations. Swearing to their own loyalty and service, aggrieved at the questioning of their constancy and dependability, their thought was a hodgepodge. In it the old patriarchal allegiance and the political theory of traditional, conservative creolism was newly animated by bitterness, and there entered a newer aggressive spirit compounded of self-assertion, Americanism, and natural rights. The customary regional patriotism was verging on embryonic nationalism. In the face of European slurs, they averred that creoles were neither cowards nor traitors. They defended Spanish Americans much as had Feijoo, and also as did the Abbé Raynal in his *Histoire des Indes* of 1770, if with more vehemence. Raynal would be well known in Spanish America by 1772, and his popular work, which began with the importance of the New World for the commerce of the Old, and which predicted the American Revolution, would have numerous editions, but the Mexicans had other sources available as well.[68]

The point is that creoles were well aware that their loyalty was of lively interest to Spain and other nations, and that even customary criollismo was taking on within its old attitudes a newly defiant spirit and some new vocabulary. Although some creoles embraced approved enlightened concepts, many of those who did and others who did not objected more than ever to political assumptions that (also more than ever) allowed domination by peninsular Spaniards. For, like English colonists, creoles of every persuasion claimed rights and privileges gained over years of relative imperial neglect. Equally important, the members of the Mexican cabildo in 1771 explicitly and emphatically declared themselves spokesmen for "a nation of America."

The careers of yet another group of Mexican creoles help fill out the picture of American relations with the Spanish empire. They date from the later 1760s and further illustrate relationships between the Bourbon reforms, the changing mental landscape, and American ambitions; and they point to a new alliance of intellectuals and government. (While a few such men also appeared in South America, more would emerge a decade or so later.) The first, Joaquín Velázquez de León, in 1765—in accord with royal approval of educational reform—was teaching (applied) mathematics in the chair of astrology at the University of Mexico. He studied mining at the same time, and in 1768, Croix and Gálvez began employing him to report on mines in Mexico and California and to map the viceroyalty. Velázquez helped to create, and became first director of, the mining guild of New Spain, founded on July 1, 1776. His career is one indication that talented creoles could and did hope and work for reform and did advance within the imperial system when other Americans were opting for independence.[69]

Another is that of José Ignacio Bartolache, his son-in-law, a physician and mathematician who substituted for him during his absences from teaching and who urged Mexicans to study applied science—astronomy, hydraulic mechanics, optics, agronomy, arithmetic, and geometry. In October 1772, Bartolache brought out the first issue of the first medical review in North America. It was written in a critical vein and one of creole self-awareness. Thus, he addressed his compatriots with mingled pride and regret: "Our *América septentional,* that great part of the world, so worthy of consideration for its riches, has not been equally renowned for the flowering of its letters, that is, for studies and useful knowledge."[70] Bartolache ardently admired Descartes and Newton, and cited the latter concerning man's becoming master of the physical world. An associate of the Basque economic society, as were a number of other Mexicans, his outlook spanned tradition and modernity, imperial attachment and regional patriotism. He dedicated a book to Croix and his doctoral thesis, as was common, to the Virgin of Guadalupe. One scholar has gone so far as to assert that in 1769, with the publication of Bartolache's *Las lecciones matemáticas,* "the modern point of view in philosophy was found complete in Mexico."[71]

Antonio León y Gama, who was Velásquez's friend and was another mathematician who read widely, including Newton, became official astronomer and adviser to two viceroys. He was also deeply interested in indigenous antiquities and wrote, in order to be useful to his patria, pieces meant to discredit calumnies against the Indians of Mexico. They were printed in the gazette edited by yet another influential creole of kindred interests, José Antonio Alzate y Ramírez.[72] Alzate, most vociferous of the circle, overflowed with a sense of self-esteem perhaps intensified by a feeling of Mexican, and personal, slight by Europeans. A great-nephew of the eminent and well-remembered seventeenth-century savant, Sor Juana Inés de la Cruz, he had been a student of Clavijero's. He had encyclopedic interests, a thirst for universal literary and useful scientific knowledge, and an inheritance which he spent on putting together a private library, a museum, a cabinet of natural history, and a collection of Mexican antiquities. He accumulated machines and instruments necessary for the practical and experimental study of astronomy and other physical sciences, his interests paralleling those of his northern contemporary, Thomas Jefferson. He was also a member of the Basque *Amigos del País,* and Gálvez used maps he made. His injudicious use of the word *tyranny,* although in an article on the theater (then also coming into vogue), was deemed by Croix, who was on guard against repercussions from the expulsion of the Jesuits, sufficiently incendiary to warrant closing down the press. Nonetheless, Alzate went on to greater heights. His career, like that of the others, was often interwoven with the reform program of Charles III, and was in the ascendant in 1776.[73]

While more traditional creoles complained of change, and more modern ones were advocating it in order to develop their home regions, another sort of response to alterations and pressures escalated during the eighteenth century and cut across the social, racial, and ethnic divisions in which Latin Americans lived. That was the popular revolt, and there were hundreds of them. Most were minor incidents, but some were more than spontaneous outbursts, if far less than revolutions for independence. They erupted sporadically and, from 1750, became more frequent. They were always calls for protecting customary usages against specific intrusions or abuses. Almost always, they involved Indians, blacks and people of mixed lineage. At least a few, though, were black slave revolts exclusively; others, in Andean regions and Mexico, were predominantly Indian. Black slaves rose, for example, in the Chocó of New Granada in 1728, and in Cuba in 1731 and 1755 in mines and against abuse by overseers; and in 1768, blacks on two Peruvian coastal haciendas formerly owned by the Jesuits revolted when the new state-directed administration, to combat lowered production, intensified work loads and cut workers' benefits, especially the customary right of slaves to cultivate their own plots.[74]

Other revolts originating among slaves spread to include various disaffected sectors of the populace. Among Indians, who were harder pressed from mid-century by rapacious corregidores and by taxes, new immigrants, the expansion of great estates, and accelerating assimilation, rebellions were usually sudden and short-lived. They were community responses to specific grievances against authorities imposed from outside. Some, however, were of broader scope. In Mexico, where a few went beyond the village to become regional, one of the largest erupted in Yucatán in 1761 and the most widespread were those in the Bajío. Discontents also tended to coalesce around a revered figure and in millenarian expectations—notably in Oaxaca.[75]

In South America, a few larger movements were led by caciques calling for restoration of the Inca empire. In 1737, Spanish authorities uncovered a conspiracy involving the leaders of seventeen provinces in southern Peru, with links to Cuzco. The next year another was exposed in Oruro; it was headed by a mestizo, Juan Velez de Córdoba. In 1740, conspirators planned to put one "Felipe Inca" on a Peruvian throne and sent an envoy to London for aid. In 1742, the dynamic Juan Santos, claiming to be the heir to Atahuallpa, the Inca ruler overthrown by Pizarro, led Indians in the central highland of Peru around Tarma in well-planned guerrilla warfare against the government. He harassed the authorities until, in 1761, he was assassinated by one of his followers. Connected was the plot of some Lima caciques in 1750 to kill the viceroy and free the slaves; reverberations of unrest spread to Indian areas in New Granada, Charcas (in present day Bolivia), and Tucumán. Again, through the 1770s, a number of localized rebellions in Upper Peru protested dishonest officials and the *mita* system of forced labor in the mines. These plots and risings, repeatedly calling for resurrection of Inca rule, gained inspiration too from Spanish and possibly British sources. Both were present within the second edition of the *Royal Commentaries of the Incas,* by Garcilaso de la Vega, known as el Inca, who was the son of a Spanish soldier and an Inca princess. That edition appeared 150 years after the first. It was printed in Madrid, and its prologue contained a prophecy, culled from the writings of Sir Walter Raleigh, that the Incas "would be restored by a people coming from the region called England."[76]

Mestizos and other mixed peoples predominated in numerous uprisings. Among the earliest was one in Paraguay in the 1720s during which one faction styled themselves *comuneros,* after Castilian townspeople who in the 1520s rose essentially against government by foreigners. In Paraguay the rebels included creoles, mestizos, and Indians. The basic cause was Asunción colonists' envy of the good lands, Indian labor, and trade in *yerba mate* of the Jesuit missions, for the Jesuits were prospering and Asunción was not.[77] Mestizos rose against Spanish authorities in Cochabamba in 1730, on rumor they would have to pay tribute—a threat to their pride as well as their purses, for doing so would class them with Indians. Peoples of mixed lineage also predominated in the increasingly frequent revolts in Venezuela, essentially against the restrictions imposed by the Caracas Company. Rebellions took place there from 1730 to 1733 (led by the mulatto Andresote) and in 1749; there were two each in the fifties and sixties, and four in the 1770s. Mestizos made up the bulk of militia deserters rising in Corrientes during 1764-65, of insurgents in Paraguay in 1764, and of rebels in Quito who in 1765 protested the newly efficient collection of customs duties and the new monopoly on rum.[78]

Among peoples of various backgrounds in Quito, Mexico, and Santiago de Chile, between 1765 and 1767 government reforms sparked violent outbreaks. In the Mexican Bajío they were directed against the tobacco monopoly, forced army levies, the extension of sales taxes and more stringent tax collection, and changes in recompense for mine work, as well as the expulsion of the Jesuits. Among the thousands of people—creoles and Indians, but mostly mulattoes and mestizos— who took to arms were mine, ranch, and field workers, vagabonds, and Indian villagers, their leaders on occasion calling for a creole or Indian king.[79] A number of peasant and slave uprisings sought to install local or regional officials in place of despised "foreign" ones, and to achieve greater autonomy under a native prince or king, but very few seem to have intended complete and permanent separation from the Spanish monarchy. Some of the more radical participants in the revolt led by Juan Santos called for complete independence, yet most of the suggestions for independence appear to have come from creoles who formed unsuccessful conspiratorial juntas and who wanted to control the affairs of their own regions. Whatever the impelling motives, the tendency of revolts has always been to become more radical once under way, and those in Latin America throughout the eighteenth century were no exception. Further, it was of course then possible, in accord with the prevailing (Hapsburg) theory of imperial attachment held by Spanish Americans, that rebels who proposed a politically autonomous kingdom could do so without seeking complete independence from the monarch.

Racial and ethnic hatreds were sometimes manifest in one form or another, particularly in slave revolts, and from time to time among rebelling Indians and mestizos, as in the Bajío in 1766-67. Regardless of the ethnic component, antagonisms were directed most immediately against overseers or administrators of whatever different race, or against masters and officials, who were mainly white. There is also evidence, however, that propertied creoles repeatedly were— at times overtly, at others secretly—behind displays of resistance to new or newly energetic supraregional authority challenging their own. In one of the earliest movements, that in Cuba in 1717 against the new royal monopoly on the island's main crop, tobacco, growers and merchants protested. Priests preached resistance, and a popular march on Havana expelled the governor. The crown, conciliatory at first, soon restored the monopoly; new uprisings in 1720 and 1723 resulted. A creole led the Paraguayan comuneros, and the revolt against the Caracas Company in the 1740s is another case in point. In inland Tocuyo, Venezuela, in 1744, recruits to mount coastal defenses refused to go, declaring it not a mission to protect Puerto Cabello and La Guaira against the British, but a Basque scheme to raise labor gangs and one bound to kill them from overwork and bad treatment. Their armed resistance, ostensibly led by mulattoes, was instigated and supported by the propertied (white) inhabitants of the town.[80] The Basques and Catalans were resented in Spanish America, just as were the Scottish in Virginia. All were viewed as canny businessmen to whom Americans frequently became indebted.

Apparent in many of these popular uprisings was cooperation of all sorts of peoples within a given region against foreigners or outsiders. Repeatedly, if briefly, a unity of common cause was forged against outside oppressors—whether government agents, non-Hispanic people, or intruders from the peninsula—who challenged accepted ways, channels of authority, and economic arrangements. Non-Hispanic foreign threat brought coalescence of an unusual degree. The rebels of Tocuyo swore they would obey as loyal vassals if they were indeed needed to fight the British. And in 1741, the people and cabildo of San Felipe el Fuerte, in revolt against the new Basque governor and the Caracas Company, opted for conciliation when they heard the English were about to invade. Juan and Ulloa reported, from their findings in Ecuador, Colombia, and Peru in that period, that although some creoles would welcome British rule, creole merchants had readied their ships for defense against Anson at their own expense and with crews of creoles and mixed races, and that Spanish Americans in general had taken much responsibility for port and coastal defenses. They had, in fact, always guarded Peru, Panama, Cartagena, and Santa Marta, showing no signs of disloyalty. Such risings and disturbances as had occurred had never gone from private factional quarrels or local outbreaks to lack of obedience to the monarch or usurpation of sovereign rights; even the movements afoot centering in Tarma and Jauja they thought at the time were not exceptions, and they were probably right.[81]

There is, further, indication of foreign (that is, non-Spanish) meddling in some popular revolts; the Dutch role in Venezuelan resistance to the Caracas Company is best known. More difficult to ascertain is the extent of English influence on Spanish American disturbances, particularly in view of British attempts, especially in wartime, to attract clients. The British, in the attack on La Guaira in 1743, sought to destroy Company property and incite the populace against Company tyranny and oppression, representing themselves as liberators. There were reports, as has been mentioned, that rebellious Indians in Oruro and on the Pacific coast on the eve of Anson's expected arrival were in contact with creoles seeking British aid, and that Juan Santos expected English assistance. Moreover, the Peruvians' representative, on his way through New Granada and Venezuela, allegedly organized insurgent juntas in the Chocó, Cartagena, and Caracas. Oglethorpe reportedly was approached in 1742 by Mexicans seeking a British protectorate, and the Puebla conspirators of 1765 had similar goals. In what was predominantly a slave revolt in Venezuela between 1771 and 1774, the chief aide to its leader was a man known as José Eduardo de la Cruz Peralta, and also as Uvaldo, who reportedly came from London. And during the American Revolution, in a Oaxaca village a parish priest led an uprising in order to emulate, he said, the British system where "everyone rules."[82]

Rebellions before 1776, in short, were in the main peasant or slave uprisings, and sometimes a blend of the two, directed against specific officials and grievances and at times stirred up or prolonged by affluent and locally powerful creoles manifesting sentiments of conservative criollismo. None of these outbreaks can be termed national in scale—although the Peruvian Indian uprisings had national content and radical adherents seeking independence from Spain—but everywhere most leaders sought local or regional freedoms, expressed as a return to a previous situation. Although many elements observable in uprisings and conspiracies before 1776 would later coalesce into broader and more intense revolts and would reappear in the revolutions for independence, in this period revolts and plots most significantly served as prime indicators of the nature and scope of Spanish American dissatisfactions and regional particularisms and, from the 1760s on, of their heightening and broadening in response to altered official policies and attitudes. Taken as a whole, eighteenth-century Spanish American revolts signified deep-rooted discontents throughout society and great mutual antagonisms among social groups, within a traditional but changing political, social, and economic imperial situation. These antagonisms were probably deepened, and some grievances were caused, by international struggles and certainly by unprecedented alterations imposed from outside or above on fragilely balanced customary social and economic arrangements. Yet, these uprisings also attest to the endurance of hierarchical society in Spanish America with a creole and peninsular aristocracy at its apex. These creoles held to a rationale for their own preeminence based upon military and, intermeshed, religious foundations, one originating in America with the Spanish conquest. The outbreaks also serve to corroborate that alterations very important to subsequent Spanish American history, occurring during the century in the attitudes and assumptions of members of all social groups, had some violent reverberations.

In sum, by 1776 the full spectrum of Latin American provinces that would, half a century later, become independent republics, could be distinguished as administrative units. Wars with England and related shifts in trade had sped the emergence of formerly peripheral areas. Provinces once dependent on the two original viceroyalties of Mexico and Peru now competed with the old hubs for attention and commerce, especially with more ports legally open to Spanish shipping, as did outlying regional centers still under those viceroys. New Spain was expanding in population, agriculture, ranching, trade, and mining. Peru's mine yields rose less dramatically. Lima was being challenged economically by its old dependencies, Venezuela, New Granada, and Buenos Aires, and by Chile, still under the Peruvian viceroy. A special case was Cuba, prospering through Mexican stipends, wartime economic boom, and the most open commerce in Spanish America. There was, over all, more trade with Spain, as well as more intraregional trade and more smuggling than ever before. There was also more regional competition, and more new personnel were entering the powerful sectors of society. Brazil, less fortunate, was undergoing recession and was the major staging area for the struggle between Portugal and Spain in La Plata from 1774 to 1777. Still, it profited from alliance with Britain and larger markets after 1776, though not without imperial tensions, as we shall see.

Some ambitious Latin Americans, largely in and through educated and government circles, were taking on an enlightened, protoliberal, modern vocabulary and the social norms of enlightened public service, including the new esteem attached to individual participation in public affairs, to being useful to one's society at a time when the concept of society was in transition. A vogue had begun among the urban educated for foreign—that is, non-Spanish—exemplars for almost every aspect of life and also one for voluntary associations—clubs, academies, societies, and civic organizations—some of which were to become the nurseries of insurgence. Even so, this trend had Spanish conduits and can best be understood as funneling through the peninsula. Among such people in the 1760s and 1770s, a rational and improvement-oriented state of mind, with many of its concepts and concerns acquired by way of Bourbon Spain, began in earnest to do battle with the old intellectual order in Latin America. They were explaining the world in scientific, rather than the old theological, terms.

Other astute, more traditionally oriented Latin Americans, wielding local power or involved in the overseas trading network, or both, were taking advantage of alterations in government, society, and international relations. They would continue to do so, and, in their local areas, seeing opportunities in conflicts in jurisdiction, would often block or hinder unwelcome new officials or measures, or would circumvent and coopt them, as self-interest and local advantage dictated.

They, too, were taking more interest in civic affairs and new pride in being both legitimate and able defenders of the land. The militia raised during the war against Britain in 1762-63 afterwards attracted propertied creoles willing to organize and outfit units in return for commissions. With rank came privileges, prestige, and a surge of pride reinforcing defensive, military elements in criollismo. While creole interest in military responsibilities ebbed quickly, the militant note in expressions of creolism did not, and that interest was to reawaken in the crises of the early nineteenth century.[83] For both the educated professionals and the propertied, the opportunity opened by readjustment, rather than revolution, appeared to hold out promise. For most of the rest of the populace, the issue remained survival.

Yet, among both groups of creoles, the more traditionally minded land and mine owners and merchants, and the more modern professionals and newer merchants, by 1776 a greater sense of being American was observable and in the ascendant. Both groups expressed sentiments which, although differing in their components, displayed a heightened regional patriotism within a *conciencia de sí,* or creolism. The overarching nature of traditional terms of imperial attachment allowed this latitude. The American regions—indeed, all America—could be and were fitted within the customary view of the imperial system. Thus, some creoles reasserted claims to regional ascendency based on Spanish ancestry while others made similar claims based upon mingled Spanish and American bloodlines. Even so, they coalesced in evidencing a growing sense of regional patriotism and a common desire for greater power and authority within their own regions of empire and in greater insistence on separateness from peninsular Spain and European Spaniards. They were Americans, was the repeated assertion; the tie was only to the crown and, less stressed as time went on, to the faith. And in both groups the sense of criollismo and Americanism was affected by events in the other Americas in the 1760s and 1770s.

From 1763, we have seen, Spanish American inhabitants—clergy, titled creoles, merchants, bureaucrats, and other professionals—knew of new books on the English colonies and on Anglo-American government and trade, and had got hold of some of them. They could also read of current events in British North America in two Spanish gazettes which, as one scholar has remarked, had wider circulation in America than in Europe.[84] They had information on Anglo-American complaints from 1765, riots in Boston against the Stamp Act, unrest in New York in 1768, appeals for domestic manufacture, and denunciations of the Navigation Acts. One Spanish gazette commented that England's only interest in America lay in the advantage to British commerce. The Stamp Act, the *Mercurio Histórico y Político* told its readers, had a most advantageous effect on the nonimportation movement, for it stimulated production of manufactures and did no harm to agriculture: "Industry and frugality reign today in all the colonies with an emulation so patriotic" that everyone tries to make more textiles and clothing.[85] Whatever Spanish Americans made of all this, a Peruvian poet then commented approvingly that newly austere viceregal inaugural ceremonies were even less elaborate than the scale on which things were done in the English colonies of North

America, and we know that from the 1760s creole interest in promoting domestic manufactures, agriculture, and commerce in home regions mounted steadily.[86]

Contact with British wares and tenets of political economy and with Anglo-American products and premises was also ongoing and mounting. Spanish Americans knew that to the government in 1776 the rebels appeared the lesser threat; still, security was tightened and jurisdiction expanded in peripheral areas and along borders almost everywhere. It is no coincidence that San Francisco was founded then and that Gálvez, becoming Minister of the Indies, in 1776 made of Nueva Vizcaya, Sonora, Sinaloa, the Californias, Coahuila, New Mexico, and Texas a separate, essentially military jurisdiction, the *Provincias Internas*. Shortly after, Venezuela received an intendant and Buenos Aires became a viceroyalty, a result of the commercial and undeclared military war with Portugal and its longtime commercial ally—indeed, mentor—Britain. The war to the north would, we shall see, provide an American exploit heightening what has been called a continental nationalism, and its outcome would present an alternative form of government and economy to imperial attachment. Before, the colonial system was common to Americans, but by 1776 it rested upon shaky and muddled principles. Nevertheless, it was still viewed by creoles as a viable system, although some of them saw it as needing correction, while others thought it had received too much.

5

"WE SEE WITH OTHER EYES":
THE NEW NATION LOOKS AT
LATIN AMERICA, 1776-1808

Englishmen came to America seeking both wealth and a more perfect society, and within the thirteen colonies there evolved the parallel values of material realism and utopian idealism—which incidentally have presented a salutary paradox to latter-day historians in quest of the American character.[1]

England's colonial policy stemmed from a primary interest in the regulation of American trade and included an interest in colonial unity. British colonists also came to feel a need for unity, but by 1776 that need had coalesced with emergent American patriotism and with personal interest in the territorial and economic expansion of the thirteen colonies, and colonists were strongly opposed to British commercial strictures. Yet, the importance England had placed on trade by 1776 had become domiciled in America, as had the knowledge that much of America's relations with the rest of the world had to do with commerce.

By 1776, understandably, relations with Europe were the principal objects of emergent American foreign policy, and European notions were joined to American experience and assumptions in its elucidation. Anglo-Americans adapted English-derived principles. They viewed as dominant goals trade (like the English) and peace (like some of the English), and they distrusted, as did the British government, Continental alliances.[2]

Early in 1776, Thomas Paine's *Common Sense* drove home certain English concepts to Americans, presenting a republican ideal and the American duty to realize it. It summed up the radical arguments made in the 1775 Continental Congress and set a radical program before the public. Like the debates of that Congress, it placed a major emphasis on issues of trade. Wrote Paine: America's "plan is commerce, and that, well attended to, will secure us the peace and friendship of all Europe; because it is in the interest of all Europe to have America as a free port." Urging American independence, insisting its declaration would bring immediate aid from France and Spain, he concluded by presenting a program for American foreign policy: "Any submission to, or dependence on, Great Britain, tends directly to involve this continent in European wars and quarrels. . . . As Europe is our market for trade, we ought to form no partial connection with any part of it. It is the true interest of America to steer clear of European contentions."[3] Paine related political independence to commercial liberty, arguing from American self-interest, from existing European relations, and within the eighteenth-century British tradition of foreign policy.

On April 6, as we have seen, Congress—well aware that confederation and declaring independence were necessary to securing the foreign aid vital to waging successful war—opened ports to all nations except Britain, thereby authorizing free trade before declaring political independence. And we recall that *free trade* had a seventeenth- and early eighteenth-century history—indeed, pedigree. The phrase included the old meanings of a direct carrying trade to and from open ports, a lack of discriminatory measures on the part of one's own national government, and an implication of low import and export duties. It also implied expectation of commercial reciprocity. Yet beyond that it signified an ideal of international trade unimpeded by governmental regulation.

In late eighteenth-century Europe, while alliances could and frequently did combine military, commercial, and economic arrangements, since Utrecht those components tended to be separated, so that the term *alliance* had taken on an ambiguity which John Adams, in drawing up the first such agreement made by the United States, in 1776 with France, chose to interpret as making possible an accord limited to trade relations—for, as Adams expressed his feelings (in 1783), "The business of America with Europe was commerce, not politics or war."[4] This was the Model Treaty for future (commercial) pacts, and it went beyond older international pacts to place a new and greater emphasis on freer trade. The Model Treaty favored commercial competition, even among fellow nationals. It evidenced the faith of the leaders of the new nation in the power of trade, and a concomitant desire to stay out of European struggles. It also, incidentally, reaffirmed the principles of the Navigation Acts and served as an instrument for Americans to make use of the European balance of power. And it indicated a belief that freedom was on the wane everywhere but in mainland Anglo-America, that America, now liberty's home, must be maintained as "an asylum for mankind," and that, while Americans must stay free from Europe's corruption, they must institute a new era in diplomacy where peace and trade with Europe were nonetheless possible and very desirable.

At the same time, during the Revolution an upsurge in profiteering and luxurious living increased old, essentially Puritan (or Calvinist) suspicions of prosperity and sparked ambivalent statements by American leaders concerning commerce. Thus, Adams decried the "excessive influx of Commerce" even while recognizing the needs for an Anglo-American carrying trade and for war matériel. His argument was not with mercantile activity itself but with immoderate thirst for individual material gain and specifically with the illicit import of British manufactures.[5]

After 1783, one issue dominated negotiations with European nations: regulating trade and settling commercial relations between the new republic and Europe. The Confederation wanted free trade and its commercial flow unhampered by foreign wars. Particularly since England dominated the seas and British blockade was the greatest threat, Americans, like Englishmen earlier, sought acceptance of principles of international law and guarantees of the safety of neutral trade. In this spirit, Thomas Jefferson drafted the first foreign policy report acceptable to Congress. It maintained the principles of the Model Treaty and suggested pacts of "amity and commerce" with other (named) states in order "to form a general system of commerce by treaties with other nations." It recommended the appointment of consuls, and the first diplomatic agent to Europe received instructions on May 7, 1784. In the same period, Jefferson spoke of the value to humanity of "the total emancipation of commerce and bringing together all nations for a free intercommunication of happiness."[6]

Although Jefferson was still writing in 1792 that in Europe "consuls would do all the business we ought to have," by then he and other Anglo-American leaders had come to realize, as Felix Gilbert put it, that "the principle of avoiding political connections proved to be incompatible with progress toward freeing commerce, which was the great hope for overcoming power politics."[7] American leaders were preeminently pragmatists, ready to deal with the world as they found it and rapidly discovering what the new nation must do to survive. By 1780, John Adams was writing that only interest decided foreign policy, that an equilibrium, a balance of powers, would be useful to his country in offsetting English tyranny of the seas, and that ministers should be sent abroad.[8]

In the 1780s, American diplomats found Europe entrenched in "the spirit of monopoly and exclusion," and Adams and Jefferson, faced with postwar depression in 1784 and belatedly recognizing that their policy of free trade had not been as eagerly reciprocated as expected, felt the United States might have to adopt stronger measures, including restrictive tariffs, in order to survive in a situation of power politics. By 1785, national leaders had endorsed tariffs for international retaliation and protection above and beyond earlier tariffs for revenue.

In England in 1780, Thomas Pownall, the former governor of Massachusetts, took for granted the separation of Anglo-America and foresaw its growth "into an independent organized being, a great and powerful empire. It has taken its equal station with the nations upon earth."[9] He also wrote that the South American colonies would break away from Europe; and, if the new American nation proceeded intelligently and used European rivalries, he thought it could establish hegemony over all the Americas. Pownall relied to some extent on Paine's *Common Sense* and, in turn, John Adams turned Pownall's pamphlet into American propaganda. In stating an early prognosis of what would come to be the dominant Anglo-American version of the Western Hemisphere idea, an American system serving as counterweight to Europe, it bridged the gap between political idealism and power politics—as did the opinion of a postrevolutionary leader inclined toward the latter, Alexander Hamilton. For tranquility and happiness at home, Hamilton wrote in *The Federalist* in 1787, sufficient strength and stability are necessary to be respected abroad; and further, commerce had replaced territory and domination as the prevailing system of nations. He, however, astutely saw commerce as no guarantor of peace, but only as changing the traditional object of war. Hamilton found a balance of power functioning, with the American system as one of four, and counseled a policy of American hegemony distinct from Europe: "Our situation invites and our interests prompt us to aim at an ascendant in the system of American affairs."[10] It was the echo of the old English policy, now applied to America, combining isolation from European politics with American domination, and it also found expression in Washington's Farewell Address of 1796. In that speech, commerce was viewed as a weapon in power politics, and, in commercial relations, nations were seen to follow their own interests, with that of the United States being the widest possible liberalization of commerce. The isolationism George Washington advocated, and for which that speech has so often been cited, referred to European power alliances only, not to relations with the other Americas and not to commerce.

Events in the nineteenth century then allowed United States foreign policy to be one of isolation from Europe, and integration of the old idealism of neutrality and peace gave United States isolationism its moralistic tone. Felix Gilbert has concluded that there was, and still remains, a basic undercurrent of tensions within American attitudes toward foreign policy: tension between idealism and realism, between gain and freedom, and between enlightened thinking and power politics. His work revised the multitude of earlier assessments of the origins of American foreign policy and, in so doing, cast light on and limned a general framework within which United States relations with Latin America can be seen to have evolved from 1776 on. As Latin Americans from then on have correctly perceived, free trade was an important part of the American revolutionary model. Moreover, as they accurately saw, it was part of a packet of working principles, including republicanism, political independence, self-government, enlightened ideas, science, domestic economic advance, and natural law and the law of nations.

The new republic from 1783 to 1808 joined France and England in competing for commercial advantage in Latin America. The three nations and Spain played balance of power diplomacy, dispatched agents, official and otherwise, to Latin America, and while watchful to make the most of every opportunity to further national interest, all were careful it should not be a rival's profit. On this international situation depended to a great extent the fate of Spain and, more indirectly, of Portugal, still a British satellite, in America. And until 1810, Spain retained its American colonies, largely because other nations were cognizant that the advantages each might gain from Spanish American independence could soon be offset by disadvantages arising should Spain's dependencies be controlled by a rival power stronger than Spain.

During this period of diplomatic sparring, British governments housed creole émigrés, encouraged their plans for Spanish American independence, and at times verged on implementing their goals.[11] France throughout its political vicissitudes until 1808 sought to maintain the Spanish alliance but also to befriend Spanish American dissidents. Napoleon in 1795 acquired the Spanish half of Santo Domingo and, in 1800, title to Louisiana. But the Haitian revolution and war with

England convinced him to forego the dream of French empire in America, and in 1803 he sold Louisiana to the United States. From the 1790s on, French agents passed through the United States, and in the propaganda they directed to Spanish America they often used the new American nation as a republican model. Napoleon's agents in New Orleans, a case in point, were instructed to inform creoles that France preferred independence for Spanish America to its current alliance with Britain through Spain.[12] In the United States also, some public officials and old revolutionaries unofficially encouraged would-be Spanish American liberators and, in at least two instances, planned to free Spanish colonies themselves. Well known is the conspiracy of Aaron Burr; less familiar is the project of Alexander Hamilton who, only second in command in the United States army in the late 1790s, wanted to be *the* liberator of Spanish American borderlands.[13] The United States, however, in the 1780s and 1790s was bound to moderation in relations with Spain and its Americas due to official concern over the questions of the Mississippi River, the frontier, and the Floridas.

The Anglo-American position within this international situation indicates some historical and strategic reasons why, regardless of the universal aspect of the opening paragraph of the Declaration of Independence, its principal author, Thomas Jefferson, manifested little direct concern with putting its principles into operation in the Americas beyond national borders. Rather, his attitude and policies toward Latin America, from the 1780s on, like those of other Anglo-American leaders, were compounded of concern for national interest, interpreted as protection and expansion of national boundaries, and increasingly—and after 1808 officially—as commercial expansion.

Jefferson, who as president exposed large gaps between his statements of republican theory and his manner of exercising power, in 1786 was momentarily carried away by the vision of the republic's population expanding throughout the hemisphere:

> Our confederacy must be viewed as the nest from which all America, North and South, is to be peopled. We should take care, too, not to think it for the best interest of that great continent to press too soon on the Spaniards. Those countries can not be in better hands. My fear is that they are too feeble to hold them till our population can be sufficiently advanced to gain it from them piece by piece.[14]

His subsequent pronouncements and policies evidenced more restricted goals for expansion but a similar regard for Spanish America remaining in Spanish hands, if only for the time being.[15]

John Adams, with much the same outlook, in that year wrote that the object of the next war would be the liberty of commerce in South America (and the East Indies) and that the United States should keep out of it, for "England would gain the most in such a turn of affairs.... And England unfortunately we can not trust."[16]

From the later 1780s, Jefferson's recognition of the importance of foreign trade and the coercive uses of commercial reciprocity, and, if necessary, retaliation, grew; conversely, he realized that a strong union was necessary for a united commercial policy. Yet he never stopped viewing commerce with ambivalence and within an agrarian frame. He saw it primarily as necessary to carry out surplus products and, although he admitted in 1785 that "our people have a decided taste for navigation and commerce," he frowned upon the wartime carrying trade as speculative and as making enemies. In the 1790s, when the issue of foreign policy was intimately tied to domestic affairs and was a prime spur to the formation of political parties, most frequently opinions concerning Latin America tended to flow from attitudes toward national concerns, and they were almost always connected to opinions on broader international relations. Thus, Jefferson's policies on Latin America were strongly influenced by his basic wish to promote United States agrarian growth, which he saw as most possible through commerce and by an expanding population, over the continent and perhaps beyond.[17]

When Spain agreed to transfer Louisiana to France in 1800, Jefferson as president bought it, mainly to protect and foster American commerce on the Mississippi; but the purchase also fit into the urge to continental expansion and adumbrated his later insistence that there be no transfer of European colonies in the Americas to other European nations: He and Madison had long desired to annex the Floridas and the Southwest, at least as far as Texas. In 1807, exasperated with the European powers and their hold on America and on its trade, he wrote to Madison:

> As soon as we have all the proofs of the western intrigues, let us make a remonstrance and demand of satisfaction, and, if Congress approves, we may in the same instant make reprisals on the Floridas, until satisfaction for that and for spoliations, and until a settlement of boundary. I had rather have war against Spain than not, if we go to war against England. Our southern defensive force can take the Floridas, volunteers for a Mexican army will flock to our standard, and rich pablum will be offered to our privateers in the plunder of their commerce and coasts. Probably Cuba will add itself to our consideration.[18]

In 1807, too, Jefferson reported approvingly to James Bowdoin, United States minister to Spain, that Aaron Burr had given up his idea of separating the West as a private domain and had "turned himself wholly towards Mexico and so popular is an enterprise on that country in this, that we had only to be still and he could have had followers enough to have been in the city of Mexico in six weeks."[19] On April 27, 1809, again writing to Madison, he indulged in some wishful thinking about the possibility of annexing Cuba, and beyond:

> ...and I would immediately erect a column on the southernmost limit of Cuba, and inscribe on it a *ne plus ultra* as to us in that direction. We should then have only to include the north in our Confederacy, which would be of course in the first war, and we should have such an empire for liberty as she has never surveyed since the creation; and I am persuaded no constitution was ever before so well calculated as ours for extensive empire and self-government.[20]

Henry Adams may not have been wrong in asserting that by 1808 the independence of the Spanish colonies was then "the chief object of American policy," but it must be added that, if so, it was because of the fear that Spain and its colonies had fallen to France.[21] Initially in that year, Jefferson reacted in hemispheric terms to Napoleon's invasion of the Iberian peninsula and to Britain's alliance with Portugal and the Spanish patriots, taking a friendly stance toward Spanish America and advocating no European influences (other than that of Spain) there. He and his cabinet only subsequently agreed to authorize United States agents to offer their nation's friendship to influential people working for independence in Cuba and Mexico. In the course of that year, too, Jefferson was generally disposed to use government agencies more actively to promote United States influence and commerce, for it was becoming clear to him and other men of affairs in the United States that Latin America, independent or not, would largely benefit Britain commercially, unless an aggressive policy was pursued to counteract British influence there.[22]

Instructions to Joel Poinsett as "United States agent to Latin America for seamen and commerce" indicated that by 1810 these hemispheric policies were official. Poinsett was to explain the mutual advantage of commerce with the United States. He was also to spread the impression that the United States cherished the most sincere good will toward the people of Spanish America as neighbors,

> as belonging to the same part of the globe, and as having mutual interest in cultivating friendly intercourse, that this disposition will exist, whatever may be their internal system or European relationships, with respect to which no interfering of any sort is pretended and that, in the event of a political separation from the parent country, and on the establishment of an independent system of National Government, it will coincide with the sentiments and policies of the United States to promote the most friendly relations, and the most liberal intercourse between the inhabitants of this Hemisphere, as having a common interest and as being under a common obligation to maintain that system of peace, justice and good will which is the only source of happiness of nations.[23]

Here is an early statement of an official desire to represent the United States as championing nonintervention and a good neighbor policy—one entrusted, significantly, to a commercial agent and in the same year that the United States annexed West Florida. In 1811 Congress, in relation to Spanish Florida, passed a No Transfer resolution, which would in 1824 be extended in the Monroe Doctrine to embrace the Western Hemisphere.

Throughout the years 1783-1808, some distinction was made between United States interests in, and policy toward, bordering Spanish lands, including Mexico and Cuba, and those directed to South America. Official concern came primarily to fix on tangential areas—Florida, Louisiana, New Spain, and Cuba. Their independence was expected to precede their passing—as strategic bases, or as areas for settlement, land speculations, and investment—to the United States, while in relations with South America friendship, possibly independence, but definitely trade preference were the goals, as Poinsett's instructions attest.

During the revolutionary war, although relatively few North Americans had contact with Latin America and although most of that interchange was com-

mercial, some of it was vital to Anglo-American independence and had ramifications beyond private business. The old trade with Spain and Portugal continued, although hampered by the British navy, and the opening of some Spanish
American ports in the Caribbean to ships of American insurgents, abetted by the
Spanish free trade act of 1778, proved profitable. From 1776, arms, military
stores, and money came secretly, and often intertwined with private commercial
transactions, to the insurgents from the French and Spanish governments by way
of those countries and the West Indies, Havana, and Louisiana. And much needed
specie was derived from commerce, particularly with the entrepôt of Havana.

Latin American trade, important to the United States at the time of the Monroe
Doctrine—when it accounted for perhaps one-fifth of United States exports and an
equal proportion of imports—was even more important in the years after 1776 and
of consequence to Atlantic coastal ports and the Mississippi region. Although a
great upsurge in exchange with Latin America came with the opening of Spanish
American ports to neutrals during Spain's war with England in 1797, indirect
commerce, contraband, and some legitimate trade increased from 1776; and after
1783, much United States wheat and flour and some re-exported manufactures
went to Spanish America and to Spain. In 1800 most United States trade was with
Latin America.[24]

Havana, long the hub of Spanish American trade and an important French and
Spanish base of operations during the war, was opened to business with the
insurgents in 1776 and became their largest Spanish American trading partner,
providing them with money and a market. The North Americans supplied Cuba,
including its garrison and expeditionary forces, its Florida dependencies, and its
numerous international traders, with flour from Philadelphia and the Chesapeake,
equipment for the sugar industry, naval stores from the Atlantic coast, and salted
beef carried from La Plata. They also provisioned New Orleans, and Mobile after
its capture, and took away sugar, military stores, and coin. American slavers, too,
traded actively with Cuba during the revolution.[25]

In the 1780s, shipments of Anglo-American wheat and flour went to Buenos
Aires and Venezuela, and a large amount to Santo Domingo, which then also
served as an emporium, particularly with New Orleans. Flour coming by that route
was essential to New Orleans, which was largely dependent on United States
provisions and shipping after 1783; smuggling flourished as never before. In the
1770's, yankee whalers had appeared off Patagonia; by 1785, the viceroy of
Buenos Aires reported a considerable number of English ships and of *bostoneses*
frequenting southern seas "on the pretext of whaling and probably with hidden
intentions."[26] While the bulk of trade was with the Caribbean and Gulf areas, by
1788 United States contraband, carried by whalers, seal hunters, and China
traders, was reaching the west coast of South America.[27] Pelts and specie for the
China trade were gathered along Spanish American coasts.

From 1789 to 1793, United States commercial emphasis shifted from Spain to
Latin America, and, with war in Europe, much carrying trade fell to United States
ships. Spain was forced to authorize neutral trade to supply the peninsula and the

colonies, and did so in piecemeal fashion, especially during war with France from 1793 to 1795, hostilities with England, 1797 to 1802, and yet again when that war was renewed in 1804–5. With the general Spanish decree of 1797 opening ports to neutrals, massive shipments of United States flour went to Havana; there was much United States investment in Cuban sugar, and United States trade with Spanish America, in general, soared. With the decree, Anglo-Americans legally supplied most Caribbean food imports and were the chief carriers to Venezuela. Large shipments of flour also went from Philadelphia to New Granada; and by 1798, the *Diario de México* reported United States vessels the most frequent visitors to the ports of New Spain. Mexican merchants appointed agents to North America, and United States houses sent representatives to Vera Cruz. The crown also used Anglo-American bottoms. They put in more often, too, at La Plata ports. From 1793 to 1799, United States exports rose steadily. They declined a bit from 1800 through 1803, then surged from 1805 to a peak in 1807 and early 1808. They fell with the embargo late in 1808 and rose again in 1809 until the war with Britain in 1812. Most commerce during the entire period was in re-exports, notably British manufactures. Although England still dominated the Brazilian trade, the ships of the new republic stopped at Brazilian ports and held first place in the carrying trade with Spanish America.[28]

In 1801, the Philadelphia *Gazette* carried advertisements for Buenos Aires hides, Caracas cacao, Cumaná cotton, and Santo Domingo coffee. With Napoleonic French-English hostilities and Spain unwisely fighting Britain from 1803 to 1805, the United States was the western world's foremost neutral trader. The Napoleonic wars allowed the American carrying trade to swell, in turn providing capital for United States commerce, manufactures, and agriculture. Anglo-Americans enjoyed profitable exchange, including in the carrying trade between Spanish and French ports, and between them and French and Spanish colonies in the Caribbean. There was much re-export of goods, including Spanish American produce and silver, through United States ports to evade British ships, to Cádiz, Hamburg, and Amsterdam, and to China, and much shipment of flour to the Iberian peninsula, especially after 1800. In 1805, the British destroyed the Spanish fleet at Trafalgar, seized many United States ships in the Caribbean, and efficiently blockaded American ports; still, Anglo-American vessels continued to sail, some under British licenses.[29] In 1806, when United States trade with Latin America was near its peak, a participant noted that "the United States was wholly in possession of the carrying trade between Mexico and Europe."[30] By 1807, Latin America was the principal source of United States specie, and the United States was Latin America's chief supplier of imports and largest market for exports, although over half of the manufactured goods North Americans carried were re-exports, largely British. The volume of United States trade with Spanish America early in 1808 has been estimated at $30 million, exceeding the British volume of commerce with that area, estimated to be $25 million. However, later that year Jefferson's embargo and Spanish alliance meant England soon gained the advantage.[31]

Outlining seminal United States policies concerning Latin America and the country's commerce with it does not tell the whole story, for in this initial period of the nation's history a wide variety of public and private relations with Latin America were often intertwined. Moreover, the lines between national and international aspects of trade relations between the Americas were often blurred. Discernible after independence as before was an international commercial and financial network within which Latin America figured as a source of raw materials and specie and as a market, and the United States both functioned as an intermediary between Europe and the Americas and forwarded its own economy. From 1776 on, as inter-American trade grew, it gave additional impetus to North American shipbuilding and internal growth and provided the new nation with capital and markets for its own products. Especially with neutral commerce, such trade was an important factor in the export sector, and it had impact on spurring and channeling early United States economic growth.

One sort of enterprise contributing to the intermixture of private and public business (and influencing military and strategic decisions) was the channeling of European funds to American insurgents. By June 1776, France and Spain had decided to extend to the rebels two million pounds sterling—one million each— secretly, without British knowledge, and to forward matériel and credits and specie as though they were loans, emanating from commercial companies and later to be balanced by American exports. The insurgents received supplies at Spanish ports and at Saint Domingue, Havana, and New Orleans. Officially in charge of expediting matters in Spain was the merchant Diego de Gardoqui of Bilbao whose firm had long had business with British America and particularly with Willing and Morris of Philadelphia and Aaron Lopez of Newport. (Gardoqui came to the United States, at war's end, as Spanish *chargé d'affaires*, and among other activities set up consuls to sell licenses to ship flour to Spanish America, the fees going to the consuls and Gardoqui.)[32]

Spanish aid also came in other ways. The victory at Yorktown was indirectly abetted by José de Gálvez's special envoy to the Caribbean, Francisco de Saavedra (from whom more will be heard), who, through expediting a loan from some residents of Havana and a transfer of army funds, got the wherewithal to enable the support of the French fleet and to finance the campaign in Virginia. Insurgent privateers sold prizes at Havana, and the South Carolina squadron got supplies and did business there. By 1782, the only circulating specie in the warring British colonies came from Cuba, and other Spanish, and some French, dependencies.[33]

Spain, upon indication of cooperation from the Anglo-Americans, mounted a campaign to retake the Floridas. The governor of Louisiana, who was Bernardo de Gálvez, the energetic young nephew of the Minister of the Indies, conquered English outposts on the Mississippi, then Mobile and Pensacola. He also protected Anglo-American ships, harbored rebel privateers, advanced funds and arms to the insurgents, and authorized their convoys on the Mississippi. He aided James Willing's expedition to capture Natchez and thwarted English plans for an Indian offensive against British American settlers in western Virginia and Kentucky.

Working closely with him was Oliver Pollock, an Irish-born businessman-adventurer who had come to Pennsylvania in his youth, gone into business in Havana during the British occupation of 1762–63, then moved to New Orleans where he acted as agent for London firms, for Willing and Morris, and for merchants shipping flour down the Mississippi. Pollock had enjoyed, in fact, a monopoly of that trade in partnership with the Spanish governor of Louisiana. He had become the representative there, too, first for Virginia and its governor, Patrick Henry, then formal agent of the committee of the Continental Congress that was charged with procuring supplies. That committee was headed by his old associate, the Philadelphia entrepreneur who in that capacity was creating an international mercantile and financial network, Robert Morris.[34] Pollock received his official commission in 1778 from Captain James Willing (the brother of Morris's business partner, Thomas Willing), who had come down the Mississippi on Morris's orders to capture British property on that river and to take charge of munitions shipped to New Orleans from Spain by Gardoqui. Pollock, as agent for Morris and his committee, from June 1778 expedited transshipping of the supplies from Spain and contracted with Bernardo de Gálvez for Spanish loans, to be repaid in goods.[35]

Morris, who had been in the contraband and slave trades with Spanish America, had a network of Spanish contacts in New Orleans, Cuba, and the West Indies, and in Philadelphia as well, where he did public and private business with Juan de Miralles, the Spanish agent who arrived from Havana in 1778. Miralles was a wealthy merchant and contrabandist connected to the Cuban branch of Aguirre, Aristegui, and Co. of Cádiz, holders of the asiento; Morris was that company's factor in Philadelphia. Miralles and Morris had had dealings during the British occupation of Havana, and Miralles, permitted by the Captain General of Cuba to trade on his own account as cover for his official mission, both sent reports in Morris's ships and with Morris did his own business in their other cargoes, duty free. When Morris got authorization from Congress to ship three thousand barrels of flour to Havana, he and Miralles, abetted by leaders in Maryland, Virginia, and North and South Carolina, worked to establish a commercial network between the eastern seaboard and Havana. Morris also planned, by borrowing on future flour shipments, to acquire specie from the Spaniards by way of Havana in order to facilitate setting up the Bank of North America. Despite some British interference, these projects appear to have met with substantial success, for Morris wrote to George Washington in July 1781: "All our ships. . . continue to be constantly employed in carrying flour to the French and Spanish islands; our port is filled in return with West India produce [and] many, many Spanish dollars."[36]

To facilitate these arrangements, in 1780 he hired Robert Smith, a native of Baltimore, and sent him to Cuba. In 1781, on Morris's recommendation (he was then superintendent of finances), Congress elected Smith consul there. His official duties, as outlined by Robert Livingston, the first secretary of foreign affairs—who had been a New York businessman and was a friend of Morris's—were "to manage the occasional concerns of Congress, to assist American traders with his advice, and to solicit their affairs with the Spanish government.'' (When in 1783 Congress chose Smith's successor, not surprisingly it appointed Oliver Pollock.)[37]

Smith also became an agent for the Spanish asentistas. In Havana, he and James Seagrove, a North American merchant who was probably also an agent of Morris's or at least a correspondent, had contact with Francisco de Miranda, the creole aide-de-camp of the Spanish commanding officer. Miranda joined Smith in smuggling goods and slaves to Havana—and specie out—and obtained ships through him, ostensibly for flag-of-truce transports, and also one as a yacht for his commander. Moreover, there is evidence Miranda was involved in illegal trade with Morris before Smith arrived. Business went well until the Spanish governor closed the port of Havana in 1781. In 1783, Miranda left surreptitiously for the newly independent states and thence to a career as the propagandist of Spanish American independence; in 1806, he was leader of the first, unsuccessful, expedition attempting liberation. During early 1782, Smith and Seagrove sent him news and information on commerce, and Miranda got Smith to insert an account of the joint Spanish and Anglo-American capture of the Bahamian island, Providence, in the Baltimore *Gazette*. Seagrove was probably responsible for securing Miranda passage northward. Both Morris and Livingston entertained Miranda during his stay in their country.[38]

Morris, who in 1782 wrote, ''A merchant as such can be attached particularly to no country. His mere place of residence is, as merchant, perfectly accidental,'' was the major correspondent in America of those international financiers, the Barings, in London, and of their collaborators on the continent, Hope and Company of Amsterdam. Sir Francis Baring belonged to the small group of merchants and wealthy landed dominating English business and politics. (His firm also did business with Thomas Willing, who from 1791 to 1807 was president of the Bank of the United States, and with the Philadelphia merchant extraordinaire, Stephen Girard.) In 1803, the Barings were general agents in London of the United States government. They and the Hopes played a crucial role in marketing a loan issued by the United States for the purchase of Louisiana, extending to the nation over ten million dollars and securing British approval for transferring the monies to Napoleon.[39] The following year the Barings, the Hopes, a number of American and some British merchants, and the English government began an involvement with the governments of Spain and France in a tremendously far-flung and successful multinational financial and commercial operation centered on Mexican silver.

In 1804, Napoleon's banker, Gabriel-Julien Ouvrard, in a complex and now incompletely understood transaction (but at least in part in return for a loan to the Spanish government), received promise of a monopoly on the commerce and the export of the stored specie of Spanish America and the sole right to collect from Mexico Spain's annual subsidy to Napoleon of nearly three million pounds sterling. All profits on trade were to be divided equally with Charles IV. The French banker called on the Hopes, who had loans outstanding to Spain, for help in transferring the silver to Europe in return for commissions and a share in the profits. They, through the Barings, secured a guarantee of safe conduct from Pitt's government. England agreed because silver was scarce in Europe, because its circulation ultimately would be valuable to the East India Company, and because, as Hope's head, Labouchère, explained, England would thus gain "a principal share in a most valuable trade...a great vent for manufactories" as well as additional duties on return products.[40]

The Hopes sent David Parish to the United States to manage the silver transfer and the trade with Spanish America through American merchants and agents in New Orleans and Vera Cruz. From 1805 to 1808, although some of the Mexican specie went directly to Europe and some arrived there by way of the United States, much of it entered United States trade channels and went through United States banks. Some was converted into American-owned goods and shipped to Europe as neutral property in neutral ships. Among United States merchants whose ships made the Mexican run were John Craig of Philadelphia, the Olivers of Baltimore, and Archibald Gracie of New York. Also involved were Thomas Willing's firm, Stephen Girard, and the Baltimore merchant and United States senator, Samuel Smith. The Olivers' agent in Vera Cruz was Pollock's son, Procopio. Before Parish arrived, Craig had received, he thought, the monopoly of trade with Mexico from the head of the Spanish *Caja de Consolidación*, which was functioning as a central bank; and with the Olivers he was shipping, principally British and German dry goods, to Vera Cruz and Venezuela. Craig and the Olivers came to an agreement with Parish. The grandiose scheme was enormously successful: It allowed the removal from Mexico of perhaps $28 million. Partially responsible for the degree of success were the speed, dependability, and low insurance rates of the Olivers' Baltimore clippers. This multinational enterprise not only provided profits to European banking houses and funds to the war-needy French, British, and Spanish governments, but it also yielded capital and impetus to the American carrying trade, upped federal income from its largest source—duties, increased the supply of specie, and contributed in particular to stimulating the North American cotton industry. Willing, presiding over the Bank, assisted United States merchants in the scheme, including through foreign exchange conversions, transferring funds among branches, advances to importers to cover customs duties, and with sixty day bank notes, treated as legal tender.[41]

Oliver Pollock and Robert Smith were among those who had set a precedent for American agents who would represent their government and become involved both in private commercial ventures of multinational scope and in politics in the regions where they served. Such men have aptly been termed "apostles of rational liberty" and "advance agents of American destiny." They represented a particular breed of commercial adventurer shaped by the American Revolution who went to Latin America and elsewhere in dual public and private capacities—the lines were sometimes none too clear. To a blend of individual and national concern with trade they often added a sense of republican mission. Most early Anglo-American agents to Latin America, oddly enough, much resembled sixteenth-century Spaniards who went there, in that both were imbued with militant zeal for their missions and bent on gaining personal wealth and esteem. These North Americans sought their own fortunes and spheres of influence confident, like those Spaniards and also like their own countryman, Robert Morris, that personal and national well-being were much the same thing and that they could work toward both at once. Some of these latter-day adventurers, too, mixed economic and political drives with a religious sense of mission, but in their case the religion was Protestantism or enlightened deism, and the political ideology was republican liberalism.

The best known of them in Latin America is Joel Poinsett, an outstanding example of the freewheeling commercial agent. He became persona non grata in Chile during its independence struggle; and after distributing the 1776 Declaration of Independence and other related documents, counseling insurgent leaders, proffering a constitution, personally leading rebel troops, and generally intruding in Chilean affairs. In Mexico in the 1820s he continued his republican pro-selytizing and meddling in internal matters.[42] Poinsett's militant patriotism was expressed as a universal republican zeal, and, while in Chile, to James Monroe as a condemnation of the Roman Catholic church. It was patriotism that gave to his activities an aspect of religious crusade, and it was a state of mind shared by other North Americans who earlier had privately dabbled in Spanish American affairs. Notable were the New Englanders Richard Cleveland and William Shaler who were in Montevideo and Buenos Aires in 1799 and again in 1801. They sailed on an international venture via Hamburg, a hub of neutral commerce, to Brazil, Chile, Ecuador, Mexico, and the California coast. Along the way they upheld the principle that free ships made free goods. They distributed Spanish translations of the Declaration of Independence to interested creoles, pointed out similarities in their countries' situations, and explained how political freedom brought com-mercial benefits.[43] The outlook of these men was one long prevalent in the thirteen colonies, at least from the time of Cotton Mather and Samuel Sewall. In short, after 1776 Anglo-Americans interested in Latin America continued to hold to earlier, commercial goals and continued to engage in international projects. And, in the process, they went on coupling these old habits with a great feeling of competition with the English. Not new, either, was their concern for their country's security and interest in its expansion. But their pride did mount through belonging to an independent and sovereign nation.

During and after the revolutionary war, Anglo-Americans not only sailed south. More of them went west or southwest toward the unclear borders between Louisiana, New Spain, the Floridas, and the western states, and some tended to use international rivalries in that vast frontier area to their own advantage. These people on occasion felt it their duty to promote republican ideals and at times functioned as United States agents, spies, and expeditionary leaders. At others, they sought independence from the United States, sometimes in league with European powers. George Rogers Clark, William Blount, James Wilkinson, Philip Nolan, and Aaron Burr at one time or another contemplated freeing Louisiana, Florida, and Mexico from Spain—not necessarily to add those areas to the union—and some of them planned to make Kentucky independent and possibly reliant upon Spain. All demonstrated to a high degree the quality of individualism, although not those of national patriotism and moderation.[44]

After the Revolution, the borderlands, including Spain's holdings there, were of continuing interest not only to Southerners and to growing numbers of Anglo-American settlers, but also to merchants in Philadelphia and New York, to easterners speculating in lands, and to their various spokesmen in the government. Jefferson as well as the Federalists understood that commercial interest in the Mississippi and the thrust for Western expansion were bound up with securing a market for agrarian products by improving trade with Spanish America and, most acute, with gaining Mexican specie. They also understood sectional rivalries, including the one between New England and frontiersmen for commerce. Moreover, Jefferson and Adams were among the few government leaders without private involvement in trade or lands. George Washington and Franklin had investments in western lands. Robert Morris overreached in land speculation as well as commerce and went to jail. Hamilton was involved in an Ohio land company. And Patrick Henry had interests in lands in West Florida, North and South Carolina, Georgia, and Kentucky dating from the revolutionary period, and wanted to buy more, on the Mississippi. Adams and Jefferson, however, were sensitive to this spectrum of interests in the West, as the diplomacy of the period attests.[45] In addition, in the arena of power politics, as the situation warranted, national leaders employed one or another of those men adjudged most disaffected, powerful, and, if neglected, potentially dangerous to national interests—thus Jefferson's relations with the inveterate intriguer, Wilkinson, his correspondence with George Rogers Clark, and his watchful waiting while Burr plotted.

A Spanish borderlands network that was devoted to land speculation and territorial expansion overlapped, even interlocked, with another engaged in international commerce. The various western intrigues make little sense outside of this intermeshed context. Moreover, international rivalries allowed enterprising opportunists to play off one government against others, deftly backing and filling as the situation appeared to demand. At least one snarled skein of mixed public and private, commercial and speculative relationships can be to some extent untangled by beginning with Oliver Pollock, who remained active after the war and returned to New Orleans in 1789. There he sought official permission to bring in large shipments of eastern tobacco and flour, promising the governor half of the profits toward repaying the jumbled public and personal debts he had incurred during the revolution. Pollock also received some general trading licenses, one of which he transferred to Joseph Ball, a Philadelphia financier. Ball then turned it over to the Philadelphia firm of Reed and Forde, who had dealings with Robert Morris; subsequently, they remained involved in trade with New Orleans and through that port with other areas of Spanish America until 1808.[46] Reed and Forde commissioned as their New Orleans agent Daniel W. Coxe, brother of Tench Coxe—assistant treasurer to Hamilton in 1790. Daniel Coxe was also recipient of the private assets unlawful for that public servant to hold. In 1793, Daniel Coxe went into partnership with Daniel Clark, Jr., who in acting as New Orleans agent for several Philadelphia firms had been a competitor, who had had private dealings with Pollock, and who in 1781 had made shipments to Amsterdam for Morris.

Land speculators, merchants, frontiersmen, Indians, Spaniards, and politicos sought to profit from British and Spanish designs in the West, especially in 1788–89 and from the late 1790s on, when the two nations were at war. Sorting out the loyalties and purposes of these conniving and ambitious men is difficult, for they played one government off against another—while those governments sometimes used them—and they particularly took advantage of the combination of Spanish desires to populate West Florida and Louisiana and Spanish fears of trouble with Anglo-American frontiersmen and of United States expansion.

Gardoqui's avowed mission in the United States was to negotiate boundaries, but his confidential instructions were to cause friction between American regions—between the West and South and the Northeast. To this purpose, and fearing western strength, he invited frontiersmen into Spanish territory, as did Spanish borderlands governors and, after 1787, the Spanish government, in order to attract them to Spain's side and possibly to attach Tennessee and Kentucky as Spanish dependencies. Gardoqui became involved in schemes initiated by eastern land speculators to separate the Cumberland settlements and Kentucky from the Confederation, and he funded some expeditions for that purpose. His fellow plotters included John Brown, Virginia's congressional representative for the Kentucky district, and Wilkinson. Brown contacted Pollock, too, in 1788, and both consulted Gardoqui. Pollock then passed on information concerning plans to separate Kentucky to Esteban Miró, the Spanish governor at New Orleans.[47]

Wilkinson had gone to Kentucky in 1784 as agent for a Philadelphia merchant— his wife, Ann's, brother, Clement Biddle—and in 1787 went down the Mississippi to New Orleans. There he arranged for Daniel Clark, Jr., to represent him in commercial matters. The next year Wilkinson registered in Richmond as an agent for Clark and entered the trade from Philadelphia and that from Kentucky, principally in tobacco, with New Orleans. He conspired with Spanish governors, off and on, and with Burr until shortly before November 1806. Then, after failing to have Burr murdered and after testifying against him, he narrowly escaped indictment for the same crimes charged to Burr. Wilkinson was chief United States military officer in the Southwest and governor of the Louisiana territory at that time; he had received secret pensions from Jefferson (who characterized him as "enterprising to excess") and from the Spanish government, and had also negotiated with the British. Wilkinson wanted power, station, and wealth—and, more specifically, to attract immigration to Louisiana and to obtain western lands for himself. By playing on Spanish hopes that the West would secede and fear that it might attack Louisiana, he was, however, instrumental in keeping the Mississippi open from 1788 until Spain formally conceded its navigation by the Treaty of San Lorenzo—Pinckney's Treaty—of 1795.

George Rogers Clark, a disgruntled revolutionary hero and western landowner who, like Pollock, was owed money for his wartime services by Virginia, was among those who proposed to Gardoqui a Louisiana colonization scheme in 1788, offering to become a Spanish subject if given a land grant to establish a settlement. Gardoqui apparently did not comply, and Clark subsequently fell in with the plan of the French minister to the United States, Edmund Genêt, during the war between France and Spain in 1793, to organize expeditions against Spanish and British colonies from United States soil; in a letter to Genêt he spoke of conquering Louisiana and Mexico. Genêt authorized Clark to lead an expedition against Louisiana, but could not fund it. In disfavor with Congress and with the Jacobin regime in France, Genêt left public life but chose to remain, and to marry, in the United States.[48]

Jefferson was originally open to Genêt's plan, probably viewing it as a way to get the Floridas. He was against recruiting in the United States but did not object to inciting insurrection in Louisiana, although he thought it unnecessary since, as he wrote to the United States commissioners in Spain in the spring of 1793 concerning Spain's American dependencies, "Time will soon enough give independence, consequently free commerce to our neighbors, without our risking the involving ourselves in a war with them."[49]

Genêt and Clark had evoked Spanish apprehension, and the new Spanish governor at New Orleans, the Baron de Carondelet, renewed negotiations with Wilkinson, preferring to turn Kentucky energies to independence rather than toward invasion of Louisiana. The government in Spain, however, chose to work through more legitimate channels and signed the 1795 treaty. Spain also renewed its alliance with France at about the same time and was soon at war with Britain—all this facilitating the additional conspiracies of William Blount and Aaron Burr.[50]

Blount, long a figure in North Carolina politics and involved in the Tennessee land company in 1785, was territorial governor and then senator from Tennessee. He promoted a colony at Muscle Shoals, and to gain for it an outlet to the Gulf he needed the Spanish out of Florida. In 1797 his scheme, exposed by the Spanish minister at Philadelphia, was to attack New Orleans with a force of Canadians, frontiersmen, and Indians, supported by the English fleet. In the course of Blount's negotiations, conversations took place between an ally of his in New York and his old friend, Aaron Burr, but they came to nothing.[51]

Burr's own schemes heightened Spanish distrust and capped some careers begun in the American Revolution and advanced by various sorts of contacts with Spain and its America. Not only did Wilkinson, after the purchase of Louisiana, become Burr's principal confidant in a plan (which predated 1803) to revolutionize West Florida and Mexico but, in New Orleans—which was, according to the plan, to be the staging area for an attack on Mexico—a not-so-secret society, the Mexican Association, was in on the plot, some of its members hoping to coordinate their activities with those of Francisco de Miranda, of whom more later. Daniel Clark, Jr., by then one of New Orleans's wealthiest merchants and in 1801 appointed United States consul there, may have been a leading mover of the Association, and at the least had friends in it and knew of its goals. He made several trips, ostensibly on private business, to Vera Cruz in 1806, bringing back data on military strength and a copy of Alexander von Humboldt's recent statistical tables of New Spain. However this may be, among Burr's supporters were easterners who objected to the Louisiana purchase and people whose speculations in Mississippi valley lands could only bear fruit if outside United States jurisdiction.[52]

While one reason for the failure of western expansion schemes may well have been that Jefferson had more interest in Florida than in Texas, another interest of his, natural science, proved useful to westward advance, much as had similar penchants to those Spanish governments sending out first Juan and Ulloa, then later eighteenth-century scientific missions and the expedition of Jefferson's contemporary and friend, the noted German naturalist, Humboldt. It should be mentioned that Humboldt's commission had some repercussions not looked for by Spain, for not only did Clark get his tables, but Wilkinson and Burr got to copy a map Humboldt, during a stop on his return to Europe, presented to Jefferson in 1804. Zebulon Montgomery Pike may have used the same Humboldt map on his march to Santa Fé—an expedition, sent out by Wilkinson, that mixed exploration and intrigue.[53] All in all, as we shall see corroborated, the net result of Humboldt's visit was to undermine Spain's hold on Spanish America.

Jefferson, whose happy ability to combine an intense and lively scientific curiosity with political and national economic purposes affected much of what he touched, including his relations with Iberia and Latin America, commissioned Meriwether Lewis and William Clark to undertake a fourfold quest in 1803. They were to seek scientific knowledge and a Northwest passage to the Pacific. They were also to establish United States influence among the Indians, to explore the possibilities of trade with those on the coast, and to assert their nation's claims to the West against the British and the Spanish.[54]

From 1797 to 1814, too, Jefferson presided over the American Philosophical Society, "held at Philadelphia for promoting useful knowledge," founded by Franklin and devoted to disseminating enlightenment. It included the city's leading clergy and principal politicians and also functioned informally as a vehicle of conciliation, a club in which to moderate factional political differences. It was a counterpart to European learned societies, including the Spanish economic and patriotic societies. Its members, like theirs, aspiring to, or recently arrived at, positions of social consequence, also like theirs shared a beneficent view of nature and science, a belief in boundless opportunity and, ultimately, one in a creator very well disposed toward humanity. Everywhere such associations disseminated both a cosmopolitanism and a fervent nationalism, their members talking in universal terms and assuming the nation-state to be the natural political and social unit as well as the natural subdivision of humankind. Active members of the American Philosophical Society went further, in mirroring the faith of their founder in the growth of enlightenment and in believing that their country, its republican virtues on the rise, must soon outshine Europe.[55]

These views permeated Jefferson's *Notes on the State of Virginia* written in 1783 expressly to refute, as he stated, the Count de Buffon's celebrated theory "of

the tendency of nature to belittle her productions on this side of the Atlantic'' and
''its application to the race of whites transplanted from Europe,'' and also to
counter Abbé Raynal, who thought America had not yet produced ''one good poet,
one able mathematician, one man of genius in a single art or single science,'' and
who believed ''the ardor of men and the size of animals'' smaller in America than
in the old world.[56] Jefferson defended all America, writing that Raynal's comments were equally invalid for North and South America, then going on to attribute
the Latin American insufficiencies he knew of to circumstances, not nature.[57]
Jefferson's involvement in the Enlightenment combined with concern for national
interest to forward the concept of a special relationship among Americans, and
incidentally lent credence and gave impetus to the broadest concept of America,
one we have seen operative in the nation's early foreign policy, what has been
termed the Western Hemisphere idea.[58] The *Notes* also came to find favor among
Latin American liberals and contributed to reinforcing among creoles the concept
of a common bond uniting all inhabitants of the New World.

This enlightened Jeffersonian attitude, common to a number of other Americans
and particularly to members of learned societies, not only fostered awareness that
the Americas shared both a locale and a relationship to Europe, but also encouraged the study of Latin American languages and culture. Thus, by 1800
Jefferson and the American Philosophical Society had established relations with
leading public figures and scientists in Spain, Mexico, and Cuba.[59] Jefferson
demonstrated a mixture of scientific curiosity and national economic and strategic
concern, as well as familiarity with enlightened Spaniards, when in 1787 he
requested of William Carmichael, the United States ambassador at Madrid,
information about the Spanish idea of a Panama canal, and suggested that
''probably the Count de Campomanes or Don Ulloa can give you information on
this head.''[60] Enlightened clubbiness cut across national lines. The Society's
members and those of other learned organizations in the United States often
combined interest in the history, flora, and fauna of Latin America with interest in
its trade.

In the United States, as indeed throughout the Americas and western Europe,
among educated and well-placed liberals scientific curiosity, material progress,
cultural fashions, and self-interest were concomitants of enlightenment. So were,
nearly always, patriotism, individual enterprise, and the pursuit of national
wealth, power, and expansion. The unique quality of this mentality was the fervor
with which some recently independent Americans believed their own republican
form of government to be the divinely chosen instrument of disseminating
enlightenment.[61]

Anglo-American interest in Latin America and friendship with individual
creoles and Spaniards, did not necessarily mean acceptance, especially of peoples
of different religions and of differing skin tones. The attitudes toward Latin
Americans manifest by Sewall and Mather and by the antipapist warhawks of 1738
continued to be expressed by a number of people, plain and prominent, in
Anglo-American society. Thus, Andrew Jackson, later popular as hero of New
Orleans and conqueror of Florida and, at length, president, speaking as a land

dealer and a leader in the western militia at the time of the Louisiana purchase, advised Jefferson to conquer all Spanish North America. He then sweepingly accused Spaniards of "acts . . . daring as well as degrading to our National Character and constitutional rights." Peripherally involved in Burr's schemes, in 1806 as general of the Tennessee militia, he avowed his goal was then to give freedom, commerce, and peace to Santa Fé and Mexico, asserting, "We can conquer not only the Floridas but all Spanish North America," and "I love my Country. I hate the Dons. I should delight to see Mexico reduced."[62] The tradition persisted among publicists and others of coupling superstition and ignorance with Catholicism and its Spanish American practitioners. William Cobbett, editor of the Philadelphia *Gazette,* for example, could play on existing popular antipathies when in 1797 he responded to the Spanish minister's criticisms of United States policies: "Gracious Heaven! Insulted by a Spaniard! Eight years of war and misery [the American Revolution] and a hundred thousand men stretched dead upon the plains of America, and all to purchase a kick from a tawny-pelted nation, which Americans had ever been taught to despise."[63]

A type of religious crusade continued, too, to be combined with republican mission by more Americans than adventurers such as Shaler and Poinsett; and within it anti-Catholicism merged with enlightened deism, yielding outlooks similar to Voltaire's. Thus, both Adams and Jefferson found in Latin American religiosity a major deterrent to political and moral liberty being able to take hold in the other Americas, and from this assessment concluded Latin Americans were not ready for self-government. In 1787, Jefferson told Congress that Mexicans must first be liberated mentally. And, more trenchant, in 1806 Adams compared Miranda's plans for free governments in Spanish America with establishing democracies "among the birds, beasts, and fishes." Jefferson wrote to Humboldt in 1812 that he had no doubt the Spanish colonies would gain independence, but because of the variety of peoples, their customs, their lack of intellectual culture, and above all their superstitions and political attitudes, it appeared impossible for them to establish democratic or republican governments; and in 1813, again to Humboldt concerning Spanish America: "History, I believe, furnishes no example of a priest-ridden people maintaining a free civil government."[64] We recall that Adams had written in 1765 that he had always looked on the settlement of North America "with reverence and wonder, as the opening of a grand scene and design of Providence for the illumination of the ignorant and the emancipation of the slavish part of mankind all over the earth."[65] And Jefferson wrote to Adams, two weeks before they both died, on the fiftieth anniversary of the signing of the Declaration of Independence, that he hoped that anniversary might "be to the world, what I believe it will be (to some parts sooner, to others later, but finally to all) the signal of arousing men to burst the chains under which monkish ignorance and superstition had persuaded them to bind themselves, and to assume the blessings and security of self-government."[66]

Jefferson and Franklin had advocated separation of church and state so that the new government and society would be free of sectarianism, but they expected society (and its system of education) to remain religious and broadly Protestant, and so it did. Alexis de Tocqueville discerned "a democratic and republican religion" in the United States and correctly thought liberty, law, morality, and religious beliefs symbiotically related.[67] In the 1950s, Will Herberg could still speak of an "operative religion of society," of all the major faiths in America disseminating similar values, and that "by every realistic criterion the American way of life is the operative faith of the American people"[68] Most recently, Henry Steele Commager has noted the tradition of civic religion in America, of "a secular faith in American mission and American destiny," and that "America herself was a religion."[69] This continuum of a close relationship between the patriotic and the spiritual both antedated and is a heritage of 1776, with continuing resonances in the Latin American relations of the United States.

In sum, while the American Revolution brought political independence and change in leaders, shifts and expansion in trade, and to some extent alterations in international alliances and in balance of power considerations, there was much that did not change. Widespread among people of all walks of life before, during, and after the Revolution was a sense of Americans having been chosen by heaven to carry the new republican faith to mankind, a complex political creed of republicanism associated with Protestantism and bound up with economic interest and the idea of progress, and often, although not always, with enlightened and liberal concepts. United States revolutionary leaders continued to exhibit an eighteenth-century, English-derived attitude linking liberty everywhere not only to the ideal of political freedom, but also to the liberal notion, developed by Adam Smith, that individual interests, virtue, political liberty, and economic freedom were all of a piece. To them, their new nation was the exemplar of this combination to the world, but principally through ensuring political and economic freedom for its own people. It was this patriotic, national primary emphasis that caused a Latin American, Francisco de Miranda, in 1792 to remark that inhabitants of the United States "no longer treated Liberty as lovers, but as husbands."[70]

Within the United States, too, old attitudes toward Spaniards in Europe and America persisted, and some new ones appeared. An adumbration of one variety of support for Latin America's revolutions can be discerned in Mercy Otis Warren's romantic play of 1790. Best known as one of the first historians of the American Revolution, Mrs. Warren in *Ladies of the Castle* wrote of the revolt of the comuneros against Charles V and drew an implicit parallel between it and the Revolution of 1776—evidence that in both Americas that sixteenth-century uprising against tyranny was looked to as a revolutionary precedent.[71] Romanticism was also present in Joel Barlow's poetry extolling America, as well as in his defense of Miranda before a French revolutionary tribunal in 1793. William Robertson's *History of America* (1777) provided material for Barlow's *The Vision of Columbus* (1787) and his *Columbiad* (1807). Creoles, too, we shall see, were influenced by Robertson, and a few of them influenced him. Barlow also read *La Araucana,* the epic poem commemorating the heroism of Chilean Indians, and the *Commentaries* of Garcilaso de la Vega, el Inca; not unexpectedly, he admired the

Indians as noble savages, was "dazzled by the conquest," but detested Spain.[72]

Another, later play roundly denounced Spanish peoples and Spanish rule in America. It was *Liberty in Louisiana,* a comedy opening in New Orleans in 1804, the year after the purchase of the Territory. James Workman, a member of the Mexican Association, wrote it, and it played afterwards in New York, Philadelphia, and Savannah, and was both well attended and widely read. Its popularity attested to the continuance of an antipathy related to competition for territory, wealth, and power.[73] Still, this attitude remained offset for some time after 1776 by that of many Anglo-Americans who, whatever their views on Hispanic culture and religion, wished Latin Americans well and hoped they, too, would eventually reap the benefits of life in secularized and independent republics. Moreover, numerous Latin Americans, like Anglo-Americans, were taking to heart the liberal and enlightened vision of possible and open-ended progress, of material advance and general prosperity, which now appeared inherent in the way of life, and attitudes toward it, current in the new American republic. Enterprising creoles and Brazilians as well as inhabitants of the United States in the late eighteenth century did not yet doubt that to encourage and to engage in inter-American economic and cultural interchange could result only in mutual benefit.

6

"A SPECIES OF REVOLUTION"

WITHIN EMPIRE:

LATIN AMERICA, 1776-1788

When the thirteen Anglo-American colonies declared independence in 1776, the most pressing and immediate effects on Spanish America came through Spanish reaction and the impact of new Spanish measures. Spain, although it joined France against Britain only in 1779, in December 1776 began secretly to aid the British American rebels, and freer intercourse was customary between the Anglo-American insurgents and Spanish American regions. From 1776, as we have seen, some Latin American ports were open for varying periods to United States ships, and individual Spanish viceroys and governors in America from time to time licensed vessels from North America to bring in badly needed provisions and war supplies. Moreover, the ongoing growth of Latin American regions coalesced with extraordinary military demand to allow greater profits both to licit Spanish and foreign ventures and to smugglers and interlopers as well. In Peru and Mexico, silver output continued to climb. Everywhere population, expenditures, consumption, and commerce all seem to have continued to rise.

In Spain, from 1776 verbal and literary attacks on Britain preceded armed conflict, but new British economic theory continued to be welcome, and it was put to use at home and in America in economic competition with the English. Thus, some of Hutcheson's ideas appeared in a tract of 1777, and Smith's *Wealth of Nations* was known and well thought of by 1780.[1] To the Spanish government, as we have seen, the contest was fundamentally economic and with Britain; the rebelling Anglo-Americans seemed, though potentially a problem, at present more an embarrassment and real loss to England than a threat to Spain. Spain's relations with the North American insurgents should be understood within this context, as subsidiary to and dependent upon those with England. Spanish ministers in Europe and America accordingly helped the United States against the British, in border areas and through the house of Gardoqui and through France, and received from the insurgents foodstuffs for Spanish troops and colonies.

Although some prominent liberal Spaniards publicly praised the rebels, Spanish statesmen, we have also noted, realized that the Revolution of 1776 might eventually loosen Spain's grip on the New World. Floridablanca, chief minister from 1777, foresaw Spanish America vulnerable to both England and Anglo-America, and George Rogers Clark's expedition into the Illinois country in 1778 heightened his awareness of the ambitions of the emerging republic. Aranda, although he admired and conversed at length with Franklin in Paris, in a dispatch of April 29, 1776 explicitly cautioned that if the Anglo-Americans revolted, rebellion could spread to "our America." And in 1779 he warned that the United States had become free to form a new empire.[2] By 1782, when Aranda wrote Floridablanca that sooner or later Spanish America would experience revolts similar to Britain's America, that opinion probably had been formed in accord with reports from America, for this dual attitude of admiration and apprehension was shared by Spanish officials in the Indies. Even though Bernardo de Gálvez was patently sympathetic to the English colonists, and the captain general in Havana, Navarro, counted on Anglo-American provisions and military cooperation and, in profusely thanking Miralles for sending portraits of Washington, gratuitously added that "his great talent ensures that his memory will pass down to future centuries," these same high authorities and others were edgy about Anglo-American expansion and commercial competition and about British rebels influencing Spanish Americans to revolt. In 1778, Navarro informed Bucareli from Havana that in Vera Cruz people were speaking of following the Anglo-American example; the Mexican viceroy replied that he knew.[3]

In 1781 Navarro, then intendant of Louisiana, warned the court of "the turbulent, ambitious Americans" and opposed granting free navigation of the Mississippi and so opening the West to them. That year, too, José de Abalos, intendant, governor, and captain general of Venezuela, saw as connected the recent rebellions in South America (to be discussed shortly) and "the sad and lamentable rising in the United States of North America," and he asked, rhetorically, of Charles III: if Great Britain could not subdue its relatively close colonies, "What prudent human would not fear greatly an equal tragedy in the astonishingly extended dominions of Spain in these Indies?" He both predicted United States independence and strongly suggested that Spanish princes be sent to govern and hold the Spanish colonies for the monarchy.[4] Meanwhile, José de Gálvez's envoy, Francisco de Saavedra, corroborated finding in Mexico unrest and resentment due to official corruption and to new and higher wartime taxes, and declared Mexicans understandably aggrieved. He predicted, in view of British American independence, catastrophe if Spanish Americans were not better treated and more closely tied to the metropolis. Spain's American dependencies were not colonies, wrote Saavedra, but an essential part of the nation. He repeated the official view articulated by Campomanes and Floridablanca in 1768, but added:

> The creoles today are in a very different state than that of some years ago. They have been enlightened greatly in a short time. The new philosophy is making much more rapid progress there than in Spain (the zeal for religion which was the most powerful brake to contain them weakens by the minute). The treatment of the Anglo-Americans and foreigners has infused them with new ideas concerning the rights of men and of sovereigns; and the introduction of French books, of which there are an immense amount there, is making a species of revolution in their mode of thinking.[5]

The "French" books he described as "thousands of copies of works by Voltaire, Rousseau, Raynal, and Robertson." The war he thought impolitic and inopportune, serving only to arouse Spanish Americans and to create a formidable enemy on Spanish borders. Louisiana—and here he cited his friend, young Gálvez—was to be the antechamber to Mexico for the North Americans, who would someday rise and be unconquerable.

Saavedra specifically scored the cutting out of planters and mule-owners by official restrictions on internal trade in grains and criticized the lack of free trade of wheat to provision other parts of Spanish America. Another forward-looking official in Mexico, Ramón Posada, the fiscal, or crown attorney, for the treasury attached to the audiencia, concurred. Such restrictions, he pointed out, abetted enriching "a neighbor powerful at its very birth" allowing *"los bostoneses"* to exchange grain at Havana for over three million pesos in silver, and he added that Venezuela too took in much United States flour in exchange for cacao, hides, indigo, and specie.[6] Posada's *informe*, also of 1781, presents a spectrum of concepts that were becoming assumptions and becoming shared by new men on both sides of the Atlantic, and also in both Americas. Adapting Campomanes' and Jovellanos' growing convictions that national prosperity depended on agriculture, Posada saw in free grain export in national or foreign ships (but not in open exports) the basis of general prosperity; agriculture and industry he defined as the wealth of New Spain. Specie alone was no help. Posada told the viceroy the country was economically a tributary of foreign nations, and especially of the English colonies supplying its armies. He complained that three million pesos in Mexican gold had been spent to buy foreign wheat for Cuba. He peppered his solicitation with enlightened and liberal phrases, among them "the obligation of office...the public interest...national interest...the happiness of the state" (more a catch-term of enlightened despotism than of liberalism), "action to promote the good of the republic....all laws should aim at the universal good," and, in an awkward reach for a statement of individual rights, "the right conceded to whomever of the People." He declared liberty of commerce a natural principle, and trade—overseen by the state, it was understood—to be the right of all peoples.[7] Although his outlook was representative, in one respect and due to differences in regional conditions it varied from that of the new breed of officials in most other areas, for many of them, including Navarro and Abalos, then eagerly welcomed shipments of North American wheat and flour.

During the war, these men and other of Gálvez's new officials throughout America continued to promote his program by attempting to impose more direct peninsular control, combat internal monopolies, and foment economic growth by spurring production in mining and on farms and ranches. The energetic governors of newly elevated La Plata and Venezuela especially, while advancing the overall economies of their regions, opened a Pandora's box of unforeseen problems in the process. Like Posada, Abalos in Caracas and Pedro de Cevallos in Buenos Aires found that expanded productivity required adequate arrangements for export, and, even earlier than Posada did, they advocated open trade within the empire. They also sanctioned the use of foreign carriers, as did the authorities in Havana.[8]

The types of changes they supported not only benefited their jurisdictions but also altered the entire Spanish American economic and political balance. The former peripheral areas reaped the immediate advantages of reform and wartime demand, while Mexico City, Lima, and their backlands bore the brunt of the expense of both, including of additional imposts, initially levied successfully perhaps only in New Spain. To Lima, whose viceroy and consulado then faced the costs of defense not only for greater Peru but also for Buenos Aires, and commercial competition from it, José de Gálvez in 1776 sent a visitador, José Antonio de Areche, to put quickly into effect measures imposed in Mexico over more than a decade. Areche established new customs houses in Peru; created a monopoly on tobacco; extended tribute charges to all Indians, mestizos, and castas; lowered military pay scales; and was soon at odds with Lima's leading creoles and their ally, Manuel de Guirior, the viceroy, and remained so with Guirior's successors.[9]

Many Spanish Americans, as well as officials, received news of events in the thirteen British colonies. The Lima *Gazeta* in 1776 discussed the course of the war—General Washington had forced General Howe to evacuate Boston—and its high cost to Britain, where there was opposition to a parliamentary bill to defray war costs, on the basis that such imposts weighed on commerce and caused artisans to emigrate; the writer referred to "the American party."[10] The Lisbon gazette, which also circulated in Brazil, in 1778 wrote of the importance of the American Revolution and printed not only the complete text of the French and American commercial treaty of 1778 but also letters of Washington, Franklin, and other leaders and criticisms of British conduct of the war; it expressed a strong sympathy for the rebels. In Buenos Aires, rapidly growing as a commercial center from 1776, the course of Anglo-American events was followed too through European periodicals and, there and elsewhere, known through books on American history published in Europe. When in 1780 Gálvez informed its viceroy, Vértiz, that he had heard that the English were secretly preparing an expedition against La Plata and Chile, Vértiz answered that military forces were weak there, a spirit of rebellion was widespread, and "a general alteration and discontent" was being spread rapidly by the "bad example of the day."[11] A prominent Chilean, José Antonio Rojas, sent information to William Robertson, whose *History of America,* published in London in 1777, was immediately translated into Spanish. Robertson, whose writings Saavedra had listed among those flooding Mexico (although the government had forbidden them to be sent to Spanish America), and, erroneously, as French, had much to say not only about Anglo-America but also about the decadence of the Spanish colonies—all with a point of view quite similar to that of Adam Smith. Rojas, in Spain from 1772, secured a license to read prohibited works and shipped to America crates of books, including new anonymous works on America, as well as sets of Raynal, "this divine man," Rojas wrote, whose books were prohibited for being so clear and truthful.[12] There appeared, too, in Madrid in 1778 Francisco Alvárez's *Noticia del establecimiento y población de las colonias inglesas en la América Septentrional,* which, while not going beyond 1775, and not being very informative, discoursed upon the economic and commercial prosperity of the thirteen colonies and told of Bacon's rebellion. And in 1781 in Mexico, the government itself printed and distributed as anti-British propaganda a pamphlet entitled *Reflexiones políticas y militares sobre la presente guerra* concerning the causes and history of the Revolution of 1776.[13]

Yet, from 1779 when Spain entered the war, Mexican inquisitors, fighting a rearguard action, more energetically condemned the growing circulation of, and the vogue for, prohibited works, a vogue also mentioned by Saavedra and Posada. The Inquisition especially scored books containing seditious political ideas and denounced as the majority of readers of such books men recently arrived in both senses—Spanish naval and army officers and a mounting number of creoles of middle social strata. Abalos too reported an influx of such works in Venezuela during 1780 and 1781, particularly copies of Raynal. (The edition of 1781 summarized the Declaration of Independence and *Common Sense*.) By 1783, the Mexican Holy Office was finding seditious materials more and more prevalent, and was dolefully inveighing against what is discerned as a growing "enchantment with novelty."[14]

Some Latin Americans are known to have had direct contact in those years with leaders of the American Revolution, as well as with their ideas and ideologies. There was, of course, much intermingling of people and projects in New Orleans, Havana, and other areas of unified war effort. Rojas, later a proponent of independence, and probably author in 1776 of a list of complaints drawn up on behalf of native born Chileans, is known to have met Franklin in France.[15] By 1777 at least one creole, José Ignacio Moreno, in Caracas, cherished copies of the proclamations made in 1774 and 1775 by the Continental Congress in Philadelphia. Recently discovered has been his commonplace book containing, along with what was undoubtedly some of his favorite poetry, handwritten transcripts of the proclamations. Moreno was either a nephew or son of a leader of the Venezuelan uprising of 1743, the Mercedarian friar, José Martínez de Porras. Moreno was also a priest and held a chair of philosophy and theology at the University of Caracas. A man of means, he owned haciendas, slaves, scientific instruments, a journeyman press, and a library—in his interests, another creole counterpart to Jefferson. And, in 1797 he would be implicated in a republican conspiracy.[16] By 1777, then, he, and undoubtedly other creoles as well, were familiar with and regarded highly some of the concepts characterizing the early stages of the movement for independence in British North America. Moreno had copied Anglo-American complaints: of slavery to Britain and of impending ruin, of arbitrary laws, of new exactions without consent, of garrisoning of troops and poor government, of the threat to commerce and the American need for markets. He preserved phrases alluding to and endorsing the blessing of liberty, individual and property rights, constitutional principles of self-preservation based upon compacts with sovereign rulers, and the cause of America.

During the American Revolution, numerous creole merchants and planters, with productivity up and change in the air, thirsted for unrestricted trade. Landowners and newer merchants then perceived a need to get directly into the world market and came into conflict with consulados and their associates in advocating liberty of commerce. The so-called free trade reglamento of 1778 opened more Spanish ports to trade with Spanish America and briefly benefited its residents in sales abroad and cheaper imports; with Spain's entry into the war in 1779, Britain blocked the sea routes and North Americans tended to replace Spanish carriers. The net result was to diminish exchange between Spain and its Americas during the war and to allow Spanish Americans even more, and more direct, access to outside buyers and sellers. Competition in exporting then grew, often cutting across designations of peninsulars and creoles, and almost everywhere the number of merchants in both external and domestic trade rose rapidly. In addition, wartime conditions, including the British blockade and climbing demand, in some Latin American regions acted as further stimulants to internal production, including in Maranhão of cotton to replace North American shipments to England and rice to substitute for Anglo-American exports to Brazil. In Mexico, the wheat and textiles of Puebla and the Bajío were in great demand, helped by the mining boom, capital invested in the country after shipping was curtailed, official stimulus, and army needs.[17] In the process of growth, the propertied found they needed more cheap labor, so that exponents of liberty of commerce were, in areas of sparse peasant population, often the same people demanding and trafficking in blacks; and they traded for other imports as well, many originating in the thirteen colonies or carried by their vessels.

We have seen that the emporium of Havana, in particular, with the Revolution of 1776 received many more North American provisions, much more trade, and a larger market for sugar that in turn spurred demand for slave labor. Havana, the Spanish commercial hub and base of operations, which was also a French base of operations and a general entrepôt, we recall supplied and traded with Anglo-American insurgents from 1778 to 1780 with the assent of local authorities, and from 1780 to 1783 under arrangements by Spanish commissioners with the Continental Congress. We remember also that Havana was the staging area for Spanish expeditions against British Pensacola, Mobile, and the Bahamas, and a center of sale for prizes brought in by Anglo-Americans. Cuba, too, received from Venezuela and Buenos Aires salt meat and traded with Campeche, exchanges in which North American ships participated. The government eased commercial restrictions there more than anywhere, and, allowing open import of blacks, ordered their internal distribution, or re-export, handled by Cubans or Spanish residents. Merchants and planters cooperated and throve, often in association with Anglo-Americans, and also through supplying military and naval requisites, through financing the sugar industry with the aid of Anglo-American capital, and through feeding and clothing slaves with licit and contraband imports brought in on North American ships. After 1776, as Franklin Knight put it, the United States became Cuba's largest trading partner. The years between 1779 and 1783 marked the true initial impulse of Cuban economic expansion. Knight also found that as of 1774 more than half of Cuba's populace was of white European ancestry; that wealthy and aristocratic Cubans were not reluctant to engage in trade, to innovate, or to push technical development; and that Cuba's main agricultural exports were still beeswax and tobacco. We recall, too, that New Orleans, another emporium for Spanish American trade, was closely connected to Havana, especially in the export of wheat and flour sent down the Mississippi from Fort Pitt and other Anglo-American depots, and that Bernardo de Gálvez permitted Pollock, as congressional agent, to pay debts in flour. As another scholar concluded, "For New Spain and the empire, the dependence of Cuba on North American markets to get foodstuffs eclipsed the significance of Spanish victories in the Caribbean."[18]

The *porteños* of Buenos Aires, by then dominating interior commerce and monopolizing Potosí's silver trade, also enjoyed greater prosperity with elevation to a viceroyalty, and with war and more open trade. Under Cevallos, they profited at the expense of both Spanish traders and interior contacts; exports of hides, often connected with imports of slaves, rose rapidly. José de Gálvez, on September 20, 1776, informed the Governor of Buenos Aires that Anglo-Americans were to be admitted into Spanish ports under their own flag; some arrived in 1777, bringing flour and carrying out salt beef to Cuba. In 1778, the Crown's order that Patagonian coasts be defended against both the English and "their insurgent colonists" undoubtedly attested to contraband activity there. Those who did best in La Plata were new merchants, former contrabandistas, who exported to, and traded through, Cuba, Brazil, and the United States. Up and down the Pacific coast, the reglamento of 1778 expanded exchange. And Chile received cargoes aboard New England ships from at least 1778.[19]

In Caracas, the cabildo cheered the dynamic leadership of Abalos, who sympathized with local problems and said idle ships were bad for the treasury. Quite possibly having learned from Britain's unhappy experience restricting trade in America, he took it upon himself to allow Venezuelans to exchange their products, except cacao, with foreign colonies. And with the Caracas Company no longer able to supply Venezuela, both Company and creole ships brought in foreign goods legally, and contraband seeped in with the authorized slave trade with foreign colonies. With war in 1779, Spain allowed any Spanish subject or any ally or neutral to import slaves from Spain except into La Plata, Chile, or Peru; and the government set a maximum price and lowered import duties. Contraband came in too, on foreign ships, some of it North American produce carried by North American ships.[20]

Not only did numerous Spanish Americans profit from economic expansion and feel opportunities were open to them, but many also joined the swelling bureaucracies and some continued to hold administrative positions.[21] And criticism of the imperial system, in the spirit of reform—that is, criticism construed as constructive—was, during the war, on several occasions consciously employed by ambitious young creoles, as it was by Spaniards in the metropolis, who were awakened to the concept of public service as a way to better their communities and gain notice and preferment. Thus, in Lima José de Baquíjano, the second son of a titled, eminent, and outstandingly wealthy creole family, provided a case in point.

He had become a doctor in civil and canon law and a legal advisor to the consulado and cabildo and, in Spain from 1774 to 1777, had been refused high office, the post of *oidor* (a judge of the *audiencia,* which was both high court and viceroyal advisory council), in Lima. Highly ambitious, Baquíjano, as professor of civil law at the University of San Marcos, bid for advancement in 1781 by pronouncing a public eulogy, subsequently published, of the new viceroy, Agustín de Jáuregui. Not only was the speech ill advised in view of the visitador's animus toward this viceroy, but it also contained oblique remarks construable as springing from subversive political concepts. In what was probably an implicit criticism—one that echoed Spanish reformers but was directed to Areche's visita and against the enemy, the English, and one that was also by inference a bow to the United States—Baquíjano opined, ''To better [the lot of] the people against its will has always been the specious pretext of tyranny.'' And, ''A people is a spring that, forced beyond what its elasticity can suffer, snaps back destroying the imprudent hand which oppresses and subjects it.''[22] The court, prodded by Areche, ordered all copies of the speech called in. Much more outspoken were the tracts published anonymously or under pseudonyms by Eugenio Espejo, a Quito physician of Quechua and *mulata* parentage, who was also an ecclesiastic of sorts and a graduate in civil and canon law; he was clearly a young man of talent. Espejo was censured in 1781 for *El retrato de Golilla,* which satirized José de Gálvez and Charles III.[23]

Although commerce quickened, although merchants, planters, and ranchers generally fared better, and although more jobs seemed to promise opportunity to people of lower and middle strata and to augur expanded internal markets, discontents of various kinds festered from 1776 to 1783. The dual advent of war and its exigencies with officials bent on reform resulted in Spanish Americans experiencing the government's opening vistas of greater commerce, economic autonomy, and prosperity; yet at the same time they felt the impact of the government's raising imports, losing control of the sea lanes, and draining capital through demanding more financial support for its international embroilments. And, while the prospect of greater opportunities for scientific, economic, and personal advance, and for trade, to some extent cheered numerous creoles, still trade was found to be far from open in any sense, even where free trade pertained, as Posada and Saavedra indicated, and reforms were more widely recognized as keyed to peninsular priorities and as limited by them. These conditions, exhilarating and enriching some creoles, frustrated, angered, or alienated many others, and large numbers of other peoples as well. Thus, the trade of older, wealthier, monopolistic merchants and their agents in particular, centered in major cities and long tied to Cádiz firms and chartered companies, suffered. New commercial patterns and routes and the greater prosperity of some provincial areas, their ports and some of their merchants, caused economic change and dislocation, further upset some customary arrangements, and drew complaints from the old monopolist families in Lima and the Mexican capital. Moreover, with the reglamento of 1778 and especially before the British blockade, greater quantities of Spanish imports—especially wines, oil, and dried fruits—and high taxes on exports hurt or ruined some formerly competitive inland domestic production. As Campomanes saw, the 1778 trade regulations tended to convert "every one of the habilitated ports, with their respective consulados, into regional Cadizes."[24]

As one result of reform, by 1779 audiencias, under Gálvez's directive of 1776, had become predominantly peninsular. This was least so in Chile, but even there discrimination against creoles had elicited a protest attributed to Rojas. The crown also had striven effectively to limit indirect local influences on authorities and to break up the traditional networks of control based upon ties of family, friends, and shared interests that so often drew in even officials from abroad.[25] Many established creoles found much of their former access to wealth and power being curtailed, and competition intensified not only from eager young businessmen but also from a swelling number of graduates of law schools, the traditional conduits to public position. Those creole bastions, the cabildos of Mexico and Lima and the cloister of the University of Mexico, responded by protests calling for preference of "descendants of conquerors and first settlers." They cited "the fundamental laws of the realm" and argued from custom—that is, prior to Bourbon innovations. Americans, they claimed, had always had the right to have substantial numbers of representatives in government.[26] The grievances they stated recalled earlier ones, those of Ahumada, the Mexican cabildo in 1765 and 1771, and Rojas; but from 1776, denunciations were more specifically directed to what creoles considered recent royal tampering with the traditional imperial system.

Everywhere new exactions were vigorously opposed. In Santiago in 1776, more efficient collection of customs and excise taxes and new taxes on agricultural commodities and retail stores, which hit all levels of society, brought on popular demonstrations and arguments from propertied creoles by way of the cabildo spokesman, Manuel de Salas. In citing earlier laws and customs in his complaint against these reforms, Salas in effect put forth constitutional arguments in claiming the right of that cabildo to be consulted on taxes, and thus by implication claimed the status for it of an advisory council to the government. He went on to propose calling a *cabildo abierto*, or open town meeting. Instead, the government, in time-honored fashion, first disavowed the measures, then introduced them, quietly, piecemeal. The same process took place elsewhere; authorities trod the thin line between discontent and resistance.[27] So did eminent creoles. Rojas successfully cleared himself in 1780 of charges of involvement with two Frenchmen who planned to create a republic.[28] More ominous, in 1779 in the northern Peruvian coastal town of Lambayeque, human rights *(derecho de gente)* were invoked in resisting new taxes. And the next year a popular insurrection, larger than ever before, began to spread throughout the Andean area and expanded to the point where some thousands of people died. Masses of people, mostly Indian but of various ethnic derivations and social strata, rose in protest in separate but linked revolts. A self-proclaimed, and probable, descendant of the last Inca ruler, calling himself Túpac Amaru II, who had been repeatedly rebuffed by the government, insisted Americans unite against peninsulars.[29] At the same time in New Granada insurgent leaders, reacting to similar stimuli, and very influenced by events to the south, appealed to a happier past and the Spanish-derived tradition of popular right of resistance to abusive central authority in taking the name comuneros (as had Paraguayans earlier), after town-centered Spanish rebels against extortionate government by foreign officials in the 1520s.

In insurgent Andean towns, some knowledge was evidenced of events in British America. Revolutionary broadsides, stating complaints similar to those of Mexicans who took arms in 1766 and 1767, also on occasion mentioned "the example of the North American colonies" then in revolt. One placard urged establishing self-governing republics, promising "they will be happy,"[30] Implicated in the revolt, as the senior royal military leader in Peru reported, were propertied Lima and Cuzco creoles who were opposed to higher taxes and influenced by the Anglo-American example.[31] It will be remembered that in 1776 Areche's high-handedness and innovations, including collecting more revenues, had caused the creole establishment to gather behind the viceroy, Guirior, who, they said, was bent on defending the country; Areche they referred to as anti-American.[32] Moreover, *cuzqueños* had long smarted under Lima's basically European ascendency and wanted more local power. Creole conspirators, the commentator added, had sought to incite castas and Indians to rebel in order to gain for whites greater autonomy and home rule under a Peruvian monarch. While perhaps overstating creole influence, his comment was valid. Even so, creoles in those areas where mass revolts occurred usually soon decided to aid government troops. Some enthusiasm in Peru too was then evident among the disaffected for the British type of constitutional monarchy and for British naval strength. And from New Granada in 1781 the viceroy, Manuel Antonio Flórez, informed Gálvez that "news of the independence of the English colonies of the north goes from mouth to mouth among everyone in the uprising."[33]

In New Granada, the revolt was led by creoles and included all classes of people. It centered on exclusion of Americans from higher offices, hatred of Spaniards, the abrasive collection of increased taxes, and stringent imposition of royal monopolies on rum, anisette, and tobacco under the new visitor-general, Juan Francisco Gutiérrez de Piñeres, sent out by Gálvez in 1778. The comunero revolt began in Socorro, where also threatened, by the free trade reglamento of 1778, was the prosperous textile industry, dominated by creoles. The forced loan of 1780, levied as a head tax, there too contributed to discontent, as did rises in the official price of tobacco. (In 1778 and 1780, impelled by desire for higher returns to offset war costs, this escalation turned away Spanish America's chief customers, the French, who instead bought more of the cheaper Anglo-American tobacco.) Gálvez and his envoy to New Granada, as one scholar has reflected, ignored Ward's advice to emulate the prosperity of the British colonies by levying low excise and sales taxes, and so lost business to them.[34]

The Andean rebellions were endorsed by a former Jesuit, Pablo Viscardo, a Peruvian in exile in Italy who requested English aid in freeing his country from Spain; one of his goals was to be able to return home. Another exiled Jesuit,

Clavijero, who had urged educational and economic reforms while in his native Mexico, published in Italy in 1780 and 1781 his *Storia Antica de Messico*, recounting his patria's glorious past and natural attributes. Scoring Raynal and other European writers for denigrating the Aztecs and all people born in America, his history preceded a similar reaction, that of Jefferson in his *Notes on Virginia*, to the same stimuli. Clavijero countered those slurs, themselves a product of the Enlightenment, with a fervent declaration of Mexican patriotism and a deep sense of Mexican nationality. As a group, the exiled Jesuits produced a literature of nostalgia, one affected by current intellectual trends. Presenting America as their homeland, they wrote expressly for their compatriots, the propertied Spanish-descended Americans, and combined religion with nationality; those from Mexico were particularly devoted to the Virgin of Guadalupe. As one American nation was coming into being, they described other American regions—to Mexicans, their *nation*—as implicitly kindred in being American and as existing in bondage. Their writings merged with indigenist expressions within Spanish America, leading authorities in Peru to outlaw all mention of the Incas and later, in Mexico, to exile the outspoken friar, Servando Teresa de Mier.[35]

At the war's end many creoles, especially those in Mexico under the new viceroy, the war hero Bernardo de Gálvez, expressed a new respect for the victorious British Americans—just as, some of them explained, Spain had done during peace negotiations at Paris. The epic contest in America and its outcome had heightened their pride and self-awareness. As Alexander von Humboldt later remarked, after the Peace of Versailles creoles preferred to say, "I am not a Spaniard; I am an American."[36]

Thus, Spanish involvement in the British American struggle, although half-hearted and primarily meant to weaken England, had reverberations in and for Spanish America. Wartime measures intensified a reform program sparked by earlier competition with Britain and emphasized the aspects of that program calculated for defense and to raise funds for Spain. Antigovernment feeling heightened, and led in South America to widespread disaffection and rebellion. And in this tense colonial situation, Spain's North American quasi allies competed with it for trade and provided an ideological and actual example subversive of Spain's own interests. Moreover, the American Revolution was indirectly responsible for Spain's double bind: the confluence of the costs and dislocations of both war and reform. These, in combination with the triumph of the new nation, then intensified among many creoles, whether of more liberal or conservative bent, and whether prospering or harder pressed, a desire for greater self-government and self-determination and an awareness of America as a unique and esteemed entity.

Spain's postwar American policy was a continuation of prewar goals, if with a certain altered tone—more defensive and more convinced of British superiority, and it emphasized cooperation between Spain and the Indies in American defense, internal development, and imperial interchange. A *consulta* of the Council of the Indies explained, "It is desirable that in America agriculture and the products which nature so lavishly bestows should be developed and should serve as raw materials for manufacturing and assembly in Spain,"—thus to lead to an exchange of mutual benefit. The commerce of both continents should be equally favored, expanded, and protected from foreigners.[37] The government took pains to instruct its American representatives to make a show of restraint in colonial taxation. And it hoped to bind the colonies through appeal to self-interest. In this vein, Americans were exhorted to help build up their regions for the benefit of the organic nation and its peoples on both sides of the Atlantic. American scientific expeditions, economic societies, and additional consulados were sanctioned, and in 1785 José de Gálvez, in permitting Saavedra to found a consulado in Caracas, remarked in an apparent about-face that he did so in order that Americans might feel they "have influence in their own happiness."[38] Ongoing ministerial fear of English subversion of Spain's colonies, now abetted by "the menace of the revolutionary spirit as represented by the United States," and United States and British ships flocking to the South Atlantic and Pacific, were major causes of the new concern with American sensibilities.[39] Floridablanca, unhappy with the Treaty of Versailles and heeding advice from America, including that of Francisco Rendón who had succeeded Miralles in Philadelphia and who saw in American smuggling and in the rapid growth of Anglo-American frontier settlements a threat to Spain, closed the Mississippi to Americans from 1784 to 1787 and pursued a policy meant both to contain them within circumscribed boundaries and to curb their trade with Spain's America.[40]

The vogue for political economy continued to spread in Spain, and translations of English and other foreign economists continued to appear, as well as tracts by Campomanes and Jovellanos. In 1784, Jovellanos spoke of the British as "the best economists in the world"; he had come during the war to urge free play of economic forces, national progress, and material accumulation, thus reinforcing the movement afoot for economic liberalism under state supervision. In 1781 in a speech to the Royal Academy of History, he gave impetus, as had Campomanes, to a liberal interpretation of Spanish history. He made explicit appeal to a national constitution, sighting its origins in medieval institutions and the workings of the Cortes, or parliament. It was a tentative step toward criticizing absolutism and advocating constitutional monarchy, and it was taken during the American Revolution. Campomanes, who was president of that Academy from 1764 to 1791, in an exchange of amenities with Franklin in 1784 proposed him for membership, while Franklin recommended Campomanes to the American Philosophical Society and wrote to him from Passy, "You are engaged in a great work, reforming the ancient Habitudes, removing the prejudices, and promoting the Industry of your Nation." Campomanes replied in kind, saying that the Academy felt honored to enroll so eminent a personage of the world of letters and one "so distinguished for the part he has played in a Revolution, the most memorable in the history of modern times."[41]

Books on England and its former colonies continued to appear, at least one of them reinforcing the concept of the constitution as the supreme law. In 1783, the *Memorias históricas de la última guerra con Gran Bretaña desde el año 1774 hasta su conclusión* by José de Covarrubias was published in Madrid. Covarrubias prodded Spaniards to compete with England. He also drew an implicit comparison between suave Spanish and despotic British colonial administration, and he scored the British "obsession with commerce." The Anglo-Americans he declared not traitors but defenders of the cause of liberty against arbitrary ministers who did not respect their constitutional rights. In addition, he presented the cause of Anglo-America as a universal one, eulogized Philadelphia as an asylum of liberty and a scientific center, and reminded his readers that "the sciences and arts are most intimately entwined with the policy of empires."[42] A creole said many of the same things. In volumes published in Madrid from 1786 to 1791, Antonio de Alsedo y Bexarano, born in Quito and a captain in the Spanish army, emulated his father, Dionisio, in writing on America, but with a difference. The younger Alsedo wrote on history north and south, criticized English colonial policies and, citing the Americans frequently in a long account of their revolution, presented concepts of individual and republican rights. His writings were known and admired at home.[43] Pedro Montengón's *Eusebio,* in imitation of Rousseau's *Emile,* also came out in Madrid in 1786. It concerned a Spanish youth, shipwrecked and cast ashore in Maryland who was adopted by a Philadelphia Quaker, and it contrasted European luxury with Pennsylvania simplicity. It extolled hard work and presented Pennsylvania as the refuge of freedom of conscience and seat of the cultivation of natural virtue. It is said over sixty thousand copies were sold in Spain and its America. Montengón was another former Jesuit living in Italy.

Unquestionably, the new nation appeared to Spaniards in Europe and America to be a going concern in the 1780s. While wartime attitudes of mixed wariness and admiration endured, as did respect for Franklin, Washington, Jefferson, and other leaders, joined to them was admiration for the nation's prosperity. The latter was seen as due largely to a sizable carrying trade and the export of farm produce and of some manufactures, all of which was made possible by access to world markets, including those of Latin America and Iberia. Authorities worried about this well-being; creoles hoped to emulate it. Spain after 1783 did reestablish control over its colonies, unlike Britain after 1763, and even took Britain's failure as a lesson, but the ongoing example and activities of the British North American republic helped to make that control tenuous.

In Spanish America after the war, economic growth in many areas and the vision of opportunity continued to raise the demand for labor, which in turn spurred the slave trade and its concomitant, commerce. So did the perceived chance for profit, taken advantage of by creoles, Spaniards, and foreigners, and by the Spanish state. In New Granada more labor was needed for mining gold, in Cuba and Peru for sugar, in Venezuela for cacao, and in La Plata and Chile for the hide industry and domestic service.[44] Latin Americans initially welcomed a surge of imports. Venezuela, Buenos Aires, and other areas profited from the inflow of private and public silver payments from New Spain and Lima, interrupted by war. Then within two years markets began to be glutted and imports to drop, and some governmental restrictions were restored. Precious metals flowed out. Growing scarcity of money slowed circulation of goods, made all forms of business and credit more difficult, and prejudiced production. The experience of boom and bust caused mutual recriminations among peninsular-associated and other merchants, numerous propertied creoles, and governing authorities, while a large postwar influx of Spanish immigrants contributed further to competition and animosities between creoles and Spaniards. United States ships and goods most often shared in this postwar market clandestinely or by way of Europe. More direct were the orders for vessels that began to come in from Spanish America, at first from Spanish authorities. By 1784, Philadelphia supplied three ships to carry monthly correspondence between Gardoqui, Spanish chargé there, and the new Mexican viceroy, young Gálvez.[45]

Mexico had three very innovative viceroys during the decade from 1783: Gálvez, whose deeds during the American Revolution Mexicans swelled to epic proportions and whose affection for French culture established a vogue; Flórez, who moved up from New Granada to institute public works, shun bullfights, patronize the theater, and welcome talented and liberal creoles to salons in the palace; and finally, the Conde de Revillagigedo. He was born in Havana and so was a nominal creole, son of the Cuban governor, the elder Revillagigedo, who had become Mexican viceroy. In later years, Mexicans acclaimed the reign of Revillagigedo the younger as the high point of the Mexican Enlightenment. Buenos Aires and New Granada had viceroys with similar outlooks. These executives and the early intendants led the campaign to secure the cooperation of Americans in developing the natural resources of their own locales and strove to work closely with cabildos and to encourage reputable creole groups who did not represent the old monopolists. Many of them also advocated or implemented setting up regional consulados, patriotic societies, and scientific institutions, as well as educational reform. A major drawback was that all of them lacked sufficient funds to float their ambitious plans for progress.[46]

A number of clergy, as exhorted by Madrid, also cooperated with other authorities and Spanish Americans in sponsoring American economic growth. Several bishops in Mexico were in the forefront of promoting and funding agricultural betterment and local industries noncompetitive with Spanish exports, and were instrumental in keeping down commodity prices in the aftermath of famine and epidemic in 1785 and 1786. In New Granada, Caballero y Góngora, who was then both archbishop and viceroy, put his funds at the disposal of victims of the earthquake of 1785 and responded to local pleas by arranging the first large legal imports of flour, which arrived in 1787 from the United States.[47]

From within the bureaucracies of church and state, or on revitalized cabildos, more creoles exhibited greater local and regional spirit, just as they did more unabashed self-interest in economic enterprise, and they expressed a heightened sense of self-worth as leaders in important regions of the monarchy. More of the educated not only collaborated with Spanish reformers but became associated with the Basque economic society, especially between 1780 and 1787. Such societies, although losing impetus then in Spain, were initiated in the 1780s for Vera

Cruz—there known as the *Sociedad Patriótica*—Santiago de Cuba, and Mompós, New Granada; and were planned in other towns, as were consulados.[48]

Interest in the natural sciences, particularly as necessary to discover, catalog, and exploit natural resources, was heightened by a number of scientific expeditions sponsored by the state. They were dispatched in much the same spirit that had been responsible for the expedition of Juan and Ulloa. Indeed, Ulloa provided continuity when, as commander of the last flota from Spain to Mexico in 1776, he carried orders to local authorities there to inventory its natural wealth. The new expeditions, however, incorporated or involved many creoles. The viceroy in Bogotá, Caballero y Góngora, in 1783 responded to a complaint from his friend, José Celestino Mutis, a physician and professor of mathematics and astronomy, that only foreigners were given permission to look into "the unknown treasures of our country," by authorizing Mutis to lead an expedition from Ecuador to the Caribbean to study plants, geography, and the heavens, and to make maps. Other such enterprises took place in Mexico and Peru.[49] Mutis had come to New Granada in the 1760s as physician to the viceroy; he then taught the first advanced mathematics in Bogotá, introducing Newton's physics. After 1770, in public lectures he cited as authorities Juan and Ulloa, Feijoo, and other enlightened men interested in America. After the expulsion of the Jesuits, Mutis worked for educational reform, but the old order was stronger in New Granada than in Lima and Mexico in the early 1770s—in Peru, Amat reorganized the university in 1771, initiating a reform program. Even so, Mutis' students spread enlightened concepts through the viceroyalty, and some of them rejoined him in the botanical expedition authorized in 1783. His closest scientific collaborator, José de Caldas, reportedly corresponded with Franklin. As we shall see, from this nucleus of creoles eager to employ useful knowledge to better their lives and those of their compatriots would come the founding fathers of Colombia.[50]

Everywhere reform of higher education begun in the late 1760s and early seventies seems to have stalled by 1783, despite continuing ferment for educational reform, which was viewed as especially indispensable to regional development. And in the mid-1780s, there were some further signs of creole dissatisfaction and even of desire to dispense with ruling Spaniards. A plot was reportedly hatched in Mexico by disgruntled creole nobles who in 1785 sent Francisco de Mendiola to England to seek assistance: they complained of Spanish imposts and bad treatment, "the tyrannical despotism which violates the constitution, and the liberty that is owed to us." They recalled, too, that Mexicans had helped Spain in the last war "with more than seventy million pesos," and they wanted to buy freely from Jamaica. Mendiola was to persuade the British that a Mexican treaty of amity and commerce would compensate them for loss of their American colonies. He went by way of New York, where he was secretly aided by the British consul, Anthony Merry, a close friend of Alexander Hamilton.[51] Although reminiscent of the Puebla conspirators of 1765, these dissident Mexicans exhibited more awareness of political currents and more specific, and commercial, goals. In 1785, too, there were rumors that the viceroy, young

Gálvez, sought to set himself up as ruler of an independent New Spain. Although they have never been substantiated, and his untimely death the next year ended speculation, yet the possibility of independence was aired, as it had been earlier by more radical people in the huge revolts in South America.[52]

A crucial nexus in contacts between the Americans in the 1780s was the Caribbean, the hub of direct and indirect trade and, during the war, a major staging area for military and naval campaigns. It was in Cuba that a creole very important to subsequent Spanish American history came into contact with Anglo-American patriots and entrepreneurs, and it was from Havana that he sailed to the United States in 1783—from there, Francisco de Miranda proceeded to England and into the history books. Miranda's career, still imperfectly known, says much about the interplay of the example of the United States, late eighteenth-century ideas and international relations, and creole aspirations. It also sheds some light on the international nature of trade arrangements in the Caribbean.

Miranda later said he first entertained ideas of Spanish American independence in 1781 when, as captain in the Spanish forces allied with those of the British American rebels, he took part in Gálvez's campaigns—when Spanish troops transported in North American ships sailed from Havana against the English in Pensacola and, again, against New Providence Island in the Bahamas. He also, as we have seen, engaged in smuggling in association with North Americans and played an as yet unquantified part in the complex multinational trading ventures of the period. He later wrote:

> When I realized on receiving the *capitulaciones de Zipaquirá* how simple and inexperienced the Americans were and on the other hand how astute and perfidious the Spanish agents had proved, I thought it best to suffer for a time in patience until the Anglo-American colonies achieved their independence, which was bound to be...the infallible preliminary to our own.[53]

While in Cuba, too, he exchanged letters with creole dissidents in Venezuela—among them Juan Vicente Bolívar, Simón's brother—who addressed him as their leader. His flight to the United States, then, and his revolutionary aspirations initially resulted from the swirling crosscurrents caused by war and rebellions and by the international situation—in particular by revolt in South America and, especially, by the success of the Revolution of 1776. Miranda took with him from Havana a letter of introduction from his superior and erstwhile protector, General Juan Manuel de Cagigal, to the man so admired by Spanish officers in Cuba, George Washington.[54]

In the course of his seventeen-month visit to the United States, he reported meeting not only Livingston and Robert Morris but also a number of revolutionary leaders, including signers of the Declaration of Independence, and he at least saw George Washington and, although not mentioned in his diary, had a number of conversations with Alexander Hamilton. John Adams later recalled that Hamilton had been "one of [Miranda's] most intimate friends and advisors."[55] Miranda greatly admired these connections; his with such men, and theirs with world-changing events. Clearly the young, attractive, intelligent, tremendously intense and energetic creole, after a life on the fringe of society in Caracas and in the Spanish army, liked being entertained and lionized as a distinguished visitor by affluent and important republicans. The abundant evidence of material prosperity, industriousness, and thriving commerce and agriculture also impressed him. He was, however, both amused and put off by displays of social equality, and very unhappy at finding his servant at table with him in a Connecticut inn. The positive aspects of life in the United States he attributed to what he termed the perseverance of the British constitution. "Good God," he commented in his diary, "What a contrast to the Spanish system!" It was in New York in 1784 that he probably conferred with Hamilton and it was there, Miranda said later, that he committed himself to work for the independence of Spanish America, in imitation of the United States and in cooperation with England.[56]

In the same period, the American Revolution had a strong impact on dissatisfied Brazilians. By 1785, Pombal's earlier and more conciliatory attitudes toward colonials were giving way to policies more like those of England toward its thirteen colonies during the 1760s. The new Portuguese government had come to trust colonials less; it sought to curb further Brazilian manufactures and to clamp down more vigorously on Brazilians involved in the large volume of contraband, offering the patently false rationale that Portugal protected Brazil. Even some wealthy and powerful Brazilians felt threatened, displayed an ever-increasing self-awareness and self-confidence, and also aired a growing enthusiasm for the North American example of political and economic change.

Unrest centered in two regions. In Río de Janeiro, some merchants wanted free commerce and desired, said one informant, to "make [of Brazil] an English America."[57] In gold- and diamond-rich Minas Gerais, dissidents were less interested in trade than in regaining prerogatives taken over by the new governor sent from Portugal and his cronies. Martinho de Melo e Castro, the minister of colonial affairs, not only disliked Brazilians but, ignoring depression and declining gold production, in 1779 had authorized a new severity in American government in order to restore high returns to Portugal. This order was kept from Brazilians until in 1788 the new governor of Minas Gerais attempted stringent reform, especially of the clergy and the fiscal system, and took effective steps to halt leakage in gold and diamonds. Thereupon, members of the entrenched, dominant native oligarchy reacted strongly against those measures and Portuguese policy for Brazil in general.

Dissidents in Minas Gerais and Río were in touch, and in 1786 a Brazilian student at the University of Montpellier, José Joaquim Maia e Barbalho, who was probably connected to the Río group, wrote to Thomas Jefferson, then United States envoy to France. Signing himself *Vendak,* he declared his country to be held in a slavery "rendered each day more insupportable since the epoch of your glorious independence."[58] Brazilians, he went on, wished to follow the North American example, to seek liberty, and to get United States help in achieving it. "Nature made us inhabitants of the same continent," he wrote in an appeal to what has since been called continental nationalism, "and in consequence in some degree compatriots." Jefferson, who also exhibited a high sense of Americanism, arranged to meet Maia, who assured him that the army in Brazil was largely native and disposed to independence and that the men of letters there "are those most desirous of a revolution." Jefferson stopped at Nîmes to talk to him, promised nothing, but, impressed favorably, wrote to John Jay that "the Brazilian dissidents consider the North American revolution as a precedent for theirs. They look to the United States as most likely to give them honest support and for a variety of considerations have the strongest prejudices in our favor. . . . In case of a successful revolution a republican government in a single body would probably be established."[59]

Other Brazilian students at Montpellier and at Coimbra in this period avidly read about and discussed the American Revolution and the possibilities of Brazil emulating it. One, who reported home the conversation between Maia and Jefferson and who was also given to enthusiasms, cited passages from Raynal that deprecated Portugal, condemned English influences there, and suggested that Brazilian ports be opened to all comers. Another was José Bonifácio Andrade e Silva, from São Paulo, who in 1785 was composing poetry attacking the "horrid monster of despotism," and who would later be responsible for the declaring of Brazilian independence and the crowning of Brazil's first emperors.[60] A third was known to buy books about the American Revolution during a year-and-a-half stay in Britain, where he studied manufacturing and vented his preoccupation with Brazilian independence in conversations with sympathetic merchants. Within Brazil, other individuals continued to gather, including in learned societies, and many of them continued to discuss and disseminate republican ideas.

In Villa Rica, Minas Gerais, when new restrictive governmental measures were announced in 1788, a small group of soldiers and literate townspeople actively planned revolt, in league with many other residents there and elsewhere, including well-placed Brazilians and some Portuguese. The conspiratorial core included a vicar and four military men who had suffered recent setbacks in their careers and fortunes due to what they considered the machinations of the governor and his friends. They intended a republic like the United States, and they derived much inspiration from the works of Raynal and from North America—not only from its example, but also from the constitutions of its new states. Americanism was a keynote; one dissident declared Brazil poor despite its natural wealth "because Europe like a sponge, was sucking all the substance."[61] These conspirators contacted a United States agent but were leery of Great Britain—thereby misjudging the United States. For, like England, its leaders were then more interested in a commercial treaty with Portugal than in trade directly with Brazil. In the end, the widespread plot failed. British dominance and Portuguese domination held, and Brazilian independence, when it came, took a very different route.

In the latter years of the decade, while more Latin Americans carried on more trade with North Americans, whose ships then circled the southern continent, many producers and newer merchants, set back by disappointments attendant upon dampened expectations, found that their earlier and very general euphoric vision of free trade needed refining; they were also discovering that free trade meant different things to different interests, and they were beginning to formulate more specifically what they themselves meant by the term.

Yet, within these circumstances and despite fluctuations, agriculture, stock-raising, and mining continued to expand in many regions and exports abroad increased, as did competition to supply them between Latin American regions. Pent-up demand due to war, the acceleration of European purchases, the thrust of reforming officials for yet higher agricultural and mining yields, continuing population growth, and more trade with both Spain and foreigners all contributed to an "Indian summer of Latin American prosperity." Land concentration in the hands of a relative few, however, tended to rise—particularly in Mexico, where wealthy miners and merchants, challenged by new men and methods and unable to trade abroad during the war, had turned to investment in land and mines. Throughout Spanish America, opportunities for employment continued to expand; still, within general economic growth, the burden of higher taxes fell largely on the bottom social groups. (So did the ravages of Túpac Amaru's revolt, those of rebellion by the comuneros, and the effects of famine and plague in Mexico during 1785 and 1786, which were accompanied by loss of land as well.) Wages did not keep pace with prices, inflated since the war years and still ascending; specie was shipped to Spain (where it contributed, along with paper money, to inflating prices higher or leaked in contraband.)[62]

On hindsight, within Spanish America it was a time of growth of both liberal and conservative components within the body of attitudes identified with criollismo. Adumbrated in previous decades, creole liberalism, associated with enlightenment and modernism by some of its adherents, was connected to regional economic progress by all of them; it gained disciples and ideological content in an era paralleling and influenced by the emergence of the United States. Creole liberalism flourished beside, or sometimes entwined with, a more entrenched and traditional creole mentality. Varieties of traditional attitudes and opinions remained strong for years to come. Creole liberalism always retained certain customary elements, and there endured among proponents of both sorts of creolism an aggressive, conservative emphasis on the prerogatives of their American birth and their privileged status, sometimes as heirs of the Spanish conquerors, and sometimes combined with a claim also based on a legacy from pre-hispanic indigenous roots; and all creole assertions of Americanism were enhanced by the appearance of an independent American nation.[63] To the more liberal and enlightened creoles, moreover, the new American republic then stood as a model of ideals in action. It stood for material well-being and for innovation itself. It made all things look possible through talent and human effort, through inhabitants of a region unifying and vigorously applying useful knowledge and the tenets of political economy to regional problems and social ills. While the use of the United States as an exemplar was then largely limited to one of economic advance and of some supporting social institutions, yet it did represent to Latin Americans liberty—political, economic, and social; a liberal liberty.

The revolutionary war itself, and Spain's involvement, had other sorts of impacts on Latin America. It had deflected reform goals in the face of an increased Spanish need for American funds, so that the first of many forced loans, in 1779, was a harbinger of a shift in Spanish relations with its America, henceforth characterized by erratic alternation in the easing and tightening up of government and of trade. That loan, too, and the curtailment of funds to maintain soldiers in Peru, contributed to the onset of Túpac Amaru's rebellion, which had its own reverberations, and that call for money exacerbated discontent and sparked conspiracies throughout Spanish America.

By 1788, the end of the reign of Charles III, Latin Americans were caught up, directly or indirectly, in several revolutions. The American Revolution and its aftermath, together with the Enlightenment and the onset of the industrial revolution, all had great impact on Spanish policies and on Spanish Americans. And certain trends observable from 1776 on would, in the next few decades, bring Spanish Americans to inaugurate another revolution.

7

"THE MOST IMPORTANT SUBJECT":

SPANISH AMERICA, 1788–1797

In 1789, Floridablanca declared that through wise policy "a happy revolution" had been achieved in the growth of Spain's trade with its America,[1] even though the government, aware that a wide divergence existed in informed opinion as to whether or not such was the case, had just concluded an investigation, publicly reported, showing contraband rampant, foreigners trading directly with the Spanish colonies, and the majority of Spain's trade with its America in re-exports. There was general recognition, as a report from a London paper reprinted in the *Gazeta de Madrid* asserted, that in its colonies Spain was "a mere commission agent of foreign factories."[2] Also generally acknowledged was a lack of significant economic progress within the empire as a whole. José de Gálvez died in 1787, Charles III in 1788. Economic malaise and weaker government coalesced with the outbreak of the French Revolution in 1789 and Spain's war with France from 1793 to 1795, to make the first decade of the reign of Charles IV a period of inflation, ideological turbulence, and administrative instability, all having ramifications for America.

Consciously or not, Floridablanca's phrase "happy revolution" echoed Adam Smith's "a revolution of the greatest importance to the public happiness." By 1788, Smith's views on political economy were being taken up by Spanish economic societies, and, in a eulogy for Charles III that year, Jovellanos, who later wrote of a debt to Smith, waxed most eloquent concerning "civil economy." Valentín de Foronda, who would become Spanish consul general in Philadelphia in 1802, and chargé d'affaires there from 1807 to 1809, made speeches to the Basque economic society, subsequently published in the *Espíritu de los mejores diarios,* the readers' digest of Madrid, which combined recommending reading Smith with publicizing political theory identified with the American Revolution. Foronda spoke of the nobility of commerce and presented Smith's version of political economy as the true science of society. He pronounced liberty the right to use as one wishes acquired goods, and opposed government's overstepping its power. He denied that enlightened despotism worked; and he and other progressives, among them Campomanes, Jovellanos, and Caburrús, Charles III's chief economic advisor, in the mid-1780s implicitly but sharply criticized absolutism and its structures and repeatedly stated as an assumption the constitutional nature of the monarchy.[3]

Although Smith, Hume, and their Spanish admirers by the late 1780s and 1790s stressed the primary importance of both production and exchange for national prosperity and power, by 1789 Spanish ministers had recognized that foreign manufactures were necessary to supply the Indies adequately and had concluded that Spain's immediate hope lay in functioning as a center of commercial exchange. In that year, Campomanes and Jovellanos were writing that the nation needed foreign manufactures and carriers, and that Spain's goal should be their regulation for Spanish profit. Royal ministers saw American products and markets as intrinsic to this arrangement, and American loyalty as a sine qua non. Thus, Campomanes stated in 1788 that "it may be affirmed that Spain's trade with the Indies is the most important subject confronting the nation."[4]

From 1787 to 1792, discussions of American matters took up a good deal of time in cabinet *(junta de estado)* meetings. As Jacques Barbier has concluded, "The importance attached to commercial affairs in this period can hardly be overestimated," and, he wrote, measures taken from 1788 to 1792 "were designed to reassure vested interests [in America], while continuing to readjust the imperial economic balance even further in the Peninsula's favor." This purpose lay behind the administration's speaking, in 1787, of promoting "the unity and equality" of Spain and the Indies. Gálvez's economic system was kept, but many of his methods of taxation and administrative reforms were abandoned. Spain then showed a new restraint in taxing America—but also in expenditures there. Civil and military bureaucracies were reduced, which meant fewer jobs for creoles, even while the state broadened the invitation to Americans to cooperate in developing their regions. Two aspects of Gálvez's system, freer trade and the shipping of American specie to Spain, gained new importance. Floridablanca headed the junta that in 1789 extended the free trade reglamento of 1778 to Vera Cruz and Lima, and that established an open slave trade to the Spanish colonies.[5]

Earlier, the cabinet had endorsed his rather quixotic plans to close the Mississippi and New Orleans to Anglo-Americans and then to form a barrier of population drawn from Anglo-American settlements to defend Spanish territory in North America, especially from commercial and territorial encroachment by the United States or the British. He termed Anglo-Americans *"aquellos diligentes y desasosegados vecinos"*—"those diligent and worrisome neighbors."[6] Still, he preferred that Spain trade with them rather than with stronger, European peoples, for, he concluded, with far less foresight than Aranda had shown, that "the discords that reign in those states because of restlessness and the love of their inhabitants for independence are favorable to us and will always cause them to be weak." His later policies undoubtedly owed something to the opinions of Gardoqui who, appointed to the new post of director of colonial trade, viewed the United States much as Carvajal had seen England at mid-century, as posing a threat to Spanish America and better serving Spanish interests if an ally; an accommodation should be reached. From 1792, government priorities shifted to an even greater concern for American defense and security, especially after the

Nootka Convention of 1790 in effect had opened the Pacific to British and United States smuggling, and when the spread of radical French ideas and activities, rebellion in Saint Domingue, and disturbances in Venezuela and Mexico indicated that those priorities were justified. By 1791, attesting to official jitters was the royal order against the entry into the viceroyalty of Peru of objects inscribed *Libertad Americana* and of "money that alludes to the liberty of the Anglo-American colonies."[7]

Two years earlier, with revolt in France, Floridablanca's domestic policies had turned more conservative, so that by 1791 economic societies were being curbed, all private periodicals suspended, and Cabarrús, Jovellanos, and Campomanes were out of favor. The situation eased in 1792 when Aranda briefly replaced Floridablanca and brought a relaxation of the official attitude. Then Manuel Godoy took charge of the government and adapted Aranda's more liberal stance, although making a more obvious attempt to attract the support of the church and the aristocracy (Floridablanca had worked with the former; Aranda belonged to the latter). Yet, events contributed to nourishing in Spain both republican sentiment centered on limited, constitutional monarchy and Catholic conservatism dedicated to absolutism; dislike of Godoy characterized advocates of each position. From 1792, beset with international woes, the government faced a decline in confidence, pleasing powerful factions of neither the left nor the right. In this climate of greater disaffection Godoy, articulating the tenets of enlightened despotism as developed under Charles III as the safest middle ground, although faith in their efficacy had eroded, continued to rely on Gardoqui through the 1790s and to avow certain enlightened American policies of the previous reign.

This period of factional sparring gave impetus among old reformers to some selective borrowing from liberal political and economic precepts and writers in Britain and the United States. Jovellanos in exile read French and English books, including Thomas Paine's *Rights of Man,* especially admired Benjamin Franklin's works, and endorsed constitutional monarchy and Adam Smith's theories of political economy, if in Spanish adaptation. Although Franklin was lauded by the Spanish press primarily for his scientific contributions, the *Espíritu* in 1798 reprinted a French epigram: "Franklin snatched the spark from the heavens and the scepter from the tyrants." And, although the text of *The Wealth of Nations* was prohibited in Spain in 1792, in 1794 the *Gazette* of Madrid announced an abridged Castilian edition and advertised it as "the best work of its class. . . very useful for public leaders and especially for propagating in the economic societies true principles which should direct their operations toward the general good of the monarchy."[8] Members of American economic societies, in particular, would heed this advice to pay attention to Adam Smith.

The first stage of revolution in France helped to popularize constitutionalism in Spain—in 1791 Jovellanos and in 1792 Cabarrús praised the French Constitution. The constitutional phase in France gave spirit and lent political philosophy to opponents of absolutism in Spain. It also helped to polarize opinion—for, in reaction, conservative spokesmen, often clergy, looked back to effective absolutism, while progressives found support for their tendency to look even further back to a medieval Spanish constitution limiting the monarch. Even so, its increasing radicalism had alienated both Spanish conservatives and progressives when a republican plot surfaced in 1795. Its leader, Juan Mariano Picornell, acknowledged not only having been influenced by the French but also having been swayed by Spain's support of the Anglo-American rebels, and, most recently, being motivated by disgust with a system allowing the rise of Godoy. Picornell was imprisoned, tried, and banished to South America. On hindsight, then, the climate in Spain of unrest and dissatisfaction during the 1790s was not, properly speaking, revolutionary, nor was it sparked principally by rebellion in France. Rather, Spanish shifts in outlook can best be understood as within the overriding, multiple varieties of revolution occurring in the Western world. These included not only the French upheaval, the earlier American Revolution, and England's industrial revolution, and the interaction of them all, but also Spain's own defensive attempt at industrial and now principally commercial revolution, itself in part resulting from the others, which incorporated a widespread enchantment among educated, more liberal Spaniards with political economy and its terminology, and which, like the political revolutions, put emphasis on an ideal of cooperation of government and people in positive and patriotic activity. Only with all these factors considered can it be said that in the late eighteenth century in Spain began "the era of the destruction of the state of mind supporting the old order."[9] A similar phenomenon occurred in Spain's colonies.

When, after the death of Gálvez, American affairs were placed topically under Spanish ministers, it meant that under Charles IV and Floridablanca, and in line with an imperial view dating to the 1760s, America was incorporated administratively into the nation-state. Further, by the advent of Godoy the pertaining American system, subsequently often designated as the Bourbon reform program, was no longer new. By then, many of the first generation of reforming administrators had moved up through lesser posts in America to high office there or had come home to direct American affairs; among the latter were Francisco de Saavedra and Gardoqui. Trained under José de Gálvez, they pushed in America the old economic reform programs languishing in Spain. They did this with renewed vigor in a partially successful attempt to develop America's resources, principally its exportable commodities and its revenues, and to make them immediately benefit the metropolis—all too as part of the ongoing defensive campaign to stave off England in America, contain the United States, and to hold international power in some sort of balance.

In order, within this policy, to implement the reinvigorated goal of American economic growth, so fervently desired by both the state and the creoles, if for varying reasons, the government authorized additional American associations, among them more economic societies. These in turn often sponsored gazettes focused on the economy and commerce, so that creoles found a forum in those societies and a wider vent for opinion in their periodicals. Patriotic societies—the preferred designation—then formed in Havana, Lima, Quito, and Guatemala. With university reform in Lima languishing, its exponents instead gathered informally in tertulias. One turned into the *Academia Filarmónica* in 1787, and in 1790 became the Amigos del País. With encouragement from the viceroy, Gil, its principal function became putting out the *Mercurio Peruano,* avowedly dedicated to political economy. To the first issue in 1791 Baquíjano, a member of the original group, contributed the significantly entitled *Historical and Political Dissertation on the Commerce of Peru,* which showed how creole goals diverged from peninsular in calling principally for a more open trade than did the government and for colonial manufactures. While he once again made critical allusions to the visitador, Areche, he now also attacked slurs against Spain by French encyclopedists; and he praised Feijoo and, above all, Jovellanos, whom he strove to emulate in tone and may have met in Seville through Olavide. That creoles were aware of the government's tenor is evidenced by the further activities of Baquíjano, who, after three years devoted to the economic society and the *Mercurio,* felt he had gathered sufficient credits to apply again for high position and returned to Spain to do so in 1793, this time with success. In 1797 he was appointed the first creole judge on the Lima audiencia in 20 years. To backtrack a bit, other issues of the *Mercurio* presented Peru as "the richest part of the globe," urged exploiting its resources, and gave much space to navigation. They offered statistics on trade with Spain and other areas and criticized the fact that Spain had few ships in American commerce. And they made cautious if obvious references to freer peoples, such as, "Our writers would be deeper and more incisive if they would have followed for instruction or amusement those who inhabit the banks of the indomitable Delaware or the freedom-filled shores of the Zuider Zee."[10]

Pérez Calama, who in 1791 had moved from Mexico to Quito as its bishop, was a founder and director of Quito's patriotic society. Voicing a point of view strikingly out of keeping with traditional clerical injunctions, he devoted his inaugural address to celebrating the newly fashionable faith in "the grand art of making money—it is the spirit and political soul," he avowed, "of cultured peoples," and he cited as examples of these the Dutch and the English. This good, and gain-endorsing, shepherd urged that regional wealth be gotten through commerce, by exchanging grains and wool for cash. Lima's *Mercurio,* in printing his speech in 1792, commented that it signified "a happy revolution of ideas!" In Mexico, Posada too used that phrase that same year in enthusing about merchants there who, by investing in mining, meat, and sugar, had yielded considerable remittances to Spain.[11] Clearly Adam Smith's phrase, and Floridablanca's using it in endorsement of alternate, economic revolution and its implementation in America, were taken up with alacrity by forward-looking men, Spanish and creole. Originally put forth as a counterproposal to what had happened in British America, and in contradistinction to any violent upheaval, this Spanish notion of a benign imperial commercial turnabout now served not only as a new rationale for Spain's civilizing mission to America, but also as one meant to offset the French concept of revolution as well, and to stir creoles to thought of participating in their own regional advance.

In the same spirit, the government dispatched more scientific expeditions to

America. In 1789, the year after Kendrick and Gray had arrived on the Pacific coast and sailed into San Francisco Bay, where British ships also anchored, the court sent out Alejandro Malespina, an Italian-born naval officer who had been a British prisoner during the American Revolution, and who vowed to surpass Cook. From 1789 to 1794, Malespina headed an expedition proclaimed scientific and instructed to investigate the flora and fauna of the Northwest coast. He had, however, secret orders to look into military arrangements and to reinforce the Spanish claim to Nootka Sound. Associated with Malespina's expedition was the creole naturalist José Mariano Mociño, who subsequently published accounts of his investigations of Mexico, also going beyond botany to criticize the political economy of the viceroyalty. Malespina himself returned to Europe favoring radical change in colonial government. By the 1790s, other Spanish expeditions had been dispatched to America, including those led by mining experts to better silver yields and processes.[12] Authorities throughout America also renewed efforts to promote technical education, to curtail clerical prerogatives, and to strengthen military forces, as well as to interest Americans in approved economic and commercial stimulus.

In this same period, Latin Americans experienced continuing ascent in the output and value of mines, farms, and ranches. This growth, a swelling overseas demand, and the decline of production in Saint Domingue of sugar and coffee brought on a boom—in sugar in Cuba; hides and wheat in Buenos Aires; sugar and cotton in Louisiana; cotton, coffee, sugar, and indigo in Brazil; and, in Venezuela, coffee. New Spain then exported six times more cotton than the United States; Mexico City and Lima were still larger than Philadelphia or New York. Yet, Latin Americans also increasingly encountered competition from other American regions, Iberian and otherwise, and from Europe in textiles and some primary products. They experienced drops in some commodity prices, including of cochineal and indigo in Guatemala and of hides in Buenos Aires, and they energetically discussed, and pushed for, more effective mechanisms for increasing and bettering output, implementing export, and finding markets. In particular, they continued to petition for American consulados and for freer trade, an appetite only whetted by the ordinances of 1778 and 1789. This situation, the progressive opening of the slave trade, and the swelling opportunities for contraband attracted more new, competitive traders, many of them agents for, or dealing with, non-Spaniards, including North Americans. Within Spanish America merchants had increased, had become increasingly powerful, and were more often either the same people or now tended to affiliate more closely with planters, hacendados, and mineowners. Social mobility rose with the higher status accorded to commerce and with opportunity provided by expanding economies and by current governmental politics; all this reinforced new entrepreneurial outlooks challenging and weakening many traditional, more static concepts and arrangements.[13]

The heady but difficult times from 1789 to 1793 presented the possibilities of greater wealth and power to ambitious Americans of property and talent. In Argentina where *estancieros,* with the viceroy's backing gained protection against hide rustlers for their herds, and farmers the right to export wheat, both hides and wheat continued to be profitably exported, often by slavers. This pattern was set by the first great entrepreneur in Buenos Aires, the audacious Tomás Antonio Romero. He outtraded the old monopolists, kept up close relations with viceroys, and he dealt directly with Boston at a time when larger markets for hides in the United States and England stimulated the desire to swell their sale not only from La Plata but from Venezuela and Brazil as well. Romero and many others throughout Latin America used the free trade in blacks as a front for contraband, or declared even the most inappropriate cargoes as necessaries for their human imports.[14]

The shifts in policy also led to some creoles regaining, and others attaining, political and social power. Gamboa, a Mexican exile of the 1760s, exemplified creole resurgence when, as *regente* of the audiencia, in 1789 with Flórez ill he wielded most power in New Spain.[15] And the new viceroy, the Conde de Revillagigedo the younger, who arrived at the end of that year, demonstrated the current official stance in circumspectly but assiduously encouraging greater cooperation of creoles with government in developing New Spain, their region of empire. The son of the previous viceroy of that name, we have seen that he had been born in Havana and thus was nominally creole. He had also distinguished himself in the late war against England, and had found favor with Floridablanca, and he brought to Mexico its last infusion of an eager, single-minded devotion to enlightened reform and economic advance. While, it has been said, "he always knew how to reconcile the good of the country with the benefit of the metropolis,"[16] his most outstanding success may have been in persuading Mexicans of the great weight he attached to the former. His measures are instructive, telling much of the last florescence of the Bourbon reforms, the obstacles encountered, and the course of imperial relations. In accord with cabinet priorities, he gave much attention to developing agriculture and mines, as well as industries not competing with Spanish, and to reforming fiscal affairs and the currency. He promoted "public works of common utility, comfort, and beauty," as he said, to keep the populace occupied and distracted from any thought of revolution. He suggested lower taxes, prizes to stimulate individual economic initiative, and overhauling the legal system and the intendancies. He was greatly concerned with commerce and with keeping an eye on the United States. In a long, confidential report home in 1793 he commented extensively on the United States's progress and its position as a competitor. While New Spain's trade abroad prospered, he pointed out, Anglo-American flour continued to shut Mexican out of Havana, and he attributed it to taxes levied both upon leaving Vera Cruz and entering Cuba. As for free trade as authorized in 1789, while "useful to the common good," it had resulted in contraband, in which Mexican merchants cooperated, and in importation of foreign textiles, which undersold native fabrics, except rough cottons, and in more revenues of New Spain being drained to Caribbean islands where they were spent on contraband. He pointed to the example of the United States; it had better roads and more ships, and it profited from a harder-working populace devoted to frugality and supplied with better farming equipment and more economic sense. Its inhabitants, he added, threatened to become greedy neighbors; they currently had designs on Texas. Like Jovellanos, Revillagigedo put aside for the time being those ideals not applicable to short-run Spanish benefit. His measures and attitudes—he was said to have wanted to alter his coat of arms, replacing heraldic symbols of the purity and virginity of Mary with allusions to Liberty and Commerce—and particularly his reliance on provincial authorities to collect information on the conditions and potential of New Spain, in the process spread and forwarded Mexican liberalism and self-awareness.[17]

During this period, Antonio Alzate, back editing a periodical from 1788 to 1795, enjoying good relations with Revillagigedo, and respected as a savant by other educated Mexicans, summed up and disseminated creole ideals, aspirations, and disappointments. He demonstrated their interplay with governmental policies, as well as some wider influences upon them. Beginning in 1788 his *Gaceta,* adumbrating the *Mercurio Peruano* and others, but ostensibly devoted to literature, reflected the mingling of two phenomena: the renewed and broadened call for active participation in economic reform and a newly vociferous liberal criollismo expressed as optimism regarding, and concern for, one's American region of birth. In the first issue, announcing himself moved to take up *"la voz Mexicana,"* he promised his readers that he would discuss European and American progress in commerce and navigation and in applied sciences. He would write of the lives and deeds of men "who have illuminated our Hispanoamerican nation," and would report on the geography, natural resources, and natural history of "our America." His prime interest, he wrote, was to be useful to fellow beings and to "la patria," which was clearly Mexico.[18] Although purportedly editing a literary journal, he would, he said, inform his readers of discoveries in experimental physics, mathematics, medicine, and chemistry, and of mining and agricultural techniques.

During 1788 and 1789, Alzate's *Gaceta* criticized selected aspects of Spanish and Spanish American life. New Spain he declared enveloped in a static state of mind, attributable in part to the peninsular government's insufficient promotion of scientific advance, but in the main to the still potent Mexican esteem for tradition-bound education and to an outmoded but still widespread tendency to disparage innovation. Familiar with European journals and the transactions of the American Philosophical Society, he totally endorsed relying upon the power of reason and holding strongly to one's own (educated) opinion, and he repeatedly praised as exemplifying the modern spirit, and even ran a series of articles on, Franklin and his scientific discoveries. He alluded to Bernardo de Gálvez's order for emergency relief during the famine of 1785 as *"una instrucción política económica,"* and the public response to it as a show of "ardent patriotic zeal." And in discussing the study of natural sciences, he concluded that "the English colonies have done more."[19] He was, we have seen, a member of the Basque Economic Society, and he was fond of citing Campomanes.

Although loyal, Alzate ever more urgently prodded Americans, by which he meant Mexicans, to shake off the fetters of every kind of obscurantism and to strengthen their own economy and society. He wrote of a Mexican patria having its own culture, past and present, formed of a unique intermixture of traditions, elements, and progenitors, indigenous and Spanish. He commented on the history of Mexico written by Clavijero, the exiled Jesuit who had been his teacher, and he planned, he said, an American edition of it; he also devoted increasing amounts of space to pre-hispanic Indian achievements, adjudging those early Mexicans good farmers and greater architects than the Spanish. He promoted agriculture and more open trade and proposed creation of a Mexican fleet "to activate commerce" with other ports in Europe and America, without specifying whose ports. He also wrote that the spinning and weaving of cotton was responsible for the subsistence of many of the poor, and that if cotton were less abundant, or too much were shipped overseas, many of them would perish; and the gazette in 1791 carried the discussion by Mociño, then with Malespina's expedition, of the problems of Mexico's internal economy, concluding that New Spain was at the mercy of foreign industry and urging reform.

Alzate, revealing the transitional condition of the creole concept of patria and implicitly examining relations between subjects and the state, sped the evolution of patria from meaning a province of New Spain to all of it, and was shifting the weight from New Spain as a region of the Spanish monarchy to it being first and foremost a region of America. While he was loyal to the monarchy, in his emphasis on being Mexican, in his patriotic zeal, directed toward immediate reform, in his impatience with aspects of the Spanish system, his optimistic assessment of Mexico's possibilities if unfettered by (Spanish) restrictions, and his use of language, he honed intellectual, rhetorical, and emotional tools others were to put to use against Spanish rule in America.

In June 1791, Alzate praised the formation of a literary society in Querétaro. It was composed, he wrote, of five men, among them a priest, a friar, a *caballero*, and a militia captain named Ignacio Allende. Their conversations, he reported with pleasure, concerned "either political innovations or some matter of erudition"; they were to be commended "for having elected to divert themselves in so amiable a way and at the same time so innocent." Alzate, who died in 1799, never heard that this friendly, wholesome gathering came to lay plans culminating in the mass uprisings of 1810, led by Allende and the priest of Dolores, Miguel Hidalgo.[20]

The first stages of the French Revolution, coalescing with the amended royal program, served as a catalyst, radicalizing broadening desires for improvement in Spanish America and intensifying the stepped up rhetoric of reform, including that of political change—raising hope, as in Spain, of the possibility of instituting that form of republicanism, constitutional monarchy. Moreover, we have seen that the outbreak of revolution in France, while only one factor within the spectrum of international relations and the complex ideological climate, coincided, and its impact intermeshed, with the increasing interest Britain and the United States displayed in Latin America and in penetrating the Pacific. This confluence caused Spanish authorities in America to tighten security and to question American loyalties and led some creoles to resent a sensed alteration in official attitudes, including a diminishing of trust. Specifically, in 1789 after the Spanish had detained the *Columbia* and a British frigate in Nootka, they held their crews at the military and naval depot of San Blas where, edgy Mexican officials claimed, with little substance, some English and American, along with French and Portuguese, sailors and technicians were spreading heretical ideas and stirring Indians to plan revolt.[21] And the Peruvian viceroy, learning of Kendrick's having put in at the Juan Fernández Islands, had Ambrosio O'Higgins, then in charge of southern Chile, not only relieve the governor of those islands but also publish the royal decree banning paraphernalia advocating the Anglo-American type of liberty. O'Higgins complied, although he had expressed joy at seeing Washington's signature on American passports, and in 1791 he warned Lima of the illegal presence of French and British, and of additional United States, ships in Chilean ports.[22] Northwards, in Louisiana the Spanish governor, the Baron de Carondelet, felt both constrained to send to Philadelphia for flour and worried that Americans in league with the French might soon invade his territory.[23]

In 1785, the Holy Office in Mexico had attested to the popularity of French books in banning some of them, notably the writings of the radical philosophe, Helvetius, Raynal's history of the Indies, and the French edition of *Fanny Hill*; even after 1789, French fashions remained much in vogue throughout Latin America among the more liberal, the educated, and the upward-aspiring, although the French Revolution had become too radical for creole tastes, with some exceptions.[24] Certain social usages, thought by their practitioners to be of French derivation, also endured—the gatherings, academies, and literary clubs emphasizing good taste and good conversation. Yet within such gatherings almost everywhere it was regional distinctions and progress that were prime topics of discussion, and although the mode was assumed to be predominantly French, these get-togethers mirrored instead a broadly Western tendency to clubbiness. Three groups in particular were or became exceptionally radical: the self-styled literary society Alzate publicized; that in Minas Gerais whose members were arrested in 1790 for plotting an independent republic, like the United States; and some members of Antonio Nariño's circle in New Granada. Most discussions in creole literary associations and social conclaves aroused what the founder of one of them termed too much patriotic enthusiasm—the sort of talk, he informed the government in 1793, that led to pondering natural rights and those of humanity, and to forgetting there were sovereign laws and religion. Such conversations, he reported, also constantly returned to admiration of the new American republic: "In fact, nothing else is discussed by the educated and the unlettered in gatherings and conversation."[25] In short, in formal and informal get-togethers, broadly European and North American influences tended to coalesce in criticism, loyal and otherwise, of Iberia and the nature of American connections to it. Gazettes undoubtedly paralleled, if with more circumspection, conversation; the *Papel Periódico of Bogotá,* for example, contained an article beginning, "The city of Washington being destined to be perhaps someday the most beautiful City of the Universe," and continuing, "Now it can be seen that General Washington will not be forgotten."[26]

In New Granada, the progress of one contributor to the *Papel* attested that rising dissatisfaction with Spanish policies and measures, the impact of initial French revolutionary sentiment, and admiration of the United States's material progress and republicanism advanced together. Pedro Fermín de Vargas had studied under Mutis, was attached to the botanical expedition from its inception in 1783, and the following year, in accord with the new policy of accommodation to creoles, was appointed to Caballero y Góngora's secretariat. In both capacities he traveled extensively and had opportunity to gain insight into the policies and problems of public administration and the country's economic and social situation. Caballero y Góngora in his final report mentioned Vargas as very able, and the new viceroy, José de Ezpeleta, in 1789 appointed him Corregidor of Zipaquirá, the old comunero center. Ezpeleta had moved up from governing Louisiana and, before that, had served as an army officer in Havana during the war under his close friend, Bernardo de Gálvez. In 1790 Vargas wrote two reports on New Granada's agriculture, commerce, mining, and population, which confirmed his ability. In both he cited the United States as a model. He wrote that it should be visited to study how to process and ship flour without spoiling. He cited "Dr. Franklin" concerning the desirability of population increase in lands where means of subsistence abounded, and referred to the United States as an example of promoting immigration. His conclusion censured Spain: "Everyone knows it is impossible for the peninsula to supply the colonies with necessities."[27] These reports show that by 1790 Vargas was fired by patriotism, enthralled with the ideal of civic duty, and distressed at seeing "the kingdom in misery" and lagging behind in innovations bringing prosperity to other Spanish American areas and to the former British colonies. The next year he sold his large library to his good friend Antonio Nariño, and fled to the United States.[28]

Two other tracts attributed to him reveal he came to conclude that "reform must be radical, one should not try to repair but to construct anew, upon new principles."[29] His *Notas* indicate the thrust of his alienation; his *Diálogo entre Lord North y un Filósofo,* his vision of independence. The *Notes* are generally thought to have been written between 1789 and 1791. The *Dialogue* was found among Nariño's papers in 1794. The notes call for radical change and blame Charles IV for being tyrannic, despotic, and keeping Spanish Americans subject, like slaves, and for stimulating class distinctions "contrary to nature, opposed to the spirit of religion, and prejudicial to society." Yet, he went on, "In America there are not obstacles to overcome to make a good revolution, as there are in Europe," and he cited the lack of grandees and of clerical abuses, and the advantage to America of its great distance from Europe. His use of *revolution* indicated a reference to Smith's and Floridablanca's concept of good revolution, but also something of the notion of radical, structural, social, political, and economic change popularized by the French Revolution. In addition, he was directly or indirectly influenced by Paine's arguments for American independence in *Common Sense* concerning George III's tyranny and America's separation by the Atlantic from the Old World. Even so, his sympathetic attitude toward the clergy in America and his upholding of the sanctity of the Catholic religion were deeply Hispanic.

The *Notas* stated what he was against; the *Diálogo*, what he proposed instead. In it the Philosopher lamented the war between England and its colonies and told Lord North that England should have declared them independent, then made alliances with their inhabitants, and he recommended that procedure for all European holdings in America as *the* way to prevent future conflict. Free trade should recompense everyone. "The good of humanity," he concluded, "is preferable to that of one nation"; and, "For 200 years blood has been spilled only for the vile interests of commerce."[30] His comments show a broad cosmopolitan sense of Americanism, and that Vargas was influenced by the American Revolution as much as by anything.

Nariño, Vargas' friend, was also an able public official, was close to the viceroy, and was in addition well-to-do. He owned the press on which the *Papel periódico* was printed and led the literary society, which he avowedly modeled after Franklin's junto. Among his papers was found a plan for decorating his study with inscriptions to Liberty, Reason, and Philosophy and with the likenesses of sages, including Newton, Washington, and Franklin—the last bearing the legend, also familiar to readers of the Madrid *Espíritu,* "He snatched the spark from the heavens and the scepter from tyrants."[31] His choice of decor and epigram bore out (or anyway provided an instance in accord with) John Adams's prophecy that the essence of the history of the American Revolution "will be that Dr. Franklin's electric rod smote the earth and out sprang George Washington."[32]

In 1794, Nariño was tried for translating and secretly publishing on that press the French *Declaration of the Rights of Man*, of 1789. He was accused, too, of plotting to put into effect "the Constitution of Philadelphia." In defending himself before the Bogotá audiencia, he argued that the declaration of the rights of man was first made by the United States of America and only afterwards by the National Assembly of France. He was correct in that the Bill of Rights was the immediate antecedent to the French declaration. The French document, he went on, with a good deal of truth, was in fact composed of eternal and universal principles within the patrimony of Western culture and very well-known to Spanish authors. While Nariño probably sought to present his radical views in their most acceptable form, and while another dissident, the Mexican friar Servando Teresa de Mier, later cited his argument when there was again need for such circumspection, both were aware that much of Spanish American revolutionary theory was indeed extremely eclectic. Nariño, in defending the doctrine of popular sovereignty, went on to say that the most important aspects of the rights of man reflected Thomistic concepts and the ideas of Heneccius and Seneca, and were to be found in *Las Siete Partidas* and other Spanish legal compilations. A creole tendency, basically scholastic, to cite eminent authorities right and left (here literally) in support of one's arguments is, incidentally, a principal reason why disagreement persists among scholars on the relative influence on Latin American independence projects of Spanish, French, English, and United States sources.[33] Nariño argued to little avail. He was sentenced to 10 years' labor in Africa and escaped en route, making his way to Paris, London, and then back to New Granada.

In Quito when Pérez Calama, the bishop, and Juan Pío Montufar, the Marqués de Selva Alegre, inaugurated the patriotic society in 1792, they appointed as its secretary the brilliant physician and essayist—whose progenitors were white, Indian, and black—Francisco Eugenio Santa Cruz y Espejo, another friend of Nariño's. Espejo was an apt choice, in that by 1787 he was corresponding with like-minded Americans in Lima, Popoyán, and Bogotá, and he looked to the society as a vehicle to cure all regional ills. He was also editor of the short-lived gazette, *Primacias de la cultura de Quito*. There were in all seven issues from January to March 1792. In its pages he lamented that local textiles were inferior to European, that they and other native products sold only regionally, and, judging the regional picture dark and embarrassing, he recommended that the crown assign to regions specific export products, noncompetitive with other Spanish American areas. He also wanted more agricultural land opened, more money in circulation, more jobs, and reform of the *obrajes,* the textile workshops, and of mining conditions. He spoke to his readers of their social obligations, writing in the *Primacias,* "We are Quiteños...through us the Patria is reborn; we are the arbiters of its felicity."[34] His mixed background undoubtedly contributed to his voicing a rather odd variation on criollismo. While sympathetic to the current plight of Indians, he declared himself disgusted by the lethargy and weakness of their temperament and pronounced the ancient Incas idolatrous, unjust, lascivious, and cruel. Spain, he wrote in 1793, had been destined and guided by God to discover and conquer Peru and its pagan and uneducated peoples. Espejo had in 1781 applied in vain for a certificate of *limpieza de sangre*, or purity of blood. It was a device, sold by the crown, guaranteeing official recognition of descent from pure white, old Christian stock, and necessary to holding public office and to entering the professions. In 1792, he placed the last vestige of his faith in abetting progress—his own and his community's—in the joint endeavor of the state and a creole elite of wealth and talent, a juncture represented in the economic society. When that group dissolved within the year, Espejo turned to more extreme remedies. He plotted a series of simultaneous uprisings throughout South America to bring about government by the native-born. He was jailed for sedition in 1795 and died in prison shortly afterwards. His career demonstrates how far intelligent and aggressive mestizos and mulattoes could, and could not, go, and it illustrates the period's Icarian effect, of raising sights to unattainable heights, then by mid-decade dashing hopes and sometimes lives as well. It also gives evidence, as do the lives of Vargas, Nariño, and others, that the 1790s were a nursery of revolutionaries. Noteworthy is the relationship of Espejo to the reforming Spaniard, Pérez Calama, and of both to the Marqués de Selva Alegre, who was also a friend of Mutis's, was later host to Alexander von Humboldt, and around whom still later, quiteños seeking self-government would rally.

From 1793 through 1794, Spain was at war with a France where revolution had lost its most beneficent aspects, and the call for constitutional monarchy had given way to regicide. That war allied Spain with Britain and brought Spain to concentrate on the security of the Caribbean, to step up measures for extracting immediate revenue from America, and primarily for that purpose, to push economic reform there with more urgency. The alliance ensured both more Spanish and more British contact with Spanish colonies. It also resulted in a surge of North American trading directly with Spanish and French colonies, bringing them more domestic exports and a tremendous amount of re-exports. The latter were mostly British, and the trade with the British West Indies flourished. Thus, it was from 1793 that British cottons became popular in Venezuela. From 1793, American ships were tolerated in the Floridas, New Orleans, and other Spanish American ports (outside of the viceroyalty of Peru), through necessity; their cargoes often substituted for provisions that had come from Santo Domingo, then rent by revolt. Moreover, much Kentucky flour then came down the Mississippi, Carondelet having lowered duties and explained that the alternative was Louisiana's falling to the United States.[35]

In this period, the redoubled efforts to have propertied Americans help in developing regional exports and revenues led to formal authorization of still more American patriotic societies and of new consulados in Caracas and Guatemala in 1793, in Buenos Aires and Havana in 1794, and in Cartagena, Vera Cruz, Guadalajara, and Santiago de Chile in 1796.[36] The consulados were expected now to promote internal growth of mining, agriculture, and transportation as well as domestic and overseas commerce. Their members also often sat on cabildos and were among the most affluent residents. All of this reinforced patriotism and economic development as creole keynotes. In one instance, the creole oidor, Jacobo de Villaurrutia, who founded the economic society in Guatemala in 1794 and also a gazette he used to win support for freer commerce, including with the United States, addressed society members as illustrious patriots. Blending Adam Smith and Bernardo Ward, he told them they must aid material progress and widen the internal market that they had a "sacred role"—that of embracing all useful knowledge—that they were working for the good of man and the glory of Guatemala, and that their work would constitute "a happy revolution."[37] That phrase, no longer popular at court, still echoed in the provinces.

In Havana, then largely supplied by United States ships, a founder of the consulado, of the economic society, and of Havana's *Papel periódico* had just returned from Spain. He was Francisco de Arango y Parreño, a spokesman for the sugar planters and an avowed follower of Adam Smith. In a speech on commercial agriculture he demonstrated that Cubans, aware of state policies linking freer trade and lower taxes to higher royal income, also saw ways those policies could be used to forward regional self-interest. Thus, Arango y Parreño suggested not only means of expanding output but also that the government open trade legally with foreign West Indian colonies, since revolt in Saint Domingue now curbed its sugar exports and since Spain could not supply Cuba. In doing so, he reminded authorities that foreign trade would stimulate treasury receipts. He, and the local officials and Cubans who were his sponsors, also sought with a good deal of success to establish regular trade with the United States, exchanging sugar for flour, and, with labor scarce and sugar mills proliferating, to have more Africans brought in. Arango y Parreño again went to Europe, to France, Portugal, and England, and to some of the British colonies; on his return, he introduced better cane and steam engines for sugar mills and became a confidant of the governor, Luis de Las Casas. The revolt in Saint Domingue did transfer much of that island's sugar business to Spanish and Portuguese America, as well as many of the whites who ran it.[38]

Just as the government pointed out to Americans the benefits to be gained from joining this early Spanish imperial version of an alliance for progress, creoles, on their part, continually reminded the authorities, making use of tenets associated with political economy, that it was to the benefit of the state to liberalize American taxes and American commercial relations with everyone. Both parties, seeking their own advantage, were careful to point out the other's. Viceroys in Venezuela as well as in Buenos Aires, where entrenched interests were weakest, understood this exchange and expertly mediated between competing groups of constituents. They favored broadening trade and consulado membership as well, in order to admit with equal representation new lesser—usually creole—merchants and growers. This equality became court policy by 1797, when a royal resolution ordered traders and planters to alternate in the offices of American consulados "so they may contribute equally to the prosperity of the state."[39]

In La Plata, the French blockade and peninsular shipping problems in general braked exports but gave impulse to greater local ship owning and increased Buenos Aires's autonomy from Lima as a commercial center. Imports rose. New meat-salting plants, promoted by the government from 1793, opened. Large estancieros, combining cattle ranching and cereal growing, gobbled land from small proprietors. Coastal growers often prospered at the expense of the interior and, while the La Plata littoral enjoyed a rapid economic rise, the interior experienced only a partial and moderate rise, accompanied by painful readjustments for its trade, agriculture and craft industries. From 1795, the crown sold export licenses to Spanish Americans and to neutrals, including permission to trade with foreign colonies. Smuggling rose, including from Brazil and in British exports. Then, during war with Britain, legitimate hide exports rose and brought new problems. Most business remained low level, high profit. Through this period, Romero and other newer men challenged the old ultraloyalist wholesalers. When those entrenched merchants made a last ditch attempt to block voting in the consulado by men outside their group and refused to sponsor the full spectrum of those reforms associated with political economy by the progressives, they infuriated the younger, more liberal creole members and their spokesman, Manuel Belgrano, a young attorney who was the consulado's secretary. These wholesalers knew, he later acridly commented, "only to buy at four and sell at eight. . . I passed my time in futile efforts to serve my country."[40]

When in 1793 the planters and estancieros of Buenos Aires had formally solicited the right to export wheat and hides freely, their representación was drawn by Belgrano, who also helped to unite them by pointing out the confluence of their interests. While studying in Spain from 1789 to 1793, as he later wrote, he had been influenced both by the rage for political economy and by the "ideas of the French revolution"—which he saw as liberty, equality, security, and property; he defined tyranny as the curbing of enjoyment of natural rights. He was also strongly, if less dramatically, taken by the theories of Ward (and thus of Campillo) and, especially, Campomanes, and was acquainted with the works of Quesnay and Adam Smith. He had returned home burning to be useful to his native land, "infatuated by the brilliant prospects for America," as he recalled, and added that he then had seen himself in glorious partnership with the government, compiling reports of the province's welfare, as, he explained, was "the intention of an enlightened minister like Gardoqui, who had lived in the United States."[41] Within the consulado, Belgrano advocated expanding agriculture by giving awards to farmers as well as by enabling the free export of ranch and field products; he reminded the crown that "interest is the only mover of the human heart and better managed can yield infinite variety."[42] The creation of the Chilean consulado in 1796 found Manuel de Salas restored to prominent position and presenting a similar representación requesting that political economy be applied to agriculture, commerce, and industry, and that the privileges accorded Buenos Aires be given to Chile.[43]

After 1793, creoles also asserted themselves on cabildos and audiencias. Cabildos exhibited more, and more mercantile, creole control, more antipathy to direction by Spanish officials, and more vigorous self-assertion. In general, friction between some Spanish authorities, especially the new intendants, and such public bodies and other officials in the Indies rose in the 1790s. Thus, Manuel Flon, intendant of Puebla and brother-in-law of Bernardo de Gálvez, was at loggerheads with the city council and at odds with the viceroy, while Victorián de Villava, as fiscal of the audiencia of Charcas in Upper Peru from 1791, was soon in conflict with intendants concerning jurisdiction and abuses in the forced mine labor, or *mita*, system. Intendants had prodded cabildos to take charge of local economic development, and they in turn were asserting a right to control expenditures. At the same time, intendants received less cooperation and fewer funds from hard-pressed viceroys ordered both to send more specie to Spain and to better defend America. Flon said he had given Revillagigedo enough information to make a dissertation on all three kingdoms—animal, mineral, and vegetable—with no results.[44]

In this atmosphere, rivalries between European Spaniards and with Americans heightened and were aired; conditions largely profited new mercantile men and they sped creole nativism, regional patriotism, and the emergence of a new and dissatisfied establishment. There was, moreover, greater friction between all social sectors within Latin America and greater signs of unrest as well as of growth in disillusionment with imperial arrangements. Both social unrest and antipathy to Spanish and to all centralized domination increased, including in areas dependent upon viceregal centers. In Upper Peru, from 1793 reports were more frequent of seditious posters and murmurings, and in both Venezuela and in New Granada, officials reported a change in the nature of popular disturbances. Caballero y Góngora concluded of the activities of Nariño and his friends, as he had not of the comuneros, that "they will shake off the yoke at the first opportunity."[45]

The reverberation in Spanish colonies of the French Revolution in Saint Domingue in 1792 contributed not only to scarcity of foodstuffs but also to racial tension and official headache, as well as to white uneasiness in areas of large black concentration, particularly in the Spanish Caribbean and Brazil. In 1795 in Coro, on the Venezuelan coast, several thousand mostly black and *pardo* (part black) cane cutters and herdsmen—slaves—revolted and killed whites. They had risen when rumors that a royal order had given them freedom proved unfounded. Rebels insisted the king had emancipated them but that the Caracas cabildo and local whites refused to obey his command. They also opposed the *alcabala*, or sales tax, and had declared all ports open. The rebellion was put down ruthlessly; unrest among blacks continued. The government had heightened racial tensions by an order of February 10 allowing pardos to apply for purchase of permission to pass, the privilege refused to Espejo, and for the rights to an education, to marry whites, to hold office, and to go into holy orders (*cédulas de gracias al sacar*); it had also revoked the *código negro* of 1789. The order was probably due to fiscal interest, since the certificates were sold; to a desire to woo the growing mulatto population and tie it to the economic program; and to the wish to offset the power of the creole elite and of traditional values. It caused a bitter backlash, especially in Venezuela, where the populace was predominantly black and mulatto. In 1796, the Caracas cabildo declared that measure against custom and a threat to colonial social organization, and it admitted whites were often distinguishable as such only by their economic situation.[46]

Authorities were most visibly uneasy in New Spain. While only two minor conspiracies were discovered there in 1794—one to seek independence with the aid of the United States, another planning an English protectorate—still, large numbers of Haitians were arriving in Guatemala and the government, as Humboldt later remarked, had come to see "the germ of revolt in every association with public illumination for its object."[47] Moreover, the new viceroy, the Marqués de Branciforte, a Sicilian and Godoy's brother-in-law, reflected the change in court attitudes and was viewed as a great, and largely unwelcome, contrast to his predecessor, Revillagigedo. He quarreled with the new consulados in Vera Cruz and Guadalajara, called them little monsters, and accused them of usurping viceregal powers; and he announced, with war against Britain in 1796, that Anglo-Americans might supply Havana with foodstuffs. Although he did strengthen Mexican defenses and expand the militia, rumor had it his interest in defense was matched by that in proliferating offices, including military ones, to enchance his power and purse through dispensing patronage. And while he gained the adherence of a number of creoles by waiving forced loans, it was public knowledge that he pocketed sizable amounts of those collected. As was being done in Spain, Branciforte arrested, interned, or deported many French residents, but he went further, in 1795 cooperating with the Inquisition in staging an auto-de-fé in which three Frenchmen went to the stake and two more were burned in effigy. Among them was Revillagigedo's pastry cook. They had been at most partisans of constitutional monarchy.[48]

Branciforte's edginess did have some basis. Authorities in Spain, Havana, Venezuela, and New Granada feared the impact of events in France and its colonies, and even Revillagigedo admitted in 1793 to being wary of the French upheaval spreading "this plague of liberty" to America. Revolutionary events were known and revolutionary literature distributed widely, despite prohibitions. Not only was Espejo arrested in Quito, and Nariño in Bogotá, and Caracas stirred by rumor of a rising in New Granada, but in 1795 the French acquired the eastern, Spanish half of Santo Domingo; then, Toussaint's armies moved in. A French invasion was feared in Buenos Aires, French and blacks arrested there for conspiracy, and discontent reported among Indians. Guatemala, Louisiana, and the Caribbean heard the French might attack Mexico. Officials in Mexico were alerted to Frenchmen and French political ideas coming in through Louisiana—which, retroceded in the peace treaty to France, in 1795 experienced an economic crisis and risings of whites and of black slaves—and also through the United States. Even an invasion from the United States through Louisiana seemed possible.[49]

Mexicans kept abreast of much of this and knew that officials both respected and worried about Anglo-American economic competition, and that the government was striving to cordon off ports and poorly defined border areas to filibusters and republicans. Thus, Branciforte and the Inquisition in 1794 condemned a tract just published in Philadelphia and financed by Genêt, Santiago Felipe Puglia's *Desengaño del Hombre (Disabusal of Man)*. Branciforte was not wrong in tying the book to proponents of free use of the Mississippi. The pamphlet advocated Spanish American independence, scored Spanish corruption, and appealed to, as authorities, the Bible, Spanish history, and Thomas Paine. Inquisition placards, in prohibiting it and in condeming Puglia for inciting Spanish Americans to rebellion and for preaching the *"homicidio de soberanos,"*[50] publicized its contents. Puglia wrote, among other things, that liberty and equality form the happiness of the nation, that the Spanish king was uninterested in supporting American merchants and their commerce, and that God would protect popular armies and send a messiah to lead Spanish America to democracy. He also repeatedly cited the United States as a model of freedom and equality, as a society where position was based on talent and strength, and as an example of military success.

Also condemned by the Mexican government and the Inquisition, as well as publicized in the *Gaceta de México*, was a virtuoso and inappropriate sermon the Dominican friar, Servando Teresa de Mier, gave in 1794 in the Church of Guadalupe on the anniversary of the death of Cortés. Mier explained that he was responding to an earlier request by Charles III to American authorities and clergy for information on "the truth of the kingdom." He preached that Saint Thomas, rather than the Indian Juan Diego, had given the image of the Virgin of Guadalupe to Mexico. By dating that event before the Spanish conquest, he retained the Old World's influence on the New, but not Spain's; and in denying Spain's religious conquest of America, he undercut a major Spanish rationale for ruling Mexico and instead presented Spaniards as overcoming other Christians. He went against the traditional criollismo rooted in the Spanish heritage alone and put himself within the ranks of those creoles claiming a mixed lineage and, within it, relegating the Spanish heritage to a subsidiary position. His explanation of the arrival of

Guadalupe followed that of the seventeenth-century creole savant and investigator of indigenous antiquities, Carlos de Sigüenza y Góngora. It was not the sort of information the government wanted, although the oration did reveal a good deal about the creole mind when it was trained in religion and attempted to synthesize the Indian past, the European heritage, the Catholic faith, an enlightened outlook, and Americanism; and when it was propelled by ambition for self-advancement to a show of talent—in this case, a pyrotechnic display of iconoclasm. Mier, sent to Spain for discipline by his order, was launched on a career as a revolutionary. His speech was part of a creole fascination with pre-Hispanic peoples and a growing— if here, tacit—acknowledgment of being of mixed Spanish and Indian parentage. This tendency was enhanced and spread by Alzate's articles and by recent histories of Mexico written by Clavijero and other exiled Jesuits. The same attitudes were also visible among indigenist limeños and were echoed in a new edition of the account of his ancestors by the mestizo, Garcilaso de la Vega, el Inca.[51]

The government, under Godoy and once more pressed by war, this time against Britain, from 1796 looked to its own fiscal interests, brought on another inflationary spiral in Spain, and managed to induce revenues from America to rise steadily that year. Yet, such were Spanish inflation, expenses, and deficit spending, that American funds became an even smaller part of the income counted upon by the treasury. Even so, within this spiral Gardoqui mortgaged the future revenues of New Spain. At the same time, the latest policy of imperial interdependence was resulting in freer interregional trade and lower duties to Spanish America and was opening more of its ports—and, in 1795, the Mississippi—to the United States. With this war Spain came to concentrate solely on schemes to defend its America and to extract from it what the traffic would bear, and royal ministers, who worried about the possibility of the United States entering on the English side, in 1797 under the pressure of British naval supremacy threw open many Spanish American ports to neutral carriers. Spanish America was governed by then by a hodgepodge of old and new institutions. Officials sold licenses to neutrals, to the profit of both, and to that of exporters and the state as well. From 1793, Spanish merchants in Venezuela had received public revenues of the colony and repaid them in Spain through a system of bills of exchange. By 1798, this sort of arrangement had been made as well with residents of Buenos Aires, Mexico, and Havana.[52]

Against this background, by 1797 a popular conspiracy in Venezuela, sparked by the exiled republican and former member of the Royal Economic Society, Juan Picornell, signaled a new coalition of peoples and of dissident movements. His chief confederates were two creoles of middle strata and bureaucratic employ, Manuel Gual, a retired officer of engineers living in La Guaira, and José María España, a minor magistrate and well-to-do merchant. The plot, Picornell later claimed, was inspired by the republicanism of the United States. (Moreno who, it will be recalled, by 1777 had transcribed the Philadelphia proclamations, was implicated in this conspiracy, as were the current Marqués de San Javier, one of León's sons, and some close relatives of the Bolívars.) Nearly all La Guaira, ran one report, was attracted to the movement, including blacks, Spaniards, militiamen, and soldiers. The conspirators' program included: a republic, the right to cultivate and raise crops freely, open trade, and equality between races. They promised abolition of slavery, of the tobacco monopoly, of the alcabala, and of tribute payments. A government spy who gained his confidence afterwards, on Curacao, reported Picornell had a contract with North Americans to introduce guns and powder into New Granada, Venezuela, and Vera Cruz, and that he had had printed on Guadaloupe booklets containing copies of the United States constitution. Copies had been brought into Spanish America by merchant sea captains, French corsairs, and *contrabandistas*. Certain creole aristocrats were in the forefront of the successful and bloody suppression of the movement.[53] Gual escaped and soon joined causes with Miranda, if he had not before. And Miranda by the late 1790s spoke for numerous propertied Latin Americans, and specifically for a network of creole conspirators who would become prominent in the independence movements, when he suggested to Gual that Spanish American revolutionaries should imitate the United States and avoid the extremes gone to in France: "Two great examples lie before our eyes: the American and the French revolutions. Let us discreetly imitate the first: let us carefully avoid the disastrous effect of the second."[54]

From the 1780s on, creole dissidents who would later spur revolts had made London a center of their activities. After Britain lost its American colonies, some of its high officials and prominent merchants, alert to the strategic and commercial advantages of an independent Spanish America, helped creoles to ready plans for divesting Spain of its Indies. Among the first to listen sympathetically to Miranda was Thomas Pownall, the former governor of Massachusetts, who during the Nootka crisis introduced him to William Pitt.[55] Although the British government was the most cordial, these creoles also found friends in high places in France and the United States—but wherever they sought aid, it was the United States republican model they most often cited. Most of them, especially after 1793, came to dread the excesses of the French Revolution. Many of them admired the British system and considered a constitutional monarchy best (as did liberal Spaniards in that decade), yet to most the United States offered a functioning, American, revolutionary analogy. All of them recognized the continuing affinities in the English and United States systems. By the late eighteenth century, then, a broad and supraregional network existed of Spanish American revolutionaries active at home and overseas.

By 1796, when Spain declared war on England, London had become the hub of those creoles working for Spanish American independence. From the 1780s, during an earlier war, men sympathetic to or involved in the revolts of Túpac Amaru and the comuneros had received British pensions. The Argentine ex-Jesuit, Juan Jośe Godoy, was in London by 1781. Luis Vidalle, an emissary of comunero leaders, was conferring with members of the British government in 1784, when Miranda arrived from the United States; the following year the Mexican, Mendiola, appeared. Miranda soon established himself as head of these dissidents in exile and in 1785 he sent the former Jesuit, Godoy, to gain aid and support in the United States and to contact sympathizers in South America.[56] Nariño, too, after escaping in Cádiz talked to Miranda and his secretary, José Caro, in Paris. He then returned to America to travel through Venezuela and New Granada, sounding out popular support for a revolution, including from old comuneros. In Bogotá in 1797, he gave himself up to the authorities, offered to work for the state, and submitted a new plan of administration for New Granada. In it he cited as inspiration his experiences in France and England and his study of Adam Smith, Jovellanos, and French philosophes, as well as contact with the region's populace; and he proposed remedies usual to members of economic societies and new consulados.[57] He was jailed until 1803.

Another former Jesuit, Juan Pablo Viscardo, a native of Guayaquil, who lived in London from 1794 until his death in 1798, also on government pension, left his papers to Rufus King, the American ambassador. King turned them over to Miranda, who extracted from them the document he subsequently published as *Carta dirigida a los Españoles Americanos*, with the place of issue listed as Philadelphia. He sent it into Spanish America in 1799 with Caro, who traveled there on and off for fourteen years as one of a number of revolutionary agents. Miranda also sent letters to the United States with Caro—one from himself to Hamilton and one from the British merchant, John Turnbull, who underwrote Miranda on behalf of the British government—to Willing and Company in Philadelphia, and that firm obligingly provided Caro with funds.[58] Viscardo's tract owed a good deal to Thomas Paine's *Common Sense*, which later became widely known in Spanish America. The *Carta* was soon circulating in Venezuela, and it was banned by the Inquisition in Mexico. Its author scoffed at the Spanish claim to have spread Union and Equality, saying that instead the government had slighted its obligations and that Americans were a different people who—in the oft-repeated phrase borrowed from Paine—nature had separated from Spain by immense seas. He pressed for independence: "The valor with which the English colonies of America have fought for liberty, which now they enjoy gloriously, covers with shame our indolence. . . . They have ceded us the palm," he went on; may their valor awaken our honor. His vision of a new free era ended on an economic crescendo: prosperity would come. The tyranny of Spanish kings and peninsulars in America would be extinguished, and then: "What an agreeable spectacle the coasts of America will present, covered with men of all nations exchanging their products for ours. They will come too to settle and enrich us with their hard work. . . . America will be a great family of brothers."[59]

Viscardo declared that Spanish rulers had honored neither Spanish nor American natural rights. They defamed Spain's constitution and broke contracts with the conquerors of America. Americans, who were descended from brave conquistadors and Indian women, had been badly treated by kings and their European-born officials, when by natural right American dominion was theirs. He cited Garcilaso de la Vega, el Inca, and Antonio de Ulloa on the escalation of prices in the Indies and on abuses by corregidores. "The augment of troops and of the navy costs us a lot and defends us not at all," he complained, and he wanted all ports open. Americans should go everywhere and buy and sell directly: "Then our riches will circulate among us and enlarge our industry." By "we" he appeared to refer to creoles, including mestizos.

After renewing a childhood friendship by 1797 with Manuel Gual, Miranda suggested to him in 1799 that he request a copy of Viscardo's letter from the governor of Trinidad. Gual replied that he had done so and praised its sentiments. In 1799 Pedro Fermín de Vargas, after a stay in Philadelphia, joined Miranda in London. The year before, the young Chilean, Bernardo O'Higgins, had been enthralled by Miranda. O'Higgin's father, who in 1797 became viceroy of Peru, had, it will be recalled, admired George Washington.[60] The difference between father and son may well have been that Ambrosio was legitimate, Caucasian on both sides, and endowed with prestigious Spanish office. However that may be, Bernardo went on to become a leader in the Chilean struggle for independence.

Miranda purportedly made plans, and signed a revolutionary pact in Paris in 1797, with fellow conspirators, among them Caro and the ex-Jesuit José del Pozo y Sucre. Olavide may have been involved but absent due to poor health. The plan called for English and United States aid in gaining independence, and afterwards for the United States to defend Spanish America in case of Spanish attack.[61] In France, working together would also be Fray Mier (from 1801), later a leader in his native Mexico as well as an influential revolutionary publicist throughout Spanish America, and Simón Rodríguez, with whom a former pupil, Simón Bolívar, would take a trip to Italy in 1805. Rodríguez, on his arrival in Paris, was greeted by the New Granadan, Francisco Zea, whom Nariño had successfully defended against charges of sedition before the Bogotá audiencia. Zea had been an aide to Mutis, and with Vargas had collaborated in the state-sponsored scientific expedition in New Granada.[62]

Dissidents also sought refuge in the United States. Godoy and Caro stopped in Philadelphia; Vargas stayed there; and living there from 1797 was Manuel Torres, a Spanish-born liberal who was the nephew of Caballero y Góngora, and who had been implicated in the Bogotá plot. In Philadelphia, Torres wrote and had published both a guide to doing business with Latin America for North American merchants and a tract to promote commerce between the Americas. He also, adumbrating Henry Clay's proposition, favored an American system. He was esteemed by Miranda and later acted as liaison among Spanish American agents.[63]

The well-educated and well-connected Brazilian, Hipólito da Costa, was also in the United States. He was sent there in 1798 by a leading royal minister, Rodrigo de Sousa Coutinho, to get information on Mexican cochineal and to obtain some insects for its manufacture. (He did send some to Brazil, but they died.) Da Costa, who like Miranda kept a diary, was less impressed with the new republic. He was scornful of the large number of braggarts he encountered—one of them had even insisted that the new university at Cambridge, Massachusetts, was better than any school in Europe. Portuguese Brazilian policy had changed after 1788, and the influential minister, Dom Rodrigo, Pombal's godson, who possessed much property in Minas Gerais, had a personal stake in Brazil. In a discourse of 1790, and thereafter, he urged that, rather than tax that mining center more heavily, mining techniques be improved and Brazil's natural resources developed. He worked in concert with Luis Pinto de Sousa Coutinho, who was from 1788 Portugal's foreign minister and, before that, governor of Mato Grosso; a man who, while ambassador to England, had given information to Robertson, and who was a believer in putting talented young Brazilians to work for the state. Luis Pinto not only wanted mining improved but also thought Brazilian manufacturing, particularly of iron, should be encouraged. Both men, like Spanish ministers, sought means to conserve the empire. Dom Rodrigo coupled enlightened optimism with guidance by "the most liberal principles," and added "if it is legitimate to adopt to our language the sense which the English attribute to the word."[64] He employed Brazilians directly and actively in inventorying their country's wealth and in seeking out new technologies, and he put even some of those implicated in the Minas conspiracy of the late eighties into responsible positions. The combination of the softened aspect of government in the 1790s, white horror at events in Santo Domingo, and good markets for exports, including high prices for sugar which brought more shipped by way of Lisbon and less to London, where high tariffs prevailed, made the monarchy and the Portuguese connection more palatable to those Brazilians flirting with republicanism before 1792. Even so, a continual irritant were the Portuguese-born who dominated overseas trade.

Through 1797 in Brazil the propertied experienced economic expansion but felt government onerous, and many of them aspired to goals not so different from those of their counterparts in British North America up to the 1770s. They sought more economic autonomy and advance—in their case, mostly markets for commodities—through more entrée to export, less internal restriction, and more control of imports. They wanted not only their social ascendency firmly assured, but also to wield the highest economic and political authority and power within their own regions.

One historian, R. A. Humphreys, thought that the acceleration of European demand in this period and not the Bourbon reforms proved the real stimulus for Spanish American economic expansion.[65] The two contributing causes are inseparable, and to them should be added internal growth, United States trade and example, the French Revolution, and war. Moreover, it will not do to speak of Spanish policy under Charles IV as simply continuing the program, known as the Bourbon reforms, instituted under his predecessor. State priorities shifted after 1787, and particularly after 1793, and even further after 1796, toward expediency and a more singleminded pursuit of revenues and defense—policies which, in avowedly responding to continuing emergency, heightened American insecurity. Spain's attempt to promote greater creole involvement in American affairs, soon coinciding with a draining off of all available American revenues and, after 1796, powerlessness on the seas, further charged the situation. The old mercantile system meant an ordered balance between fiscal need and economic interest, and that balance was destroyed in Spain in the 1790s.

Evidence from Latin America may indicate that Clifford Geertz, when he wrote that the French Revolution was "the greatest incubator of extremist ideologies to the time because the central organizing principle of political life, the divine right of kings, was destroyed," was less on target than was Lord Acton in stating that the French Revolution primarily "taught people to regard their wishes and wants as the supreme criterion of right."[66] Yet, the two conclusions mesh, in that the French Revolution, as did the American, demonstrated that the nation made the state rather than the other way around. Thus, in Mexico between 1794 and 1797, the Inquisition rooted out and prosecuted men expressing views corroborating both effects. Radicals elsewhere in Latin America voiced such sentiments, and the rise of constitutionalism and the avowal of natural rights and their concomitant, the moral worth of self-interest, owe a debt to them. The radicalization of Vargas, Nariño, Espejo, and *afrancesados* in Mexico between 1790 and 1794 occurred in large part through a combination of the French Revolution and Spain's war with France.[67] Throughout Latin America, two concepts reinforced by the French uprising and bearing out both conclusions gained currency from 1789 on, building up their own heads of antipeninsular steam. One was the idea that the duty and dignity of the citizen lay in political activity. The other, related notion was that if the citizens of a state no longer approved of political arrangements, they could alter or replace them. In all this, the French Revolution intensified and spread the same discontents fanned by the revolt of 1776, although some were exacerbated too by contact with theories and advocates of political economy, and it radicalized and disseminated the concepts of natural rights and popular sovereignty emanating earlier from North America—indeed, it romanticized them, and even heightened creole pride in being American. To many creoles, as to Jefferson, the French upheaval initially had seemed to broaden the promise of the American Revolution, and as the French example became less acceptable to propertied creoles and Brazilians, it was the Anglo-American that emerged with even greater luster, as related but preferable.

It is probable that numerous Latin Americans, as did Europeans, during the 1790s favored a constitutional monarchy, if for varying reasons. Both Iberian and Latin American reformers usually tended to view Spain or Portugal, and their own regions of empire, as ailing, but they felt the sick body could be cured through their own ministrations and—still a majority view—in connection with the monarch. There was, though, growing social unrest, racial and ethnic tension, and the broadening of a radical network dedicated to achieving absolute independence; and in Spanish America, governmental and leading creole attitudes and actions from 1793 did little to allay any of them. While generalizations are difficult, and great variations existed among different groups and in different locales, the majority of Latin Americans experienced numerous and accelerating changes. These were occasioned by international relations and internal reactions to them, population growth and shifts, including increased numbers of blacks and mestizos, higher prices, natural disasters, greater pressure exerted by the government, and a tendency to greater inequality in land holding. There were attendant disruptions in traditional communal life, the reappearance of old abuses, such as the *re-partimiento*, the system whereby local officials forced villagers to buy unwanted goods at high prices, and the mita system of forced labor in Mexico and Peru, and a heavier load of tribute, taxes, and monopolies. More opportunity for employment and wages more frequently paid in money sometimes helped. Yet generally wages did not keep pace with costs, and unrest and vagrancy soared. Uprisings became larger and more widespread and were no longer solely addressed to specific regional grievances, but to economic, political, and social change as well. The

French Revolution and that of Santo Domingo gave new form, content, and hope to broad-based popular movements.

For our purposes, it is important to know that for many Latin Americans, accelerating changes affected their lives and livelihoods. And, in all this, United States trade and United States example and ideological influences had an impact felt most directly by numerous (mainly middle and upper strata) people, and especially by those touched by empathy for enlightenment, constitutionalism, and liberalism. A number of these people then held responsible positions in their own regions and constituted a resurgent creole establishment. A few—disenchanted, impelled by personal situations and proclivities and by regional conditions and concerns, or enamored of the ideas and example of the French as well as the American Revolution—then turned to more extreme political solutions to their own and their compatriots' problems. But most, by late 1796 and the war with Britain, saw earlier dreams of an American progress to be achieved hand in hand with the government dimming, that the policy of unity and equality was a sham. They saw a political situation lacking direction, in Spain a corrupt court, new wars and huge expenses, less effective and, even when better liked, often less respected officials, a restless and potentially threatening multiracial populace, and their own entry to domestic authority and to outside markets clogged. From the late 1790s such people, putting new value on their own self-interest and on that of their home regions and repeatedly voicing frustration and the sense of being shackled or at least burdened by a decrepit imperial system, more often employed language used by discontented Anglo-Americans in the decade preceding 1776, and they sought similar goals for themselves and their countries.

8

TOWARD AN AMERICAN SOLUTION:
LATIN AMERICA, 1797–1808

When war with Britain brought a closing of sea lanes, particularly from 1797 when Nelson blockaded Cádiz and Russian ships appeared on the Pacific coast, Spain became even more kindly disposed to the United States as a counterweight to Britain. A biography of Benjamin Franklin was then published in Madrid, and the *Gazeta* advertised as anti-British the writings of Thomas Paine. That year, as we have seen, the *reglamento de comercio libre* allowed neutral ships into Spanish American ports, a measure to some extent after the fact and primarily favoring North Americans, and from then on the crown sacrificed economic development in Spain and Spanish America to fiscal exigencies. Francisco de Saavedra, who had become an architect of Spanish policy, advocated neutral commerce with wide powers of discretion to local authorities in Spanish America, and he looked forward to cheap imports killing colonial industry so that with peace Spain could dominate American markets. Neutral trade was not only needed for supplying Spanish America but it also enabled financing the war, for by 1798 the crown was issuing in Spain to its better connected creditors bills of exchange (*libranzas*), payable for cash, on American treasuries, and foreign ships were vital for capital flow and for this system to attract investors.[1]

While viewing trade with United States firms as necessary, more Spaniards in government were becoming more apprehensive than ever about Anglo-American expansionist intentions. Thus in 1798, the year of the Blount conspiracy, the Mexican viceroy, Azanza, was concerned about the possibility of the United States allying with Britain in a joint attack on New Spain through Louisiana and Florida. Authorities throughout Spanish America subsequently welcomed United States carriers and supplies but ordered close watch for subversive materials and signs of unrest. Some by then also saw greater autonomy for America as inevitable. One who did was Victorián de Villava, fiscal of the audiencia of Charcas, who in 1797, in a manuscript enjoying wide circulation in South America, declared that the spirit of liberty animating the world was the *motor* of progress. He also foresaw democracy in Spanish America and feared it would cause anarchy, rivers of blood, and domination by despots. Like earlier Spanish officials, Villava spoke of America's immensity and distance from Europe, but unlike them, he suggested that one crowned head and a supreme council, an elected parliament, govern America; that is, he echoed liberal Spanish currents in advising a constitutional monarchy on republican and federative principles in order to preserve the empire.[2]

With the ordinance of 1797, not only did North American trade with Latin America swell and massive shipments of United States flour go to Havana, where before large, legitimate, regular shipments had come only through Spain, but there was even more United States investment in Cuban sugar. Ships from the United States supplied most Caribbean food imports and did business with Venezuelan ports, Cartagena, La Plata, and the Pacific coast. By 1798, the Mexican press reported most ships into Vera Cruz North American.[3] Among creoles, the attendant upsurge of commerce, in which they saw United States carriers predominate, whetted appetites for more, and more direct, trade. Creoles actively solicited trade and United States merchants responded, until market gluts of imports once again soon dampened rosy expectations.

In Havana, the new consulado favored greater legitimacy for its commerce with the United States, even then taking half of the tonnage Cuba exported and a third of its exports in value; in 1799, Arango y Parreño wrote that Cuba needed foreign imports and was completely dependent upon sugar exports.[4] In Caracas, disagreements rent the consulado. They were part of wider quarrels, which would intensify in the following years, between planters and established wholesalers, and by extension between hinterland and port. Planters, with exports halved, and prices down, strapped by a scarcity of labor and worried by the Coro revolt and general unrest, while socially conservative were economically liberal. In accord with the intendant, they welcomed ports opened to direct commerce with friends and neutrals, particularly with North Americans, in order to market their products and because there too United States flour had come before legally by way of Spain and had arrived stale and often spoiled. Wholesalers too wanted to use neutral carriers. They urged naval protection and suggested an agent be sent to the United States to get its ships to carry out cacao and bring in flour, other provisions, and naval stores, but complained on patriotic but not unselfish grounds that Anglo-Americans must stop bringing in British textiles. It was here that they parted company with the hacendados, who argued for importing dry goods without restrictions.[5]

In Mexico, too, trade with Spain had nearly ceased, and, in Vera Cruz wheat, sugar, and indigo awaiting export had perished on the docks. Riots ensued and prices of European goods rose steeply until the authorities approved neutral carriers. Then, although the consulado objected to Anglo-Americans putting into port, some Vera Cruz firms began dealing with them, and some merchants acted as agents for North Americans. Even after the revocation in 1799 of the 1797 reglamento, Azanza permitted neutral trade and favored Tómas Murphy, a merchant married to the viceroy's cousin. Murphy had advised Revillagigedo, was friendly with Godoy, and had connections to United States houses and to dealers in Jamaica. While Azanza wrote home that Anglo-Americans would profit most from current arrangements, there were Mexican merchants too who prospered as never before. Although Mexican grains could not compete with United

States wheat and flour in Havana, or in Santo Domingo, Puerto Rico, Louisiana, or Venezuela, growers saw that neutral trade enabled some export; without it there would be none. Vera Cruz then supplanted the capital as the commercial center of New Spain, yet merchants of the Mexican consulado did well too. Unable to ship funds to Spain, they once again invested them internally, especially profiting the textile industry, which during the war grew extraordinarily. Smuggling too continued to flourish; Humboldt estimated a quarter of New Spain's imports then arrived as contraband.[6]

Porteños experienced general mercantile upsurge. More of them turned to more speculative trade. Exchange rose with the United States and with the Portuguese as well, and more of them invested their own capital and began acquiring their own vessels. Local shipyards were busy, and in 1798 the entrepreneur Romero ordered ships from New England, as did other merchants. He continued to buy blacks from dealers in Newport and Boston, and he and others established an important commercial network in both permitted exchange and in contraband with North Americans. Medium quality textiles then appeared, mostly German and imitating luxury fabrics. Among their carriers, it will be recalled, were Shaler and Cleveland, who introduced cargoes from Hamburg. Even so, interior textiles revived during the war. La Plata did lose markets for hides, but more wheat went out to Cuba and Brazil, and the preponderant export remained silver.[7]

War and the loosening of trade did bring greater cooperation on some issues within consulados, usually at Spanish expense. Thus, not only did Caracas growers and some wholesalers agree on the need for United States carriers, but in 1797 Argentine merchants and estancieros of the littoral and the interior united against the old Cádiz interests, and Belgrano dispatched another memorandum to the crown. Chile had long been dependent on Lima and Buenos Aires for imports and for commodity markets and restricted in what could be grown, but it was now more frequently visited by outsiders, including North American ships. There it was a liberal Spaniard, José de Cos Iriberri, who spoke for the consulado as its secretary in a series of reports from 1797 to 1802. In 1797 he welcomed the opening of trade as promising Chile "protection, promotion, and expansion," but within a year he was disabused. Upon finding exports still piling up and ensuring the stagnation of all economic activity, he pronounced as root cause that the trade of Chile and other South American regions, including Brazil, was ultimately controlled by North Americans and by British merchants. The specific remedy he proposed was a Chilean-run trading company. His general suggestions— protection of domestic agriculture and of embryonic industries, and the right to determine the country's economic policies free of Lima, Buenos Aires, and Cádiz domination—became and remained Chilean desiderata.[8] At the time, Cos spoke for a minority, for with the exception of men tied to the Cádiz consulado, and some (often the same people) who were profiting through smuggling, numerous officials, ranchers, planters, and merchants in Latin America then tended to approve with less reservation of doing business with Anglo-Americans.

The war, inflation, and reliance on neutral trade both irritated antagonisms between Spanish Americans and the metropolis and intensified numerous frictions among Latin American regions and within Latin American society. First of all, although more interregional trade was sanctioned (and was often carried on in Anglo-American vessels), yet ultimately regional competition for markets sharpened. Within Mexico, Puebla wheat and textiles competed with those of the Bajío. In La Plata, a struggle went on between rural Buenos Aires, Entre Ríos, and the Banda Oriental in exporting hides. Moreover, as soon as Buenos Aires was cut off by blockade, Tampico sent salt beef to Havana. And in Mexico, as we have seen, Havana's thriving trade with the United States was resented, especially since it undercut Mexican exports of wheat and sugar.

Secondly, although cooperation grew in some areas, in general rivalry heightened within consulados. The clash intensified between the old mercantile aristocracy and newer interests—those usually younger, smaller, more adventurous traders allied with producers. They favored more open, speculative trade and smaller profit margins, and their goals often dovetailed with those of regional officials. It was new men and hacendados who profited most when the viceroy in Buenos Aires, and in Caracas the intendant, authorized trade with neutrals even before receiving the order of 1797. They were spurred by a need for provisions and carriers to export commodities, and for revenues resulting from legitimate trade. It was not only Azanza who got around the revocation decree: The intendant in Caracas initially refused to publish it, explaining he wanted "to avoid forwarding the attempts being made by the king's enemies to revolutionize these provinces."[9] He also wanted to sell and ship out the government-owned tobacco.

Thirdly, competition between consulados stiffened. While in Cuba an equilibrium obtained within the consulado and generally among planters, merchants, and producers of finished products, all profiting from Havana's favored position in sugar exports and as an entrepôt for neutral trade, that consulado was often at odds with the merchant guild of Vera Cruz. In Lima and the Mexican capital, where older consulados and other entrenched corporations existed, those guilds not only clashed with newer ones but also they and high clergy often quarreled with viceroys and other public officials. In Guatemala, with indigo exports dwindling due to increasing competition from Caracas and the East Indies, Jacobo de Villaurrutia, as president of the audiencia, continued to side with planters in repeatedly pleading for freer commerce and specifically for opening legitimate trade with the United States, thereby arousing the ire of the consulado and other officials. The consulado protested his allowing Guatemalans to deal with an Anglo-American contrabandista, one Andrew Burk. It was probably also responsible for Madrid closing down the local economic society, which it viewed as competitive, even though the directorates of both overlapped. Villaurrutia who, it will be recalled, had founded that society and its gazette, shared a secretary with the society and the consulado, Alejandro Ramírez, who also edited the *Gazeta*. The consulado probably responded with mixed feelings when Villaurrutia sent Ramírez to the United States to study its agriculture and industry, yet one Guatemalan merchant certainly agreed with Villaurrutia's commercial views. Juan Bautista Irisarri had earlier dispatched Ramírez on another commission to Philadelphia, where as Irisarri's agent he sold indigo, and from where he sent a frigate laden with clothing to Chile.[10]

Events between 1797 and 1800, despite some points of agreement between authorities and creoles, nevertheless tamped down lingering hopes of honest reform in league with the government in Madrid, and they intensified a creole *conciencia de sí*,—a self-awareness as creoles—compounded of separation and difference from Spain and a feeling of more pressing need to shoulder responsibility for the specific region of one's birth. One noticeable concomitant was the end of the honeymoon between many intendants and cabildos in the interior; cabildos increasingly requested viceregal support in their contests for power against officials who had aroused them to active governance and self-awareness in the first place. These frictions reflected, too, the traditional appeal to distant authorities against immediate ones.[11] Spanish Americans accurately perceived that Spain's colonial policy was adrift. Thus Belgrano, in his memoria of 1797, struck a new note, one of dissatisfaction with the monarchy, in arguing that Charles IV had changed Charles III's ideas of free trade. He requested more local autonomy in economic matters and made an implicit allusion to the importance of fostering private self-interest, reminding the crown that without recompense there is no talent.[12] Chileans then watched with dismay their old champion, Ambrosio O'Higgins, as viceroy of Peru advance policies benefiting Lima at their expense, while factional strife continuing among Guatemalan leaders nearly caused a popular uprising in 1803. In Peru from 1801 on creoles, if less displeased with viceroys, manifested greater pressure for position, more resentment, touchiness in response to peninsular discrimination, and greater contact with the non-Spanish world.

While internal power struggles between competing propertied groups were prevalent and potent, among such people there prevailed not only a heightening awareness of those economic interests they had in common, but also an ongoing fear of social revolution and of government contributing to it. Plots and uprisings were occurring more frequently among artisans, peasants, and blacks, in reaction to taxation, to more oppressive working conditions, and to hopes stirred most directly by revolt on Santo Domingo. In Venezuela again, in 1799, after the uncovering of one plot and with others rumored planned on the coast, landed proprietors applauded free trade but criticized the protection magistrates gave to "*mulatos, pardos*, and all inconsequential people, in order to lower esteem for old, distinguished, and honored families." The cabildo, agreeing, again refused to enforce the royal order of 1795 permitting the sale of certificates of whitening.[13] Of no reassurance to such men were the rumblings among creoles and castas in 1799 in Cartagena, Maracaibo, Río Hacha, and the Antilles, as well as insurrections at New Barcelona in 1802, and among Indians in Riobamba in 1803, with discontents played upon by incitement, and promise of aid against Spain, from Trinidad, British since 1797. From New Granada the viceroy reported home word of a North American "General Maytenland" plotting on Jamaica to inflame minds against "our Spanish rule."[14]

Artisans, slaves, and enlisted men were arrested in Bahia for conspiring to free Brazil. It was in Bahia that planters and city dwellers saw that government measures were directing the benefits of agricultural expansion and a rise in the value of exports chiefly to Portuguese-born merchants. The direct cause of the plot of 1798 was high food prices, exacerbated by putting land into cotton and sugar. Those arrested were mostly mulattoes who were, it was said, "infected by the abominable French principles and attached to the absurd French constitution." A second revolutionary group, not prosecuted, was white and socially prominent; it included members of a secret masonic society of French inspiration, and probably the economist and future statesman José da Silva Lisboa. Both groups proposed free trade with foreign nations as a panacea for economic ills. Plotters, citing the experience of the United States, spoke of their expectations of French aid. Yet, the white and propertied feared race war, the influence of France and Haiti, and radical demands then made for abolishing legal and social hindrances to racial equality. At the same time, as we have seen, Rodrigo de Sousa Coutinho offered them a more favorable alliance, a new general Brazilian policy based on lighter taxes and a federative imperial system. The dominions, especially those of America, he told the council of state, "are properly the base of the greatness of the throne."[15]

In the Mexican capital in 1799, another plot by artisans was discovered. These men had taken the name *Convención Nacional Americana*. They blended French and American elements, adopted military ranks and uniforms, called for independence from peninsular oppression, and promised government by a congress like that of the United States. Dismissed by the viceroy, Félix Berenguer de Marquina, as young, poor, and uneducated, they were only reprimanded. He was more concerned about rumored Indian disaffection, British complicity, and the security of Mexican coasts and borders.[16]

That year, most authorities in Latin America, if jittery about unrest among a variety of groups, recognized that the need for the traditional crown policy of rule through arbitration between social divisions, and its converse, maintaining social divisiveness in order to rule, had become more compelling than ever. Still, a few prescient commentators, in reporting both class and racial rancor growing, saw beyond to an overarching American unity emerging out of common grievances and transcending the mutual hatreds of American groups. Attesting to this spirit, San Miguel, the reforming bishop of Michoacán, presented a representación to the king written by his young aide, Manuel Abad y Queipo.[17] This priest would later point out that the allure of Americanism had been heightened by conditions during the 1790s, exposing Spanish Americans to Spanish weakness and governmental inconsistency and to inflation and rising exactions—and, he might have added, growing governmental distrust of the American-born. Officials had become reluctant to place strategic defenses in the hands of the inhabitants. In Peru, militia and indigenous army recruits had not been trusted since 1780. In New Spain, although Branciforte called a militia cantonment of thousands of Mexicans in 1798, when rumor reached him of a British attack imminent on Vera Cruz in conjunction with an invasion from North America, he saw in the vast throng he had assembled a situation potentially more dangerous than outside aggression.[18]

By 1801, with all habitual resources at home exhausted, Spain turned to the colonies for funds. At the same time, fiscal exactions became more onerous, Spanish communications with America became more difficult, and weakness and corruption patent, all within an atmosphere combining two parts of despair with

one of hope until 1805. In 1801, the unauthorized presence of Philip Nolan's small
band of horse traders and smugglers in Texas raised outsized fears in Mexico, as
did attempts by agents coming from Santo Domingo to subvert slaves in Spanish
America through the early 1800s. Rumors of Indian risings and of conspiracy in
Mexico, and continuing worry about Gual and Picornell on Trinidad, disturbed the
government and many propertied Latin American residents. With the Peace of
Amiens in 1802, Madrid attempted to return to prewar policies, including ending
licensing of foreign ships, with little success. Duties were again lessened,
intercolonial trade promoted, and new ports opened. Then in 1803, when Spain
pledged an annual tribute to France, British attacks on Spanish ships carrying
subsidies to Napoleon revived the war. Again, neutral trade was permitted and was
even more necessary to Spain's deficit funding. In 1803, much specie left Vera
Cruz in the name of the government, transported by neutrals or the enemy. By
1804 it was clear to everyone that neutral commerce was "designed to maintain the
revenues from that trade without consideration of the economic impact. . . in the
Americas or Spain itself."[19]

Legitimate United States commerce with Latin America, we recall, reached a
new high in 1800. Although Spanish American ports were again officially closed
to neutrals, due to the ongoing pressure in Spain from the consulado of Cádiz,
there were secret orders to the contrary and, for much of 1801, local authorities
made exceptions, licenses were granted and honored, and United States merchants
and their captains resorted to various ruses, including false registries. Spanish
agents in the United States were then authorized, including by the *Caja de
Consolidación de Vales Reales*, or Consolidation Fund for Royal Bonds, which
was engaged in funding the national debt, to sell bills of exchange on Spanish
American treasury receipts, as well as trading permits, and some firms were in fact
licensed to trade with Spanish America as a means to redeem those bills. The
crown was also bestowing upon "court figures" licenses for neutral trade, which
those people then resold to merchants, and by 1801 the government too was selling
these permits directly to traders. That year neutral trade was again authorized, but
principally to license-holders in order to facilitate royal fiscal arrangements.
Authorities in Spain, as long as the state profited, sanctioned exchange with
foreigners and non-Spanish imports; an inflow of contradictory public and secret
orders to American authorities resulted, sometimes confusing their recipients, and
often making relations with their charges or other Spanish dependencies more
difficult. In Caracas, the intendant had both to conciliate the consulado and find
ways to sell and export the tobacco piled up in government warehouses. There,
licensed carriers were allowed in during 1801 and 1802, but in Cuba the intendant
would not honor Branciforte's license to import flour and did his own business in
trade permits with North Americans.[20] One result was that Arango y Parreño, then
head of the Amigos del País in Havana, received shipments of books from the
American Philosophical Society, read its transactions in meetings, and distributed
copies in Spanish. He was also speaking out against abolition of slavery. (Some
ninety-three thousand blacks arrived between 1790 and 1805, one Cuban historian
has estimated.) Anglo-American residents increased too, and a sentiment began to
form for annexation to the United States.[21]

From 1800, as we have seen, there were more United States ships in Pacific waters, and more of them put into major and minor ports everywhere.[22] Trade with southern South America continued to increase between 1802 and 1805, and, although the court complained in 1801 that shipments from the United States and Jamaica flooded Mexico, Vera Cruz too was opened by Spain to licensed neutrals until 1803 and again, with renewed hostilities against Britain, in 1805, and officials in Mexico issued permits to United States citizens to introduce merchandise into Vera Cruz in the interval.[23] There were twenty-nine United States citizens residing in Buenos Aires in 1804, including David de Forest, who from 1801 was involved in contraband and unofficially acted as United States consul there. Other ports had consuls authorized by Congress.[24]

In Venezuela, by 1805 consulado members were accusing Francisco Caballero Sarmiento of controlling overseas trade and the country's economy. Sarmiento was the agent in La Guaira, and son-in-law, of John Craig, the Philadelphia merchant involved too in the Mexican silver scheme. Craig had in 1803 received a license to sell flour to Venezuela from Manuel Sixto Espinosa, treasurer of the Consolidation Fund, who in turn had bought the privilege from Branciforte, the former Mexican viceroy and Godoy's brother-in-law. Craig brought in Robert Oliver of Baltimore, his brother-in-law. He also had contracted with the Marqués de Casa Irujo, Spanish Minister to the United States, in 1799 to transport Venezuelan tobacco owned by the state monopoly. The intendant in Caracas, however, had made his own arrangements. That same year he negotiated the sale and trade of that tobacco with William Davis Robinson, a Philadelphia trader, and his associates, Benjamin H. Phillips, United States consul on Curacao, and John Corser, a naturalized Dutch resident there. Robinson handled the tobacco business from 1799 to 1806. Initially he promised to pay a fifth in flour and the rest in gold, silver, and textiles; then in 1803 he contracted to take out the leaf in exchange for slaves, bringing in with each five barrels of flour. Craig, who reached some sort of agreement with Robinson, at any rate arranged to bring in powder, ball, muskets, and foodstuffs, and reputedly introduced less legal flour than smuggled textiles. Even so, the consulado of Caracas complained that Craig made huge profits on the wheat monopoly. The amounts he imported and exported were not indicated by the number of North American ships putting in, although there were a great many, for Craig also hired vessels under Danish, French, Dutch, and Swedish flags; and some North American wheat arrived by way of Trinidad.[25]

Although commercial activity accelerated, mine output declined. Spanish American regions expanding in agriculture and ranching continued to find insufficient markets for their products; imports continued either scarce or overabundant. A large rise in sugar production in Cuba, Mexico, Louisiana, Venezuela, and in Brazil as well, all profiting from the troubles of Santo Domingo, required customers. And not only Mexican wheat suffered: Although in 1791 New Spain had exported six times as much cotton as had the United States, by 1805 Mexicans recognized that the United States was way ahead. Thus, in Mexico alone, exports of wheat, cotton, and sugar, as well as mining, suffered in the early 1800s from a combination of Anglo-American competition, Havana's rise at the expense of Vera Cruz, British blockade, the use of the cotton gin in the United

States, and Spain's policies, specie requirements, and debility.[26] Not surprisingly, a large sugar and cotton grower in 1808 led the movement deposing the viceroy.

More open trade and the effects of royal policy after 1800 contributed to depressing further much of the interregional trade of Spanish American products. The cheaper manufactured cotton goods from England and Germany, often imported in United States ships, competed more successfully in South America with trade in interior textiles. Thus, the Ecuadorian and general Andean highland exchange with Lima now suffered keenly, as did analogous interior trades with Chile and Buenos Aires. Rivalry mounted between ports or administration centers and hinterlands. And a decree in 1801 forbade Mexican exchange with other parts of Spanish America. Regional isolation and sense of particularism were rising, undoubtedly sped by Latin Americans finding their regional economies more often in competition with one another and ever more geared to foreign exchange. The rage to export aggravated these conditions. So did United States exports and re-exports, carriers, and republican influence. And so did its use as an economic exemplar and its proximity, for in 1803 Jefferson acquired Louisiana.[27]

In these circumstances, creoles saw their own well-being as more closely tied to that of their provinces and regional productivity and its protection as more urgent, often as *the* key to progress; They saw their local economies expanding or having the potential to expand, yet their economic problems only multiplying. They exerted, too, more pressure for position, expressed more resentment and a greater awareness of discrimination, and displayed greater competition with and antipathy toward European Spaniards, who were perceived as venal but increasingly favored. Accordingly, from 1800 to 1808, many more creoles slid from the heights of optimism, even overoptimism, concerning the immediate prospects of their regions to an anguished seeking to discover why in fact conditions were getting worse. New gazettes were revealing and disseminating the descent from great expectations to disappointment and soul-searching. The creole goal was still to find the way to progress, certain that it existed.[28] In this endeavor, not only the North American example of the efficacy of combining economic with greater political liberty was at hand. There were also available numerous sources corroborating the advantages of public control of economic and political affairs. From Madrid in 1801, for example, the consulado of Vera Cruz received from its resident agent a list of books for a proposed library. Mentioned were works by Spanish economists, periodicals, the 1784 Spanish edition of *The Wealth of Nations*, a French book on the constitutions of Europe and the United States, and much on North American trade; and one volume concerned the influence of republican government on Anglo-American prosperity. At the time other, private libraries in Latin America had the same or similar contents, and some accounts of the American Revolution as well. And a new generation of the propertied native-born were more conscious of being Americans and were seeking innovative and more practical sorts of education. Thus members of the Caracas consulado, in a notable instance, did stop bickering in 1798, long enough to underwrite one Fray Francisco de Andujar's teaching a mathematics class in the house of an orphan of prominent family, Simón Bolívar. In 1799, young Bolívar was on his way to Spain to pursue further studies, primarily in mathematics and foreign languages. He returned to Caracas at the age of nineteen, in 1802, recently married, and that year became a member of the consulado and opened a place of business. His wife's death in 1803 left him grief-stricken, ended his commercial career, and sent him back to Europe and on to other pursuits.[29]

Porteños saw the revocation of neutral commerce loosely imposed, and competition for contraband trade between mercantile groups winked at by viceroys, especially with renewal of war with England, from 1802. Yet complaints, voiced by Belgrano and others in the 1790s, echoed in the new *Telégrafo Mercantil*, which noted the mutual dependence of producers and merchants, then urged exporting in porteño-owned vessels and promoting finishing industries—in this discussion suggesting importing master tanners from the United States and also emulating that country in exporting wheat and flour. Yet more trenchant were essays in the *Semanario de agricultura, industria, y comercio*. The interests of its editor, Juan Hipólito Vieytes, aligned with those of more liberal consulado members and Belgrano; they were solely economic, with little pretense of literary content. Vieytes reprinted articles by Franklin, and he admired British power and prosperity and cited reputable authorities on political economy, including Jovellanos, Campillo, Ward, Foronda, and Hume. And in 1804, in a long exposition of Adam Smith's ideas, he concluded that capital should be invested in America in order to develop, in consecutive stages, cultivation, manufactures, and foreign trade, and he viewed economic freedom as a step to greater political liberty.[30]

Chileans, as had Cos Iriberri, were coming to associate the Spanish interpretation of free trade with too many foreign imports and too few benefits to themselves. Manuel de Salas, a leading member of the consulado, had in the early 1790s—much as had his friend Belgrano—counted on the monarchy to be the chief instrument of Chilean and American progress, and had been enthusiastic about cooperating with royal officials. Salas too had spoken of "the passion or mania that dominates me of being useful to the nation and my country." And, as had the exiled Jesuits and Jefferson, he also chose to defend America against repeated European slurs, in 1801 asserting Americans vindicated by, among others, Franklin. By then, still convinced that Chile had immense natural and human resources that only needed releasing, and that its basic problems were slow population growth and limited opportunity to market produce, he had come to blame lack of progress on the government's misguided commercial policy. He was still loyal and was more sanguine than Cos about the efficacy of more open trade, proposing it as the solution of first order, necessary to expand exports. By 1804, however, Salas and other members of the Santiago consulado were both requesting more authority to direct the development of the country and distinguishing between varieties of free trade. They were protesting United States contraband and criticizing most severely the sort of commercial liberty the state imposed. It was then that Salas complained that Chile had too much trade. And, in 1805, in a letter to Belgrano, he spoke of the decline of royal policy into realpolitik, indicating creole understanding of Spain's stance: "The hope of reform having disappeared," he wrote, "there has come to substitute for it the execution of a fiscal project."[31] Cos, who had complained of too many imports since 1796, noted that the only change since then was one of more merchants and more consumption, its net result the extraction and consequent scarcity of metals.[32]

The court-sponsored fact-finding tour of Spanish America by Alexander von Humboldt, from 1799 to 1804, coincided with the ascent of creole concern about regional economies and with a winding down of governmental energies directed toward reform. In South America, the Caribbean, and then in Mexico in 1803 and 1804, as the possibility for reform in cooperation with Spain was receding, Humboldt pointed out the illustrious native past, the nature of current problems, and some glowing possibilities open to Spanish Americans. Inventorying natural resources, in Mexico especially, and foreseeing great progress if only hindrances were removed, he fed creole aspirations and furthered Mexican self-consciousness. There and everywhere he travelled—in Cuba, Venezuela, New Granada, and Peru as well—he spoke to leading officials, to residents, and especially to scientists. To them all he imparted his vision of material progress as a natural occurrence and a cure-all for social ills, and he coupled civilization and culture with economic awakening. Spanish Americans could not advance under present political principles, he wrote; government must improve. Industry was suffering from current Spanish policies. Taxes impeded trade, and although Mexico's public revenues had risen from six million pesos in the 1760s to over 20 million in 1802, its wealth was chiefly benefiting Spain.[33] Many Spanish institutions, he concluded systematized oppression, and he also noted that Mexican society unfortunately lacked an "intermediate estate."

In support of these observations Humboldt cited at length the 1799 report written by Abad y Queipo, describing how present policies maintained social divisions and predicting social conflict.[34] In explicit comparison, Humboldt called attention to an American prodigy, the United States' growth in population, agriculture, and industry, as an example of unfettered progress. And he warned the Spanish government, and coincidentally reminded creoles, that "in the eye of the law every white creole is a Spaniard. The abuse of the laws, the false measures of the colonial government, the example of the United States of America, and the influence of the opinions of the age, have relaxed ties which formerly united more closely the Spanish creoles to the European Spaniards."[35] He went on to explain that inhabitants of remote provinces thought *European* and *Spaniard* synonymous, and Spain to be still *the* European power. In the capitals, however, creoles acquainted with French or English literature went to the other extreme, preferring strangers to European Spaniards, and "they flatter themselves with the idea intellectual cultivation has made more rapid progress in the colonies than in the peninsula."[36]

Humboldt's ideas and encyclopedic writings on the New World were tinged with scientific romanticism. They revealed a great faith in human endeavor and a Germanic emphasis on national folk history; and they emphasized as attainable: ideals of political and economic freedom, rational enquiry, informed criticism, individual worth, civic responsibility, and constructive innovation. Humboldt's visit and views inspired or reinforced creoles' dreams of taking their country's destiny into their own hands, and also strengthened their belief that they could do it. He introduced creoles to their own lands, as the Mexican historian and statesman Lucas Alamán commented, and they then "formed an extremely exaggerated concept of the wealth of their patria, and considered that it, being independent, could come to be the most powerful nation of the universe."[37] Abad y Queipo, with a reciprocal admiration, cited Humboldt in 1805; so did a Mexican dissident in New Orleans, another José Antonio Rojas, in 1807, and the baron was later a favorite source for Fray Mier.[38]

Humboldt, preeminently a naturalist, was himself like a bee carrying pollen. In his travels from region to region he spread, or at least reinforced, a sense of an American network among like-minded, educated people engaged in a wide spectrum of professions or careers—government, the press, the clergy, the military, science, education, mining, agriculture and ranching, and commerce, and frequently in more than one of them. His stay in Cartagena in 1801 with José Ignacio de Pombo points up the inclusion among such people of a creole business-man at once entrepreneurial, intellectual, and patriotic, with a cosmopolitan awareness of events and of the role, actual and potential, of America and Americans in them. Pombo, who came of a distinguished provincial family of Popayán, and who had studied philosophy and jurisprudence for six years at the Colegio de Rosario in Bogotá, in 1784 began what became a highly successful, many-branched export-import firm. He was a confidant of Mutis and cor-responded with him, with Zea, and with Caldas, whose research he often underwrote.

Pombo founded Cartagena's economic society and wrote reports to its con-sulado and to the government on economic, fiscal, and scientific matters relating to the development of New Granada. In the early 1800s, he scanned gazettes from Havana, Lima, Buenos Aires, Madrid, Philadelphia, and Charleston for infor-mation, and he quoted Jefferson, Edmund Burke, Jovellanos, Campomanes, and Adam Smith in support of his own views. He defended liberty of commerce and assumed property rights to be the foundation of social order. He hated England, declaring the English "arrogant, the natural enemy of other industrious peoples, and always ours."[39] He called them pirates who used neutral ships to introduce their wares and traders. In contradistinction, he wrote of the United States as a nation which by simple and just means and by cultivation and trade had rapidly achieved power and greatness, as well as a spread of wealth and public felicity, and he foresaw commercial alliances with it as necessary "in order to brake the despotism of the English," and to drive them from all America.[40] It should be safe to assume he did business with the North Americans and found the British on Trinidad and Jamaica strong competitors.

From New Granada Humboldt went to Quito, where—along with Aime Bon-pland, the French natural scientist, and Caldas—he stayed with Montúfar, Pombo's friend, a leading proponent of reform, and, earlier, Espejo's ally. Montúfar's son, Carlos, accompanied Humboldt back to Europe. Traveling on, in Lima in 1802 the baron enjoyed the company of Hipólito Unanue, the principal Peruvian man of science and publicist of the Enlightenment. Unanue was a

member of the Lima literary salon that had become the economic society. Unanue
had also been a confidant and adviser to the progressive viceroys, O'Higgins and
Francisco Gil de Taboada, and among his correspondents, in 1802 and 1803, was
Dr. Samuel Mitchell of New York, with whom he discussed the need for
commerce between the Americas. Mitchell, an active enthusiast for closer relations between the United States and Latin America, belonged himself to learned
societies, enjoyed high political connections and influence, and wrote the letter
published as a preface in 1806 to the New York edition of DePons's account of
Venezuela. This document evidenced his proclivities in stating, ''To many it may
be a recommendation that the author writes more like a man of business than a man
of science.'' In 1806, perhaps through Mitchell, Unanue knew Jefferson's *Notes
on Virginia*, and he cited it.[41]

Humboldt himself visited the United States in 1804, became associated with the
American Philosophical Society, and as we have seen, befriended and continued
to correspond with Jefferson. The German savant was indeed part of a multinational network of educated people interested in material advance, including
economic progress and commercial interchange, and convinced that it was
realizable through utilizing natural and applied science, and that it promised
greater social well-being. Bernardo O'Higgins later thought Humboldt's opinions
worth repeating, as did another admirer, Simón Bolívar. Humboldt, after his
return from America, conversed with Bolívar in France. Bolívar, who subsequently wrote to him and quoted him, was told by him that Spanish America and
its peoples were unique and worthy of a separate existence. Humboldt's writings
remain a principal source on Spanish America during this period.[42] They were a
link in forging a spirit of cosmopolitan and continental Americanism, and they still
stand as one major interpretation of the assumptions and content of political
economy, and of enlightened assumptions, as applied to America. In short,
Humboldt was among those Europeans visiting America who combined scientific,
political, and economic interests, whose views encouraged creoles to free themselves from all perceived obstacles to progress, and who singled out as the major
hindrance the disarray of the current Spanish imperial system.

With the brief peace between Spain and England, in early 1804 European goods
flooded in and British traders proliferated, as did North American carriers. Again,
this hurt domestic manufactures and interregional trade and did not help exports
much. And this time the respite from war brought little cheer to producers, for that
year the court decreed that certain church funds be turned over to the state in
Spanish America, and that a stipulated large group of church properties be sold and
the returns paid to the Consolidation Fund—all to refinance government notes
issued in the subsidy to Napoleon and the Ouvrard arrangement and to be
compensated for by other government bonds. This was an extension and variation
of a similar process carried out in Spain, where, however, it had smaller impact on
the economy. The decree was enforced effectively only in Mexico and, to a
degree, in Peru. In New Spain it resulted in the calling in of most church mortgages
on agricultural and, to a lesser extent, urban, property belonging to many land and
mine owners and to some merchants; the recalling of many subsidiary debts as

well; and to a specie drain. When published there in 1805, it provoked the first broad spectrum reaction against the state. It caused widespread consternation and financial loss, affected every level of society, from members of the aristocracy to day laborers, and deepened discontents. It brought numerous written protests from municipal councils, including that of the capital—which spoke of injustice on behalf of the entire kingdom—from the mining tribunal, and from Michoacán farmers and merchants and the ecclesiastical cabildo in Valladolid (now Morelia). Among those most directly affected were nobles—titleholders who were property owners with multiple investments in agriculture, livestock, mines, and commerce, and whose titles had usually come with wealth during the past half-century. It contributed to a fall in land values and a rise in agricultural prices, reduced circulating capital, and acted adversely upon mining, trade, and employment. Especially hard hit was the Bajío, where the church had immense agricultural holdings, and, hardest of all, Valladolid, which became a center of resistance to that law. Bajío wheat prices fell initially, and one hacienda attached as a result of the sequestration process belonged to the priest of Dolores, Miguel Hidalgo. A militia captain in nearby San Miguel, Ignacio Allende, also had a mortgage outstanding. In the south, in Oaxaca, hacendados and merchants suffered and blamed local administrators, the intendants and, ultimately, Godoy. There a very large debt was owed by Gabriel Yermo, whose wealth was in lands, sugar, cotton, and herds, and who in 1808 had revenge of sorts in leading the coup overthrowing Godoy's appointee, José de Iturrigaray, the viceroy responsible for implementing the act of 1804. It was common knowledge that over a third of the proceeds were siphoned as graft, including to the viceroy, the archbishop, and the royal collector, and that in May 1806 at least five million pesos collected under this act were sent to subsidize the French.[43]

Abad y Queipo, who had written in 1799 of simmering hatreds between various social groups, composed in 1805 the representación of the farmers and merchants of Michoacán. In it he coupled the impossibility of competing with United States exports with the onus of the decree of 1804, and explained the act's effect to be an impossible exaction on an already overburdened economy. Mexicans had to rely on foreign capital as it was, he explained, and even then never had much on hand. They had few funds of their own and little money in circulation. Business transactions were slow; war raised prices, even tripled them. Internal communications and commerce had decayed, specie was being shipped abroad, Mexicans paid heavy duties and taxes, and United States flour continued cheaper in Havana, attesting to poor state policies. "Nothing," he concluded, "increases discontent so much as a demand for money."[44] Many Mexicans, agreeing with the liberal Spanish priest, also concluded that progress was at an end by 1805. From then on, widespread disenchantment, spurred by the decree and its implementation, coalesced and became an important factor in provoking a resentment unifying powerful groups and the populace in one shared sentiment—opposition to continuing domination by the present government of Spain.

The loyal but aggrieved attitudes embodied in protest by Abad y Queipo, and the protests themselves, can be viewed as a response to Spanish policies from the later

1790s. In those policies the Enlightenment had been merged with a resurgent, state-supervised Catholicism. Thus, churchmen throughout the empire were encouraged to lead approved reform, while at the same time the state moved to restrict more closely clerical privileges and power and to extend its authority over church property. The government, in effect, then both exhorted clergy in Spain and America to become active social leaders in reform and was felt to hinder their doing so. Most pronounced was a growing disaffection among the lower clergy, who in America were mostly native-born. Mier and Hidalgo are outstanding cases in point.[45]

Defeat at Trafalgar in 1805, destroying the navy, removed Spain from the seas. By then, liberals and conservatives opposing Godoy were rallying behind Prince Fernando, and liberal laws and periodicals were being banned. By 1804, Charles IV and Godoy saw America slipping away and were considering holding it through setting up four princes there, "in a feudal sovereignty of Spain with certain obligations to pay a certain quantity in recognition of vassalage and to supply troops and ships where they are needed."[46] They doubted the loyalty of Spanish Americans, Godoy in his memoirs ascribing blame for the Spanish American thirst for autonomy to the Revolution of 1776.[47] Spanish Americans knew of Spanish disgust with the royal court, often shared it, and were aware of the repression in Spain of the thrust for liberal constitutional monarchy. Spanish weakness and divisiveness deepened American disaffection, and it reinforced a creole sense of Americanism in the face of a corrupt and fissiparous Europe. Thus, in Peru certain *cuzqueños*, objecting to the moral corruption of the Spanish court, also opposed bad local government and European Spaniards, or *chapetones*, spur-wearers, in general. They were familiar with the contents of the Mexican cabildo's petition of 1771, admired the writings of Jovellanos, and plotted against Spain. Their leader was a creole mineowner who was also a romantic indigenist. The principals included a friar and an Indian who had heard of Raynal's views on America. They had also heard that the captain of a Boston frigate had told creoles at Callao they would soon be unburdened of European rule, just as the people of the United States had been. Their manifestoes invoked the precept of Túpac Amaru, and one of them, in ascribing their tie to the throne to an oath only, implied a view of monarchy as contractual and constitutional. The plot had ramifications in Upper Peru; in La Paz, leaders demanded a republic.[48]

In Mexico, respect for viceroys, who were seen as Godoy's appointees, noticeably declined, so that dissidents could refer to them as objects of animus. The Mexican Rojas declared Branciforte a robber and looked back nostalgically to the days of that creole appointed by Charles III, *"el virtuoso Revillagigedo."*[49] Azanza's favoritism toward his contrabandista relatives was common gossip. His successor, Marquina (whose mother was a FitzGerald), was rumored to have purchased his post from Godoy and was known to have been captured by the British en route to America and taken to Jamaica; he was known, too, to permit smuggling with England and the United States. And his replacement, Iturrigaray, was seen to have arrived to take up office laden with goods to sell, duty free. Iturrigaray went on to sell mercury—vital to processing silver—to selected favorites, and to be recognized as profiting from Spain's hand-to-mouth fiscal policies and involved international commitments—much as did other traders and the royal treasury. Thus, when reprimanded in 1806 for allowing contraband in with neutral trade, he reminded the court that it had in confidential directives sanctioned just that. The crown, as we know, permitted and profited from the network (still imperfectly understood) involving the Ouvrard contracts and the Consolidation Fund, and including the Hopes, the Barings, Parish, and the consortium selling trading licenses and bills of exchange through representatives in North American ports. Also involved were the mercantile houses of Reid, Irving, and Gordon, Tómas Murphy, and others, who engaged in direct trade between Europe and Mexico, as well as in commerce between Jamaica and Vera Cruz. They were provided with British safe-conduct passes and permission to ship under neutral flags. They too collected specie to offset bills of exchange. Some large sums were even destined for London and delivered to British warships waiting offshore.[50]

Exchange between Latin America and the United States peaked from 1806 until Jefferson's embargo took effect late in 1808. The governor of Havana in 1806 received a very secret royal order to permit Craig and Company to introduce flour into Cuba, and many other licenses to private firms not involved in the silver caper assured continued great North American contact.[51] In 1807, the New York *Daily Advertiser* could speak of "our extensive commercial intercourse with Caracas."[52] Buenos Aires then dominated the trade of La Plata, Chile, and Peru, and its entrepreneurs, Spanish and creole, dealt with North American merchants, including DeForest, and used ships and captains from the United States. Thus one resident Spaniard, Julián Hernández Banuso, who contacted yankee merchants through John Stoughton, then liberally issuing letters-patent as Spanish consul for New England, did business in association with merchants in Lima and Montevideo, loading cargoes in Boston on United States ships destined for Chile and Peru. Two other residents of Buenos Aires, Tómas O'Gorman, nephew of the personal physician who arrived with the first viceroy in 1777, and Tómas O'Reilly, employed North American frigates. O'Gorman attempted trade, in a Portuguese ship out of Lisbon, with Chile, where he was blocked by Spanish merchants. North American vessels, escaping that fate, traded along the coast without local permission. In 1806, the Chilean consulado complained of North American captains having an "enormous propensity to contraband."[53] Moreover, at least one of the North American frigates then trading with Chile had been fitted out by Spanish merchants and loaded at Cádiz. The multinational nature of neutral trade during this period is inescapable, as we have noted, and, it often involved exchange, direct or indirect, with non-neutral Britain. Thus, the Chilean consulado complained, too, of English and North Americans using double patents. Some creole merchants were making arrangements with London, and at Cartagena during 1806 and 1807 an English warship took on specie in an arrangement similar to that pertaining in Vera Cruz.[54] Pombo, an informed, established creole merchant, then fired another verbal volley against both the British and Spanish for retaining monopolies and not allowing Cartagena neutral trade, in an informe addressed to the local consulado and meant for the viceroy. In it he continually referred to the United States as an example of wise economic and commercial policies, even citing Albert Gallatin's address to Congress of December 5, 1806, which sustained theories of free trade. North American cotton, he pointed out, was exempt from imposts, and the North American population throve along with its agriculture. Pombo, genuinely concerned with the future of New Granada and reacting to the unholy alliance of Spanish monopolists, crown agencies, Napoleon's bankers, and the British government and traders, appealed to the United States' experience and suggested commercial alliance with that nation as an alternative. Yet everywhere, while more United States ships put in, British imports and competition swelled. Jamaica, Trinidad, and Brazil served as emporiums. Cotton textiles, exports and re-exports, from Britain surged from 1804. British exports to Latin America rose from an estimated three hundred thousand pounds sterling in 1805 to an estimated value of over six million in 1809.[55]

In Buenos Aires, by 1805 Belgrano was reading Washington's farewell address, perhaps a gift from DeForest, who was then busy as a commission agent and in smuggling. They had a mutual friend in Juan Larrea, the syndic of the consulado who was in addition a business associate of DeForest's. DeForest's finances were managed by another North American, William P. White, who also had dealings with a British admiral, Sir Home Popham, who owed him money. Popham was interested in La Plata and its commercial advantage to Britain by 1804, as a memorandum he signed that year attests.[56] It suggested invading Buenos Aires and cited the former United States minister in London, Rufus King, as believing conquest the only way to save La Plata from the French; the plan was approved by Pitt, then postponed. Popham went in on his own upon returning from South Africa, where he had talked to an American sea captain, one Captain Waine, who had showed him Buenos Aires gazettes critical of the government, including Vieytes's weekly and the *Telégrafo*. Waine had told him that if the city could trade freely with Britain, its inhabitants would hold it for the English, and had played on Popham's fear of the French beating him to it.[57] The British government had made repeated plans for attacks on South America during the wars of the eighteenth century and were now at it again, in the struggle with Napoleon. Popham's ventures, though unauthorized, pleased George Canning, secretary of state for foreign affairs, since Napoleon was closing European ports and the United States threatening to close its own.[58] Yet, arriving as conquerors in La Plata, the British aroused creole patriotism and military ardor. Belgrano and the rising young attorney, Mariano Moreno, stunned and mortified at the ease of British entry and occupation, emerged as defenders of the patria, driving out the English forces by 1808. An observer reported that in 1807 creoles had become "so enthused with military service they heard of new enemy disembarkations with jubilation."[59]

The fiasco convinced the British that creoles wanted an open trade but would not tolerate foreign domination. It aroused a broad spectrum xenophobia among porteños. One representación to the cabildo, approved by many merchants and other residents, not only called for expelling foreigners, but stipulated, "Colonial commerce is no longer tolerable, nor is the entry of North American expeditions, which have come with royal permission."[60] The invasion brought creoles to prefer, if domination was necessary, Spain's under a limited monarchy; but, if domination could be shucked off, they would rather have independence. The British encouraged talk of all sorts of liberty through political and commercial example, as well as in discussion—and, after invading Montevideo in 1807, through the English-backed *La Estrella de Sur*, which championed creole rights.[61] A British officer there reported finding creoles were "entirely turned toward independence, and the establishment of a Republic or Federal Government similar to that of North America."[62] Belgrano recalled that porteños in 1807 were anti-French, distrusted the British, and were ready to bide time under Spain until the opportune moment. That moment arrived, he added, in 1808, when creoles saw and took their chance for leadership. Belgrano was in their forefront, arguing for working for the liberty of America.[63]

During the English occupation of La Plata, more United States ships came in, but British traders and imports triumphed, finally and decisively. United States ships brought in Africans, Cuban sugar, and tobacco, and took away hides, and tallow and jerked beef for the Caribbean, but mostly silver. British ships, goods, commission agents, and adventurers poured in, flooding markets. They competed with local merchants and did not forward Britain's popularity.[64] Moreover, Belgrano, seeing consulado merchants offering the English no resistance and even welcome in 1806, commented with bitterness, "The merchant recognizes no country, no king, and no religion other than his own interests."[65] Unwittingly, he echoed Robert Morris, but in diametrically opposed spirit, and he adumbrated a Latin American viewpoint that would spread in reaction to a very unfavorable balance of trade combined with ascending economic nationalism.

In Mexico, where from 1805 the sequestration program and the silver transfer scheme were under way, where old and new consulados agreed in opposing Godoy's policies and Iturrigaray—although certain inhabitants, mainly creoles whom he favored, were drawn to him—the viceroy and many others were aware of Miranda's schemes and of his expedition being readied, and of British plans of 1804, 1806, and 1808 to invade Vera Cruz, in which they thought collaboration from the southwestern United States probable. Iturrigaray announced in the *Gaceta de México* the imminent threat of foreign invasion and made public statements decrying the hypocritical liberal mask of England and its former colonies—and he alluded specifically to the continuation of black slavery in the United States. He thereby, attempting to discredit a growing respect for both governments, inadvertently reassured propertied Mexicans of the moderate character of social change after the Revolution of 1776.[66] It was then, in northern Mexico, that José Melchor Sánchez Navarro, heir to a huge landed estate and in 1810 actively opposed to Hidalgo's revolt, enjoyed conversing with Zebulon Pike as Pike was leaving New Spain under escort. The Sánchez Navarro had "built the latifundio primarily to make money," and commerce was of great interest to them, as it was to Pike.[67] Iturrigaray also called cantonments of the native-born militia, three of them in Vera Cruz from 1805 to 1807, and two in Jalapa in 1806 and 1808, to hold military maneuvers. The sight of fourteen thousand armed compatriots marching through the streets of the capital en route impressed its residents, as the gazette reported. It also announced creole triumph in 1808 in La Plata, smugly concluding that "the American creole has not degenerated in spirit, in heart, or in generosity."[68]

Some Mexican officers, among them Allende, returned home from the war games brimming with Mexican patriotism and a swollen pride in being leaders and defenders of their country, as were porteños of theirs.[69] Allende had seen duty in Texas, having been sent there in expectation of Burr's expedition. Indeed, Mexicans of every political stripe, especially after the loss of Louisiana, thought the United States might advance into New Spain. They knew, as Godoy had rather offhandedly put it, that you can not lock up an open field. Fray Mier, at the time of the purchase, saw such expansion as inevitable since, he stated, United States power was built upon industry, commerce, liberty, and growth in population.[70] In 1807 he argued that Anglo-Americans' domination of the Northwest coast made them masters of the fur trade and the commerce with "India" and that "they will become with time for us the most terrible neighbors."[71] Yet, Mier was to change his mind, and Allende to attempt to reach refuge in United States territory. The United States would continue to be an economic exemplar and competitor, a political mentor, and a haven for creole dissidents.

It was those years in which materialism and a new radicalism, voiced by some of the clergy and the more educated creoles and frequently combined with opposition to the regime, came to bedevil the authorities and the Inquisition, that the Mexican Rojas escaped from that tribunal's prison to New Orleans. Rojas had attended the relatively new School of Mines, read extensively in the library owned by Posada, taught architecture, botany, and chemistry, practiced medicine (on his friends and the poor), and held the chair of mathematics at the new University of Guanajuato. His bent toward useful knowledge and his avowal of a natural morality and scorn of established institutions and conventions precipitated his detention and flight. From Louisiana in 1807 he wrote inflammatory letters to Mexican friends, among them Hidalgo, insisting the Spanish political system was undesirable and unnecessary. He held out the United States, instead, as a model for change, lauded its economic progress, and sent them copies of its Constitution and other republican documents.[72]

At the same time in Chile, among the Americans jumping ship was Procopio Jacinto Pollock, Oliver's son, now a medical doctor by profession but most recently at Vera Cruz involved with the huge multinational transfer of silver. He passed about to receptive chilenos his so-called *Gacetas*, mostly résumés of journals in English and, when ordered out of the country, he went to Buenos Aires and continued to send messages of republican inspiration to Chilean friends. One of them was Juan Martínez de Rozas, the political mentor of Bernardo O'Higgins.[73]

An outstanding historian has concluded, in speaking of Argentina, that there was no general indication of the coming collapse of the imperial system up to 1806; that before then a hidden crisis existed, one that included new ideological currents harbored within classical thought, and a veneration of republican values.[74] He is right only in part. The new ideological currents were indeed present—sometimes combined with classical concepts and sometimes not—and the crisis included not only imperatives drawn from new currents but also Spain's inability to continue to pose as champion of "a happy revolution." Moreover, intermeshed with new currents and values—indeed, a principal component of them—were economic tenets thought of as indissolubly linked to political life and taken up as guides by Latin Americans who wanted markets and felt the impact of new foreign demand and new imported wares. By 1806, many Spanish Americans were convinced the government would not, and could not, benefit them further. Their exposure to concepts of republican virtue and constitutionalism then acted as a solvent in emotional separation from a court seen as morally corrupt and impotent in its authoritarianism. Still, it was Spanish liberalism and constitutionalism as much as anything that bridged the gap for creoles between the old imperial order and independence.

By 1808, that the idea of complete independence from Spain had as yet gained much popularity anywhere is far from certain, but republicanism and constitutionalism had, and in support of them numerous allusions were made to the general state of well-being enjoyed by North Americans. Moreover, North American interest, benign and otherwise, had given a number of leading creoles the idea that the new republic, whatever its aspect, would help them to rid themselves of European domination. Miranda, after all, had sailed from New York in 1806 on his liberating expedition; among his men were two hundred United States citizens, and in his manifestoes he cited the success of the United States. Although his venture failed, its attempt gave other creoles hope.[75] And shortly afterwards, Simón Bolívar, en route home from Europe, spent four or five months on the eastern seaboard, visiting Lexington, Concord, New York, Philadelphia, and Washington, before sailing from Charleston on January 1, 1807.[76] He was returning to a part of the globe where the socially powerful inhabitants were open to new directions.

By 1808, too, not only was the Spanish regime bankrupt and the propertied in America seeking effective change, but numbers of Latin Americans of all backgrounds, prodded by inflation and economic insecurity, by the American and—especially tantalizing to blacks—the French and Santo Domingo examples, were ready to implement revolutionary rhetoric. Creoles, losing much of their naiveté concerning the Spanish concept of liberty of commerce, nevertheless retained belief in some of its underlying principles, concepts also common to liberal Europeans and Americans. Important among these beliefs was the idea of population as wealth: It heightened interest in bringing all Latin Americans into the political economy, which was thought of as regional and as best directed by its propertied and entrepreneurial, largely or purportedly white, and resourceful native sons.

A new generation was maturing, born after Gálvez inaugurated reform, and within it were people who would take charge of revolution and guide the new republics. Most of them came from areas that had been outside geographical and social centers of power until the 1760s, so that they saw current conditions in 1808 as the shipwreck of the old imperial order; that is, of the heyday of the Bourbon reforms. They and their regions felt the impact of the court's rudderless policies, measures, and attitudes, now dictated by fiscal expedience. They were economically affected and deeply embarrassed by its loss of international stature; they kept abreast of world events and, at home, of surging population growth and expanding but inhibited economies. In this situation, to many of them the closest guide, in proximity and experience, appeared to be an American one, the progress of the United States.

9

"EMBRACE INDEPENDENCE":

1808—1826

Events in Spain were the immediate cause of the convolutions in America from 1808 on. Napoleon's invasion and capture of the royal family, the formation of a number of provincial patriotic juntas against the French and in the name of Ferdinand VII in May 1808, and British military and naval aid to the patriots all influenced attitudes and events in America. A central junta, formed in September 1808, called for a cortes, including American deputies; by January 1810, it was confined to Cádiz and then dissolved, leaving a regency that did achieve a cortes, and that parliament in 1812 produced a constitution. In Portugal when the French invaded, the royal family boarded a British warship and moved the imperial court to Brazil. Yet behind immediate responses, and also influencing the course of what became independence movements, were Iberian and Latin American interaction over time and the full spectrum of relations within the broader eighteenth-century Atlantic world. Especially observable from 1808 to 1810 was the cumulative impact of political and economic liberalism upon Latin Americans. There existed in America a great desire for autonomy, and thus for limiting monarchical authority, and for power there, on the part of both right and left, in 1808, including among some resident Spaniards. It was a desire that had been aired even earlier in terms of seeking constitutional limitations on government. This situation makes it difficult to separate liberal and conservative political theory except relatively and in relation to specific attitudes and issues, or to draw sharp lines between creole attitudes before and after 1808. Two themes then predominated in the rhetoric and goals of the propertied, urban men who took charge of their regions: constitutionalism—still spoken of as self-government within constitutional monarchy—and more advantageous commercial exchange. And in these years it was the United States that was most often invoked as a prime symbol of these twin liberties, as a precedent and as a model for emulation. It was also looked to as a source of aid and protection and as a commercial partner. Still, Latin Americans—particularly those in bordering regions—were aware of its less beneficent aspects, recognizing it as a territorial and economic competitor, and so as a possible threat to those liberties, so ardently desired, that it represented.[1]

193

We have seen that, although Jefferson's embargo remained in effect until March 1809, exports from the United States increased to the Iberian peninsula, where wheat products flowed to French and especially to British armies and fed civilians as well; now, reversing earlier trade routes, they also went through Cuba. In 1808 Spanish America and Portugal were the largest consumers of exported United States grain. Trade with both Iberia and its America rose even higher with the raising of the embargo, but from then on that to the peninsula remained greater. In 1812, British hostilities with the United States notwithstanding, Wellington wrote from Portugal that "all this part of the peninsula has been living this year on American flour"; and Admiral Lord Keith commented dolefully on the ineffectiveness of the British blockade of the Bay of Biscay: "The Americans are running in and out like rabbits."[2] Only Congress was able, in 1813, to stop that commerce with the enemy. In addition, United States trade in domestic exports rose in relation to re-exports, always dominantly British. The War of 1812 gave further impetus to the emerging United States cotton textile industry and to exports of cotton goods.

After 1808, too, American trade spurted with Brazil, where euphoria prevailed at becoming the hub of empire, and where absolutists and constitutionalists then cooperated. Britain received favored trading privileges, and the British envoy, Lord Strangford, exercised great influence at court. Brazilians, too, had influence, and they prospered. Finishing industries based on cotton, sugar, beef, wheat, and hemp did well, and a bank was founded. Thus Río merchants and Northeast planters, profiting from rising sugar prices, espoused laissez faire, and the opinion of José da Silva Lisboa, the liberal Brazilian political economist, had weight in the Prince Regent's decision to open ports in 1808. This measure allowed North Americans initially to outsell the British and to saturate the markets of Bahia, Río, and São Vicente. That year Jefferson, in a letter in effect welcoming the prince, John VI, to America, made an early statement of the Western Hemisphere idea: "Inhabitants now of the same land, of that great continent which the genius of Columbus has given to the world, the United States feels sensibly that they stand in new and closer relations with your Royal Highness . . . They see in prospect a system of intercourse between the different regions of this hemisphere of which the peace and happiness of mankind may be the essential principle."[3]

The French invasion of Spain, British alliance with the Spanish and the Portuguese, rumors through New Orleans that Mexicans would declare independence if the United States would recognize them, and overtures from Cuban dissidents combined to elicit not only from Jefferson an early expression of commonality of interests and hemispheric solidarity, but also from his cabinet, in October of 1808, a broad statement of policy in the course of authorizing agents to indicate friendship to proponents of independence in Spanish America, and in opposition to political or commercial domination there by France or England.[4] Americans and their government continued to be influenced by growth in the grain trade to Spain, by interest in domestic shipping, commercial agriculture, and nascent manufacturing, and by an expansionist urge; but they held on to old habits of looking down upon Latin Americans—upon their skin tones, religion, and capabilities. Jefferson's main concern through 1809 remained expansion into the

Floridas and Cuba, while Madison, in an exchange of letters with him, felt the nation's trade with Latin America was more important.[5]

By late 1809 Napoleonic agents were using the United States, and especially Baltimore, as a base for revolutionizing Spanish America, for dispatching men and pamphlets. They played on creole antipathy toward peninsular Spaniards; appealed to localism and to the desire to protect church, community, and economic affairs; and proclaimed the United States, Napoleon, and God on the side of the colonists. In addition, they were instructed to make a point of informing Spanish Americans of "the comforts which [Anglo-]Americans enjoy," their progress in commerce, agriculture, and navigation, and their freedom. Napoleon most probably favored creating new Spanish American states, which coming under United States hegemony would shift the international balance of power, to England's loss.[6] His agents were told to appoint lieutenants throughout the continent and particularly to contact clergy. One provocateur, Octavio D'Alvimar, was in Mexico in 1808. He came in through Texas, was captured in Chihuahua, and en route to Mexico City briefly lodged with the curate of Dolores, Miguel Hidalgo.[7]

In 1808 within Spanish America, the strongest and most immediate reaction of many political, social, and economic leaders, and aspirants, to events in Spain and to internal ramifications of international events was one of multiple opportunities to be seized. There, as in Spain, regional and local juntas "of prudent men" formed in a chain reaction and in the name of the absent Ferdinand VII. In America they replaced Spanish-designated authorities and took over cabildos. Creoles, whether of liberal or conservative bent and while genuinely concerned about the possibility of the fall of the peninsula to France, wanted no domination by French, English, or Spaniards. Very quickly they recognized that claiming to represent the monarchy, of a constitutional sort and with an absent incumbent, could achieve their ideal of peaceful, evolutionary change, yielding them their most immediate desires: regional autonomy and the opening of their ports and products to international trade under their own aegis and regulation.[8] Like the Spanish juntas of 1808, those in America functioned fundamentally as traditional community councils, as assemblies of notables called in gravest emergencies to resolve "the will of the community" (with community always understood as a corporate, organic entity, and often as the repository of sovereignty). Originally institutions of the Spanish reconquest, such juntas appeared in America with the conquistadors and had become part of American tradition as well. Moreover, with the appearance of juntas in Spain in 1808, not only is it true, as has been said, that the state was destroyed and a nation emerged, but in addition Americans were repeatedly told that they were an integral part of that nation and were expected to govern themselves within the system of relative regional autonomy then prevailing. The Junta Central in January 1809 went further, asking each American viceroyalty and captaincy-general to send deputies with instructions from their cabildos, and then in May speaking of a cortes with American participants. Both occurrences aroused discussion that vented grievances and advertised the depth and breadth of American desire for autonomy. Proclamations from Spain added fuel: That of early 1810 from the regency to Americans, published in Mexico and Peru, told them their destiny was in their hands, that now they were "raised to the dignity of free men."[9]

Mexico provided one early example of parallelism and interaction with these trends. In the capital in the summer of 1808, liberal creole members of the audiencia and cabildo claimed, as had peninsular juntistas from June on, that according to the (medieval) Spanish constitution, sovereignty had reverted to the people. Interpreting "people" as the corporate bodies, the nobility, the church, and the representatives of communities, they called for a congress of the kingdom, made up of notables and cabildo representatives, to act as a variety of Mexican regency, and even as head of empire should the peninsula fall.[10] The viceroy, Iturrigaray, with his protector, Godoy, gone, concurred, apparently counting on his popularity with those Mexicans he had favored, on winning over others, and probably, too, on arms from the United States. Statements he made at the time were directed to arousing xenophobia, largely against the French, but they also called attention to the United States's threat, along common borders and to Vera Cruz. He informed the junta of Oviedo that there was a good deal of sentiment abroad in Mexico for an independent and republican government, its proponents taking their cue from the Anglo-Americans.[11] Spanish residents, reacting to all this, deposed him in September. These events both spread hatred of Spaniards throughout Mexico and drew protests from the provinces against the claims of the cabildo of the capital to speak for all the viceroyalty. The events of 1808 also added fuel to autonomist sentiments, and to creole determination to control government in New Spain.

During that summer, some Mexicans predicted that Spain would fall to France and that the United States might then join France in invading New Spain; such presentiments were repeated frequently during the next few years. The United States was also cited in both positive and negative contexts in some of the replies of the provincial cabildos to the call for discussion of a national congress. From Vera Cruz, understandably, came a warning against opening (other) ports and an ambivalent view of the United States—as prosperous, still under English economic domination, competing with Mexico, and enjoying advantages Mexicans lacked. Mexico, that town council stated, had only this bad port, no navigable river or canal, no mercantile spirit, no capital—and worse, no understanding of how to manage capital. The United States had them all. Mexico could not compete in agriculture, and even if it could, it needed industry or it would never be opulent. The report urged development of interior trade, manufactures, and self-sufficiency: "This is the only way to attain our independence." It declared contraband to be a crime against the state and that the English favored Mexican independence in order to treat the country as the Dutch did Japan—to denude it—and its authors suggested closing ports to prohibit trade with all industrial nations.[12] It is impossible for historians to assert any longer that in 1808 Latin Americans had no grasp of economic or international affairs.

Further impetus to provincial fears and ambitions in New Spain was given in 1809 by the archbishop-viceroy, Francisco Javier de Lizana y Beaumont, when he expanded the military and, wary of the infiltration of Napoleonic agents and the possibility of invasion from the United States, concentrated troops north of the capital—thereby arousing greater fears and hopes among creole officers. In the same period, the bishop-elect of Michoacán, the reform-minded Spaniard, Abad y

Queipo, warned the government that a joint French and American invasion might occur. In his city, Valladolid (now Morelia), a plot surfaced whose participants voiced these same fears and which represented an essentially nativistic and regional reaction to events. The conspirators—members of the militia and the clergy, and other, mostly young and well-educated, creoles—planned a junta to defend New Spain in the name of Ferdinand VII. Some of them, including Allende, later joined Hidalgo and Morelos in revolt; others became deputies to the Spanish Cortes before finally choosing independence. The Valladolid dissidents were linked to groups in Querétaro, San Miguel, Guanajuato, and other regional centers. From 1808 on, complex patriotic reactions, merging with self-interest and lacking a clear cut concept of the geographical boundaries of patriotism, were the nurseries of the independence movements. It was then in Caracas that Simón Bolívar, along with other leading creoles and consulado members, called for freer trade, with or without Spain, and a conspiracy formed to replace Spanish authorities with a junta. And in Havana Arango y Parreño then suggested forming a junta, but European Spaniards and creoles demurred, undoubtedly influenced by the need for English shipping with Jefferson's embargo in effect. Cuba's trade was halved from late 1807 through 1809, and the sugar industry pinched. Yet Cubans, prosperous and relatively free of commercial restrictions, opposed the stand taken by the United States and Britain against the slave trade. By 1813, well-to-do Cubans preferred to remain as they were. So, by and large, did limeños.[13]

In Buenos Aires, where porteños had ousted the British, by 1809 Spaniards with ties to Cádiz, who controlled governing institutions and the consulado and who favored monopoly and profited from contraband, were losing ground to creoles, who were bent, as were some prominent Mexicans, on liberalizing trade and limiting monarchy. Particularly vocal and active were a group of young radicals finding leaders in Belgrano, Juan José Castelli, Mariano Moreno, and Vieytes. Some of them, while considering what is often termed the mask of Ferdinand VII necessary to retain popular adhesion and British protection against France, flirted with an American regency under Ferdinand's sister, Carlota, the wife of John VI of Portugal, recently arrived in Río de Janeiro. These radicals and some of the more moderate creoles convinced the new viceroy, Baltasar Hidalgo de Cisneros, to open ports to British trade in order to keep afloat the creole merchants and the royal treasury.[14] In this endeavor, another representation was drawn, probably by Moreno and Belgrano, in the name of the ranchers and farmers of La Plata, stating that only the consulado profited under the old closed system of trade, and declaring that well-treated colonists would not revolt, that it was not excess of riches and prosperity that had caused British colonists to rebel, but excess of repression, which—and here the analogy was implicit to creoles who had turned away the invading English—had made them take up arms so often before employed in defense of the motherland. The authors refuted the assertion that Britain and the United States protected their own citizens and national economies through preferential duties. They cited Jovellanos (making him sound like a true believer in the invisible hand), Foronda's opinions, and an issue of the Baltimore *Gazette* of 1809 announcing all Spanish consuls authorized to issue patents to "Anglo-American ships to trade with Puerto Rico, Cuba, Maracaibo, La Guaira, and St. Augustine"—intimating that the viceroy should institute the same practice in Buenos Aires.[15] In 1809, too, a subversive tract, circulating in that city, repeated Viscardo's argument, beginning, "The valor with which the English colonies of America fought for their freedom . . . "[16]

Elsewhere, in Chuquisaca (now Sucre), La Paz, Quito, and Bogotá, provincial juntas were set up in 1809 in moves principally for regional autonomy and against both Carlota's pretensions and Spanish administrative and economic centers in America.[17] In Bogotá juntistas, much like earlier comuneros in New Granada, advocated equality with European Spaniards and economic reform, and they cited North America as a model. Camilo Torres, who was then an adviser to the cabildo and is known as the ideologue of the New Granadan movement, in a widely circulated tract called for "a restitution of our monarchy to its primitive constitutional bases, a federation of provinces" and for an American cortes. He pronounced the United States Constitution "the wisest under heaven," and suggested imitating North American government and especially the union of small and big provinces. Torres also blamed Spain for squandering American wealth which, he said astutely, "goes to nourish peoples more industrious, better governed, better educated, less oppressed, and more liberal" (a probable reference to England and the United States), to make Europe more arrogant, and to be buried in China, Japan, and "Indostan."[18] His compatriot and former student, Ignacio de Herrera, repeated the old criticisms, made by the comuneros and others, of Spanish law in the Indies and its complexities, of administrative abuses, Indian tributes, and monopolies. Yet, Herrera's outlook also attested to a growth in sophistication concerning economic affairs, for although he wanted monopolies abolished, rather than free trade he urged that the government protect commerce for the benefit of Spanish Americans, and protect their industries in order to lessen the large number of unemployed vagrants.[19] Here and elsewhere, such appeals for emulation both reflected a desire to attract North American approval and were often tinged with assertive competitiveness. Thus, during the unsuccessful revolt in Potosí that year, a proclamation directed to the populace repeated the old cry, "Let us show our brethren of North America that we are equally as free, as independent, and as happy as they, or perish in the attempt!"[20] And from Quito—where Montúfar, the Marqués de Selva Alegre, was the core of the junta of 1809, whose members advocated eventual constitutional monarchies in America and opposed government by the Spanish-born—a creole wrote that the change had occurred with a peacefulness that was a triumph for the revolution and outshone the example of Philadelphia.[21]

Chilenos during 1808 and 1809 looked to the new Spanish junta for freedom from Buenos Aires, and especially from Lima. Although the *Gacetas* of Procopio circulated, Chileans then preferred and expressed, says one scholar, a heady sense of a new equality within the empire. He might have added they saw theirs was a liberal interpretation of the imperial system. Salas and Rojas were then among those sustaining "the constitution of monarchy" and the cabildo of Santiago as *the* royal representative. Yet by 1809 Cruz, secretary of the consulado, was advocating balanced and truly free trade, saying that although it would hurt Spain, most Chilean imports were not Spanish anyway. Yet when in that year Chileans got a whiff of open trade, they found shops overflowing with British merchandise coming from Buenos Aires. And Cruz then remarked, "Can one see without rancor that England returns our copper to us finished?"[22] By the end of 1809, only La Plata was independent of Spanish governors, and it was intent upon extending its authority to Paraguay, Uruguay, the internal provinces, and to Chile, if possible. In a statement intended to attract Chile to the patriot cause, Dr. Antonio de Alvear, referring to the beauty of federation, used the North American analogy: "Thus New York, Philadelphia. . . all the United States peoples, and provinces," he wrote, "is the only target. . . the only love, of Anglo-American patriotism"[23]

In Spain, the regency, having called for a cortes including deputies from the American colonies and faced with Spanish America having thirteen million people while Spain had a population of ten and a half million, decided each peninsular province should elect four deputies and each overseas province one. It thereby gave the lie to continued expression of complete equality. It added fuel to American autonomist sentiments, fed anger at Spanish arrogance, and gave further impetus to Americans establishing their own governing juntas independent of the regency and to their setting up some independent even of the monarchy.[24]

A chain of American revolts during 1810 ousted Spanish authorities. Caraqueños deposed their captain-general in April, creoles in Buenos Aires their viceroy in May, bogotaños theirs in July, and in September Chileans achieved the resignation of the Spanish captain general (inaugurating the *patria vieja* of 1810 to 1814), while in the provinces of New Spain Hidalgo called into being what became a nationwide social revolution. The following year Quito rose and Venezuela and New Granada declared absolute independence. Paraguay was independent from 1811.

Some Spanish liberals in 1811 and 1812 advocated force against American dissidents, and in September 1811 the regency agreed to accept the help of the Cádiz consulado in funding and transporting troops to America to quell revolt, in exchange for clamping down on Spanish America's freedom to trade. Ferdinand VII, returning in 1814, abolished the Constitution of 1812 and reasserted the principles of Bourbon legitimacy and authoritarian monarchy. By late 1815, Spanish authority was being reimposed in America. Decisive viceroys from Mexico City and Lima, with Spanish and American troops, had defeated Morelos as well as Hidalgo and had reconquered New Granada and Venezuela, although not Caracas. Yet those creoles—mostly lawyers and priests—who had sat in the Cortes of Cádiz and worked on the liberal Constitution of 1812, carried American complaints to Spain and aired them during deliberations which, publicized in the official gazette and other accounts, continued to circulate widely in Spanish America.[25]

During Spain's experiment with a constitution, Americans had found they held grievances in common. They had felt hopes rise for equality within a constitutional monarchy, then die when, before 1814, purportedly liberal Spaniards did not grant them either equal political representation or equality in the trade between America and Cádiz and Madrid. Americans had appropriated Spanish revolutionary language. They had come to realize that American survival did not depend on Spanish, and they saw Spaniards continuing to view Americans, humiliatingly, as colonists. Americans had enjoyed a taste of self-government, political and social supremacy, and greater economic freedom. The Spanish swing to the right in 1814, and severe treatment of American insurgents, pushed Spanish Americans more decidedly to the left, or at least to an America right—in both senses.

During this first round of Spanish American revolts, as the Spanish emissary, Luis de Onís, who succeeded Foronda in 1809, reported, the United States treated the situation in Spain and its colonies as civil war, and its citizens traded with all factions. From 1810 to 1816, United States policy unofficially favored the insurgents, as did public opinion; yet, New England and New York then dealt largely with Spain, and Baltimore with Spanish America, and sentiments in those areas roughly correlated with commerce. From 1809 to 1813, those commercial sectors with more interest in the peninsular trade were at odds with Madison's policy—in part based on viewing Britain as chief competitor—of cooperating with France in Spanish America. Moreover, this cooperation aroused British hostility and took his country toward the War of 1812. Although American trade with Latin America picked up after 1809, it never regained its ascendancy. British exports to America had tripled in 1808 and continued to expand through the 1820s. The war did heighten national feeling and unity in the United States and contribute to the continuation of rapid growth of manufacturing, especially cottons, which had begun with Jefferson's embargo.[26]

In 1810, as we have seen, in line with official policy Jefferson appealed to a hemisphere-embracing mystique, and United States agents were sent to Latin America—Robert K. Lowry to La Guaira; Joel Poinsett to Buenos Aires, Chile, and Peru; and William Shaler, who had a decade earlier carried republican propaganda to South America and up the Pacific coast, was to go to Havana and Vera Cruz. Spanish American agents were permitted to purchase supplies in the United States. Manuel Torres, in Philadelphia since the 1790s, acted as liaison between newly arrived creoles and a number of North Americans—merchants, bankers, publicists, and mercenaries—as well as the United States government. In 1810 he introduced an agent from Venezuela, Juan Vicente Bolívar, Simón's brother, to Stephen Girard, who got the caraqueños a cargo of arms and subsequently sponsored attempts by Torres and Venezuelan and Buenos Aires agents to buy stockpiled weapons from government arsenals—a sale Monroe refused.[27]

Another Venezuelan in Philadelphia, Manuel García de Sena, in 1811 published his *La independencia de la Costa Firme, justificada por Tomás Paine treinta años ha*. It included excerpts from Paine, the Declaration of Independence, the Articles of Confederation, the United States Constitution, and the constitutions of Massachusetts, Connecticut, New Jersey, Pennsylvania, and Virginia. His purpose, he announced in the preface, was "nothing contrary to our religion," but was to enlighten his fellow citizens regarding the legitimacy and the benefits of independence, as demonstrated in the social, political, and economic system of the United States. The state constitutions, he went on, gave "man in society the place corresponding to his class, leaving him in entire liberty... which before had appeared to me incompatible with public tranquility and order,'' and that the United States had ''a government near the most beautiful that has ever existed on earth.'' His *Historia concisa de los Estados Unidos* came out in the same city the following year, its prologue asserting that ''our cause is identical'' and that the present circumstances of Spanish America were ''analogous to those of this country when it tried to remove the yoke of Great Britain''; and ending ''Happy then when from the cold land of Labrador to the far end of Tierra del Fuego nothing will be seen but congresses.''[28] Sena's compendiums had a powerful impact, as we shall see, on political thought and constitutions in Spanish America. Also published in Philadelphia in 1811 were demands made by American delegates in the Spanish Cortes for equal political representation and for free trade with Cádiz and Madrid. Their editor was a Cuban, José Alvárez de Toledo, who had represented Santo Domingo in the Cortes and had come to America, he said, on behalf of the creole deputies to promote revolution in northern Mexico.[29]

In 1811 Monroe and Madison unofficially backed and abetted revolution in Texas and Mexico, in a plan that had probably taken shape with the arrival in Washington that fall of the Mexican José Bernardo Gutiérrez de Lara, a merchant from Revilla and emissary from Hidalgo, who spoke to Monroe.[30] William Shaler, refused admission as United States agent in Vera Cruz, and then barred from Cuba on suspicion of being a French spy, proceeded to New Orleans where the governor, W. C. C. Claiborne, lodged him with Gutiérrez. There Toledo joined them, and introduced the old revolutionary, Picornell. These men then began another series of attempts from the United States to separate Mexico from Spain. Gutiérrez, with Shaler's advice and help, recruited mostly North Americans in Natchitoches; then with them he took San Antonio where, Shaler subsequently heard, he had massacred Spanish officers and was looting and living like a pasha. Shaler saw to it that Toledo replaced the Mexican, until a Spanish reoccupation ended the ephemeral republic of Texas. This fiasco, like previous and future ones, does not seem to have dimmed the hopes of Mexican dissidents that the United States would yet prove a source of liberation.[31]

With war in 1812, United States official and public interest, except in the Texas area, waned. The United States had by then taken Baton Rouge and much of Spanish West Florida, and by 1813 it had advanced as far east as Mobile. In 1814 Jackson invaded East Florida, in order to keep Pensacola from the English, and by 1815 his country occupied all of the Spanish Floridas west of the Perdido River. The first North American war against Britain had brought Latin America closer to the new nation; the second one, other than geographically, reversed the process. Yet, although it lessened commercial and political contact, some influential Americans, especially Baltimore merchants, and some periodicals continued to keep the other Americas in the public eye. Spanish American agents, and Torres in particular, had a good press, and they wrote and lobbied aggressively and ceaselessly.[32] An official attitude of benevolent neutrality toward Latin America continued with the end of the war in 1815. Arthur Whitaker sees it as a policy of nonbelligerency and watchful waiting, deliberately intended to aid the separatists—a policy based on the realization that Europe after Vienna presented a potential threat to the United States.[33] It should be added that in 1815 and 1816, with Spanish American patriot fortunes at their nadir, only Buenos Aires seemed to have a cause worth supporting. Yet with peace, public interest in Spanish American affairs mounted. North American ships and men were at liberty. Spanish American agents issued letters of marque. Vessels were fitted out in United States ports under the flags of Cartagena, Venezuela, Mexico, and Buenos Aires.

Although in September 1815 Madison, wary of the upsurge in enthusiasm for revolutionary enterprise, forbade exporting arms and ammunition to Spanish America, still, as Monroe informed Onís, the country's laws allowed private commerce with the separatists and permitted patriot ships to enter its ports. Moreover, in the Southwest sentiment was still strong for Mexican independence; and with South America in dissarray, its agents in the United States decided upon a joint venture to promote separation of Mexico as the first step toward that of all Spain's dominions. Among the distinguished creoles who had come north on behalf of Bolívar were the Venezuelans Manuel Palacio Fajardo and Pedro Gual; Gual's father and uncle had conspired against Spain in 1797. Gual was in touch with Toledo in late 1815, and the Mexican agent José María de Herrera was in contact with William Davis Robinson, who had become a publicist for the separatists, and with José Miguel Carrera, the Chilean leader then in exile in Bueno Aires, and *his* friend, Poinsett.[34] As United States officials grew more cautious, these creoles, with little left to lose, in 1816 would initiate a series of expeditions from the United States meant to free their homelands.

Conversely, within Spanish America in the years from 1810 to 1816, North Americans, including official agents who went beyond their instructions, promoted independence. Insurgent leaders sought United States aid and supplies, and that country continued to represent a complex of aspirations and fears. In Venezuela, in April 1810 landed aristocrats—called by one historian *"los grandes cacaos"*—consulado members, and small proprietors joined in revolt. They were certain that the intendant was a contrabandista who would never put into effect the Spanish order for opening trade with neutrals, and furious because their products for export were piling up and rotting and their funds being expropriated through forced loans. Probably egged on by the Englishman John Robertson (a provocateur and entrepreneur sent by the English governor of Curacao) and by Lowry of the United States, they deposed the intendant and formed a junta centered on the cabildo. Made aware by their agent in Philadelphia, José Rafael Revenga—and probably by Lowry as well—that separation from Spain was a precondition of United States aid, and under pressure from radicals, including Miranda, centered in the patriotic society, in 1811, on July 5, they declared independence. In an earlier act, on April 25, 1810, that junta had established trade with neutrals, subject to stipulated tariffs. It had been requested and drawn up by the consulado, which had also joined in protesting to the Cádiz government new forced loans, as well as in requesting commerce with neutrals.[35] Consulado influence remained strong in the junta during its first year. It was then that Juan Vicente Bolívar and Orea, who had been born in Tenerife and was an exporter, ships' agent, and retailer, were immediately sent to the United States to arrange "a lasting alliance and treaties of commerce"; simultaneously with their arrival in North America, the junta abolished export and import duties, only to restore them shortly afterwards.[36]

Venezuela's Declaration of Independence, which followed reports by Orea from Washington that attitudes in the United States were favorable, closely adhered to the language of that of 1776, so closely that Onís thought it had originally been written in English and edited and sent down by Jefferson—an intriguing notion. Onís saw Jefferson's hand too in the Venezuelan federal constitution of December 1811, its preamble beginning, "We the representatives of the United Provinces...." However that may be, by 1811 Venezuelans were becoming familiar with seminal United States documents, including through Sena's widely distributed compilation. Between 1810 and 1812, too, an Irish resident in Caracas, William Burke, in his series of articles, *"Derechos de la América del Sur y México"* ("Rights of South America and Mexico"), published in the *Gazeta* (printed on a press two British entrepreneurs bought in Trinidad) in order to gain support for the Venezuelan federal constitution, praised North America's progress and its "increase in population, agriculture, manufactures, trade, resources, arts, sciences, and morals, in short in all the means which constitute the power, civilization, happiness, and real glory of a nation."[37] But when he advocated "the Philadelphia Constitution" as a guide to religious toleration, he drew angry rebuttals, also printed in the *Gazeta*, declaring the United States, although it enjoyed certain advantages, a government without God or religious law, and its people "a vast lodge of freemasons" occupied only with material matters.[38] Religious toleration, actively promoted by North Americans in Latin America, remained a touchy issue. The view of the United States as principally materialist also continued to be voiced in support of varying domestic positions within Latin America.

Attitudes surfacing during the first stage of revolution in Venezuela and elsewhere in Latin America delimited the general range of sentiments concerning the United States held by Latin Americans throughout the nineteenth century. In 1813, in a letter published in the *Gazeta* and redressing the balance, Simón Bolívar's secretary of state suggested that other Spanish American states employ as models both the United States's and Venezuela's declarations of independence. He also compared Bolívar to Washington (and to William Tell) in bringing a nation suddenly into existence.[39] In 1814, in the ceremony recognizing Bolívar as dictator for the duration of the struggle for independence, the governor of Caracas likened him to Washington and Franklin, as did other speakers.

Bolívar himself, in speaking later of his "short visit to the United States" in 1806, said it was there that "for the first time in my life I saw national liberty."[40] Yet the opinions he expressed concerning the United States varied; they were to prove ambivalent and often expedient, depending on circumstances of time and place. In 1813 he looked to that republic and England as sources for recruits, credit, arms, and supplies, sending agents to both. Dispatched to London was the United States citizen William Walton, whose books subsequently publicized the patriot cause. North Americans, too, privateered under Bolívar's flag and those of other insurgent governments. Yet as early as 1812 he warned, in implicit reference to North American institutions, among others, against emulating foreign or ideal republics instead of viewing government as a pragmatic science, and we shall see shortly how his opinions developed. He did consistently hold to the broad, mystical—indeed, romantic and cosmopolitan—view of America, as he stated it in 1814: "For us, the Patria is America."[41] It was synonymous with his vision of Gran Colombia, and with Miranda's of Colombia, and it embraced only by extension and on occasion Brazil, Haiti, and the United States.[42] Yet, when it suited him Bolívar referred to the common assumption of an inter-American relationship, to the United States and his America as brothers.

In Buenos Aires, radical young members of the patriotic society, disciples of Mariano Moreno who were influenced by the French republic and the example of the United States and who were unhappy with British interference in the port's politics and economy, made the revolution of May 1810. Still, more moderate young freetraders, supported by established creole merchants favoring self-government, soon dominated the new governing junta. Moreno, on May 22, had called a general congress, or cabildo abierto. It had led to replacing the viceroy with that junta, of which he was a member and Belgrano the secretary, and which quickly passed commercial legislation true to the interests of its constituents. It allowed the export of precious metals and export duties on cattle products. Its members in 1811 wrote to President Madison, suggesting treaties of commerce "between nation and nation" and referring to "the two states," thereby, in broaching relations with the United States, elucidating porteño aspirations to sovereignty and nationality.[43] With the lifting of Jefferson's embargo, more North American ships had put in than British, and Poinsett arrived to counter British influence energetically during what, by hindsight, proved to be the high point of United States popularity.[44]

Revolutionary attitudes, and much of the rhetoric dispensed to the public and employed in attempts to assert hegemony over neighboring regions, then coincided and meshed with a positive image of North America. Thus Moreno, explaining the value of propaganda within the course of outlining a plan of operations for porteño agents to follow in exporting revolution to Brazil, mentioned the popular appeal inherent in that well known and respectable revolutionary, Washington. Yet Moreno was far from a consistent admirer of all things North American. In his essentially centralist plan for La Plata, while he wrote glowingly of the federated system of the United States, and of that of the Swiss, he thought them unsuitable to South America. (In much the same spirit, one of limited imitation, he published a translation of Rousseau's *Social Contract*, but wanted voting limited to the educated.) It was the old style of Hispanic argument, made through appeal to the right authorities, with modifications appropriate to time and place, a scholastic device continually employed by peninsular and creole lawyers and publicists. Moreno went on to make an apparent about-face in November, in the *Gaceta de Buenos Aires*, when, in citing Jefferson's *Notes on Virginia* describing Indian social and political organization as federative, he declared that system admirable. In August 1811, disenchanted and ill, his power eroded, he returned to an earlier theme, but now in lament: "Where, noble and great Washington, are the lessons of your policy?"[45]

By 1813 Buenos Aires envoys had returned from the United States with one thousand guns obtained, it was commonly thought, through the agency of Monroe. Sena's book, translating North American constitutions and Paine's writings, was well known, and his translation of the Articles of Confederation and the Constitution of 1787 had appeared in the *Gaceta*; a radical republican, Bernardo Monteagudo, in his "Reflection," published during July and August that year, averred the institutional mechanisms of the United States were dominant in La Plata.[46] Stephen Girard's and John Jacob Astor's ships en route to Canton had put in; DeForest returned, purchased nutria pelts for Astor, and found his old associate, the Catalan-born Larrea, in favor under Bernardo Rivadavia, and he himself became an honorary citizen. Similarly, William P. White and the United States consul, Thomas Lloyd Halsey, were dabbling in commerce and local politics. Halsey, who had resided in Buenos Aires since 1807, invested in privateers and issued blank commissions. Although the War of 1812 stopped trade between the Americas, these men continued to prosper. When White was commissioned by Larrea, the secretary of the treasury, to raise a navy to blockade the royalists holding Montevideo, DeForest joined in. White and DeForest acquired United States merchant ships and the services of British deserters and of an Irish captain, and this assemblage took Montevideo. Well supplied with booty, DeForest afterwards expanded into retailing. And on his return to the United States, he sold Argentine letters of marque for privateers.[47]

Yet, from the end of 1813 porteños reversed their position of seven years earlier. Now, fearing a Spanish invasion, they counted on British protection, and Britain, shut out of Europe and the United States in 1812, and pushing its Latin American trade, received preferential treatment in Buenos Aires, as well as in Venezuela and Brazil. Masterminded by the minister to Brazil, Lord Strangford, the British kept up a counterattack on American influence, in general abetted by Carlota and by the fact that from 1814 porteño leaders favored a constitutional monarchy like Britain's in order to ensure unity and stability. During the War of 1812, British merchants and retailers took over in Buenos Aires and the interior; reliance on England probably held up the declaration of Argentine independence, until 1816. Although United States vessels returned after 1815, and DeForest resumed shipping out nutria skins to Astor in exchange for cargoes of munitions and naval supplies, United States prestige and trade were on the wane. By then, too, its competition was evident for Havana's wheat market.[48]

Yet, while political and economic considerations turned porteños from the United States, provincial leaders in La Plata, as some did elsewhere, found its example a bulwark of precedent for regional autonomy against the port's bid for hegemony. José Gervasio Artigas, now hailed as father of Uruguayan independence, was in Buenos Aires with Moreno in 1810. It was Artigas who, in instructing provincial delegates to the La Plata convention of 1813 to support absolute independence and strong regional autonomy, thereby brought on their exclusion from that congress by porteño centralists. He looked to United States models in those instructions and in his project of a constitution for the *banda oriental*, now Uruguay. Artigas was probably influenced by Sena's compendium, and from 1813 he was close to Halsey. His proposed constitution cited those of Massachusetts and Pennsylvania and began, "Since all men are born free and equal...." and it listed as rights, which it was the duty of the government to ensure, the enjoying and defending of life and liberty; acquiring, possessing, and protecting property; and seeking and obtaining security and happiness.[49] What these excerpts reveal of both the differences from and similarities to United States models is instructive, particularly the quasi-patrimonial view of government and the emphasis on property and security. Up river, in Paraguay, a congress rebuffed porteño overtures and sent to Buenos Aires on July 20, 1811 a constitutionlike reglamento declaring Paraguay "autonomous or independent within the Spanish Amerian empire." It may have influenced Artigas's instructions of 1813 and, like them, may have itself had some North American precedents. That year too in Asunción Dr. Francia took an engraving of Franklin from a wall of his study and presented it to the porteño envoys, Belgrano and Echevarría.[50]

In Chile, the first echo of North American political credos sounded in a commercial document. On November 9, 1810 the national junta instructed the consulado to propose a plan for "free trade," directing that "it should not imperil our industries" but should provide outlets for products. The resulting law, of February 21, 1811, allowed but regulated more open trade; it permitted the government broad powers to rule and regulate in order to benefit and promote the country's industry, and it also bore more than a slight resemblance to United States precedents, for it began, "All men have certain inalienable rights which the Creator has given them in order to ensure their happiness, prosperity, and well being...."[51] That junta exhibited a great enthusiasm for United States institutions, and it had Juan Egaña draw up a project for a constitution. His consequent *Declaración de los derechos del pueblo de Chile* ("Declaration of the Rights of the People of Chile") contained a plan of confederation for all America.[52] Bernardo O'Higgins, who then emerged as a national leader, supported the calling of a congress and free trade, valuing both as preludes to interesting Chileans in revolution. He received a letter from Juan McKenna expressing similar sentiments, McKenna reminding him that Chilean interest was not in "warlike deeds and miraculous escapades, but in the amounts of wheat and potatoes, cheese and butter a man could produce."[53] During this initial period of Chilean independence, O'Higgins cited the United States Constitution on the election of representatives and went on to make his own amalgam of the Bill of Rights and other North American governing documents.[54]

Two of Girard's ships put in at Chile in 1811; other United States vessels brought in dry goods, spirits, playing cards, and naval stores and took away copper and bullion. Although the war stopped merchant shipping, whalers continued to ply southern waters. From 1812 through 1814, too, a United States warship under Captain David Porter patrolled the coasts, endeavoring to protect American whalers from the British and their loyalist allies in Peru.[55] Poinsett journeyed on to

Santiago and was soon close to Salas and to O'Higgins's rival, José Miguel Carrera, among others, and he collaborated with them in preparing the Chilean Constitution of 1812. Poinsett urged Carrera to buy supplies from United States merchants, was responsible for the purchase of two North American ships to be used as privateers, and, in April 1813, rode in with Chilean troops, in Chilean uniform, to free Nantucket seamen held by Spaniards at Talcahuano. An irate Englishman in La Plata reported home, "That Firebrand Mr. Poinsett is as busy as a Fiend in contaminating the whole population on that side of the continent."[56] A press and three printers imported from the United States then turned out the major gazette, the *Aurora de Chile*. Its editor, Camilo Henríquez, another friend of Poinsett's, educated in Lima with Baquíjano and other liberals, passionately espoused liberty and praised the United States in nearly every issue. He dilated on the glories of North America and held up the American Revolution to Chileans as "a sacred fire of liberty illuminating the continent."[57]

Colombian independence began as a coup in Bogotá in 1810, by men affiliated with the botanical expedition and literary societies who, in a style becoming customary, formed a junta (nominally dependent upon the Spanish Council of Regency), which called a constitutional electoral assembly. In a document explaining why they did it, two juntistas, Camilo Torres and Frutos Joaquín Gutiérrez de Caviedes, stated as reasons the failure of the Bourbon reforms coupled with widespread economic misery. They cited Augustine on the contractual origin of political society and its concomitant, popular sovereignty, and Aquinas in asserting that it was the right of people, according to the law of nations, to unite against oppression in a just, defensive war—arguments echoing those put forth from 1808 by earlier creole separatists and by Spanish juntas. The manifesto went on to describe Spanish America much as had critical residents for a long while, and as did dissident creoles everywhere, as "an immense land where government does not permit the sciences, nor arts, nor agriculture, nor commerce, where schools, factories, industry, and work are lacking, and where people are reduced to a servile state, not free except to sow a little wheat or maize, and to raise some cattle. Americans must buy all goods at highest prices instead of producing them."[58] Its authors recalled that Spanish commercial monopoly, breached only by contraband, had isolated the colonies economically and regionally until the eighteenth century, when Spain had tried to diversify colonial economies in order to expand its own trade. Economic barriers in European markets and Spain's lack of capacity to supply the colonies with manufactures had doomed the reforms, making it necessary for Americans now "to resume the rights of sovereignty." This clearsighted look at the nature of American disaffection is one more indication that leading colonial separatists, while appealing to respected political theory, also voiced their grievances, and couched their manifestoes and appeals for support, strongly in economic terms and most urgently sought relief from economic distress. They foresaw rapid material and moral advance with self-government.

In New Granada, as in other areas long dependent on Spain and its older viceregal centers, Mexico and Peru, where in 1810 and 1811 the domestic centralist-federalist controversy had not yet crystallized, the recent history of the

United States was often invoked. José Ignacio de Pombo, as prior of the consulado of Cartagena, drew up a plan concerning the commerce of all New Granada and presented it to the Bogotá junta. It paralleled that body's sentiments, as expressed by Torres and Gutiérrez. In opposing export taxes on agricultural products, Pombo referred to "the wise system of the United States, its prosperity and rapid growth, and the happiness of its inhabitants," and he cited a message of Jefferson's to Congress in support of abolishing internal duties. He counseled removing governmental monopolies, citing the untrammeled growth of Cuba's sugar industry. He urged promoting raising coffee, as well as expanding cotton production through using machines to clean it like those recently invented in the United States.[59] His nephew, Miguel de Pombo, who had participated in the botanical expedition, and had distinguished himself as an orator and fervent partisan of emancipation, became a member of the Bogotá junta and published there in 1811 a book containing a translation of the United States Constitution, other North American governing instruments, and economic data. He asserted the superiority of New Granada's condition over that of the thirteen colonies in 1776 and claimed their subsequent growth to be a result of federalism. His attitude was agrarian, romantic, and broadly American. That Constitution, he wrote, "has promoted the happiness of our brothers of the North and will promote our happiness also, if we imitate their virtues and adopt their principles."[60] He praised Washington and Franklin as "legislators of the New World" and invoked their examples and a spirit of broad hemispheric patriotism.

The confederation the provinces of New Granada formed in 1811 was avowedly modeled on the early United States. Each province drew up its own constitution, with many borrowings from North America. But by 1811 Nariño, once so ardent in his admiration of United States as well as French republican political institutions, was among the centralists opposed to so loose a system. He governed in Bogotá in 1811 with dictatorial powers, and in October, adumbrating Bolívar, expressed a change of heart: "The Constitution of the United States is the most perfect which until now has been known; a constitution so perfect in order to be adopted requires enlightenment, virtues, and recourses which we do not have."[61] Again in 1813, when Bogotá declared independence and the New Granada provinces, centered in Cundinamarca, followed its lead on their own, he wrote, "We are not in a condition of comparison with some peoples who are always free." Yet, later he came full circle, pronouncing, "Federalism is an epidemic sickness [affecting] all Spanish America through the contagion of English America."[62]

While the old viceregal centers, Mexico and Peru, remained under Spanish viceroys through the early years of general revolt in Spanish America, in both of them uprisings took place and independence gained adherents.[63] The revolt led by Hidalgo in September 1810 began as a popular, regional rising in the Bajío, a variant on the tendency toward provincial autonomy, but it was more populist and ethnically mixed, and it was more inspired by xenophobia, hatred of peninsular Spaniards, and fear of invasion than were South American creole coups of that year, and it became national in scope. It grew more radical, frightened creoles, and ultimately failed. Hidalgo, a middle-aged priest, was less an enlightened liberal than a holdover from the more radical social visionaries of the 1780s and 1790s. And Allende, who shared direction of the movement, was of the creole gentry, a militia officer and gentleman of dwindling fortune, who had taken part, it will be recalled, in war maneuvers and in protecting border areas expecting invasion from the United States.

The Mexican insurgents initially expressed admiration for the United States—its heroes and institutions—and they sought its help. Their periodical, the *Despertador Americano*, in its first issue and frequently thereafter proclaimed Hidalgo *''el nuevo Washington''* sent to Mexico by God.[64] Hidalgo not only dispatched agents to the United States for support and aid, but in defeat attempted to reach refuge there. Allende, in the last days of the revolt, during February 1811, declared that the only hope of success lay in help from the United States. Both he and Hidalgo were captured and executed. José María Morelos carried on in much the same spirit, also sending emissaries to Washington. When the Mexican government failed to put into effect the Constitution of Cádiz, he was joined by some of the creoles who had participated in popular municipal elections during 1812 and were determined to form a nativistic government. They collaborated in drafting the 1813 declaration of independence and the Constitution of Apatzingán. The latter reflected some influence from the United States and more from France, but was primarily fashioned on the Spanish Constitution of 1812. Among these men was Carlos María Bustamante, who then hoped for help from the United States; and, even after Morelos was captured and executed in 1815, such hopes lingered among Mexicans seeking independence.[65]

By the end of 1815, Spain had regained power in much of America. Bolívar then stated with some truth his opinion that warfare between the United States and Britain was responsible for that sad state of affairs—for the conflict had interrupted Spanish American commerce with the United States, depriving patriots of supplies and matériel. But for United States involvement in the War of 1812, he concluded, ''Venzuela singlehandedly would have triumphed, and South America would not have been devastated by Spanish cruelty nor destroyed by revolutionary anarchy.''[66] It is, while too simple a conclusion, an interesting conjecture.

The tide turned in 1816. Separatists attracted widespread support and, in 1824, under Bolívar in the north and José de San Martín in the south, fought their way to complete independence from Spain. On July 9, 1816, in a document emulating the Philadelphia decree, the United Provinces of Río de La Plata, headed by Buenos Aires, declared independence. In 1818, winning the battle of Maipú, San Martín freed Chile. In 1819, Bolívar was named President by the Venezuelan Congress at Angostura, and New Granada announced its liberation. Quito followed in 1822 and, with the defeat of the Spanish army in Peru in 1824, all Spanish America was free. Brazil took another, bloodless route, when the prince, Dom Pedro, proclaimed independence in 1822 and became Pedro I, Emperor of Brazil. In this second stage of revolution there was a retreat from radical democracy and much elaborating of constitutions, as well as of political and philosophical theory, and much drawing upon United States institutions. As we have seen, a widespread knowledge of North American republicanism and constitutive documents preceded these developments, and Sena's books and other publicity for United States institutions may well have been the source for the texts of most of the written instruments bringing into formal existence the Spanish American nations.[67] Yet the concept of constitution itself had Spanish provenance as well, and British. From 1816, too, leaders became more authoritarian in response to the demands of war and, preferring strong executive authority both as part of that response and within hispanic centralist tradition, even championed monarchy, most often on the British model.

During this period in the United States, where the sort of protection furnished by war and the protective tariff of 1816 had spurred larger-scale manufacturing, a more general interest again arose in Latin America, especially as a market for the growing textile industry and for surplus war supplies. And, as a speaker in Congress put it, rather optimistically, "United States textiles plus rational liberty equals the exclusion of European influence from Latin America."[68] Even in New England, which had previously found economic advantages in attachment to the Spanish cause, the new *North American Review* exclaimed with gusto, "Our example has animated the Spanish American provinces to declare themselves independent!"[69] Its editors undoubtedly took into account the absolutist regime in Spain and its ties to the reactionary concert of Europe, and perhaps were also responding to the rising vogue for romanticism. The new administration—Monroe was president—remained benevolent toward the rebels. He pointedly informed Onís that United States laws allowed private commerce with separatists and patriot ships to enter United States ports.[70]

Spanish American agents in Philadelphia—among them Orea, Manuel Torres, Gual, Roscio, Revenga, Toledo, and later Vicente Pazos Kanki, an Aymará from Upper Peru, and Vicente Rocafuerte, best described as a cosmopolite from Guayaquil—continued to publicize the cause. In 1816, some of them agreed on an invasion of Mexico from the United States, to be led by Javier Mina, a Spanish liberal and a hero of the patriot struggle against France, who had been recruited by Mier. Mina's expedition, although initially successful, ultimately failed. The agents then turned to an alternate project: to gain strategic control of the Caribbean and the Gulf of Mexico through occupation of Amelia Island off Florida.[71] Monroe and his secretary of state, John Quincy Adams, initially conceded to Gregor McGregor, a soldier of fortune retained by the Spanish American agents, a commission to take Amelia, but when slaves and contraband flowed from the island to Georgia and it became a haven for raids on United States shipping, Monroe ordered McGregor's occupation ended by United States troops. An immediate result was that in 1817 Monroe signed a neutrality act prohibiting belligerents buying arms from private individuals in the United States; but, reconsidering, on April 20, 1818 he issued a new neutrality act, its terms more favorable to the patriots.[72]

Insurgent victories in La Plata and Chile (presented to the American government by the porteño agent Aguirre as "following the example of their brothers and natural friends of North America") by then had brought officials in Washington to consider using commercial treaties as an indirect form of recognition, much like the procedure France had inaugurated fifty years earlier with the incipient United States.[73] The cabinet, however, demurred when certain leading Cubans proposed independence, annexation, and statehood, for its members foresaw that the result might be war with Spain and Britain. Adams, on a divergent tack, felt the eventual annexation of Cuba "indispensable to the continuance and integrity of the Union itself," but that the rest of Latin America would become economically competitive with his country.[74] In the same period, during the congressional debates on the neutrality law of 1817, Samuel Smith of Maryland, who had begun taking a commercial interest in Latin America as an aide to Robert Morris during the American Revolution, opposed promoting Spanish American independence, arguing that the United States suffered from competition even then with the new regimes, and that Chilean flour was underselling American in Brazil and the West Indies. Henry Clay, who was gaining a name as champion of the cause of Spanish American independence through advocating hemispheric American freedom from despotism in Europe, countered by implying that Smith had just received a valuable trading license from the Spanish government.[75]

These differences, the airing of Spanish American factional disputes, and rumor of the audacious guarantee of a two million dollar loan to La Plata—made by Halsey in the name of the United States—caused Monroe, in a play for time, to send a special commission to southern South America. Its three members returned from visiting La Plata and Chile in 1818 with differing reports, achieving little in promoting either better relations or mutual understanding. Its most voluble spokesman, Henry M. Brackenridge, wrote books on South America before and after the journey. In his first, published in 1817, he referred to "a common American continental interest" and proposed that the United States gain the honor of recognizing the new states, thereby forwarding both republicanism and North American commerce; he also prophesied that "the United States will be the natural head of the New World." As such, he was certain, it could not offend anyone, but would remain an elder state with a more numerous, homogeneous, active, and enlightened population, its leadership resulting "from a greater disinterestedness and regard to justice and love of peace."[76] Yet upon his return, he and the other commissioners, all of whom initially had favored Spanish American independence, did agree in recommending no immediate recognition of the faction-ridden regimes of Buenos Aires and Chile.

In 1818 Clay campaigned to have the new governments recognized. His plea included the argument that recognition would provide markets for American shipping and manufactures. Although Western members supported the measure, it was voted down by Congress. The press, in approving the vote, cited the following reasons for preferring a wait-and-see stance: Clay's political designs, disputes among Spanish American agents, monarchist tendencies among patriots, continuing doubts of Spanish American ability for self-government, public disillusion due to commission reports, and the great importance of trade with Cuba and Spain. It was, too, a time of negotiation with Spain over acquisition of the Floridas (of special interest to the South and West) and adjustment of commercial claims (sought by the East).[77] Then in 1819 the Adams-Onís treaty was signed, in 1821

Clay gained a congressional vote of sympathy with Latin America, and in 1822 the government resolved to recognize the de facto independence of new American states. Recognition by then could be construed as a neutral act—for Adams it was an extending of disengagement from Europe—where in 1817 and 1818 it would have been obviously interventionist. Yet seen in broadest perspective, official delay in recognition was due primarily not to the government's desire to secure Florida first, but to assessments of the international situation and the position within it of the United States.[78] Moreover, from 1820, protection and promotion of the country's trade with Latin America was a major governmental concern, as was Britain's successful competition for that trade. For by 1822, the volume and value of United States commerce with Latin America was less than half England's. The United States only conserved its advantage with Cuba. British trade was accompanied by a good deal of capital. None was forthcoming from the United States, then turning its energies to the West.[79]

By the 1820s the idea of two spheres, Europe and America, was commonplace in both the United States and Latin America, and it was undoubtedly fed by United States commercial rivalry with Britain and by Spanish American fear of renewed European domination. The Monroe Doctrine of 1823 evolved naturally from this idea and other current assumptions, and was an immediate and unilateral response to a combination of international concerns and domestic issues. Monroe, Adams, and Clay, among others, then favored territorial expansion on the continent and commerce, especially to find markets for United States goods. They feared not only British commercial dominance in Latin America but also European aggression there, including an English assault on Cuba and Puerto Rico.

European aggression was also of concern to the United States in the form of connections and influence on institutions, especially in Buenos Aires. The doctrine, conceived by Monroe and Adams, was an announced stand against not only territorial designs but also European commercial and ideological penetration of the other Americas. It went beyond de facto recognition of Latin American independence to assert the proposition, contained in the instructions to Richard Rush, minister to England, of November 20, 1823, that it was "the unaltered determination" of the United States not to interfere in European affairs, but that "American affairs, whether of the Northern or the Southern Continent, can henceforth not be excluded from the interference of the United States." It was both a warning to Europe that would set precedent for future relations with Latin America and the asserting of an independent balance of power.[80] Privately, in September of 1820, Adams had vented his feelings: "As to an American system, we have it; we constitute the whole of it; there is no community of interests or of principles between North and South America. Mr. Torres and Bolívar and O'Higgins talk about an American system...but there is no basis for such a system."[81] Yet his instructions of May 27, 1822 to Richard C. Anderson and Caesar Rodney, who headed the first legations in Latin America, modified that outburst and affirmed the idea of "a combined system of total and unqualified independence of Europe."[82] In others to Rodney, dated May 18, Adams preferred that all American nations be governed by republican institutions and, again, be politically and commercially independent of Europe. The United States wanted no special privileges, but did want to be a most-favored nation. He then opposed the United States presiding over a meeting of the Americas, but subsequently favored sending representatives to the Pan-American Congress of 1826, as we shall see.

After 1823, commercial rivalry with England intensified, as did the new European rage for Latin American investments. And the principle of open trade suffered when, at the behest of Clay and others, Congress enacted a high tariff to protect manufactures, particularly in order to compete with Britain in Latin America. For peace and liberty brought a decline of Latin American purchases of North American food and matériel—Buenos Aires excluded American flour, and only Colombia, the United Provinces of Central America, and Brazil signed reciprocal commercial treaties—and in fact Latin America was becoming more of a competitor in producing foodstuffs and raw materials. Brazil, however, at war with Argentina, needed provisions so that in 1825 only United States trade with Cuba, still Spanish, exceeded that with Portuguese America. Brazil also, responding to the Monroe Doctrine, was the first Latin American nation to request recognition. It was forthcoming, but Adams and Clay hedged in response to a Brazilian request for clarification of the Doctrine, and they would not be drawn into a Pan-American league against Portugal or into other overt acts of intervention.[83]

Although both men preferred that their nation remain an interested spectator when in 1823 Gual suggested it be included in an American confederation, they responded positively to invitations to attend the Panama conference for a number of reasons. These were listed by Adams in his message to Congress in 1825, and included among them the hopes that the United States might be in a position to advise Spanish Americans, receive commercial advantages, define boundaries and neutral rights, work for the abolition of the slave trade, and advocate religious liberty. He opposed formal United States ties to any individual Latin American nation or to any congress of them. The press agreed. In Congress northern manufacturing and commercial interests favored attendance; proslavery southerners, who were also competitors for markets, opposed it.[84] Moreover, the debates on the issue became a rallying ground for political opposition to Adams, and that opposition got ammunition when Poinsett, as United States minister to Mexico, again rashly blundered in referring to the Doctrine as a pledge to protect Spanish America. Clay, corresponding with Poinsett concerning a commercial treaty with Mexico, first implicitly supported that presentation, then, when antiadminstration forces seized on the issue, declared the Doctrine limited to protecting only United States interests, another diplomatic blunder.[85] The entire incident gave the Doctrine unwise, contradictory interpretations, and, in relation to the spirit of its promulgation, two overly radical and reductionist readings.

Within Latin America in the 1820s not only Poinsett, but other United States emissaries principally grounded in commerce, were unable to resist meddling in politics, and they repeatedly encountered, and chafed under, swelling British predominance in trade and English influence on the new governments. The American chargé in Brazil, Condy Raguet, was only outstandingly brash (and was soon recalled).[86] The problems met in Mexico deserve closer attention. There a spectrum of attitudes toward the United States observable immediately after independence mirrored the interplay of internal politics, economic pressures, and outside influences, much as they did elsewhere in Latin America. When in 1821, a coup brought to power a government in Madrid liberal but dedicated to keeping the colonies dependent, a broad social and political coalition in Mexico agreed on independence. Nobles and high clergy reacted adversely to "the tyranny of the liberal Spanish government"; so did insurgents and the general public. Creole officers, certain that Spain could not maintain stability or protect their country, with general approval installed Agustín Iturbide as a constitutional monarch. It was not solely a conservative reaction to liberal Spain, but was also a broadly national reaction among widely varying social, political, and economic groups united, for differing reasons, in the desire to be free of Spain. Mexicans tended to view the recognition of their independence by the United States as very important, as appearing to confirm that independence in public and world opinion, and as leading to alliance. The news of that recognition was, incidentally, brought to Mexico in the first ship purchased by Iturbide's government in the United States for the new imperial navy.[87]

Iturbide himself, much like Iturrigaray and then the insurgents of 1810, appealed to xenophobia. He warned of encirclement by the Russians in California, the Spaniards in Vera Cruz, and the Indians and the United States to the northeast—although once in power he opened the Mexican north to colonization by Stephen Austin. He also favored close relations with the United States, admired Clay, and accepted advice from the old superagent, James Wilkinson. Wilkinson, in Mexico in 1822—he died there in 1823—published in Spanish his observations on commerce and his reflections on the province of Texas.[88]

Mexican periodicals mentioned the republic to the north in various contexts. In November 1821 the *Semanario Político y Literario*, attempting to influence Iturbide, began a series of Spanish translations of United States political documents. In September Bustamante, in his *La Abispa (The Bee) de Chilpancingo*, excerpted from John Marshall's life of Washington the farewell address and pointedly suggested Iturbide take Washington, rather than classical heroes, as his model, and that he heed how Washington had both resigned his military command and withdrawn from public office. In Mexico City *El Sol*, edited by Alamán, and the offical *Gaceta de Gobierno Imperial de México* printed Monroe's message to the House, of March 8, 1822, on revolution in Spanish America. On May 15, in discussing whether or not Mexicans could achieve a government like that of their northern neighbor, *El Sol* adroitly concluded the nation would be served best by hereditary monarchy. Four days later Iturbide became Agustín I, Emperor of Mexico, and *El Sol*, despite his fancy footwork, was soon suppressed; it reappeared after Iturbide's forced abdication and in its first issue compared him, unfavorably, to Washington.[89]

While absolute monarchy and authoritarianism threatened, Mexican gazettes frequently mentioned the United States government and Washington as a republican symbol, but even before Iturbide's fall, reservations were voiced by the liberal opposition; afterwards, they intensified. When Wilkinson in 1823 gave the Mexican Congress a portrait of Washington by Gilbert Stuart, Bustamante wrote in his diary that he hoped the likeness would inspire imitation; later, in his supplement to the history of Mexico of the exiled Jesuit, Andrés Cavo, he presented the United States as a nation of adventurers.[90] Mier, in Philadelphia in 1821, published his *Memoria política instructiva* to present to Mexicans the United States as a model of republican government and progress and as "our compatriots." Opposing both monarchy and great provincial autonomy, he offered a compromise, republican system he based on adaptation of some United States precedents. Two years later his position had shifted; he described the proposed Mexican constitution of 1823 as a monstrous graft of that of the United States on to that of Cádiz of 1812, and he stated that while the United States was then at the height of its social perfection, Mexicans must change before they could adopt its form of government, and that any mechanical copy was bad.[91]

To the course of Mexican politics and the spectre of United States expansion must be added Britain's rivalry for Mexican trade as souring relations between Mexico and the United States. Poinsett, in Mexico City in 1825 as United States minister, vied for power—unwisely, aggressively, and publicly—with his British counterpart, Henry G. Ward, who had the ear of the government. Poinsett cultivated the liberal opposition and influenced the formation of York Rite masonic lodges, affiliated with the Grand Lodge in New York City, as chief liberal rallying points and political mechanisms, and he may well have engineered an October cabinet revolution through which partisans of the United States temporarily gained the upper hand. *Yorkinos* and the liberal coalition then favored strong protection; powerful among them were representatives of cotton textile workers threatened by imports of cheap British cloth.

Ward, on his part, prevented a commercial treaty and boundary agreement with the United States, impressed Mexicans with the danger of American designs on Texas, played on their fear of United States expansionist ambitions in general, and put it about that Poinsett was instructed to embroil Mexico in civil war in order to ease his nation's acquisition of the provinces north of the Río Bravo. Mexicans resented Poinsett's flatfootedness as well as derogatory remarks Adams had made about their country and American ambitions regarding Cuba and Texas. Britain, preeminent in finance, commerce, and seapower, in the 1820s won the struggle for economic supremacy in Mexico and contributed to escalating hostility toward the former English colonies.[92] Such international jockeying for power was a telling factor in the formative years of United States relations with Mexico, and with all of the Latin American nations.

Earlier, from 1816, relations between La Plata and the United States had followed a similar pattern. That year, the Declaration of Independence of the United Provinces of the Río de La Plata of July 9 closely adhered to its North American prototype. That year, too, DeForest advertised for sale Sena's history of the United States, and, on San Martín's suggestion, copies were used to further the cause in Chile. Brackenridge reported in 1818, if with some exaggeration, that both of Sena's books were known by everyone able to read and produced an extravagant admiration of his country. In letters to North American authorities La Plata leaders stressed the United States as symbol, as well as a common American-ness and a shared cause, love of liberty.

Yet by 1817 a reaction against some specific decisions of the United States was setting in. Its government had disavowed the loan guaranteed in its name by Halsey and had attempted to stop Aguirre's dispatch of two warships to Buenos Aires. Aguirre, whose credentials had compared the United States to "a luminous constellation which indicated the career traced by Providence for the other people of this part of the globe," then wrote to the Supreme Director, Juan Martín Pueyrredón, that the nation's actions favoring South America "will be for the purpose of enriching their merchants."[93] A preference for constitutional monarchy was on the ascendant, with England its obvious model. In 1816 Belgrano proposed, in the tradition of Túpac Amaru and Miranda, an American monarch descended from the Incas.[94] From that year, too, most Buenos Aires trade was with Britain. The enterprising Robinson brothers and other British merchant-adventurers went into the interior. Porteños adopted British dress and decor, and between 1820 and 1822 Bernardo Rivadavia advocated English-type government and corresponded with Jeremy Bentham.[95] In La Plata as a whole, although United States republican ideals remained valued and were employed to fan revolutionary ardor and promote unity, and although the Constitution of 1819 sounded a lot like the Declaration of Independence, the Buenos Aires centralists dominated, and they preferred British trade and protection and the British political system. San Martín, in customary centralist manner, then mentioned the United States in a less complimentary context: "If a country like the United States, with an established government, well-populated, and [skilled in industry,] agriculture, and commerce had so many difficulties under a federal system during the last war with England, what would happen if the provinces of La Plata should become jealous of one another?"[96] One answer to that question is the nineteenth-century history of Argentina, for Buenos Aires continued to fight to establish hegemony over many of the provinces formerly under the viceroy, and it gave most business to England, but many Argentinians, especially provincial ones, continued to pay homage to North American ideals and to be inspired by them.[97]

United States commercial strength and influence in Chile, too, reached a zenith in 1817 and 1818; the republicans there were then spoken of as the North American party, and a number of deserters from United States vessels joined the Chilean navy, some to become its highest officers. From 1818 American influence ebbed. Some of the reasons why, as explained in letters to Monroe from a keen yankee observer, Jeremy Robinson, were unstable customs duties discouraging Ameri-cans, Chilean disappointment in not getting a loan from the United States government, and suspicions of its designs on Florida. The factionalism and high-handedness of members of the commission of 1818 had aroused resentment, as had the activities of other Americans, who were dealing with royalists in Peru and along Chilean coasts, protected by United States warships. So had word that one of those ships, at least—the *Ontario*, commanded by James Biddle—was transporting specie for royalists in Lima. Robinson himself, although without official standing, worked for commercial treaties between Chile and the United States, and he engaged in private speculation. He and the formal representatives of his government in Chile, the special agent, John B. Prevost (who was Burr's stepson), and the consul, William G. D. Worthington, if with less bravado than Poinsett had, meddled in Chilean affairs. Worthington submitted a constitution to O'Higgins and, by 1820, John Quincy Adams recognized Prevost as quite able but fervently partisan toward recognition of Chilean independence. The attempt by Prevost, Biddle, and Robinson to secure the release of two whaling ships impounded by royalists in Chile, one of them sent out by Astor and captained by Richard Cleveland, involved Biddle in unwisely carrying a viceregal agent to Chile aboard his ship. Moreover, by 1820, as Robinson explained, although American merchants were predominant in arming and supplying Chilean patriots, British merchants were more able and willing to extend credit to individuals, and British mercantile shipping was prevailing, the English trade volume expanding, and the majority of Chilean naval officers were British.[98]

In 1818 O'Higgins preferred Alexandre Petion's Declaration of Independence and its affirmation of military and moral power to that of the United States, and by 1822, the last year of his administration, protectionist sentiment was high. The legislature raised duties on imports, and he and others favored a strong state role in the economy. That year Henríquez, once a premier exponent of emulating the United States, observed to Salas that the study of political economy was growing in Buenos Aires and Chile, and he founded the *Mercurio de Chile*, expecting to promote sophistication concerning public finances, debt management, and a national system of public credit—all on English models. Robinson then found that O'Higgins no longer gave importance to the North American connection. He and other Latin American leaders had come to substitute a general concept of America for what the United States had signified earlier. O'Higgins wrote to Henríquez in 1824: "It is evident that the republics of the New World carry the vanguard of liberty of the entire world. . . in the example of America is the highest hopes of philosophy and patriotism."[99] Emerging on the other side of liberty, these men combined republican rhetoric with a new hard look at international relations.

In Lima after 1817, war taxes and loss of Chile and its wheat had forced the viceroy to open Peru's trade to foreign shipping; United States ships not only transported specie, but also supplied both sides with grain and arms. In providing coastal exchange between Chile and Peru, their captains often declared they were clearing for Río, then put in at Callao. In 1821 the viceroy, Joaquín de Pezuela, and his followers abandoned Lima for the interior. By then, young separatists had the backing of some army officers and old constitutionalists, including Unanue. Both loyalists and separatists, however, were rent by factions—the royalists by absolutist and constitutionalist subdivisions, the separatists by monarchists and republicans. Unity was imposed only briefly by San Martín, who was soon out of favor for his aristocratic and monarchist preferences, and then by Bolívar; at independence, personalism was the strongest political cement within the country.[100]

Greater economic sophistication, growing British influence, and greater complexity in relations with the United States were also evident in Gran Colombia, made up of Venezuela, New Granada, and Ecuador. A large number of British volunteers, men and officers, fought in its armies; and from 1817 on, there too Britain and British merchants gained exclusive concessions, although sometimes in cooperation with Anglo-Americans. They installed street lights, operated pearl fisheries and steamboats on the Orinoco, ran the Zipaquirá salt mines, and advised national leaders. In 1824 the American minister to Bogotá, Anderson, reported that quite a few newspapers were being published "under the auspices and at the expense of Colombian stockholders in London."[101] Not surprisingly, very little was printed in them about the United States. An exception was the *Correo del Orinoco*, established by Bolívar and directed by Zea, which from 1818 to 1822 from time to time praised "the glorious Americans of the North" and their leaders, especially Clay. It identified Bolívar with Washington, cited William Robinson, who had traded there until 1806, on the possibility of a transoceanic canal through the Chocó, and recalled the American Revolution, which, it said, in now familiar terms and imagery, had sought to "break the chains of slavery and snatch the scepter from the despot, to erect an altar on the sepulchre of the Inquisition, raise a people to a belief in liberty, found temples to science and commerce, and create a constitution under whose wide arc any human being. . . can hold himself erect and sublime in the dignity of man."[102] In 1821 it took an article from the Baltimore *Gazette* endorsing the idea of a great American destiny and foreseeing South America becoming "a great and opulent empire."[103] In this instance the United States press served as a vehicle for an essentially Latin American variety of Americanism.

American commerce flourished despite tariff restrictions. Colombia signed a commercial treaty giving the United States equal trade advantages with Britain—a momentous decision in a country where, as in the other new republics, customs duties were the nation's main source of income. In addition, in Bogotá the Monroe Doctrine was applauded and excerpted in a special edition of the *Gaceta de Colombia*, and, in a message to the Congress, its president, Francisco de Paula Santander, called that pronouncement "an act worthy of the classic land of liberty"—although he admitted uncertainty as to its scope and intent. Pedro Gual, who was then his secretary of state, went further, to declare it had made the two nations allies. Shortly afterwards, when Santander invited the United States to the Pan-American conference at Panama, it was, however, not an offer to join an inter-American federation but was extended only in order to discuss problems of common interest.[104]

Among the earliest, most outstanding Spanish American separatists to express ambivalence in his attitudes toward the United States was Simón Bolívar. Relatively early, by 1815, he viewed both England and that country as favoring Latin American independence and desiring Latin American trade and markets, but he deplored their lack of active aid. In 1814 he employed the United States as a model within a realistic assessment of international power:

> If, then it is well established that the independence of the United States is of greater benefit to England than was its dependence, what shall we say of our countries, whose

political importance will never compare with that of the United States? The results of United States independence set such a clear example for all to see that, without doing violence to reason, it is impossible to imagine that England would prefer to adopt conservative ideas which have always resulted in misery and oppression.[105]

The following year, in his most complete early statement, known as the Jamaica Letter, he vented opinions similar to those of Nariño, Moreno, and other centralists, writing that events in Venezuela had shown that purely republican institutions were inappropriate to the character, customs, and education of its inhabitants; that "until our patriots acquire those talents and political virtues which distinguish our North American brethren, I am very much afraid that our popular systems... will occasion our ruin."[106]

At the same time, after Britain did not respond to his request for aid, he turned to the north for it. He wrote to Gual, who was in Philadelphia, that "mercantile relations between Venezuela and the United States will be advantageous to both" and would be lucrative, and that frequent trade with the North Americans and "the protection which government will concede to honest foreigners who want to establish themselves among us will offset our depopulation and give us virtuous citizens," and he instructed Gual to advertise these sentiments.[107] Although supplies continued to come from private sources in the United States, when in 1817 its government objected to privateering and took Amelia Island, and when that same year Venezuelan patriots captured two North American ships supplying Spanish forces on the Orinoco, Bolívar complained the United States was not truly neutral—that laws should not be for the weak to uphold and the strong to abuse.[108]

By 1819, the North Americans had angered Latin Americans by withholding recognition—in part because of, and thereby intensifying, the problems plaguing insurgents of instituting functioning governments. In his Angostura discourse on February 15 of that year, at the inauguration of the second national congress of Venezuela, Bolívar, asserting the federal constitution of Venezuela was excellent but inapplicable to the current situation, commented:

> It is a prodigy that its model in North America has subsisted so prosperously and that it has not changed its aspect at the first embarrassment or danger. In spite of this that people is a singular model of political virtue and of moral enlightenment.... Liberty has been its cradle, it has been raised in liberty, and has been nourished on pure liberty.... This people is unique in the history of the human race.[109]

He declared it remarkable that so weak and complicated a system as the federative should survive and flourish, and continued:

> The idea never even remotely entered my head to liken the situation and nature of two states so distinct as the Anglo-American and the Spanish-American. Would it not be very difficult to apply to Spain the code of political, civil, and religious liberty of England? Well then, even more difficult would it be to adopt in Venezuela the laws of North America.

He urged that government be rooted in reality and, citing Montesquieu's *Spirit of the Laws*, he once again told Venezuelans to look at the current situation in their own lands, at the condition of their peoples, and at their religion, wealth, numbers, commerce, and customs. They should reflect upon the degree of liberty they could manage. "Here," he concluded,—"is the code we ought to consult and not that of Washington!"

The following year, although Torres in a report to Bolívar's secretary on May 20 said, "The United States will always be our friend and ally, and joined with them we can laugh at the designs of Europe," Bolívar on May 26 wrote to a merchant on Trinidad, William White: "North America, pursuing its arithmetical conduct of business, will avail itself of the opportunity to gain the Floridas, our friendship, and a great domination of commerce."[110] And just the day before he had written to José Rafael Revenga concerning Monroe's policy: "Never has conduct been more infamous than that of the Americans to us . . . now that through its anti-neutrality America has vexed us so greatly. We extend to them services which they repay in humiliation and fratricide."[111] By 1823 he had located the real villain elsewhere, in a letter of August 5 to Monteagudo from Guayaquil announcing: "I believe that Portugal is no more than the instrument of England, which never sleeps; in order that its confederates do not fear its name it invites the United States, so it may appear detached and to spread conviviality, as to a banquet. After we are gathered, it will be the feast of the lambs, the lion will enter and eat them."[112] He had no desire to invite the North Americans to Panama.[113]

Although in 1824 and 1825 more North American than British ships entered Venezuelan ports, and although Bolívar had put his nephew Fernando in school in Germantown, Pennsylvania, the Liberator repeatedly demonstrated he felt that Britain was most powerful and could prove a more stable friend than would the United States, but also indicated he thought that they would eventually ally, making it politic to maintain friendly relations with both. It was then he questioned the staying power of the United States's political system, according to a report made to the British admiralty by Captain James Malling, in saying that in the United States little "can be done for the benefit of the state. I certainly doubt whether the present situation in the United States can be much prolonged."[114] Yet, by 1826 he was repeatedly lauding North American institutions, undoubtedly in order to connect his own image and policies to democratic usages. So in January in his message to the Congress at Chuquisaca, in explaining the lifetime presidency in his proposed constitution he made too close an analogy in asserting he had taken for Bolivia the executive and "the example and so sublime lesson" of "la república americana."[115] And although continuingly critical of United States foreign policy in private correspondence, he continued publicly to applaud that nation as a model republic. In 1826 he made much ado about Washington, in an implicit comparison with himself, mentioning to the president of Colombia "the honrosa lección that has been left me by the hero citizen, the Father of the Great American Republic."[116] And in November, during a reception for the North American chargé in Colombia, he managed both to salute the United States and nod to Britain: "The United States, children of England, were the first who showed us the way to independence," and, he went on, this land "imitates the examples of glory, liberty and virtue that it receives from the United States."[117] Privately, however, he fell back upon his position of 1816; in a letter of 1827, after complaining of "this mania for provincial federalism," he remarked, "We wish to imitate the United States without considering the difference in elements, people and things. . . . Our composition is very different from that nation's, whose existence can be counted among the marvels produced by politics from century to century."[118]

In May 1829 he wrote to a former aide, Belford Wilson, of his resolve to retire to the United States, where Wilson then was: "Very soon, my dear Wilson, you will see me up there."[119] Two months later he complained to General Rafael Urdaneta, "Wilson writes me that in all the United States he has encountered no one who will speak in my favor, particularly because of the business of Santander."[120] That August, his health broken, his power gone, wary of Britain, annoyed at North American policies, perceiving himself rejected by the United States, and hurt by the attitudes of the rest of Latin America, his unfailingly mordant sense of irony suffused an outburst to Patrick Campbell, the British chargé at Bogotá. Its immediate cause was a new scheme of Poinsett's: "Don't you think that England would be jealous of the election of a Bourbon [as king of Gran Colombia]? How it would be opposed by all the new American states and the United States, which seem destined by Providence to plague America with miseries in the name of Liberty! I think I see a general conspiracy against this poor Colombia [now too much envied] by as many republics as America has."[121] He went on to mention anti-Colombian attitudes of specific Spanish American republics. It was six weeks later that he made the frequently quoted statement, to another former aide, Daniel O'Leary: "I think it would be better for [our] America to adopt the Koran than the government of the United States, although it is the best in the world."[122]

Shortly before his death in 1830 he again revealed, to a friend, both his high respect for the United States and disappointment in it, and his general sense of sadness. Stating he then saw Colombia on the verge of civil war, he said he would not object if its Congress established a monarchy but that he would never wear a crown. He had been much misunderstood, he went on, including in the United States, where he had hoped to be done justice.[123]

By the late 1820s, a mutual disillusionment prevailed in many facets of relations between the United States and Latin America. To North Americans, trade, institutions, and British predominance in Latin America were disappointments. For Latin Americans, North American arrogance, high tariffs, and either expansionism or lack of interest had dashed earlier, higher hopes. Still, cultural interest and interchange, some commerce, a small amount of investment, and a broad sentiment of Americanism endured. As long as the idea of progress held them, many Latin Americans would continue to admire that of the United States. Its example would remain coupled with the founding concepts and institutions of all the American republics, and a rather mystical sense of common interest would survive.

10

SOME OBSERVATIONS

I.

Some years ago David Potter wrote, concerning the United States, "We were right in supposing that we wielded a revolutionary force, but were wrong in supposing it to be an ideological one, when it was in fact, material . . . not an ideal of democracy but our export of goods and gadgets."[1] Potter himself was right in part, but his view is too restrictive, for the revolutionary force was in the interplay of the material and the ideational. Much the same thing can be said about a very different approach, Immanuel Wallerstein's much broader, theoretical model of a capitalist world-system, in which England in the eighteenth and early nineteenth centuries was presented as within the core, Iberia as semiperiphery, Latin America as periphery, and the new United States as moving from periphery to semiperiphery.[2] Pierre Chaunu, in his summing of the material aspects of Latin American independence, and Fernand Braudel, in his concern with material life and its sweeping underlying structures, are both instructive, as have been some of the studies of the dependency of Iberia and its America on the more developed countries,—notably, for our period, the Steins' essays on *The Colonial Heritage of Latin America*. Ronald Edward Robinson and John Gallagher have written on the imperialism of free trade, and although they focus on Asia in the nineteenth century, Richard Graham has extended their discussion to Latin America.[3]

Still other historians, in the fashion of political scientists, have commented on linkage groups within and among domestic societies and economies in Latin America, and the ties of commercial, intellectual, and military elites with the outside world, and they speak in terms of penetrated societies.[4] For Latin America, Gallagher, Robinson, and Graham are essentially correct in finding British imperialism ongoing; yet not so in placing the moral onus for colonial exploitation mainly on indigenous leaders, for the interchange between English and Anglo-American entrepreneurs and those in Latin America was at first desired on all sides, and only later qualified. Initially it was viewed by them all as of individual and national value, even as a boon to mankind. Spanish Americans and Brazilians saw combined public and private worth in free trade. By the end of the eighteenth century, free trade meant to them direct commerce with foreigners, but modified by attitudes necessarily of a very complex nature concerning what they wanted from outsiders. Certainly all this puts initial United States relations with Latin America in a new light, if in an ongoing context from at least 1713, and adds a strong materialist component to Felix Gilbert's discussion of the sources and inception of United States foreign policy. Moreover, clearly the American colonies as a whole participated in the general wave of eighteenth-century prosperity, if unevenly. Their leaders wanted to participate even more, and that desire became one cause of revolution in the Americas. That desire too was an important nexus between material and ideational factors in the history of the period. It came of, and was nurtured by, both.

No one study of ideological perspectives embracing the entire area and time comes to mind, but those by Ernst Cassirer and Peter Gay on the Enlightenment in Europe, Henry May on its ramifications in the United States and Arthur Whitaker on those in Latin America, Bernard Bailyn on the thrust to revolution in 1776, Michael Kammen on North American colonists as people of paradox, and Harry Bernstein on cultural interchange between the United States and Latin America have all contributed to the general picture. J.G.A. Pocock has shown the continuity of British, and fundamentally classical, political theory. Ideology concerned with material factors during our period has been, however, neglected, although Joyce Appleby has discussed interconnections of economic theory, business, government, and politics—most successfully for England. And most recently and successfully, Gary Nash has limned the interplay of society, economy, and the ideational climate in colonial Philadelphia, New York, and Boston. This interplay emerges in Drew McCoy's book on republicanism and political economy in America and, largely implicitly, in some works on Latin America. Notable among them are Tulio Halperín-Donghi's *Historia Contemporánea de América Latina*, Kenneth Maxwell's contributions on Portugal and Brazil, Charles Harris's tracing of the history of one family of entrepreneurs, the Sánchez Navarro, of northern Mexico. More explicit is Richard Morse's article in the collection by Louis Hartz, *The Formation of New Societies*. Much, however, remains to be done on the social impact of the tenets of political economy and emergent liberalism.

We have seen entrepreneurs, intellectuals, and patriots to have shared similar outlooks, goals—even, at times, pursuits—and a variety of sorts of leadership as well, in England, Iberia, and the Americas from 1713 to 1826, and many people to combine these roles, as they believed harmoniously. In this they were abetted by the coalescence developing in fact and theory in the eighteenth century between the material and the ideological, so that business, public life, and leading philosophies and approaches to science reinforced one another in our theater of the West. This allowed energetic pursuit of careers in any or all of them by talented and ambitious men—the role of women in the period is another story.

Throughout much of the West, the earlier scientific revolution and the rise of rationalism converged in the Enlightenment, which in turn meshed with emergent liberalism and with concepts of—indeed, the notion itself of—political economy. Men with weight in trade and affecting government came to be strongly influenced by all these trends and by the age's strong emphasis on overarching, temporal universalism and cosmopolitanism—if in varying ways and while retaining a large, old, enduring stock of more traditional notions. Here, as in so much of life, as Lord Acton noted and Fernand Braudel has abundantly corroborated, the higher history is the record of the abiding. And with regard to this general frame of mind, in the American colonies, although the British and Iberian substratas of background and outlook differed, as did the time, methods, and results of initial colonization and the dates of revolutions, the years between 1713 and 1826 yield a good deal of similarity.

In both Americas, among many entrepreneurs, intellectuals, and patriots there prevailed the idea that social change for the better depended on economic development, and (an extension) that self-regard was a starting point for general advance. This happy confluence between belief and preference, reconciling self-interest with benevolence, allowed enterprising men to see their own and their societies' interests as one and to believe that in pursuing intelligent and enlightened self-interest they could better their communities, thought of first in regional and later in national terms. Even more, these patriots could look at their own activities as of great importance to their societies, and could even conclude that social betterment depended on their actions. As early as 1752, David Hume spoke to this conjunction in commenting that "industry, knowledge, and humanity [were] linked together by an indissoluble chain [once men were roused from their lethargy and] put into a fermentation."[5]

In the thirteen colonies and Latin America, people with similar outlooks, sharing a sense of active patriotic participation and a penchant for voluntary association, and propelled by the vision of combined public and private progress, came to reach for a rose they viewed as having few or no thorns. Combating inner doubts with faith in the human capacity to conquer and mold the environment, many of them eagerly embraced political independence and the future. The intensity of that faith was all-important, and faith it was. Not only did a combination of enlightened thought, civic humanism, and liberal political economy become a sort of secular scripture, but Thomas Jefferson originally described the truths for which we stand as "sacred" rather than "self-evident."[6] And Jacob de Villaurrutia in 1794 succinctly summed up the elements of the new belief among creoles when he proclaimed that "the sacred role" of the Guatemalan economic society was to embrace useful knowledge for the good of man and the glory of Guatemala, thus to effect "a happy revolution."[7] The phrase, we recall, echoed Adam Smith and the Conde de Floridablanca. In the same decade in New Granada, José Félix de Restrepo, in urging reform of education, reminded his compatriots of the words of Cicero, "We are born for God and the Patria."[8] And there on January first, 1810, Joaquín Camacho, a respected theorist on law and economics, wrote in Caldas's *Diario Político* of "holy revolution" that gives man back his rights and comes to destroy usurpers and to "remove the shackles from industry and protect the personal property of work."[9] In the same vein, José Ignacio Pombo, in his 1810 plan for commerce, opposed regulations violating "the most sacred rights of the citizen, those of respect for his property and for his individual liberty."[10] Here, then, in the nexus of concepts identified with the Enlightenment, civic humanism, and the nascent liberalism embedded in political economy, we have some ideological origins of, or at least background to, revolution in the Americas.

Such people also welcomed that liberal invention, the individual, as well as the new value put on the middle class and on its values of talent and achievement. In so doing, they echoed David Hume who, in his *History*, declared the middling rank of men both "the best and firmest basis of public liberty" and important to the growth of commerce and industry; though middling, from their ranks, was the implication, emerged a form of natural aristocracy. As Sacvan Bercovitch and others have commented, the American Revolution enshrined the middle class.

These men echoed, too, Hume's assertion that European history taught that order and good government, individual liberty, and the progress of commerce, manufactures, and society all went hand in hand. Believing in their own abilities to mold the future, they held as an article of faith the possibility of the harmonious development of the economic and social structures and their own crucial role in both. It was an evolutionist view of the universe. It embraced the cosmos, life, and society, and it interacted with the rise of relativism in ethics and social thought, as well as with belief in liberty, change, and progress. It was an outlook dating at least from the appearance early in the eighteenth century of Bernard de Mandeville's "The Fable of the Bees, or Private Vices, Public Benefits."

In all this Adam Smith's *Wealth of Nations*, in joining, expanding, and putting system into existing theories of political economy, served as conduit, and did more. As one scholar put it, "He crystallized the social outlook of civilization";[11] and, as another reminds us, "In every proposal of economic policy there lies an often undisclosed preference for a society integrated in one way rather than another."[12] Yet a third, H. J. Habakkuk, has added, "The influence of economic ideas was less in molding specific measures of politics than in creating certain presuppositions about politics."[13] These were the presuppositions, he went on to say, supporting economic liberalism and he compared the force of its ideas to that of Keynesian economics at the time he wrote, the mid-1960s.

By the 1760s in Europe, *nation*, long a component of *empire*, had begun to separate from and to succeed that concept as a preferable political organizing principle. In Spain the organic nation, replacing dynastic empire but still headed by a hereditary monarch, became in reform-minded, relatively liberal government circles *the* political unit. Patriotism was endorsed and stimulated as inseparable from economic advance; witness the alternative designations for those self-help organizations, the patriotic or economic societies.[14] In America, the birth of a new nation a decade later placed nationality and nationalism in a new, democratic light. That nation was then thought of by its citizens as the sum total of individuals comprising it, as guarantor of their individual freedom, and nationalism itself became the American ideology.[15] In Latin America from the 1780s, customary and Iberian usages made easy the transition from the concept of patria as region of one's birth and, in the light of the North American precept, made seem possible, by 1810, new American nations based on old imperial units but now grounded in principles of liberty and the virtue of constitutional, republican form. In Spanish

America, moreover, the traditional concept of empire had protected regional particularism and sanctified the notion of patria preserved in creolism, and it gave to breaking away from Spain, when combined with circumstances from 1808, a reorganizing rather than an innovative aspect.

At the same time, the presence of continental and cosmopolitan concepts enabled a supraregional sentiment of Americanism to facilitate independence. Being American came to replace attachment to an empire spanning the Atlantic; but like that empire, America was seen as made up of smaller, distinct components (and the sentiment of being American allowed the possibility of, and sometimes the belief in, a special relationship existing with the United States). In Mexico in the 1720s Ahumada, citing the law of nations in asserting that office in the Indies belonged to the native-born heirs of the conquistadors, referred to creoles as Americans. In the 1760s, the exiled Mexican Jesuit Diego Abad entitled his epic poem *Musa Americana*. Humboldt commented on the heightened pride in being American after Versailles, and by 1788 in a report to the government, the consulado of Mexico City showed that it simply accepted that designation. In upland Quito four years later Eugenio Espejo was repeating, in the first issue of his gazette, a defense of "all America and the Americans" against the slurs of European philosophes, writing of "an immaculate and cultured nation, being *American*"[16]—the emphasis was his. By then, in Europe, the exiled Jesuit, Viscardo, had written his call for independence, which included a vision of all Americans as brothers.

Beyond this, the new assumption was that people were organized within a world community made up of nation-states. It was new in that it expected nations to be synonymous with political entities and precluded imperial arrangement—and it was, of course, especially favored by those concerned with throwing off the (old imperial) yoke, as they put it, with a nod to Rome. Moreover, the concept of nationality was used, as has been noted, as an invitation by some men to others to join them in a common enterprise, from the call in the Spanish royal council of 1768 through that of the founding fathers of the United States to the *gritos* of the insurgents of 1810. Nationality underlay Hidalgo's efforts to arouse a sleeping Mexican nation made up of all born on its soil; nationality was used by Moreno in an attempt, essentially imperial, by Buenos Aires to gain hegemony over Brazil. The French Revolution carried on what that of 1776 began; it coupled populism with nationhood. But it had an added appeal to Spaniards on both sides of the Atlantic because it initially made synonymous *republic* and *constitutional monarchy*. Thus, it provided a bridge to self-government as well as a stirringly romantic, organic example—one presented in a more familiar tone, one identified with religious intensity. Even so, it claimed descent from the Revolution of 1776. Throughout almost all of these invitations, too, ran concepts of the sanctity of liberty, life, and property and a commitment to the ideal of equality of opportunity. There was, however, no belief in the equality here and now of the propertied and the propertyless. (The outline of the history of social thought, and an examination of social relations, should be fleshed out for this period and these parameters, but will not be here, for to do so properly will require another book the heft of this one.)

Liberalism, says Kenneth Minogue, "depends upon a consciousness of being modern."[17] In Spain and its America, *lo moderno* was promoted by the state from mid-century on in line with endorsing tenets also becoming associated with political economy. Concurrently, it was advanced in forward-looking cultural and educational circles. From the1740s, while Benjamin Franklin was popularizing modernity in the United States, there formed in Mexico a small circle of young, self-proclaimed moderns, explicitly advocating modernism in cultural matters in reaction to *misoneísmo*, or intransigent traditionalism; that they were Jesuits indicates the complexity of the modernizing impulse. As we have seen, at mid-century the royal minister, Carvajal, urged that Spain not try to recoup wartime losses but "let go the old and turn toward *lo moderno*." While in England industrialization and modernization advanced together, their connection, as E. A. Wrigley has pointed out and situations elsewhere corroborate, was contingent, not necessary. Throughout the West, commerce was bringing people of all nations into contact—indeed, into a single network. The rise of industry in one powerful nation—England—gave that nation a further preeminence within the commercial system and changed that system itself into one geared to British predominance in both production and on the seas, except during the Napoleonic Wars, when the United States was given an opportunity it took to advantage.

The point here is that modernity was then an umbrella term for many of the newer currents of the eighteenth century. It now is used about that period to signal technological advance and a spectrum of ideas, and often for getting around interpreting history in Marxian terms. For our purposes the word makes sense only in that knowing it was used then, and how it was employed, sheds light both on the mentality of that period and on inter-American—indeed, world—relations during it. Here what is important is that a number of the people who directed American societies claimed to be modern, that the word was used interchangeably with *enlightened* and later with *liberal*, and that it implies a dynamic view of history and a faith in progress and in human ability to harness and direct natural forces.

Against this background, David Barry, the London publisher of the first edition of the *Noticias Secretas*, by Juan and Ulloa, could write in 1826, in the prologue: "half of the terraquous globe presented itself suddenly to the energetic Europeans, offering them an immense theatre where they might exercise their talents and their valor, their activity and constancy . . . the vast Ocean is now no more than a lake for mariners and the four quarters of the world form a general market for the merchants." It should be mentioned that Barry was a merchant.

In a similar vein, the Spaniard Covarrubias reflected that "the sciences and arts are most intimately entwined with the policy of empire," a remark closely echoing the observation made two hundred years before by Antonio de Nebrija, in the dedication to Queen Isabella of his Castilian grammar, that language is a companion to empire. John Adams, who owned a copy of Nebrija's grammar, implicitly agreed with its emphasis on imperial expansion in his own visions of America's future, set down in the 1750s and 1760s.

Jefferson also made all these cultural and imperial connections. Thus while, as Garry Wills said, "His world was full of untagged specimens and infant sciences. His model was Newton, charting the universe,"[18] and while in much of Europe and

America his dispatching of Lewis and Clark's expedition was admired as a contribution to science, some observers recognized the indissoluble blend of Jefferson's interests. In the *Correio Braziliense*, published in London, one of them, Hipólito da Costa, fretted:

> With respect to America's ambitious plans to become great, we see that this began to develop during the administration of Mr. Jefferson, who, as president of the United States, sent an expedition entrusted with crossing the continent of North America to the western coast, to discover the rivers which originate in the lakes of the West and flow into the Pacific Ocean, and to search there for the most suitable seaports for commercial depots for the East Indian archipelago and China. The character of Mr. Jefferson, a man dedicated to the natural sciences, made people in Europe believe that this voyage was merely for philosophical ends, searching for exact knowledge of the geography of the country, information on its natural products, etc. But he who knows well the American government suspected early on the political aims of the President. They were more suspect when American ships bound for China rounded Cape Horn, touched at ports in Peru to obtain silver, and then went to California before going on to China, from whence they returned by way of the Cape of Good Hope.[19]

"Imperialism," as David Landes has concluded, "is a multifarious response to a common opportunity that consists simply in the disparity of power."[20] Da Costa erred concerning American expansion. It can, of course, be traced back before 1776, to colonists, and further, to England and to Spain as well. There empire was formal, legally defined, and territorial in that deputies of the monarch governed and Spaniards settled overseas, initially in kingdoms connected only through the imperial crown, colony-kingdoms ultimately meant to provide Spain with bullion. Later, after 1750, the Spanish tendency was toward, as Vicens Vives phrased it, "imperial liberalism."[21]

For both Iberia and Britain by the eighteenth century, overseas commerce was of overriding imperial concern, though their reasons for such interest were not identical. Both also directed attention to keeping an eye on rivals and to acquiring territory, principally for strategic value (and, in England's case, in response to public opinion). Within this context, Britain and its mainland American colonies extended the concept of free trade to the right to interloping in that of rival empires—thus, in a sense, extending the range of one's own empire, at least economically. Free trade, that is, initially helped make preferable and promote informal empire—at first that of Britain in the Americas, and then also that of the United States. Iberia followed England in coupling empire with free trade: At mid-century this meant commercial ties and expansion, with goals beyond bullion, but within the empire and primarily for the benefit of the state and the home economy. In Spain, Bernardo Ward reiterated that "freedom is the soul of trade," in an attack directed against monopoly within the imperial system, and Jovellanos commented that, "the political principle of first importance is that of leaving men the greatest possible freedom, in whose wake trade, population, and wealth will follow."[22] *Freedom* and *liberty* were first championed in the Hispanic lands in the eighteenth century in connection with commerce.

Connected to commerce, too, were early references to revolution. Even before

Adam Smith's "happy revolution," Campomanes, in reflecting on Spanish trade with the Indies, held up England as a model: "All the nations believe," he wrote in 1762, "that wealth by means of commerce, navigation, and industry is the only source of public felicity"; he went on to speak of England benefiting from "this mercantile revolution that inclines the balance on its side."[23] Yet, in 1776 an anonymous critic of José de Gálvez was coupling revolt with unhappiness and the concept of America as a separate empire: "He has destroyed more than he has built . . . his destructive hand is going to prepare the greatest revolution in the American empire."[24] By 1810, as we have seen, the sacred, and these secular, senses of revolution merged in Latin America, much as they had in the Revolution of 1776, if with the added heat lent by the French upheaval.

II.

The American revolutions occurred within a forty-year span, a matter of two generations; they had more in common, and more connections, than has been assumed. In both hemispheres they were outgrowths of internal expansion and changing attitudes, international struggles, shifting international economic arrangements, and new outlooks on colonies by the metropoli and the other way around. A number of influential people in Latin America who were conversant with contemporary trends and events sought to bring their lands abreast of Anglo-America in material progress and social well-being through encouraging agricultural, industrial, and commercial development, and through intelligently and directly joining the international trading system on the best terms possible. In all this they were not unlike the founding fathers of the United States—a comparison they themselves made in their frequent admiring references to Franklin and Washington, and to Jefferson's thoughts on America. And with them they shared certain goals and views abetting revolution.

Both areas had a history, marked in the eighteenth century, of divergence in custom from their metropoli. Both enjoyed a greater amount of autonomy in the earlier portion of the century, and from mid-century on underwent greater restriction while experiencing economic expansion and population growth. Religion also altered, although clergy advocating reform touched much broader segments of the populace in Anglo-America, where some spoke out against impingements by institutions—including by the state and established clergy—on belief and conscience. In North America, the Great Awakening had an impact upon popular and elite outlooks, and later, in 1774, the Quebec Act, confirming certain prerogatives of the Roman Catholic Church in Canada, intensified anti-Catholicism in the thirteen colonies. In Latin America, enlightened opinion and policies and regalism did affect the few but influential self-proclaimed moderns, and it aroused a vocal traditionalist reaction. The expulsion of the Jesuits cut across both groups and it gave rise to protests against new policies, newly energetic European authorities, and the concept of change itself as inimical to religious principles and as therefore destructive of the legitimating bases that up until then had defined most human relations. In Anglo-America by the 1770s, as Edmund Morgan has said, politics replaced theology as "the most challenging area of human thought and endeavor."[25] In Spanish America, politics challenged old orthodoxies. In Michoacán the Bishop, San Miguel, lauded "the two useful sciences, economics and politics." Pérez Calama and Abad y Queipo urged secular progress through political changes, as did Hidalgo. It was accepted—in fact, was a Spanish and Hispanic American tradition—that men of the cloth might engage directly in politics, indeed, should do so. In both North and South America, many clergy promoted independence.

Deference to authority was traditional throughout the New World, but so was the custom of evading the law—as Sir Lewis Namier, the elder Arthur Schlesinger, Samuel Eliot Morison, John Leddy Phelan, and most observers of the Hispanic world have demonstrated. In one sense, both revolutions stemmed from new administrative efficiency and tax increases. From 1688 in the thirteen colonies, colonial assemblies had consolidated their claims to legislation over taxation; in the same period to the south, bureaucracy was decentralized and had become linked to regional societies. In Anglo-America in the 1760s, the pained cry was no taxation without representation; in Latin America it was none without negotiation by royal authorities.[26] The taxes then levied in both regions were symbolic to inhabitants of attempts to centralize government and to augment its power; to assert, in the thirteen colonies, British legislative dominance and, in Spanish America, royal bureaucratic preeminence; in both, the reaction was a call for restoration of what was seen as the traditional constitution. Reaction in both, that is, invoked dissenting traditions of the metropolis which had earlier become domesticated in America.[27]

In both regions, a sense of Americanism swelled. It implicitly opposed Europe and domination by metropolitan Europeans or by their American cohorts. There was a related avowal of holding to American customs and traditions, particularly in matters political and legal, in accord with an understood pact with the monarch dating back to the conquests and first settlements. Beyond this agreement two other, related pacts were understood: that of individuals with one another, which had formed the republic or social community, and that of community with God, a covenant to uphold the Law. The latter compact was seen as binding even the monarch and was a rationale for popular sovereignty.[28] Thus, the Preamble to the Massachusetts Constitution ran: "The body politic is formed by a voluntary association of individuals. It is a social compact by which the whole people covenants with each citizen, and each citizen with the whole people, that all should be governed by certain laws for the common good."[29] The exiled Mexican Jesuit Francisco Javier Alegre averred that the immediate origin of authority lay in the consent of the community, in accord with the law of nations, and that royal sovereignty was only mediate, obtained through its delegation by common voice. Writing in 1789, he cited Samuel Pufendorf while implicitly concurring with the earlier political theory of the Spanish Jesuit Francisco Suárez, who has been said to be the John Locke of Latin American republicanism.[30] However that may be, by the late eighteenth century some or all of these pacts were assumed to be synonymous with the constitution, in both Americas. Thus in both, as R. R. Palmer in reiterating Thomas Paine said of English colonists, Americans could solve the problem of constituting a new government by means of a constitutional convention. This new device with traditional roots embodied in theory the sovereignty of the people.[31] And in both Americas, people could find continuation of legitimacy in the principle of the constitution.

The juntas coming into being in 1808, which William Shaler explained not incorrectly as "provincial legislatures," were at bottom constitutional institutions. At the least they tacitly corroborated the principle of monarchy limited by natural law. They also endorsed explicitly traditional references made in the Laws of the Indies and the Spanish code, *Las Siete Partidas*, to community as a pact between sovereign and people, an endorsement lent even by their opponents, who upheld one or more Spanish juntas instead. Mier wrote of this pact with the king as "the American constitution" and of Europeans violating it.[32] Juntas everywhere said much the same thing. The *Memorial del Agravios* of the Bogotá cabildo of 1809 cited the Partidas in opposition to tyrants and repeated the call by Jovellanos for "the restitution of our monarchy to its primitive and constitutional bases." And in 1810 Camilo Torres, an author of the memorial, wrote of a broken pact, of "the sovereignty that resides in the mass of the nation," which he said "has been reasserted," and spoke of the *nation* and the *constitution*.[33] Constitutional government was common throughout Spanish America in one form or another, and came to mean a form of government limited by law, Spanish and American custom, and natural rights (derived from the law of nature and, ultimately, God), a government representing the best interests of the community.

In addition, both Americas were during the first stages of revolution still viewed by most inhabitants as important regions of empire, separate from but equal to European communities, tied politically only to the king. England and Spain, trying to tighten American adherence by closer imperial integration, unwittingly tampered with the traditional terms of empire embedded in law, custom, and religion—terms that had allowed colonists a good deal of latitude. In this sense, Europe in both cases was the first to abolish the old imperial order and to force consideration of the newer political desideratum, the nation-state; this in turn led to thought of the inappropriateness of that entity to overseas union. In addition, such seemingly dissimilar men as Spanish bureaucrats and Massachusetts Puritans and politicians presented the nation as a moral and political being, a concept flowing into religious beliefs and, in effect, becoming one, leading into sanctifying the idea that the nation rather than the king was sovereign, and raising questions concerning the composition and boundaries of the nation and of patriotism. Related were modern republicanism and the belief that government derives from the consent of the governed—just as were many of those assumptions written into, even making possible, the American Declaration of Independence, a document much admired and imitated in Latin America.[34] As Franklin Ford observed of Europe during the revolutionary-Napoleonic era, in the Americas, too, language, especially rhetoric and terms that came to be closely identified with revolution, served as a conditioning factor.[35] Patriotic leaders throughout the Americas both embraced similar ideologies and carefully tailored their presentation of them to their audiences, starting from familiar bases, such as customary language and appeal to custom, and going on to invest old terms with new meaning.

Concomitant with avowals of popular sovereignty, a major change was that from more passive to active government, and then from vassal to active subject to citizen. A rise in voluntary associations—public, literary, scientific, philanthropic, and social—and civic pride fits here, as does the fact that inhabitants of both Americas discovered (or thought they had) their own military capabilities and their competence to defend their native lands against foreign aggression. They began as well to take charge of civic government, at first within the empires. Witness, in Mexico, the assertions of Ahumada in the 1720s and of the cabildo of the capital in 1771, and recall Franklin's attitude by 1750 and subsequent evidence of popular sentiments. Some prominent or ambitious men in the colonies saw themselves pushed aside with the help of government. An effect of wars and change was to throw up new men and work against entrenched merchants, who tended as one scholar says, to ossify. In addition, Iberia and England supported merchants of the metropolis at American expense; the practice of British merchants bypassing American wholesalers was a prime cause of the Boston Tea Party.[36] In British America, governors reasserted power; to the south, viceroys and visitadores did so. With good reason, Americans felt themselves to be distrusted. Creoles were eased off audiencias; North American legislatures were circumscribed. In both regions, political and social alliances coalesced and shifted, then converged sufficiently to win independence.

It has been said that an Anglo-American colonial agreement was founded on racial consensus. The sense of national belonging and common purpose was far stronger in the emergent United States, and race was a less important factor there, largely probably because it was not so important in the makeup of the population. Certainly creoles in Mexico or South America made no jokes, as did yankees, about being Indians. While among creoles a real process of *mestizaje* (racial or ethnic intermixture) did occur, especially in the later eighteenth century, it was to them no laughing matter, nor would it have been to Anglo-Americans.[37] Yet some creoles, especially in Mexico, did base a sense of Americanism on cultural *mestizaje*. And others, although humiliated at being viewed as mestizo, nevertheless recognized the need to attract to their cause people of mixed background and felt the necessity of discovering a unique, American heritage. Accordingly, they too pointed with pride to the pre-Hispanic indigenous empires, and used as symbols of America and for Americans of all backgrounds the Inca and Aztec empires. The enlightened notion of population as wealth fed into this current.

By 1810 a powerful group of merchants, lawyers, clergy, medical men, scientists, intellectuals and other educated people lamented the political, economic, and social reality—usually viewed through the lens of enlightened principles and political economy—of their parts of Latin America. They were the same sorts of men who had spurred and then led revolution in 1776. Although in Spanish America the movements were complicated by more factions, yet between 1808 and 1810, as in the early 1770s in the thirteen colonies, they found common cause in a number of factors: in constitutional crisis; in a perceived need for self-defense; and in economic plight manifested in lack of markets, inability to protect their products from imports, a drain of specie, financial crisis in Europe, and so on.

They also bid for greater political power and greater legal equality: They chafed under lack of equality with their European brethren and under feelings of neglect, abuse, and humiliation by the metropolitan government. All in all they experienced the misery of (as J. R. Pole said of British America) injured self-esteem. Creoles vociferously demonstrated it in responding to European slurs, while Anglo-Americans vented it in reaction to being treated wretchedly by Englishmen, most blatantly and widely during the wars.

III.

The social history of the Latin American independence movements remains to be written, although Charles Griffin and Tulio Halperín-Donghi have sketched it in. Accelerating general changes, including population expansion, had brought more people in contact with larger societies, with a larger market economy, and with unsettling changes in their own lives attendant upon: new and higher taxes, altered trade routes and demands, competition from imports, new chains of authority, rumors of greater freedom and greater well-being, and the very possibility of a better life. Racial and social antagonisms had built up in areas of multiracial composition. The risings of the 1760s and 1780s had left a legacy of united action against oppression from without. The men who emerged as leaders after 1808 came to know all this and to value numbers, and they understood that their own success must be tied to general support and to a shared vision of a rosier future. As steps in those directions they frequently issued proclamations of social reform, promising, in accord with eighteenth-century precepts, freedom from old burdens. They abolished slavery and Indian servitude and tribute, and announced more equitable distribution of lands and better education. They sometimes cited the United States model, but seldom held out social revolution.

Some of the great leaders—Miranda, Hidalgo, Bolívar—who charted the course of the movements deeply affected their course and direction. While their personal model was most probably a romanticized Napoleon, in a larger sense it was also the heroic defiance of him by the Spanish people and, beyond that, the era's impulse to self-expression and to nationhood through revolution. Without Napoleon, Latin American independence might have been delayed. Without the revolution of 1776, the ideological content of the movements for independence and the construction of the new governments would have been very different. Napoleon did not invent the pursuit of fame; it was a touchstone for leaders of the first rank in North America, as it had been throughout the history of Western Europe. Bolívar, the foremost liberator of Spanish America, had models aplenty to draw from, going back to classical times—which he did for his vision of "an authoritarian kingdom [or republic] of virtue."[38] For many other regional leaders, their revolutionary cradle was a mixed and intense involvement with the Bourbon reform movement and the late eighteenth-century protoliberal mentality.[39]

Relative stability followed upon the revolution of 1776; banditry—described by Halperín-Donghi as "a local prerogative"—and greater violence ensued upon those of 1810.[40] In Spanish America, public life became militarized; and the military, privileged. Local families—clans—important in the revolutionary movements, held on and continued feuding among themselves and with the new capitals for power and spoils, within a heritage of small civil wars. In Latin America the old tradition endured of proclaiming allegiance to the least pressing authorities. Chief cities and ports on one hand and upcountry regions on the other continued to vie for power and profits, seemingly in traditional Spanish American fashion, whereas in England and the United States integration of cities and their hinterlands in the period is frequently mentioned.[41] The old controversies between centralists and federalists remained prime political issues, provincial federalists still citing the United States example, having in mind its organization before 1787.

There was some social rearrangement. The composition of the elites altered, and a new mestizo creole aristocracy emerged. Slaves were emancipated in many regions and Indians freed from tribute, but also from the old patrimonial state's protection, and sometimes from their lands. Only in Venezuela did an urban sector based on commerce and credit remain dominant; elsewhere, in seaports whole-salers, as they had been in colonial British America, were bypassed by British merchants and goods. The British were becoming, says Halperín-Donghi, the new Spaniards. Domestically, the army and the landed consolidated effective power and tightened their control of the labor force; in spite of a blurring of caste lines, social demarcations held firm. Power came to reside with the landed in the countryside and the provinces, abetted by their cohorts in the capitals and ports; such were the new entrepreneurs and patriots. "Public life was for those who had no other way of prospering."[42] Those more liberal creoles who foresaw eminence and esteem through directing society, and who led the revolutions destroyed the very administrative processes, the old system, upon which their vision had been built, and had relatively little potency in the new political situations, so that bitterness characterized many of the brightest and most responsible. Thus, Bolívar pronounced his own epitaph: "I have ploughed the sea." The leaders who survived Latin America's revolutions ended their days not as Washingtons or Jeffersons, but contemplating retirement in Europe or the United States.

Latin Americans had believed by 1810, as did leaders in the United States, that necessary to a society's well-being was economic advance, which they associated with industrial revolution, as in England, and with national growth and prosperity as experienced by the United States—that is, with improvement in agriculture and transport, industry, a sophisticated monetary system, capital accumulation, and intellectual precepts and an educational system suitable to bringing about a new orientation of society. And, like British colonists opposed to the Navigation Acts, they endorsed more open trade. With the Napoleonic Wars, numerous Latin Americans with a stake in overseas trade advocated using foreign carriers and welcomed foreign imports, but by 1810 some of them had seen British textiles and United States wheat and flour have adverse effect on their regional economies and they thought better of their earlier unqualified espousal of commercial liberty.

By 1810, then, Latin Americans showed an economic sophistication not usually ascribed to them. This may be, in large part, because with revolt and then independence the new governments, as had Spain, negotiated foreign loans to disadvantage, and, relying on taxing the volume of trade, did not discourage imports. Britons, with a huge surplus of manufactures, looked harder than ever for large and quick cash profits and expected an expanding market in Latin America—a growth they believed would in part be prodded by supplying the Latin Americans with motivation to work in order to acquire the wherewithal for those wonders, manufactured goods. Britain also further integrated Latin America into the world trading circuit, carrying out not only specie and raw materials as before, but also much more copper, to India. Luxuries, as Halperín-Donghi points out, now became necessities—windowpanes, good shoes, tableware—and the dispersion of capital was aggravated by these trends and by continued domestic instability and the allure of British investments. By 1830 market limits were obvious, as was the loss of entrepreneurial spirit among creoles.

Historians have noted the divergence of eastern and western Europe in early modern times; the same sort of divergence, if for varying reasons, accelerated between the United States and Latin America in the 1800s. The United States became more urban and industrialized and politically broader-based. Latin America grew in latifundia, neoserfdom, fissiparous regionalism, and autocracy. In all this the colonial heritage of both played a large part, but so did the world situation at the time each became independent. The North Americans were ideally suited and positioned to take advantage of the Napoleonic Wars and new industrial technology, and to expand frontiers; it is interesting to conjecture what would have been the history of the United States had it not become independent until the 1820s, or had the revolution there lasted, as it did in Spanish America, for sixteen years.

In the United States after independence the agrarian, yeoman ideal, and the individualism reminiscent of the country dissenters of England—an individualism that had been called upon by Adams, Jefferson, and others in the revolutionary era, then had become enshrined in American law and reflected in the Bill of Rights and in those frequent appeals to natural rights, individual property, minimum government, and an agrarian economy—soon gave way to a more corporate sense of property and of the nation, and came to support business rights and active central government. It gave way, that is, to the Federalist, unitary view of society and the image of commercial man taken up by the republicans and sanctified in the Constitution of 1787 and in ongoing judicial process.[43] Even so, in the popular mind old yeoman ideals and imagery endured and came to mesh, not always harmoniously, in some rationales for wealth and power. This evolution was very much in evidence by 1815 when, with the end of the artificial protection provided by the War of 1812, there was general support for tariff barriers and for spurs to industrial growth as well as territorial expansion. Here would be the nineteenth-century playgrounds for what Alexander Hamilton had referred to as "the adventurous spirit, which distinguishes the commercial character of America."[44] By the 1820s, classical liberalism had in Europe and America replaced Adam Smith's "simple and natural liberty," and the state was viewed within it, as Jeremy Bentham expressed it, "as the great agency for achieving happiness."[45] Not only did the American judicial process reflect these developments, but also John Adams came to praise Daniel Raymond's *Thoughts on Political Economy*, published in Baltimore in 1820 and closest in outlook to the national, protectionist, organic theories of the German Friedrich List.[46] A corporate mentality became more pervasive in operative United States institutions and supporting theory than is usually acknowledged. In invocations of an American system the emphasis was on both words. The rugged individualism of the nineteenth century belonged to social imagery, business, and the frontier.

These trends had parallels in Latin America. There, both the Americas were fit within a post-Napoleonic Atlantic climate compounded of a retreat from enlightened cosmopolitanism, a romanticism extolling the outstanding individual, and a romantic patriotism centered on the individual nation as a mystical body. The state was not seen as an agent of society, but as a separate, independent, moral entity meant to take charge of society. Although liberalism was "born as a penchant for non-bureaucratic methods," in the 1830s economic liberalism was ascendant and linked to utilitarian concepts: Desire for free flow of goods included favoring administrative regulation to facilitate that freedom, thus achieving the paradox of a liberal bureaucracy. Romanticism embellished this venture while glorying in such abstractions as the people, the nation, liberty, and progress. The tone of metropolitan governments in the 1760s found echo in those of the new nations.

The liberalism of the Latin American independence movements, a liberalism akin to that of Spain in 1812—somewhere between the formulations of Adam Smith and Jeremy Bentham, if with French overtones and Iberian overlays—was invoked by insurgent leaders and publicly disseminated; thus, *El Peruano Liberal* appeared in 1813.[47] And it was in this liberal spirit that many of the formal governing institutions of Latin American republics were inaugurated. Legitimacy, which as we have seen formerly resided in the crown, became located in the very act of constituting a nation. An epidemic of constitutions ensued, all espousing principles of federation and popular sovereignty; they have elicited perhaps an equally abundant commentary. Yet it was even earlier, by the late eighteenth century in Latin America, that constitutionalism was allied to republicanism and had come to refer to government (not excluding monarchy) limited by law, custom, natural rights, and the best interests of the community. Within this context, law was thought to have a life of its own and be derived from a higher natural law, and ultimately from God, and thus was superior to decrees made by incumbents, even in high office and including the king.

There was a related belief in the interlocking nature of economic and political life and of both as embodied in a functioning if unwritten constitution. Cabarrús packaged it thusly in 1785: "The economy of a kingdom does not consist of partial reform of such and such a branch, but of such and such a constitution."[48] With independence, people of similar mentality preferred formal instruments in the tradition of the United States and France, especially after creoles had seen the Spanish Constitution of 1812 assert moral authority without hampering the wielders of power. Russell Fitzgibbon has said that the approach to constitutions for the new republics, "was ritualistic"; so was that to government, which was viewed as formalistic, remote, even alien and antagonistic. "We" seldom went beyond regional patria. Many of the written constitutions originated more as pronunciamentos against opponents, as justifications, than as guides to political life. Even those closest to United States models put more emphasis upon religion, a strong executive, and upon the moral restraint exercised by virtue in the old Roman sense. Glen Dealy describes these constitutions as "a second catechism."[49] Again, none of them can be understood without taking into account the movement in Iberia and its Americas, afoot by the 1780s, for constitutional monarchy.

Some time ago George Blanksten concluded that these written instruments were unrealistic and bore little relation to the constitutions in force, rather than, as in the United States, harmonizing reasonably with a consensus of generally held assumptions. Dealy agrees that they embodied a wish, an ideal as had old Spanish law, while tradition and custom sanctified the continuingly effective unwritten constitutions, which had such a consensus and, it should be added, incorporated elements of medieval frontier theory and of the Spanish conquest in America. In short these traditions upheld militant individualism as a means to power and reinforced oligarchic domination within a patriarchal system wherein administrators wielded delegated authority. These traditions were further supported by a religiously derived corporate view of society, of Augustine's earthly city annexed to the Roman concept of *res pública* as the ultimate residence of sovereignty. It was a view reiterated by people of every political faction; such people differed chiefly on where and to what extent sovereignty had been delegated or conferred. Spanish patriots had revitalized this ubiquitous theory of residual sovereignty; American constitutionalists and patriots had taken it up. Moreover, and often overlooked, these Hispanic tendencies toward corporate thinking were reinforced in Latin America in the early nineteenth century not only by intellectual trends in Europe but also by the evolution in the United States of constitutional, legal, and economic thought, including a trend toward more corporate concepts.

In addition, with independence creoles found in the writings of Bentham a most congenial, kindred outlook on society. It was one that advanced the old enlightened emphasis on utility, and that of political economy on material progress, one that supported the written and unwritten interpretations of the constitutions, at will—all in all, it put the new republics on the road to what would become their favorite rationales for asserting social betterment would come through state-directed economic progress, the principles of positivism. Their adaptations of Bentham's ideas resulted in a British overlay on political theory akin to their dressing in English clothing.[50] Even so, it was often the United States, in its nineteenth-century aspect, that Bentham and his followers glorified as a utilitarian utopia, and though at first glance the sorts of individualism and liberalism advocated by the new entrepreneurs and patriots in Latin America, and by many Europeans, was far different from the content of those terms as understood in the United States, on closer examination, as we have seen, the distance was not as great. By hindsight too we can see that Latin Americans then were shrewder in their appraisals of exactly what they were borrowing from the North American republic than the judgments of many subsequent commentators have indicated. For to the extent that the activities and outlooks of entrepreneurs, intellectuals, and patriots had altered, they had done so more or less across the board, throughout the

Atlantic world. And if the unwritten constitutions in Latin America became the more effective ones, they had the support not only of their own traditions but of some broadly Western tendencies.

People in the United States from the 1820s on looked at Latin America with sundry assumptions, much as they always had—as politically chaotic; as the dark underside of the hemisphere, religiously benighted; as a mass of humanity held down by servitude and ignorance; as a region of inferior peoples (especially with the rise in popularity of theories of white supremacy and racial purity); as a region of vast resources and much gold and silver. More positively, they saw it as a potential trading partner, as a fascinating and strange world of jungles, rivers, lost cities, and exotic cultures; and, most sanguinely, as a part of the Americas capable of great strides, if provided with the proper education and technology. And the idea of the United States exercising an informal protectorate over Latin America endured.[51] Even so, United States relations with Latin America nearly always have been filtered through a concern with broader international foreign policy and balance of power politics, on one hand, and through the prism of their relation to domestic issues, on the other.

Latin Americans continued to view the United States as a land of entrepreneurs and a source of republican traditions—as the astute, conservative, and disapproving Chilean Melchor Martínez put it, as "the republic that opened the first door to American liberty and broke the chains which joined it to Europe."[52] Yet, emulation of the United States had its limits; as Garcia de Sena remarked in 1811, creoles would borrow nothing against "our religion and man's place in society, according to his class and which leaves him in entire liberty."[53] They continued, too, never quite to separate it from Britain in their thinking during a time when England exercised greatest international power and maintained closest economic ties to Latin America. In Mexico, and elsewhere, the early United States republic remained an exemplar referred to by out-of-power liberals advocating an agrarian democratic ideal, while in the 1820s traditionalists like Lucas Alamán admired the current political and economic order in that country. Yet, by the 1830s Mexicans and other Latin Americans felt misled and had become embittered; their criticism of Anglo-American settlement in Texas came to a head with war in the 1840s. By then, too, many liberals had become narrowly nationalistic.[54]

With the rise of positivism wielded as a rationale by governments seeking foreign capital and technology, the United States became both an ideal of material advance to a greater degree than ever before, and a focus for criticism by opponents advocating economic nationalism. Antonio José de Irisarri, in 1819 Chilean minister in London, had voiced a reaction intensifying among such people as the century wore on; he noted "the contempt with which this nation as well as the United States have viewed us; they send their merchant ships to our ports as they would send them to an uninhabited coast, threatening it with their warships as they would the blacks of Senegal."[55] In addition, that complaint came to include foreign investment, and all of these attitudes fed into twentieth-century nationalism, the impulse to Third World alignment, and concepts of dependency.[56] Simón Rodríguez, Bolívar's sometime mentor, was among the first to note a dilemma for patriots, one inserting a wedge between entrepreneurs and intellectuals, when he wrote: "The wisdom of Europe and the prosperity of the United States are two enemies of the liberty to think in America."[57]

IV.

The birth of the American nations began within a multinational network and within an international trading system. Its history goes back before 1713, but that system gained strength with war, England's commercial thrust, and the dissolution of dynastic empires. Jacques Barbier speaks to this point in mentioning "the Spanish surrender of its imperial trade into the hands of multinational commercial interests."[58] The words that Juan and Ulloa's English editor, Barry, put down in 1826 form a refrain: "The vast Ocean is now no more than a lake for mariners and the four quarters of the world form a general market for merchants." Relations between the United States and Latin America have always taken place within a multinational context, as we have seen, as Mira Wilkins, while primarily concerned with American companies operating abroad from the 1800s, implies, and as formulators of policy in both Americas have usually been well aware.[59] Men with some interest in a sophisticated international trading network, in fact and theory, and proponents of revolution for independence in both Americas were often the same people. And afterwards, international involvement in both trade and investment loomed large throughout the nineteenth century—indeed, swamped its orginal advocates in Latin America. In the twentieth, the heirs of people like the FitzGeralds maneuver large multinational corporations adroitly around state bureaucracies, and states appear once more to be losing the contest for greater control of the activity of their nationals outside the country, and often of other nationals within it. The argument that Latin America is overwhelmingly dominated by that monolithic entity, the United States, has been and remains simplistic. Immanuel Wallerstein is among those who have noted a decline in United States state hegemony and an increased freedom of capitalist enterprise for larger, now multinational, corporations able to maneuver against state bureaucracies.[60]

With the demise of the old empires, the full impact of the industrial revolution, the advent of the new nations, and their entry as such into the international system, national leaders who tended to justify collaboration with foreigners as a means to higher patriotic ends were attacked, and sometimes succeeded, by populists who disavowed their opponents' emphasis on material development first and with outside help. Populists used distrust of foreigners and appeals to their country's sad international posture as rallying devices, to invoke popular unity and gain popular support. These appeals had their counterparts in the concurrent uses of patriotism to mold public opinion, in England, Iberia, and the United States. In them all, new dissenting traditions were in the making. Entrepreneur-adventurers persisted, but were probably most effective if directing large companies. Never again has the outlook of entrepreneurs, intellectuals, and patriots been so in accord throughout the Atlantic world as it was from 1713 to 1826, when few of them gave any thought to the fragility of progress or to resources as limited, and many of them were united in a great campaign, still being waged, to harness the environment.

In sum, this has been a look at certain aspects of the mental and material network comprising international relations in the Atlantic world between Utrecht and the first Pan-American conference. We have seen that economic concepts and conditions were integral to political and social attitudes and occurrences, and the other way around, including in the causes of the Revolution of 1776. Also very evident is the economic content of the revolutions of 1810, and that many of the people who made them began by espousing theories of political economy useful in advancing the agriculture, commerce, industry, and population of their regional patrias, which became the new republics. And a greater liberty to trade was an important political issue in both Americas. The vantage point of this book has not only permitted sighting both new similarities among American revolutions and a new spectrum of initial relations between the United States and Latin America, but has allowed seeing that these relations traversed a continuum from at least 1713, and that they were and continued to be thought of on all sides, and carried on, within an international framework. It has permitted, too, four observations in regard to the question of dependency and colonial exploitation.

First, we have seen that the industrial revolution brought a need for markets and materials but also sped Iberian competition with England, and that it fired the energies and aspirations of entrepreneurs, intellectuals, and patriots throughout much of the Atlantic world. Such people probably also fired it, and certainly provided a felicitous and nourishing environment for its growth. It well may be that the advent of mass production depended, as Ralph Davis has said, on a relatively small amount of capital. Even so, its debt must be acknowledged to the impetus of the existing network of attitudes and desires and to supportive theories of political economy and the Enlightenment. The interplay of the mental and the material, and of public and private interests, was propitious to this revolution, as it was to those for independence,

Second, during the eighteenth century, Latin America and the United States participated in the broadly Western growth of economy and population. Leaders in both were touched by the Enlightenment, by the new "science" of political economy, and by its concomitant, nascent liberalism. They foresaw harmonious progress for their societies—happy revolution—as possible and beneficial to everyone, although Anglo-Americans were less positive and more prone to raise ifs and buts.

Third, in Latin America then, although some entrepreneurs, intellectuals, and patriots were indeed ruthless, there as elsewhere on the whole they should not be viewed simply as *vendepatrias*, callously selling out their countrymen to more developed nations. From the later eighteenth century through independence, we have seen that such people repeatedly recognized and commented on the dangers of British economic dominance and dumping of imports and were unhappy at the prospect of United States territorial expansion and commercial competition. But, they also realized that their countries needed trading partners and saw that the range of options open to them was narrow. Leaders in the United States had faced similar decisions in relation to France and Britain. For Latin America, economic dependency and exploitation, varying over time and in place under Iberia, endured after 1810, fueled by the need for tax revenues and markets, the overwhelming pressure of British industry, and by the influx of British investment capital and technology. It was only after the First World War that people and institutions of the United States overtook the British in Latin American trade and investment. Yet before that a number of Latin American patriots and intellectuals had raised the standard of economic nationalism in association with their appeals to xenophobia, and some held up the United States as a symbol of the heartless materialism infecting their America. They viewed the industrial nations, including the United States, much as Charles III had viewed Britain, and when such men did come to power they usually launched programs reminiscent of the Bourbon reforms.

Finally, and all this said, economic exploitation in fact has been less national than either multinational or individual: Exploitation has been the province, that is, of international traders and investors or groups of them, on the one hand, and of certain people and groups within the country on the other. Nor has it been simply conscious and self-serving. Through independence, entrepreneurs in Latin America—José Ignacio Pombo and some other members of consulados, economic societies, and so on—saw a felicitous juncture between the social advantages of national development and their own profits and prestige, much as did John Hancock, Robert Morris, and even Benjamin Franklin. Moreover, the roots of the multinational character of commerce by 1713 can be discerned in the old custom of trading within an international network despite war, a custom common to many peoples, including the ancient Greeks and the Mexican civilizations the Spaniards first encountered. The FitzGeralds, a multinational family, Morris, Miranda, the participants in the Mexican silver transfer scheme, and many other people, including untold smugglers, took up this hoary practice. With the Napoleonic wars, the Latin American independence movements, and the flourishing of the industrial revolution, Latin America became the focus of more multinational wheeling and dealing than ever before. Foreign entrepreneurs in many instances cooperated there despite competition between their nations, as in the case of the United States and Britain, and some of these same people tended to see themselves as patriots devoted to the cause of liberty at home and abroad. Concomitantly, it can no longer be claimed that people who planned and brought about Latin American independence were not an integral part of a vast and loose international network involving, once again, entrepreneurs, intellectuals, and patriots. These transnational goings-on were most important not only to Atlantic trade and revolution, but also to the beginnings of relations among the Americas, as many Americans realized at the time.

LIST OF ABBREVIATIONS

AEA	Anuario de Estudios Americanos
AHA	American Historical Association
AHR	American Historical Review
AQ	American Quarterly
BAE	Biblioteca de Autores Españoles
BAGN	Boletín del Archivo General de la Nación (Mexico)
CSIC	Consejo Superior de Investigaciones Científicas
CSSH	Comparative Studies in Society and History
DNA	Documentos Relativos a la Independencia de Norteamérica existentes en Archivos Españoles
EA	Estudios Americanos
EcHR	Economic History Review
EEHA	Escuela de Estudios Hispano-Americanos
EnHR	English Historical Review
FCE	Fondo de Cultura Económica
HAHR	Hispanic American Historical Review
HM	Historia Mexicana
INAH	Instituto Nacional de Antropología e Historia
IPAGH	Instituto Panamericano de Geografía e Historia
JEcH	Journal of Economic History
JIAS	Journal of Inter-American Studies
JIH	Journal of Interdisciplinary History
JLAS	Journal of Latin American Studies
JMH	Journal of Modern History
LARR	Latin American Research Review
MMC	Memorias del primer coloquio mexicano de historia de la ciencia
MVHR	Mississippi Valley Historical Review
PAGN	Publicaciones del Archivo General de la Nación (Mexico)
PAPS	Proceedings of the American Philosophical Society
RHA	Revista de Historia de América
RI	Revista Iberoamericana
RIn	Revista de Indias
TAm	The Americas
UNAM	Universidad Nacional Autónoma de México
WMQ	William and Mary Quarterly

NOTES

Full citations to sources are given only at the first appearance of each. References to first citations are listed in the index.

PREFACE

1. James A. Henretta et al., *"American Historical Review* Forum: Social History as Lived and Written," *AHR* 84 (1979): 1314.

2. Paul J. Dietl, "Deduction and Historical Explanation," *History and Theory* 7 (1968) 167-188.

3. Georges Lefebvre, *The French Revolution from Its Origins to 1793,* trans. Elizabeth Moss Evanson (New York: Columbia University Press, 1962), p.121.

4. Perry Miller, *Nature's Nation* (Cambridge: Harvard University Press, 1967), p.12.

5. Fernand Braudel, *Capitalism and Material Life, 1400-1800,* trans. Mariam Kochan (New York: Harper & Row, 1975), p.x.

CHAPTER 1

1. Cited in Henry Kamen, *The War of Succession in Spain, 1700-15,* (Bloomington: University of Indiana Press, 1969), p.135. Frédéric Mauro, in "Towards an 'Intercontinental Model': European Overseas Expansion between 1500 and 1800," *EcHR* (2d ser.) 14 (1962): 1-2, states that Western civilization from 1500 to 1800 was distinguished by commercial capitalism, that it is "possible to speak of a revolution in sea-trade." Also see his *L'expansion européenne, 1600-1870* (Paris: Presses Universitaires de France, 1964); and Ralph Davis, *The Rise of the Atlantic Economies* (Ithaca: Cornell University Press, 1973).

2. England feared, justifiably, French trade expansion in the late seventeenth century, as did the Spaniards. French commercial interest in Spanish American trade was a cause of the War of Spanish Succession. England competed with France in that trade during the war. For a summary, see Bailey W. Diffie, *Latin American Civilization: Colonial Period* (Harrisburg, Pa.: Stackpole & Sons, 1945).

3. Max Savelle, *Empires to Nations: Expansion in America, 1713-1824* (Minneapolis: University of Minnesota Press, 1974), p.142. He adds, "Thereafter Britain followed a reasonably constant policy of preserving the internal integrity of the Spanish American empire."

4. Eric J. Hobsbawn, *Industry and Empire* (New York: Pantheon, 1968), p.17.

5. See Charles Tilly's contributions to the book he edited, *The Formation of National States in Western Europe* (Princeton: Princeton University Press, 1975); Leonard Krieger, *Kings and Philosophers, 1689-1789* (New York: Norton, 1970); Jacob Viner, "Man's Economic Status," in J. H. Plumb et al., *Man versus Society in Eighteenth-Century Britain* (Cambridge, 1968), pp. 22-53; and Joyce Appleby, "Ideology and Theory: The Tension between Political and Economic Liberalism in Seventeenth-Century England," *AHR* 81 (1976): 499-515.

6. Sir Lewis Namier, *England in the Age of the American Revolution,* 2d ed. (London: Macmillan, 1961); Hobsbawm, *Industry,* 16-17; Kamen, *War,* 46-47; and Richard Koebner, *Empire* (New York: Grosset & Dunlap, 1965), p. 79.

7. Namier, *England,* p. 33.

8. Cited by Robert Ashton, reviewing Charles Wilson, *England's Apprenticeship, 1603-1763* (London: Longmans, Green & Co., New York: St. Martin's Press, 1965), in *EcHR* 19 (1966):203.

9. William Letwin, *The Origins of Scientific Economics* (Garden City, N. Y.: Doubleday, 1965), ch. 8.

10. Cf. G. N. Clark, *The Wealth of England* (New York: Oxford University Press, 1946), p. 144; and R. Ashton, review of Wilson, p. 202.

11. George Lichtheim, *Imperialism* (New York: Praeger, 1971), pp. 37-38. D. C. McClelland, *The Achieving Society* (Princeton: Van Nostrand, 1961); and E. E. Hagen, *On the Theory of Social Change* (London: Tavistock, 1964) have pointed out the importance of attitudes and have advanced theories on the psychological formation of the eighteenth-century English emphasis on entrepreneurial achievement.

12. Even in Puritan England, religion was no longer the primary consideration in foreign policy, if it ever had been. International alignments frequently crossed religious lines, paticularly in the mid-seventeenth century English-Dutch rivalries (Lichtheim, *Imperialism,* p. 43). See Bernard Semmel, *The Rise of Free Trade Imperialism, 1750–1850* (Cambridge, 1970), pp. 3 ff., for the historiography of British imperialism.

13. Koebner, *Empire,* p. 77.

14. Glorification of English sea power was one response to the Peace of Utrecht and gave rise to Matthew Prior's lines [in *Poems* (1720) 260–75; cited in Koebner, *Empire,* p. 81]:

Where, by the Strength of this Idea charm'd,
Lighten'd with Glory and with Rapture warm'd,
Ascends my Soul? What sees She White and Great
of Pow'r and Plenty; Her Imperial Throne,
For Justice and for Mercy—sought and known....
...her Armed Fleets she sends
To Climates, folded yet from human Eye;...
From Pole to Pole, She hears her Acts resound,
And rules an Empire by no Ocean bound;
Knows her Ships anchor'd, and her Sails unfurl'd
In other Indies, and a second World.
Long shall Britannia (That must be her Name)
Be first in Conquest, and preside in Fame.

15. See William S. Maltby, *The Black Legend in England: The Development of Anti-Spanish Sentiment, 1558–1660* (Durham: Duke University Press, 1971).

16. James Thomson in *Britannia, A Poem* (1727), cited in Koebner, *Empire,* p. 82.

17. From *Alfred, A Masque,* in James Thomson, *Works,* 2, cited in Koebner, *Empire,* p. 83. Cf. Daniel Defoe, *Defoe's Review* (March 6, 1705), ed. C. M. Andrews, Facsimile. Text Society Publication no. 44, vol. 2, no. 3 (New York, 1938), p. 9:

England is a Trading Nation...and the Blood of Trade is mixed and blended with the Blood of gallantry, so that Trade is the Life of the Nation, the soul of its Felicity, the Spring of its Wealth, the Support of its Greatness and the Staff on which both King and People lean, and which (if it should sink) the whole Fabrick must fall, the Body Politick would sicken and languish, its Power decline, and the figure it makes in the world, grow by degrees, most Contemptibly mean.

18. Klaus E. Knorr, *British Colonial Theories, 1570–1850* (Toronto: University of Toronto Press, 1944), pp. 128–33. He finds that before 1660 English colonial theories were like the Spanish: colonies were then thought useful to search for precious metals, Christianize Indians, and reap glory for the nation and the crown. Cf., for example, Daniel Defoe, *A Plan of English Commerce* [1728] (Boston:

Houghton Mifflin, 1928), pp. 271–73; "The Manufactures support the Poor, Foreign Commerce supports the Manufactures, and planting Colonies supports the Commerce." For theories of colonies then held by British colonists in America, see Max Savelle, *Seeds of Liberty: The Genesis of the American Mind* (Seattle: University of Washington Press, 1965), p. 206.

19. Written in 1728 by Sir William Keith, *A Collection of Papers and Other Tracts Written Occasionally on Various Subjects* (London, 1740), pp. 168–84, cited in Jack P. Greene, ed., *Great Britain and the American Colonies, 1606–1763* (Columbia: University of South Carolina Press, 1970), p. 195. And see Colin Steele, *English Interpreters of the Iberian New World from Purchas to Stevens: A Bibliographical Study, 1603–1727* (Dyfed, Wales: Dolphin, 1976).

20. In William L. Payne, ed. and comp., *The Best of Defoe's Review* (1951; reprint ed., Freeport, N.Y.: Books for Libraries Press, 1970), pp. 176–79.

21. G. N. Clark, *Wealth*, p. 145; Lichtheim, *Imperialism*, p. 36. The Navigation Acts barred foreign ships from British colonial ports, monopolized the intraempire carrying trade for Britain and colonial shipping, and designated Britain as the entrepôt for colonial trade.

22. *The Wealth of Nations* (New York: Modern Library, 1937), p. 460.

23. See Appleby, "Ideology"; Caroline Robbins, " 'When It is that colonies may turn Independent,' an Analysis of the Environment and Politics of Francis Hutcheson (1694–1746)," *WMQ* 11 (1954):214–51. D. K. Fieldhouse, "Imperialism: an Historiographical Review," *EcHR* 14 (1961): 209, says of nineteenth-century imperialism: "It can be seen that imperialism owed its popular appeal not to the sinister influence of the capitalists, but to its inherent attractions for the masses." Appleby finds that this attraction was visible earlier, but was consciously heightened to abet certain economic and political interests. Walpole, during his ministry (1721–48), went so far as to suggest that colonials be encouraged in commercial activity, in this sense becoming a precursor of the free trade thought aired after midcentury. He also, however, sponsored protection for English manufactures.

24. Eli F. Heckscher, "Revisions in Economic History: Mercantilism," *EcHR* 7 (1936):44–54; and see D. C. Coleman, ed., *Revisions in Mercantilism* (London: Methuen, 1969). David S. Landes, *The Unbound Prometheus: Technological Change and Industrial Development in Western Europe from 1750 to the Present* (Cambridge, 1969), p. 32, puts it this way: "Mercantilism was, in short, pragmatism gilded by principle."

25. C. Wilson, *Apprenticeship*, p. 269.

26. See Jacob Viner, "Power versus Plenty as Objectives of Foreign Policy in the Seventeenth and Eighteenth Centuries," *World Politics* 1 (1948):1–29. An earlier mercantile assumption had equated wealth solely with bullion; Spain subsequently became *the* horrible example of bullionism: see Thomas Mun, *England's Treasure by Forraign Trade or the Balance of Our Forraign Trade is the Rule of Our Treasure* (London, 1664), pp. 5–23.

27. See Knorr, *Theories*, p. 71.

28. Thus, governmental interference in the course of industrial development was expected to be slight. See Appleby, "Ideology"; and for weaknesses in mercantile thought; M. Blaug, "Economic Theory and Economic History in Great Britain, 1650–1776," *Past and Present* 28 (1964):111–12; and Peter Mathias, *The First Industrial Revolution* (London: Methuen, 1969), pp. 84–103.

29. Erasmus Philipps, *The State of the Nation in Respect to her Commerce, Debts, and Money* (London, 1725), pp. 2–3.

30. A. P. Thornton, *Doctrines of Imperialism* (New York: Wiley, 1965), p. 114.

31. Landes, *Unbound Prometheus*, p. 32; and see Arnold Thackray, "The Industrial Revolution and the Image of Science," in Arnold Thackray and Everett Mendelsohn, eds., *Science and Values* (New York: Humanities Press, 1974), pp. 3–18.

32. Namier, *England*, p. 32.

33. See Ernst Cassirer, *The Philosophy of the Enlightenment* (Boston: Beacon, 1955) and Peter Gay, *The Enlightenment*, 2 vols. (New York: Knopf, 1966, 1969), Cf. J. H. Plumb, "Reason and Unreason in the Eighteenth Century: the English Experience," in J. H. Plumb, *In the Light of History* (Boston: Houghton Mifflin, 1973), pp. 3–24; and Robert Darnton, "In Search of the Enlightenment: Recent Attempts to Create a Social History of Ideas," *JMH* 43 (1971):113–32. Both articles make the point that the great majority of Europeans were unenlightened.

34. Newton, Hobbes, and Locke are now generally regarded as within the Enlightenment rather than, as they used to be, as its progenitors within an earlier Age of Reason. Moreover, both David Hume and Adam Smith fall within the compass of the Enlightenment; see Gay; Krieger, *Kings*.

35. Alfred North Whitehead, *Science and the Modern World* (New York: Mentor, 1948), p. 56.

36. Namier, *England,* pp. 32–33; "Possibly the reducing of all values to one common money denominator was to some extent stimulated by the discovery of the atom, a common unit in an infinitely diversified creation—social and moral discipline, having no exact measure of their own and yet trying to stimulate precision, are singularly liable to be influenced by terms and conceptions borrowed from science. The quantitative theory of happiness of the English utilitarians was, no doubt, psychologically connected with this habit of reducing moral values to the money unit." Cf. J.G.A. Pocock, *The Machiavellian Moment: Florentine Political Thought and the Atlantic Republican Tradition* (Princeton: Princeton University Press, 1975), p. 577.

37. R. Ashton, review of Wilson, p. 203. Landes, *Unbound Prometheus,* p. 60, mentions the shift in attitudes toward the laboring poor in the late seventeenth and early eighteenth centuries. Dissidents there were, though, among pietists and the landed, a Country or Commonwealth faction opposed to the new value placed on money and commerce: see Pocock, *Machiavellian Moment;* and Caroline Robbins, *The Eighteenth-Century Commonwealthman* (Cambridge: Harvard University Press, 1961).

38. Ralph Davis, *The Rise of the English Shipping Industry in the Seventeenth and Eighteenth Centuries* (New York: St. Martin's Press, 1962); Davis, *Atlantic Economies;* and Mauro, *L'expansion*.

39. J. Sperling, "The International Payments Mechanism in the Seventeenth and Eighteenth Centuries," *EcHR* 14 (1962):446–68.

40. The carrying trade was expected to yield that sine qua non, a favorable balance of trade: see, for example, William Wood, *Survey of Trade* (London, 1722), pp. 81–82. G. N. Clark, *Wealth,* p. 166, found three thousand English ships in the colonial trade in 1698 and, by 1774, fifteen thousand. The relatively static English woolen industry was protected, the infant cotton manufacturers discriminated against, although they benefited from protection of woolens through the closing of the English market to East Indian cottons. Finished English cotton goods did not figure prominently among main overseas exports in the first half of the century. Woolens comprised an estimated 30 percent of English exports around 1700 and over half of all national exports in 1740 (Wilson, *England's Apprenticeship*, p. 276). And see A. H. John, "Aspects of English Economic Growth in the First Half of the Eighteenth Century," *Economica* 28 (1961):168.

41. Ibid.; Ralph Davis, "English Foreign Trade, 1700-1774," *EnHR* (2d ser.) 15 (1962):289; and G. N. Clark, *Wealth,* pp. 164-67.

42. See Jean O. McLachlan, *Trade and Peace with Old Spain, 1667-1750* (1940; reprint ed., New York: Octagon, 1974); H. E. S. Fisher, "Anglo-Portuguese Trade, 1700-1770," *EcHR* 16 (1963): 219-33; his *The Portugal Trade: A Study of Anglo-Portuguese Commerce, 1700-1770* (London: Methuen, 1971); C. R. Boxer, *The Golden Age of Brazil, 1695-1750* (Berkeley and Los Angeles: University of California Press, 1962); and his *The Portuguese Seaborne Empire: 1415-1825* (New York: Knopf, 1969). John Cary, in *A Discourse on Trade* (London, 1745) 86-87, stated that to Spain went all sorts of "woolen Manufactures, Lead, Fish, Tin, Silk, and Worsted Stockings, Butter, Tobacco, Ginger, Leather, Bees-Wax, and sundry other things." From Spain came fruits, wines, oil, cochineal, indigo, and a large return in silver and gold. William Wood, in *Survey of Trade,* also mentioned items in the Spanish trade (pp. 86-87).

43. *The British Sailor's Discovery* (London, 1739).

44. Richard Pares, *War and Trade in the West Indies, 1739-63* (London: Oxford University Press, 1936), p. 5. During the War of Spanish Succession the English derived an estimated six million pesos from the trade with Port Bello and Cartagena by way of Jamaica, roughly half in gold and silver, half in produce. And see Gedalia Yogev, *Diamonds and Coral: Anglo-Dutch Jews and Eighteenth-Century Trade* (Leicester: Leicester University Press, 1978); and above, n. 26.

45. George Scelle, "The Slave Trade in the Spanish Colonies of America: The Asiento," *American Journal of International Law* 4(1910): 612–61; José Antonio Saco, *Historia de la esclavitud de la raza africana en el nuevo mundo, y en especial en los países américo-hispanos,* 4 vols. (Havana, 1938-40), 4; Arthur S. Aiton, "The Asiento Treaty as Reflected in the Papers of Lord Shelburne," *HAHR* 8 (1928): 167-77; George H. Nelson, "Contraband Trade under the Asiento, 1730-39," *AHR*

51 (1945): 57; Vera Lee Brown, "The South Sea Company and Contraband Trade," *AHR* 31 (1926): 662-78; her "Contraband Trade: A Factor in the Decline of Spain's Empire in America," *HAHR* 8 (1928): 178-89; and Judith B. Williams, "The Establishment of British Commerce with Argentina," *HAHR* 14 (1934): 43-64.

46. Nelson, "Contraband," pp. 58, 64-65. Aiton found "enormous profits" ("Asiento," p. 173) and that the Company's operational losses at the end of its tenure were due largely to excessive dividends declared and unpaid claims from Spanish seizures (p. 174). He adds that everyone was involved in smuggling, from factors to crews, and had contraband interests in cargoes, even in blacks, and that large quantities of illicit goods were also exported (p. 175). Cargoes from Spanish America were sold and exchanged in other ports in Spain or English America or taken to Europe, and they included gold bullion, pieces of eight, cocoa, snuff, tobacco, sarsaparilla, balsam, sugar, hides, tallow, cochineal, indigo, and dyewood (p. 173). Nelson stated that by 1738 profits were almost a hundred percent and the trade had been even more lucrative earlier. He estimates contraband totaled at least £5,500,000 annually (p. 63). Profits were almost approximately £1,500,000 annually from the trade in blacks (p. 64). The fullest report on peculation of directors, from information gained from papers at Simancas, is in V. L. Brown, "South Sea Company." Peculation and contraband indicate the difficulty of ascertaining now the extent of British trade with Latin America, the profitability of chartered companies, the gains reaped from the trade in blacks, or the correct statistics of that trade and conclusions based upon them.

47. C. Wilson, *Apprenticeship*, p. 271; McLachlan, *Trade;* Nelson, "Contraband," p. 62, stated that South Sea Company contraband activities decreased in the late 1730s, due to the competition of private Dutch and English traders, to the vigilance of the Spanish coast guard, and to increasingly severe regulation of the asiento trade by Spain. For earlier interlopers and their methods, see Clarence H. Haring, *Trade and Navigation between Spain and the Indies in the Time of the Hapsburgs* (1918; reprint ed., Gloucester, Mass.: Peter Smith, 1964). For patterns of trade, see Savelle, *Empires,* pp. 262-98. For smuggling by way of the Portuguese colonies, see Boxer, *Golden Age.* For the FitzGeralds of London, see Jacob M. Price, *France and the Chesapeake,* 2 vols. (Ann Arbor: University of Michigan Press, 1973), 1:559-61.

48. George L. Cherry, "The Development of the English Free-Trade Movement in Parliament, 1689-1702," *JMH* 25 (1953): 103–19. Letwin, *Origins*, app. IV, pp. 271–94 calls Sir Dudley North's *Discourses upon Trade*, published in 1691, the first great exposition of free-trade doctrines, and he thinks Roger North, Sir Dudley's brother, wrote them. North, at the time an exception, stated that "the whole World as to Trade is but one Nation or People, and therein Nations are as Persons."

49. Interlopers illegally (from British and Spanish points of view) engaged in trade with Spanish America. Smuggling also involved avoiding duties in and out of ports, national and foreign. The distinction is that interloping in Spanish America involved cutting into the South Sea Company's monopoly by other British ships; smuggling had to do with all illegal buying and selling. See. W. A. Cole, "Trends in Eighteenth Century Smuggling," *EcHR* 10 (1958): 395–410; and H.W.V. Temperley, "The Relations of England with Spanish America," *AHA, Annual Report* (1911; Washington, 1913), who cites the Duke of Newcastle: "The trade to the Spanish West Indies, although illicit by treaties, is so very lucrative, that the Parliament will never pass a law [prohibiting it], and the English merchant will run the hazard of carrying it on in spite of treaty" (p. 236). Temperley added the majority of smugglers were from the thirteen colonies and that half of the articles consumed by Mexico and Peru came from British North America.

50. See William L. Schurz, *The Manila Galleon* (New York: Dutton, 1939) especially Ch. 11; Serafin D. Quiason, "English Trade Relations with the Philippines, 1644–1765," (Ph. D. diss., University of Pennsylvania, 1962); Richard Pares, *Yankees and Creoles* (1956; reprint ed., Hamden, Conn.: Archon Books, 1968); Pares, *War*; and McLachlan, *Trade.*

51. Pares, *War*, pp. 28, 61–65; Davis, "English Foreign Trade," p. 29; Sperling, "International Payments," pp. 447–48; and see H.W.V. Temperley, "The Causes of the War of Jenkins' Ear, 1739," *Royal Historical Society Transactions* (3rd ser.) 3 (1909); 197–236; and Ernest H. Hildner, Jr., "The Role of the South Sea Company in the Diplomacy Leading to the War of Jenkins' Ear," *HAHR* 18 (1938): 322–41. Jenkins, a smuggler violating the asiento, lost his ear in 1731 (during King George's War in North America).

52. J. H. Plumb, *England in the Eighteenth Century (1714–1815)* (Baltimore: Penguin Books, 1950), p.25

53. Cited in Felix Gilbert, *The Beginnings of American Foreign Policy* (New York: Harper & Row, 1965), p. 23.

54. Defoe, *Evident Advantages to Great Britain and its Allies from the Approaching War* (London, 1721), p. 15.

55. Thomas S. Ashton, *An Economic History of England: the Eighteenth Century* (New York: Barnes and Noble, 1954), and C. Wilson, *Apprenticeship,* 276–80, think wars deflect energies. Pares does not agree, nor does A. H. John, in "War and the English Economy, 1700–1763," *EcHR* 7 (1955): 329–44. And see J. M. Winter, ed., *War and Economic Development* (Cambridge, 1975), especially Phyllis Deane, "War and Industrialization," pp. 91–102.

56. Penfield Roberts, *The Quest for Security, 1715–1740* (New York: Harper & Bros., 1947), pp. 258–60.

57. Cole, "Trends," p. 395.

58. Defoe, *Evident Advantages,* pp. 21–22, and see p. 43.

59. Pares, *War,* pp. 65–74.

60. Ibid.

61. "Santiago and the Freeing of Spanish America, 1741," *AHR* 4 (1899): 323–28, contains the text; and see James A. Robertson, "The English Attack on Cartagena in 1741 and Plans for an Attack on Panama," *HAHR* 2 (1919): 62–71. Robertson cites an anonymous British official's opinion concerning plans for a secret expedition to Panama shedding light on the prevalence of contraband: "First. That if anything should be debated in council of Proceeding to Panama it might be done with utmost secresy because we have so many vessels that trade from this place [Jamaica] to that coast that should the Affair in any manner come to be known the Traders certainly would acquaint them of it."

62. Glyndwr Williams, ed., *Documents Relating to Anson's Voyage Around the World, 1740–1744* (London: Navy Records Society, 1967), p. 20; and Vera Lee Brown, "Anglo-Spanish Relations in America in the Closing Years of the Colonial Era," *HAHR* 5 (1922): 390–94.

63. Pares, *War,* pp. 65–74.

64. V. L. Brown describes Anson's opinions on the expedition. Also see Pares, *War,* pp. 65–74; and Ch. 4, concerning eighteenth-century Peruvian uprisings.

65. In this spirit, too, Sir Charles Wager, First Lord of the Admiralty, was interested in starting a revolt in Guatemala until he realized it was hardly a grand scheme.

66. Pares, *War,* p. 86; and Julio J. Le Riverend Brusone, "Desarrollo Económico y Social," in Ramiro Guerra y Sánchez, et al., *Historia de la Nación Cubana* (Havana: Editorial Historia de la Nación Cubana, 1952), 2:137–80. Under the asiento English trade with Cuba, by way of Jamaica, had increased and it included Cuban salt pork and hides, mules, and tobacco (p. 233). In 1740, when the Spanish Royal Havana Company took over the importation of slaves to Cuba, it purchased them in Jamaica and had them transported in English vessels. This trade was relatively small from 1740 to 1760; perhaps one thousand blacks went to Cuba in this way.

67. Pares, *War,* pp. 126, 96, 115. An attempt to found an English colony in the strategically located bay of Guantanamo failed, but certainly established precedent.

68. T. Ashton, *Economic History;* Hobsbawm, *Industry,* pp. 10-19; E. J. Hobsbawm and R. M. Hartwell, "The Standard of Living during the Industrial Revolution: A Discussion," *EcHR* 16 (1963): 119–46; David Landes, "Technological Change and Industrial Development in Western Europe, 1750–1914," in J. H. Clapham and Eileen Power, eds., *Cambridge Economic History of Europe,* 7 vols. (Cambridge; 1941–1977), vol. 6, *The Industrial Revolution and After,* ed. H. J. Habakkuk and M. Postan (1965), pp. 274–585; and his *Unbound Prometheus.*

69. G. N. Clark, *Wealth,* p. 141.

70. Ibid., p. 181. War had exposed the poor state of the navy, and Anson, who headed the Admiralty—effectively from 1748 and as its First Lord from 1751 until his death in 1762—did much to rectify it.

71. Davis, "English Foreign Trade," p. 295.

72. See H.E.S. Fisher, *Portugal;* Kenneth R. Maxwell, *Conflicts and Conspiracies: Brazil and Portugal, 1750–1808* (Cambridge, 1973), chs. 1–2; Allan Christelow, "Economic Background to the

Anglo-Spanish War of 1762," *JMH* 18 (1946): 22–36; and his "Great Britain and the Trades from Cadiz and Lisbon to Spanish America and Brazil, 1759–83." *HAHR* 27 (1947): 2–29. Malachy Postlethwayt, *Britain's Commercial Interests explained and improved* (London, 1757), 2: 462–63, notes the large number of British ships still seen in Spanish harbors. Pares, *War,* p. 61, states that royal ministers almost always ignored the English trade to Spain, for the merchants involved in it were Roman Catholics and Jews; cf. H.E.S. Fisher, *Portugal,* pp. 55–56; Yogev, *Diamonds,* and see above concerning the FitzGeralds.

73. Landes, "Technological Change"; and his *Prometheus Unbound*; Phyllis Deane, *The First Industrial Revolution* (Cambridge, 1965); and Phyllis Deane and W. A. Cole, *British Economic Growth, 1688-1959: Trends and Structure* (Cambridge, 1967), p. 45. While they find a spectacular advance in the British economy in the 1790s, Deane and Cole think the greatest growth took place in the third quarter of the century. In the same vein, Hobsbawm (in *Industry*, p. 32) sees 1750 to 1770 as "the runway for industrial 'take-off,' " and Robin M. Reeve, *The Industrial Revolution, 1750–1850* (London: University of London Press, 1971) moves the older later starting date for the industrial revolution back to mid-century. See also T. S. Ashton, *The Industrial Revolution*, 1st ed. rev. (New York: Oxford University Press, 1964); R. M. Hartwell, ed., *The Industrial Revolution and Economic Growth* (London: Methuen, 1971), p. 30; and Michael W. Flinn, *Origins of the Industrial Revolution* (New York: Barnes and Noble, 1966) for a well-balanced survey and a discussion of social, intellectual, and psychological factors involved. Ralph Davis, *The Industrial Revolution and British Overseas Trade* (Leicester: Leicester University Press; New York: Humanities Press, 1979), p. 9, says Deane and Cole, while granting overseas trade a considerable role in the course of the industrial revolution, incline toward the view that increased domestic spending, progressively cheaper food, and a rise in the number of middle-level incomes was responsible. Rather, Deane and Cole see all these factors as interrelated, unlike Davis who argues that the industrial revolution was not an outgrowth of earlier trade, "take-off," or capital accumulation, but resulted simply from a new industry, cotton textiles. The industry needed little capital; its rapid advance in and through productive techniques owed something only to the practical help of the skills of craftsmen and, he acknowledges, to a huge domestic market. His deus ex machina conclusion is based largely upon statistics showing which manufactures were most valuable (cotton) in the great spurt of the late eighteenth century and where they sold most initially. He does not discuss the industrial revolution's sources of expanding population and purchasing power, of commercial and financial expertise, and governmental cooperation, or the effects of a relatively stable economy and of cheap food, or mention any of the generally accepted contributing factors. And cf. Peter Lane, *The Industrial Revolution; the Birth of the Modern Age* (New York: Barnes and Noble, 1978) who says, "From the controlled system of colonial trade Britain gained necessary imports, a larger merchant navy, and an expanded commercial class with the capital for risk-taking, which became richer and gained the expertise and experience invaluable in the industrial revolution (p. 105). Also see Davis for a recent bibliography.

74. Then, besides woolens, England sent, including to Iberia and Latin America, its nails, axes, firearms, buckets, coaches, clocks, saddles, handkerchiefs, buttons, cordage, and so on, and there was still a bounty on what had been its major export, grain. Landes, "Technological Change," p. 288, says cotton now had clout that woolen interests could no longer squelch. Cf. Davis, *Industrial Revolution,* p. 65, who argues that acceleration of growth in cottons in the 1750s and early 1760s was only temporary.

75. Richard B. Sheridan, "The Commercial and Financial Organization of the British Slave Trade, 1750-1807," *EcHR* 11 (1958): 249-63, says that triangular trade to Barbados only took place early; afterwards, bills of exchange were used. Planters began to undertake the marketing of their own produce, notably sugar, so that by the 1750s slave-merchant ships often sailed home in ballast or with some minor staples. Jamaica was more favorable to the triangular trade until 1760, for there Spanish colonies brought in large amounts of currency, much of which was spent "on purchasing produce to load back the Guiney ships and make returns to Great Britain" (253-54). In the 1750s, Jamaica's annual slave imports averaged over five thousand five hundred; between 1763 and 1775, over eight thousand annually (p. 258). Roger Anstey, *The Atlantic Slave Trade and British Abolition, 1760-1810* (Atlantic Highlands, N. J.: Humanities Press, 1975) attacks the thesis that the slave trade was generally profitable and thus a basis for the industrial revolution, a thesis supported in Eric Williams, *Capitalism*

and Slavery (1944; reprint ed., New York: Russell and Russell, 1961); and cf. Flinn, *Origins*. In view of the complexity of trade involving Africans, the distortions of profits reported, for example, by the South Sea Company directors (see above, n. 46), and a tendency by some commentators to rely on data for too short a period as evidence for the entire century, the last word on the subject has yet to be said.

76. Deane, *First Industrial Revolution*, p. 58, discusses the significance of the re-export trade to British economic growth and industrialization, as well as ways foreign trade helped to precipitate the industrial revolution (pp. 66-68). See table in Landes, *Prometheus*, p. 8; Hartwell, *Industrial Revolution;* Davis, *Industrial Revolution*, p. 64; and W. E. Minchinton, ed., *The Growth of English Overseas Trade in the Seventeenth and Eighteenth Centuries* (London: Methuen, 1969). Minchinton's conclusion that "trade was a limited source of industrial finance" (p. 47), while valid, can be compared with Paul Bairoch, "Commerce international et gènese de la révolution industrielle anglaise," *Annales* 28 (1973) 541-71, who notes, "Home demand increased but foreign demand multiplied. If a spark was needed, this is where it came from" (p. 542), Cf. Flinn, *Origins*, pp. 45-46, 57; Clark, *Wealth;* T. Ashton, *Industrial Revolution;* E. A. Wrigley, "Modernization and the Industrial Revolution in England," *Journal of Interdisciplinary History* 4 (1972): 225-59; and Charles P. Kindleberger, "Commercial Expansion and the Industrial Revolution," *Journal of European Economic History* 4 (1975): 613-54.

77. H. W. V. Temperley, "The Age of Walpole and the Pelhams," in *The Cambridge Modern History*, ed. Sir A. W. Ward, Sir G. W. Prothero, and Sir Stanley Leathes, 13 vols. (New York: Macmillan, 1934), vol. 6, *The Eighteenth Century*, pp. 40-89. The Molasses Act put a high duty on importing molasses into English colonies from the non-British West Indies, thus protecting the production of the British islanders. Mainland Anglo-Americans, depending on cheaper French and Spanish molasses for their rum distilleries, evaded the act, sometimes purchasing a false Jamaican bill of lading.

78. See Ian R. Christie, *Crisis of Empire: Great Britain and the American Colonies, 1754-1798* (New York: Norton, 1966) for an account of the political and constitutional background to 1776. J. R. Pole, in conversation, has suggested that renewal of warfare in the 1750s delayed that reorganization. Also see Michael Kammen, *Empire and Interest: The American Colonies and the Politics of Mercantilism* (Philadelphia: Lippincott, 1970); Kammen, *A Rope of Sand: The Colonial Agents, British Politics and the American Revolution* (Ithaca: Cornell University Press, 1968); and Greene, *Great Britain*, who, on pp. 267-300, prints the liberal opinion of Thomas Pownall, former governor of Massachusetts. While Pownall wanted colonial as well as British ideas of empire taken into account, he thought all reform measures should be compatible with the true commercial spirit from whence the empire arose.

79. Letwin, *Origins*, pp. 229-33. Semmel observes that political economy was a kind of secular scripture with a moral and scientific sanction.

80. G. N. Clark, *Wealth*, p. 187.

81. Tucker argued that colonial suppliers depended on the British market and that without the colonial tie Britain could purchase in the cheapest market and avoid the expense of governing and defending territories; see Donald Winch, *Classical Political Theory and Colonies* (Cambridge: Harvard University Press, 1965), p. 18; George Anson, *A Voyage Around the World* (London, 1948); Octavio Gil Munilla, "Malvinas. El conflicto anglo-español de 1770," *AEA* 4 (1947): 275-77; Julius Goebel, *The Struggle for the Falkland Islands* (1927; reprint ed., New York: Kennikat Press, 1971); and above, n. 61–62.

82. See Koebner, *Empire*, pp. 101-4; Postlethwayt, *Britain's Commercial Interests*. Cf. Savelle, *Empires*, 99-100, 187-88, who however gives an off-balance interpretation of Postlethwayt's opinions on England's American colonies.

83. R. J. White, *Europe in the Eighteenth Century* (New York: St. Martin's Press, 1965), p. 163; and see C. Wilson, *Apprenticeship*, p. 281; and Allan Christelow, "Contraband Trade between Jamaica and the Spanish Main, and the Free Port Act of 1766," *HAHR* 22 (1942): 313-14, for pamphleteers' aims during that war.

84. G. N. Clark, *Wealth*, p. 191.

85. See Namier, *England*, p. 33; Plumb, *England*, pp. 105-25; Landes, "Technological Change"; Hobsbawm and Hartwell, *"Standard";* and Deane, *First Industrial Revolution*.

86. *Europe*, p. 169.

87. Herminio Portell Vilá, *Cuba en sus relaciones con los Estados Unidos y España . . .* 3 vols. (Havana: Jesus Montero, 1938), 1:55-61; Davis, "English Foreign Trade," p. 257; and see *Papeles sobre la toma de la Habana por los ingleses en 1762* (Havana: Publicaciones del Archivo Nacional de Cuba, 1948); and Nelson Vance Russell, "The Reaction of England and America to the Capture of Havana, 1762," *HAHR* 9 (1929): 307-10. The *Papeles*, p. 116, include secret instructions to Count Albemarle from George III, dated February 15, 1762, to take Havana and garrison it, to attack Vera Cruz, Pensacola, Saint Augustine, or Santiago de Cuba, and to concert with Lord Amherst who was to continue on to attack Louisiana. In "Observations on the (proposed) siege of Havana," Knowles, writing in 1761, named, as advantages, stopping the Spaniards' receiving treasure from the West Indies during the war, and ending commerce from Caracas and all ports to Vera Cruz. He added: "We should then command the whole West Indies and I may venture to add, carry on what trade we pleased to every port in it, while the war lasted . . . And (it) is not to be doubted, that so soon as the Americans hear of it being taken, it will be well supplied with everything those countries afford" (Ibid., pp. 188-89).

88. See V. T. Harlow, *The Founding of the Second Empire, 1763-1793,* 2 vols. (London: Longmans, Green, 1952, 1964); and his commentators: Richard Pares's review of vol. 1 in *EnHR* 48 (1953): 282-85; Ronald Hyam, "British Imperial Expansion in the Late Eighteenth Century," *The Historical Journal,* 10 (1967): 113-24; and Peter Marshall, "The First and Second Empires: A Question of Demarcation," *History* 59 (1964): 13-23. Cf. Semmel, *Rise*, p. 13; and Namier, *England,* p. 250, who set the foundation of an empire based on trade in 1760, and so too late. "The big changes in British expansion," says Hyam rightly, "stemmed from the industrial revolution, not the American revolution" ("British Imperial Expansion," p. 124). The American Revolution can no longer be said to demarcate a sharp cleavage in the nature of British imperialism. Changes in policy toward America underwent greater alteration in the late 1740s.

89. John, "War," p. 344.

90. Namier, *England;* and see Kammen, *Empire;* and Thomas C. Barrow, "Background to the Grenville Program, 1757-1763," *WMQ* 22 (1965): 93-104. Spain, Portugal, and England all now kept regular army contingents in their American colonies.

91. Christelow, "Contraband," p. 313.

92. Arthur Young, *Political Arithmetic* (London, 1774), p. 87; and see Richard B. Sheridan, *Sugar and Slavery: An Economic History of the British West Indies, 1623-1775* (Baltimore: Johns Hopkins University Press, 1974); and Christelow, "Contraband," p. 316. In 1764, a reporter wrote from Jamaica regarding trade with Spanish colonies:

> That part of trade which was the support of this island and its credit at home is entirely subsided by orders from home to suppress all commerce with the Spaniards who were the only people that brought us money here for our British manufactures, and enabled us to make our remittances to England. Not a Spanish vessel can now come with money to this island, but what is seized by officers either under the admiral or Governor. We have been prevented receiving on this island (since I arrived) nearly a million dollars.

From *The Gentleman's Magazine* (1764), p.337; cited in Sheridan, *Sugar,* pp. 459-60.

93. For Portugal, see Maxwell, *Conflicts;* and H. E. S. Fisher, "Anglo-Portuguese Trade," p. 231; and for Spanish and Portuguese attitudes toward Britain, below, Ch. 3.

94. See Christelow, "Great Britain."

95. In 1763 British Dominica had been opened to French West Indian commerce as a free port. The Dutch and Danes had pioneered the system, and there were French and Spanish precedents for it. A combination, in itself unusual, of British West Indian and North American interests put the act through Parliament. They were abetted by the Rockingham ministry, then seeking to reverse the policies of Grenville with this measure and to gain the repeal of the 1765 Stamp Act, a repeal seen by merchants as a means to recover returns from trade. See Frances Armytage, *The Free Port System in the British West Indies* (London: Longmans, Green, 1953); Christelow, "Contraband Trade," pp. 334, 338. Namier, *England,* pp. 234-41, found thirteen West Indian members of Parliament in 1766 and forty with West Indian connections, while only ten MPs had North American ties. The (more usual) clash of interests came with West Indians wanting the British monopoly maintained on sugar and molasses, while New

Englanders wanted to import the cheaper sugar from the French, Dutch, and Spanish islands and when forbidden, they smuggled—"The bootlegger can claim a more distinguished ancestry than the prohibition agents" (p. 238). Here a compromise was reached. West Indians, Namier went on to explain, were helped by "their commercial demands being in accord with mercantilist doctrines of trade then universally accepted and punctiliously adhered to in Great Britain." They were also helped by not being, as were the New Englanders, more and more in competition with metropolitan carriers.

96. Christelow, "Great Britain," p. 16.

97. Sheridan, *Sugar,* pp. 46-65; and see above, n. 75.

98. Cited in Christelow, "Great Britain," p. 28. See Goebel, *Struggle.*

99. In 1765 a "M. Guiller" (Wheeler?) reported to the Spanish government a plot by some Puebla landowners, merchants, and a priest to free Mexico from Spain and make an alliance with Britain in exchange for commercial advantages in Vera Cruz. The British, he said, were interested but wanted a trade monopoly in Mexico and the cession of Vera Cruz. See "Plan de independencia de México en 1765," in *Documentos para la Guerra de Independencia de México de 1808-1821,* Juan Hernández y Dávalos, comp., 6 vols. (Mexico: Sandoval, 1877), 2: 620-23; "Notas acerca de una pretendida conspiración . . . " *BAGN* 9 (1938): 769-79; and "Proyecto singular de Marqués D'Aubarède sobre formar una República en México por los años de 1770," in *Archivo del General Miranda,* 24 vols. (Caracas: Parra León Hmnos., Ed. Sur-América, 1929-50), vol. 15 (1938), pp. 5-27. Christelow, "Great Britain," pp. 24-25, cites a 1771 London document, "State of the Services of the Marquis d'Aubarède," implying that that Frenchman, who was involved in the plot, was employed by the English. John Rydjord, in *Foreign Interest in the Independence of New Spain* (1935; reprint ed., New York: Octagon, 1972), p. 64, thought the British were prepared to act on the Puebla plan. And see below, Ch. 4, n. 53. Between 1765 and 1767, the English government evidenced great interest in the nature of disturbances in Quito and Mexico and in ascertaining the amount of discontent general throughout the Spanish dependencies. Moreover, an eminent Briton, Alexander Dalrymple, in 1768 voiced the current revitalized enthusiasm for Latin American trade in proposing "an amicable intercourse for mutual benefit." He argued against conquest and colonization in Spanish America, and specifically against England emulating Spanish conquest and pillage there. Had the Spanish but followed "the humane policy of trading" with the numerous peoples of Mexico and Peru from the Conquest on, he was certain they would be far wealthier. From Howard T. Fry, *Alexander Dalrymple (1737-1808) and the Expansion of British Trade* (Toronto: University of Toronto Press, 1970), p. 24.

100. Christelow, "Great Britain," p. 24.

101. V. Brown, "South Seas," pp. 187-88; cf. Gil Munilla, "Malvinas"; and J. Goebel, *Struggle.*

102. *The Merchant of Manchac: The Letterbooks of John Fitzpatrick, 1768-1790,* ed. Margaret Fisher Dalrymple (Baton Rouge: Louisiana State University Press, 1978), p. 9; and see below, Ch. 2 and 4.

103. Christelow, "Great Britain," p. 24.

104. Robin Humphreys, "Historical Revision: British Colonial Policy and the American Revolution, 1763-1776," *History* 19 (1934): 44.

105. Christie, *Crisis,* p. 66. Pitt's ministry was cut short by mental illness and he was succeeded by less politic men.

106. Ibid., p. 80. Kammen, *Rope,* shows that after the Stamp Act crisis of 1765 American lobbyists were virtually ignored by the British government.

107. Knorr, *Theories,* p. 130, cites a 1775 opinion. P. D. G. Thomas, *British Politics and the Stamp Act Crisis* (New York: Oxford University Press, 1975) points out that British ministers failed to understand that postwar depression in America was responsible for diminished trade and partly for colonial reluctance to shoulder further financial responsibilities. Also see Christie, *Crisis;* Jack P. Greene, "Plunge of Lemmings," *South Atlantic Quarterly* 47 (1968): 141-75; Greene, "An Uneasy Connection: An Analysis of the Preconditions of the American Revolution," in Stephen G. Kurtz and James H. Hutson, eds., *Essays on the American Revolution* (Chapel Hill: University of North Carolina Press; New York: Norton, 1973), pp. 32-80; J. R. Pole, *Foundations of American Independence, 1763-1815* (Indianapolis: Bobbs-Merrill, 1972); and Carl Ubbelohde, *The American Colonies and the British Empire* (New York: Crowell, 1968).

108. See Adam Smith, *The Wealth of Nations;* Knorr, *British Colonial Theories,* ch. 6 and p. 156 for a bibliography.

109. J.G.A. Pocock, "Machiavelli, Harrington, and English Political Ideologies in the Eighteenth Century," *WMQ* 22 (1965): 582. See J. M. Clark, "Adam Smith and the Currents of History," J. M. Clark, et al., *Adam Smith, 1776-1976* (Chicago: University of Chicago Press, 1976), pp. 53-76; R. H. Coase, "Adam Smith's View of Man," *Journal of Law and Economics* 19 (1976): 529-46; and Terence Hutchinson, "Adam Smith and the Wealth of Nations," Ibid., 507-28.

110. See Andrew S. Skinner, "Adam Smith: an Economic Interpretation of History," Andrew S. Skinner and Thomas Wilson, eds., *The Market and the State: Essays in Honour of Adam Smith* (London: Oxford University Press, 1976), pp. 154-78; R. Koebner, "Adam Smith and the Industrial Revolution," *EcHR* 11 (1959): 381-91; and Duncan Forbes, "Sceptical Whiggism, Commerce, and Liberty," in Skinner and Wilson, *Essays,* pp. 179 ff., who reminds us that Smith himself did not assume that progress was natural and led to freedom.

111. Winch, *Theory,* p. 19. Hume, who in 1769 looked forward to American independence, by 1774 had become more cautious and then thought "Benjamin Franklin wanted to emancipate them too soon." When in 1774 Edmund Burke spoke in Parliament against American colonial taxation but for returning to the restrictions of the old colonial system and asked Parliament to "be content to bind America by laws of trade; you have always done it" (Burke spoke for the merchants of Bristol), Josiah Tucker opposed his argument, stating that American trade rested rather on the superiority of British capital. Tucker in 1766 had made the often repeated observation that England was a shopkeeping nation, and he had added that among its best customers were the Anglo-Americans. As Semmel, in *Rise,* pp. 15, 20-22, points out, Tucker was both "a free trader and a nationalist, a prophetic combination." So was Adam Smith, who questioned the utility of colonies, indicating Britain did not gain from dominion, for government and defense were costly, and that, seeking a monopoly of trade, she got only a monopoly on maintenance. His views on what to do about existing colonies, however, were not explicit and have been interpreted by various scholars as ranging from independence to federated empire. Asa Briggs, in Wilson and Skinner, *Market and the State;* p. 28, cites Smith's "Memorandum of 1778" on "The State of the Contest with America," where Smith predicted Americans would rue a change of government if they made one. Smith also wrote that North America prospered because of "the genius of the British constitution which protects and governs (it)," and contrasted the American situation to government by mercantile company in the East Indies (ibid., p. 40). Smith appears to have counseled gradual transition in colonial status.

112. See Pocock, *Machiavellian Moment;* his "Machiavelli"; and his "The Machiavellian Moment Revisited: A Study in History and Ideology," *JMH* 53 (1981): 49-72.

113. John Roberts, *Revolution and Improvement: The Western World, 1775-1847* (Berkeley and Los Angeles: University of California Press, 1976), p. 21.

CHAPTER 2

1. Samuel E. Morison, *The Maritime History of Massachusetts, 1783–1860* (Boston: Houghton Mifflin, 1941); Bernard Bailyn, *The New England Merchants in the Seventeenth Century* (Cambridge: Harvard University Press, 1955), p. 80; Diffie, *Latin American Civilization,* pp. 408, 413; Max Savelle, *The Origins of American Diplomacy* (New York: Macmillan, 1967), pp. 291–99; Savelle, *Empires;* Harry Bernstein, *Origins of Inter-American Interest, 1700–1812* (1945; reprint ed., New York: Russell & Russell, 1965), p. 16; and see Gary B. Nash, *The Urban Crucible: Social Change, Political Consciousness, and the Origins of the American Revolution* (Cambridge: Harvard University Press, 1979) for an outstanding overview.

2. William H. Baxter, *House of Hancock* (Cambridge: Harvard University Press, 1945), pp. 52–53.

3. Charles M. Andrews, "Colonial Commerce," *AHR* 20 (1914): 43–63; Charles M. Andrews, *The Colonial Period of American History,* rev. ed., 4 vols. (New Haven: Yale University Press, 1938); Bailyn, *Merchants,* p. 85; Morison, *Maritime History,* p. 19; Byron Fairchild, *Messrs. William*

Pepperrell (Ithaca: Cornell University Press, 1954), p. 50; Dorothy S. Towle, "Smuggling Canary Wine in 1740," *New England Quarterly* 6 (1933):144–54; and Bernstein, *Origins*, pp. 16, 180. A trade in equipment for the new West Indian sugar mills, along with slaves who worked them and provisions, expanded with those mills in the 1700s.

4. Pares, *War*, pp. 395–97, said West Indian sugar planters needed flour, horses, fish, and lumber. Merchants paid few duties in North American ports on West Indian goods and often got false clearances in the British West Indies for cargoes from foreign islands. See Bailyn, *Merchants*, p. 129; Frank W. Pitman, *The Development of the British West Indies, 1700–1763 (1917*; reprint ed., Hamden, Conn.: Archon, 1967), pp. 150–52, 281–82, Savelle, *Empires*, pp. 262–98; Gary Walton, "New Evidence on Colonial Commerce." *JEcH* 28 (1968): 363–89; Bernstein, *Origins*, pp. 16–17; and above, Ch. 1, n. 49.

5. Georgia was settled in 1733. Among other things, the Carolinas shipped limburger cheese to New Orleans, supposedly for the Indians. There was a flourishing trade between Charleston and Saint Augustine from 1732 to 1763. See Joyce E. Harman, *Trade and Privateering in Spanish Florida, 1732–1763* (Jacksonville: Saint Augustine Historical Society, 1969), p. 2; Pitman, *Development*, pp. 449–63; N.M. Miller Surrey, *The Commerce of Louisiana during the French Regime* (1916; reprint ed., New York: AMS Press, 1968), p. 448: and John G. Clark, *New Orleans, 1718–1812: An Economic History* (Baton Rouge: Louisiana State University Press, 1970). Arthur L. Jensen, *The Maritime Commerce of Colonial Philadelphia* (Madison: State Historical Society of Wisconsin, 1963), p. 42, found that Philadelphia traded from the 1680s on with the West Indies.

6. Arthur M. Schlesinger, *The Colonial Merchants and the American Revolution* (1918; reprint ed., New York: Facsimile Library, 1939), pp. 39–49.

7. Saco, *Historia*; Pitman, *Development*, p. 64; and Peter Duignan and Clarence Clendenen, *The United States and the African Slave Trade, 1619–1862* (Stanford: Hoover Institute, 1963), pp. 1–7. Bernstein, *Origins*, pp. 73–74, speaks of a slave uprising in New York in 1741 led by "Spanish negroes," of a 1746 complaint concerning Cubans enslaved in Rhode Island, and of a case in New York where the admiralty freed seventeen Indians, mulattoes, and blacks taken by slavers from a Spanish vessel, and there were others. Also see Nash, *Urban Crucible*, 107 ff. ; and James G. Lydon, "New York and the Slave Trade, 1700 to 1774," *WMQ* (3d ser.) 35 (1978): 375–94; and James G. Lydon, *Pirates, Privateers, and Profits* (Upper Saddle River, N.J.; Gregg Press, 1970).

8. Aiton, "Asiento," 174–76; John Tate Lanning, "The American Colonies in the Preliminaries of the War of Jenkins' Ear," *Georgia Historical Quarterly* 11 (1927): 136; and A. L. Jensen, *Maritime*, pp. 57 ff.

9. Christelow, "Contraband," p. 329; T. S. Ashton, *Economic History*, pp. 140–42, adds that many English ships were built along the North American seaboard, where timber, sites, and skills were available. Parliament sanctioned docks and other facilities built by companies and commissioners.

10. During the war, the English government unofficially permitted and abetted the Spanish trade but not the French: see Pares, *War*, pp. 411–13, and above, Ch. 1.

11. V. L. Brown, "South Sea," p. 184; Towle, "Smuggling," p. 152.

12. Lanning, "American Colonies," p. 144; Nash, *Urban Crucible*, pp. 166 ff. Morison, *Maritime History*, p. 20, writes with some satisfaction that in 1748 a Massachusetts-built privateer owned by the Quincys captured a large and laden Spanish treasure ship.

13. Harman, *Trade*, pp. 35–37, 40–41; Pares, *War*, pp. 446–51, adds that on occasion prisoners for exchange were purchased; and Nash, *Urban Crucible*, recounts they were sometimes in short supply.

14. Price, *France*, p. 347.

15. Charles A. Barker, *American Convictions: Cycles of Public Thought, 1600–1850* (Baltimore: Johns Hopkins University Press, 1970), pp. 67–77; and see Nash, *Urban Crucible*, pp. 161 ff. The Massachusetts Staples Act prohibited shipping all provisions to English possessions except under bond. Early in 1745 embargoes were laid on all shipping in four New England colonies. Both measures were gotten around. Baxter, *House*, pp. 79–97, tells how Hancock maintained agents in Amsterdam for his trade between there and Boston. From 1745 until the war's end, his fortune grew too with government contracts to provision Newfoundland and Louisberg, captured from Spain's ally, France.

16. Lawrence Gipson, *The British Empire before the American Revolution*, 15 vols. (Caldwell, Idaho: Caxton, 1936–1970; vols. 4–15, New York: Knopf), vol. 2 (1946), pp. 232–33; John H. Andrews, "Anglo-American Trade in the Early Eighteenth Century," *Geographical Review* 45 (1955): 101; A. M. Wilson, "The Logwood Trade in the Seventeeth and Eighteenth Centuries," in D. C. McKay, ed., *Essays in the History of Modern Europe* (1936; reprint ed., Freeport, N. Y: Books for Libraries Press, 1968). Logwood, a dyestuff from the heartwood of a tropical tree, *Haematoxyion campechianum*, was re-exported from North America to England and was the second most valuable colonial mainland export after tobacco. Virginia Harrington, *The New York Merchants on the Eve of the Revolution* (New York: Columbia University Press, 1935), found woods the most valuable New York cargo to Britain (p. 167), and that New York merchants did a good trade in mahogany and logwood with Honduras and the Mosquito Coast. The trade was usually indirect; produce from the mainland was sold elsewhere and wood was bought with the proceeds. New York's Caribbean commerce was largely with Jamaica, Curacao, and Honduras. Also see above, n. 3; and Pitman, *Development*, pp. 271–96.

17. George L. Beer, *British Colonial Policy, 1754–1765* (1907; reprint ed., New York: Peter Smith, 1933): p. 73, cites Knowles's report of December 6, 1750. Also see Pares, *War*, pp. 446–55; and Surrey, *Commerce*, p. 457.

18. William S. Sachs and Ari Hoogenboom, *The Enterprising Colonials* (Chicago: University of Chicago Press, 1965), p. 40; Pitman, *Development*, p. 297; Stuart Bruchey, *The Roots of American Growth, 1607–1861* (New York: Harper & Row, 1968), p. 149; A. L. Jensen, *Maritime Commerce*, p. 51; and Geoffrey N. Gilbert, "Baltimore's Flour Trade to the Caribbean, 1750–1815," *JEcH* 37 (1977): 259–61.

19. Le Riverend Brusone, "Desarrollo," p. 231. In 1757 the New York merchant, William Walton, had contracts to supply the Saint Augustine garrison and other Havana Company areas: Harman, *Trade*, pp. 52–56. Lydon, "New York," p. 389, mentions that Walton owned shares in three African slavers and that his Caribbean traders commonly carried blacks to New York for sale. For the Waltons, also see Bernstein, *Origins*, pp. 19–20, 76.

20. A. L. Jensen, *Maritime Commerce*, pp. 57 ff; and James G. Lydon, "Fish and Flour for Gold; Southern Europe and the Colonial American Balance of Payments," *Business History Review* 39 (1965): 171–83.

21. Dorothy B. Goebel, "The 'New England Trade' and the French West Indies, 1763–1774: A Study in Trade Politics," *WMQ* 20 (1963): 331–72; Herbert C. Bell, "The West Indian Trade before the Revolution," *AHR* 22 (1917): pp. 272–87; Pares, *War*, pp. 388, 456; Christelow, "Contraband Trade," pp. 313, 321–22, 332; Savelle, *Empires*; Harrington, *New York*, p. 192; and Philip L. White, *The Beekmans of New York in Politics and Commerce, 1647–1877* (New York: N.Y. Historical Society, 1956), pp. 326, 400–1. Trade with the French through Monte Christi is frequently emphasized; for our purposes, it is the Spanish trade that needs recalling.

22. Schlesinger, *Merchants*, p. 46; Baxter, *House*, p. 129: in Boston, Thomas Hancock received large government contracts once again, enabling him to emerge from the war the richest man in the city.

23. Harman, *Trade*, p. 57. The flag of truce trade was again brisk. In Pennsylvania in 1759, Governor Denny openly sold flag of truce passes (Pitman, *Development*, p. 328); see Victor L. Johnson, "Fair Traders and Smugglers in Philadelphia, 1754–1763," *Pennsylvania Magazine of History and Biography* 83 (1959): 125–49; and Pares, *War*, pp. 188, 356, 388–89.

24. Ibid., p. 409.

25. Harman, *Trade*, pp. 68–72; at least one privateer out of Saint Augustine was a New England-built sloop.

26. Le Riverend Brusone, "Desarrollo," p. 210; and see above, Ch. 1.

27. Schlesinger, *Merchants*, pp. 46–47. In 1760 the governors of New York, Massachusetts, and Rhode Island were writing home to little avail that contraband in the last analysis benefited England, for its merchandise was sold in the trade and its profits ultimately went to Britain for manufactures for the colonies: Savelle, *Origins*, pp. 304–5; and Pitman, *Development*, pp. 320–26.

28. Ibid., pp. 326–31; Schlesinger, *Merchants*, pp. 47–48; Baxter, *House*, p. 150; V. Johnson, "Fair Traders"; Savelle, *Origins*, pp. 455–69; Joseph A. Ernst, "Economic Change and the Political

Economy of the American Revolution,'' in Larry R. Gerlach et al., eds., *Legacies of the American Revolution* (Logan: Utah State University Press, 1978); and Nash, *Urban Crucible*, pp. 236 ff.

29. Christelow, ''Contraband Trade,'' p. 341; Pitman, *Development*, pp. 332–33.

30. Schlesinger, *Merchants*, pp. 47–48; Baxter, *House*, pp. 129–46, 168; Sachs and Hoogenboom, *Enterprising Colonials*, p. 41; A. L. Jensen, *Maritime Commerce*, p. 67, and pp. 107–33 for routes; and Bernstein, *Origins*, p. 20, who mentions that Rhode Islanders supplied slaves to Puerto Rico. Harrington, *Trade*, pp. 200–202, found New York trade, like Philadelphia's, soared with Iberia. Between 1754 and 1772 New York's increased eight-fold; some went to Barcelona and Cádiz, more to Lisbon, and most to the wine islands—Madeira and the Canaries. Anglo-American trade with Iberia was very small from 1759 to 1763, affected by war and English policy.

31. A. L. Jensen, *Maritime Commerce*, p. 136; and see Fisher, *Portugal*, pp. 87, 91–92, 129.

32. Sergio Villalobos, *El comercio y la crisis colonial* (Santiago de Chile: Universidad de Chile, 1968), p. 138; Sachs and Hoogenboom, *Enterprising Colonials*, pp. 41–43; Savelle, *Empires*, pp. 5–57; S. E. Morison, ''The Commerce of Boston on the Eve of the American Revolution,'' *Proceedings of the American Antiquarian Society* 32 (1922): 24–51. In 1774, Aaron Lopez of Newport sent 30 ships to the Falklands for whale oil and had earlier traded with Spain, Portugal, and the Caribbean (Bernstein, *Origins*, p. 26); and see Stanley F. Chyet, *Lopez of Newport* (Detroit; Wayne State University Press, 1970).

33. Daniel P. Mannix and Malcolm Cowley, *Black Cargoes: A History of the Atlantic Slave Trade, 1518–1865* (New York: Viking, 1962), p. 169, and Charles L. Chandler, *Inter-American Acquaintances* 2d ed., ext. (Sewanee: Tennessee University Press, 1917), p. 20. Rice and indigo booms in the Carolinas and sugar in Cuba in the years between 1764 and 1777 contributed to the surge in the Atlantic slave trade. See above, Ch. 1, n. 75.

34. James F. Shepherd and Gary M. Walton, *Shipping, Maritime Trade, and the Economic Development of Colonial North America* (Cambridge, 1972), pp. 160–61; A. L. Jensen, *Maritime Commerce*, p. 60.

35. Arthur P. Whitaker, ''The Commerce of Louisiana and the Floridas at the End of the Eighteenth Century,'' *HAHR* 8 (1928): 190–203; Christelow, ''Contraband Trade,'' pp. 331–32, 339; J. Leitch Wright, Jr., *Anglo-Spanish Rivalry in North America* (Athens, Ga.: University of Georgia Press, 1971), pp. 115–16; and J. G. Clark, *New Orleans*, pp. 173–75, 233.

36. Shepherd and Walton, *Shipping*, pp. 160–66; cf. Bell, *West Indian Trade*; Marc Egnal, ''The Economic Development of the Thirteen Continental Colonies, 1720 to 1775,'' *WMQ* 37 (1975): 191–222, and Walter E. Minchinton, ''The Triangular Trade Revisited,'' in Henry A. Gemery and Jan S. Hogendorn, eds., *The Uncommon Market* (New York: Academic Press, 1979), pp. 31–52. Spanish, British, and French free ports escalated rivalries helpful to Anglo-Americans. From 1767 New Englanders frequented the French free port of Mole St. Nicholas, Saint Domingue, and did a lively business there, including in indirect exchange with Spanish colonies (D. Goebel, ''New England,'' pp. 354–57).

37. See Cotton Mather, *Religión pura to which is added La fé christiano; en veynte quarto artículos de la institución de Christo. An essay to convey religion into the Spanish Indies* (Boston, 1699), which explained on the title page, ''Sent to the Spaniards so that they will open their eyes and be converted from darkness to light and from the power of Satan to that of God.'' Also see Pares, *Yankees*, p. 150; Harry Bernstein, *Making an Inter-American Mind* (Gainesville: University of Florida Press, 1961); and Bernstein, *Origins*, pp. 66–71.

38. Corsairs out of Cuba roamed as far as the port of New York: Portell Vilá, *Cuba*, 1:52–53. Colonists in the Carolinas and Georgia, only recently settled, felt especially threatened by the Spanish: Lanning, ''American Colonies,'' pp. 138–42. From 1719 to 1721, South Carolinians had feared a rumored invasion during the undeclared war fought by England against Spain and Portugal: Savelle, *Empires*, p. 119.

39. Cited in José de Onís, *The United States as Seen by Spanish American Writers (1776–1890)* (New York: Hispanic Institute, 1952), pp. 9–10. John Shy, in *Toward Lexington: The Role of the British Army in the Coming of the American Revolution* (Princeton: Princeton University Press, 1965), p. 3, reminds us that *governor* was a military title in British America.

40. Pares, *War*, p. 82. British North American interest in taking Cuba or other foreign islands in order to expand markets was opposed by sugar interests in the islands under England, who feared competition and depopulation.

41. Savelle, *Seeds*, p. 571. There was also a popular, and justified, fear of Catholic conversions occurring on the New England frontier.

42. Cited in Ernest Lee Tuveson, *Redeemer Nation: The Idea of America's Millennial Role* (Chicago: University of Chicago Press, 1968), p. 101.

43. In his novel, *Roderic Random* (1748), Tobias Smollett, who served as a ship's surgeon's assistant on the expedition against Cartagena, commented on these provisions and their quality, or lack of it:

> our provision consisted of putrid salt beef. . . salt pork of New England which though neither fish nor flesh savoured of both; bread from the same country, every biscuit of which like a piece of clockwork moved by its own internal impulse, occasioned by the myriads of insects that dwelt within it, and butter served out by the gill, that tasted like train oil thickened with salt.

Cited in Lanning, "American Colonies," p. 155. Also see Albert Harkness, Jr., "Americanism and Jenkins' Ear," 37 (1950): p. 61–90; Towle, "Smuggling."

44. Pares, *War*, pp. 92–93; Portell Vilá, *Cuba*, 1: 49–53; John T. Lanning, "American Participation in the War of Jenkins' Ear," *Georgia Historical Quarterly* 11 (1927): 191–215; Harkness, "Americanism," pp. 75–76, 88–89; and Carl Bridenbaugh, *The Spirit of '76: The Growth of American Patriotism before Independence, 1607–1776* (New York: Oxford University Press, 1975), pp. 92–93.

45. Marc Egnal and Joseph A. Ernst, "An Economic Interpretation of the American Revolution," *WMQ* 29 (1972): 10; Marc Egnal, "The Pennsylvania Economy, 1748–1762: An Analysis of Short-run Fluctuations in the Context of Long-run Changes in the Atlantic Trading Community" Ph.D. Diss., University of Wisconsin, 1974); and Egnal," Economic Development." Foreign trade was slow in the early 1750s and had its ups and downs thereafter, with long-run growth. And see Nash, *Urban Crucible*, 236 ff., for society and the economy from the 1750s.

46. Greene, "Uneasy Connection," p. 36; and see James Henretta, *The Evolution of American Society, 1700–1815: An Interdisciplinary Analysis* (Lexington, Mass.: D. C. Heath, 1973). Cf. Michael Kammen, *People of Paradox* (New York: Knopf, 1972) for the complex of hopes and fears expressed by Americans.

47. Nash, *Urban Crucible*, 178 ff.; Jack P. Greene, "The Social Origins of the American Revolution: An Evaluation and an Interpretation," *Political Science Quarterly* 88 (1973): pp. 1–22; Kenneth Lockridge, "Social Change and the Meaning of the American Revolution," *Journal of Social History* 6 (1973): pp. 403–39.

48. Henry May, *The Enlightenment in America* (New York: Oxford University Press, 1976), p. 26; and see Donald H. Meyer, *The Democratic Enlightenment* (New York: Putnam, 1976).

49. See Meyer, "Uniqueness"; Bernard Bailyn, "Political Experience and Enlightened Ideas in Eighteenth-Century America," *AHR* 67 (1962): pp. 339–51; Meyer Reinhold, "The Quest for Useful Knowledge in Eighteenth-Century America," *PAPS* 119 (1975): pp. 108–33; Bernard Fay, "Learned Societies in Europe and America in the Eighteenth Century," *AHR* 37 (1932): pp. 255–66; and for the Enlightenment and its relationship to the sweep of colonial culture also; Barker, *American Convictions*; Louis B. Wright, *The Cultural Life of the American Colonies, 1607–1763* (New York: Harper & Row, 1962); Otho T. Beall, Jr., "Cotton Mather's Early 'Curiosa Americana' and the Boston Philosophical Society of 1683," *WMQ* 18 (1961): pp. 360–72; and Raymond P. Stearns, "Colonial Bedfellows of the Royal Society of London, 1661–1778," *WMQ* 3 (1946): pp. 208–68, who shows that colonial members included merchants, scientists, physicians, colonial governors, politicians, lawyers, diplomats, and soldiers.

50. See Perry Miller, "From Covenant to Revival," in *The Shaping of American Religion*, James W. Smith and A. Leland Jamison, eds. (Princeton: Princeton University Press, 1961), pp. 322–68; H. May, *Enlightenment*; Nash, *Urban Crucible*, 205 ff; Sacvan Bercovitch, *The American Jeremiad* (Madison: University of Wisconsin Press, 1978); William G. McLoughlin, "The Role of Religion in the Revolution," in Kurtz and Hutson, *Essays*, pp. 197–255.

51. See Pocock, *Machiavellian Moment;* Robbins, *Eighteenth-Century Commonwealthman;* Jerald C. Brauer, "Puritanism, Revivalism, and the Revolution," in Brauer, ed., *Religion and the American Revolution* (Philadelphia: Fortress Press, 1976), pp. 1–27; and Sacvan Bercovitch, *The Puritan Origins of the American Self* (New Haven: Yale University Press, 1975).

52. Nash, *Urban Crucible*, 340 ff., presents a schematic survey of political outlooks and who held them. See Henretta, "Evolution," p. 83, who speaks of a "modal personality" in subjected societies, encouraged by childhood training, embodied in role expectations, induced by values, and passed from generation to generation, so that in this fashion members are persuaded or conditioned to behave in culturally prescribed ways; cf. Peter Berger and Thomas Luckmann, *The Social Construction of Reality* (Garden City, N.Y.: Doubleday, 1966).

53. See Joseph A. Ernst, *Money and Politics in America, 1755–1775* (Chapel Hill: University of North Carolina Press, 1973). Spanish coins were valued; the United States dollar derives from the peso: See William G. Sumner, "The Spanish Dollar and the Colonial Shilling," *AHR* 3 (1898): 619.

54. J. E. Crowley, *This Sheba, Self: The Conceptualization of Economic Life in Eighteenth-Century America* (Baltimore: Johns Hopkins University Press, 1974), pp. 76–85, 112, 114, 122–23; and see J.G.A. Pocock, "Virtue and Commerce in the Eighteenth Century," *JIH* 3 (1972): pp. 119–34; and Joseph Dorfman, *The Economic Mind in American Civilization, 1606–1865*, 5 vols. (1946–59; reprint ed., vols. 1–3, New York; A. M. Kelley, 1966–69): 1.

55. J. R. Pole, *The Pursuit of Equality in American History* (Berkeley and Los Angeles: University of California Press, 1978), p. 37.

56. Savelle, *Origins;* and his *Empires;* Sachs and Hoogenboom, *Enterprising Colonials;* Richard L. Merritt, *Symbols of American Community, 1735–1775* (New Haven: Yale University Press, 1966); Crowley, *Sheba*, pp. 86, 96–99; Kammen, *People;* and Drew R. McCoy, "Benjamin Franklin's Vision of a Republican Political Economy for America," *WMQ* 35 (1978): 605–28.

57. Franklin, *Observations concerning the Increase of Mankind, the Peopling of Colonies* . . . This treatise has been called the first systematic Anglo-American analysis of relationships among population, available land, the economy, and the politics of North America; see Koebner, *Empire*, pp. 87–89; and Savelle, *Seeds*. There were five new colonies founded between 1745 and 1775. Population growth was sustained through the century, mostly by natural increase, and where in 1700 there were twenty Englishmen for every American white, by 1775 the ratio was three to one (Henretta, *Evolution*, p. 9).

58. Cited in Koebner, *Empire*, p. 107; and see McCoy, "Franklin's Vision," and Gerald Stourzh, *Benjamin Franklin and American Foreign Policy*, 2d ed. (Chicago: University of Chicago Press, 1969).

59. Also see Savelle, *Seeds*, p. 326.

60. Mayhew, *A Sermon Preach'd in the Audience of His Excellency William Shirley, Esq . . . May 29, 1754* (Boston, 1754), pp. 32–47; cited in Savelle, *Empires*, p. 147.

61. Edmund S. Morgan, ed., *Puritan Political Ideas* (Indianapolis: Bobbs-Merrill, 1965) pp. 304 ff.

62. Burr, *A Discourse Delivered in New-Ark, in New Jersey, January 1, 1755* (New York, 1755), pp. 29, 40; cited in Savelle, *Empires*, p. 147.

63. To Nathan Webb, October 12, 1755, in *Works of John Adams*, C. F. Adams, ed., 10 vols. (1850–56; Freeport: Books for Libraries, 1969), 1:23. And see James Truslow Adams, "On the term British Empire," *AHR* 27 (1921–22): pp. 485–89; Paul Varg, "The Advent of Nationalism, 1758–1776," *AQ* 16 (1964): pp. 169–81; and Bridenbaugh, *Spirit*.

64. See Bercovitch, *American Jeremiad;* Bercovitch, *Puritan;* Richard H. Niebuhr, *The Kingdom of God in America* (Chicago: University of Chicago Press, 1937); and Nathan O. Hatch, *The Sacred Cause of Liberty: Republican Thought and the Millennium in Revolutionary New England* (New Haven: Yale University Press, 1977).

65. *Papeles*, pp. 130–31; and David Syrett, comp. *The Siege of Havana, 1762* (London: Navy Records Society, 1970), pp. 253, 261, 264, 272, 275, 282, 290–95. British officers also complained of "that iniquitous trade" carried on from North America throughout the war (p. 301).

66. Russell, "Reaction"; Bernstein, *Origins*, p. 22; and see Joseph Sewall, *A sermon . . . . on the reduction of the Havannah* (Boston, 1762).

67. Cited in Russell, "Reaction," p. 314.

68. Savelle, *Seeds*, p. 578. Merritt, *Symbols*, states that after 1763 the press encouraged colonists to think of themselves as Americans.

69. Richard W. Van Alstyne, *Empire and Independence* (New York: Wiley, 1965), chs. 1–2.

70. Robert M. Weir, "Who Shall Rule at Home: The American Revolution as a Crisis of Legitimacy for the Colonial Elite," *JIH* 6 (1976): 679-700; Alan Rogers, *Empire and Liberty: American Resistance to British Authority, 1755-1763* (Berkeley and Los Angeles: University of California Press, 1975); Savelle, *Seeds,* p. 577; Kammen, *People;* Ernst, "Economic Change," pp. 109 ff.; and Jack P. Greene, "The Seven Years War and the American Revolution," in Peter Marshall and Glyn Williams, eds., *The British Atlantic Empire Before the American Revolution* (London: Frank Cass; distributed by Biblio Distribution Center, Totowa, N.J., 1980), pp. 85-105.

71. Cited in Arthur M. Schlesinger, "The American Revolution Reconsidered," *Political Science Quarterly* 34 (1919): 63. For the years 1760-1776 see Christie, *Crisis;* Nash, *Urban Crucible,* 236 ff.; Pole, *Foundations;* Kammen's works; Bernard Bailyn, *The Ideological Origins of the American Revolution* (Cambridge: Harvard University Press, 1967); Bernard Knollenberg, *Origin of the American Revolution, 1759-1766* (New York: Macmillan, 1960); and cf. J. M. Bumsted, "'Things in the Womb of Time'; Ideas of American Independence, 1633-1763," *WMQ* 31 (1974): 533-64. Also see Edmund S. Morgan, *The Birth of the Republic, 1763-1789* (Chicago: University of Chicago Press, 1956); Ubbelohde, *American Colonies;* Kurtz and Hutson, eds., *Essays;* Egnal and Ernst, "Economic Interpretation"; J. G. A. Pocock, "1776: The Revolution Against Parliament," in Pocock, ed., *Three British Revolutions: 1641, 1688, 1776* (Princeton: Princeton University Press for the Folger Institute of Renaissance and Eighteenth-Century Studies 1980); and Jack P. Greene, ed., *The Reinterpretation of the American Revolution, 1763-1789* (New York: Harper and Row, 1968).

72. V. Johnson, "Fair Traders," 144. That Assembly also reminded the governor, Denny, writes Johnson, that it "had counted upon receipts from the trade with Portugal and the Wine Islands to help support bills of credit recently issued in response to the Crown's appeal for aid in carrying on the war." Portuguese salt, it added, was essential for provisions (p. 142). Thomas Willing then complained, "Irreparable damage [has been done] to this Collony where [there] has been the greatest plenty of Grain ever known and no export for it" (p. 143).

73. Otis, *A Vindication of the Conduct of the House of Representatives of the Province of Massachusetts-Bay* (Boston, 1762), p. 20. Otis was upholding that body's opposing the governor's appropriation of defense funds without prior consent. His argument against the writs of assistance in a Boston court John Adams later saluted as the first blow of the American Revolution. See Andrew J. Reck, "The Declaration of Independence as an Expression of the American Mind," a paper presented at the Fourth International Congress on the Enlightenment, Yale University, July 1975; Andrew J. Reck, "The Philosophical Background of the American Revolution," *Southwestern Journal of Philosophy* 5 (1974): 179-202; Christie, *Crisis*, pp. 36-37; Nash, *Urban Crucible,* 277 ff.; and Morton G. White. *The Philosophy of the American Revolution* (New York: Oxford University Press, 1978).

74. Humphreys, "Revision," pp. 45, 44.

75. Ernst, "Economic Change," p. 106; Christie, *Crisis,* pp. 39-48; Edward C. Papenfuse, *In Pursuit of Profit: The Annapolis Merchants in the Era of the American Revolution, 1763-1805* (Baltimore: John Hopkins University Press, 1975); and see Nash, *Urban Crucible,* regarding the disparity in prosperity between Boston and Philadelphia.

76. Christie, *Crisis,* p. 69.

77. Edmund S. and Helen M. Morgan, *The Stamp Act Crisis, Prologue to Revolution,* rev. ed., (New York: Collier, 1963); Edmund S. Morgan, "Colonial Ideas of Parliamentary Power, 1764-66," *WMQ* 5 (1948): 311-42; Ernst, "Economic Legacies."

78. Dickinson, "The Late Regulations Respecting the British Colonies" (Dec. 7, 1765), in *The Writings of. . .Paul L. Ford,* ed. (1895; reprint ed. New York: Da Capo, 1970), pp. 209-45. See Stephen E. Lucas, *Portents of Rebellion: Rhetoric and Revolution in Philadelphia, 1765-1776* (Philadelphia: Temple University Press, 1976), pp. 32-35, 47, 56; Robert F. Oaks, "Philadelphia Merchants and the Origins of American Independence," *PAPS* 121 (1977): 407-36; and Nash, *Urban Crucible.*

79. Robert M. Calhoon, "William Smith Jr.'s Alternative to the American Revolution," *WMQ* 22 (1965): 118.

80. William S. Sachs, "The Business Outlook in the Northern Colonies, 1750-1775" (Ph.D.

Diss., Columbia University, 1957); Christie, *Crisis,* pp. 59, 68-69; Bailyn, *Ideological Origins,* pp. 120-21; and see Nash, *Urban Crucible;* and Pole, *Pursuit,* 39 ff., concerning social unrest from 1765 on.

81. Bland, *An Inquiry into the Rights of the British Colonies* (Williamsburg, 1766); C. F. Adams, ed., *Works of John Adams,* 1:66; and Bailyn, *Ideological Origins,* pp. 140, 198-229.

82. Ernst, "Economic Change," 116 ff.; Carl Ubbelohde, *The Vice-Admiralty Courts and the American Revolution* (Chapel Hill: University of North Carolina Press, 1960). Ernst explains: "Colonial merchants, planters, and mechanics alike judged their possibilities of making a profit according to traditional short-run indicators, namely: prices, exchange rates, the state of the market, the availability of credit and currency, and the cost of freight and insurance."

83. Christie, *Crisis,* pp. 71-72; Nash, *Urban Crucible,* p. 352.

84. Cited by Reck, "Declaration," p. 11.

85. Bailyn, *Ideological Origins,* p. 305, says that defiance of constituted authorities in 1768 was most intense among local religious dissenters.

86. Richard B. Sheridan, "The British Credit Crisis of 1772 and the American Colonies," *JEcH* 20 (1960): 182. In 1772, America underwent what Sachs calls "a sharp economic downturn"—just how sharp is a matter of dispute. Ernst thinks very, with economic collapse: See Joseph Ernst, "Political Economy and Reality: Problems in the Interpretation of the American Revolution," *Canadian Review of American Studies* 7 (1976): 109-18; his other writings, and Egnal and Ernst, "Economic Interpretation"; cf. Nash, *Urban Crucible,* 351 ff. who develops Ernst's opinion. Other scholars are less certain: Among them is J. R. Pole, in "The Revolution of the Radicals" *Reviews in American History* 5 (1977): 503-509. He is reviewing Joseph Ernst, " 'Ideology' and an Economic Interpretation of the Revolution," in Alfred F. Young, ed., *The American Revolution* (DeKalb: Northern Illinois University Press, 1976). Disruptions of 1772 proved profitable to some American merchants: Papenfuse, *Pursuit,* pp. 59 ff.; and see Baxter, *House,* pp. 269, 280; and Schlesinger, "American Revolution," p. 70.

87. In Schlesinger, *Merchants,* appendix, pp. 607-13. Nash, *Urban Crucible,* pp. 317 ff. notes that the Tea Act was perceived as English intervention in the American economy.

88. Crowley, *Sheba;* and Calhoon, "William Smith."

89. Bailyn, *Ideological Origins,* pp. 140, 305 ff.

90. Adams, *Novanglus and Massachusettensis* (Boston, 1819); and see Charles H. McIlwain, *The American Revolution: A Constitutional Interpretation* (New York, 1923).

91. Cited in Henry Steele Commager, *Jefferson, Nationalism, and the Enlightenment* (New York: Braziller, 1975), p. 163.

92. Cited in Max Savelle, "Nationalism and other Loyalties in the American Revolution," *AHR* 67 (1962): 901-23.

93. H. Trevor Colbourn, "Thomas Jefferson's Use of the Past," *WMQ* 15 (1958): 56-70; cf. Bailyn, *Ideological Origins,* pp. 81-83.

94. Christie, *Crisis,* p. 94.

95. Cited in Bailyn, *Ideological Origins,* p. 188; and see Reck, "Declaration," pp. 26, 28.

96. Pole, *Pursuit,* p. 41; cf. Thomas Fleming, *1776: Year of Illusion* (New York: Barnes & Noble, 1975).

97. See Pocock's writings; Greene, "Uneasy Connection"; Bernard Bailyn, "The Central Themes of the American Revolution: an Interpretation," in Kurtz and Hutson, *Essays,* pp. 3–31; Bailyn, *Ideological Origins*; Edmund S. Morgan, "The American Revolution Considered as an Intellectual Movement," in Esmond Wright, ed., *Causes and Consequences of the American Revolution* (Chicago: Quadrangle, 1966), pp. 172–92; and Nash, *Urban Crucible.*

98. Quoted in Morison, *Maritime History,* p. 27; and see Henretta, *Evolution*; Merrill Jensen, *The American Revolution within America* (New York: New York University Press, 1974); Gordon S. Wood, "Rhetoric and Reality in the American Revolution," *WMQ* 23 (1966): 332; Greene, "Social Origins"; and Nash, *Urban Crucible.*

99. Robert C. Middlekauff, "The American Continental Colonies in the Empire," in Frank Otto Gatell and Allen Weinstein, eds., *American Themes* (New York: Oxford University Press, 1968), p. 20. cf. Pocock, "Machiavellian Moment Revisited," pp. 70–71.

100. Julian P. Boyd, et al., eds., *The Papers of Thomas Jefferson* (Princeton: Princeton University Press, 1950–), 1:123–24. Oliver M. Dickerson, *The Navigation Acts and the American Revolution* (Philadelphia: University of Pennsylvania Press, 1951); Ubbelohde, *American Colonies*; Lawrence A. Harper, "Mercantilism and the American Revolution," *Canadian Historical Review* 23 (1942): 1–15, 29–34; and G. M. Walton, "The New Economic History and the Burdens of the Navigation Acts," *EcHR* 24 (1971): 533–42. Benjamin Franklin stated the case: "Freedom and protection are most indisputable principles whereon the success of trade must depend...nor is there a greater enemy to trade than constraint."

101. The phrase is from James B. Hedges, *The Browns of Providence Plantation* (Cambridge: Harvard University Press, 1952), p. 240.

102. Crowley, *Sheba*, pp. 136–37, 125–26; Pocock, "Machiavellian Moment Revisited"; Ernst, "Ideology"; and McCoy, "Franklin's Vision." One pamphlet, of March 1776, told of the "advantages of buying linens, woolens, cottons, silks and hardware in France, Spain, and Portugal...cheaper, in exchange for our lumber, naval stores, tobacco, flax seed, etc." (cited in Schlesinger, *Merchants*, p. 595). A study of the ideas of political economy in colonial America would be very valuable.

103. Bernstein, *Origins*, mentions Spanish holdings of the New York Library Company between 1764 and 1770, a Spanish grammar published in New York in 1751, and a Spanish course taught in Philadelphia in 1771—all coalescing with great mercantile interest in Spain and its American colonies. And see Stanley T. Williams, *The Spanish Background of American Literature*, 2 vols. (New Haven: Yale University Press, 1955), 1:23.

CHAPTER 3

1. Stanley G. Payne, *A History of Spain and Portugal*, 2 vols. (Madison: University of Wisconsin Press, 1973), 2:373; and see Antonio Domínguez Ortiz, *Sociedad y estado en el siglo XVIII español* (Barcelona: Ariel, 1976); Leonard Krieger, *An Essay on the Theory of Enlightened Despotism* (Chicago: University of Chicago Press, 1975); and William N. Hargreaves-Mawdsley, *Eighteenth-Century Spain, 1700-1788* (Totowa, N.J.: Rowman and Littlefield, 1979). Philip V had little administrative control of the country and had first to unify it, which wartime measures helped to do; see Kamen, *War;* and also Gonzalo Anes Alvárez, *El antiguo regimen: los borbones,* 4th ed. (Madrid: Alianza, 1979).

2. R. C. Blitz, "Mercantilist Policies and the Pattern of World Trade, 1500-1700," *JEcH* 27 (1967):43.

3. Fisher, "Anglo-Portuguese Trade," pp. 227-28, explains why England dominated Portugal and that the Methuen treaty of 1703 was not *the* cause.

4. In the first half of the century, Spain was divided into eight *reinos,* or kingdoms, each headed by a military captain-general assisted by an *audiencia*—a combination of council and magistracy. In some regions intendants—royal overseers—were installed for security and economic stimulation. Tax collection was made more centralized and efficient, and many but not all internal customs duties removed. The government began creating an administrative bureaucracy and set up factories producing luxury goods, to rival French imports. Catalonia, assisted by trade in Venezuelan cacao and Cuban sugar, recovered earliest. The amount of economic advance is sometimes overstated, as in Richard Herr, *The Eighteenth Century Revolution in Spain* (Princeton: Princeton University Press, 1958). Compare Jaime Vicens Vives, *An Economic History of Spain,* trans. Frances López Mòrillas (Princeton: Princeton University Press, 1969); Jaime Carrera Pujal, *Historia de la economia español,* 5 vols. (Barcelona: Bosch, 1943-47), 3,4; Juan Plaza Prieto, *Estructura económica de España en el siglo XVIII* (Madrid: Cajas de Ahorro, 1976); Payne, *History,* 2; Earl J. Hamilton, "Money and Economic Recovery in Spain under the First Bourbons, 1701-46," *JMH* 15 (1943):192-206; and Hamilton, *War and Prices in Spain, 1651-1800* (Cambridge: Harvard University Press, 1947).

5. Clarence Haring, *The Spanish Empire in America* (New York: Harcourt, Brace, and World, 1947), pp. 293, 318; and for the war period: Kamen, *War,* pp. 130-40; Roland D. Hussey, *The Caracas*

Company (1728-1784) (Cambridge: Harvard University Press, 1934), chs. 1, 7. Undeclared hostilities erupted with England in 1718, 1727, and formally, in 1739. The British favored the fleet system for Spain, since the fleets carried largely English goods while many of the registros were French. For commercial treaties between Spain and England from 1711 to 1716, see McLachlan, *Trade*, ch. 3. Also see Jerónimo Becker, *España y Inglaterra. Sus relaciones desde las Paces de Utrecht* (Madrid: A. Pérez, 1906); Vicente Palacio Atard, "El equilibrio de América en la diplomacia del siglo XVIII," *EA* 3 (1949); and Geoffrey J. Walker, *Spanish Politics and Imperial Trade, 1700-1789* (London: Macmillan, 1979).

6. See Uztáriz; there is an English edition: *The Theory and Practice of Commerce and Maritime Affairs*, trans. J. Kippax, 2 vols. (London, 1751); and also see Herr, *Eighteenth-Century Revolution*, pp. 47 ff.; Marcelo Bitar Letayf, *Economistas españoles del siglo XVIII* (Madrid: Editoriales Cultural Hispánica, 1968), pp. 75–97; Earl J. Hamilton, "The Mercantilism of Gerónimo de Uztáriz: A Reexamination (1670-1732)," in *Economics, Sociology, and the Modern World: Essays in Honor of T. N. Carver*, ed. Norman E. Himes (Cambridge: Harvard University Press, 1935); Carrera Pujal, *Historia*, 3:206-31; Lucas Beltrán Flórez, *Historia de las doctrinas económicas*, 3rd ed. rev. (Barcelona: Teide, 1976); Robert S. Smith, "Spanish Mercantilism: A Hardy Perennial," *Southern Economic Journal* 38 (1971):1-11; Stephen K. Ainsworth, "Commerce and Reform in the Spanish Empire during the Eighteenth Century" (Ph.D. diss., Duke University, 1975); Vicens Vives, *Economic History*, p. 526; José Múñoz Pérez, "El comercio de Indias bajo los Austrías y la crítica de proyectismo del siglo XVIII," *AEA* 13 (1959):90; and Múñoz Pérez, "Ideas sobre comercio en el siglo XVIII español," *EA* 19 (1960):57.

7. Walker, *Spanish Politics*, pp. 95 ff; Patiño studied to be a Jesuit, then became a lawyer, administered intendancies, and came to specialize in naval construction (McLachlan, *Trade*, pp. 149-54). As H. V. Temperley observed in the foreword to McLachlan, "Both diplomacy and politics rested on a solid commercial foundation in the eighteenth century. Indeed, commerce really was the steel framework of the political machine." For other companies, see Vicens Vives, *Economic History*, pp. 572-75.

8. Walker, *Spanish Politics*, pp. 150-54; Antonio García-Baquero González, *Cádiz y el Atlántico, 1717-1778*, 2 vols. (Seville: EEHA, 1976); José Joaquín Real Díaz, *Las ferias de Jalapa* (Seville: EEHA, 1959).

9. Rafael Antúñez y Acevedo, *Memorias históricas sobre la legislación y gobierno del comercio de los españoles con sus colonias en las Indias Occidentales* (Madrid, 1797), Pt.V: 297-304.

10. Ibid., V: 267.

11. Arthur P. Whitaker, *The Mississippi Question, 1795-1803* (New York: Appleton-Century, 1934), p. 191.

12. Antúñez y Acevedo, *Memorias*, V: 297.

13. Juan and Ulloa, *A Voyage to South America* (London, 1758); their *Noticias Secretas de América* (1826; reprint ed., Madrid: Editorial-América, 1918). It has been translated by John J. TePaske and Besse A. Clement as *Discourse and Political Reflections on the Kingdom of Peru* (Norman: University of Oklahoma Press, 1979); and see Arthur P. Whitaker, "Antonio de Ulloa," *HAHR* 15 (1935):155-94. Peru then included Ecuador, Bolivia, Argentina, Paraguay, and Uruguay; in addition, the captaincies of Chile, Santa Fé de Bogotá (Colombia)—until 1739—and Venezuela were dependent upon it. Ulloa was the son of an economist-royal minister, Bernardo de Ulloa, whose *Restablecimiento de las fábricas, y comercio español...* of 1740 generally followed Uztáriz, but put greater emphasis on manufacturing and on active naval, commercial, and industrial competition with other European nations. In his detailed suggestions the elder Ulloa praised the English Navigation Acts and urged Spain to emulate them. Only forty Spanish ships traded with America annually, he noted, compared to three hundred foreign ones. Dionisio Alsedo y Herrera also wrote several published reports on New World trade including smuggling. They were firsthand, but not of the high caliber of Juan's and Ulloa's: See Walker, *Spanish Politics*, p. xi.

14. Juan and Ulloa, passim.

15. Ibid.; and Bernal Díaz del Castillo, *Historia verdadera de la conquista de la Nueva España*, 2 vols. (Mexico: Editorial Porrúa, 1968), 2:39-40.

16. See Peggy K. Liss, *Mexico Under Spain, 1521-1556* (Chicago: University of Chicago Press, 1975), ch. 4; and J. H. Elliott, *The Old World and the New, 1492-1650* (Cambridge, 1969).

17. Ciriaco Pérez Bustamante, *España y sus Indias a través de la obra de Feijoo* (Madrid: Imp. Ed. Magisterio Español, 1965), p. 12. And for Feijoo as an introducer of English thought, see Susi Hillburn Effros, "English Influence in Eighteenth-Century Spanish Literature, 1700-1808" (Ph.D. diss., Columbia University, 1962).

18. G. Delpy, *L'Espagne en l'esprit européen: l'oeuvre de Feijoo (1725-1760)* (Paris, 1936), p. 293; and see Ivy L. McClelland, *Benito Jerónimo Feijoo* (New York: Twayne, 1969). Luis Vives (1492-1540) was an outstanding humanist. Melchor Cano (1525-60), a Dominican, gained and retained fame for his *De locus theologicus* (1562)—renovating scholasticsm, urging scientific rigor and critical analysis in methodology, and supporting the royal prerogative.

19. See J. A. Pérez-Rioja, *Proyección y actualidad de Feijoo* (Madrid, 1965), pp. 40-41, 163; Luis Sánchez Agesta, *El pensamiento político del despotismo ilustrado* (Madrid, 1953), p. 6, and Effross, "English Influence." Feijoo preferred Bacon's experimental method and he introduced Spaniards to skepticism and to the value of experimental science. Over four hundred thousand copies of his works were published.

20. See Pérez Bustamante, *España*, pp. 5-21; Agustín Millares Carlo, "Feijoo en América," *Cuadernos Americanos* 3 (1944):139-60; Hermenegildo Corbato, "Feijoo y los Españoles Americanos," *RI* 5 (1942):59-70; and Anthony Tudisco, "América en la literature española del siglo XVIII," *AEA* 11 (1954):565-85.

21. Hussey, *Caracas*, pp. 77-79; Pares, *War*, pp. 114-21; Becker, *España*; and George R. Dilg, "The Collapse of the Portobelo Fairs: a Study in Spanish Commercial Reform, 1720-1740" (Ph.D. diss., Indiana University, 1976).

22. *Nuevo sistema de gobierno económico para la América* [1743] (Madrid, 1789), pp. 64, 156, 11.

23. Ibid., 9; and see Juan Beneyto Pérez, *Los orígenes de la ciencia política en España* (Madrid, 1949); and Liss, *Mexico,* for other uses of the simile, at times as metaphor.

24. Campillo, *Nuevo sistema,* pp. 172-76.

25. Ibid., pp. 171-72, and see 1 ff., 25, 33, 60; and Miguel Artola, "Campillo y las reformas de Carlos III," in *RIn* 50 (1952):685-714.

26. Campillo, *Nuevo Sistema,* pp. 166-67, 210 ff., 270, 284; and Josefina Cintrón Tiryakian, "Campillo's Pragmatic New System: a Mercantile and Utilitarian Approach to Indian Reform in Spanish Colonies of the Eighteenth Century," *History of Political Economy* 10 (1978):237-38, 245. She concludes that "Campillo's enthusiasm for property and freedom was based on what he believed to have been the results of their adoption·in England."

27. Cited in McLachlan, *Trade,* p. 204; and see Vicens Vives, *Economic History,* pp. 475, 557-64; Múñoz Pérez, "Ideas," p. 49; Mark A. Burkholder and David S. Chandler, *From Impotence to Authority: the Spanish Crown and Appointments to the American Audiencias, 1687-1808* (Columbia: University of Missouri Press, 1977), pp. 85-86; García-Baquero, *Cádiz,* especially 1:273 ff.; and Pierre Vilar, *La Catalogne dans l'espagne moderne: Recherches sur les fondements economiques des structures nationales* (Paris, 1962).

28. Hussey, *Caracas,* 56 ff., pp. 108, 166-68. The Caracas Company established processing factories in Spain—flour mills, distilleries, and weaving shops (p. 169).

29. Ibid., pp. 104-8, 136-56.

30. Cited in Miguel Artola, "América en el pensamiento español del siglo XVIII," *RIn* 29 (1969):63.

31. Ibid., p. 67, and see 71 ff.

32. Ibid., p. 59.

33. J. O. McLachlan, "The Seven Years' Peace and the West Indian Policies of Carvajal and Wall," *EnHR* 53 (1938):457-77. And see Hussey, *Caracas,* p. 112; and Christelow, "Economic Background," p. 22.

34. In a letter of May 18, 1748; cited in McLachlan, *Trade,* pp. 204-7.

35. McLachlan, "Seven Years Peace," pp. 466-75; Lawrence H. Gipson, "British Diplomacy in

the Light of Anglo-Spanish New World Issues, 1750-1757,'' *AHR* 51 (1946):638-47; and, on Wall: Nigel Glendenning, ''Influencia de la literatura inglesa en España en el siglo XVIII,'' offprint from *La literatura española del siglo XVIII y sus fuentes extranjeras* (Oviedo: Universidad de Oviedo, 1968), p. 15.

36. Payne, *History*, 2:405.

37. The Portuguese Queen Regent, Maria Ana, was also Austrian. See Maxwell, *Conflicts*, pp. 2-4; Boxer, *Portuguese Seaborne Empire*, pp. 178-79; and H. V. Livermore, *A New History of Portugal*, 2d ed. (Cambridge, 1976), pp. 205-38.

38. Cited in Maxwell, *Conflicts*, p. 12; and see Kenneth Maxwell, ''Pombal and the Nationalization of the Luso-Brazilian Economy,'' *HAHR* 48 (1968):608-31.

39. Maxwell, *Conflicts*, pp. 12-18; and Colin M. MacLachlan, ''The Indian Directorate: Forced Acculturation in Portuguese America (1757-1799),'' *TAm* 28 (1972):357-87. Jesuits in Spanish America, too, dealt with the British, including in Cartagena, and those of Paraguay who smuggled gold and silver out in arrangement with the South Sea Company (V. L. Brown, ''South Sea Company,'' pp. 666, 669; Nelson, ''Contraband,'' p. 58).

40. Payne, *History*, 2:405-7.

41. Boxer, *Golden Age, passim;* Boxer, *Portuguese Seaborne Empire*, p. 192; Herbert S. Klein, ''The Portuguese Slave Trade from Angola in the Eighteenth Century,'' *JEcH* 32 (1972):894-918.

42. *DNA* (Madrid: Ministerio de Asuntos Exteriores, 1976-77), IV:1, 87.

43. Pombal did nothing for Portuguese agriculture with the exception of promoting national control of wines for export through a chartered company. For intellectual trends during his regime: Boxer, *Portuguese Seaborne Empire*, pp. 356-66; E. Bradford Burns, ''Concerning the Transmission and Dissemination of the Enlightenment in Brazil,'' in A. O. Aldridge, ed., *The Ibero-American Enlightenment* (Urbana: University of Illinois Press, 1971), pp. 141-207; and Manoel Cardozo, ''The Internationalism of the Portuguese Enlightenment: The Role of the Estrangeirado,'' in Ibid., pp. 141-207. For a judicious verdict on that regime: Payne, *History*, 2:408.

44. Dauril Alden, *Royal Government in Colonial Brazil, 1769-79* (Berkeley and Los Angeles: University of California Press, 1968); and Dauril Alden, ''The Marquis of Pombal and the American Revolution,'' *TAm* 17 (1961):369-82.

45. Charles signed the third Family Compact in 1761—the first was in 1733, the second in 1743—and entered the war, pressured by France to do so and, too late, recognizing French defeat would ruin the equilibrium of power in America, exposing Spain's colonies. See Christelow, ''Economic Background''; Palacio Atard, ''Equilibrio''; Carrera Pujol, *Historia* IV:310 ff. and, for English commercial treaties, Vicens Vives, *Economic History*, p. 568. A new treaty was signed with England in 1769, in which the British received trade and tax preferences. They were allowed to export gold and silver from Spain and Portugal, and British ships could not be searched. In America during the war, however, Spanish officials did lower contraband by keeping stricter account of bullion movements.

46. Bernardo Ward, *Proyecto Económico*, 4th ed. (Madrid, 1787), pp. 135, 144, 149. The formulation of the Spanish reform program recalls the Newtonian method of analysis and synthesis, that of breaking up phenomena into primary qualities and reconstructing them into a formal coherent system. Adherents of enlightenment everywhere tended to apply Newtonian method to human values and to all sorts of problems. Charles III had twenty years of administrative experience ruling Naples and held his ministers in tighter rein than had his predecessors. For details of the drawing up of the program: Arthur S. Aiton, ''Spanish Colonial Reorganization under the Family Compact,'' *HAHR* 12 (1932):269-80; and Herbert I. Priestley, *José de Gálvez, Visitor-General of New Spain* (Berkeley and Los Angeles: University of California Press, 1916).

47. Barbara H. Stein and Stanley J. Stein, ''Concepts and Realities of Spanish Economic Growth, 1759-1789,'' in Pierre Vilar, et al., *Historica Iberica* (New York: Anaya/Las Américas, 1973). 1:103-5.

48. Jean Sarrailh, *L'Espagne eclairée de la seconde moitíe du XVIIIème siècle* (Paris: Imprimaire Nationale, 1954); translated into Spanish as *La España ilustrada de la segunda mitad del siglo XVIII* (Mexico: Fondo de Cultura Económica, 1957), p. 181.

49. Campomanes's *"Respuesta fiscal sobre abolir la tasa y establecer a comercio de granos"* (Madrid, 1764). See Payne, *History,* 2:364; Sarrailh, *España,* pp. 546-47; Herr, *Eighteenth-Century Revolution;* Glendenning, "Influencia," pp. 51-52; Marcelin Defourneaux, *Pablo de Olavide ou L'Afrancesado (1725-1803)* (Paris: Presses Universitaires de France, 1959); and Estuardo Núñez, *El nuevo Olavide* (Lima: Villanueva, 1971). From 1756 on, royal decrees had supported internal and external free trade in grains but had not been enforced. In 1758 there appeared the *Discurso económico-político...* of Ramón Miguel Palacio.

50. Vicens Vives, *Economic History,* pp. 537-38.

51. See Pedro Rodríguez de Campomanes, *Dictamen Fiscal de Expulsión de los Jesuitas de España (1766-1767),* Jorge Cejudo and Teófanes Egido, eds. (Madrid: Fundación Universitaria Española, 1977); my thanks to Charles E. Ronan, S. J., for calling this, Campomanes's own account (recently discovered) of the reasons for the expulsion, to my attention. Campomanes was *fiscal,* or crown attorney, for the Council of Castile. Also see Earl J. Hamilton, "Monetary Problems in Spain and Spanish America, 1751-1800," *JEH* 4 (1944):21-48; Herr, *Eighteenth-Century Revolution,* pp. 14-31; and Magnus Mörner, "The Expulsion of the Jesuits from Spain and Spanish America in 1767 in the Light of Eighteenth-Century Regalism," *TAm* 23 (1966):156-64.

52. Sarrailh, *España,* p. 179.

53. Pedro Rodríguez de Campomanes, *Discurso sobre la Educación Popular de los artesanos y su fomento* (Madrid: Sancha, 1775), p. 35; and see Herr, *Eighteenth-Century Revolution,* pp. 167-69; Antonio Alvárez de Morales, *La "ilustración" y la reforma de la universidad en España del siglo XVIII* (Madrid: Escuela Nacional de Administración Pública, 1971); Richard L. Kagan, *Students and Society in Early Modern Spain* (Baltimore: Johns Hopkins University Press, 1974); Defourneaux, *Olavide;* and Mario Góngora, *Studies in the Colonial History of Spanish America,* trans. Richard Southern (Cambridge, 1975), ch. 5.

54. Cited in Ricardo Donoso, *Un letrado del siglo XVIII, el Dr. José Perfecto de Salas,* 2 vols. (Buenos Aires: Facultad de Filosofía y Letras, 1963), 1:378.

55. Luis Angel García Melero, comp., *La Independencia de los Estados Unidos de Norteamérica a través de la prensa española ("Gaceta de Madrid" y "Mercurio Histórico y Político"). Los precedentes (1763-1776)* (Madrid: Ministerio de Asuntos Exteriores. Dirección General de Relaciones Culturales, 1977).

56. Stein and Stein, "Concepts," p. 104. The London Society was founded in 1660. See Sarrailh, *España;* Domínguez Ortiz, *Sociedad;* Ricardo Krebs Wilckens, *El pensamiento histórico, político, y económico del Conde de Campomanes* (Santiago: Universidad de Chile, 1960); Gonzalo Anes Alvárez, *Economía y "ilustración" en la España del siglo XVIII* (Barcelona: Ariel, 1969); Paula de Demerson, et al., *Las sociedades económicas de Amigos del País en el siglo XVIII* (San Sebastian: CSIC, 1974); Robert J. Shafer, *The Economic Societies in the Spanish World (1763-1821)* (Syracuse: Syracuse University Press, 1958); and Ernesto Ruiz y González de Linares, *Las sociedades económicas de los amigos del país* (Burgos, 1972).

57. Herr, *Eighteenth-Century Revolution,* pp. 228-29.

58. See Vicente Rodríguez Casado, "Comentarios al decreto y real instrucción de 1765 regulando las relaciones comerciales de España e Indias," *Anuario de Historia del Derecho España* (Madrid) 13 (1936-41):100-135. To compete with contraband trade in blacks and to allow Spanish America ample labor to build up its agriculture, in 1759 Charles III inaugurated a new slave trade policy, to encourage free importation into the Indies by both Spanish subjects and foreigners. The king had wanted a single great Spanish company; it was chartered in 1765; see Priestley, *Gálvez,* pp. 32-37. The new Spanish asentistas were to trade Spanish goods for blacks on the African coast, then use Puerto Rico as an entrepôt to other ports, including Cartagena, Porto Bello, Cuba, Honduras, and Campeche. In practice however, most slaves going to Puerto Rico were purchased from the British, including from Anglo-Americans. The company, Aguirre, Aristeguí and Co., was set up in 1768 and with it Puerto Rico replaced Jamaica and local asentistas; consequently, the company was resented by them, and by colonial officials. It was also hamstrung by high duties retained on sale of slaves and in 1772 declared bankrupt. In 1773 its license was renewed and the high duties, as well as the Puerto Rican entrepôt, abandoned. The company's chief factory then became Havana. It was from the start a chimerical

endeavor, for the 1766 British Free Port Act allowed blacks purchased in Jamaica to be exported in Spanish ships, so that the Puerto Rican emporium proved unnecessary. Puerto Rico, though, was freighted by British North Americans and may have given newcomers a way into the Spanish trade and a way around entrenched Jamaican interests. The asiento of the company ended in 1779, with the war. In southern South America, La Plata continued, despite the lowering of import duties for slaves brought by Spanish ships directly from Africa, to do a brisk business in blacks supplied mostly from Río de Janeiro; see James F. King, "Evolution of the Free Slave Principle in Spanish Colonial Administration," *HAHR* 22 (1942):36-45.

59. See William W. Pierson, "The Establishment and Early Functioning of the *Intendencia* of Cuba," in his *Studies in Hispanic American History* (Chapel Hill: University of North Carolina Press, 1927), pp. 74-112.

60. Cited in Múnoz Pérez, "Ideas," p. 57.

61. See Priestley, *Gálvez*; Hussey, *Caracas*, 230-31; Aiton, "Spanish Colonial Reorganization." V. L. Brown, in "Anglo-Spanish Relations," states that Gálvez was recommended for the position by one Carrasco, a member of the French faction who strongly influenced the plan for Mexico. Carrasco said trade was in the hands of four bodies: the royal audiencia, the magistracy, the military, and secular priests. He wanted "to gain by intrigue two. . .and crush the other two and restore a more centralized form of control" (p. 340). The visita, which went way beyond the fact-finding mission envisioned by Campillo, was preceded by the sending of an army to Mexico in 1764 and by plans for a militia to be recruited there.

62. See Priestley, *Gálvez; Instrucción del Virrey Marqués de Croix que deja a su sucesor Antonio María Bucareli (1771)*, Norman F. Martin, S. J., ed. (Mexico: Editorial Jus, 1960); Eduardo Arcila Farías, *Ed siglo ilustrado en América* (Caracas, 1955); Luis Navarro García, *Don José de Gálvez y la comandancia general de las provincias internas del norte de Nueva España* (Seville, 1964); María del Carmen Velásquez, *El estado de guerra de Nueva España, 1760-1808* (Mexico: Colegio de México, 1950); Velásquez, *Establecimiento y pérdida del septentrión de Nueva España* (Mexico: Colegio de México, 1974); Bernard E. Bobb, *The Viceregency of Antonio María Bucareli in New Spain, 1771-1779* (Austin: University of Texas Press, 1962); Rómulo Velasco Cevallos, *La administración de don Frey Antonio María Bucareli y Ursúa*, 2 vols. (Mexico, 1936); Maria Lourdes Concepción Pajarón Parodey Díaz-Trechuel and Maria Luisa Rodríguez Baena, "Don Antonio María Bucareli," in José Antonio Calderón Quijano, ed., *Los virreyes de Nueva España en el reinado de Carlos III*, 2 vols. (Seville: EEHA, 1967, 1970); "Papel instructivo de Virrey Bucareli al Caballero de Croix, 1777," *BAGN* 6 (1965):445-76; Peggy K. Korn [Liss], "Topics in Mexican Historiography, 1750-1810: The Bourbon Reforms, the Enlightenment, and the Background to Revolution," in *Investigaciones Contemporáneas sobre Historia de México* (Mexico: Universidad Nacional and University of Texas Press, 1971), pp. 159-210; Peggy K. Liss, "México en el siglo XVIII—algunos problemas e interpretaciones cambiantes," *HM* 27 (1977):273-315; Burkholder and Chandler, *Impotence;* Lyle N. McAlister, *The Fuero Military in New Spain, 1764-1800* (Gainesville: University of Florida Press, 1957); Christon Archer, *The Army in Bourbon Mexico, 1760-1810* (Albuquerque: University of New Mexico Press, 1977); and David A. Brading, "Government and Elite in Late Colonial Mexico," *HAHR* 53 (1973):389-414. David A. Brading, *Miners and Merchants in Bourbon Mexico, 1763-1810* (Cambridge, 1971), is weak on the intent and efficacy of the reforms but excellent on the Mexican situation; cf. his "El mercantilismo ibérico y el crecimiento económico en la América Latina del siglo XVIII," in Enrique Florescano, comp., *Ensayos sobre el desarrollo económico de México y América Latina, 1500-1975* (Mexico: Fondo de Cultura Económico, 1979), pp. 293-314.

63. In 1755 Mexican children were forced to learn Spanish in village schools, and a royal decree a year earlier had stipulated that Indians must have Spanish to hold communal offices: Elisa Luque Alcaide, *La educación en Nueva España en el siglo XVIII* (Seville, EEHA, 1970), pp. 235 ff.; Edmundo O'Gorman, "Enseñanza del Castillo como factor político colonial," *BAGN* 17 (1946): 165–71; Shirley B. Heath, *Telling Tongues: Language Policy in Mexico, Colony to Nation* (New York: Columbia Teachers College Press, 1972); Tiryakian, "Campillo"; Magnus Mörner, "Bourbon Reform and Social Racial Policy," in his *Estado, razas y cambio social en la hispanoamérica colonial* (Mexico: Sepsetentas, 1974), pp. 136-50, says that in 1767 Gálvez suspended

269

the old laws of Indian-Spanish separation as a result of riots when the Jesuits were expelled, and that the Spanish minister, the Conde de Aranda, instructed on March 1, 1767 that Spaniards be permitted to reside in Indian villages in order to open and facilitate reciprocal trade. Francisco Antonio Lorenzana, regalist Archibishop of Mexico, was in the 1760s another champion of castilianization of Indians. He both suggested that Indian languages be suppressed because they were a source of hatred of the conquerors and of idolatry, as Góngora recounts in his *Studies* (p. 161), and viewed Indians as the natural wealth of Mexico and of value to the Spanish economy. See Francisco Antonio Lorenzana, *Cartas pastorales y edictos del...*(Mexico: Hogal, 1770). Opposition by the viceroy, Bucareli, and village priests in the 1770s on grounds of lack of funds and disturbing the status quo doomed the project.

64. Priestley, *Gálvez,* pp. 388-89; and see Luis Navarro García, "Destrucción de la oposición política en México por Carlos III," *Anales de la Universidad Hispalense* 24 (1964):13-46; and Múñoz Pérez, "Ideas," p. 57.

65. The Earl of Rochford to Conway, Nov. 11, 1765; in V. L. Brown, "Anglo-Spanish Relations," p. 343.

66. See, for a rather splenetic account of the regalist 1769 Mexican church council: Manuel Giménez Fernández, *El concilio IV provincial mejicano* (Seville: Gavida, 1939). Lorenzana was its moving spirit. Also see Nancy M. Farriss, *Crown and Clergy in Colonial Mexico, 1759-1821* (London: Athlone Press, 1968); and Javier Malagón-Barceló, "La obra escrita de Lorenzana como arzobispo de México," *HM* 23 (1974):437-65.

67. Luque Alcaide, *educación;* Rafael Moreno, "La filosofía moderna en la Nueva España," in Miguel León-Portilla, et al., *Estudios de historia de filosofía en México* (Mexico, 1963); English trans., Robert Caponigri, *Major Trends in Mexican Philosophy* (Notre Dame: University of Notre Dame Press, 1966), pp. 130-83; Bernabé Navarro, *Cultura mexicana moderna en el siglo XVIII* (Mexico: UNAM, 1964); Pablo González Casanova, *El misoneísmo y la modernidad cristiana en el siglo XVIII* (Mexico: Colegio de México, 1948); John Tate Lanning, *Academic Culture in the Spanish Colonies* (New York: Oxford University Press, 1940); and below, Ch. 4. For Spain: Sarrailh, *España;* Sánchez Agesta, *pensamiento;* and Herr, *Eighteenth-Century Revolution,* pp. 163-80.

68. See Pedro Rodríguez de Campomanes, *Juicio Imperial* (Madrid, 1768; rev. ed., 1769); Vicent Llombert, "Mercantilismo tardío, 'liberalización' comercial y explotación colonial americana: las reflexiones sobre el comercio español a Indias (1762) del Conde de Campomanes," in Alberto Gil Novales, ed., *Homenaje a Noël Saloman: Ilustración española e independencia de América* (Madrid: Porrúa Turanzas, 1979), pp. 333-43; Ricardo Krebs Wilckens, *pensamiento;* Ricardo Krebs Wilckens, "Pedro Rodríguez de Campomanes y la política colonial española en el siglo XVIII," *Boletín de la Academia Chilena de la Historia* 53 (1955); Herr, *Eighteenth-Century Revolution,* pp. 25-26; and Sarrailh, *España,* pp. 209-11.

69. Richard Konetzke, "La condición legal de los criollos y las causas de la independencia," *EA* 2 (1950):45; Ricardo Levene, *El mundo de las ideas y la revolución hispanoamericana de 1810* (Santiago: Editorial Jurídica de Chile, Facultad de Derecho de la Universidad de Chile, 1956); Navarro García, "Destrucción," p. 21.

70. Neither creoles nor crown had much to say about the (British) category of colonies of settlement, although Campomanes thought the English colonies of North America a new species, characterized by absence of indigenous population and inhabited by Europeans with the same customs and laws as people of the Old World, so that such colonies were in reality a European nation transplanted to America. This view facilitated Spain's aiding the Anglo-American insurgents of 1776. The term *colony,* in reference to Spain's America, appeared often in late eighteenth-century Spanish documents, according to Carlos Deustúa Pimentel, "Concepto y término de 'colonia' en los testimonios documentales del siglo XVIII," *Mercurio Peruano* 35 (1954):687-92; cf.: Ricardo Levene, *Las indias no eran colonias* (Buenos Aires and Mexico; Espasa-Calpe, 1951). For imperial theory: Sarrailh, *España;* Sánchez Agesta, *pensamiento;* Krebs Wilckens, *pensamiento,* 262-71; Liss, *Mexico;* and José Múñoz Pérez, "La idea de América en Campomanes," *AEA* 10 (1953):232.

71. Antonio Domínguez Ortiz, *La sociedad española en el siglo XVIII* (Madrid: Instituto Balmes de Sociológia; Consejo Superior de Investigaciones Cientificas, 1955); his *Sociedad y Estado;*

García-Baquero, *Cádiz,* 1:565-67; Sarrailh; *España;* and H. R. Trevor-Roper, "The Spanish Enlightenment," in his *Historical Essays* (New York: Harper and Row, 1957), pp. 260-72. Herr has understated the strength of tradition in this period.

72. Campomanes, *Discurso sobre el fomento de la industria popular* (Madrid, 1774); Campomanes, *Discurso sobre la educación popular;* and Campomanes, *Apéndice a la educación popular,* 4 vols. (Madrid, 1775-77); Robert Ricard, "De Campomanes á Jovellanos," *Les lettres romanes* (Louvain) 11 (1957):31-52; and see Marcelo Bitar Letayf, "El conde de Campomanes y el comercio español con Indias," *Cuadernos Hispanoaméricas* (Madrid) no. 205 (1967):91-97.

73. Gaspar Melchor de Jovellanos, "Informe del Real Acuerdo de Sevilla al Consejo Real de Castilla sobre la extracción de aceites a reinos extranjeros," (May 14, 1774) in *Obras publicadas é inéditos de G. M. de Jovellanos,* 2 vols. BAE, vols. 46-50 (Madrid: M. Rivadeneyra, 1859), vol. 50, p. 3. See John H. R. Polt, "Jovellanos and his English Sources," *Transactions of the American Philosophical Society* 54 (1964):5-74; and Polt, *Gaspar Melchor de Jovellanos* (New York: Twayne, 1971). Sarrailh, *España,* p. 549, says Jovellanos exclaimed after reading *Wealth of Nations* through three times, "¡Cómo prueba las ventajas del comercio libre con las colonias!" Jovellanos was very aware of the multiple uses of liberal concepts.

74. See C. Alan Hutchinson, *Frontier Settlement in Mexican California* (New Haven: Yale University Press, 1969), ch. 1.

75. Cited in Michael A. Otero, "The American Mission of Diego de Gardoqui, 1785-1789" (Ph.D. diss., UCLA, 1948), p. 12; and see *DNA,* passim; Manuel Conrotte, *La intervención de España en la independencia de los Estados Unidos de la América del Norte* (Madrid, 1920); Juan F. Yela Utrilla, *España ante la independencia de los Estados Unidos,* 2 vols., 2d ed., rev. (Lerida, 1925), 1:78, 83, 183; F. Morales Padrón, *La participación de España en la independencia de los Estados Unidos* (Madrid, 1963); and María Pilar Ruigómez de Hernández, *El gobierno español del despotismo ilustrado ante la independencia de los Estados Unidos de América; una nueva estructura de la política internacional* (Madrid: Ministerio de Asuntos Exteriores; Dirección General de Relaciones Culturales, 1978).

76. Cabarrús, "Discurso sobre la libertad de comercio concedida por S. M. a la América meridional" (read in a junta of February 28, 1778), in *Memorias de la Sociedad Económica* (Madrid) 3 (1787):282-94.

77. Cited in Warren L. Cook, *Flood Tide of Empire: Spain and the Pacific Northwest, 1543-1819* (New Haven: Yale University Press, 1973), p. 99. And see J. W. Caughey, *Bernardo de Gálvez in Louisiana, 1776–1783* (1934; reprint ed., Gretna, La: Pelican, 1972); Guillermo Porras Múñoz, *Bernardo de Gálvez* (Madrid: Instituto Gonzalo Fernández de Oviedo. Consejo Superior de Investigaciones Científicas, 1952). And see James A. Robertson, comp., "Spanish Correspondence Concerning the American Revolution," *HAHR* 1 (1918):299-316: Royal instructions of December 24, 1776 to the governor of Louisiana were to declare secretly to Americans that the king would be glad to see them seize Pensacola and other English settlements, in order to transfer them to Spain, and that the governor was to aid the English colonists through Havana with arms, ammunition, clothing, and quinine, using private traders as intermediaries (pp. 304-6); and, for Spanish aid, below, Chs. 5, 6.

78. On October 4, 1782, Aranda wrote to Floridablanca from Paris, suggesting that sooner or later Spanish America would experience revolts similar to British America's (Conrotte, 166). The authenticity of Aranda's "Dictamen reservado que el conde de Aranda dió al Rey sobre la independencia de los colonias inglesas, después de haber firmado el tratado de paz ajustado en Paris en el año de 1783" (a copy is in the Yale University Library) has been questioned; Arthur P. Whitaker, in "The Pseudo-Aranda Memoir, 1783," *HAHR* 17 (1937):287-313, found spurious this note in which Aranda purportedly set out his fear of the United States' growth threatening Spanish America and suggested that three Spanish princes be given American kingdoms and that the Spanish king take the title of emperor. Boleslao Lewin, in *Los movimientos de emancipación en Hispanamérica y la independencia de Estados Unidos* (Buenos Aires: Raigal, 1952), pp. 43, 54, is among those who think the *memoria* genuine. He notes its contents are consistent with Aranda's views from the 1760s on. Whitaker concedes that in 1786 Aranda did propose imperial reorganization, in reaction to "the menace of the revolutionary spirit represented by the United States" (p. 311). Cf. below, Ch. 6, for views similar to Aranda's coming from Spanish authorities in America from 1781 and lending credence to the case for authenticity—which appears to be at least as strong as the case against it. Also see Lucas Alamán,

Historia de Mejico, 5 vols. (Mexico: Lara, 1849-52), 1 (1849), pp. 126-27; Rydjord, *Foreign Interest,* pp. 17, 81, 94; and Almon R. Wright, "The Aranda Memorial: Genuine or Forged?" *HAHR* 18 (1938):445-60.

79. See *Reglamento y aranceles reales para el comercio libre de España a Indias. 12 Octubre 1778. Madrid.* (Seville: *EEHA,* 1979); José Múñoz Pérez, "La publicación del Reglamento de comercio libre a Indias de 1778," *AEA* 4 (1947):615-64; García-Baquero, *Cádiz,* passim.

80. Giménez Fernández, *concilio;* cf. Maxwell's and Payne's views on Pombal.

81. Stanley J. and Barbara H. Stein, *The Colonial Heritage of Latin America* (New York: Oxford University Press, 1970), p. 99; and see Liss, "Topics"; Liss, "Mexico"; Leon G. Campbell, "Recent Research on Bourbon Enlightened Despotism," *The New Scholar* 7 (1979):29-50; and Jacques A Barbier, *Reform and Politics in Bourbon Chile, 1755-1796* (Ottawa: University of Ottawa Press, 1980) among newer accounts.

82. Cited in Herr, *Eighteenth-Century Revolution,* p. 50.

83. Cf. Pocock, *Machiavellian Moment;* and his "Machiavellian Moment Revisited."

CHAPTER 4

1. See Juan and Ulloa, *Noticias Secretas;* V. L. Brown, "Contraband," pp. 178-84; Demetrio Ramos, *Minería y comercio interprovincial en Hispanoamérica (siglos XVI, XVII, y XVIII)* (Valladolid: Universidad de Valladolid, 1970), p. 258, who, however, underestimates contraband; García Baquero, *Cádiz;* Walker, *Spanish Politics;* Lydon, *Pirates;* Real Díaz, *feria;* Vicens Vives, *Economic History,* pp. 540 ff. Diffie's *Latin American Civilization* is still the best general colonial account; Savelle, *Empires,* is good on products exchanged. While Hussey, *Caracas,* stated that not more than five ships went from Spain to Venezuela between 1700 and 1728 (p. 41), Eduardo Arcila Farías, in *Economía colonial de Venezuela* (Mexico: FCE, 1946) found some 170 ships went between Spanish and Spanish American ports between 1701 and 1715 (p. 169). There is a second, revised edition in 2 vols.: Caracas: Halgráfica, 1973. And see the general survey: Luis Navarro García, *Hispano-América en el siglo XVIII* (Seville: Universidad de Seville, 1975).

2. See above, n. 1 and Ch. 1; Sergio Villalobos, *Comercio y contrabando en el Río de la Plata y Chile* (Buenos Aires: Editorial Universidad de Buenos Aires, 1965), pp. 37-56; Villalobos, *Comercio y crisis:* Gonzalo Aguirre Beltrán, *La población negra de México,* 2d ed. rev. (Mexico: FCE, 1972); and Haring, *Trade,* pp. 117-18.

3. Saco, *Historia,* 1:312; Villalobos, *Comercio y contrabando,* p. 19. Over 40 ships rounded Cape Horn from 1700 to 1713, and although the port at Buenos Aires was officially closed, they were allowed to provision and water there.

4. Juan and Ulloa, in *Noticias Secretas,* add that the Peruvian market was found glutted by foreign goods when galleons arrived in 1715, although only thirty French ships had entered the South Seas legally. All evidence points to a small market and much contraband. See Schurz, *Manila Galleon;* Eduardo Arcila Farías, *Comercio entre Venezuela y México entre los siglos XVII y XVIII* (Mexico: Instituto de Comercio Exterior, 1975); Julio J. Le Riverend Brusone, "Relaciones entre Nueva España y Cuba (1518-1820)," *RHA* 37-38 (1954):45-108; Miguel Lerdo de Tejada, *Comercio exterior de México, desde la conquista hasta hoy* (Mexico: R. Rafael, 1853; facsimile edition: Mexico, 1967); María E. Rodríguez Vicente, *El Tribunal del consulado de Lima en la primer mitad del siglo XVIII* (Madrid: Ediciones Cultura Hispánica, 1960); and see above, Ch. 3, n. 11.

5. Hussey, *Caracas,* p. 94.

6. See above, Chs. 1, 2, for English and British North American trade with Latin America during the war.

7. Le Riverend Brusone, "Relaciones," p. 67; see below, n. 12; Pares, *War,* pp. 110-126; Hussey, *Caracas,* pp. 79-85; Manuel Moreyra Paz-Soldán, "La toma de Portobelo por el almirante Vernon y sus consecuencias económicas," *Mercurio Peruano* 20 (1948):289-329; John Campbell, *A Concise History of Spanish America* (1741; reprinted ed., New York: Barnes and Noble, 1972); and Juan and Ulloa, *Noticias Secretas,* pp. 30, 78-88, 106. They commented (pp. 137-38) on the *irregular* construction common to merchant ships built on the Pacific, noting that when an English shipwright in Peru a few years earlier, after looking over a privately owned vessel, had been requested to advise on

improving it, he responded he had first to determine which was the bow and which the stern. Ramos, *minería,* p. 274, states that Guayaquil cacao nearly dislodged Venezuelan beans in Vera Cruz and brought on governmental action returning the market to Venezuela.

8. *Noticias Secretas,* pp. 220-44.

9. Ibid., p. 248.

10. See above, n. 1; and Schurz, *Manila Galleon,* pp. 287 ff.

11. Góngora, *Studies,* pp. 165-66; Hussey, *Caracas,* pp. 101, 171; Arcila Farías, *Economía;* Claude Morin, "Sentido y alcance del siglo XVIII en América Latina: el caso del centro-oeste mexicano," in Florescano, ed., *Ensayos,* pp. 154-70; and François Chevalier, *La Formation des grands domaines au Mexique* (Paris: Institut d'Ethnologie, 1952); the translation into English, by Alvin Eustis, *Land and Society in Colonial Mexico* (Berkeley and Los Angeles: University of California Press, 1963; paperback, 1970) is cited below. Hussey thinks the Company contributed substantially to the economic growth of Venezuela, Arcila Farías argues it did not; the problem remains of how much Venezuela developed under it and, the unanswerable, how it would have done without the Company. Michael Conniff, "Guayaquil through Independence: Urban Development in a Colonial System," *TAm* 33 (1977):393, found that Company activity in Venezuela gave Guayaquil cacao an advantage with the Dutch.

12. Le Riverend Brusone, "Desarrollo," pp. 226-27; and John TePaske, *The Governorship of Spanish Florida, 1700-1763* (Durham: Duke University Press, 1964), p. 97.

13. Harman, *Trade,* pp. 52-56; Herminio Portell Vilá, *Los "otros extranjeros" en la revolución norteamericana* (Miami: Ediciones Universal, 1978), pp. 112-13; and see below, n. 41.

14. *DNA* I:1:290; Hussey, *Caracas,* p. 86; Villalobos, *Comercio y contrabando,* p. 49; and María del Pópulo Antolin Espino, "El virrey Marqués de Cruillas," in Calderón Quijano, ed., *Carlos III,* 1:128.

15. Le Riverend Brusone, "Desarrollo," p. 235; his "Relación," p. 73; and see *Papeles;* Franklin W. Knight, "Origins of Wealth and the Sugar Revolution in Cuba, 1750-1850," *HAHR* 57 (1977):231-53; Stein and Stein, *Colonial Heritage,* p. 97; Encarnación Rodríguez Vicente, "El comercio cubano y la guerra de emancipación norteamericana," *AEA* 11 (1954):61-106; J. G. Clark, *New Orleans,* p. 175; and above, Chs. 1, 2.

16. British trade with Spanish America, in a slump in 1764, revived and had a boom year in 1771, but channels altered. Dominica then rivaled Jamaica, and much Spanish American trade funneled through Trinidad. See Brown, "Contraband," pp. 186-88; and Hussey, *Caracas,* pp. 253-55.

17. See above, Ch. 3, n. 58.

18. Alonso Carrió [Concolorcorvo], *El Lazarillo de ciegos caminantes* (Lima, 1775-76); in an English translation by Walter D. Kline, as *El Lazarillo* (Bloomington: Indiana University Press, 1965), p. 63. He went on: "There is a great wealth of (retail) merchants. . . . four times as many as in Lima, only one large farmer and no family estates." See Mercedes M. Alvárez F., *Comercio y comerciantes y sus proyecciones en la independencia venezolana* (Caracas: Vargas, 1963), p. 17; Troy S. Floyd, "The Guatemalan Merchants, the Government, and the *Provincianos,* 1750-1800," *HAHR* 41 (1961):90-110; Brading, *Miners;* Brading, "Government"; and Charles H. Harris, 3d, *A Mexican Family Empire* (Austin: University of Texas Press, 1975).

19. Tulio Halperín-Donghi, *Politics, Economics, and Society in Argentina in the Revolutionary Period* (Cambridge, 1975), p. 29.

20. Arcila Farías, *siglo,* 72; his *Economía,* pp. 271,349, and ch. 12, explaining Spanish freer trade from 1765; and *DNA* I:1:3.

21. See Ibid.; Arcila Farías, *Comercio;* Ramos, *minería,* pp. 273-80; Le Riverend Brusone, "Nueva España."

22. Haring, *Spanish Empire,* p. 320; Le Riverend Brusone, "Desarrollo," pp. 203-5, 241-43; Hussey, *Caracas,* p. 232; and Christelow, "Contraband," p. 340.

23. Carrío, *Lazarillo,* p. 53.

24. Guillermo Céspedes del Castillo, *Lima y Buenos Aires* (Seville, 1947); and J. H. Parry, *Trade and Dominion* (New York: Praeger, 1971), pp. 301, 309.

25. Priestley, *Gálvez,* pp. 173-74, 304-05; V. L. Brown, "Anglo-Spanish Relations," 377 ff.; Aguirre Beltrán, *El contrabando y el comercio exterior en la Nueva España* (Mexico: Banco Nacional

de Comercio Exterior, 1967); Antolin Espino, "Cruillas," in Calderón Quijano, ed. *Carlos III,* I:95, 239, found that the viceroy, the Marqués de Cruillas, had tolerated English ships in Vera Cruz after the 1763 armistice, then with Villalba's arrival in 1764 they were turned away. Cruillas objected when Gálvez cracked down on such contraband and caused the arrest of officials and merchants involved. Among items then smuggled in were rum from British North America and Hungarian mercury via Pensacola. Arcila Farías, *siglo,* discusses the large number of British asentistas in Mexico before the 1730s.

26. Gálvez, cited in Brading, *Miners,* p. 26; and see Priestley, *Gálvez,* p. 283; William B. Taylor, "Town and Country in the Valley of Oaxaca: 1750-1812," in Ida Altman and James Lockhart, eds., *Provinces of Mexico* (Berkeley and Los Angeles: University of California Press, 1976), pp. 93-95; William B. Taylor, *Landlord and Peasant in Colonial Oaxaca* (Stanford: Stanford University Press, 1972); Charles Gibson, *The Aztecs Under Spanish Rule* (Stanford: Stanford University Press, 1964); John K. Chance, *Race and Class in Colonial Oaxaca* (Stanford: Stanford University Press, 1978); Richard L. Garner, "Zacatecas, 1750-1821: The Study of a Late Colonial Mexican City," (Ph.D Diss., University of Michigan, 1970); and above, Ch. 3, for specific reforms.

27. Carrió, *Lazarillo,* p. 226. He specifically mentioned that British baizes, linens, and woolens were displacing Cuzco textiles.

28. See above, Ch. 3; Maxwell, "Pombal"; Roberto C. Simonsen, *História Econômica do Brasil, 1500-1820,* 5th ed. (São Paulo: Companhia Editôra Nacional, 1967); Dauril Alden, "Vicissitudes of Trade in the Portuguese Atlantic Empire during the First Half of the Eighteenth Century," *TAm* 32 (1975):282-91.

29. By the 1730s, over twenty thousand blacks, it is estimated, were being imported annually into Brazil (Boxer, *Portuguese Seaborne Empire,* p. 171). See too: A. J. R. Russell-Wood, *Fidalgos and Philanthropists* (Berkeley and Los Angeles: University of California Press, 1968), p. 338; Pierre Verger, *Flux et reflux de la traite des négres entre le Golfe de Bénin et Bahia de Todos os Santos du XVIIe au XIXe siècle* (Paris, 1968); Colin M. MacLachlan, "African Slave Trade and Economic Development in Amazonia, 1700-1800," in Robert B. Toplin, ed., *Slavery and Race Relations in Latin America* (Westport: Greenwood Press, 1974), pp. 112-45; and above, Ch. 3, n. 41.

30. Some smuggling was unofficially sanctioned in southern Brazil, buying livestock from Spaniards in exchange for European goods, or exchanging blacks for Spanish silver and hides. Colônia was the center until the 1760s, when Spain closed it down. Spanish ships from the south were well treated in Brazilian ports (Alden, *Royal Government,* pp. 390-91).

31. Ibid.; Dauril Alden, "The Coming of the Yankee Sperm Whalers to Brazilian Waters and the Decline of the Portuguese Whale Fishery (1773-1808)," *TAm* 20 (1964):267-68; H. E. S. Fisher, "Anglo-Portuguese Trade," p. 232; Alexander Marchant, "Aspects of the Enlightenment in Brazil," in Arthur P. Whitaker, ed., *Latin America and the Enlightenment,* 2d ed. rev. (Ithaca: Cornell University Press, 1961), pp. 95-118; and Savelle, *Empires,* pp. 75-76.

32. See Alden's works, including his "Manoel Luis Vieira: An Entrepreneur in Río de Janeiro during Brazil's Eighteenth-Century Agricultural Revolution," *HAHR* 39 (1959):521-37; Maxwell, *Conflict;* Boxer, *Golden Age;* John N. Kennedy, "Bahian Elites, 1750-1822," *HAHR* 53 (1973):415-39; Stuart B. Schwartz, "Family, Friends, and Empire: Magistracy and Society in Colonial Brazil," *HAHR* 50 (1970):715-30, who notes the marked rise after 1730 of urban merchants (p. 728); and Klein, "Portuguese Slave Trade," p. 915.

33. Chevalier, *Land,* pp. 27, 294; François Chevalier, "The North Mexican Hacienda: Eighteenth and Nineteenth Centuries," in Archibald R. Lewis and Thomas F. McGann, eds., *The New World Looks at Its History* (Austin: University of Texas Press, 1963), pp. 95-107; and Harris, *Mexican Family Empire.*

34. Francisco López Cámara, *La génesis de la conciencia liberal en México* (Mexico: Colegio de México, 1954), pp. 29-39; Burkholder and Chandler, *Impotence,* pp. 36-79.

35. López Cámara, *génesis,* pp. 20-46; Juan and Ulloa, *Noticias Secretas,* pp. 415, 428; John P. Moore, *The Cabildo in Peru under the Bourbons* (Durham: Duke University Press, 1966).

36. José Rogelio Alvárez, "Ideas económicas de Oliván Rebolledo," *HM* 5 (1956): 433-39. The tract was dedicated to the viceroy, Juan de Acuña, Marqués de Casa Fuerte. And see Villalobos, *comercio y crisis,* pp. 11-45; García-Baquero, *Cádiz,* 1:129-30; Real Díaz, *fería.*

37. Hussey, *Caracas,* pp. 208-11. Auditors in 1748 found fraud and mismanagement, but despite protests by Spaniards, Cubans continued to run the company. When England seized its assets in 1762, fraud among the Cuban directors had again been uncovered, and, after the Cuban shareholders ransomed company property, they refused to divide profits with shareholders in Spain (ibid., pp. 214-15). For its trade with the New York merchant, William Walton: Harman, *Trade,* p. 53; and above, Ch. 2.

38. Arcila Farías, *economía,* pp. 331-35; and cf. Hussey, *Caracas,* whose account is outlined here. Cacao imports to Spain increased from 1750 to 1764, so that by then twice as much went to the peninsula as to Vera Cruz (Arcila Farías, *economía,* p. 256).

39. IPAGH, *Documentos relativos a la insurrección de Juan Francisco de León,* preliminary study by Augusto Mijares (Caracas, 1949); Hussey, *Caracas,* pp. 122-34, 154-55; Arcila Farías, *economía,* pp. 218-53. Arcila Farías argued against Hussey's attributing the León revolt to a standing Canarian-Spanish split and specifically to Spanish curtailing of contraband. Rather, he stated, all planters were creoles and were generally opposed to the company. He cited the ties between the Canarian León and the Conde de San Javier, who was of Spanish descent, and he declared the revolt a truly national movement, one also involving small planters, laborers and peasants, militia members, some artisans, and mostly blacks, mulattoes, and Indians. Also see Carlos Felice Cardot, *Rebeliones, motines y movimientos de masas en el siglo XVIII venezolano, 1730-1781* (Madrid, 1961); Francisco Morales Padrón, *Rebelión contra la Compañía de Caracas* (Seville, 1955); and above, Ch. 3. The elderly Conde de San Javier eased the situation by dying soon afterwards. He had also been implicated in a 1745 conspiracy against the *guipozcaños,* in plotting a revolt meant to look like it began among the lower classes and Canarians (Arcila Farías, *economía,* p. 223; and see 439-41; and below for other revolts).

40. Ibid., pp. 255, 466-72; Hussey, *Caracas,* p. 166; and Alvárez F., *Comercio,* pp. 10-11.

41. Hussey, *Caracas,* p. 179. A similar accusation of inadequate supply of clothing by the Company came from the governor of Puerto Rico in 1759. To alleviate such shortages, the governors of Puerto Rico and Margarita allowed in supplies from foreign colonies. With the Seven Years' War, the Company verged on bankruptcy.

42. Sergio Villalobos, *Tradición y Reforma en 1810* (Santiago: Universidad de Chile, 1961), pp. 89 ff., 99; Hussey, *Caracas,* p. 218.

43. Néstor Meza Villalobos, *La conciencia política chilena durante la monarquía* (Santiago: Universidad de Chile, 1958), p. 164; Barbier, *Reform,* pp. 23-45.

44. Llano Zapata, *Memorias* (Lima, 1904); cited in Jorge Basadre, "Historia de la idea de Patria en la Emancipación del Perú," *Mercurio Peruano* no. 330 (September 1954): 647.

45. E. Bradford Burns, *Nationalism in Brazil* (New York: Praeger, 1968), pp. 21-23. He cites a paragraph from the *História da América Portuguêsa, 1500-1724,* of Sebastião da Rocha Pita, published in Lisbon in 1730, terribly romantic in its vision of Brazil. The author was a charter member of the first, ephemeral, Brazilian literary academy, founded in Bahia in 1724 to write the history of Brazil; cf. Burns, "Transition."

46. In Xavier Tavera Alfaro, *El nacionalismo en la prensa mexicana del siglo XVIII* (Mexico: Club de Periodistas de México, 1963), pp. 37-38; and see pp. i-liii; and Liss, *Mexico,* for the origins of creolism there.

47. Juan José Eguiara y Eguren, *Prólogos de la Biblioteca Mexicana,* trans. Agustín Millares Carlo (Mexico, 1944; rev. ed., Maracaibo, 1963). And see Millares Carlo, "Feijoo"; Juan Hernández Luna, "El iniciador de la historia de las ideas en México," *Filosofía y Letras* 25 (1953): 65-80; Bernabé Navarro, "La cultura mexicana frente a Europa," *HM* 3 (1954): 547-61; Navarro, *Cultura;* and Tavera Alfaro, *nacionalismo,* xlvii-viii.

48. See Francisco de la Maza, *El guadalupanismo mexicano* (Mexico: Porrúa y Obregón, 1953); Liss, *Mexico;* González Casanova, *misoneísmo;* Jacques Lafaye, *Quetzalcóatl et Guadalupe* (Paris: Gallimard, 1974; English translation by Benjamin Keen, Chicago: University of Chicago Press, 1976); Peggy K. Liss, "A Cosmic Approach Falls Short: a Review of Jacques Lafaye's *Quetzalcóatl and Guadalupe: The Formation of Mexican National Consciousness, 1531-1813,*" *HAHR* 57 (1977): 707-11; and, for an excellent summary of the history of Guadalupe as Lafaye should have written it, J. H. Elliott's review of the book in *New York Review of Books* 24 (May 26, 1977), pp. 28-30. Among Spaniards who were attracted to the cult was the regalist archbishop, Lorenzana. He also wrote a

history of Hernando Cortés, extolling him as a man destined by God to present the Catholic King with another empire.

49. See Juan Luis Maneiro and Manuel Fabri, *Vidas de mexicanos ilustres del siglo XVIII* (Mexico: UNAM, 1956), pp. 1-51; Gabriel Méndez Plancarte, *Humanistas del siglo XVIII* (Mexico: UNAM, 1941); Rafael Moreno, "filosofía"; and Navarro, *Cultura*. Campoy was born in Sinaloa of a prominent family. His precosity was admired by Ignacio de la Rocha who later, as Bishop of Michoacán, gained renown as an enlightened reformer. Campoy taught at the Jesuit colegio in Vera Cruz and there became interested in navigation and astronomy. He corresponded with the Spanish Jesuit and satirist, José Isla, received numerous books from Spain, and his friendship with Vera Cruz merchants resulted in their supporting the Jesuit school there.

50. Christelow, "Great Britain," pp. 20-21; "Inventorio de la correspondencia entre el virrey Marqués de Cruillas y el gobernador de la plaza de Veracruz," *BAGN* 30 (1959): 49-129; and Alamán, *Historia* 1:107.

51. Cited in Farriss, *Crown,* p. 134.

52. See Monelisa Pérez-Marchand, *Dos étapas ideológicas del siglo XVIII en México a través de los papeles de la Inquisición* (Mexico: Colegio de México, 1945), p. 98; and José Miranda, *Las ideas y las instituciones políticas mexicanas,* 2d ed. (Mexico: UNAM, 1978), pp. 158-60. A marked rise in Inquisition cases in New Spain, although resulting partially from denunciations of irreverent Spanish soldiers, demonstrated the wariness of authorities, especially now, about political deviance and subversion of Spain's economic arrangements. The presence of new, non-Catholic, aggressive neighbors added incentive to both insubordination and its repression.

53. These creoles, overestimating disaffection, expected "a universal rising" in Mexico but admitted that the wealthier inhabitants feared for their property. The conspirators were well aware that "a popular furor is easy to excite but difficult to contain within its just limits." They approached one "M. Guiller," reportedly a French architect, for military advice and for help in formulating a plan of government. It could not be a monarchy, they told him, since there were too many great families of equal rank for any one of them to assume command. Further, they were certain that they could carry out the revolution without shedding a drop of blood. M. Guiller, in reporting the plot to the Spanish government, declared that the plan would prove repugnant to other Mexicans, principally because it would give Protestant England a foothold in New Spain. He also said that the Mexicans misunderstood Britain, for it religiously observed treaties and would not weaken itself through overextension of territory but would expand by augmenting its commerce and navigation. Britain was interested, he stated, in a trade monopoly in Mexico and the cession of Vera Cruz: Hernández y Davalos, *Documentos* 2:62-63; and see above, Ch. 1, n. 99.

54. See Burkholder and Chandler, *Impotence* 85 ff.; but cf. Barbier, *Reform,* for Chile as an exception. Also see above, n. 44, and Doris Ladd, *The Mexican Nobility at Independence* (Austin: University of Texas; Institute of Latin American Studies, 1976); cf. Priestley, *Gálvez;* Brading, *Miners;* Mark A. Burkholder, *Politics of a Colonial Career: José Baquíjano and the Audiencia of Lima* (Albuquerque: University of New Mexico Press, 1980), ch. 1; and John F. Wilhite, "The Enlightenment and Education in New Granada, 1766-1830" (Ph.D. Diss., University of Tennessee, 1976). Immigrants and businessmen from Northern Spain were more in evidence throughout Spain's America. For an interesting example of the career and attitudes of one: Manuel R. Pazos, "Un español ilustre en el México colonial: Don Roque Yáñez, 1735-1787," *Archivo Ibero-Americano* 31 (1971): 97-172.

55. Maneiro and Fabri, *Vidas,* p. 145.

56. See ibid; Miranda, *ideas;* Efraín Castro Morales, ed., *Documentos relativos al historiador Francisco Javier Clavijero y su familia* (Puebla, 1970); Navarro, *Cultura;* Bernabé Navarro, *La introducción de la filosofía moderna en México* (Mexico: Colegio de México, 1948); R. Moreno, "Modern Philosophy," pp. 166-78; Charles E. Ronan, S. J., *Francisco Javier Clavijero, S. J. (1731-1787)* (Chicago: Loyola University Press, 1977); and Allan Deck, *Francisco Javier Alegre* (Tucson: Kino House, 1976).

57. Morales, *Documentos,* pp. 23-39; Ronan, *Clavijero,* ch. 1; and Edith B. Couturier, "Family Economy and Inheritance in Eighteenth-Century Puebla: A Study of Five Families," a paper presented at the Middle Atlantic Conference on Latin American Studies, Philadelphia, April 2, 1981, pp. 15 ff.

58. In Mariano Cuevas, S. J., ed., *Tesoros documentales de México: siglo XVIII* (Mexico:

Editorial Galatea, 1944), pp. 321-33; and see too Clavijero's "Frutos en que comercia o puede comerciar la Nueva España," and "Proyectos utiles para adelantar el comercio de la Nueva España," ibid., pp. 363-98.

59. See Carlos María de Bustamante, ed., and supplement to, Andrés Cavo, *Los tres siglos de México* (Mexico: Navarro, 1852); Francisco Javier Clavijero, *Storia antica del Messico* (Cesena, 1781), and its most recent edition: *Historia antigua de México*, Mariano Cuevas, S. J., ed., 4 vols. (Mexico: Porrúa, 1958); Francisco Javier Alegre, S. J., *Historia de la Provincia de la Compañía de Jesús de Nueva España*, ed. Ernest J. Burrus, S. J. and Félix Zubillaga, S. J., 4 vols. (Rome: Institutum Historicum Societatis Iesu, 1956-60); Diego José Abad, *Musa Americana* (Madrid, 1769); Juan Ignacio Molina, *The Geographical, Natural and Civil History of Chile*, trans. William Shaler and Richard Alsop (Middletown, Conn., 1808); originally published in Bologna, 1776; Antonello Gerbi, *The Dispute of the New World* (Pittsburgh: University of Pittsburgh Press, 1973); and above, n. 56.

60. Priestley, *Gálvez*, p. 170; Bustamante, supplement to Cavo, *Tres Siglos*, p. 145; Manuel Orozco y Berra, *Historia de la dominación española en México*, 4 vols. (Mexico: Biblioteca Historia Mexicana de Obras Inéditos, 1938), 4:111-31; Arcila Farías, *siglo*, pp. 204-9, 245; Luis Chávez Orozco, *Conflicto de trabajo con los mineros de Real del Monte, año de 1766* (Mexico: Biblioteca del Instituto Nacional de Estudios Historicas de la Revolución Mexicana, 1960); Rubén Vargas Ugarte, S. J., *Historia de la Compañía de Jesús en el Perú*, 4 vols. (Burgos: Aldecoas, 1963-65), 4 (1965); Chevalier, *Formation;* Manuel de Amat y Junient, *Memoria de Gobierno* (Seville: EEHA, 1947); Nicholas P. Cushner, *Lords of the Land: Sugar, Wine, and Jesuit Estates of Coastal Peru, 1600-1767* (Albany: SUNY Press, 1980); Herman W. Konrad, *A Jesuit Hacienda in Colonial Mexico, 1576-1767* (Stanford: Stanford University Press, 1980); Gibson, *Aztecs*, 190; James D. Riley, *Hacendados Jesuitas en México* (Mexico: SepSetentas, 1976); and cf., for Brazil, n. 28, above.

61. John Tate Lanning, *The Eighteenth-Century Enlightenment in the University of San Carlos de Guatemala* (Ithaca: Cornell University Press, 1956), pp. 68, 148.

62. Lanning, *Academic Culture;* Whitaker, *Latin America;* Brading, *Miners;* Priestley, *Gálvez;* Luque Alcaide, *educación;* Wilhite, "Enlightenment"; and Luis Martín, S. J., *The Intellectual Conquest of Peru: The Jesuit College of San Pablo, 1568-1767* (New York: Fordham University Press, 1968), pp. 216-35. For an outstanding Mexican example: Juan Benito Díaz de Gamarra, *Elementos de filosofía moderna*, trans. Bernabé Navarro (Mexico: Centro de Estudios Filosóficos, UNAM, 1963); and see Victoria Junco de Meyer, *Gamarra o el eclecticismo en México* (Mexico: FCE, 1973).

63. Manuel Giménez Fernández, *Las doctrinas populistas en la independencia de Hispano-América* (Seville: EEHA, 1947), p. 24; Luis Navarro García, "El Marqués de Croix," in Calderón Quijano, *Carlos III*, 1:161-381; and Priestley, *Gálvez*, p. 170.

64. Cited in Rydjord, *Foreign Interest*, p. 65.

65. J. G. Clark, *New Orleans*, pp. 166-68; and see Caughey, *Bernardo de Gálvez;* John P. Moore, *Revolt in Louisiana, the Spanish Occupation, 1766-1779* (Baton Rouge: Louisiana State University Press, 1976).

66. See Toribio Esquivel Obregón, *Biografía de Don Francisco Javier Gamboa* (Mexico, 1941); Malagón, "obra", p. 438; Navarro García, "Destrucción," pp. 20-23; Farriss, *Crown*, p. 132; and Brading, *Miners*, p. 70.

67. "Representación que hizó la ciudad de México al rey Don Carlos III en 1771 . . . ," Hernández y Dávalos, *Documentos* 1:427-55; and see Arcila Farías, *siglo*, p. 204; Brading, *Miners*, p. 36; and Ladd, *Mexican Nobility, passim.*

68. See Gerbi, *Dispute;* Salvador de Madariaga, *The Fall of the Spanish American Empire*, rev. ed. (New York: Collier, 1963), pp. 222-25; Benjamin Keen, *The Aztec Image in Western Thought* (New Brunswick: Rutgers University Press, 1971); and Pérez-Marchand, *Dos étapas*, p. 25.

69. Santiago Ramírez, *Estudio, biográfico del señor don Joaquín Velázquez Cárdenas y León, primer director general de Minería* (Mexico, 1888); Roberto Moreno, *Joaquín Velázquez de León y sus trabajos científicos sobre el Valle de México* (México: UNAM, 1977); Walter Howe, *The Mining Guild of New Spain and Its Tribunal General (1770-1821)* (Cambridge: Harvard University Press, 1949); Iris W. Engstrand, *Royal Officer in Baja California, 1768-1777; Joaquín Velásquez de León* (Los Angeles: Dawson's Book Shop, 1976).

70. Francisco Fernández del Castillo, "El Doctor Don José Ignacio Bartolache, médico, escritor e

innovador," in *MMC*, 2 vols. (Mexico: Sociedad Mexicana de Historia de la Ciencia y la Tecnología, 1964), 2:207-20.

71. Rafael Moreno, "Modern Philosophy," p. 158.

72. See Carlos R. Margain, "Don Antonio León y Gama (1735-1802). El primer arqueólogo mexicano. Análisis de su vida y obra," in *MMC*, 2:149-84.

73. See José Antonio Alzate y Ramírez, *Gacetas de Literatura de México*, 4 vols. (Puebla: Oficio del Hospital de San Pedro, 1831); Alexander von Humboldt, *Essai Politique sur le Royaume de la Nouvelle Espagne*, 5 vols. (Paris: Chez F. Schoell, 1811), 2:19. The English translation, by John Black, is *Political Essay on the Kingdom of New Spain*, 4 vols. (London, 1811); and see Tavera Alfaro, *Nacionalismo;* Juan Hernández Luna, ed., *José Antonio Alzate, 1738-1799* (Mexico: Secretaría de Educación Pública, 1945); his "José Antonio Alzate, hombre de la Ilustración," *MMC* 2:201-66; Rafael Moreno, "Alzate, educador ilustrado, *HM* 2 (1953):37-89; his 'Creación de la nacionalidad mexicana," *HM* 12 (1963):531-51; Francisco López Cámara "La conciencia criolla en Sor Juana y Sigüenza," *HM* 6 (1957):350-73; and Peggy K. Korn [Liss], "The Problem of the Roots of Revolution: Society and Intellectual Ferment in Mexico on the Eve of Independence," in Fredrick B. Pike, ed., *Latin American History: Select Problems* (New York: Harcourt, Brace, 1969), pp. 100-32. For the theater and the eighteenth-century revolution in morals, see González Casanova, *misoneísmo,* ch. 3. Maneiro and Fabri mention that several of the Jesuit "moderns" knew Sor Juana's writings. Antonio Alcedo was writing in Ecuador.

74. Wilfredo E. Kapsoli, *Sublevaciones de esclavos en el Perú. Siglo XVIII* (Lima: Universidad Ricardo Palma, 1975), pp. 50-59; in Peru, the rebels threatened to kill the administrators and *mayordomos*. Troops sent by the viceroy put down the rising. Another broke out on the same haciendas in 1779. Also see Federico Brito Figueroa, *Insurrecciones de esclavos negros en la Venezuela colonial* (Caracas: Cantaclaro, 1960); and William F. Sharp, *Slavery on the Spanish Frontier: the Colombian Chocó, 1680-1810* (Norman: University of Oklahoma Press, 1977). Slaves rising in the mines at Santiago de Cuba in 1731 were convinced a royal order freeing them was being withheld by local authorities: Elias Entralgo, "Los fenomenos raciales en la emancipación de Cuba," in *El movimiento emancipador de hispanoamérica. Actas y ponencias. Academia Nacional de Historia. Mesa redonda de la Comisión de Geografía e Historia*, 4 vols. (Caracas: IPAGH, 1961), 3:329-30. He adds that when the English squadron [1762] was off Havana there were some revolts in the sugar mills southeast of the city. Also see Ernesto Alvarado García, "La independencia de América," in ibid., p. 294.

75. See William B. Taylor, *Drinking, Homicide, and Rebellion in Colonial Mexican Villages* (Stanford: Stanford University Press, 1978); and above, n. 26, 55. Araucanians rose in Chile in 1766: Alvarado García, "independencia," p . 294. And see Luis Navarro García, La sublevación yaqui de 1740 (Seville, 1966); and Gibson, *Aztecs*.

76. John H. Rowe, "El movimiento nacional Inca del siglo XVIII," *Revista Universitaria* (Cuzco) 43 [2do. semestre 1954 (1955)], pp. 17-47. The prophecy appeared in Raleigh's relation of a voyage to Guiana, written to convince Queen Elizabeth to sponsor South American conquest. Also see Amat, *Memoria*, pp. 288-307; J. H. Rowe, "The Incas under Spanish Colonial Institutions," *HAHR* 37 (1957): 155-99; Leona Ruth Auld, "Discontent with the Spanish System of Control in Upper Peru, 1730-1808" (Ph.D. diss., University of California at Los Angeles, 1963; Lewin, *movimientos,* especially pp. 101-7; Roberto María Tisnes J., *Movimientos pre-independientes gran-colombianos* (Bogotá: Academia Colombiana de Historia, 1962); Eric Hobsbawm's criteria for peasant revolutions in *EcHR* 27 (1974):707; Francisco Loayza, *Juan Santos, el invencible* (Lima, 1942); Simeón Orellana Valeriano, "La rebelión de Juan Santos," *Anales Científicos de la Univ. del Centro del Perú* (Huancayo) 3 (1974):513-51; Karen Spalding, "The Colonial Indian: Past and Future Research Perspectives," *LARR* 7 (1972):47-76; and Leon G. Campbell, "Recent Research on Andean Peasant Revolts, 1750-1820," *LARR* 14 (1979):3-49. Juan Santos was educated by the Jesuits, then in his early twenties spent five years abroad, in Spain and possibly England. He was rumored to have been in Angola as well and to have talked to Englishmen there about help by sea for the rebellion.

77. See Adalbert López, *The Revolt of the Comuneros, 1721-1735* (Cambridge, Mass.: Schenkman, 1976); James S. Saeger, "Origins of the Rebellion of Paraguay," *HAHR* 52 (1972):215-29; his "Institutional Rivalries, Jurisdictional Disputes, and Vested Interests in the Viceroyalty of Peru: José de Antequera and the Rebellion of Paraguay," *TAm* 32 (1975):99-116; and Hildegard Krüger, *Der*

Cabildo von Asunción (Frankfurt am Main: Peter D. Lang, 1979). Similar situations existed in Sonora and Brazil.

78. See Brito Figueroa, *insurrecciones;* Felice Cardot, *sublevaciones.*

79. Priestley, *Gálvez;* Taylor, *Drinking;* Villalobos, *Tradición,* pp. 90-96.

80. Felice Cardot, *sublevaciones,* pp. 25-48; A. López, *Revolt;* and cf. Rafael Gómez Hoyos, *La revolución granadina, ideario de una generación y una época,* 2 vols. (Bogotá: Temis, 1962), 1:160-61, who mentions a popular uprising in Vélez, New Granada in 1740 against a forced loan levied in order to pay troops at the time of the siege of Cartagena by the English.

81. Juan and Ulloa, *Noticias,* pp. 120-21, 199-200, 219, 253-54, 306, 308, 333; Felice Cardot, *sublevaciones,* pp. 29, 34-41. Cf. Amat, *Memoria,* pp. 305-7.

82. Brito Figueroa, *insurrecciones,* pp. 46-59; Taylor, *Drinking,* p. 123; above, n. 81; and see Ch. 1 concerning British interest in disturbances in Quito and Mexico in the 1760s.

83. Cf. Leon G. Campbell, *The Military and Society in Colonial Peru, 1750-1810* (Philadelphia: *Memoirs* of the American Philosophical Society, v. 123, January 1978); Allan J. Kuethe, *Military Reform and Society in New Granada, 1773-1808* (Gainesville: University of Florida Press, 1977); Archer, *Army;* McAlister, *Fuero;* and M. Velásquez, *estado.*

84. Luis Miguel Enciso Recio, *La Gaceta de Madrid y El Mercurio Histórico y Político, 1776-1781* (Valladolid, 1957), pp. 83-86.

85. García Melero, *Independencia,* p. 66.

86. Chandler, *Inter-American Acquaintances,* p. 4.

CHAPTER 5

1. For general interpretations of the period see, among others: M. Jensen, *American Revolution;* Bercovitch, *Puritan;* Forrest McDonald, *E Pluribus Unum: The Formation of the American Republic, 1776–1790* (Boston: Houghton Mifflin, 1965); Gordon C. Bjork, ''The Weaning of the American Economy: Independence, Market Changes, and Economic Development,'' *JEcH* 24 (1964): 541–60; George A. Billias, ''The Revolutionary Era: Reinterpretations and Revisions,'' in G. A. Billias and Gerald N. Grob, eds. *American History: Retrospect and Prospect* (New York: Free Press, 1971), pp. 34–84; J. Greene, ed., *Reinterpretation;* Jackson Turner Main, *The Social Structure of Revolutionary America* (Princeton: Princeton University Press, 1965); Henretta, *Evolution;* Pole, *Foundations;* William A. Williams, *The Contours of American History* (Chicago: Quadrangle, 1966), pt. 1; Gordon S. Wood, ''Rhetoric'';' and his *The Creation of the American Republic 1776–1787* (Chapel Hill: University of North Carolina Press, 1969); Esmond Wright, ed., *Causes;* and Arthur Schlesinger, Jr., ''America: Experiment or Destiny?'' *AHR* 82 (1977): 505–22. The title quotation is from Paine, letter to Abbé Raynal, Philadelphia, August 21, 1782: ''Our style and manner of thinking had undergone a revolution . . . we see with other eyes, we hear with other ears and we think with other thoughts than those formerly used.'' Thomas Paine, *Writings,* collected and edited by Moncure Daniel Conway, 4 vols. (1894–96; New York: AMS Press, 1967), 2:105.

2. With some reservations, noted in passing, I follow in this discussion Felix Gilbert, *To the Farewell Address;* the edition cited here has the title *The Beginnings of American Foreign Policy.* I also refer to Alexander DeConde, *A History of American Foreign Policy,* 2d ed. (New York: Scribners, 1971); Lawrence S. Kaplan, *Colonies into Nation: American Diplomacy, 1763–1801* (New York: Macmillan, 1972); and Van Alstyne, *Empire.* See too Lloyd C. Gardner, Walter F. LaFeber, and Thomas J. McCormick, *Creation of the American Empire: United States Diplomatic History* (Chicago: Rand McNally, 1973); Edward Weisband, *The Ideology of American Foreign Policy* (Beverly Hills: Sage, 1973)—who, however, overstates Lockean influence; William A. Williams, ed., *The Shaping of American Diplomacy* (Chicago: Rand McNally, 1956), and his ''The Age of Mercantilism: An Interpretation of the American Political Economy, 1763 to 1828,'' *WMQ* 15 (1958): 419–37. Cf. William H. Goetzmann, *When the Eagle Screamed* (New York: Wiley, 1966), ch. 1, and his bibliographical remarks, pp. 107–8. Goetzmann correctly indentifies Thomas Jefferson and John Adams as the prime makers of the foreign policy of the new nation. He and others remind us that influences on foreign policy included domestic issues (as well as international ones), popular ideas and moods, and local or sectional sentiments.

3. Thomas Paine, *Common Sense*, ed. M. D. Conway (Franklin Square, Pa.: Franklin Library, 1979), pp. 21–22, and see p. 40.

4. Gilbert, *Beginnings*, pp. 42–45. He cites John Adams to Secretary Livingston, February 5, 1783. Gilbert says Adams took the idea of separation of commercial and political treaties from the Treaty of Utrecht. See Kaplan, *Colonies*, for a general narrative, especially pp. 87–91.

5. See Edmund S. Morgan, "The Puritan Ethic and the American Revolution," *WMQ* 24 (1967): 5; Curtis P. Nettels, *The Emergence of a National Economy, 1775–1815* (New York: Holt, Rinehart, and Winston, 1962), p. 10–15; and cf. Crowley, *Sheba*; and H. May, *Enlightenment*, pp. 155–57.

6. Cited in Gilbert, *Beginnings,* p. 71. In 1784 Jefferson wrote to George Washington that he would not speculate on whether commerce contributed to the happiness of mankind but that "all the world is becoming commercial," that it would be impossible for the republic to remain aloof from that trend, and that it was important to gain as large a share as possible of this modern source of wealth and power. Washington agreed that "from trade our citizens will not be estranged." (Cited in Crowley, *Sheba*, p. 137).

7. Gilbert, *Beginnings*, p. 75. He overstates *philosophe* influence, particularly on Jefferson's policies and on the element of utopian idealism—specifically of pacific internationalism—in initial United States foreign policy. Cf. James H. Hutson, "Intellectual Foundations of Early American Diplomacy," *Diplomatic History* 1 (1977): 1–19, whose criticism, however, goes too far, misrepresenting Gilbert; and, better, William D. Grampp, "A Re-examination of Jeffersonian Economics," *Southern Economics Journal* 12 (1946): 263–82, who emphasized the development of Jefferson's ideas and policies in accord with perceived national needs and desires. Grampp stated (p. 267) that Jefferson, though an agrarian, was not a physiocrat but more of a British classicist, most influenced by the economics of Adam Smith. To this should be added and by the philosophy of the Scottish school, especially that of Smith's mentor, Hutcheson. Cf. Merrill D. Peterson, "Thomas Jefferson and Commercial Policy, 1783–1793," *WMQ* 22 (1965): 584–610; and Drew R. McCoy, *The Elusive Republic: Political Economy in Jeffersonian America* (Chapel Hill: University of North Carolina Press, 1980). Bercovitch, *Puritan*, outlines particular strains of the utopian idealism long evident among Southern colonists and those among New Englanders, and Henry May explains American utopianism as a component of the revolutionary Enlightenment. Gilbert (p. 22) notes Walpole's earlier insistence on peace as necessary to promoting English trade and his desire to keep clear of continental European entanglements; cf. above, Ch. 1. The real question here is why peace and internationalism were also thought to be to the new republic's interest in 1783. And the most obvious answer is its leaders thought freedom necessitated peace—that is, no conflict with England's superior naval forces—and trade with other nations, much the same sort of international situation desired by the British until the 1830s and by some of them after that.

8. Gilbert, *Beginnings*, p. 86.

9. Ibid., pp. 107–11; and see John A. Schutz, "Thomas Pownall's Proposed Atlantic Federation," *HAHR* 26 (1946): 263–68.

10. Gilbert, *Beginnings*, pp. 112–14.

11. In 1770 a British expedition was planned against New Orleans during the Falklands dispute. Britain continued to toy with Spanish American independence during wars with Spain, especially in 1798–99, and took Trinidad in 1797. Some British officials in 1805–1807 favored Aaron Burr's schemes, discussed below. Admiral Sir Home Riggs Popham invaded Buenos Aires without orders in 1806 and Arthur Wellesley, afterwards Duke of Wellington, was preparing an expedition against Mexico in 1807 when Napoleon's invasion of Spain diverted it there. See William S. Robertson, *The Life of Miranda*, 2 vols. (Chapel Hill: University of North Carolina Press, 1929); W. W. Kaufmann, *British Policy and the Independence of Latin America* (New Haven: Yale University Press, 1951); J. Leitch Wright, *Britain and the American Frontier, 1783–1815* (Athens, Ga.: University of Georgia Press, 1975); and cf. John Lynch, "British Policy and Spanish America, 1783–1808," *JLAS* 1 (1969): 1–30.

12. See Rydjord, *Foreign Interest*; Enrique de Gandia, *Napoleón y la independencia de América* (Buenos Aires: Antonio Zamora, 1955), pp. 210–12; Rayford W. Logan, *The Diplomatic Relations of the United States with Haiti, 1776–1891* (1941; reprint ed., New York: Kraus, 1969); and William S. Robertson, *France and Latin American Independence* (1939; reprint ed., New York: Octagon, 1967). Napoleon's chief agent in this business, Desmôlard, operated from the United States. Earlier, in 1793,

Edmund Genêt came to the United States as Girondin emissary from France and, with Britain allied to Spain, vainly sought official United States cooperation in revolutionizing Spanish America: see below and n. 48. Even after the project fizzled, a Jacobin society in Philadelphia circularized Louisiana (Rydjord, *Foreign Interest*, pp. 115–16), and France continued to introduce revolutionary literature and agents into Spanish America and especially Mexico through the United States.

13. Ibid, pp. 164–65; Bernstein, *Origins*, p. 83. Hamilton and Rufus King, United States minister to England, were Federalists favoring promoting revolution in Latin America. They privately supported Francisco de Miranda, who corresponded with (or only wrote to) Presidents and other well-placed people in the new nation. King was much interested in opening American trade with Mexico and Manila and had ties to New York merchants. See *Works of Alexander Hamilton*, ed. Henry Cabot Lodge, 9 vols. (New York: Putnam, 1885–86), 7:97; Rufus King, *Life and Correspondence of . . .* 6 vols. (1894–1900, reprint ed., New York: DaCapo Press, 1971), 2:300; Robertson, *Life*, pp. 166 ff.

14. Jefferson to Archibald Stewart, Paris, January 25, 1786; in Paul R. Ford, ed., *Works of Thomas Jefferson*, 12 vols. (New York: Putnam, 1904–1905) 5:75; and cf. ibid., 10:381–82.

15. See Arthur P. Whitaker, *The United States and the Independence of Latin America, 1800–1830* (1941; reprint ed. New York: Russell & Russell, 1962); Whitaker, *The Spanish American Frontier, 1783–1795* (Boston: Houghton Mifflin, 1927); Samuel F. Bemis, *The Latin American Policy of the United States* (New York: Harcourt, Brace, 1943) pp. 26 ff.; Rydjord, *Foreign Interest*; and DeConde, *History*. For Jefferson on Brazilian independence: below Ch. 6, and see Raul D'Eca, "Colonial Brazil as an Element in the Early Diplomatic Negotiations Between the United States and Portugal, 1776–1808," in A. Curtis Wilgus, ed., *Colonial Hispanic America* (Washington: George Washington University Press, 1936), pp. 551–57. In 1787 Jefferson told Congress he wanted to postpone Latin American independence until the United States instead of Britain would benefit, and, as President, he suggested that James Wilkinson warn Latin Americans against Europe and encourage their friendship with the United States.

16. John Adams to John Jay, May 28, 1786, in *The Diplomatic Correspondence of the United States, 1783–1789*, 7 vols. (Washington: F. P. Blair, 1833–34), 5:123–30. And see Rydjord, *Foreign Interest*; and Robertson, *Life*.

17. See Grampp, "Re-examination," p. 274; Burton Spivak, *Jefferson's English Crisis* (Charlottesville: University of Va. Press, 1979) ch. 1; and Donald D. Jackson, *Thomas Jefferson and the Stony Mountains* (Urbana: University of Illinois Press, 1981). Unlike Washington, who in 1791 wanted to aid in quelling the "alarming insurrection of negroes on Hispaniola," Jefferson, although disturbed by the possibility of reverberations in the form of slave revolts in the United States, steered a neutral course and was not opposed to the growing United States carrying trade to the island. The British presence there, however, undoubtedly affected his favoring its retention by France. Yet Napoleon in 1802 did persuade him to stop trade and supplies to Haiti, probably as prelude to the Louisiana purchase. It was after French defeat in Haiti that Napoleon sold Louisiana, and probably because of it, so that Haitian independence (declared in 1804) spelled the end of French imperial hope in America and enabled the continental expansion of the United States. Logan, *Diplomatic History*, pp. 38–41, 112, 130; Kaplan, *Colonies*, pp. 286–87; and, for Washington and Spanish America, see Marshall Smelser, "George Washington Declines the Part of El Libertador," *WMQ* 11 (1954): 42–51.

18. Jefferson to Madison, August 16, 1807; in Ford, ed., 9:124–25; and see Whitaker, *Mississippi*; and Alexander DeConde, *This Affair of Louisiana* (New York: Scribners, 1976).

19. April 2, 1807, in Ford, ed., 10:381–82.

20. H. A. Washington, ed., *The Writings of Thomas Jefferson*, 9 vols. (Washington, 1853) 5:444–45. I am indebted to Robert F. Smith for this citation. See his "The American Revolution and Latin America: An Essay in Imagery, Perceptions, and Ideological Influence," *JIAS* (1978):421–41.

21. Cf. Whitaker, *United States*, p. 49.

22. Ibid.; and see Arthur P. Whitaker, *The Western Hemisphere Idea* (Ithaca: Cornell University Press, 1954; paperback ed., 1965, cited here); and Jared W. Bradley, "W.C.C. Claiborne and Spain: Foreign Affairs under Jefferson and Madison, 1801–1811," *Louisiana History* 13 (1972): 16–17. On May 17, 1808 Jefferson wrote to Gallatin concerning Cuba: "I shall sincerely lament Cuba's falling into any hands but those of the present owners. Spanish America is at present in the best hands for us."

(Washington, ed., 5:290). He developed the Western Hemisphere idea after leaving the presidency, but it was certainly implicit in his statement of 1786, above, and it appeared in a more developed form in his letter to the Prince Regent of Portugal in 1808, cited below, Ch. 9.

23. Cited in J. Fred Rippy, *Joel R. Poinsett, Versatile American* (Chapel Hill: University of North Carolina Press, 1935) p. 36.

24. Vicens Vives, *Economic History*, pp. 561–80; Whitaker, *United States*, p. 38; Bernstein, *Origins*, p. 100; Roy F. Nichols, *Advance Agents of American Destiny* (Philadelphia: University of Pennsylvania Press, 1956), who attempts statistics; Charles L. Chandler, "United States Commerce with Latin America at the Promulgation of the Monroe Doctrine," *Quarterly Journal of Economics* 38 (1924): 466–86; Fernando Barreda y Ferrer de la Vega, *Comercio marítimo entre los Estados Unidos y Santander (1778–1829)* (Santander: Centro de Estudios Montañeses, 1950); Earl C. Tanner, "South American Ports in the Foreign Commerce of Providence, 1800–1830," *Rhode Island History* 14 (1955); 15 (1956); 16 (1957); Pierre Chaunu, *Histoire de l'Amérique Latine* (Paris: Presses Universitaires, 1949), translated into Spanish by Federico Monjardín: *Historia de América Latina* (Buenos Aires: EUDEBA, 1964); and Logan, *Diplomatic Relations*. Contraband flourished so that statistics are suspect and quantities hard to assess.

25. Forrest McDonald, *We, the People* (Chicago: University of Chicago Press, 1958), p. 366: "Havana was such a good market for American wheat that many felt it had saved the United States economy during the hardest war years." See Bernstein, *Origins*, 36 ff., 49–50; Le Riverend Brusone, "Desarrollo," pp. 232–39; Nettels, *Emergence*, p. 18; Knight, "Origins," p. 249; and Albert J. Gares, "Stephen Girard's West Indian Trade, 1789–1812," *Pennsylvania Magazine of History and Biography* 72 (1948): 311–42. During the Revolution, Girard sailed as mate on a New York-New Orleans run. Americans were allowed to bring provisions to Havana, but not merchandise, until 1782, when all imports were prohibited. But special permission was extended repeatedly and the Spanish decree allowing neutrals to import slaves to Spanish America from 1789 facilitated smuggling, much as had the British asiento. Then with Spain at war with France in 1793 Havana was again opened to United States shipments of food, and from then on generally was open, so that by 1797 Havana trade was virtually a United States monopoly. Americans also carried provisions to Cuba from St. Eustatius, St. Croix, and New Orleans from 1776, and sold prizes and their cargoes in Havana. Also see *DNA* I:2; no. 5777, and pp. 659–61, 669; I:1:6.

26. Hernán Asdrúbal Silva, "The United States and the River Plate: Interrelationships and Influences Between Two Revolutions," in Joseph S. Tulchin, ed., *Hemispheric Perspectives on the United States.* (Westport: Greenwood, 1978) p. 24. And see *DNA* I:1, pp. 21, 24, 46, 111–12, 114, 99–100, and passim.

27. Anglo-American ships put in down the South American coast, rounded Cape Horn, and appeared in Pacific ports up to Nootka. See Eugenio Pereira Salas, *Las primeros contactos entre Chile y los Estados Unidos, 1778–1809* (Santiago: Editorial Andrés Bello, 1971); E. Pereira Salas, *Buques norteamericanos en Chile a fines de la era colonial (1788–1810)* (Santiago: Universidad de Chile, 1936); above, n. 24; and below, n. 43 and Charles Griffin, *The United States and the Disruption of the Spanish Empire, 1810–1822* (1937; reprint ed., New York: Octagon, 1968), pp. 43–44. From 1784 Nantucketers especially joined or captained whaling expeditions of multinational nature, some sailing from Dunkerque or England, and some going into the China trade. The diary of Captain Cook inspired a Boston group, its prime mover Charles Bulfinch, to send out two patriotically named ships to collect sealskins in the Northwest. They sailed from Nantucket, in 1788. The *Columbia* was captained by John Kendrick, a privateer hero of the Revolution; the *Lady Washington*, by Robert Grey. Spanish authorities in Chile and Peru were uneasy at the Columbia's arrival. In Nootka, the Spanish seized it, along with a British frigate, and the detention of their crews in San Blas (Mexico) led to an English protest and, in 1790, the Nootka Convention. Jefferson aided whaling by lowering customs duties in 1788; much followed, principally from Nantucket and New Bedford, leading to huge profits, to rivalry between the United States and England in the 1790s, and to especially tense relations with Spanish authorities from 1796: see Pereira Salas, *primeros contactos*, pp. 24, 33–34, 38, 73; J. G. Clark, *New Orleans*, p. 227; DeConde, *History*; Gares, "Girard"; and *DNA* I:passim.

28. The best account at present is John Coatsworth, "American Trade with European Colonies in the Caribbean and South America, 1790–1812," *WMQ* 24 (1967): 243–65; and see Bierck, "Impact."

Nettels, *Emergence*, pp. 227–28, says that after 1789 there was less United States trade with the British West Indies than with the Spanish and French islands. He reminds us that 1793–1807 was a golden age of American shipping (p. 233), and that shipbuilding throve from 1789 to 1812 (p. 242). Cf. Pereira Salas, *primeros contactos*, pp. 17–18. R. A. Humphreys, in *Tradition and Revolt in Latin America* (London: Weidenfeld and Nicolson, 1969), p. 142, adds that Britain complained that British manufactures re-exported from the United States undersold direct imports, since they were bought cheaply in the United States auction system and freight and charter rates were also lower. Anna C. Clauder, *American Commerce as Affected by the Wars of the French Revolution and Napoleon, 1793–1812* (1932; reprint ed., Clifton Heights, N.J.: Augustus M. Kelley, 1972), estimated that a little less than a quarter of U.S. exports in 1792 went to Spain and Portugal and their colonies (pp. 21–22). C. L. Chandler, "List of United States Vessels in Brazil, 1792–1805, Inclusive," *HAHR* 26 (1946): 599–617, found that between 1792 and 1805, 83 United States ships put into Brazilian ports. As Asdrúbal, "United States," remarks, after 1797 United States trade with La Plata went through intermediary German (and sometimes French) ports as well, carrying United States products to northern Germany and cheap German textiles (and French and British goods) to Spanish America, where they undersold Spanish and British imports. Whitaker, *Mississippi*, pp. 130–54, observed that between 1797 and 1802 Louisiana went from little export to shipping out cotton, sugar, and flour, as well as much specie from the annual subvention from Mexico. By 1802 most sailings from New Orleans were direct to the United States. In this period, too, many of the ships in Vera Cruz flew the U.S. flag. See Herr, *Eighteenth-Century Revolution*, pp. 388–89; Whitaker, *United States*, p. 8; Nichols, *Advance Agents*, pp. 39, 225; Velásquez, *estado*, p. 215; Brian R. Hamnett, *Politics and Trade in Southern Mexico, 1750–1821* (Cambridge, 1971) p. 102; Michael T. Hamerly, *Historia social y económica de la antigua provincia de Guayaquil, 1763–1842* (Guayaquil: Publicaciones del Archivo Histórico del Guaymas, 1973), pp. 125, 134; Bernstein, *Origins*, p. 77; E. Taylor Parks, *Colombia and the United States, 1765–1934* (Durham: Duke University Press, 1935); C. L. Chandler, "United States Merchant Ships in the Río de la Plata, as Shown by Early Newspapers," *HAHR* 2 (1919):26–54; Chandler, "The River Plate Voyages, 1798–1800," *AHR* 23 (1918):816–26; Tanner, "South American Ports"; Benjamin Keen, *David Curtis De Forest and the Revolution of Buenos Aires* (New Haven: Yale University Press, 1947); Robert S. Smith, "Shipping in the Port of Veracruz, 1790–1821," *HAHR* 23 (1943); 5–20; Javier Ortiz de la Tabla Ducasse, *Comercio exterior de Veracruz (1778–1821)* (Seville: EEHA, 1978); Arcila Farías, *siglo*, pp. 107–17. Some United States ships went to Spain and Portugal with forged British passports, and some to the West Indies under Spanish registry (A. L. Jensen, *Maritime*, pp. 199, 212).

29. Whitaker, *United States*, pp. 18–23; DeConde, *History*, pp. 86–94; Nettels, *Emergence*, pp. 226–27; and Logan, *Diplomatic History*, p. 126.

30. Vincent Nolte, *Fifty Years in Both Hemispheres* (1854; reprint ed., Freeport, N. Y.: Books for Libraries Press, 1972), p. 78.

31. Whitaker, *United States*; Chaunu, *Historia*, pp. 121–22; Norman Guice, "Trade Goods for Texas: An Incident in the History of the Jeffersonian Embargo," *Southwestern Historical Quarterly* 60 (1957): 3–15. Congress in 1806 forbade trade with Haiti, permitting Britain to monopolize that commerce: Rayford Logan, *Haiti and the Dominican Republic* (New York: Oxford University Press, 1968) p. 99.

32. See royal instructions of December 24, 1776 to the Governor of New Orleans, in Robertson, "Spanish Correspondence," pp. 304–7; Whitaker, *Spanish American Frontier*, for Spanish attitudes towards the United States and Gardoqui's instructions of 1784; *DNA* I:1, passim; Van Alstyne, *Empire*, p. 125; Alden, "Coming of Yankee Sperm Whalers," p. 276 (for López, and above, ch. 4); Nichols, *Advance Agents*, pp. 32–33; Robert East, *Business Enterprise in the American Revolutionary Era* (1938; reprint ed., Gloucester, Mass.: Peter Smith, 1964); Conrotte; *intervención;* Yela Utrilla, *España*, Thomas Perkins Abernethy, *Western Lands and the American Revolution* (1937; reprint ed., New York: Russell & Russell, 1959), p. 203; and Harold D. Williams, "Bernardo de Gálvez and the Western Patriots," *RHA* 65–66 (1968): 53–70.

33. See James A. Lewis, "Las damas de la Havana, el precursor, and Francisco de Saavedra: A Note on Spanish Participation in the Battle of Yorktown," *TAm* 37 (1980): 83–101; Yela Utrilla, *España*, I:377; Rodríguez Vicente, "comercio," p. 102; *DNA* I:1:131; and above, Ch. 3, n. 75.

34. See Pedro Torres Lanzas, *Independencia de América: Fuentes para su estudio,*6 vols. (Madrid; Estab. tip. de la Sociedad de Publicaciones Históricas, 1912) 1:26–43; Nichols, *Advance Agents*; J. G. Clark, *New Orleans*, pp. 173, 183, 203; James Alton James, *Oliver Pollock* (1937; reprint ed., Freeport, N. Y.: Books for Libraries Press, 1970); and Robertson, "Spanish Correspondence." Caughey, *Bernardo de Gálvez*, p. 132, says Willing circulated the Declaration of Independence in Mobile.

35. Caughey, *Bernardo de Gálvez*; Torres Lanzas, *Independencia*, 1:15–43; Yela Utrilla, *España*, 1:376–79; East, *Business*, p. 138; Nichols, *Advance Agents*, pp. 15–19; J. Leitch Wright, Jr., *Florida in the American Revolution* (Gainesville: University of Florida Press, 1975); and Portell Vilá, *Cuba* 1:86. Morris and Patrick Henry, with Bernardo de Gálvez, favored a campaign against British Pensacola and Mobile, but were opposed by John Adams, Arthur Lee, and a Congressional majority. Morris had sent James Willing without Congressional approval. Later, Morris wanted Congress to surrender the navigation of the Mississippi and the southwestern territories to Spain, forcing areas north of the Ohio to trade with and to rely on the East. In this he was in accord with the Spanish agent, Juan de Miralles, and with the French, but not with Henry and other Americans interested in western lands (Abernethy, *Western Lands*, pp. 203–4; *DNA* 1:2, pp. 773, 783, 898).

36. Morris cited in Bierck, "Origins," p. 10. See Torres Lanzas, *Independencia*, 1:47; Light T. Cummins, "Spanish Agents in North America during the Revolution, 1775–1779" (Ph.D. Diss., Tulane University, 1977); and Helen M. McCadden, "Juan de Miralles and the American Revolution," *TAm* 29 (1973): 359–75, who says as part of the bargain Miralles had sought for Spanish aid, on September 17, 1779 Congress unenthusiastically agreed to guarantee the Floridas to Spain, if it could take them. Portell Vilá, *Cuba*, 1:79–84, adds that Miralles stopped in Charleston en route to Philadelphia and bought a ship and rice there. He talked to Patrick Henry regarding a joint Spanish-United States project to take British Florida, and also made loans to the government of South Carolina (*DNA* I:2:898; and see Portell Villá, "Otros," p. 65). Morris not only sent North American wheat but offered to send what he could buy in the Dutch and Danish islands to the Spanish in Havana.

37. Pollock was not welcomed by the Spanish, who closed Havana in 1783 and objected to his extensive smuggling activities (see Otero, "American Mission," pp. 92–97; *DNA* I:1:893–94, and passim). But when, with the Spanish order of 1797 allowing neutral trade, United States commerce with Spanish America doubled within the year, the consular system, languishing since 1783, expanded. Procopio Jacinto Pollock, Oliver's son, was commissioned to New Orleans and Daniel Hawley to Cuba. When Hawley was removed in 1799 for tending only to his own business affairs, his successor, John Morton, whose brother, George, was in business in Havana, was approved on the recommendation of New York and Philadelphia businessmen. In 1800, a United States consul was named to La Guaira: see Nichols, *Advance Agents*, pp. 23, 27–28; Yela Utrilla, *España*, 1:396; Rodríguez Vicente, "comercio," pp. 72, 95, 97; Nettels, *Emergence*, pp. 31–34; East, *Business*, p. 172; Bernstein, *Origins*, pp. 35–36; and J. G. Clark, *New Orleans*; and see Cummins, "Spanish Agents," for the other side of the coin.

Clarence L. Van Steeg, *Robert Morris, Revolutionary Financier* (1954; reprint ed. New York: Octagon, 1974) notes Morris was born in England and came to America at thirteen. His father was a tobacco agent. In the 1760s he shipped to the West Indies as a supercargo, and traded, in partnership with Thomas Willing, with Britain, Portugal, and Spain. During the Revolution, Willing and Morris employed the official Congressional envoys to Europe, Silas Deane and William Bingham, as agents, thus merging private and public credit arrangements, and were also linked in business to a number of other merchants along the Atlantic seaboard. They were involved in getting a monopoly for Philadelphia to supply France with tobacco since the Spanish American price went up in 1778. Complaints in Congress against Morris, and against Deane and Franklin, were spearheaded by Richard Henry Lee and Arthur Lee, but Morris's private and public business was hard to disentangle because, he claimed, of subterfuges used against Britain. In 1777 Morris wrote, concerning American merchants: "Their own interest and the publick good goes hand in hand" (p. 346). And to Silas Deane he ventured, "It seems to me the present opportunity of improving our Fortunes ought not to be lost, especially as the very means of doing it will contribute to the service of our country at the same time." [In Elmer James Ferguson, *The Power of the Purse: A History of American Public Finance, 1776–1790* (Chapel Hill: University of North Carolina Press, 1961) pp. 70 ff.] He mixed patriotism and profit, occasionally traded with the enemy, and in 1781 became *the* Congressional financier. Morris was involved with Deane in an informal international trading company which included Charles Willing in the Barbados, and Pollock as Morris's agent at New Orleans (Ibid.; East, *Business*, p. 130; Abernethy, *Western Lands*, p. 183). Ellis P. Oberholtzer, *Robert Morris* (1903; reprint ed. New York: Burt Franklin, 1968); and Van Steeg mentions the heavy losses of Morris, and the United States, in Spanish trade due to British seizures. Morris headed the committee controlling foreign policy until, as Secretary of Foreign Affairs, Robert Livingston superseded its authority in 1781—although Livingston and his immediate successors did not wield any sort of decisive power. Livingston, in office for twenty months, assigned salaries to diplomats, whom he forbade to engage in trade; up until then, this was the customary way of covering expenses. Consuls to Spanish America continued, however, to carry on public and private business simultaneously, and when Livingston was asked by an agent of José de Gálvez in 1782 if the United States would help Spain stop the smuggling to Cuba, he answered no: (Portell Vilá, *Cuba*, 1:96). After a year's hiatus, John Jay succeeded Livingston. Kaplan, *Colonies*, p. 157, concludes of Jay: "He gave preferment to those groups and classes most clearly involved in international commerce," believing it a matter of national interest. Livingston, in his instructions of February 26, 1782 to Robert Smith asked for reports: on naval and military strength, "the population, commerce, husbandry, and revenue of the island, the sentiments of the people with respect to this war, and everything else you may deem curious or interesting." In Jared Sparks, ed., *Diplomatic Correspondence of the American Revolution*, 12 vols. (Boston, 1830), 11: pp. 237–38. Nichols, *Advance Agents*, p. 27, says Smith died in the spring of 1782, but Smith wrote to Francisco de Miranda from Cap Français on December 6 of that year: *Archivo del General Miranda*, t. V:*Viages. Documentos, 1781 a 1785. Cartas a Miranda: 1775 a 1785*, p. 234.

38. Nichols, *Advance Agents*, pp. 23, 27–28; Robertson, *Life*, 1:23–28, cites Miranda's correspondence with "R. Smith" in Baltimore. Also see Miranda, "Diario de Panzacola," *Archivo...Miranda*, 1:141–91; ibid., 5:233–34, 255, 262; Madariaga, *Fall*, pp. 383–89; J. H. Parry, "Eliphalet Fitch: A Yankee Trader in Jamaica during the War for Independence," *History* 40 (1955):84–98; and *The New Democracy in America: Travels of Francisco de Miranda in the United States, 1783–84*, trans. Judson P. Wood, ed. John S. Ezell (Norman: University of Oklahoma Press, 1963). Miranda (p. 49) was favorably impressed by Morris who, he wrote, "seems to me, without doubt, the official of greatest capacity and performance in his line that the United States has had during the past strife, in any department!"

39. Morris, cited in A. L. Jensen, *Maritime*, p. 213; and see DeConde, *History*, p. 82; Marten G. Buist, *At Spes non Fracta: Hope and Company, 1770–1815* (The Hague: Martinus Nijhoff, 1974); and Ralph W. Hidy, *The House of Baring in American Trade and Finance* (Cambridge, Mass.: Harvard University Press, 1949). Labouchère, head of the house of Hope, and Sir Francis Baring's daughter Dorothy married in 1796; another Baring married a Philadelphia Bingham.

40. Stuart W. Bruchey, *Robert Oliver, Merchant of Baltimore, 1783–1819* (Baltimore: Johns Hopkins Press, 1956), pp. 274–75; and see Nolte, *Fifty Years;* John H. Jackson, Jr., "The Mexican Silver Schemes: Finance and Profiteering in the Napoleonic Era, 1796–1811" (Ph.D. diss. University of North Carolina, 1978); John Rydjord, "Napoleon and Mexican Silver," *Southwestern Social Science Quarterly* 19 (1938): 171–82; and José Joaquín Real Díaz and Antonia M. Heredia Herrera, "El virrey José de Iturrigaray," in Calderón Quijano, *Carlos IV*, 2:236, 243.

41. J. Jackson "Mexican Silver," p. 280. The scheme probably contributed (in ways yet to be explored) to United States relations with Latin America. Procopio Jacinto Pollock had been United States consul in New Orleans in 1797. His way in Vera Cruz was eased by a note of introduction from the Spanish minister in Philadelphia, the Marqués de Casa Irujo, to the Mexican viceroy, Iturrigaray. Expected to act jointly for the Olivers with the Vera Cruz resident merchants, the Murphys, Pollock and they kited prices for their own profit. Matthew and Tómas Murphy were nephews of a previous viceroy, Azanza. See ibid., pp. 108, 116; Bruchey, *Oliver*, pp. 253, 265–69, 295–315; Ortiz de la Tabla, *comercio*, pp. 322, 327; Nichols, *Advance Agents*, p. 36; and Sandra Sealove, "The Founding Fathers as Seen by the Marqués de Casa Irujo," *TAm* 20 (1963):37–42. Members of the Vera Cruz consulado complained of the silver scheme: R. S. Smith, "Shipping" p. 13. Repercussions of the transaction within Mexico require further investigation. Despite the Embargo of 1807, it was arranged with the Secretary of the Treasury, Albert Gallatin, to work the transfer by way of New Orleans. Also

see P. G. Walters and R. Walters, Jr., "The American Career of David Parish," *JEcH* 4 (1944):149–66; and *DNA* I:1:38, 168 ff.

42. See Rippy, *Poinsett*; and Dorothy M. Parton, *The Diplomatic Career of Joel Roberts Poinsett* (Washington: Catholic University, 1934). His name became attached to a bright red plant, also very seasonal and often shipped out of the country.

43. See Richard J. Cleveland, *A Narrative of Voyages and Commercial Enterprises*, 3d ed. (Cambridge, Mass.: John Owen, 1850); William Shaler, "Journal of a Voyage between China and the Northwestern Coast of America," *American Register*, 1808; John C. Pine, "The Role of United States Special Agents in the Development of a Spanish American Policy, 1810–1822" (Ph.D. Diss. University of Colorado, 1955), pp. 178–83; Roy F. Nichols, "William Shaler, New England Apostle of Rational Liberty," *New England Quarterly* 9 (1936):72 ff.; Nichols, *Advance Agents*, pp. 51–74; and cf. Pereira Salas, *Buques*, p. 31; and Pereira Salas, *primeros contactos*, pp. 99–100, 121–22. In 1801 they carried principally British goods. Shaler was captain, Cleveland supercargo. Shaler's father, Timothy, had turned his merchantman into a privateer during the revolution. Simon Collier, *Ideas and Politics of Chilean Independence, 1808–1833* (Cambridge, 1967), p. 42, cites the diary of another sailor from the United States in Chile in 1802, who advocated independence to interested creoles. Shaler later, like Poinsett, became a United States agent; see below, Ch. 9.

44. See Whitaker, *Spanish American Frontier*; Whitaker, *Mississippi*; J.L. Wright, *Rivalry*; his *Frontier*; Alamán, *Historia*, 3; Alberto María Carreño, *La diplomacia extraordinaria entre México y Estados Unidos 1789–1947*, 2d ed., 2 vols. (Mexico: Jus, 1961), 1; Griffin, *United States*; Lillian E. Fisher, "American Influence upon the Movement for Mexican Independence," *MVHR* 18 (1932): 463–78; and L. E. Fisher, *Background of the Revolution for Mexican Independence* (Boston: Christopher, 1934), pp. 373–82.

45. Whitaker, *Spanish American Frontier*, stresses frontier particularism and does not give enough weight to land speculation in borderlands relations with Spanish America; cf. Abernethy, *Western Lands*, pp. 193–204, 360; Richard R. Beeman, *Patrick Henry* (New York: McGraw-Hill, 1974), pp. 181–82; and East, *Business*, pp. 206–23, for the general speculative outlook after the war. Clifford L. Egan, reviewing DeConde's *This Affair of Louisiana*, in *AHR* 82 (1977):1069, mentions the role of land speculators in the Louisiana Purchase and that land speculation, as much as anything, may have motivated Livingston, when, as American representative to France (along with Monroe), he negotiated the purchase. As Bernard Bailyn said in a paper presented at the annual meeting of the American Historical Association in 1977, "Land speculation was the most common way of making a fortune in the colonies." He added the West "was no agrarian preserve"; rather, that part of gaining profit was settling the land. It should be remembered that contributing to colonial frustrations on the eve of revolution, and especially to those of Massachusetts, Virginia, and Pennsylvania land speculators, had been the Quebec Act of 1774, putting the Ohio Valley and Canada under the authority of Quebec.

46. See Arthur P. Whitaker, "Reed and Forde: Merchant Adventurers of Philadelphia," *Pennsylvania Magazine of History and Biography* 41 (1937): 237–62; and C. Richard Arena, "Philadelphia-Spanish New Orleans Trade in the 1790s," *Louisiana History* 2 (1961): 431, who only mentioned Pollock's debt on behalf of the states, while Whitaker only noted his private one. James A. James, in *The Life of George Rogers Clark* (Chicago: University of Chicago Press, 1929), pp. 155, 293–97, says that in 1785 Congress awarded Pollock $90,000 on the debt owed him by Virginia but that it was not paid for another six years. Also see James, *Pollock*.

47. Abernethy, *Western Lands*, pp. 328, 342–44; Whitaker, "Reed," p. 243; Whitaker, *Spanish American Frontier*, p. 127; Kaplan, *Colonies*, pp. 168–70; José Navarro Latorre and C. F. Solano, *¿Conspiración Española, 1787–1789?* (Zaragoza: Instituto Fernando el Católico [C.S.I.C.] de la Diputación Provincial, 1949); William R. Shepherd, "Papers Bearing on James Wilkinson's Relations with Spain, 1787–1789," *AHR* 9 (1904):748–66; Shepherd, "Wilkinson and the Beginnings of the Spanish Conspiracy," *AHR* 9 (1904):490–506; and Manuel Serrano y Sanz, *El Brigadier Jaime Wilkinson a sus tratos con España para la independencia del Kentucky (años 1787 a 1797)* (Madrid, 1915). Cf. Otero, "American Mission," who whitewashed Gardoqui in this connection.

48. Frederick J. Turner, "Correspondence of Clark and Genêt," *American Historical Association Annual Report, 1896* (Washington, 1897), 1:945 ff; Turner, "The Mangourit Correspondence in Respect to Genêt's Projected Attack on Louisiana and the Floridas," ibid., 1897 (Washington,

1898), pp. 569–79; Turner, "The Origin of Genêt's Projected Attack on Louisiana and the Floridas,"
AHR 3 (1898): 650–71; Whitaker, *Spanish American Frontier*, pp. 128–33, 143 ff., 187–88;
DeConde, *History*, pp. 61–71; Logan, *Diplomatic History*, pp. 40–41; James, *Clark*, pp. 417 ff.; and
Jackson, *Jefferson*, p. 78.

49. March 23, 1793, Ford, 6:206; Whitaker, *Spanish American Frontier*, pp. 187–88.

50. See Thomas P. Abernethy, *The Burr Conspiracy* (1954; reprint ed., Gloucester, Mass.: Peter
Smith, 1968); George Dargo, *Jefferson's Louisiana* (Cambridge, Mass.: Harvard University Press,
1975), p. 197, for a recent bibliography; Isaac Joslin Cox, "The Pan-American Policy of Jefferson and
Wilkinson," *MVHR* 1 (1914): 212–39; Cox, "General Wilkinson and His Later Intrigues with the
Spaniards," *AHR* 19 (1914): 794–812; Cox, "Hispanic-American Phases of the Burr Conspiracy,"
HAHR 12 (1932): 145–75; Ernesto de la Torre Villar, "Dos proyectos para la independencia de
Hispanoamérica: James Workman y Aaron Burr," *RHA* no. 49 (1960): 1–83; and Whitaker, *Spanish
American Frontier*, pp. 108 ff., 175–80.

51. Whitaker, *Mississippi*, pp. 104–10; Walter Brownlow Posey, "The Blount Conspiracy,"
Southern College Bulletin 21 (1928);11–21. As governor of the Southwest Territory, Blount had
contact with the United States agent among the Creeks, James Seagrove, who had been Miranda's
friend in Cuba: Whitaker, *Spanish American Frontier*, p. 166. And see Ibid., and Abernethy, *Lands*,
for discussion of the various land companies.

52. Abernethy, *Burr*; Whitaker, *Mississippi*, concerning D. Clark, Jr., Wilkinson, Philip Nolan,
and Burr's interest in New Orleans, 1802 on; and see E. E. Hale, "The Real Philip Nolan,"
Publications of the Mississippi Historical Society 4 (1901): 281–329. Abernethy, *Burr*, pp. 54, 74–75,
noted that Burr, D. Clark, and Wilkinson speculated in lands, but Wilkinson's possibilities lay within
United States jurisdiction, while the others' ventures would only be profitable outside it. Abernethy
cites William Duane in the *Aurora*, 1806: The conspiracy appealed to land debtors, those with bad and
specious titles, and those with thwarted political ambitions. Clark turned evidence on Wilkinson in
1808, but Jefferson protected Wilkinson, who claimed Spanish payments to him had been for
purchases of tobacco.

53. Conversely, Humboldt, *Political Essay*, 4:304–18, reprinted statistical tables he got from
Albert Gallatin, drawn up from United States customs house books, concerning the value of United
States exports 1799–1803, which he compared with those of Mexico.

54. In a note to G. R. Clark, of December 4, 1783, Jefferson had thanked him for specimens of
shells and seeds, and he mentioned English interest in exploring from the Mississippi to California as
prelude, he thought, to colonizing, commenting, "They pretend it is only to promote useful knowledge." He then sounded him out on leading an expedition west (*AHR* 3 [1898]: 672–73). Cf.
Goetzmann, *When the Eagle Screamed*; and William H. Goetzmann, *Exploration and Empire: The
Explorer and the Scientist in the Winning of the American West* (New York: Knopf, 1966), who
remarks: "Down to the Mexican War, the trade of Santa Fe and Chihuahua was the lodestone that drew
Americans into the Southwest. Indeed, any close examination of the Mexican War and of the whole
Manifest Destiny movement will indicate that Santa Fe and its trade was one of the basic American
objectives" (p. 52); and see D. Jackson, *Jefferson*.

55. See H. May, *Enlightenment*, pp. 212–17.

56. Jefferson, *Notes on the State of Virginia*, ed. William Peden (New York: Norton, 1972), pp.
64–65, 275–76.

57. "... the glimmerings which reach us from South America enable us all to see... inhabitants
held down by slavery, superstition, and ignorance. Whenever they shall be able to rise under their
weight and to shew themselves to the rest of the world, they will probably shew they are like the rest of
the world." Ibid, p. 276.

58. Whitaker, *Western Hemisphere*; and see Whitaker, "The American Idea and the Western
Hemisphere: Yesterday, Today, and Tomorrow," *Orbis* 20 (1976):161–78.

59. The American Philosophical Society had thirteen Spanish corresponding members between
1784 and 1804 (Shafer, *Economic Societies*, pp. 40, 59). Franklin successfully sponsored Campomanes for membership. Valentín de Foronda, an honorary member, who was Spanish consul-
general and then *charge d'affaires*, in the United States from 1801 to 1809, was also a friend and
correspondent of Jefferson, and a member of Spanish economic societies. Foronda was of ency-

clopedic bent, republican views, and liberal disposition. He translated Spanish plays into English and had them put on in Philadelphia. In a study he wrote of the United States, *Apuntes ligeros sobre los Estados Unidos de la América Septentrional*, he declared the country's economic prosperity the fruit of freedom. Although praising its religious liberty and widespread education, the privileged position of women relative to Europe, its citizens' health and its simple taxes, he criticized the state of the arts and sciences, found too great a freedom of the press, a lack of true democratic spirit, and a dominating passion—to make money. He explained in mixed admiration and disapproval, "Ten thousand vessels upon the seas! In truth, this is a wealth greater than the famous mountains of Potosí." There is a copy in the New York Public Library, and see José de Onís, "Valentín de Foronda's Memoir on the United States of North America, 1804," *TAm* 4 (1948):351–87. Foronda also wrote a tract counseling Spain to free Spanish America: *Sobre lo que debe hacer un principe que tenga colonias a gran distancia* (Philadelphia, 1803). Therein he suggested Spain sell her colonies to independent companies or to another nation in order to allow Spain's economy to be more oriented to commerce, more similar to that of the United States. (A copy exists in the rare book collection of the Library of Congress.) Foronda favored social and economic reform within Spain as well. See Robert S. Smith, "A Proposal for the Barter and Sale of Spanish America in 1800," *HAHR* 41 (1961):275–86; Bernstein, *Origins*, pp. 44, 53, 55, 59–60; Bernstein, *Making an Inter-American Mind*; and Harry Bernstein, "Some Inter-American Aspects of the Enlightenment," in Whitaker, ed., *Enlightenment*, pp. 53–69. Foronda's writings were censored or prohibited in Spain: Herr, *Eighteenth-Century Revolution*, p. 55; J. R. Spell, "An Illustrious Spaniard in Philadelphia," *Hispanic Review* 4 (1936):136–41; and below, Ch. 7.

60. Cited in Claude G. Bowers, "Thomas Jefferson and South America," *Bulletin of the Pan American Union* 77 (1943):189. Jefferson gave Campomanes a copy of his *Notes on Virginia*. (Bernstein, *Mind*, p. 18). And for his interest in Spanish and Portuguese literature, see D. Jackson, *Jefferson*, pp. 88–89.

61. Shaler and Cleveland said they wanted to make enough money to be able to devote themselves to literary pursuits (and they did write). John Stoughton, Spanish consul in Boston and Gardoqui's brother-in-law, attached prestige to membership in learned societies and also, licensed by Gardoqui, either conducted a private trade with Spanish America, or resold licenses (Bernstein, *Origins*, pp. 43–44). Shaler wrote to James Monroe in 1812: England and the United States "seem destined by Providence to be the guardians of the liberties of mankind." (Cited in Joseph Lockey, "An Early Pan-American Scheme," *Pacific Historical Review* 2 [1933] 445). Cf. the attitudes of Joel Barlow, in H. May, *Enlightenment*, pp. 192, 239; and M. Jensen, *American Revolution*. And see Helmut De Terra, "Alexander von Humboldt's Correspondence with Jefferson, Madison, and Gallatin," *PAPS* 103 (1959):783–806; and Joseph Ellis, "Habits of Mind and an American Enlightenment," *AQ* 28 (1976):150–64.

62. Robert V. Remini, *Andrew Jackson and the Course of American Empire, 1767–1821* (New York: Harper & Row, 1977), p. 149; and see Whitaker, *Mississippi*, p. 14.

63. Writing under the pseudonym, "Peter Porcupine," cited in Whitaker, *Mississippi*, p. 121; and passim for anti-Spanish sentiment to 1803.

64. Rydjord, *Foreign*, p. 104; Robertson, *Life of Miranda*, 2:246; Levene, *mundo*, p. 168; and Ford, ed., *Jefferson*, 11:351. Also see H. May, *Enlightenment*; Bercovitch's writings; Herbert Morais, *Deism in Eighteenth Century America* (1943; reprint ed., New York, Russell & Russell, 1960); and William Gribbin, "A Matter of Faith: North America's Religion and South America's Independence," *TAm* 31 (1975):470–87. Gilbert, in his discussion of the origins of American foreign policy, neglected the religious and racial components. Instead, he found a high-toned moralism first appearing in the nineteenth century. I would argue that such moralism appeared in colonial British America and in foreign policies under England and continued through 1776; cf. Bailyn, *Ideological Origins*; Crowley, *Sheba*; and Bercovitch's corpus.

65. C. F. Adams, ed., *Works*, 1:66.

66. Cited in Arthur Ekirch, *Ideas, Ideals, and American Diplomacy* (New York: Appleton, Century, 1966), p. 31.

67. For a comment on Tocqueville's thesis: Cushing Strout, *The New Heavens and New Earth: Political Religion in America* (New York: Appleton, Century, 1966) p. 31; and see McCoy, *Elusive Republic*.

68. Herberg, *Protestant, Catholic, and Jew*, rev. ed. (Garden City, N. Y.: Doubleday, 1960), p. 75.

69. Commager, *Jefferson*, p. 190. And see Robert N. Bellah, "Civil Religion in America," *Daedalus* 96 (1967):1–21; Bellah, "The Revolution and Civil Religion," in J. E. Brauer, ed., *Religion and the American Revolution* (Philadelphia: Fortress Press, 1976), pp. 55–73; and Catherine L. Albanese, *Sons of the Fathers, the Civil Religion in the American Revolution* (Philadelphia: Temple University Press, 1976).

70. Turner, "Correspondence," 1:945–53.

71. See F. P. Hill, *American Plays, Printed, 1714–1830* (Stanford: Stanford University Press, 1934).

72. See S. T. Williams, 1:26, 38, 40; *Archivo del General Miranda*, 7:158; and Frederick S. Stimson, *Orígenes del hispanismo norteamericano* (Mexico: Ediciones de Ancrea, 1961).

73. See Charles S. Watson, "A Denunciation on the Stage of Spanish Rule: James Workman's *Liberty in Louisiana*, 1804," *Louisiana History* 11 (1970):245–58.

CHAPTER 6

1. Glendenning, "Influencia," pp. 50–51, 395; he mentions that the poetry of James Thomson, to whom *Rule Britannia* is attributed, was often cited in Spain. And see Robert S. Smith, "*The Wealth of Nations* in Spain and Hispanic America, 1780–1830," *Journal of Political Economy* 65 (1957): 104–25.

2. Cf. the sentiments of Cabarrús in Ch. 3 and its n. 76. He both admired the rebels in 1778 and advocated expansion of free trade as ultimately beneficial to Spain, citing Cuba, then free of monopoly, as an example. Cabarrús was involved as a principal in a group of mixed French, Dutch, and Spanish financiers. He raised large loans for the state during the war, from abroad and principally through Hope and Co. of Amsterdam, and it was on his advice that Charles III established the Banco de San Carlos in 1782 as a form of central bank. Research is needed on Cabarrús and this international network. See, too, Buist, *At Spes*, p. 279.

3. *DNA* I:1:52; Portell Vilá, *Cuba*, 1:488; and Alfred H. Siemens and Lutz Brinckmann, "El sur de Veracruz a finales del siglo XVIII: un análisis de la "Relación de Corral," *HM* 26 (1976):263–324.

4. Abalos in *Documentos para la historia de América* (Mérida, Venezuela: Universidad de los Andes, 1961–65); and Carlos E. Múñoz Oraá, "Pronóstico de la independencia de América y un proyecto de monarquías en 1781," *RHA* 50 (1960):439–73. Navarro is cited in Whitaker, *Spanish American Frontier*, p. 9; and see *DNA* I:1:52.

5. Francisco Morales Padrón, "México y la independencia de Hispano-américa en 1781 según un comisionario regio: Francisco de Saavedra," in *Homenaje a D. Ciriaco Pérez-Bustamante* (Madrid: Instituto Gonzalo Fernández de Oviedo; CSIC, 1969), pp. 335–58. Saavedra went on to sum up succinctly: If an uprising were to occur, especially in maritime provinces, the rebels would have English help, out of vengeance and because "we have declared indirectly, in favor of their colonies." The French want our trade, he added, and they spread sedition. Generally, Americans were persuaded that Spain wanted to take all it could from them, particularly hated the greed of officials put over Indians, and saw official impunity resulting from the system. Contraband, they believed, could only be destroyed by free trade. Cf. Corral, above, n. 3.

6. Arcila Farías, *Comercio*, pp. 96–97; Eduardo Arcila Farías, "Ideas económicas en Nueva España en el siglo XVIII," *El Trimestre Económico* 14 (1947):74–77; and José Joaquin Real Díaz and Antonia M. Heredia Herrera, "Martín de Mayorga," in Calderón Quijano, *Carlos III*, 2:122–23. It will be recalled that after 1770 British North American wheat was replacing Mexican in Havana.

7. Arcila Farías, "Ideas," pp. 74–76. Cf. Posada's outlook on liberty of commerce to that of Cabarrús above, n. 2; and see James A. Lewis, "Nueva España y los esfuerzos para abastecer la Habana, 1779–1783," *AEA* 33 (1976):101–26, for problems in getting Mexican wheat to Havana.

8. *DNA* I:1, passim; Arcila Farías, *Economía*, pp. 259–91; Alvárez F., *comercio*, pp. 16, 35, 38, 117; J. A. Arellano Moreno, *Orígenes de la economía venezolana*, 2d ed. (Caracas and Madrid: Editoriales Edime, 1960), p. 273; Emilio Ravignani, "El virreinato del Río de la Plata (1776–1810),"

in Ricardo Levene, ed., *Historia de la Nación Argentina*, 2d ed., 10 vols. (Buenos Aires: El Ateneo, 1936–42), 4(1940):185–93; and Ricardo Levene, "Riqueza, industrias y comercio durante el virreinato," in ibid., 4:287–88.

9. See Céspedes del Castillo, *Lima;* Burkholder, *Politics;* Brading, *Miners,* p. 116; and Bobb, *Viceregency,* pp. 98–99. Cevallos and his successor, Juan José Vertiz y Salcedo, also had Buenos Aires compete successfully for the interior trade of southern South America, formerly monopolized by the consulado of Peru: Levene, "Riqueza," pp. 287–93; Ravignani, "virreinato," pp. 185–89. See Vicente Palacio Atard, *Areche y Guirior: Observaciones sobre el fracaso de una visita al Perú* (1776–1794) (Seville, 1946); Eunice J. Gates, "Don José Antonio de Areche: His Own Defense," *HAHR* 8 (1928):14–42; and Campbell, "Colonial Establishment." Cf. the visita to Chile, from 1778 to 1786, of a subordinate of Areche, in Barbier, *Reform,* p. 113 ff.

10. Ella Dunbar Temple, *La Gaceta de Lima del siglo XVIII. Facsimiles. . . .* (Lima: Universidad Nacional Mayor de San Marcos, 1965), October 27–December 16, 1776.

11. Donoso, *Antecedentes,* p. 187; Henry Hunt Keith, "Independent America through Luso-Brazilian Eyes: the 'Gazeta de Lisboa' (1778–1779) and the 'Correio Braziliense' (1808–22) of London," in Keith, et al., *Portugal and America: Studies in Honor of the Bicentennial of American Independence* (Lisbon: Luso-American Educational Commission and the Calouste Gulbenkian Foundation, 1976), pp. 31–34.

12. Donoso, *letrado,* 1:339 ff., 399–405, 473; Ricardo R. Caillet-Bois, "La revolución de las colonias Inglesas de la América del Norte. La colaboración prestada por España y la repercusión del movimiento en el Río de la Plata," in Levene, ed., *Historia,* 5:142, 147. Cf. R. A. Humphreys, "William Robertson and his *History of America,*" in Humphreys, *Tradition,* pp. 18–36. Skinner, in Skinner and Wilson, *Essays,* p. 175, mentions that Robertson stated the main propositions of Adam Smith. And see below n. 43, for another of Robertson's creole collaborators.

13. See James A. Lewis, "New Spain during the American Revolution, 1779–1783: a Viceroyalty at War" (Ph.D. Diss., Duke University, 1975).

14. Torres Lanzas, *Independencia,* 1:22–23, 44; Pérez-Marchand, *Dos étapas,* pp. 83, 98, 96, 127; Mariano Picón Salas, *Dependencia e Independencia en la historia hispanoamericana* (Caracas: Editorial de la Librería Cruz del Sur, 1952), p. 14. Pérez-Marchand thinks that 1779 began a stage of more intense interest in prohibited political books. She may, however, confuse intensity of desire to prohibit such works with a change in reading habits, and in that case the latter need not have occurred in 1779.

15. Donoso, *letrado* 1:411–13; Collier, *Ideas,* pp. 16–20; Villalobos, *Tradición,* pp. 120–22.

16. *Los Proclamas de Filadelfia de 1774 y 1775 en la Caracas de 1777,* edited by Mauro Páez-Pumar (Caracas: Centro Venezolano Americano, 1973). I am indebted to León Helguera for calling my attention to this book. The Bolívars had a neighboring *finca,* or country place, close to Moreno's. And see Pedro Grases, *Libros y Libertad* (Caracas: Ediciones de la Presidencia de la República, 1974), pp. 3–4. Thomas Jefferson kept a similar book: Gilbert Chinard, ed., *The Literary Bible of Thomas Jefferson: The Commonplace Book of Philosophers and Poets* (Baltimore, 1928).

17. Readying for war in 1778, Spain declared trade permissible from thirteen ports of the peninsula to twenty four in its America, excluding Venezuela and Mexico, and lowered some duties. In older histories, the upsurge of Spain's trade with its America is emphasized, from the 1778 *reglamento de comercio libre* to the English wars beginning in 1796—Haring, *Spanish Empire,* p. 320, estimates that this trade increased seven-fold—while the rise in contraband, harder to document, has received too little attention. Nor has much attention been paid until recently to the question of re-exports. The Steins, in *Colonial Heritage,* noted an increase and broadening in peninsular trade with America, but not that in smuggling, and they implied static growth in Spanish America and overlooked wartime demand and changes; in that book they (like Brading, in *Miners,* p. 115, and passim) laid the influx of European goods in the 1780s only to this reform. The Steins changed their minds in "Concepts." Barbara Stein there (p. 108) cited Campomanes, who in 1788 wrote that these regulations, like the trade of Cádiz, were indeed very flawed, and concluded that Cádiz in fact held on to its monopoly and to the bulk of trade with America. Moreover, that trade was still mostly in re-exported foreign goods, and mostly shipped to Mexico in return for silver. Humboldt remarked of this reglamento, in *Political Essay* 4:97, "In affairs of commerce, as well as in politics, the word freedom expresses merely a

relative idea." Also see Antúñez, *Memorias,* p. 304; Múñoz Pérez, "publicación;" *DNA* I:1:264; de la Tabla Ducasse, *Comercio;* John Fisher, "Imperial 'Free Trade' and the Hispanic Economy, 1778–1796," *JLAS* 13 (1981); Pierre Chaunu, "Interpretación de la Independencia de América Latina," in Heraclio Bonilla, et al., *La Independencia en el Perú* (Lima: Instituto de Estudios Peruanos; Campodónico, 1972), p. 131; and cf. Chaunu, *Historia,* 56. For Mexico: Hamnett, *Politics,* found that Mexican consulado funds then went into cotton and dye trades and into textile production and distribution; Richard E. Greenleaf, "The Obraje in the Late Mexican Colony," *TAm* 23 (1967):227–50, found that textile workshops began to expand from 1776; Richard J. Salvucci, "Enterprise and Economic Development in Colonial Mexico: the Case of the Obrajes," *JEcH* 61 (1981):197–99, a summary of his Ph.D dissertation (Princeton University, 1980); Brading, *Miners,* speaks of consulado members then investing in mines, too; and see Arcila Farías, *siglo,* 131 ff.; Arcila Farías, *comercio;* and Eric Wolf, "The Bajío in the Eighteenth Century: An Analysis of Cultural Integration," in *Publications of the Middle American Research Institute of Tulane University* 17 (1955):177–200. For Brazil: MacLachlan, "African Slave Trade."

18. Lewis, "Nueva España," p. 524; Knight, "Origins," p. 249; Julio Le Riverend, *Historia Económica de Cuba* (Havana: Instituto Cubano del Libro, 1974), pp. 113, 133, 144; Torres Lanzas, *Independencia* 1:39, 47; and see *DNA* I:1:21.

19. Tulio Halperín-Donghi, *Politics, Economics, and Society in Argentina in the Revolutionary Period* (Cambridge, 1975), p. 30; Susan M. Socolow, *The Merchants of Buenos Aires, 1778–1810: Family and Commerce* (Cambridge, 1978); Jonathan Brown, *A Socioeconomic History of Argentina, 1776–1860* (Cambridge, 1979); Diffie, *Latin American Civilization,* pp. 428–31; Haring, *Spanish Empire,* p. 320; Asdrúbal Silva, "United States," pp. 23–24; Pereira Salas, *primeros contactos;* Villalobos, *comercio;* Hernán Ramírez Necochea, *Antecedentes económicas de la independencia de Chile* (Santiago: Editorial Universitaria, 1959), pp. 40–54; and n. 8, 9 above.

20. *DNA* I:1:264; Arcila Farías, *Economía,* pp. 314, 300, 342, 452, 466–70. Anglo-American ships were also active in the carrying trade between Spain and its American colonies: *DNA* I:1:6, 264–68; Barreda, *comercio;* and above, Ch. 5, n. 24.

21. Brading, *Miners,* pp. 239, 257, says that most creoles in the Bajío worked for the government, and that reforms had quadrupled the Mexican bureaucracy.

22. Félix Denegri Luna, et al., *Antología de la independencia del Perú* (Lima: Comisión Nacional del Sesquicentenario de la Independencia del Perú, 1972), pp. 25–34; Lewin, *movimientos,* p. 93; Eduardo Arcila Farías, "El pensamiento económico hispanoamericano en Baquíjano y Carillo," in *Extremos de México. Homenaje a Dr. Daniel Cosío Villegas* (Mexico: Colegio de Mexico, 1971); Guillermo Lohmann Villena, *Los ministros de la audiencia de Lima en el reinado de los Borbones (1700–1821)* (Seville: EEHA, 1974); Burkholder, *Politics,* passim; L. Campbell, "Establishment"; and Maria Luisa Rivara de Tuesta, *Ideólogos de la Emancipación Peruana* (Lima: Comisión Nacional del Sesquicentenario de la Independencia del Perú, 1972), pp. 46 ff.

23. See Francisco Eugenio Santa Cruz y Espejo, *El nuevo Luciano de Quito, 1779* (Quito: Imprenta de Ministerio de Gobierno, 1943); Philip L. Astuto, *Eugenio Espejo* (Mexico: Tierra Firme, 1969), pp. 54–63; and Antonio Montalvo, *Francisco Javier Eugenio de Santa Cruz y Espejo* (Quito, 1947).

24. Ainsworth, "Commerce," p. 15; and see Julio César Guillamondegui, "La repercusión inmediata del Reglamento de comercio libre de 1778: una solicitud de creación del Consulado de Buenos Aires, 1779," in III *Congreso del Instituto Internacional de Historia de Derecho Indiano* (Madrid, 1972). *Actas y estudios jurídicos,* 1973, pp. 985–1012; John Fisher, *Silver Mines and Silver Miners in Colonial Peru, 1776–1824* (Liverpool: University of Liverpool, Centre for Latin American Studies, 1977); Halperín-Donghi, *Politics,* pp. 5–6, 12, 22; Ramos, *minería;* Céspedes del Castillo, *Lima,* pp. 129, 139–40, 143, 152, 185–86; Levene, *Investigaciones,* 2:302; Amat's *Memoria* of 1779; Brading, *Miners;* Brading; "Government"; Enrique Florescano and Isabel Gil, comps., *Descripciones económicas generales de Nueva España, 1784–1817* (Mexico: INAH, 1973) 1:75–90; Hamnett, *Politics;* and above, n. 18.

25. The petition said that governmental measures had been insufficient to reestablish education after the expulsion of the Jesuits, that creoles were on unequal footing with other Spaniards and discriminated against in appointments, and that young Chileans felt stifled and disinherited. They

wanted to hold responsible posts and be useful in government. See Donoso, *letrado,* p. 411; Villalobos, *Tradición;* Barbier, *Reform,* pp. 92 ff, and Burkholder and Chandler, *Impotence,* p. 109.
26. Ibid., pp. 99–121.
27. Miguel Luis Amunátegui, *Don Manuel de Salas,* 3 vols. (Santiago: Imprenta Nacional, 1895) 1:23–29; Barbier, *Reform,* 92 ff.; Ruben Vargas Ugarte, S. J., *Historia del Perú virreinato (siglo XVIII)* (Lima: Gil, 1956), pp. 300, 347, 353, 402. Salas, his brother-in-law, Rojas, and his father, José Perfecto de Salas, president of the audiencia, who began his rise assisting the innovating viceroy, Amat, first in Chile and then in Peru, and who had recently returned with a fortune of several million pesos and a library previously owned by the Jesuits, were thought to be the authors of seditious broadsides against the tobacco monopoly and the new tax collector. In 1776 Gálvez in effect ordered the exile of the elder Salas by appointing him fiscal of the House of Trade in Cádiz, probably both because of his unsettling influence in Chile and reports of his defrauding the treasury while in Lima. Other creole officials were sent to the audiencia of Lima, the result being to turn a predominantly creole audiencia into a predominantly European one between 1776 and 1778. Enrique de Gandia, in *Conspiraciones y revoluciones de la independencia americana. Movimientos precursores* (Buenos Aires: Orientación Cultural Editores, 1960), p. 21, says that Gálvez responded to the cabildo protest by ordering it to abstain from such opinions and advised its *syndic* that only through pure commiseration was he spared from spending, as merited, some years in the Malvinas. In Venezuela in 1781 the intendant, Abalos, lowered duties, and he did not implement new monopolies in order, he explained, to avoid uprisings, for there were new and intense complaints against taxes and the tobacco monopoly "where before there had been silence": Alvárez F., *comercio,* p. 33. Workers in the government's tobacco factory in the city of Mexico struck in 1780; for Mexico, see Real Díaz and Heredia Herrera, "Mayorga," in Calderón Quijano, *Carlos III,* 2:142–49, 163, 175, and 246.
28. Cf. Miguel Luis Amunátegui, *Un conspiración en 1780* (Santiago: Impenta del Progreso, 1853) with Villalobos, *Tradición,* pp. 129–45. The forced loan of 1780 raised little cash in South America and caused much complaint. It was suspended by the governor of Buenos Aires in 1781: Céspedes del Castillo, *Lima,* p. 152. It was also suspended in Chile, according to Meza Villalobos, *Conciencia,* p. 205, because of the rebellion of Túpac Amaru.
29. In 1779 free mulattoes who were militia leaders in Lambayeque succeeded in resisting registration for tribute payment because the government, fearing British invasion by sea, would not deploy troops from coastal defense. Accounts of this resistance spread and heartened aggrieved residents of Cuzco, Arequipa, La Paz, Tarma, and Cochabamba, initially including creoles against current taxes and for Guirior. The revolt of Túpac Amaru, one of a number of peasant community leaders who felt his powers and prerogatives were being undermined, followed and swelled. See L. Campbell, "Military"; his "Recent Research," pp. 37–38; Leon G. Campbell, "Black Power in Colonial Peru: The 1779 Tax Rebellion in Lambayeque," *Phylon* 33 (1972):140–52; L. Campbell, "The Army of Peru and the Túpac Amaru Revolt, 1780–83," *HAHR* 56 (1976):31–57; Magnus Mörner, *Perfil de la sociedad rural de Cuzco a fines de la Colonia* (Lima: Universidad del Pacífico, 1978) 109–32, 155, who questions older interpretations; Céspedes del Castillo, *Lima;* John Fisher, "La rebelión de Túpac Amaru y el programa de la reforma imperial de Carlos III," *AEA* 28 (1971):405–21; Lewin, *movimientos,* pp. 100–113; Boleslao Lewin, *La rebelión de Túpac Amaru* (Buenos Aires: Hachette, 1957); Rowe, "Movimiento"; Tisnes, *Movimientos,* pp. 51–59; Carlos Daniel Valcarcel, *La Rebelión de Túpac Amaru,* 3d ed., rev. (Lima, 1970); Carlos Daniel Valcarcel and Guillermo Durand Flórez, comps., *La rebelión de Túpac Amaru* (Lima: Comisión Nacional de Sesquicentenario de la Independencia del Perú, 1971); and Ricardo Levene, "Intentos de independencia en el virreinato del Plata (1781–1809)," in Levene, *Historia,* 5:424.
30. Lewin, *movimientos,* pp. 124, 142, 145; Tisnes, *Movimientos,* p. 189; Melchor de Paz y Guini, *Guerra separatista: rebeliones de indios en sur América; la sublevación de Túpac Amaru, crónica,* ed. Luis Antonio Eguiguren (Lima, 1952), facsimiles of 2 vols. of the original 3 vols. The text of the manuscript is in the Rich Collection, New York Public Library.
31. Demetrio Egan, cited in Leon G. Campbell, "A Colonial Establishment: Creole Domination of the Audiencia of Lima during the Late Eighteenth Century," *HAHR* 52 (1972):15; and see Campbell, "Army," p. 51. Areche and Gálvez by 1781 voiced their dislike and distrust of, and disdain for, Peruvians. Moreover, Areche's economy drive, in good part made necessary by the costs of war

against Britain, perhaps allowed Túpac Amaru's revolt to gain impetus, in that troops were sparse and many recruits unhappy with pay cuts: L. Campbell, "Military." Túpac Amaru's manifestos solicited mestizo and creole support and emphasized Peruvian unity against foreign (Spanish) domination, but not against the king. There are indications that some of the more radical participants toward the end of the movement sought total independence and race war.

32. See above, n. 9.

33. Cited in Fransciso Posada, *El movimiento revolucionario de los comuneros neogranadinos en el siglo XVIII,* 2d ed. (Mexico: Siglo XXI, 1975), p. 24.

34. John L. Phelan, *The People and the King: the Comunero Revolution in Colombia, 1781* (Madison: University of Wisconsin Press, 1978); and see Gómez Hoyos, *revolucion,* 1:115–204; Tisnes, *movimientos;* Pablo E. Cárdenas Acosta, El *movimiento comunal del 1781 en el Nuevo Reino de Granada,* 2 vols. (Bogotá: Editorial Kelly, 1960), and Jane M. Loy, "Forgotten Comuneros: The 1781 Revolt in the Llanos of Gasanare," *HAHR* 61 (1981):235–57. In Socorro, people also suffered from a smallpox epidemic in 1776, and poor harvests: Phelan, *People,* p. 44. There, aggrieved Indians spoke of proclaiming their own king, a descendant of the Zipas, and creoles used this tradition to manipulate Indian discontent. By 1780, too, there was much ethnic mixture and categories, including whites, were blurred (pp. 42, 79). Creoles, mainly middle-strata planters, merchants, and artisans, united all groups and rebel demands were drawn up in the *capitulaciones de Zipaquirá,* in the name of explicitly defending old peninsular juridical and political traditions by which the king could not impose tributes without the consent of his subjects, as represented in cabildos. Phelan (*People,* p. 158 ff.) described the rebel demands as a long list of specific grievances on behalf of New Granada, which was spoken of as a *corpus mysticum politicum.* Among them were seven articles concerning trade calling for free trade and simplified duties, to be spent at home, and suggesting deep merchant and planter discontent with the visitador's new measures, mentioning too that most credit came from the church so that the crown, in calling in church trust funds and substituting bonds for them, was drying up viceroyalty credit and capital. Also visible was provincial rivalry with Bogotá. The provincial creoles wanted a monopoly on offices and restoration of customary privileges; they wanted to rule the kingdom in the king's name and excoriated European disdain for and power over Americans. Still, there were marked reverberations within Bogotá (Gómez Hoyos, *revolucíon,* I:205 ff.) The revolt was defused by the archbishop, Antonio Caballero y Góngora, de facto viceroy from May 1781 and de jure from mid-1782, by adroit negotiation. Leaders hoped for British aid and had contact with men in the English government and much with Túpac Amaru.

35. Miguel Batllori, *El Abate Viscardo* (Caracas: IPAGH, 1953), pp. 41 ff.

36. Humboldt, *Political Essay* 1:154.

37. *Consulta* of the Council of the Indies, July 5, 1786, cited in Ramírez Necochea, *Antecedentes.* And see A. García-Baquero González, "Comercio colonial y producción industrial en Cataluña a fines del siglo XVIII," in Jordi Nadel and Gabriel Torrella, eds., *Agricultura, comercio colonial y crecimiento económico en la España contemporánea* (Barcelona: Ariel, 1974), p. 288; and Miguel Izard, "Comercio libre, guerras coloniales y mercado Americano," in ibid., pp. 295–321. Jacques A. Barbier and Herbert S. Klein, "Revolutionary Wars and Public Finances: the Madrid Treasury, 1784–1807," *JEcH* 61 (1981):315–39.

38. Eduardo Arcila Farías, *El Real Consulado de Caracas* (Caracas: Instituto de Estudios Hispanoamericanos, Facultad de Humanidades y Educación, Universidad Central de Venezuela, 1957) p. 34; Angel López Cantos, *Don Francisco de Saavedra, Segundo Intendente de Caracas* (Seville: EEHA, 1973).

39. Aranda, cited in Whitaker, "Pseudo-Aranda," p. 311. See *DNA* V:2:598; Ricardo Donoso, "Bosquejo de una historia de la independencia de la América Española," in *Movimientos Emancipadores* (Caracas: IPAGH, 1961), 4:199; and above, Ch. 5, n. 35. Miguel Luis Amunátegui, *Los precursores de la independencia de Chile,* 3 vols. (Santiago: Imprenta Barcelona, 1909–10), 3:261, cited Aranda to Floridablanca, March 12, 1786:

> I have got it in my head that South America is slipping from our hands. . . . Do not think that our America is as innocent as in past centuries nor as unpopulated, nor believe it lacks educated people who see that those inhabitants are forgotten on their own soil and its substance sucked away by

those born in the metropolis. . . . Nothing of what happens here is hidden from them; they have books that instruct them in the new maxims of liberty; and they do not lack propagandists who are going to persuade them if the situation arises.

40. Whitaker, *Spanish American Frontier*, pp. 10 ff.; *DNA*:I:2:888–94.

41. *Writings of Benjamin Franklin*, ed. Albert Henry Smith, 10 vols. (1907; reprint ed. N.Y.: Haskell House, 1970), 9:22–23; Polt, "Jovellanos," pp. 9–11; John E. Englekirk, "Franklin en el mundo hispano," *RI* 21 (1956): 319–71; Ricardo Krebs Wilckens, "La visión de historia española en el pensamiento de Campomanes," *Miscelánea Vicente Lecuna, homenaje continental* (Caracas: Cromotip, 1959), pp. 237–51. In 1785 the anonymously published *Cartas político-eonómicas al Conde de Lerena* (there is a 1968 Madrid edition, by Antonio Elorza), now attributed to León de Arroyal, who held office in the Spanish treasury, concluded that Spanish decline was due to the emergence of absolutist monarchy with the Habsburgs, destroying the balance between crown, people, and aristocrats in the medieval constitution, and that economic reform was impossible without constitutional reform. And see the Steins, "Concepts."

42. Cited in Mario Rodríguez, *La revolucíon americana de 1776 y el mundo hispánico. Ensayos y documentos* (Madrid: Tecnos, 1976), p. 165. Antonio de Nebrija, three hundred years earlier, had written the same thing to Isabella: see Liss, *Mexico*, p. 163, n. 31.

43. See Jefferson R. Spell, *Rousseau in the Spanish World before 1833* (reprint ed., New York: Gordion, 1969), pp. 12–13. Antonio de Alcedo y Bexarano, *Diccionario geográfico-histórico de las Indias, o América*, 5 vols. (Madrid, 1786–89); it was translated as *The Geographical and Historical Dictionary of America and the West Indies*, ed. G. A. Thompson, 5 vols. (London, 1812–15). And see Ciriaco Pérez Bustamante, *Antonio de Alcedo y su "Memoria" para la continuación de las "décadas" de Herrera* (Madrid: Instituto Gonzalo Fernández de Oviedo, 1968); and José de Onís, "Alcedo's *Biblioteca Americana* [1791], HAHR 31 (1951):530–41; who says the *Diccionario* was very popular in Spanish America, admired by Mier, and consulted by Miranda. Volume Two contains the account of the Revolution of 1776 and its antecedents. It had been published in Quito in 1765. Alcedo also sent Robertson data on Spanish America: Charles Ronan, S. J., "Antonio de Alcedo: His Collaborators and His Letters to William Robertson," *TAm* 34 (1978):490–501. His collaborators were various Jesuit exiles who sent him information.

44. Alvárez F., *comercio*, pp. 139–40, cites Francisco de Saavedra, then intendant of Caracas, writing to José de Gálvez, May 25, 1785, to report that with imports of blacks came naval stores, barrels, and tools for indigo, coffee, and cotton growers, and parts for brandy stills. See Aguirre Beltrán, *población*, King, "Evolution," pp. 45–54; Miguel Acosta Saignes, *Vida de los esclavos negros en Venezuela* (Caracas: Hesperides, 1967); Hubert H. S. Aimes, *A History of Slavery in Cuba, 1511–1868* (1907; reprint ed., New York: Octagon, 1967); Kenneth K. Kiple, *Blacks in Colonial Cuba, 1774–1899* (Gainesville: University of Florida Press, 1976); Jaime Jaramillo Uribe, "Esclavos y señores en la sociedad colombiana del siglo XVIII," *Anuario colombiano de historia social y cultura* 1 (1963); Sharp, *Slavery;* MacLachlan, "African Slave Trade"; and Rolando Mellafe, *La esclavitud en Hispanoamérica* (Buenos Aires: Editorial Universitaria de Buenos Aires, 1964); translated as *Negro Slavery in Latin America* (Berkeley and Los Angeles: University of California Press, 1975); in the latter, pp. 107–109, he notes a continuing increase in severity of treatment of black slaves in Latin America in the second half of the century. Some ameliorative legislation prompted by it had little effect, for owners then had greater interest in production. There were more vagabonds and bandits, among them blacks and part-blacks, and an increase in *cimarrón*, or fugitive, villages. There were also more laws to discourage interbreeding among races.

45. See *DNA* I:1:382; I:2:659; Céspedes de Castillo, *Lima*, pp. 177–79; Socolow, *Merchants*; Barbier, *Reform*, pp. 113 ff.; Villalobos, *comercio y crisis*; Ramírez Necochea, *Antecedentes*, p. 54; Ramos, *minería*, p. 281; J. Fisher, *Silver*; Brading, *Miners*, p. 126; Hamnett, *Politics*; Humboldt, *Political Essay* 4:23. Harris, *Mexican Family*, pp. 85–86, found those northern Mexican hacendados, the Sánchez Navarro, prospering, principally through supplying sheep and wool to the Bajío and Mexico City, until 1785, then suffering because of glutted markets. They also invested, along with the consulado of Mexico, in the new Royal Philippine Company (p. 106) whose chief advocate was Cabarrús. It ultimately failed, but not before, as successor to the Guipúzcoa monopolists, flooding the

Venezuelan market in 1785: King, "Evolution," p. 48; Arcila Farías, *Economía*; Alvárez F., *comercio*, p. 139; Ortiz de la Tabla Ducasse, *Comercio*; William L. Schurz, "The Royal Philippine Company," *HAHR* 3 (1920): 491–508; and Ch. 5, n. 24 and 25.

46. Gálvez, while in Louisiana, married Felice St. Maxent, daughter of New Orleans' wealthiest merchant. Two of his brothers-in-law, who also married while on military duty in New Orleans, were among Mexico's first intendants—Manuel Flon in Puebla and José Antonio Riaño in Guanajuato. The presence of *los Gálvez* in the palace and of these career officers and their wives in provincial capitals disseminated newer Spanish concepts of political economy and a new cosmopolitanism, and ensured that Frenchified culture would become fashionable. Flórez sponsored the creation of a botanical garden and an academy of fine arts, backed the mining reforms of Fausto de Elhuyar, the expert sent from Spain in 1786, and approved the founding of the *Sociedad Patriótica* in Vera Cruz. He was also advanced in years, and so arthritic the audiencia, headed by Gamboa, had at length to govern in his stead. For Revillagigedo, see below. Between 1777 and 1784, a number of intendancies were established: in Louisiana, Chile, Peru, Quito, Bogotá, and so on, and in New Spain in 1786. See John R. Fisher, *Government and Society in Colonial Peru: The Intendant System, 1784–1814* (London: University of London, Athlone Press, 1970); John Lynch, *Spanish Colonial Administration, 1782–1810: The Intendant System in the Viceroyalty of the Río de la Plata* (London: University of London, Athlone Press, 1958); Luis Navarro García, *Intendencias en Indias* (Seville: EEHA, 1959); Lillian E. Fisher, *The Intendant System in Spanish America* (Berkeley and Los Angeles: University of California Press, 1929); J. Miranda, *Ideas*, pp. 194–206; Brading, *Miners*, pp. 64–92; David Hugh Edwards, "Economic Effects of the Intendancy System in Chile: Captain General Ambrosio O'Higgins as Reformer" (Ph.D. Diss., University of Virginia, 1973); Barbier, *Reform*, 124 ff.; Gisela Morazzini de Pérez Enciso, *La intendencia en España y América* (Caracas: Universidad Central de Venezuela, 1966); Reinhard Liehr, *Ayuntamiento y oligarquía en Puebla, 1787–1810* (Mexico: SepSetentas, 1976); Horst Pietschmann, "La introducción del sistema de intendencias en el virreinato de Nueva España dentro del marco de la reforma administrativa general de monarquía española en el siglo XVIII," *Jahrbuch fur Geschichte von Staat, Wirtschaft und Gesellschaft Lateinamerikas* (1970), pp. 411–16; and W. W. Pierson, "La intendencia de Venezuela en el régimen colonial," *Boletín de la Academia Nacional de Historia* (Caracas) 24 (jul-set. 1941): 259–75.

47. See José Manuel Pérez Ayala, *Antonio Caballero y Góngora: virrey y arzobispo de Santa Fé, 1723–1796* (Bogotá, 1951). In the Bajío, from 1776 José Pérez Calama, a priest who came to Mexico with the regalist bishop of Puebla, Francisco Fabián y Fuero, in the 1760s, was aide to the reform-minded bishops of Michoacán, Rocha and Antonio de San Miguel, and was also an associate member of the Basque economic society. He urged clerical and educational reforms, in the process sponsoring a contest in 1784 on "the true method of studying scholastic theology." It was won by an acute critic of current texts and methods, accurately reflecting Pérez Calama's own ideas, the young priest and teacher, Miguel Hidalgo y Costilla, who in 1810 would launch a revolution. In 1784 and 1785 Pérez Calama, his bishop, and the bishop of Guadalajara, Ruiz Cabanas, instituted emergency measures to offset the severity of plague, famine, and ensuing vagrancy, as did Bernardo de Gálvez and the archbishop in the capital. This experience of church and state intervention in society, disquieting to many propertied creoles, incidentally publicized concepts of being useful to fellow citizens, of patriotism and civic duty, and of regional and communal self-help in achieving material progress. In 1789 Pérez Calama went to Quito as bishop, continued to work for reform, and vented his opinions in the patriotic society and the *Mercurio Peruano:* see below, Ch. 7. The 1785 relief program also publicized the philosophy underlying the Bourbon reforms, including a new attitude toward the poor, in which idleness was viewed as a social disease and charity as a source of idleness, and public works and workhouses were seen as solutions. Reformers manifested a desire to broaden the economic base through manufacture of other than luxury items or goods competing with Spanish. They saw improving the lot of the laboring poor both as saving lives and as finding producers and consumers, and they believed that the state depended upon them, its clergy and leading citizens, to manage society. San Miguel then wrote of "his obligations as a man, a faithful vassal, a bishop, and a good citizen," and in a neat blend of old and new went on: "With the Apostle Saint Paul, my conscience shouts to me: that although I might possess in the highest degree the two useful sciences, economics and politics, all would be vanity, clanging bell, and thundering air, if I did not employ and give my rents to the benefit of the poor and the public cause." Cited in Aguilar Ferreira Melesio, "Fray Antonio de San Miguel

anuncia la construcción de Acueducto de Morelia," *Anales de Museo de Michoacán* (Morelia) 4 (1946):79–91. See Germán Cardozo Galué, *Michoacán en el siglo de las luces* (Mexico: Colegio de México, 1973); and Miguel Hidalgo y Costilla, "Disertación sobre el verdadero método para estudiar teología escolástica," appendix to Julian Bonavit, *Historia del Colegio de San Nicolás* (Morelia: Universitaria Michoacana, 1958), pp. 413–35. Their activities too reflected Floridablanca's continuing reliance on the clergy.

48. Shafer, *Economic Societies;* Cardozo Galué, *Michoacán,* pp. 41–43, found that in Mexico members of the Basque society occupied political, military, and ecclesiastical positions, high and low, in the capital and the provinces, and were creoles and Spaniards. José Miranda, *Humboldt y México* (Mexico: UNAM, 1962), p. 30, says there were 312 members of the Basque society in New Spain by 1792, and Socolow, *Merchants,* p. 113, remarks that in the 1770s some porteño merchants sent funds to the Basque society.

49. Pérez Ayala, *Caballero;* Astuto, *Espejo,* p. 48; Gómez Hoyos, *revolución;* John F. Wilhite, "Foreign Ideas in New Granada, 1760–1830," *Annals of the Southern Conference on Latin American Studies* 8 (1977):5–18; and see, among others, Arthur P. Whitaker, "The Elhuyar Mining Missions and the Enlightenment," *HAHR* 31 (1951):558–85; Clement Motten, *Mexican Silver and the Enlightenment* (Philadelphia: University of Pennsylvania Press, 1950); Rose Marie Buechler, "Technical Aid to Upper Peru: the Nordenflicht Expedition," *JLAS* 5 (1973):37–77; Diffie, *Latin American Civilization,* pp. 547–50; Cook, *Floodtide;* Humboldt, *Political Essay,* 2:362; Juan Carlos Arías Divito, *Las expediciones científicas españolas durante el siglo XVIII* (Madrid: Ediciones Cultural Hispánica, 1968); Hipólito Ruiz, *Travels of Ruiz, Pavón and Dombey in Peru and Chile (1777–1788),* trans. B. E. Dahlgren (Chicago: Field Museum of Natural History, 1940); Arthur R. Steele, *Flowers for the King* (Durham: Duke University Press, 1969); and Francisco de las Barras y de Aragón "Notas para una historia de la expedicion botánica de Nueva España," *AEA* 7 (1950):411–59.

50. Gómez Hoyos, *revolución;* Wilhite, "Foreign Ideas"; Joaquín Piñero Corpas, ed., *Real Expedición Botánica del Nuevo Reino de Granada, 1783–1816* (Bogotá: Caja de Crédito Botánica, 1973); and Javier Ocampo, *El proceso ideológico de la emancipación: Las ideas de génesis, independencia, futuro e integración en los orígenes de Colombia* (Tunja: Universidad Pedagógica y Tecnológica de Colombia, 1974).

51. *DNA* V:2; Carlos Villanueva, *Napoleón y la independencia de América* (Paris, 1911), p. 44; and see below, Ch. 7, n. 56.

52. See Caughey, *Bernardo de Gálvez;* Otero, "American Mission"; María del Carmen Galbis Díez, "Bernardo de Gálvez," in Calderón Quijano, *Carlos III,* 2:327–59; José Maria Luis Mora, *México y sus revoluciones,* 3 vols. (Mexico: Porrúa, 1950), 2:248–55; and Joaquín Fernández de Lizardi, "Testamento Político del Pensador mexicano (1827)," *Revista Mexicana de Estudios Históricos* 1 (1927):184–85. His diary on the siege of Pensacola was published in Madrid in 1781 and became popular there and in Mexico, where in 1785 there appeared an epic poem exaggerating his heroism (Onís, *United States,* pp. 21–22). His plan may have been similar to that of Abalos in 1781, and the one of 1783 attributed to Aranda, suggesting that three *infantes* rule as American kings and that the Spanish monarch take the title of emperor, except that he, Bernardo de Gálvez, rather than a Spanish prince, was to rule Mexico. Yet, his father-in-law had had dealings with Miranda (see Whitaker, *Spanish American Frontier,* p. 41) and the possibility exists that Bernardo de Gálvez, like Iturbide later, did contemplate a throne.

53. *Archivo de Miranda,* 8:9. For *capitulaciones de Zipaquirá:* above, n. 34.

54. Robertson, *Life,* 1:23–28; Robertson, *Miranda,* pp. 235–41; *Archivo de Miranda,* 1:92— Miranda came to the United States on the American whaler, *Prudence;* and see Madariaga, *Fall,* pp. 383 ff.; and above, Ch. 5, n. 38.

55. Adams to James Lloyd, March 6, 1815, in C. F. Adams, ed., *Works,* 10:134 ff.

56. Miranda, *New Democracy,* pp. xx, 5, 19, 30–32, 46, 81, 147, 156. He assiduously investigated the fortifications and battlegrounds of the recent war, and admired the beauty and intelligence of the well-to-do women he met, but not their usual devotion to home and family. He did not like and was perhaps jealous of George Washington (ibid., pp. 44, 58, 116). He wrote in the *Edinburgh Review* in 1809 of his thoughts in 1781. Nicolás García Samudio, *La Independencia de Hispanomérica* (Mexico: Fondo de Cultura Económica, 1945), p. 17, says that in a letter to the French deputy Gerisoné of October 10, 1792, Miranda mentioned that on arriving in New York City in 1784 he had organized a

project for achieving Spanish American independence with the cooperation of England. García Samudio, p. 18, adds that on August 20, 1785 the *Morning Chronicle* (London) lauded Miranda's work toward Latin American independence and told of plans underway by Spanish Americans, "among whom the principal theme and model of imitation is the example of the United States." Cf. Robertson, *Miranda*, pp. 249–51; *DNA* V:2.

57. Maxwell, *Conflicts*, p. 136. My account here principally follows Maxwell. In the 1780s, Portugal enjoyed a favorable balance of trade with England for the first time, due to large exports of Brazilian cotton (H. E. S. Fisher, *Portugal*).

58. Maxwell, *Conflicts*, p. 80.

59. Jefferson to John Jay, Marseilles, May 4, 1787; in Maxwell, *ibid.*, pp. 80–81. Jefferson wrote further:

> The royal revenue from the fifth and diamonds, as well as the rest of the gold production could be counted on. . . . They have an abundance of horses. . . . They would want cannon, ammunition, ships, sailors, soldiers and officers, for which they are disposed to look to the U.S., always understood that every service and furniture will be well paid. . . . They would want of us at all times corn, and salt fish.

Maxwell continues: "Apparently Río de Janeiro, Minas Gerais and Bahia would instigate the uprising and the other captaincies were expected to follow their example." Edward Dumbauld, *Thomas Jefferson, American Tourist* (Norman: University of Oklahoma Press, 1946), p. 88, mentions the interview at Nîmes and adds Jefferson had had a similar interview with a Mexican in Paris but been noncommittal, suspecting he was a Spanish spy.

60. Maxwell, *Conflicts*, p. 82, comments: His poetry was "heavy with a bewildering profusion of heroes, including Rousseau, Voltaire, Locke, Pope, Virgil, and Camoes." Dauril Alden, in "Yankee Sperm Whalers," pp. 287–88, mentions that in 1790, in discussing the decline of whaling, José Bonifacio opposed the monopoly on that enterprise and urged free competition in order to combat American and British whaling off South America. Another young Brazilian, Hipólito José da Costa Pereira, later editor of the *Correio Braziliense,* who was sent by the government to investigate United States know-how, in 1798, suggested inviting several Nantucket families to settle in Brazil; see below, Ch. 7.

61. Maxwell, *Conflicts*, pp. 125–35, 181–85. It is known as the conspiracy of Tiradentes, from the nickname of one of the soldiers, referring to his moonlighting as a tooth-puller.

62. See Alvárez F., *comercio*, p. 16; Bernstein, *Origins*, p. 41; Levene, *Investigaciones*, 2:60; Socolow, *Merchants*, pp. 159, 128 ff.; Asdrúbal Silva, "United States"; Barbier, *Reform*, p. 113 ff.; Portell Vilá, *Cuba*, 1:114; Arcila Farías, *siglo;* Brading; *Miners;* D. A. Brading, *Haciendas and Ranchos in the Mexican Bajío: León, 1700–1860* (Cambridge, 1978), pp. 184–96; Priestley, *José de Gálvez;* Hamnett, *Politics;* Hamerly, *Historia;* Gibson, *Aztecs*, pp. 212, 253–66; Hamilton, *War;* and Hamilton, "Monetary Problems." Hamilton says that Spain doubled its paper money *(reales vales)* in 1782, for war had drained the treasury. Estates swelled by engrossment and purchase of Jesuit properties: see above, Ch. 4, n. 60; J. Fisher, *Silver*, pp. 99–102, compares merchant investment in Peruvian mines to Brading's conclusion that in Mexico large merchants invested directly in mines. In Peru, mining credit and supplies came through *aviadores,* middlemen, relying on Lima capitalists in turn tied to Spain, and these arrangements may have widened retention of creole support for Spanish rule. In Guatemala, although indigo exports peaked in the 1780s, merchants complained of contraband and British influence and pressed for free trade, and in 1786 complained of the quantity of silver sent to Spain, leaving individuals and commerce strapped: Miles Wortman, "Government Revenue and Economic Trends in Central America, 1787–1819," *HAHR* 55 (1975):251–86; and Miles Wortman, "Bourbon Reforms in Central America, 1750–1786," *TAm* 32 (1975):222–38. In 1786 throughout New Spain, tribute assessments were raised and people moved about to avoid payment. Spanish authorities in America continued to decry the lack of shipping and declared ships necessary for regional prosperity. In 1785 Saavedra wrote Gálvez that while agriculture swelled, much was lost for lack of vessels. He also said that trade with foreign colonies was necessary and lucrative to Venezuela, which thereby exported fruits, cows, and mules, for after all, "what can we do with more than 10,000 mules?" (Alvárez F., *comercio*, p. 139).

63. For the continuation of traditional influences, see Góngora, *Studies;* González Casanova, *misoneísmo;* and Carlos Stoetzer, *The Scholastic Roots of the Spanish American Revolution* (New York: Fordham University Press, 1979).

CHAPTER 7

1. Conde de Floridablanca, "Memoria presentado al Rey Carlos III y repetido al Rey Carlos IV. . . . renunciado al ministerio," in *BAE* (Madrid: Ediciones Atlas, 1952), 59:336. He reported that free commerce had tripled Spanish trade with the Indies and more than doubled royal duties there; this was "the happy revolution." But he also admitted that imports were swamping Spanish trade and industry, and foreign goods were flooding Spain and its America. Also see above, Ch. 6, n. 17.

2. S. Stein, "Concepts," p. 112, and passim. Stein (citing T. S. Ashton, *Economic History*, p. 125) says that a sharp, sustained rise in English textile exports to the British Caribbean began in 1787, and that between 1785 and 1800 such exports went up 16-fold, implying that a good deal came to Spanish America (pp. 118–19). Woodward, "Origins," p. 552, notes that in 1783 and 1786 Charles III granted the British at Belize legitimate logcutting concessions, and that that region flourished as an illicit emporium for trade with Guatemala, and, it should be added, Mexico. And even before the trade was opened in 1789, a British company was licensed to import slaves to Cuba.

3. José Antonio Maravell, "Las tendencias de reforma política en el siglo XVIII español," *Revista de Occidente*, 2d ser. 5 (1967): 53–82; and J. A. Maravell, "Cabarrús y las ideas de reforma política y social en el siglo XVIII, *Revista de Occidente*, 6 (1968): 273–300; Antonio Elorza, *La ideología liberal en la Ilustración* (Madrid: Tecnos, 1970); Herr, *Eighteenth-Century Revolution*, pp. 53–57, 71–72, 337 ff. Hume's *Discursos políticos. . .* too appeared in Madrid in 1789. And see Cabarrús in Ch. 3, above, n. 76; Polt, "Jovellanos"; R. S. Smith, *Wealth*; R. S. Smith, "English Economic Thought in Spain, 1776–1884," *South Atlantic Quarterly* 67 (1968):312–13, who explains that much of Adam Smith's renown in Spain came later and was due to the French economist, Jean Baptiste Say, that in 1784 economics was taught in a school founded by the Aragonese Economic Society, and that other such societies instituted similar courses. Also see B. Stein, "Concepts," pp. 108–9; and for Foronda in the United States, above, Ch. 5, n. 59.

4. Cited in S. Stein, "Concepts," p. 118; and Villalobos, *comercio*, pp. 236–37. See Artola, "América," p. 74; and Jovellanos's *dictamen* in *BAE* 50:72–73.

5. Jacques Barbier, "The Culmination of the Bourbon Reforms, 1787–1792," *HAHR* 57 (1977):57–58, 62; Barbier, *Reform*, pp. 157–58; and see his exchange with John Fisher in *HAHR* 58 (1978):87–90; Barbier, "Peninsular Finance and Colonial Trade; the Dilemma of Charles IV's Spain," *JLAS* 12 (1980):21–37; and Mark A. Burkholder, "The Council of the Indies in the Late Eighteenth Century: A New Perspective," *HAHR* 56 (1976): 404–23. A current debate questions whether 1788–92 saw reaction setting in or was the height of the Bourbon reform program. Barbier, "Culmination," opts for the latter; Brading, *Miners*, p. 73, said that reform faded with the death of José de Gálvez. The question is unnecessary, for both are right.

The royal cédula of 1789 opened to foreigners the slave trade with the Spanish Caribbean and stipulated low duties, stating that it was necessary in order to encourage agriculture. This concession was granted first for Cuba—Cubans had requested it in 1788—and then for Santo Domingo, Puerto Rico, and Caracas. The obvious goal was to bring in more blacks at low prices so that the Spanish colonies could compete with the sugar of Saint Domingue, Jamaica, and Guadeloupe. The act was then progressively extended to La Plata ports in 1791, Callao and Paita in 1795, and Guayaquil and Panama in 1804, and terms liberalized for importation. Contraband went in with blacks; profits were enormous; most shippers were foreign. The British profited most, but United States vessels and dealers had a great but as yet undetermined share in the profits; see Ch. 6, n. 44.

6. Floridablanca, "Instrucción reservada que la Junta de Estado, creada formalmente por mi decreto de este día 8 de julio de 1787, deberá observar en todos los puntos y ramos encargados a su conocimiento y examen," in *BAE*, 59:227–28.

7. Pereira Salas, *primeros contactos*, p. 212, for the order of 1791. Whitaker, *Spanish American Frontier*, p. 149; and Otero, "American Mission," pp. 282–93, for Gardoqui; appointed in 1789, he stated that opinion in 1791. Also see Cook, *Floodtide*, p. 69.

8. Herr, *Eighteenth-Century Revolution*, pp. 45–46, 260–69, 317–21, 361, 373; and see R. S. Smith, *Wealth*, pp. 108–17; Polt, "Jovellanos," pp. 9–11; and also for Jovellanos: above, Ch. 3, n. 73. Polt says that in 1784 Jovellanos spoke of the English as "the best economists in the world!" and by 1790 he favored Hutcheson's system of moral philosophy. Jacques Turgot made the epigram, in 1776.

9. Herr, *Eighteenth-Century Revolution*, pp. 348–59, 321–25, 267. Herr, however, sets too late a date, 1792, and gives too much credit for causation to the French Revolution: cf. Saavedra, above, and Maravell, "tendencias," who explicitly disagreed with Herr and found Spanish changes, rather, within more general European trends. For Picornell: Iris M. Zavala, "Picornell y la revolución de San Blas, 1795," in Vilar, *Historia*, pp. 35–58; and her "Cabarrús y Picornell: un documento desconocido," *Cuadernos Hispanoamericanos* 78 (1969):744–82.

10. *Mercurio peruano de historia, literatura, y noticias públicas que da á luz la Sociedad academica de amantes de Lima. Y en su nombre D. Jacinto Calero y Moreira*. T. 1–12. January 1791 (1794) (Lima: Imprenta real de los Niños huérfanos [etc. 1791] 1795); Ella Dunbar Temple, "Idea económica del Perú colonial a través de los periódicos limeños del siglo XVIII," *Cultura Peruana* 2 (1942); and in Denegri Luna, *Antología*, pp. 84 ff; also see Alberto Tauro, ed., *Los ideólogos* (Lima: Comisión Nacional del Sesquicentenario de la Independencia del Perú, 1971); Josefina Cintrón Tiryakian, "The *Mercurio peruano*: Herald of Modernization of Peru in the Eighteenth Century" (Ph.D. diss., Harvard University, 1969); Shafer, *Economic Societies*, pp. 157 ff.; Miguel Maticorena Estrada, "José Baquíjano y Carillo, reformista peruano del siglo XVIII," *Estudios Americanos* (Seville), nos. 76–77 (1958); Gerbi, *Dispute*, pp. 302–13, 412; Emilia Romero del Valle, "El *mercurio Peruano* y los ilustrados limeños," in *MMC*, pp. 335–78; José Ignacio López Soria, *Ideología económica del "Mercurio Peruano"* (Lima: Comisión Nacional del Sesquicentenario de la Independencia del Perú, 1972); Elisa Luque Alcaide, *La sociedad económica de Amigos del País en Guatemala* (Seville: EEHA, 1962); and above, Ch. 6, n. 22.

11. Posada, *Dictamen* of January 27, 1792, in Enrique Florescano and Fernando Castillo, comps., *Controversia sobre libertad de comercio de Nueva España, 1776–1818*, 2 vols. (Mexico: Instituto Mexicano de Comercio Exterior, 1975), 1:264; cf. Arcila Farias, "ideas"; and Cardozo Galué, *Michoacán*, pp. 49, 91–92.

12. See above, Ch. 6, n. 49, 50; Alejandro Malespina, *Viaje al Río de la Plata en el siglo XVIII* (Buenos Aires, 1938); Donald C. Cutter, "Spanish Scientific Exploration along the Pacific Coast," in *The American West: An Appraisal* (Sante Fe: Museum of New Mexico Press, 1963), pp. 151–60; H. W. Rickett, "The Royal Botanical Expedition to New Spain," *Chronica Botanica* 11 (1947); Michael Weber, et al., *The Malespina Expedition* (Sante Fe: Museum of New Mexico Press, 1977) which catalogs our ongoing indebtedness to that group. Revillagigedo, too, favored Mociño's research. Malespina came a cropper, not in trying to outdo Cook, but in attempting to supplant Godoy in Maria Luisa's affections. Also see Arthur P. Whitaker, *The Huancavelica Mercury Mine* (Cambridge, Mass.: Harvard University Press, 1941).

13. Lima still controlled the economy of Chile, Ecuador, and some of upper Peru: see Ramírez Necochea, *Antecedentes*; and Barbier, *Reform*, pp. 159–63, for Ambrosio O'Higgin's report of 1789; cf. Ramos, *minería*, pp. 289–92, who, however, assumes that crown policy and consulado activities were in complete harmony. See, too, Federico Brito Figueroa, *La estructura social y demográfica de Venezuela colonial* (Caracas, 1961); Arellano, *Orígenes*, pp. 396–97; Portell Vilá, *Cuba*, 1:116–19; Shafer, *Economic Societies*, p. 181; Alan K. Manchester, *British Preeminence in Brazil, Its Rise and Decline* (1933; reprint ed., New York: Octagon, 1964), pp. 52 ff.; Diffie, *Latin American Civilization*, p. 346; Hamnett, *Politics*, passim; R. S. Smith, "Indigo Production and Trade in Colonial Guatemala," *HAHR* 39 (1959):181–211; Brading, *Miners*, pp. 116–17; Brading, *Haciendas*, pp. 193–94; Florescano and Castillo, *Controversia*; Ladd, *Mexican Nobility*; Harris, *Mexican Family*; David Brading, "Los españoles a México hacia 1792," *HM* 23 (1973):142; Chance, *Race*; John K. Chance and William B. Taylor, "Estate and Class in a Colonial City: Oaxaca in 1792," *CSSH* 19 (1977):454–87; Robert McCaa, Stuart Schwartz, and Arturo Grubessich, "Race and Class in Colonial America: A Critique," *CSSH* 21 (1979):413–33; and Chance and Taylor's rejoinder, Ibid., pp. 434–42; Woodward, "Economic and Social Origins"; Woodward, *Class Privilege*; Ann Twinam, "Enterprise and Elites in Eighteenth-Century Medellín," *HAHR* 59 (1979):391–417; and Sharp, *Slavery*, who says that in 1789 perhaps half of the gold of the Chocó left as contraband. In this period,

too, both the contraband and legitimate slave trades were brisk: cf. Acosta Saignes, *vida*; Philip Curtin, *The Atlantic Slave Trade* (Madison: University of Wisconsin Press, 1969); and D. R. Murray, "Statistics of the Slave Trade to Cuba, 1790–1867," *JLAS* 3 (1971):131–49, who criticizes Curtin for accepting custom house figures of 1790 with no allowance for contraband; also see above, Ch. 6, n. 18; and this chapter, below, n. 36.

14. Ravignani, "virreinato," pp. 197–201; J. Brown, *Socioeconomic History*; Socolow, *Merchants*; and Germán O. E. Tjarks, *El consulado de Buenos Aires y sus proyecciones en la historia del Río de la Plata*, 2 vols. (Buenos Aires: Universidad de Buenos Aires, 1962), 1:374–85.

15. Brading, *Miners*, p. 70.

16. Joaquín García Icazbalceta, *Opúsculos y biografías* (Mexico: Universidad Nacional, 1942), p. 177.

17. Juan Vicente de Güemes Pacheco de Padilla, Conde de Revillagigedo, *El comercio exterior y su influjo en la economía de la Nueva España (1793)* (Mexico: Banco Nacional de Comercio Exterior, 1960), pp. 36–37. Revillagigedo had Fabián de Fonseca and Carlos de Urrutia draw up their monumental *Historia General de Real Hacienda*, completed in 1791 and published in Mexico City in six volumes from 1845 to 1853. It was followed by Urrutia's "Noticia geográfica del Reino de Nueva España y estado de su población, agricultura, artes y comercio" of 1794, in Florescano and Gil, *Descripciones*, 1:68–127, and by the *Compendio de la historia de la real hacienda de Nueva España* of Joaquín Maniau y Torquemada, that same year (an edition by Alberto M. Carreño was printed by the Secretaría de Industria y Comercio in 1914). *Real hacienda* means royal treasury. Urrutia's works were consulted by Humboldt; data for them and for Revillagigedo's census of 1792 were collected at local levels.

Revillagigedo wrote that Mexicans should be allowed to fish and whale instead of leaving those enterprises to the English and Anglo-Americans, and he noted much confusion in Spanish administration in Mexico. While in 1791 he defended the intendancies—authorized for Mexico in 1786—by 1793 he had decided that their workings combined the defects of the old system with those of a new, imperfect one; that intendants' projects were vast, resources slight, and disenchantment setting in at local levels. That year he mentioned that many French in Mexico maintained contact with their homeland by way of Philadelphia, but only at the end of his administration did he express fear that "the madnesses of the French" might undermine Mexicans' loyalty. He was also concerned about the plight of the poor, warred on drunkenness and dirt, and complained to Flórez that it was difficult to find a bathtub in Mexico City. See Conde de Revillagigedo, *Informe sobre las Misiones* (1793) e *Instrucción Reservada al Marqúes de Branciforte* (1794) (Mexico: Jus. 1966); Ignacio J. Rubio Mañé, "Síntesis histórica de la vida del II Conde de Revillagigedo, virrey de Nueva España," *AEA* 6 (1949):451–96; Miranda, *ideas*, pp. 198–206; Nicolás Rangel, comp., *La vida colonial: Precursores ideológicos de la guerra de Independencia*, 1789–1794, 2 vols. (Mexico: PAGN, 1929, 1932), 1 (1929): 15; Luis Muro, "Revillagigedo y el comercio libre (1791–1792)," in *Extremos de México*, pp. 229–344; Brading, *Miners*, pp. 81–83; Hamnett, "Obstaculos"; María Díaz-Trechuelo, Concepción Pajarón Parody, and Adolfo Rubio Gil, "El segundo Conde de Revillagigedo," in Calderón Quijano, *Carlos IV*, 1;85–366; David Bushnell, "El marqués de Branciforte," *HM* 2 (1952): 391–93; and Archer, *Army*, pp. 28, 82–111.

18. Alzate, *Gaceta*, 1, reprinted in Tavera Alfaro, *nacionalismo*, pp. 55–58; and in English in Korn (Liss), "Problem," pp. 115–17. Earlier, in 1784, the printer Manuel Antonio Valdés had put out the *Gaceta de México*; León y Gama edited numbers 16 through 20 of it. See above, Ch. 4, n. 73; and Luis González y González, "El optimismo nacionalista como factor de la independencia de México," in Isabel Gutiérrez del Arroyo, et al., *Estudios de historiografía americana* (Mexico: Colegio de México, 1948), pp. 155–215.

19. *Gacetas*, 2:74–77; and see vols. 2 and 3, passim, and also Tavera Alfaro, *nacionalismo*, p. lxxxii. He referred to the work of Alexander Garden, the South Carolina botanist, on cochineal and tobacco.

20. See Korn (Liss), "Problem," p. 119; and Roberto Moreno, "Las Notas de Alzate a la Historia Antigua de Clavijero," *Estudios de Cultura Nahuatl* 10 (1972):359–92.

21. Richard Greenleaf, "North American Protestants and the Mexican Inquisition," *Journal of Church and State* 8 (1966):192; Cook, *Floodtide*, pp. 177, 192, 198–99. José de Gálvez had made San

Blas a port in 1766, to facilitate shipping to and from California (Bobb, *Viceregency*, p. 166). American shipwrights were there by 1787.

22. Pereira Salas, *Primeros contactos*, pp. 56–57; and Victor Andrés Belaunde, *Bolívar and the Political Thought of the Spanish American Revolution* (1938; reprint ed., New York: Octagon, 1967), p. 27. Known were two picture cards, one of Liberty breaking with one hand the chains of a man representing the people, while in the other holding scales of Justice; the other card depicted a king, at his feet a herd of sheep with human heads. He was holding with one hand a bloody crown and with the other giving a favorite a sack of pounds sterling.

23. *DNA* I:1:442–43; Whitaker, *Spanish American Frontier*, p. 163.

24. Pérez-Marchand, *Dos étapas*, pp. 24–25, 127–34. Raynal's interpretations altered in his successive editions—1770, 1774, 1780—and he later became, as Onís, in *United States*, p. 42, put it, a Bible to revolutionaries during the independence struggles. And for Raynal in Latin America see: Madariaga, *Fall*; Whitaker, ed., *Latin America and the Enlightenment*, passim; and François R. J. DePons, *A Voyage to the Eastern Part of Tierra Firme* . . . , 3 vols. (New York: I. Riley, 1806), 2:318 ff.; and above Ch. 4, n. 68.

25. Tisnes, *Movimientos*, pp. 116–22, and Antonio Cacua Prada, *Don Manuel del Socorro Rodríguez* (Bogotá: Banco de la República, 1966), pp. 79, 86. I am indebted to John Wilhite for the last citation. See Maxwell, "Generation," for the Minas Gerais group, an influential cultural elite and adherents of Raynal and the North American model; and above, Ch. 6.

26. *Papel periódico de la Ciudad de Santafé de Bogotá, 1791–1797*, 7 vols. (Bogotá: Banco de República, 1978) 5:1027—no. 93, May 22, 1795.

27. Vargas, "*Pensamientos políticos*" y "*Memoria sobre la población del Nuevo Reino de Granada*" (Bogota: Biblioteca Popular de Cultura Colombiana, 1944), pp. 104, 15, 98–99; cf. *Papel periódico* of March 9, 1792 (2:34) which, echoing Alzate, urged sowing wheat and underselling that brought from Europe and the United States. And see Roberto María Tisnes, *Un precursor: don Pedro Fermín de Vargas* (Bogota: Editorial Kelly, 1969); Tisnes, *Movimientos*, pp. 119, 126, 140, 145; Gómez Hoyos, *revolución*, I:275 ff.; Eric Beerman, "José de Ezpeleta," *Revista de Historia Militar* 21 (1977):97–118; Angel Grisanti, *El precursor Neograndino Vargas* (Bogota: Iqueima, 1951); and Lewin, *movimientos*, p. 92.

28. One reason, at least, for Vargas's flight was his entanglement with a married woman, Barbara Forero, later a heroine of independence.

29. *Notas*, in Gómez Hoyos, *revolución*, 1:290–99.

30. *Diálogo*, cited in ibid., pp. 296–99. Tisnes, *precursor*, p. 64, mentions that Vargas wrote "Notas al escrito de Juan Bautista Picornell." If these are those, then Gómez Hoyos is probably wrong in dating them between 1789 and 1791. Internal evidence does indicate that they may have been written later. Their arguments, it is worth mention, closely parallel those of Paine as adapted by Viscardo in his *Carta* (see below).

31. Eduardo Posada and P. M. Ibañez, eds., *El precursor: Documentos sobre la vida pública y privada del General Antonio Nariño* (Bogotá: Imprenta Nacional, 1903); José Manuel Pérez Sarmiento and Luis Martínez Delgado, eds., *Causas célebres a los Precursores: "Derecho de Hombre" / Pesquisa de sublevación / pasquines sediciosas*, 2 vols. (Bogotá: 1939); Guillermo Hernández de Alba, comp., *Cartas íntimas de General Nariño*, 1:1788–1823 (Bogota: Sol y Luna, 1966); Thomas Blossom, *Nariño* (Tucson: University of Arizona Press, 1967); José María Vergara, *Vida y escritos del General Nariño* (Bogotá: Imprenta Nacional, 1946); and John F. Wilhite, "The Disciples of Mutis and the Enlightenment in New Granada," *TAm* 37 (1980):179–92.

32. Cited in Ellis, "Habits," p. 150.

33. Servando Teresa de Mier, *Memorias*, 2 vols. (Mexico: Porrúa, 1946), 1:26. As Picón Salas mentioned, in *Dependencia*, pp. 2–3, the United States was thought by a number of creoles to put into practice the ideas of Rousseau; Franklin was spoken of in nearly every European gazette, and in European courts projected an image of an envoy extraordinary of a free and virtuous Rousseauian world. See Louis Gottschalk, "The Place of the American Revolution in the Causal Pattern of the French Revolution," in E. Wright, ed., *Causes*, pp. 293–305; and Durand Echeverria, *Mirage in the West: A History of the French Image of American Society to 1815* (1957; reprint ed., New York: Octagon, 1966); Ricardo R. Caillet-Bois, "El Río de la Plata y la Revolución Francesca, 1789–1800,"

in Levene, *Historia*, 5:27–50; Levene, *mundo*, pp. 179 ff.; and Melchor Martínez, *Memoria histórica sobre la revolución de Chile, desde el cautiverio de Fernando VII, hasta 1814* (Valparaiso, 1848). Martínez is cited by Onís, *United States*, pp. 30–31; a conservative Chilean, Martínez looked back on the relative influences of the American and French revolutions during the Spanish American insurrections; and below, n. 48, 49.

34. *Primacías de la cultura de Quito* (1792), 2d ed. (Quito: Imprenta Municipal, 1958); Miguel Albórnoz, "Eugenio Espejo, medico de Quito del siglo XVIII y hombre de ciencia," *MMC*, 379–90.

35. *DNA* I:1:442–43; Barbier, "Culmination," p. 66; Coatsworth, "American Trade," p. 252; Whitaker, *Mississippi*, pp. 84–85; Whitaker, *Spanish American Frontier*, pp. 175–80, and see Francois Crouzet, "War, Blockade, and Economic Change in Europe, 1792–1815," *JEcH* 24 (1964):567 ff.

36. See Robert S. Smith, "A Research Report on Consulado History," *JIAS* 3 (1961): 41–52; R. S. Smith, "The Institution of the Consulado in New Spain," *HAHR* 24 (1944): 61–83; Ortiz de la Tabla Ducasse, *comercio*, Ch. 3 ff., R. S. Smith, "Origins of the Consulado of Guatemala," *HAHR* 26 (1946): 150–61; José Ramírez Flores, *El Real Consulado de Guadalajara* (Guadalajara, 1952); Arcila Farías, *Real Consulado*; Mercedes M. Alvárez F., *El Tribunal del Real Consulado de Caracas*, 2 vols. (Caracas: Ediciones del Cuatricentenario de Caracas, 1967), Arellano, *Orígenes*, 394 ff.; Humberto Tandrón, "The Consulado of Caracas and Venezuela's Overseas Trade, 1793–1811" (Ph.D. Diss., Columbia University, 1970); H. Tandrón, *El Real Consulado de Caracas y el comercio exterior de Venezuela* (Caracas: Universidad Central de Venezuela, 1976): Hamnett, *Politics*, pp. 95–104; G. Tjarks, *consulado*; and see above, n. 10. For Peru: cf. Burkholder, *Politics*; and John E. Woodham, "Hipólito Unanue and the Enlightenment in Peru" (Ph.D. Diss., Duke University, 1964), p. 228.

37. Shafer, *Economic Societies*, pp. 353–54; Dewitt S. Chandler, "Jacobo de Villaurrutia and the Audiencia of Guatemala, 1794–1804," *TAm* 32 (1976):402–12; Yves Aguila, "Don Jacobo de Villaurrutia, criollo ilustrado," in Gil Novales, *Homenaje*, pp. 39–47; R. S. Smith, "Indigo"; R. S. Smith, "Origins"; Carlos Meléndez, *La Ilustración en el Antiguo Reino de Guatemala* (San José: EDUCA, 1970); Woodward, *Class Privilege*; Woodward, "Origins"; Miles Wortman, "Government, Revenues, and Economic Trends in Central America, 1787–1819," *HAHR* 45 (1965): 544–66; and Luque Alcaide, *sociedad*. For Villaurrutia's later career on the Mexican audiencia: José Guerra (Servando Teresa de Mier) *Historia de la Revolución de Nueva España*, 2 vols. (1813; reprint ed., Mexico: Imprenta de la Cámara de Diputados, 1922).

38. See Francisco de Arango y Parreño, *De la factoria a la colonia* (1808) (Havana: Talleres de Cultural, 1936), which includes his "Discurso sobre la agricultura en la Habana y medios de fomentarla," of 1792; Julio Le Riverend Brusone, "Los ideas económicas en *El Papel Periódico de la Havana* (1790–1805)," in Homenaje a Silvio Zavala, *Estudios Históricos Americanos* (Mexico: Colegio de México, 1953), pp. 9–29; W. W. Pierson, Jr., "Francisco de Arango y Parreño," *HAHR* 16 (1936): 451–78; Herbert S. Klein, *The Middle Passage: Comparative Studies in the Atlantic Slave Trade* (Princeton: Princeton University Press, 1978), Ch. 9, and see William R. Lux, "French Colonization in Cuba, 1791–1809," *TAm* 29 (1972):57–61.

39. Ravignani in Levene, *Historia*, 4; Arcila Farias, *Economía*, pp. 374–80; Ladd, *Mexican Nobility*, p. 51.

40. Manuel Belgrano, *Estudios Económicos* (Buenos Aires: Editorial Raigal, 1954), pp. 13–47; Ravignani in Levene, *Historia*, 4:197–204; G. Tjarks, *Consulado*, 1:408; Socolow, *Merchants*, pp. 110, 161–62; and 111, for the conservatism of Spanish wholesalers; Levene, "Riqueza," pp. 266–71; 275–78; Clifton B. Kroeber, *The Growth of the Shipping Industry in the Río de La Plata Region* (Madison: University of Wisconsin Press, 1957).

41. Belgrano, *Estudios*, p. 49.

42. Ibid., pp. 86, 63, 70, 81 ff.; and cf. Jovellanos and Floridablanca above, Ch. 3.

43. Villalobos, *comercio y crisis*, p. 166; Sergio Villalobos, "El comercio extranjero a fines de la dominación española," *JIAS* 4 (1962):523; Donoso, "Bosquejo"; Amunátegui, *Salas*; and in *precursores* 3:343 ff., he notes that Salas correspondió con Belgrano.

44. J. Miranda, *ideas*, pp. 194–206; Liehr, *Ayuntamiento*; Taylor and Chance, "Estate"; Hamnett, *Politics*; Moore, *Cabildo*; J. Fisher, *Government*; Burkholder and Chandler, *Impotence;* Lynch, *Spanish Colonial Administration*, pp. 247–65; Díaz-Trechuelo, et al., "Revillagigedo," in

Calderón Quijano, *Carlos IV*, 1:142; Carlos Deustua Pimentel, *Las intendencias en el Perú* (1790–1796) (Seville: EEHA, 1965); and so on, and for intendants, above, Ch. 6, n. 46.

45. Francisco A. Encina, *Historia de Chile desde la prehistoria hasta 1891*, 20 vols. (Santiago: Editorial Nascimento, 1941–52), 6:39–44. Encina, mistakenly, says Caballero y Góngora was viceroy when he wrote this, on August 19, 1797, to Manuel Godoy. Cf. Torres Lanzas, *Independencia*, 1:106, 108–9, on creole indignation, aroused by European overreaction, to imprisoning Nariño and the others; and ibid., p. 156, wherein the viceroy at Bogotá said dangerous factions were forming between creoles and Europeans; and also see Caracciolo Parra-Pérez, *Historia de la primera república*, 2 vols. (Caracas: Tipografia Americana, 1939), 1.

46. Arellano, *Orígenes*, pp. 405–407. See DePons, *Voyages* 3: 129 ff.; Pedro M. Arcaya, *Insurrección de los negros de la serrano de Coro* (Caracas: Comife de la Emancipación: IPAGH, 1949); Torres Lanzas, *independencia*, 1:137, 146, 155; Acosta Saignes, *Vida*; Brito Figueroa, *insurrecciones*; Eleazar Córdoba-Bello, *La independencia de Haiti y su influencia en Hispanoamérica* (Caracas: IPAGH, 1967); Mörner, *Race Mixture*; and John Lynch, *Spanish American Revolutions, 1808–1826* (New York: Norton, 1973), pp. 20–21. Maxwell, "Generation," and below, Ch. 8, for trouble in Bahia in 1798. Richard B. Sheridan, in "The Crisis of Slave Subsistence in the British West Indies during and after the American Revolution," *WMQ* 33 (1976): 641, advances the interesting thesis that with 1776 "American foodstuffs and materials helped to fuel the expansion of sugar and slavery in Cuba and St. Domingue and possibly led to the great slave revolt in St. Domingue"—thus pointing to a chain reaction from 1776 to Coro.

47. Humboldt, *Political Essay*, 4:236–37.

48. See Bustamante, *suplemento*, p. 39; Miranda, *ideas*, pp. 184–85; Luis Navarro García and María del Pópulo Antolin Espino, "El virrey marqués de Branciforte," in Calderón Quijano, *Carlos IV*, 1:369–625; Bushnell, "Branciforte"; Pérez-Marchand, *Dos étapas*, pp. 128–32; Torres Lanzas, *independencia*, 1:81–83; Jacques Houdaille, "Frenchmen and Francophiles in New Spain from 1760 to 1810," *TAm* 13 (1956): 1–30; Spell, *Rousseau*; Brian Hamnett, "Mercantile Rivalry and Peninsular Division: The Consulados in New Spain and the Impact of the Bourbon Reforms, 1789–1824," *Ibero-Amerikanishes Archiv* 2 (1976): 283; John Rydjord, "The French Revolution in Mexico," *HAHR* 9 (1929): 60–98; Rydjord, *Foreign Interest*, 179 ff.; Rafael Heliodoro Valle, "Algunas Franceses en México," *Filosofía y Letras*, 2 (1943): 153–59; Greenleaf, "Mexican Inquisition"; and Miranda, *Humboldt*. Humboldt said this repression aroused Mexican discontent and public criticism which went unheeded by the government. He thought agitations would have been more frequent but for "the mutual hatred of the castes, and the dread which whites and the whole body of freemen entertain of the great number of blacks and Indians" (4:263–66). Revillagigedo was much more conciliatory. When on January 13, 1794, one thousand men and four hundred women employed in the tobacco factory had demonstrated in front of the palace against an increase in work, he sent an aide to negotiate, and they dispersed (García Icazbalceta, *Opusculos*, p. 179). Alvárez F., *comercio*, p. 117, mentions that from 1779 to 1783 Branciforte had held the exclusive right to import wheat into Venezuela.

49. As part of the reaction in 1793 San Miguel, the bishop of Michoacán, in a pastoral letter, warned of France, of the *filósofos libres* who were bent on destroying the Catholic religion, the priesthood, and the empire, and of "the pernicious maxims of Descartes." His new aide, Miguel Abad y Queipo, in protesting infringement of privileges of the clergy, spoke of "*el siglo pretendido de las luces,*" which mixed truth and error (Cárdozo, Galué, *Michoacán*, p. 96). Both these men were, and are, thought of as liberal and enlightened Spaniards. In Mexico City, on January 17, 1795, an anonymous broadside circulated saying the destinies of America should be given to Americans (Torres Lanzas, *Independencia*, 1:105). In 1796 in Guatemala, the oidor Jacobo de Villaurrutia was denounced to the Inquisition for owning sixteen volumes of Condillac and Montesquieu's *Persian Letters*, neither very revolutionary: see Jacques Houdaille, "Les Français et les Afrancesados in América Centrale, 1700–1810," *RHA* 44 (1957): 305–30. Also see Brading, *Miners*, pp. 85–86; Burkholder and Chandler, *Impotence*, pp. 88–89; Villalobos, *Tradición*, pp. 145–50; Woodward, "Origins," p. 554; Lynch, *Spanish Colonial Administration*; Ernest Liljegren, "Jacobinism in Spanish Louisiana," *Louisiana Historical Quarterly* 22 (1939): 47–97; and Rangel.

50. *DNA* I:1; p. 426; Pérez-Marchand, *Dos étapas*, pp. 128–32, 164; Lucia Fox, "Dos precursores de la Independencia Hispanoamericano y sus obras editadas en Filadelfia entre 1794 y 1799,"

Inter-American Review of Bibliography 19 (1969): 407–14; González Casanova, *misoneísmo*, p. 222; Elorza, *Ideología*, pp. 297–300; and Merle E. Simmons, *Santiago F. Puglia, an Early Philadelphia Propagandist for Spanish American Independence* (Chapel Hill: University of North Carolina Press, 1977).

51. "Causa formada al Dr. Fray Servando Teresa de Mier por el sermon que predicó en la Colegiata de Guadalupe el 12 de diciembre de 1794," Hernández y Dávalos, *Documentos* 3:5–17. Mier declared the Mexican Indians descended from workers on the Tower of Babel. He assimilated indigenous goddesses to Guadalupe and pronounced her especially precious to America, "now that the Philistines of France have attacked Israel." For Clavijero: Bustamante, *suplemento*; John D. Browning, "Cornelius de Pauw and Exiled Jesuits: the Development of Nationalism in Spanish America," *Eighteenth Century Studies* 11 (1978): 289–307; and see above, n. 20; and Ch. 4, notes 56–59. Similarly, in Lima the *Mercurio* proposed a study of Inca mining methods. In 1789 the Council of the Indies censored passages of Clavijero's history of Mexico, including one comparing the Spanish to the Turks and the Mexicans to the Greeks oppressed by the Mohammedans.

52. Jacques A. Barbier, "Venezuelan *Libranzas*, 1788–1807: From Economic Nostrum to Fiscal Imperative," *TAm* 37 (1981):457–78; Barbier, "Peninsular Finance"; and Tandrón, *real consulado*.

53. Alvárez F., *comercio*, pp. 70–72, 91, 103–04. Directly implicated were seventy nine conspirators: twenty five Europeans, forty nine creoles, thirty nine blacks, and thirty three mulattoes, according to DePons, *Voyage*, 1:45–54. See Hector García Chuecos, estudio preliminar, *Documentos relativos a la Revolución de Gual y España* (Caracas: Instituto Panamericana de Geografía e Historia, 1949); Casto Fulgencio López, *Juan Bautista Picornell y la Conspiración de Gual y España* (Cadiz and Caracas: Ediciones Nuevas, 1955); I. Zavala, "Picornell"; Herr, *Eighteenth-Century Revolution*, p. 317 ff.; Torres Lanzas, *Independencia*, 1:182–86, 202; Harris Warren, "The Early Revolutionary Career of Juan Mariano Picornell," *HAHR* 22 (1942): 57–81; Tisnes, *movimientos*, p. 246, who states that Picornell expected help from the English, who had just taken Trinidad; Pedro Grases, *La conspiración de Gual y España y el ideario de la independencia* (Caracas: IPAGH, 1949); who says a republic was planned on the four foundations of the rights of man, which were listed as equality, liberty, property, and security; Enrique de Gandia, *Conspiraciones*, 96 ff., who declared the conspirators not separatists but liberal Spanish republicans; and Parra Pérez, *Historia*, 1:50, who says the plotters spoke in the name of the "American people" for independence and a republic. The plot may have included advocates for both autonomy and independence. Parra-Pérez, 1:82, also mentions that Gual's father was Mateo Gual, commandant of La Guaira when Knowles attacked in 1743. And see Harold A. Bierck, *Pedro Gual* (Caracas 1947); García Samudio, *independencia*, p. 65; Humboldt, who wrote that Gual favored an independent Venezuela, to be called *Las siete provincias unidas de la América meridional* (*Political Essay*, 4:265); and above, n. 30.

54. *Archivo del General Miranda*, 15:404; and Onís, *United States*, pp. 43–44.

55. Parra-Pérez, *Historia*, 1:26.

56. Godoy was tricked onto a Spanish ship in Charleston in 1786 by an agent of Caballero y Góngora, taken to Cartagena, and jailed, and died in a Cádiz prison in 1788: see *DNA* V:2, passim; Robertson, *Life*, 1:201; Batllori, *Abate Viscardo*; Levene, *mundo*, pp. 120–21; Cárdenas Acosta, *movimiento*, pp. 17, 226–36; Tisnes, *movimientos*, pp. 45, 88–93; Lewin, *movimientos*, p. 95; and José Toribio Medina, *Un precursor chileno de la revolución de la independencia de América* (Santiago de Chile: Cervantes, 1911).

57. Antonio Nariño, "Ensayo de un nuevo plan de Administración en el Nuevo Reino de Granada" (November 16, 1797), in Vergara, *Vida;* and Gómez Hoyos, *revolución*, 1:207–42.

58. A royal order of August 21, 1978 described Caro as having a black disguise, and warned Spanish American coastal authorities to detain any foreign black: L. A. Eguiguren, "Colaboradores del procer Miranda," in *Miscelánea Lecuna*, pp. 88–143; Parra-Pérez, *Historia*, 1:33, 111; and see Smelser, "Washington."

59. Viscardos's *carta* is printed in Batllori, *Abate Viscardo*; as an appendix to Giménez Fernández, *doctrinas;* and in "Documentos históricos," *BAGN* 3 (1932): 167–73. See Robertson, *Life*, 1:173–76; Rydjord, *Foreign Interest*, pp. 149–89; Angel Grisanti, "La personalidad de Juan Pablo Viscardo y Guzmán..." (Arequipa: Colmena, 1948), offprint of the *Revista*, Universidad de Arequipa, no. 27. Viscardo, who was educated by the Jesuits in Cuzco, in 1780 wrote the British

consul in Rome applauding Túpac Amaru's revolt and said he hoped for Peruvian Independence and to be able to go home. Torres Lanzas, *Independencia*, 1:296, gives evidence of correspondence between Viscardo and Clavijero. Gerbi, *Dispute*, p. 196, says Miranda bought Clavijero's *Storia de Messico* in Rome in order to have it translated into English. It did appear in English in the early 1800s, in London and New York.

60. Robertson, *Life*, 1:192–98; Whitaker, *United States*, p. 224; Tisnes, *movimiento*, pp. 213, 267; Grases, *Gual;* Onís, *United States*, p. 22; Rydjord, *Foreign Interest*, pp. 319–38; Bernstein, *Origins*, p. 77. Bernado O'Higgins then went to Madrid and while there conferred with other creole dissidents. On December 18, 1798, the Spanish envoy Carlos Martínez de Irujo wrote to Francisco de Saavedra that Vargas had been living in Philadelphia for some time as Don Fermín Sarmiento; in 1799, Vargas left New York for Europe: Torres Lanzas, *Independencia*, 1:213, 239.

61. Robertson, *Life*, 1:166–67; Tisnes, p. 48; Rydjord, *Foreign Interest*, pp. 149, 156; Parra-Pérez, *Historia*, 1:42, 61–62; Villanueva, *Napoleón*, pp. 325–33, includes the alleged text of the *Acta* of 1797. The signers remind England that it lost its colonies through Spanish intervention and now can reciprocate, offer England commercial advantage and, to the United States, the right to join in the venture by providing five thousand infantry and two thousand cavalry to liberate Spanish America. Robertson thought Olavide was involved. Eguiguren, "colaboradores," gives the explanation cited. Defourneaux, *Olavide*, pp. 99, 105, thinks Olavide was not involved. A royal order of 1799 to authorities in America said Miranda, Pozo, Salas, and Olavide were among those participating in a London plan to make Spanish America independent (Torres Lanzas, *Independencia*, 1:255).

62. Mier, *Memorias*, 1:25–26, 46; and see Eguiguren, "colaboradores"; Roberto Botero Sal-darriaga, *Francisco Antonio Zea*, 2 vols. (Bogotá, 1969)—Zea later became president of the Congress of Angostura; Gómez Hoyos, *revolución*, 1; and above, n. 31.

63. Onís, *United States*, pp. 33–35; Griffin, *United States*, pp. 252–53; Charles H. Bowman, Jr., "Manuel Torres: a Spanish American Patriot in Philadelphia, 1796–1822," *Pennsylvania Magazine of History and Biography* 94 (1970): 26–53. In 1799 Miranda mentioned Torres (known too as D. Manuel Trujillo) as among the distinguished people in Philadelphia who because of involvement in disturbances had fled South America (*Archivo de Miranda*, 15:402).

64. Maxwell, "Generation," p. 134; and see his account of Brazilian attitudes and new Portuguese imperial policy. Da Costa, *Diario de Minha Viagem para Filadelfia* (Río de Janeiro: Academia Brasileira de Letras, 1955). Imprisoned as a dissident after his return to Brazil, he fled to London and there edited the liberal *Correio Braziliense* from 1808 to 1822. He was also a Mason who as a student at Coimbra in 1793–94 had been initiated into a Portuguese lodge, and he associated with lodges in the United States and Britain. The question of Masonic influences in Latin America from the 1760s on needs further investigation. There is good evidence that the eighteenth-century tendency to clubbiness was manifest not only in literary, economic, and philosophical societies there: Masonic-type lodges we know were instruments of revolutionaries. See Carlos Rizzini, *Hypólito da Costa e o Correio Braziliense* (Sao Paulo, 1957); H. H. Keith, "Independent"; Jane Herrick, "The Reluctant Revolutionist: A Study of the Political Ideas of Hipólito da Costa (1774–1823)," *TAm* 7 (1950): 171–81; Halperín-Donghi, *Politics*, pp. 122–23; Patricio José Maguire, "Algunos antecedentes para evaluar la influencia de la masonería en la liberación de hispanoamérica," *Boletín de la Universidad Nacional* (Instituto de Historia Argentina "Doctor Emilio Ravignani," Buenos Aires) 10 (1968): 47–68; 11 (1969): 127–81: Da Costa is discussed in pt. II. Cf. Richard Greenleaf, "The Mexican Inquisition and the Masonic Movement, 1751–1820," *NMHR* 42 (1969): 93–117; and Rangel, *Vida*, vol. 2.

65. R. Humphreys, "Economic Aspects of the Fall of the Spanish American Empire," *RHA* no. 30 (1950): 450–56.

66. John Emerich Edward Dahlberg-Acton, First Baron, *Essays on Freedom and Power* (New York: Meridian, 1955), p. 142; Clifford Geertz, "Ideology as a Cultural System," in David E. Apter, ed., *Ideology and Discontent* (London: Free Press of Glencoe, 1964), p. 63.

67. Juan Francisco Ramírez, a Franciscan in Mexico, was accused of saying man is free, we have left the century of ignorance, and that the French were the political redeemers of the human race and Voltaire *"el santo padre del siglo."* The French also had done well in suppressing absolute monarchy, he went on, for it was not just that so great a multitude of men should be ruled by a single head, for all kings were tyrants, including those of Spain. Cited in Elías Martínez, "Los franciscanos y la

independencia de México,'' *Abside* 24 (1960): 139. Also see Pérez-Marchand, *Dos étapas*; and J. Miranda, *ideas*, pp. 150–53, 170–71.

CHAPTER 8

1. Barbier, ''Peninsular Finance'', passim. By 1800, he adds, Spain and Britain were negotiating to enable both to trade with Spain's America; and see Herr, *Eighteenth-Century Revolution*, p. 361; W. E. Lingelbach, ''Commercial History in the Napoleonic Era,'' *AHR* 19 (1914):257–81; and Hamilton, ''War''.

2. Victoriano de Villava, ''Apuntamientos para la reforma del Reino España e Indias'', in Ricardo Levene, *Vida y escritos de Victorián de Villava* (Buenos Aires: Instituto de Investigaciones Históricos de la Facultad de Filosofía y Letras, 1946), pp. 103–12; Lynch, *Spanish Colonial Administration*, p. 247; José Luis Romero, *A History of Argentine Political Thought*, trans. Thomas F. McGann (Stanford: Stanford University Press, 1963) p. 54; Robertson, *Miranda*, pp. 311–13; María del Carmen Galbis Díez, ''El virrey Miguel José de Azanza'', in Calderón Quijano, *Carlos IV*, 2:54; Christon Archer, ''The Keys to the Kingdom: The Defense of Veracruz, 1780–1810'', *TAm* 27 (1971):426–49, cites Flon in 1801: ''The walls of Vera Cruz would not be sufficient to stop the assaults of a group of boys against an orchard'' (p. 439). Barbier, ''Peninsular Finance'', n. 19, makes the point that *comercio neutral* of 1797 ''did not legally open the Spanish colonial trade to foreign merchants nor (save in Venezuela and Mexico)'' allow in more foreign goods. But ''given its mechanics . . . it became far harder to keep out the foreigner and his products''—which the Spanish ministry foresaw and accepted. (It could, of course, tax all trade occurring through proper channels.) The purposes of the 1797 regulation, he notes, were ''to provide vital services to the colonies, restrain establishment of colonial factories, discourage contact with foreign ports of the New World, and sustain some level of Spanish export to the Indies'' (p. 13).

3. Le Riverend Brusone, ''relaciones'', pp. 77-79; Ramos, *minería*, p. 299; Velázquez, *estado*, p. 215; Hamnett, *Politics*, p. 102; and see above, Ch. 5.

4. Alexander von Humboldt, *Personal Narratives of Travels to the Equinoctial Regions of the New Continent* . . . 1799–1804, 7 vols. (London, 1822–29), 7:221–48; Ortiz de la Tabla Ducasse, *Comercio*, Ch. 5; Le Riverend Brusone, ''relaciones'', p. 81; Bernstein, ''Inter-American Aspects,'' p. 57; and above, Ch. 7, n. 38.

5. Arcila Farías, *Economía colonial*, pp. 360–61; Robertson, *Miranda*, pp. 220–21; Torres Lanzas, *Independencia*, 1:235; Tandrón, ''Consulado'', pp. 99–117; Arellano, *Orígenes*, p. 394 ff., 412, 414–15, who says (pp. 414–15) Venezuelan exports from 1796 to 1800 dropped 47 percent relative to 1793–96. Also see above, Ch. 7.

6. Humboldt, *Political Essay*, IV:94, 109, 115 ff., 123, 125, 131; Bustamante, *suplemento*, pp. 224–26; Lerdo de Tejada, *comercio*, pp. 21 ff.; Quiros, in appendix to Lerdo de Tejada, pp. 204–14; *Instrucción reservada que dió el virrey don Miguel José de Azanza a su sucesor don Félix Berenguer de Marquina* (Mexico: Jus, 1960); Eduardo Arcila Farías, comp. and intro. to José Donato de Austria, ''Noticias y reflexiones acerca del comercio que en el año de 1800 ha hecho el puerto de Veracruz con los de la metrópoli y con las Américas españolas, para conocimiento de la balanza...'', *Revista de Historia* (Caracas) no. 21 (1964): 16–34; Alamán, *Historia*, 1:142–43; Abad y Queipo in Hernández y Davalos, *Documentos*, 2:863–64; Hamnett, ''Mercantile Rivalry,'' pp. 287–88; Hamnett, *Politics*, 99–102; Galbis Díez, ''Azanza,'' in Calderón Quijano, *Carlos IV*, 2:15, 27; R. S. Smith, ''Shipping''; Arcila Farías, *siglo*, pp. 111–13; and Ortiz de la Tabla Ducasse, *Comercio*, pp. 183–212, 298, 303, 320–28.

7. Asdrúbal Silva, ''United States,'' p. 28; G. Tjarks, *consulado*, 1:133–34, 378, 385; Ravignani in Levene, *Historia*, 4:127–28; Levene, ''Riqueza,'' p. 281; Ricardo Caillet-Bois, ''Las corrientes ideológicas europeas del siglo XVIII y el virreynato del Río de la Plata,'' in Levene, *Historia*, 5:21–36; Ricardo Caillet-Bois, ''Los ingleses y el Río de la Plata, 1780–1806,'' *Humanidades* 23 (1933):193–202; Bernstein, ''Origins,'' pp. 32, 41; Halperín-Donghi, *Politics*, pp. 11–34, 89; and Tulio Halperín-Donghi, *Historia Contemporánea de América* (Madrid: Alianza Editorial, 1969) pp. 22–36.

8. Villalobos, *comercio y crisis*, pp. 201–18; Villalobos, *Tradición*, pp. 85–89; Ramírez Necochea, *Antecedentes*, p. 171; José de Cos Iriberri, "Memoria de 1797," in Miguel Cruchaga, *Estudio sobre la organización económica y la hacienda pública de Chile*, 3 vols. (Madrid; Editorial Reus, 1929), 3:248; and cf. Nariño's plan of 1797 for New Granada, above, Ch. 7.

9. Alamán, *Historia*, 1:142–43; Arcila Farías, *Economía*, pp. 360–62, 368–69; Le Riverend Brusone, "relaciones," p. 82; DePons, *Voyage*, 3:317 ff.; Alvárez F., *comercio*. A representación to the crown by the growers in 1798 identified the monopolistic merchants, as did supporters of Gual and España, as "the oppressors of these lands" (Arellano, *orígenes*, p. 415; Tandrón, "Consulado," pp. 113 ff.). Eguiguren, "colaboradores," p. 118, says that José Caro reported to Miranda, on February 1, 1799, on English Americans frequenting La Guaira and being well received "due to the hatred of the French."

10. Bernstein, *Mind*, p. 23; Bernstein, *Origins*, p. 56; Chandler, "Villaurrutia," pp. 407–11; Shafer, *Economic Societies*, pp. 195–96, 210, 221; R. S. Smith, "Indigo," 208 ff. On their parts, Philadelphians were sufficiently impressed by Ramírez to name him, in 1801, a corresponding member of the American Philosophical Society, the first creole so honored. Shafer, p. 205, notes that José Flores, a founding member of the Guatemala economic society stopped in Philadelphia en route to Spain in 1796 and visited Joseph Priestley, British scientist and nonconformist minister. Irisarri maintained accounts with houses in London, Cádiz, Madrid, Philadelphia, Boston, Baltimore, Jamaica, Havana, Mexico City, Vera Cruz, Lima, Guayaquil, Valparaiso, Santiago de Chile, and Coquimbo, and with the governments of Mexico and Peru: Ricardo Donoso, *Antonio José de Irisarri, escritor y diplomatico*, 2d ed. (Santiago: Prensas de la Universidad de Chile, 1966): p. 13. This Irisarri is his son, who settled in Chile. And see Pereira Salas, *primeros contactos*, pp. 153–54; and Wortman, "Government," p. 259.

11. Lynch, *Spanish Colonial Administration*, pp. 287–88; Burkholder and Chandler, *Impotence*, pp. 114 ff.; and cf. Nariño, "Ensayo."

12. *Estudios*, pp. 98 ff.

13. Arcila Farías, *Economía*, p. 370. Members of this cabildo had in 1764 complained of Sebastian de Miranda, Francisco's father, being made a militia captain and showing himself in the streets in the same uniform as men of superior quality and proven whiteness (*limpieza de sangre*). Miranda was a Canarian. Agents from Saint Domingue worked to subvert slaves in Spanish American colonies through the decade: Torres Lanzas, *Independencia*, 1:278 ff., 299. See Aguirre Beltrán, *Población*; Mörner, *Race Mixture*, and above Ch. 7, and its n. 36.

14. Torres Lanzas, *Independencia*, 1:239, 248, 253–55, 307, 319, 328; Brito Figueroa, *insurrecciones*, pp. 78–79. Gual was on Trinidad, where the governor, Picton, promised him aid. Picton's letter of 1797 to South American inhabitants, written on order of the British government, circulated widely. It recommended liberation "from the oppressive and tyrannic system which supports, with so much vigour, the monopoly of commerce," offering British aid of troops, arms, and ammunition: William Walton, *An Exposé on the Dissentions of Spanish America* (London, 1814) app., Doc. A, p. 481, and see pp. 67, 69. Cf. Viscardo's *Carta* (above, Ch. 7). Yet, Britain was not backing Miranda's plan in 1798–99, for it feared the effect of French revolutionary spirit in Spanish America (Lynch, "British Policy," pp. 13–14) and was content with Spanish rule as long as France stayed out of Spain's America.

15. Maxwell, "Generation," pp. 137–39; Luis Henrique Dias Tavares, *Historia da Sedição Intentada na Bahia em 1798* (São Paulo: Pioneira/MEC, 1975); Donald Ramos, "Social Revolution Frustrated: The Conspiracy of the Tailors in Bahia, 1798," *Luso-Brazilian Review* 13 (1976): 74–91; and Klein, "Slave Trade," p. 915.

16. Alamán, *Historia*, 1:133; Ramón Mena, comp., "Conspiración de los machetes," *BAGN* 4 (1933): 74–86; Mariana Rodríguez del Valle, "El Virrey Félix Berenguer de Marquina," in Calderón Quijano, *Carlos IV*, 2:162–67; Christon Archer, "Pardos, Indians, and the Army of New Spain; Interrelationships and Conflicts, 1780–1810," *JLAS* 6 (1974): 246 ff., mentions an attempted rising of Indians in the Tepic area on the Pacific coast in 1801, perhaps with British collusion; and see Torres Lanzas, *Independencia*, 1:294.

17. Abad y Queipo, "Representación sobre la inmunidad personal del clero," December 11, 1799, in Hernández y Dávalos, *Documentos*, 2:823–52.

18. Navarro García and Antolin Espino, "Branciforte," in Calderón Quijano, *Carlos IV*, 1:528; and Ladd, *Mexican Nobility*, p. 56. Branciforte, with some reason, worried about an English blockade of Havana, seizure of Roatan, and attempts on the Mosquitos, Nicaragua, and Yucatán, and about a war with Russia: cf. Robert Stewart Londonderry, Viscount Castlereagh, *Memoirs and Correspondence*, 12 vols. (London: Shoberl, 1845–53), 7:344. In 1798 the British under Abercrombie did attempt to take Puerto Rico (DePons, *Voyage*, 1:xix).

19. Barbier, in an earlier draft of "Peninsular Finance," cited throughout; Barbier and Klein, "Revolutionary Wars," p. 331; Torres Lanzas, *Independencia*, passim; Real Díaz and Heredia Herrera, "Iturrigaray," in Calderón Quijano, *Carlos IV*, 2:230.

20. Barbier, "Peninsular Finance." The bestowing of such permits on favorites and their resale was a Spanish tradition, resorted to particularly under Ferdinand of Aragon and Charles V. Barbier (p. 31) comments that when *comercio neutral* was again legalized in 1801, "the decision was narrowly financial," reflecting altered priorities. "The crown prepared to throw open its colonial possessions to British manufactures in return for being allowed to draw nourishment from the Indies *cajas*". Cf.: *DNA* I:2:820–21; III:1:77 ff., 91–92, 348; Coatsworth, "United States." pp. 252, 255; Torres Lanzas, *Independencia*, 1:291, 298; Whitaker, *United States*, pp. 6–9; Pereira Salas, *primeros contactos*, pp. 26–27; and Villalobos, *comercio y crisis*, p. 117. Humboldt estimated that three-fifths of Spanish American exports were then in gold and silver. In 1801 the crown specifically permitted United States houses to take silver out of La Plata "with the probability of remitting in equivalent value" (Asdrúbal Silva, "United States").

21. Portell Vilá, *Cuba*, 1:132, 147, 149; Nichols, *Advance Agents*, p. 225; Nichols, "Trade," p. 303; Bernstein, *Origins*, p. 100; and Bernstein, *Mind*, pp. 22–25.

22. Shaler on July 11, 1802 was at San Blas, selling goods and taking on otter skins and spreading the republican word to disgruntled inhabitants. He then sailed to San Diego, the Sandwich Islands (Hawaii), Canton, back to the West Coast in 1804, to Guaymas, Sonora, and Honduras, California again, and, in another ship, to Havana and then to China once more (Nichols, *Advance Agents*, p. 51). See Villalobos, *comercio y crisis*, p. 149; and DePons, *Voyage*, 2:313–14, who said that in the six months of 1801 that ports were legally open, "The Americans from the United States proceeded in crowds to Laguaira."

23. Alamán, *Historia*, 1:143–44; R. S. Smith, "Shipping," p. 13; Real Díaz and Heredia Herrera, "Iturrigaray," in Calderón Quijano, *Carlos IV*, 2:275–81, 242, Humboldt, *Political Essay*, 4:52, said with peace 1802 was a boom commercial year for exports, then in 1803 exporting stopped with threat of war; and see above, Ch. 6.

24. Nichols, "Trade"; and see Asdrúbal Silva, "United States"; and Keen, *DeForest*.

25. Tandrón, "Consulado," pp. 108–9, 139–40, 153–54, 165, 176–77, 180–82, 194, n. 42; Harold A. Bierck, "Tobacco Marketing in Venezuela, 1798–1799: An Aspect of Spanish Mercantilistic Revisionism," *Business History Review* 39 (1965):489–502; Clauder, *American Commerce*, p. 132; Bruchey, *Oliver*, pp. 260–69.

26. J. R. Fisher, *Silver*, states that registered Peruvian silver production peaked in 1799, while Brading, *Haciendas*, p. 137, notes that Mexican silver output declined after 1797, and lays it to the lack of mercury attendant upon British blockade. See Hamnett, "Mercantile Rivalry," pp. 287–92, who observes that by 1803 United States cotton exports outstripped Mexican, but that Mexican obrajes were helped by lack of export of raw cotton; and see Enrique Florescano, *Precios del maíz y crisis agricolas en México* (Mexico: Colegio de México, 1969), p. 197 and Diffie, *Latin American Civilization*, pp. 343–46.

27. Ramos, *minería;* Hamerly, *Historia;* Villalobos, *comercio y crisis;* Conniff, "Guyaquil," pp. 406–7—in 1803 Guayaquil was put back under Peru. In 1801 the captain general in Caracas reported collecting forced loans, and that commerce was obstructed, agriculture in decline, and "all branches of the public felicity interrupted and affected adversely" (Arellano, *Orígenes*, p. 415).

28. See Burkholder and Chandler, *Impotence*, pp. 114 ff.; Jacobo de Villaurrutia, transferred to the Mexican audiencia, founded the *Diario de México* in 1804. In 1808 in Caracas, wealthy merchants began the *Gazeta de Caracas*, giving information on ship arrivals and departures, commodity prices, and city and consulado elections (Alvárez F., *consulado*, p. 108); and below for others.

29. Julio Febres Cordero G., "Estudios del joven Bolívar en Caracas," *Boletín de la Academia*

Nacional de la Historia Venezolana 27 (1944):260–62; Alvárez F., *Comercio*, 2d ed., pp. 94–97; R. S. Smith, "Institution," pp. 78–102; R. S. Smith, *Wealth*; Irving Leonard and R. S. Smith, "A Proposed Library for the Merchant Guild of Vera Cruz, 1801," *HAHR* 24 (1944):84–102. Irving Leonard, "A Frontier Library, 1799," *HAHR* 23 (1943):21–51, found that the library of Manuel Gayoso de Lemos, governor of Louisiana and West Florida, contained Jefferson's *Notes on Virginia*, Robertson's *History of America*, Ramsey's *American Revolution*, a Spanish version of Raynal, and a number of books too on English literature, science, mathematics, and history, as well as Juan and Ulloa's *Voyages*. Harry Bernstein, "A Provicial Library in Colonial Mexico, 1802," *HAHR* 26 (1946):162–83, catalogs the collection of José Pérez Becerra, administrator of the inland *aduana*, the customs house, at Guanajuato, who owned 394 volumes; they ranged widely and included Spanish economists, Mexican histories, Buffon, Feijoo, Raynal, and a book on the history and commerce of the English American colonies. Ladd, *Mexican Nobility*, p. 68, says that the powerful Fagoaga family had several hundred volumes, including Buffon, Adam Smith, the *Mercurio Peruano*, and that the Marqués de Rayas too had a large collection. Most of these libraries were an eclectic blend of traditional and more recent works. The Fagoaga, for instance, had books too in Greek and Latin. See Whitaker, ed. *Latin America and the Enlightenment*, passim; and Maxwell, "Generation," pp. 112–15, and his n. 25.

30. *Telégrafo Mercantil* (facsimile) (Buenos Aires: Junta de Historia y Numismática Americana, 1914–15); *Semanario de agricultura, industria y comercio* (facsimile) (Buenos Aires: Junta de Historia y Numismática Americana, 1928, 1937); Juan Hipólito Vieytes, *Antecedentes económicos de la revolución de Mayo. Escritos publicados en el* Semanario de agricultura, industria, y comercio (Buenos Aires: Raigal, 1956), preliminary study of Félix Weinberg; Ravignani in Levene, *Historia*. The Semanario between 1804 and 1806 ran four articles taken from Franklin, one on "luxury, laziness, and work," one on how to make people enjoy work, one on how to have pleasant dreams, and one on "Benjamin Franklin's Whistle." Levene, "Riqueza," pp. 272–78, mentions that by 1802 the increment of salt beef was so great that there were insufficient ships to export it. Ricardo Caillet-Bois, "El Real Consulado y una tentativa para contratar maestros curtidores en los Estados Unidos in 1801," *Boletín de Instituto de Historia Argentina Americana* (2d ser.) (Buenos Aires: Universidad Nacional), 1 (1956):265–68, noted the attempt failed because the fiscal refused on the grounds they were foreign and Protestant. Also see J. Brown, *Socioeconomic History*; Halperín-Donghi, *Politics*; and Pereira Salas, *primeros contactos*, pp. 196, 216, and passim.

31. Amunátegui, *precursores* 3:449, 445 ff.; *Escritos de don Manuel de Salas,* 3 vols. (Santiago, 1910–14); Amunátegui, *Salas*, 1:243 ff.; Villalobos, *tradición*, p. 48; Robert M. Will, "The Introduction of Classical Economics into Chile," *HAHR* 44 (1964):1–21. Picón-Salas, *Dependencia*, p. 5, remarked that Manuel de Salas learned English in order to read Franklin's books and maxims, and that he founded the Academia de San Luis in Santiago as a technical school on a model recommended by Franklin.

32. Villalobos, *comercio y crisis*, pp. 188–200, 216; Pereira Salas, *primeros contactos*, pp. 249, 293 ff., 310 ff.; and S. Collier, *Ideas*.

33. Humboldt, *Political Essay*, 1:223, 259. The first, Paris edition of this work was sold in 1808, and his *Tablas Geográfico-políticas del Reyno de Nueva España* were presented to Iturrigaray in Mexico in 1804 and printed in London in 1805. In May 1803 Bustamante had published extracts from them in the *Diario de México*. Many copies circulated among functionaries and men interested in the sciences in New Spain, and a modified version of the *Tablas* with added economic statistics was published by the tribunal of the Mexican consulado in 1805: Florescano and Gil, *Descripciones*, reprint the *tablas*, pp. 128–71, and the *noticias*, pp. 172–230. In 1811, William White, spokesman in London for the Spanish American revolutionaries, in his *El Español* dated independence sentiment in Mexico "from the time Baron de Humboldt was there." Guaranteed to raise creole conciencia de sí were such statements by Humboldt as, "No city of the continent, not even excepting those of the United States, can display such great and solid scientific establishments as the capital of Mexico" (*Political Essay*, 2:11); and see ibid., 2:258–62; J. Miranda, *Humboldt*; González y González, "Optimismo"; and Edmundo O'Gorman, *La idea de descubrimiento de América* (1951; reprint ed., UNAM, 1976). The Spanish government had not so much sent Humboldt as given him permission to visit its America. His tour can not be viewed, as it so often is, as ensuing from the benevolence of the court. Humboldt's

censure of Spanish policies is reflected in his views on American conditions. In the *Political Essay* (4:115) he reported that "at present 30 million of piastres worth of goods imported into Mexico are exchanged for six millions of piastres in produce of Mexican agriculture, and 14 millions of piastres in specie," and, "commerce tends to unite countries which a jealous policy has long separated"—in *Personal Narratives*, 3:123; and see Humboldt, *The Island of Cuba* (New York, 1856).

34. Humboldt, *Political Essay*, 1:91, 196.

35. Ibid., 1:154. He continued, "A wise administration may yet reestablish harmony, calm their passions and resentments, and yet preserve for a long time the union among the members of one and the same great family."

36. Ibid., 1:158.

37. Alamán, *Historia*, I:141–42; and see González y González, "optimismo."

38. José Antonio Rojas, "Cartas biográficas y filosóficas de un materialista," appended to Pablo González Casanova, *La literatura perseguida en la crisis de la colonia* (Mexico: Colegio de México, 1958), p. 166. Abad y Queipo referred to Humboldt's statistical tables: October 24, 1805: Hernández y Dávalos, *Documentos*, 2:864.

39. Gómez Hoyos, *revolución*, 2:266, 250 ff.

40. Ibid, 2:267–68.

41. DePons, *Voyage*, 1; Bernstein, "Inter-American Aspects," pp. 59–62; Luis Alayza Paz Soldán, *Unanue, geógrafo, médico y estadista* (Lima: Editorial Lumen, 1954); and Woodham, "Unanue," pp. 78, 228.

42. See S. Collier, *Ideas*, p. 371; J. Fred Rippy and E. R. Brann, "Alexander von Humboldt and Simón Bolívar," *AHR* 52 (1947):697–703; for Humboldt's influence in the United States, above, Ch. 5; and on England: Calvin P. Jones, "The Spanish American Works of Alexander von Humboldt as Viewed by Leading British Periodicals, 1800–1830," *TAm* 29 (1973):442–48; Jones claims reviews of Humboldt's essays "were among the foremost influences interesting Britons in speculating in Spanish America" (p. 448).

43. Alamán, *Historia*, 1:139–41, 348–49; Bustamante, *suplemento*, pp. 213, 242–43; Quiros, app. to Lerdo de Tejada, *Comercio*; Florescano and Gil, *Descripciones*, pp. 222–30; Barbier, "Trade," p. 2; Brian Hamnett, "The Appropriation of Mexican Church Wealth by the Spanish Bourbon Government: The 'Consolidación de Vales Reales,' 1805–1809," *JLAS* 1 (1969):85–113; Hamnett, "Dye," pp. 66–68; Asunción Lavrin, "The Execution of the Law of *Consolidación* in New Spain: Economic Aims and Results," *HAHR* 53 (1973):27–49; Roméo Flores Caballero, *Counter-revolution: The Role of the Spaniards in the Independence of Mexico, 1804–38* (Lincoln: University of Nebraska Press, 1974), Chs. 1–2; R. Flores Caballero, "La representaciones de 1805," *HM* 20 (1971):477–510; Ladd, *Mexican Nobility*, pp. 96–103; cf. Mark Burkholder, "Titled Nobles, Elites, and Independence: Some Comments," *LARR* 13 (1978):290–95, who notes that the act had lesser impact in Peru; cf. Timothy E. Anna, *The Fall of the Royal Government in Peru* (Lincoln: University of Nebraska Press, 1979), pp. 11–13. Also see Manual Abad y Queipo, "Representación a nombre de los labradores y comerciantes de Michoacán," Hernández y Dávalos 2:853–66; David Brading, "La situación económica de los hermanos don Manuel y don Miguel Hidalgo y Costilla, 1807," *BAGN* 11 (1970):5–82; D. Brading, "Noticias sobre la economía de Querétaro y de su corregidor don Miguel Domínguez," *BAGN* 11 (1970):273–78; Reinhard Lïehr, "Staatsverschuldung und Privatkredit: Die 'Consolidación de Vales Reales' in Hispanoamerika," *Ibero-Amerikanisches Archiv* 6 (1980):149–85; Geoffrey A. Cabat, "The Consolidación of 1804 in Guatemala," *TAm* 28 (1971):20–38; Villalobos, *Tradición*, pp. 97–99; and Inge Wolff, "Algunas consideraciones sobre causas económicas de la emancipación chilena," *AEA* 11 (1954):178, who says the captain-general there suspended the order on complaint of the cabildo of Santiago. The same sort of thing occurred elsewhere in South America. More study is needed of the edict and its repercussions within the context of Spain's international financial transactions. John J. TePaske, *La real hacienda de Nueva España: La Real Caja de México (1576–1816)* (Mexico: INAH, 1976), in his tables for 1805 includes large *préstamos patrióticos*, or war loans, also collected.

44. Abad y Queipo, *Representación* of 1805; L. E. Fisher, *Background*, pp. 194–98.

45. See Herr, *Eighteenth-Century Revolution*, for Spain; Farriss, *Crown*; J. L. Mecham, *Church*

and State in Latin America (Chapel Hill: University of North Carolina Press, 1934), p. 34; Abad y Queipo, Hernández y Dávalos, *Documentos*, 2:823–52; Mier, *Memorias*, 1:187:88; and Cardozo Galué, *Michoacán*; and cf. above, Ch. 7, n. 67.

46. Charles IV to the Bishop of Orense on October 6, 1806, in Eugenio López-Aydillo, *El Obispo de Orense en la regencia del año 1810* (Madrid, 1918), p. 189. The "princes" the king mentioned as suitable were his younger sons, his nephew, his brother-in-law, and Godoy. The project was mentioned in 1804, 1806, and 1807 by Godoy, reviving earlier plans put forth by Carvajal and Aranda: Demetrio Ramos, "Los proyectos de independencia para América preparados por el Rey Carlos IV," *RIn* 28: no. 111–12 (1968):85–123; Manuel Godoy, "Proyecto de... para a gobierno de las Américas (1808)," in Ernesto de la Torre Villar, *La constitución de Apatzingán y los creadores del Estado Mexicano* (Mexico: UNAM, 1964), pp. 107–11; and Godoys's *Memorias de Principe de la Paz, BAE*, 38:419.

47. Ibid. Spain's aid to the Anglo-American rebels, he said, opened Pandora's box.

48. *Antología*, pp. 99–106; Caillet-Bois, "Ingleses," pp. 187–88; Gandia, *conspiraciones*, pp. 146–61, 187 ff.

49. González Casanova, *literatura*, p. 172; and see Hamnett, "Mercantile Rivalry," p. 288.

50. Torres Lanzas, *Independencia*, 1:278–99; Barbier, "Trade," pp. 1, 14–15; Quiros, *Nota* of February 24, 1806 and that of January 24, 1807, in app. to Lerdo de Tejada, *Comercio*; Ladd, *Mexican Nobility*, p. 103; Enrique Lafuente Ferrari, *El virrey Iturrigaray y los orígenes de la Independencia de México* (Madrid: Instituto Gonzalo Fernández de Oviedo, 1941), p. 294; Ortiz de la Tabla Ducasse, *comercio*, pp. 322, 327–29; Jackson, "Mexican Silver"; above, Ch. 5; Real Díaz and Heredia Herrera, "Iturrigaray," in Calderón Quijano, *Carlos IV*, 2:230, 236, 243; and on p. 244 is mentioned a secret royal order of December 12, 1806 to Iturrigaray: The London houses, Gordon, Murphy, and Reid, and Irving and Co. were to carry mercury, cigarette paper, and such for the government and, to Cádiz, colonial products to the royal account and with these could go up to ten million pesos in private goods, all under neutral flags. Iturrigaray was to turn over three million pesos to the agents of those houses.

51. *DNA* I:1:38, 168 ff.; Coatsworth, "United States," pp. 253–57; Nichols, *Advance Agents*, p. 225; R. S. Smith, "Shipping," pp. 13–14; Villalobos, *comercio y crisis*, p. 118; Whitaker, *United States*, pp. 18–19, 23, 142; and see above, Ch. 5.

52. Bernstein, *Origins*, p. 82; Alvárez F., *consulado*, p. 113; and cf. Diffie, *Latin American Civilization*, p. 431.

53. Villalobos, "comercio," pp. 530–32; Pereira Salas, *buques*; his *primeros contactos*, pp. 177, 195, 216, 256, 293–94, who mentions one 1807 voyage—a ship from New York flying a French flag, manned by a Portuguese crew, and carrying mostly British textiles; and see Villalobos, *comercio y crisis*, p. 124; and, for Stoughton: *DNA* as cited above, n. 20.

54. Real Díaz and Heredia Herrera, "Iturrigaray," in Calderón Quijano, *Carlos IV*, 2:236–43; Caillet-Bois, "Ingleses," pp. 186–87.

55. Gómez Hoyos, *revolución*, 2:268–72; R. R. Palmer and Joel Colton, *A History of the Modern World*, 3rd ed., (New York: Knopf, 1965), p. 400; R. Davis, *Industrial Revolution*, pp. 38, 90, 92, 96, 104, 114–15. In 1810 the consulado of Vera Cruz complained foreign imports had soared over two and a half million pesos in value between 1806 and 1809, benefiting only the Havana company: Alamán, *Historia*, 1:42; L. E. Fisher, *Background*, p. 113.

56. "Miranda and the British Admiralty, 1804–1806," *AHR* 6 (1901):508–30; John Street, *Gran Bretaña y la independencia del Río de la Plata* (Buenos Aires: Paidos, 1967), pp. 19–25, 50–51; Belgrano, *Estudios*; and Manuel Belgrano, *Introducción a la Despedida de Washington a Pueblo de los Estados Unidos* (Buenos Aires: Tip. Dalmazia, 1906).

57. Street, *Gran Bretaña*, pp. 31–48; R. A. Humphreys, *Liberation in South America, 1806–1827: the Career of James Paroissien* (London: University of London/Athlone Press, 1952), pp. 4–16.

58. Ibid., p. 4; cf. Lynch, "British Policy"; and see Whitaker, *United States*, pp. 29–32; C. F. Mullett, "British Schemes and Spanish America in 1806," *HAHR* 27 (1947):269–78; Caillet-Bois, "Ingleses," pp. 183–87. W. W. Kaufmann, *British Policy*, p. 41, said British agents were in Mexico by 1806, stirring up revolt among creoles and Indians. Lynch, p. 28, noted that by 1807 Peruvian ports were "infested with British vessels."

59. Donoso, "antecedentes," pp. 215–16; Mariano Moreno, *Escritos políticos y económicos*, Norberto Piñero, comp. (Buenos Aires, 1915); Eugene M. Wait, "Mariano Moreno: Promoter of Enlightenment," *HAHR* 45 (1965):359–83—who thinks Moreno, while studying law at Chuquisaca, was influenced by Villava; Ricardo Levene, "Significacción histórica de la obra económica de Manuel Belgrano y Mariano Moreno," in *Historia*, 5:489–520; and Asdrúbal Silva, "United States," p. 30.

60. Ibid.

61. Facsimile ed. (Montevideo: Instituto Historia y Geografía de Uruguay, 1942). The *Southern Star* discussed the economic and commercial situtation of the Spanish colonies, the weakness of the Spanish monarchy, creole rights, and freedom of the press.

62. Ricardo Levene, ed., *Los sucesos de Mayo contados por sus actores* (Buenos Aires, 1928), pp. 60–71.

63. Manuel Belgrano, *Autobiografía*, 2d ed. (Buenos Aires: Emecé, 1945) p. 23. Belgrano recalled that he talked to the English Brigadier General, one Crawford, who told him of possibilities for Argentine independence under English protection. Belgrano concluded that England wanted trade and would leave the winning of independence to Spanish Americans. The British also established two masonic lodges in Buenos Aires, where an earlier one existed, an offshoot of a grand lodge in Philadelphia (Maguire, "antecedentes" [1969], p. 138) in what was probably the same desire to compete with United States influence as occurred in Mexico in the 1820s (see below, Ch. 9); and see J. Canter in Levene, *Historia*, 5:245–422.

64. J. Brown, dissertation, pp. 53–55; Chandler, *Inter-American Acquaintances*; Dorothy B. Goebel, "British Trade to the Spanish Colonies, 1798–1823," *AHR* 43 (1938):288–320; Humphreys, *Liberation*; and above, n. 53.

65. *Autobiografía*, cited in Halperín-Donghi, *Politics*, p. 125.

66. Lafuente Ferrari, *Iturrigaray,* pp. 428–33; Real Díaz and Heredia Herrera, "Iturrigaray," in Calderón Quijano, *Carlos IV*, 2:205, 230, 248, 269, 275 ff.; Hamnett, "Mercantile Rivalry," p. 292. Iturrigaray wrote to Pedro de Cevallos at court, on March 12, 1807, that he had heard from Wilkinson, who claimed credit for protecting Mexico from Burr. Wilkinson said Burr had planned to attack Vera Cruz and might have reached Mexico City. Wilkinson wanted money. Iturrigaray claimed he was not alarmed for he had long been prepared: Walter F. McCaleb, *The Aaron Burr Conspiracy* (New York, 1903), pp. 168–69.

67. C. Harris, *Mexican Family*, p. 312, and passim.

68. *Gaceta* of January 13, 1808, cited in Ladd, *Mexican Nobility*, p. 95; see Alamán, *Historia*, 1:146–47; Bustamante, pp. 238–40. Comment on creole degeneracy carried on the American defense against European slurs: see Gerbi, *Dispute*; Jefferson's *Notes on Virginia*; and González y González, "Optimismo."

69. Alamán, *Historia*, 1:146–47; Bustamante, *suplemento*, pp. 238–40; and Velázquez, *estado*, agree on this manifestation of praetorianism among creoles. Archer, *Army*, disagrees, commenting that cantonments from 1797 to 1810 soured some creoles on military service and strained officers' resources. Probably so, but Archer posits too lineal a thesis, not allowing for ebb and flow in the popularity of belonging to the militia, nor for varying attitudes, and perhaps not for generational differences. Thus, Campbell, *Military*, pp. 217–25, writes in 1803 that the Peruvian viceroy Avilés found morale low in the militia (Campbell cites his memoirs and Humboldt corroborated them), but with the energetic José Fernando de Abascal y Sousa in 1806 spirits rose and an American army was recognized as such, even though Abascal had a low general opinion of creoles. See Vicente Rodríguez Casado and José Antonio Calderón Quijano, eds., *Memoria de gobierno del virrey Abascal*, 2 vols. (Seville; EEHA, 1944). Creoles in Buenos Aires before 1806 disdained military careers, according to Tulio Halperín-Donghi, "Revolutionary Militarization in Buenos Aires, 1806–1815," *Past and Present* 40 (1968):85; and Kuethe, *Military Reform*, found no elitist military tradition in New Granada.

70. Mier, *Memorias*, 2:27.

71. Ibid.; and, for his later views, below, Ch. 9.

72. González Casanova, *literatura*, pp. 166–89; Nicolás Rangel, "José Antonio Rojas, victima celebre de la Inquisición," *BAGN* 2 (1931); Alamán, *Historia*, 1; Bustamante, *suplemento*, p. 238; and Whitaker, *United States*, p. 145, n. 8, who mentions that Dr. Benjamin Rush wrote, on February 6, 1810, to a member of the House, Walter Jones, introducing "José Roxas" (whom he had met through

Dr. Alexander Watkins of New Orleans), as of excellent character, great literary and scientific attainments, a friend of liberty and an enemy of superstition in religion. Rush said he had known Rojas for several months and suggested that President Madison might learn "something useful" from his knowledge of New Spain. Whitaker commented, "Thus again, as in Samuel Latham Mitchell's case, was science the handmaiden of international politics."

73. Jaime Eyzaguirre, "Las Gacetas de Procopio," *Revista Chilena* no. 121, 122, (1930):499–501; Pereira Salas, *primeros contactos*; Eugenio Pereira Salas, *La influencia norteamericana en las primeras constituciones de Chile* (Santiago, 1945); and above, Ch. 5, n. 41.

74. Halperín-Donghi, *Politics*, p. 119.

75. In New York Miranda's friend, Col. William Smith, surveyor of that port, and Samuel D. Ogden, a merchant, helped ready the ship and find recruits. His attempted landing on April 28 at Puerto Cabello was foiled by Spanish troops, and sixty of his men, among them United States citizens, were captured. Miranda and most of his force escaped to Trinidad from where, on August 17, he exhorted Venezuelans to separate from Spain "and follow the example of the United States, whose 300,000 inhabitants have broken the yoke of powerful England," and he again sent out copies of Viscardo's *carta* (Garcia Samudio, *independencia*, pp. 24–25).

76. Salvador de Madariaga, *Bolivar* (New York: Schocken, 1969), p. 97.

CHAPTER 9

1. For the peninsula: Raymond Carr, *Spain, 1808–1939* (London: Oxford University Press, 1966), Ch. 3; William S. Robertson, "The Juntas of 1808 and the Spanish Colonies," *EnHR* 31 (1916):573–85; A. F. Zimmerman, "Spain and its Colonies, 1808–1820," *HAHR* 11 (1931):439–63; Gabriel Lovett, *Napoleon and the Birth of Modern Spain*, 2 vols. (New York: New York University Press, 1965). For the international context: Chaunu, *Historia*; J. H. Pirenne, "L'influence de la politique européenne sur l'accession de l'Amérique latine à l'independance (1808–1825)," in Academie Royale des Sciences d'Outremer, *Bulletin des Seances* 4 (1964):742–63; and below. For the internal situation: Torre Villar, *constitución*, 169 ff.; William S. Robertson, *The Rise of the Spanish American Republics* (New York: Free Press, 1965); Lynch, *Revolutions*; Halperín-Donghi, *Historia*; and Burkholder and Chandler, *Impotence*.

2. G. E. Watson, "The United States and the Peninsular War, 1808–1812," *Historical Journal* 19 (1976):859–76; Coatsworth, "United States," p. 256; cf. Whitaker, *United States*, p. 52; above, Ch. 5, n. 24; and see *DNA* III:1:302–03, 312; Chaunu, *Historia*, pp. 121–22; José Luis Sul Mendes, "Introductory Notes to Balance Sheets for Trade between Portugal and the United States, 1783–1831," in Keith, *Portugal*, pp. 61–63; and Christopher Lloyd, *The Navy and the Slave Trade* (London, 1949), pp. 45–62, who says that after the United States signed the Treaty of Ghent abolishing the slave trade in 1808, many American slavers sailed under the Spanish flag. Spain first prohibited that trade to its nationals in 1817, but then only north of the equator.

3. Bemis, *Policy*, p. 26. See Sul Mendes, "Notes"; Manchester, "Rise," 54 ff.; G. Tjarks, *consulado* 1:340; Chandler, *Inter-American Acquaintances*, p. 23; Maxwell, "Generation," p. 143. Silva Lisboa supported the court's treaty with Britain in 1810 granting commercial concessions, on the grounds that it gave Brazil experience in the credit system and would expand its foreign trade (Manchester, p. 69). From Río, Carlota, wife of John and sister of Spain's Ferdinand VII, employed Englishmen and Americans as agents, from 1808, in intrigues for personal power (Torres Lanzas, *Independencia*, 1:445, 447, 454, 557–59; Street, *Gran Bretaña*; and John Street, "Lord Strangford and the Río de la Plata, 1808–1815," *HAHR* 33 [1953]:477–510). And in London, Hipólito da Costa began publishing the *Correio Braziliense*, with approval of the English government and probably a subvention from it, although in 1808 he did warn Brazilians against a preferential trade treaty with Britain. The *Correio* urged adopting constitutional monarchy in the Portuguese empire and opposed Brazilian independence, but proposed revolution in Spain's America. From 1809, young creole radicals in Buenos Aires borrowed from its pages. Da Costa admired the United States and its political institutions, its commerce, and its religious toleration, but said they owed much to England, and in 1816 he was warning of United States territorial designs on Spanish America, and also of the pitfalls of

open trade: Keith, "Independent America"; and Manchester, "Rise," p. 93. Brazilian planters backed independence only when the Portuguese Cortes opposed free trade and differed on concepts of monarchy: see José Honório Rodrigues, *Independencia: Revolução e Contra-revolucão*, 5 vols. (Rio de Janeiro: Livraria Francisco Alves Editora, 1975), 5.

4. See above, Ch. 5 and its n. 22. Continuing Spanish domination, if not directed by France or England, was of no great moment. Whitaker, *United States*, p. 43, cites Wilkinson to Jefferson, advocating, a few days before the cabinet's statement, formation of a distinct American community.

5. Grampp, "Re-examination," p. 279, adds that in 1809 Jefferson also favored "a natural equilibrium" of agriculture, manufactures, and commerce, and desired exchanging surplus, and that all raw materials be manufactured in the United States. Jefferson sent Wilkinson to Cuba in 1809 to tell the captain-general that the United States would prevent Cuba or Florida being used by any European power except Spain: Whitaker, *United States*, p. 63, and pp. 93–94, criticizing scholars expressing simplistic views concerning United States policy toward Latin America drawn along clear-cut agricultural, commercial, and industrial lines; and see Portell Vilá, *Cuba*, 1:150–61.

6. Joseph Napoleon [Bonaparte], "Instructions...," in Manuel Palacio Fajardo, *Outline of the Revolution in Spanish America* (London, 1817), pp. 55–58; and as Document B appended to Walton, *Exposé*; Isidro Fabela, *Los precursores de la independencia mexicana* (Mexico, 1926; 1970), pp. 156–65, noting the agents were Spaniards and creoles and included three women; Belgrano in Levene, *Historia*, 5:96; Rydjord, *Foreign Influence*; Gandia, *Napoleon*; Garcia Samudio, *Independencia*, pp. 86–89; William S. Robertson, *France and Latin American Independence* (Baltimore: John Hopkins Press, 1939); Villanueva, *Napoleon*; Lovett, *Napoleon*; *DNA* III:1 and 2, passim. In 1808 Joseph Bonaparte was made king of Spain—José I—by his brother, and the French called an assembly of notables in Bayonne, of 150 members, including 6 from the colonies, who accepted a constitution granting the colonists rights equal to peninsular provinces, including representation and freedom in agriculture and industry, and recognizing America as distinct political entities. A proclamation which José I instructed French agents to circulate, promised to create in Spanish America independent, constitutional states on the United States model.

7. Alamán, *Historia*, 1:296–97; and *DNA* I:2:737–38; III:1:259 ff.; III:2:passim.

8. See Gómez Hoyos, *revolución*, 2:92–93; above, n. 1; and Torre Villar, *constitución*, 38 ff., for numerous links among the revolts, so that from 1808 they spurred one another on and can be seen as a single movement.

9. Hernández y Dávalos, *Documentos*, 2:34–38, and see pp. 22–27, 886; Basadre, "Historia," p. 651; Gómez Hoyos, *revolución*, 2:92; Pierre Vilar, "Nation et patrie dans le vocabulaire de la guerre d'independance espagnole," *Annales Historiques de la Révolution Francaise* 72 (1972); and for the junta held by Cortés in Vera Cruz: Liss, *Mexico*, pp. 24–26.

10. Iturrigaray's actions can be construed as carrying through Spanish plans for princes to govern America, with himself in the role of prince. See Alamán, *Historia*, 1; Genaro García, ed., *Documentos históricos mexicanos*, 7 vols. (Mexico: Museo Nacional, 1910–12), 2(1910):136–46, 302: and vol. 7; Ladd, *Mexican Nobility*, pp. 106–109; Luis Villoro, *El proceso ideológico de la revolución de Independencia* (Mexico: UNAM, 1967); Hugh M. Hamill, Jr., "Un Discurso formado con angustia: Francisco Primo Verdad el 9 de agosto de 1808," *HM* 28 (1979):439–74. Jacobo de Villaurrutia, then a member of the Mexican audiencia, advised calling a congress in order to grapple with the constitutional crisis: Hernández y Dávalos, *Documentos*, 1:534–44; Guerra [Mier], *Historia*, 1:85, 112. A United States merchant ship on July 17 had brought for Iturrigaray from Cuba manifestoes and proclamations published by the Junta Central, including a declaration of war against the French emperor: Guadalupe Nava Oteo, ed., *Cabildos y Ayuntamientos de la Nueva España en 1808* (Mexico: SepSetentas, 1973), pp. 177–78.

11. Anastasio Zerécero, *Memorias de las Revoluciones en México* (Mexico: Gobierno, 1869), 25n; "Documentos históricos," *BAGN* 3 (1932):161–73; Nava Oteo, *Cabildos*, pp. 101–102; Ladd, *Mexican Nobility*, p. 109; Genaro García, *Documentos*, 2:91–94, 136–46; and see Lafuente Ferrari, *Iturrigaray*.

12. Hernández y Dávalos, *Documentos*, 1:490–92; Nava Oteo, *Cabildos*, pp. 159–61; Miranda, *ideas*, pp. 323–28; Hamnett, *Politics*; and Liehr, *Ayuntamiento*.

13. Portell Vilá, *Cuba*, 1:150–51; Torre Villar, *constitución*, pp. 32, 69–71; Alamán, *Historia*,

1:279 ff.; Hernández y Dávalos, *Documentos*, 2:880 ff.; and see Genaro García, *Documentos*, 1:xviii, 60 ff., 103, 253 ff., 340, 356–58, 467–71; Archer, *Army*, pp. 293–95; John E. Bachman, "Los panfletos de la independencia," *HM* 20 (1971):522–38; Timothy Anna, *The Fall of the Royal Government in Mexico City* (Lincoln: University of Nebraska Press, 1978); Ladd's discussion, in *Mexican Nobility*, of the amount of independence sentiment; and Brian R. Hamnett, "Mexico's Royalist Coalition: the Response to Revolution, 1808–1821," *JLAS* 12 (1981):55–86, for a thoughtful explanation of social divisions, interests, and attitudes over this period for and against independence. See, too, Hamnett, *Revolución y contrarevolución en México y el Perú. Liberalismo, realeza, y separatismo (1800–1824)* (Mexico: FCE, 1978); and Hamnett, "New Viewpoints on the Mexican Independence Period, 1810–1821," paper read at the 96th meeting of the American Historical Association, Los Angeles, 1981. In Lima, relative tranquility in 1808 and 1809 can in part be attributed to a recognition of growing provincial challenges to its authority and an understanding that that authority depended on the Spanish connection. For provincial unrest: John Fisher, "Royalism, Regionalism, and Rebellion in Colonial Peru, 1808–1815," *HAHR* 59 (1979):232–57. It mattered too that the viceroy in Lima, Fernando de Abascal y Sousa, was more adroit than Iturrigaray, and parried criticism through a sagacious show of representing a constitutional monarchy. Still, in 1808 the radical aristocrat, José de la Riva Agüero, then a royal functionary and later first president of Peru, presented to England a plan for Peruvian separation; in 1809 he was involved with some other creoles and peninsulars in a Lima conspiracy headed by a creole noble, and secret lodges formed in opposition to the government: Daniel Valcarcel, "Perú Borbónico y emancipación," *RHA* no. 50 (1960):315–78; Rubén Vargas Ugarte, S. J., *Historia del Perú Emancipación* (1809–1825) (Buenos Aires: López, 1958); Abascal, *Memoria*; Denegri Luna, *Antología*; Anna, *Peru*, pp. 40–46. In Caracas in 1809 old revolutionaries thought numerous Mexicans of circumstance and wealth, both creole and European-born, were, in league with the United States, planning independence, and that in Havana prominent whites only awaited the success of that attempt: cf. Ladd, *Mexican Nobility*, and above, concerning Mexican separatists. Grases, *Libros*, cites Manuel Cortés Conde, the principal collaborator of Picornell in Madrid in 1795 and then involved too with Gual and España, writing to Miranda in 1809 to say Wilkinson had troops ready on the Mississippi, and, in a letter of December 30, 1809, Cortés Conde praised the Mexican Marqués de Apartado, his brother, and "a nephew named Villaurrutia" as "true creoles." Also see Alvárez F., *comercio*, 2d ed., pp. 94–100; Parra Pérez, *Historia*, 1:184 ff.; Robertson, *Life*; and *Conjuración de 1808 en Caracas para la formación de una junta suprema gubernativa* (Caracas: IPAGH, 1949).

14. Halperín-Donghi, *Politics*; Street, *Gran Bretaña*.

15. Its authors declared they were "raising the voice of the patria to promote its felicity," to gain export of local products, and to repair the treasury, and for these ends a free commerce was necessary with the English. An abundance of imports would mean low prices to consumers; "commerce will seek equilibrium of circulation." We can only be happy through agriculture, they went on, and Spanish ships can neither take out our products—and they included silver as simply another product—or supply our needs: Representación of September 30, 1809 in Moreno, *Escritos*, pp. 107–73; and in Henry G. Ward, *Mexico in 1827*, 2 vols. (London, 1828), 2:479–83. G. Tjarks, *consulado*; and Germán Tjarks and Alicia Vidaurreta de Tjarks, *El comercio inglés y el contrabando* (Buenos Aires, 1962), p. 44, think Belgrano the author. Lynch, *Spanish American Revolutions*, assumes Moreno wrote it, as does Halperín-Donghi, *Historia*, p. 117. In answer to the Spanish monopolists' charge that the interior provinces would suffer from the entry of competitive British goods, the representación responded, too optimistically, they would instead lower prices and abet the export of surpluses, that English cloths would never undersell ponchos: cf. Halperín-Donghi, *Politics*, pp. 81–91, who says that they did, but not as immediately as often supposed. Tjarks and Tjarks note that the representación was first printed in Río, in 1810 in a Portuguese translation by Silva Lisboa, and afterwards in London in the *Correio Braziliense*, in 1810 (p. 43). Keen, *DeForest*, p. 73, indicates that DeForest was involved in the Río printing. Cf. Street, "Lord Strangford"; and Humphreys, *Liberation*, p. 235.

16. Cited in Chandler, *Inter-American Acquaintances*, p. 54. Viscardo's *Carta* was found circulating, and was publicly burned, in Mexico that year.

17. See Halperín-Donghi, *Historia*; Lynch, *Spanish American Revolutions*; and Roberto Etchepareborda, "¿Qué fue el carlotismo?" (Buenos Aires: Plus Ultra, 1971).

18. Camilo Torres, "Memorial de Agravios," in Gómez Hoyos, *revolucion*, 2:19 ff.; and in Manuel José Forero, *Camilo Torres* (Bogotá: Iris, 1960), pp. 29–31; and see Ocampo, *proceso*, pp. 97, 103, 110–11, 324–25.

19. Ibid, pp. 548–62, prints Herrera's "Reflexiones de un americano imparcial sobre la legislación de las colonias españolas"; and see Gómez Hoyos, *revolución*, 2:90–121.

20. Laura Bornholdt, *Baltimore and Early Pan-Americanism* (Northampton: Smith College Studies in History 34, 1949), found the Potosí placard cited in the Baltimore *American* of April 23, 1810, and that other Spanish American declarations urging emulation of the United States were printed in various United States newspapers. See also Bruce B. Solnick, "American Opinion Concerning the Spanish American Wars of Independence, 1808–1821" (Ph.D. Diss., New York University, 1960).

21. Cited in Robert L. Gilmore, "The Imperial Crisis, Rebellion, and the Viceroy: Nueva Granada in 1809," *HAHR* 40 (1960):8; and see Michael T. Hamerly, "Selva Alegre, President of the *Quiteña* Junta of 1809: Traitor or Patriot?" *HAHR* 48 (1968):642–53.

22. North Americans, he went on, did not separate from their metropolis because of the growth of agriculture, industry, commerce, and skills, but for lack of equality and justice—because of deprivation of rights and prerogatives belonging to citizens. His thrust was that the same thing would not happen where Spanish vassals of both hemispheres were governed by the same laws, united by a single religion, and tied with equality and justice to the crown. Cited in Villalobos, *comercio y crisis*, pp. 358–64; and see Villalobos, *Tradición*, ch. 4; Meza Villalobos, *conciencia*, pp. 264–68; and Collier, *Ideas*, pp. 24–27, 56.

23. Cited in Meza Villalobos, *conciencia*, pp. 262–63.

24. The Cortes of Cádiz first met September 24, 1810; it was composed of liberal Spaniards and included sixty three Americans. It drew up the Constitution of 1812, modeled largely on the French of 1791, yet, as Torre Villar, *constitución*, pp. 81–82, and others have noted, while the form and formulas of constitutions in the hispanic world were always modern, they tended principally to find legitimacy in renovated national traditions, so that tradition and revolution were always amalgamated. The Spanish Junta in 1809 moved to expel English and Americans from its America, for "some of them foment revolutionary ideas which have begun to germinate" (Pereira Salas, *primeros contactos,* p. 312). By 1810 Jovellanos, grand old man of the Cortes, was warning another elder statesman, Francisco de Saavedra, of British and American ambitions; even though he was well disposed toward Britain, "that country of liberty," he wanted closer relations with the United States, since it was, he said, the natural enemy of England, but it was also ambitious to join Mexico to its empire, and held out temptations to Mexicans, Floridians, and habañeros to make common cause: Jovellanos to Francisco de Saavedra, February 3, 1810, in *BAE* (Madrid, 1956), 86:492–94; Polt, "English Influence," p. 15, also pp. 7–8, 13; Ocampo, *proceso*, p. 98; Demetrio Ramos, "Las Cortes de Cádiz y América," *Revista de Estudios Políticos* (Madrid) no. 126 (1962):433–639; and Payne, *History*, 2:425, who remarks that the Cortes romanticized "the Spanish tradition of liberty." The word *liberal* has been said to have originated in Spain in this period: see Juan Marichal, "From Pistoia to Cádiz: a Generation's Itinerary, 1786–1812," in Aldridge, *Ibero-American Enlightenment*, pp. 107–8, who found that liberal originated as a political term among constitutionalists of 1812, but had long meant a generous man or ideal gentleman in Spain, and in the 1790s had been used for a middle-of-the road republican. Also see Brian R. Hamnett, "Constitutional Theory and Political Reality: Liberalism, Traditionalism, and the Spanish Cortes, 1810–1814," *Journal of Modern History* (demand article D1071 1977). For some American reactions and discussion of exclusion of American blacks from representation: James F. King, "The Colored Castes and American Representation in the Cortes of Cádiz," *HAHR* 33 (1953):33–64; and Ocampo, *proceso*, p. 228, who cites Nariño in 1811 saying Spain's struggle against France disseminated ideas of liberty and independence, but that Spain, fighting its own revolution for independence, was at the same time repressing Americans espousing those ideas; and see above, n. 1; Onís's reports (n. 7); Alamán, *Historia*, 3; Anna, *Peru*, pp. 43 ff; and J. Fisher, "Royalism," pp. 242–43, 248.

25. Interim deputies and then duly elected ones presented similar petitions to the Cortes. They requested, in order of importance, liberty for agriculture and to develop industry, freedom of commerce, suppression of monopolies, freedom to mine, equality with peninsulars in high appointments, and the return of the Jesuits, followed by other specifics. King, "Colored Castes," p. 61,

remarks that the deputies' "tenderness for the castes stemmed in large part from their desire for maximum representation." See American deputies to the Cortes, August 1, 1811, in Hernández y Dávalos, *Documentos*, 3:826 ff.; Walton, *Exposé*; Nettie Lee Benson, ed., *Mexico and the Spanish Cortes, 1810–1822* (Austin: University of Texas Press, 1966), especially John H. Hann, "The Role of the Mexican Deputies in the Proposal and Enactment of Measures of Economic Reform Applicable to Mexico," pp. 153–84. Among the most trenchant reports was that of Miguel Ramos de Arizpe, of 1811, who wanted "to inspire the respect of the United States," yet urged that Texas be strongly governed and its Indians kept friendly "in case of a rupture with the United States." He envisioned a federation of provinces, with most power in strong provincial governments. Since other, Spanish deputies viewed such federalism, correctly, as a bid for autonomy, like early United States federalism, and in conflict with the monarchy, the United States Constitution was seldom cited, although another Mexican, José Miguel Guridi e Alcocer, during debates concerning subordinating the power of the king to that of the Cortes, mentioned, probably unwisely, the United States Constitution as precedent for such subordination: Nettie Lee Benson, "Comparison of the American Independence Movements," in *Dos Revoluciones: México y los Estados Unidos*, Josefina Zoraida Vázquez, *et al.* (Mexico: edición especial para El Colegio de México y la American Historical Association, por Fomento Cultural Banamex; Jus, 1976), pp. 117–27; Anna, *Mexico*, pp. 47–50; and see N. L. Benson, ed., *Report that Dr. Miguel Ramos de Arizpe . . . presents to the Congress on the Natural, Political, and Civil Condition of the Provinces of Coahuila, Nuevo Leon, Nuevo Santander, and Texas* (1950; reprint ed. Westport, Conn.: Greenwood, 1971). The report was printed in Mexico, London, and Philadelphia by 1814, in Cádiz in 1812. Also see Jaime E. Rodríguez O., *The Emergence of Spanish America: Vicente Rocafuerte and Spanish America, 1808–1832* (Berkeley and Los Angeles: University of California Press, 1975); Mario Rodríguez, *The Cádiz Experiment in Central America, 1808 to 1826* (Berkeley and Los Angeles: University of California Press, 1978); and below, n. 29.

26. Douglass North, "Industrialization in the United States," in *Cambridge Economic History*, ed. H. J. Habakkuk and M. Postan, (Cambridge, 1965), 6:673 ff; Whitaker, *United States*, pp. 53–62 79–81: In 1811 James Monroe, as Secretary of State, wrote United States ministers in Europe that their government looked with favor on Spanish American revolutions, although it advised caution in provoking Britain. Congressional appropriation of $50,000 that year for Venezuelan relief following an earthquake was not unalloyed philanthropy: ibid., p. 86; and see Alamán, *Historia*, 3: app. 45, doc. 12: Onís to Francisco Javier de Venegas, viceroy of Mexico, in 1812 on what he thought the United States wanted—continental expansion and Cuba; and Onís in n. 7, above. Yet, even after 1812 the American grain trade to Iberia continued through the intercession of the Barings, although by 1815 British blockade and United States customs had stopped it: W. Freeman Galpin, "The American Grain Trade to the Spanish Peninsula, 1810–1814," *AHR* 28 (1922):24–44; a case in point appears in Carl Seaburg and Stanley Paterson, *Merchant Prince of Boston: Colonel T. H. Perkins, 1764–1854* (Cambridge, Mass.: Harvard University Press, 1971), pp. 234–35. Said Perkins on May 5, 1811: "Will not all Spanish America be bitten by the Tarantula of Liberty and set to dancing?" Davis, *Industrial Revolution*, p. 17, mentioned that Britain closed off raw cotton to European manufacturers, so that power spinning was curtailed on the continent by its shortage until 1815, when the practice became to import British cotton yarns. Britain's re-exports from Latin America soared, and cotton exports from 1814 to 1816 to Latin America swelled, more than doubling from the decade since 1804–1806, and they continued strong to the United States; so did English imports of Latin American foodstuffs from about 1814 (ibid., pp. 116–17, 19, 96, 92). Earlier, after Britain abolished slaving in 1806–7, Liverpool shipping turned to other trade with Latin America. And see R. A. Humphreys, "British Merchants and South American Independence," and "Anglo-American Rivalries and Spanish American Emancipation" in *Tradition and Revolt in Latin America and Other Essays* (London: Weidenfeld and Nicholson, 1969), pp. 106–53; D. C. M. Platt, *Latin America and British Trade, 1806–1914* (New York: Harper and Row, 1972); Frank R. Rutter, *The South American Trade of Baltimore* (Baltimore: Johns Hopkins University Studies in History and Political Science, ser. xv:9; Johns Hopkins Press, 1897), pp. 13–14; Emiliano Jos, "Juan Vicente Bolívar. Notas sobre su misión diplomática a los Estados Unidos, 1810–1811," *Boletín de la Academia Nacional de la Historia* (Caracas) 26 (1943):147; Keen, *De Forest*, p. 88; D. Goebel, "British Trade"; J. Fred Rippy, *Rivalry of the United States and Great Britain over Latin America (1808–1830)* (1929; reprint ed, New York: Octagon, 1961); Charles C. Griffin, "La opinión pública norteamericana y la independencia de

Hispanoamérica, 1810–1822," *Boletín de la Academia Nacional de la Historia* (Caracas) no. 93 (1941):12, who says that the public initially supposed the rising in Caracas a European plot, the Federalists suspected the French (as did Onís), and Republicans the English; Griffin, *United States*; Bornholdt, *Baltimore*; Solnick, "American Opinion"; and Brendan C. MacNally, "La prensa de los Estados Unidos y la Independencia hispanoamericana," *HM* 3 (1954):521–26, who found that by 1810 seaboard papers favored independence, and they saw adhesion to Spain nominal, but some expressed doubts of Spanish American aptitude for self-government and, on June 22, the Richmond *Enquirer* said an "ideological revolution" was needed first. MacNally found that they foresaw in Latin American events expansion for United States trade, a successful imitation showing the world the United States as an example of republicanism, and great benefit to Spanish Americans in their taking up the sword of Washington and the pen of Jefferson.

27. Bowman, "Torres," pp. 33–43; Jos, "J. V. Bolívar"; Cristóbal Mendoza, ed., *Las primeras misiones diplomáticas de Venezuela*, 2 vols. (Caracas: Biblioteca de la Academia Nacional de la Historia, 1962); C. L. Mendoza, comp., "Las primeras relaciones diplomáticas de Venezuela con los Estados Unidos. Correspondencia de Orea," *Boletín de la Academia Nacional de la Historia Venezolana* 27 (1944):346–73. Torres wrote several pamphlets, including *An Exposition of the Commerce of Spanish America: With some Observations upon its Importance to the United States* (Philadelphia: G. Palmer, 1816), which glowingly described Spanish American products. Cf. Parra-Pérez, *Historia*, 1:328–29, who said that the Caracas junta knew the spirit of Poinsett's instructions, so sent Bolívar and Telésforo Orea, that they found it hard to buy arms since outbid by the Spanish authorities in Mexico and Peru, and that Bolívar sent home farm machinery and presses for printing paper money instead; and *DNA* III:1:300 ff. for Onís's influence on J. V. Bolívar.

28. Grases, *Libros*, pp. 21–32. Grases says the *Historia* was a translation of a text by an emigrant Scot, William M'Culloch, mostly explaining independence and governmental organization. See Pedro Grases and Alberto Harkness, *Manuel García de Sena y la Independencia de Hispanoamérica* (Caracas: Vargas, 1953), pp. 51 ff. for the great influence of Sena's book on Spanish America.

29. José Alvárez de Toledo y Dubois, *Manifesto o satisfacción pundonorosa a todos los buenos españoles europeos, y a todos los pueblos de la América*...(Philadelphia, 1811); in English as an appendix to Walton; *Exposé*; and see above, n. 25.

30. Monroe, Gutiérrez wrote in his diary, told him that if the United States declared war on Britain it would send troops to liberate Mexico, and Monroe encouraged him to form a provisional government and had raised the possibility of a Pan-American confederation. Gutiérrez also got the impression from him that the United States wanted control of Texas: Elizabeth H. West, intro., "Diary of José Bernardo Gutiérrez de Lara," *AHR* 34 (1928):55–77; and see Alamán, *Historia*, 3, and its app. 45; and Fabela, *precursores*, pp. 33–41.

31. In 1813 Monroe ordered Shaler not to interfere in affairs in the Spanish colonies, for he wanted to give Spain no pretext to join the British: Whitaker, *United States*, p. 95. Richard W. Gronet, "The United States and the Invasion of Texas, 1810–1814," *TAm* 25 (1969):281–306, specifically questioning Whitaker and Nichols *(Advance Agents)*, argues that the filibustering expedition had administration backing. Yet Whitaker does present administration attitudes and Gronet neglects to explain them within broader policy context, or how official policy too changed. See too, *DNA* III:1:353–54, 505–6, 626, 634–35; Isaac Joslin Cox, "Monroe and the Early Mexican Revolutionary Agents," *AHA Report*, 1911; V. Vital-Hawell, "El aspecto internacional de las usurpaciones americanas en las provincias españolas limítrofes con los Estados Unidos de 1810 a 1814," *RIn* 25 (1965):115–53; Harris G. Warren, "José Alvárez de Toledo's Initiation as a Filibuster, 1811–1813," *HAHR* 20 (1940):56–82; H. G. Warren, *The Sword Was Their Passport* (Baton Rouge: Louisiana State University Press, 1943) 18 ff.; Lockey, "Shaler's Pan-American Scheme." Picornell was in the United States between 1799 and 1801 or 1802, and again in 1806, and was involved in the movement in Caracas between 1810 and 1812, returning again with Pedro Gual, an emissary of Simón Bolívar, by 1814, but that year Picornell married a *pensionada* of Spain in New Orleans and by 1816 had obtained a pardon and was working for Ferdinand VII: *DNA* III:1:95, 98, 505–06, 512, 605–06, 626, 664; Torres Lanzas, *Independencia*, 4:168.

32. Bowman, "Torres," overstates in saying Torres swung public opinion to Spanish American independence, but he did favorably impress leading members of the United States government: cf. Whitaker, *United States*; Bornholdt, *Baltimore*; Griffin, *United States*, and Peter Zahendra, "Spanish

West Florida, 1781–1821'' (Ph.D. diss., University of Michigan, 1976), pp. 295–307. Onís reported the United States had supported France in Latin America in 1811 and this policy had led it to war in 1812 on the side of France: see Whitaker, *United States*, pp. 58–60; Robertson, *France*, pp. 84, 86, 93–95; *DNA* III:1, passim.

33. Whitaker, *United States*, Ch. 7, for the "cautious, unheroic" policy of 1815 and 1816.

34. See Bemis, *Latin American Policy*, 33 ff.; Palacio Fajardo, *Outline*; Bierck, *Gual*; Charles C. Griffin, "Privateering from Baltimore during the Spanish American Wars of Independence," *Maryland Historical Magazine* 35 (March 1940):1–25; García Samudio, *Independencia*, pp. 134–35; Onís, *United States*, p. 81; Torres Lanzas; *Independencia*, 4:64–70; and William D. Robinson, *A Cursory View of Spanish America* (Georgetown, D.C., 1815).

35. Parra Pérez, *Historia*, 1:189–222, 2:11 ff.; García Samudio, *Independencia*, pp. 111–13; Arellano, *orígenes*, pp. 408–9, 420–21; Arcila Farías, *Económia*, p. 372; Palacio Fajardo, *Outline*; Parks, *Colombia*, p. 79, says by 1810 there were British commercial houses in La Guaira and the British paid 25 percent less duty than all other foreigners. In 1811 Lowry explained the earthquake relief funds to Venezuelans as a gesture of friendship and interest, and went on to speak of the mutual advantages to commercial interchange. Arcila Farías, in "pensamiento," p. 82, remarks that Caracas merchants by 1813 still wanted liberty of trade with all the islands and to welcome British ships at La Guaira, but not English establishments, and they sought to retain their monopoly on cacao to Vera Cruz. In 1824 Lowry, in a venture with three Englishmen, John Myers and the brothers of Admiral Cochrane, John D. and Charles S., leased Aroa copper mines from Simón Bolívar. Also see *DNA* III:1:299–300; Halperín-Donghi, *Historia*, pp. 99–101; William H. Gray, *Early Trade Relations between the United States and Venezuela* (Mexico: IPAGH, 1949); and William C. Olson, "Early North Americans in Venezuelan Commerce, 1810–1830'' (Ph.D. diss., University of North Carolina, 1974), pp. 41–48.

36. Bornholdt, *Baltimore*, 22, sees their abolition, probably correctly, as propaganda directed toward the United States. Mendoza, "primeras relaciones," p. 346, cited Orea to Monroe, May 17, 1811: "The United States pointed out to Venezuela the road to liberty and social virtues." Orea reported finding Monroe friendly and disposed toward Venezuelan independence, knowing it would increase the power of the United States; but Orea himself preferred close ties to England, for his major concern was Venezuelan commerce, and he thought England wanted markets for manufactures and would take his country's products: ibid., pp. 349, 354–55, 364; and see *DNA* III:1:283, 287–88, 294; Alvárez F., *consulado*, p. 118; Onís, *United States*, p. 24; Griffin, *United States*, pp. 56–57; Gray, *Early Trade*, 88 ff.

37. William Burke, *Derechos de la América del Sur y México*, 2 vols. in *Biblioteca de la Academia Nacional de la Historia. Sesquicentenario de la Independencia*, 125 vols. (Caracas, 1959), X;10–11; Mariano Picón-Salas, ed., *Gazeta de Caracas*, 1–2:1808–1812, 2 vols., facsimile (Caracas: Academia Nacional de Historia, 1960); Grases, *libros*, pp. 55, 103, ff.; Grases and Harkness, *García de Sena*, p. 11; Olson, "Early North Americans," p. 39; Onís, *United States*, pp. 65–66; Parra Pérez, *Historia*, 2:26, who states that Burke was probably a spokesman for Miranda, and pp. 38–50; Javier Malagón, ed., *Las Actas de Independencia de América* (Washington: Pan American Union, 1955); Palacio Fajardo, *Outline*; Jos, "Juan Vicente Bolívar," p. 145; *DNA* III:1:291, concerns "the President's friend, Dr. Thornton, giving the Caracas deputies "a kind of constitution;" and see above, n. 27.

38. Cited in Griffin, *United States*, p. 66; cf. Onís, *United States*, pp. 49, 65, who refers to an essay by Antonio Gómez opposing religious toleration and with a variant criticism of the United States government. Gómez conceded a national religion did unify the United States, but said its Constitution while now young and vigorous would age, and, was the implication, deteriorate. His source was French, Gabriel Bonnet de Mably.

39. Antonio Múñoz Tebar to Bolívar, December 31, 1813, in Vicente Lecuna, comp., and Harold Bierck, ed., *Selected Writings of Bolivar*, 2 vols. (New York: Banco de Venezuela/Colonial Press, 1951) 1:51–58. Lecuna and Bierck think Bolívar may have written this piece himself.

40. Ocampo, *proceso*, pp. 326–27; Chandler, *Inter-American Acquaintances*, p. 90; and Manuel Pérez Vila in notes prepared for an address to the Southern Historical Association's annual meeting, Atlanta, November 1977.

41. Ibid.; Parks, *Colombia*, p. 117; William R. Shepherd, "Bolívar and the United States,"

HAHR 1 (1918):270–98; Chandler, *Inter-American Acquaintances,* p. 158; Whitaker, *United States*, pp. 169 ff.; A. C. Wilgus, "Some Activities of United States Citizens in the South American Wars of Independence, 1808–1824," *Louisiana Historical Quarterly* 14 (1931):182–203.

42. Pérez Vila, *notes*; and see below, n. 112; and Córdova-Bello, *independencia*, p. 164.

43. Kroeber, *Growth*, p. 87.

44. Street, *Gran Bretaña,* pp. 164, 218–19; Keen, *DeForest*.

45. Moreno, *Escritos*, pp. 297, 34–49, 289, 291, 298–310; Wait, "Moreno," p. 380; García Samudio, *Independencia*, pp. 103–04; and see Belgrano, *Estudios*, pp. 147–52, 212, 22, 264, 268, ff.; C. L. Chandler, "United States Shipping in the La Plata Region, 1809–1810" *HAHR* 3(1920): 159–76. Chandler, in *Inter-American Acquaintances,* pp. 63, 114, remarks that there were more United States vessels putting in at Buenos Aires in 1810 than in 1910, more American than English ships in that harbor in 1824, and "far more on the west coast of South America in 1813 than in 1913." In 1811 a triumvirate was in power in Buenos Aires and in 1812, in a military coup, the army took charge of government: see Halperín-Donghi, *Politics*.

46. Ariosto D. González, *Las primeras fórmulas constitucionales en los paises de la Plata (1810–1814)* (Montevideo: Barreiro and Ramos, 1962), pp. 134, 147, 151; Chandler, *Inter-American Acquaintances*, p. 73; Wilgus, "Some Activities," p. 194; and Levene, *mundo*, pp. 159–60, who says that the Buenos Aires edition of Sena's book on Paine included a long, eulogistic comment on the revolt in Venezuela.

47. Keen, *DeForest*, pp. 88–96.

48. Whitaker, *United States*, pp. 67–74. Fray Mier, who was in London in 1810 with José de San Martín, Alvear, and other men who, banded together in the Lautaro Lodge, from 1812 came to determine policy in Buenos Aires and to direct military operations, in 1813 warned that declaring absolute independence would cause difficulties with the British government: Ricardo Caillet-Bois, "Noticias acerca de los vinculaciones de Fray Servando Teresa de Mier, Guillermo Walton y Santiago Perry con el gobierno de Buenos Aires (1812–1818)," *RHA* 35 (1953):119–20; See Torres Lanzas, *Independencia*, 3:44; Street, "Lord Strangford"; Street, *Gran Bretaña*; Asdrúbal, "United States," p. 34, cited Strangford to Wellesley, June 10, 1810, saying Britain should try to exclude United States intervention in Spanish colonial affairs by all means possible; G. Tjarks, *Consulado* 1:367; Keen, *DeForest*, p. 96; Platt, *Latin America*; Halperín-Donghi, *Politics*; Humphreys, *Liberation*; Humphreys, *Tradition*; D. Goebel, "Rivalry"; J. Brown, *Socioeconomic History*; Vera Blinn Reber, *British Mercantile Houses in Buenos Aires, 1810–1880* (Cambridge, Mass.: Harvard University Press, 1979); and Robert G. Albion, "British Shipping and Latin America, 1806–1914," *JEcH* 11 (1951):361–74, who says (p. 371) that "between 1815 and 1830, Britain poured into Latin America some 20 million pounds sterling."

49. González, *primeras fórmulas*, pp. 347–74. La Plata was full of constitutional proposals, its leaders explaining them as devices to keep the confidence of the populace; most used the United States as the point of departure. See P. A. Martin, "Artigas: the Founder of Uruguayan Nationality," *HAHR* 9 (1939):2–15; Grases and Harkness, *García de Sena*, pp. 56–57; Kroeber, *Growth*, p. 87. Buenos Aires's duties on hides from the interior hurt the latter. Artigas in Montevideo, like creoles earlier in Buenos Aires, favored trade with Britain but stipulated consignees must be native. In the same period, Montevideo's cabildo remarked that trade "constitutes the sinews of the state: John Street, *Artigas and the Emancipation of Uruguay* (Cambridge, 1959), p. 236.

50. Chandler, *Inter-American Acquaintances*, p. 67.

51. Villalobos, *comercio y crisis*, p 373, ff., prints the decree; and see Rámírez Necochea, *Antecedentes*, p. 103; John L. Rector, "Merchants, Trade, and Commercial Policy in Chile, 1810–1840" (Ph.D. diss., Indiana University, 1976); and S. F. Edwards, "Chilean Economic Policy Goals, 1811–1829; A Study of Late Eighteenth-Century Social Mercantilism and Early Nineteenth-Century Reality" (Ph.D. diss., Tulane University, 1971).

52. García Samudio, *Independencia*, pp. 109–10; Villalobos, *Tradición*, pp. 87–93, 104, 162–66; and cf. Whitaker, *Western Hemisphere Idea*.

53. Meza Villalobos, *conciencia*, p. 308, cites McKenna, February 20, 1811; and see Villalobos, *Tradición*, pp. 182 ff., 254.

54. See Luis Valencia Avaria, ed., *El pensamiento de O'Higgins* (Santiago: Editorial del Pacífico,

1974), letter to José María Benavente, of February 13, 1811, for an example; also see Collier, *Ideas*, p. 80; Roger M. Haigh, *The Formation of the Chilean Oligarchy, 1810–1821* (Salt Lake City: Historical S. and D. Research Foundation, 1972); and Mary Lowenthal Felstiner, "Kinship Politics in the Chilean Independence Movement," *HAHR* 56 (1976):58–80.

55. David Porter, *Journal of a Cruise made to the Pacific Ocean . . . in the United States Frigate Essex, in the Years 1812, 1813, 1814* (Philadelphia, 1815); Onís wrote home on July 28, 1812 that he was certain Porter had gone to subvert Chile: *DNA* III:1:528; Eugenio Pereira Salas, *La actuación de los oficiales navales norteamericanos en nuestras costas (1813–1840)* (Santiago: Prensas de la Universidad de Chile, 1935); and Estuardo Núñez, "El comodoro Porter y el tipógrapho Johnston en los prodomos de la emancipación hispanoamericana," in *movimiento emancipador*, 3:295–305.

56. Captain Peter Heywood to Viscount Melville, December 4, 1812, cited in Collier, *Ideas*, p. 98; and see Pereira Salas, *Buques*, pp. 35–43.

57. García Samudio, *Independencia*, p. 109; Chandler, *Inter-American Acquaintances*, p. 74. Henríquez subsequently edited the *Semanario Republicano*, which he took over from Antonio José de Irisarri, the son of the Guatemalan merchant, shipowner, and contrabandista. (See above Ch. 8, n. 10.) Both editors drew on Paine's *Common Sense*. Irisarri wanted a republican government; Henríquez, by 1813, a limited monarchy: see Felstiner, "Kinship," pp. 68–70; and A. Owen Aldridge, "Camilo Henríquez and the Fame of Thomas Paine and Benjamin Franklin in Chile," *Inter-American Review of Bibliography* 17 (1967):51–67. Henríquez also owned a copy of the United States Declaration of Independence, given him by Poinsett, and in the *Aurora* printed a Fourth of July address delivered by Madison and Washington's Farewell Address. The United States, he then insisted, was "the Beacon which we should follow" [Griffin, *United States*, p. 61; and Bernard Moses, *The Intellectual Background of the Revolution in South America, 1810–1826* (1926; reprint ed., New York: Russell and Russell, 1966), pp. 96–107, 155–56]. The press belonged to Mathew Hoevel, the American vice-consul, later a captain in the Chilean militia and treasurer of its navy (Wilgus, "Some Activities," p. 196). The three printers, Garrison, Burbridge, and Johnston, celebrating the Fourth of July in 1812 at a party honoring Poinsett became too drunk and too jolly with the ladies and landed in jail (Onis, *United States*, p. 28). Johnston, soberer later, became a lieutenant in the Chilean navy (Wilgus, "Some Activities," p. 194). Hoevel arrived in 1805 as supercargo on a New York frigate belonging to John R. Livingston and condemned for contraband (Pereira Salas, *Buques*, p. 35). Poinsett was expelled from Chile in 1814, the year the Spanish regained control. That year the conservative Chilean Fray Melchor Martínez, a delegate to the Cortes, wrote scathingly of the *bostoneses* and their adherents in Chile in his *Memoria*.

58. Gutiérrez and Torres, "Motivos que han obligado al Nuevo Reino de Granada a resumir los Derechos de la Soberanía, remover los autoridades del antiguo gobierno e instalar una Suprema Junta bajo la dependencia del Consejo de la Regencia y cualquier otra representación" (Santafé de Bogotá, September, 25, 1810), in *Proceso histórico del 20 de julio de 1810 (documentos)* (Bogotá: Banco de la República, 1960), pp. 210–49. Four thousand copies were put on sale, advertised in the *Diario Político* (no. 11); sale was slow: Gómez Hoyos, *revolución*, 2:74 ff., and see passim. Torres, heading the Federalists in 1811, wrote Madison for guidance: Wilhite, "Foreign Ideas" pp. 10–11; and see Gómez Hoyos, *revolución*, 2: Chs. 1, 3. New Granada followed the same process as Venezuela. A junta, set up on July 20, 1810, sent a circular to provincial cabildos calling for a congress. It was convened a year later and approved an act of confederation embracing provinces of the old audiencia and "those provinces or municipalities which did not belong to New Granada . . . but still were connected to it by ties based on geographical position, commercial relations, or similar reasons," who wished to join (Belaunde, *Bolívar*, pp. 142–47). Caldas, editing the *Semanario del Nuevo Reino de Granada* from 1808 to 1811, provided statistical and ideological fuel to economic separatists. His outlook epitomized the convergence of creole optimism, regional patriotism, rationality, and proto-nationality: see Caldas, *Semanario . . . 3* vols. (Bogotá, 1942), 1:51–54; and Caldas, *Obras Completas* (Bogotá: Universidad Nacional, 1968). In 1811 he initiated correspondence with the American Philosophical Society (Bernstein, "Aspects," pp. 58–61).

59. Gómez Hoyos, *revolución*, 2:275–97.

60. Miguel de Pombo, *Constitución de los Estados Unidos de América, precedida de los actas de*

independencia y federación. . . .(Santa Fé de Bogotá: Nicolás Cavo, 1811); and Gómez Hoyos, *revolución*, 2:178 ff. Miguel Pombo exhorted, "Let us imitate the conduct of the Anglo-Americans and like them divide the lands. . .multiply everywhere the proprietors and facilitating by this means subsistence, very shortly we will see our population augmented (ibid., p. 181). In July 1810 the proclamation of the junta of Socorro, center of the comuneros 30 years before, to the Bogotá audiencia spoke of "that character of virtue which history points out to us as a political phenomenon of which there is no example before the revolution of North America, and which seemed to be reserved to the happy inhabitants of Philadelphia" (cited in Griffin, *United States*, p. 63).

    61. Cited in Ocampo, *proceso*, pp. 370, 373.

    62. Ibid., pp. 329–30, García Samudio, *Independencia*, pp. 104–7; in 1810–11 Nariño in his *La Bagatela* included a "Sketch of William Penn" and an explanation of the Constitution of the United States: Wilhite, "Foreign Ideas," p. 17. In 1813 he mentioned "the celebrated Esmit [Adam Smith] in his immortal work on *The Wealth of Nations* makes us look to the evidence that from the division of labor is born the perfection of [industrial] arts and their low price" (cited in Ocampo, *proceso*, p. 570). Although some enlightened revolutionaries and their attitudes endured in New Granada—Francisco Zea joined Bolívar in 1814 and later became vice-president of Gran Colombia and its ambassador to England—many were victims of war. In 1816 the Spanish General Morillo executed six of the eleven members of the botanical expedition for, he reportedly explained, "This is a revolution of doctors and, to put it down, it is necessary that their heads must roll": cited by Thomas F. Glick, "Science and Independence in Latin America," a paper presented at the American Academy of Arts and Sciences annual meeting, Boston, February 20, 1976.

    63. In Lima in 1811 the cabildo pushed for commercial and economic autonomy, Abascal permitted a free press, and liberalism and *conciencia de sí* ran rampant in many of the periodicals. They extolled the constitution, deplored royal despotism and Spanish misgovernment in America, and in 1812 the most incendiary of them, *El Satélite del Peruano*, was shut down for a piece beginning, "By patria we understand the vast extenstion of both Americas," and going on to say, in opposing provincial rivalries, that "all inhabitants of the New World are brothers, all of one family, all have some of the same interests"; united they would be "invincible, happy, industrious, and worthy of being a nation." Cited in Raúl Porras Barrenchea, *Los ideólogos de la Emancipación* (Lima: Ed. Milla Batres, 1974), pp. 119–21; see Abascal, *Memoria*; Valcarcel, "Peru," p. 384; Rivara de Tuesta, Ideólogos, pp. 49 ff., 97; and Anna, *Peru*, p. 50. The ninth issue of the *Gaceta* carried an article stating that if Spain succumbed, the New World should be "the port and asylum" from Bonaparte, and the *Satélite* saw America as the future empire of reason, happiness, and philosophy; and, in a supplement, "Spain free of the French is our *madre patria*; America is our patria in all the literal rigor of the word" (cited in Basadre, "Historia," pp. 661–62). Liberal constitutionalists such as Baquíjano and Cisneros wrote for the papers under pseudonyms. (In 1813 *El Peruano* became *El Peruano Liberal*.) Unanue that year proposed freedom of exports and suggested imitating the governor of Havana in 1808, by permitting taking Peruvian surplus in Peruvian ships to the United States (Bernstein, "Some Inter-American Aspects," p. 66; Diffie, *Latin American Civilization*, pp. 415–16). Risings in Tacna and elsewhere in 1811 and 1813, stimulated by porteños, and one in Cuzco in 1813, spread through southern Peru, the rebels challenging Lima's ascendency, protesting maladminstration, and fueled by the curbing of American rights advocated in the constitutional debates in Spain. One Peruvian deputy, Manuel de Vidaurre, who had been in the Cortes, returned in 1812 to sit on the Cuzco audiencia, declined a request that he head the dissident junta there, and instead made his way to Philadelphia, where, he said, he studied the country's laws and came to revere its customs (Rivara de Tuesta, *Ideólogos*, pp. 97 ff., Fisher, "Royalism"). Another representative to the Cortes, Manuel Rivero, was arrested in Cuzco in 1813 for ties to the rebels. See, too, Valcarcel, "Perú," pp. 395–96; Fisher, *Government*, p. 227; Denegri Luna, *Antología*; and Anna, *Peru*, pp. 45 ff.

    64. *El Despertador Americano* (Mexico: INAH, 1964). Its full title was *El Despertador Americano. Correo Político Económico de Guadalajara*; see Xavier Tavera Alfaro, "Hidalgo y el *Despertador Americano*," *Filosofía y Letras* 24 (1952):259–73; and Hugh Hamill, *The Hidalgo Revolt* (Gainesville: University of Florida Press, 1966). Hidalgo, in the *Despertador*, proposed a general congress consisting of urban representatives who were to maintain religion and govern as fathers. He

foresaw minimal government, and was certain a short relatively bloodless coup would usher in a political and social situtation enabling general well-being ("Manifiesto del Sr. Hidalgo contra el edicto de Tribunal de la fé," Hernández y Dávalos, *Documentos*, 1:125. And see Gutiérrez de Lara, "Diary."

65. Torres Lanzas, *Independencia*, 3:351, 376, 444. See Torre Villar, *constitución*; J. Miranda, *Ideas*, pp. 362–63; Benson, *Cortes*; Anna Macias, *Génesis del gobierno constitucional en México, 1808–1820* (Mexico: SepSetentas, 1973); Ernesto Lemoine Villacaña, *Morelos* (Mexico: UNAM, 1965); José R. Guzmán Rodríguez, "La misión de José Manuel Herrera en Estados Unidos," *BAGN* 10 (1969):253–88; Fabela, *precursores*, pp. 42–45, 64–70; Alamán, *Historia*, 3, and its app. 45–52; and J. Rubio Mañé, "Iturbide y sus relaciones con los Estados Unidos," *BAGN* 6:1 (1965):65–67, citing the letter written to the government of the United States introducing Herrera. Also see Ernesto de la Torre Villar, *Los "guadalupes" y la independencia* (Mexico: Jus, 1966), concerning liberals in touch with the United States, and Torres Lanzas, *Independencia*, 3:240, 332. For Guatemala, part of the viceroyalty of New Spain, see Mario Rodríguez, *Cádiz*.

66. To the Editor of the Royal Gazette, Kingston, September 28, 1815; in *Cartas del Libertador*, 2d ed., ed. and intro. Vincente Lecuna (Caracas: Banco de Venezuela. Fundación Vicente Lecuna, 1964–), 1:238.

67. See Torre Villar, *constitución*, p. 78, for a listing; Belaunde, *Bolívar*, pp. 29–30, 153–55, 173; A. González, *primeras formulas*; Collier, *Ideas*, p. 152; and Glen Dealy, "Prolegomena on the Spanish American Political Tradition," *HAHR* 48 (1968):37–58 who, however, overstates the rejection of eighteenth-century liberalism.

68. Whitaker, *United States*, pp. 111–13. Grampp, "Re-examination," p. 280, reminds us that by 1816 Jefferson had declared that manufactures were necessary to United States independence, for the country could be shut out of international commerce.

69. Edith F. Helman, "Early Interest in Spain in New England (1815–1835)," *Hispania* 29 (1946):343. The *City of Washington Gazette* in 1817 excerpted Abad y Queipo's letter of May 30, 1810 to the Spanish Regency, urging free trade be extended to all Spanish American ports and inter-Spanish American commerce be opened (Whitaker, *United States*, p. 173; and see Griffin, *United States*; and Bornholdt, *Baltimore*).

70. Bierck, *Gual*, pp. 107–8; A. Curtis Wilgus, "Some Notes on Spanish American Patriot Activity along the Atlantic Seaboard, 1816–1822," *North Carolina Historical Review* 4 (1927):172–81; Whitaker, *United States*, pp. 126–27, who concurs with Vernon G. Setser, *The Commercial Reciprocity Policy of the United States, 1774–1829* (Philadelphia; University of Pennsylvania Press, 1937), pp. 243–44; and A. Curtis Wilgus, "Spanish American Patriot Activity along the Gulf Coast of the United States, 1811–1812," *Louisiana Historical Quarterly* 7 (1925):193–215.

71. Mina while in England had been introduced by Lord Holland, the opposition leader, to General Winfield Scott, who assured Mina and Mier he could get arms and recruits in the United States (Bierck, *Gual*, 116–21). A group of Baltimore merchants, headed by Dennis and Alexander Smith and gambling on large profits, agreed to help Gual outfit the expedition. Toledo appears the villain of the enterprise. Secretly reconciled with Spanish representatives in New Orleans and Philadelphia in 1816, he misled Mier, who went with Mina and was captured and imprisoned in Mexico, and Toledo dissuaded the Baltimoreans and even Joseph Bonaparte, then living in New Jersey, from their inclinations to aid the scheme. See Warren, *Sword*; Vital-Hawell, "aspecto," pp. 141 ff.; Fabela, *precursores*, pp. 64–70; Onís, *United States*, pp. 72–77; Torres Villar, *constitución*, p. 45; William D. Robinson, *Memoirs of the Mexican Revolution* (Philadelphia, 1820); Hernández y Dávalos, *Documentos*, 6:807; Torres Lanzas, *Independencia*, 4:168; William R. Manning, *Diplomatic Correspondence of the United States relating to the Independence of Latin American Nations* (New York: Oxford University Press, 1925); F. J. Urrutia, *Páginas de historia diplomática; los Estados Unidos y las repúblicas hispanoamericanas de 1810 a 1830* (Madrid, 1918); and Greenleaf, "Mexican Inquisition and the Masonic Movement," concerning Mier's trial.

72. Dr. William Thornton, long a dabbler in Latin American relations—see above, n. 37—and a close friend to acting Secretary of State Richard Rush, acted as intermediary, possibly self-styled, between Rush and Gual and McGregor. Thornton expected the Spanish American group to conquer

Amelia Island and then sell it to the United States: Whitaker, *United States*, p. 227; Bierck, *Gual*, pp. 139 ff.: Thornton was said to be descended from an Irish family named Wall, changed to Gual in Spanish. One agent involved, Pazos, was in touch with Stephen Girard, Astor, David Porter, and the New York politician DeWitt Clinton: Charles H. Bowman, Jr., "Vicente Pazos and the Amelia Island Affair, 1817," *Florida Historical Quarterly* 53 (1975):273–95; Onís, p. 80; and see Vicente Pazos, *Letters to Henry Clay on the Revolution in South America* (New York, 1819). Embittered, Gual wrote from Amelia to the United States government that "since we think of the people of the United States as the only free people on the face of the globe, we can not admit that you may now be turned into partisans of a tyrant" (Bierck, *Gual*, p. 154). And see Whitaker, *United States*, pp. 237, 245, 290–91; and Torres Lanzas, *Independencia*, 4:261–62, 303, 314.

73. Garcia Samudio, *Independencia*, p. 137.

74. Parks, *Colombia*, p. 135; Whitaker, *United States*, p. 161, n. 39.

75. Ibid., pp. 244–45; Griffin, "Opinion," pp. 15, 21: G. Gilbert adds that during these years Baltimore merchants opened a vast new flour trade to Brazil.

76. Helman, "Early Interest," p. 344, cites his *Letter to James Monroe upon the Present State of South America*; and see H. M. Brackenridge, *Voyage to South America...*, 2 vols. (Baltimore, 1819); Watt Stewart, "The South American Commission, 1817–1818," *HAHR* 9 (1929):31–59; Bornholdt, *Baltimore*, pp. 50 ff., 132; and Whitaker, *United States*, pp. 178 ff., 241.

77. See Randolph B. Campbell, "The Spanish American Aspect of Henry Clay's American System," *TAm* 24 (1967):3–17; and Ernest R. May, *The Making of the Monroe Doctrine* (Cambridge, Mass.: Harvard University Press, 1975), pp. 55 ff. By 1818 Clay was addressing the House of Representatives in favor of Latin American independence: "This interest concerns our politics, our commerce, our navigation." He foresaw United States hemispheric hegemony and new Spanish American governments "guided by an American policy.... We are their great example." He went on: "The precious metals are in South America and they will command the articles wanted in South America, which will purchase them. Our navigation will be benefited by the transaction and our country will realize the mercantile profits." The cause of the patriots, he added, was just, "and we have a great interest in its success" (cited in W. A. Williams, *Shaping*, pp. 157–58).

78. Whitaker, *Latin America*, pp. 273–74; Setser, *Commercial Reciprocity*; William S. Robertson, "The Recognition of the Hispanic-American Nations by the United States," *HAHR* 1 (1918):239–69. Monroe proposed the first minister be sent to Mexico, then a monarchy, but was right in thinking it would soon be a republic (Whitaker, *United States*, pp. 371–72). Among the data Adams sent to Congress was the correspondence of Torres, who, while he did not originate the doctrine of pan-American confederation or inspire the Monroe Doctrine, did propose by 1820 to Adams, who liked and respected him, a broad American stance distinct from Europe, and especially from England, a *causa Americana* (Garcia Samudio, *Independencia*, pp. 171–77, 185; Chandler, *Inter-American Acquaintances*, p. 164; Bowman, "Torres"; Whitaker, *United States*, pp. 326–27, 407). Torres did explain to Adams that despite liberal control in Spain in 1820, the regime there was excluding from representation everyone of African origin, thereby disenfranchising the liberation armies, and that it was curbing the privileges of the church and the army, and at the same time alienating colonial upper classes by strongly reasserting Spanish authority in the colonies.

79. Davis, *Industrial Revolution*, pp. 18–19, says, "From the 1820s the Latin American market outgrew that of the United States by a wide margin," that then almost half the total of British cotton exports went to America, and that Latin America was the single largest market through the 1830s; and see Bernardine Pietraszek, "Britain and Direct Spanish American Trade, 1815–1825," *Mid-America* 37 (1955):67–100; and above, n. 26. Chaunu, *Historia*, pp. 121–22, mentions the advent of the steamship as giving Britain further advantage. The *New York American* of March 11, 1822, noted manufacturers in the United States could not yet supply South America but that American ships could carry re-exported goods and wanted no transit duties on such cargoes (Whitaker, *United States*, p. 387; and cf. p. 600). Chandler, "United States Commerce," did find a sharp increase in United States trade with Latin America in 1823.

80. Whitaker, *United States*, pp. 479, 520; Whitaker, *Western Hemisphere*; E. May, *Monroe Doctrine*, pp. 19–20, 55. The immediate cause of the Doctrine was à result of France invading Spain in

1823 to help Ferdinand against the constitutionalists. Britain proposed a warning to both against retaking Latin America. Americans, knowing that England opposed intervention and dominated the seas, seized the opportunity to appear independent of Britain, denounce the Holy Alliance, warn Russia off Alaska, present the United States as protector of Latin America, and delimit a United States sphere of influence. Whitaker, *United States*, pp. 147 ff., 396–412, 474 ff., attempted unconvincingly to minimize Adam's role in propounding the Doctrine. Cf. Dexter Perkins, *The Monroe Doctrine, 1823–1826* (1927; reprint ed., Gloucester, Mass.: Peter Smith, 1965) who overstates fellow feeling, underemphasizes commercial interest; E. May who, in discussing the Doctrine as a result of internal political issues and ambitions, fails to delineate sufficently the international context; and see Walter LaFeber, ed., *John Quincy Adams and American Continental Empire: Letters, Papers, and Speeches* (Chicago: Quadrangle, 1965), pp. 97–116.

81. *The Memoirs of John Quincy Adams*, ed., C. F. Adams, 12 vols. (Philadelphia: Lippincott, 1874–77), 5:176.

82. William S. Robertson, "The First Legations of the United States in Latin America," *MVHR* 2 (1915):195–96.

83. See William R. Manning, "An Early Diplomatic Controversy between the United States and Brazil," *HAHR* 1 (1918):123–45; Stanley E. Hilton, "The United States and Brazilian Independence," in A. J. R. Russell-Wood, ed., *From Colony to Nation* (Baltimore: Johns Hopkins University Press, 1975), pp. 109–29; Joseph B. Lockey, *Pan-Americanism, Its Beginnings* (New York: Macmillan, 1920); D. Perkins, *Monroe Doctrine*, 144 ff; above, n. 3; and William S. Robertson, "South America and the Monroe Doctrine, 1824–1828," *Political Science Quarterly* 30 (1915):82–105. Brazilian independence, superficially exotic, was only a variant on the general Latin American situation. There a republican revolt in the north had been put down in 1817. With the liberal rebellion in Portugal in 1820, the king returned home, leaving his son Pedro to govern. In London da Costa's *Correio*, while opposing independence, had long urged adoption of constitutional monarchy by the Portuguese king in Brazil. When it came in Portugal with liberal revolt, it did not bring equality for the colonies, just as liberal government in Spain had not, and when the Portuguese Cortes signaled a return to the old system of monopoly, the Portuguese in Brazil, merchants in the main, and the native aristocracy of planters looked to the prince, Dom Pedro, to protect their gains through declaring independence. He did so in 1822. A rift soon split Portuguese favoring absolute monarchy, Brazilians advocating constitutional kingship, and the few republicans. The native oligarchs triumphed. Pedro I was expelled by the constitutionalists and his infant son, Pedro II, under the tutelage of José Bonifácio Andrade, entered upon what would be a long reign. See A. K. Manchester, "The Rise of the Brazilian Aristocracy," *HAHR* 11 (1931):145–68; and R. A. Humphreys, ed., *British Consular Reports on the Trade and Politics of Latin America, 1824–1826* (London: Royal Historical Society, 1940).

84. Said Adams, "The principles of a liberal commercial intercourse should be exhibited to them [the nations assembled at Panama]; and urged with disinterested and friendly persuasion upon them." His interest here, as elsewhere, was also in the carrying trade—"Free ships make free goods": Lefeber, *John Quincy Adams*, pp. 131–36; Whitaker, *United States*, pp. 574–75, 580, who stated that this speech advanced the rhetoric of hemispheric cooperation and its supporters said the main purpose of the mission was to promote national, and mainly economic, interests of the United States within the traditional policy of neutrality. See Frances L. Reinhold, "New Research on the First Pan-American Congress, held at Panama in 1826," *HAHR* 18 (1938):342–63; Frederick J. Turner, *Rise of the New West, 1819–1829* (New York: Harper, 1907), pp. 280–85; García Samudio, *Independencia*, p. 212; Portell Vilá, *Cuba*, 1:288, who mentions United States influence in restraining the Spanish American republics at Panama from revolutionizing Cuba (for Cuba, 1823, also see Córdoba Bello, *Independencia*, pp. 151, 164, concerning fear by Cuban whites of another Haiti). Lockey's verdict on the conference rings true: "The greatness, the benevolence, the humanity of its design appeared to make no appeal to men's imaginations" (*Pan-Americanism*, p. 317).

85. Turner, *Rise*, pp. 280–85, shows the congressional debate from 1825 on, on sending a mission to Panama, to have been primarily a rallying ground for political opposition to Adams: and see Randolph Campbell, "Henry Clay and the Poinsett Pledge Controversy of 1826," *TAm* 28 (1972):429–46.

86. Manning, "Early Diplomatic Correspondence," 129 ff.

87. See W. S. Robertson, *Iturbide of Mexico* (Durham: Duke University Press, 1952); Ladd, *Mexican Nobility*, pp. 121–31; E. Martínez, "franciscanos," p. 157; and Manuel Carrera Stampa, "Nota a Quiros' 'Reflexiones sobre el comercio libre'" (1817) *BAGN* 19 (1948):171–215, for some attitudes of the nobility, clergy and Vera Cruz merchants, respectively.

88. Rubio Mañé, "Iturbide," 6:1:65–79, 124–25; 6:2:256–57; and Herbert E. Bolton, comp., "General James Wilkinson as Advisor to Emperor Iturbide," *HAHR* 1 (1918):163–80; Ladd, pp. 129–31. In 1822 the Mexican emissary to the United States, José Manuel Bermúdez Zozaya, denounced in a dispatch home United States arrogance and territorial ambitions, partially at least in response to what he sensed as general hostility to empire in Mexico (Whitaker, *United States*, p. 390; Fabela, *Precursores*, pp. 150–53).

89. Nettie Lee Benson, "Washington: Symbol of the United States in Mexico," *Library Chronicle of the University of Texas* 2 (1947):178–89, who adds that also put forth in Mexico City in 1823 was Washington's Circular Letter of June 8, 1783 to states' governors favoring disbanding the army.

90. Bustamente, *suplemento*, p. 241, included a diatribe against slavery in the United States. Fabela, *Precursores*, p. 31, cites him as writing elsewhere: "If Hidalgo would have gained the practical understanding we have, he would have preferred to invoke the help of the emperor of the Morroccos, before that of these people." Cf. Charles Hale, *Mexican Liberalism in the Age of Mora, 1821–1853* (New Haven: Yale University Press, 1968) Chs. 1–2; David Brading, *Los orígenes de nacionalismo mexicano* (Mexico: SepSetentas, 1973); Rubio Mañé, "Iturbide," 6:2:256–57; and Jesús Reyes Heroles, *El liberalismo mexicano*, 3 vols. (Mexico: UNAM, 1957–61), 1.

91. See Edmundo O'Gorman, "Fray Servando Teresa de Mier," in O'Gorman, *Seis estudios históricos de tema mexicano* (Jalapa: Universidad Veracuzana, 1960), pp. 57–97; N. L. Benson, "Servando Teresa de Mier, Federalist," *HAHR* 28 (1948):514–25; Hale, *Mexican Liberalism*, 194 ff; J. M. Miquel i Vergés and Hugo Díaz-Thomé, eds., *Escritos inéditos de Fray Servando Teresa de Mier* (Mexico; Colegio de Mexico, 1944); Brading, *orígenes*; and J. Rodríguez, *Emergence*, 47 ff. Vicente Rocafuerte was with Mier in Philadelphia, published, bound with Mier's *Memoria política*, his *Bosquejo ligerísimo de la revolución de Mégico*...went to Mexico with Mier, and then became president of Ecuador. Torre Villar, *constitución*, p. 83, noted the Mexican constitution of 1824 was influenced by institutional forms of the United States.

92. Whitaker, *United States*, p. 589; Rippy, *Poinsett*; Ward, *Mexico*; Parton, *Poinsett*, who mentions that Alamán was friendly with Ward (pp. 182–83) and in *El Sol* spoke of the United States having designs on Cuba; J. F. Rippy, "Britain's Role in the Early Relations of the United States and Mexico," *HAHR* 7 (1927):2–24; J. F. Rippy, "Latin America and the British Investment 'Boom' of the 1820s," *JMH* 19 (1947):122–29; J. F. Rippy, "Early British Investments in Latin America," *Inter-American Economic Affairs* 6 (1952):40–51; Brading, *orígenes*, pp. 178–83, 145–46; and Barabara A. Tenenbaum, "Merchants, Money, and Mischief: The British in Mexico, 1821–1862," *TAm* 35 (1979):317–40.

93. Whitaker, *United States*, pp. 212–33; Chandler, *Inter-American Acquaintances*, pp. 80, 99–101; González, *primeras fórmulas*, pp 148–50; Brackenridge, *Voyage*; Pine, "Role," pp. 315–38. In 1817 Buenos Aires firms trading with the United States were divided into two rival factions, one led by Halsey, the other by DeForest. That year DeForest was appointed consul-general from the United Provinces to the United States, left for home, and took with him blank letters-of-marque, privateering licenses, ensuring his fortune. He lobbied in Washington for the Argentine cause and died in New Haven in 1825, a respectable citizen, known as very liberal in his gifts to Yale (Keen, *DeForest*, 95 ff., 125–29).

94. Street, *Gran Bretaña*, p. 254. See Romero, *History*, pp. 83 ff.; Thomas M. Davis, Jr., "Carlos de Alvear and James Monroe: New Light on the Origin of the Monroe Doctrine," *HAHR* 23 (1943):632–49; Whitaker, *United States*, pp. 102–9, 345, 559–60; Watt Stewart, "Argentina and the Monroe Doctrine, 1824–1828," *HAHR* 10 (1930):26–32. Halperín-Donghi, *Historia*, pp. 112–14, sees Belgrano's autobiography as an apology for his monarchist leanings.

95. Street, *Gran Bretaña*, pp. 258–63; E. J. Pratt, "Anglo-American Commercial and Political Rivalry on the Plata, 1820–1830," *HAHR* 11 (1931):302–35; H. S. Ferns, "The Beginnings of British Investment in Argentina," *EcHR* 4 (1952):341–52; Charles K. Webster, *Britain and the Independence of Latin America, 1812–1830: Select Documents from the Foreign Office Archives*, 2 vols. (New York:

Oxford University Press, 1938); Kaufmann, *British Policy*; Humphreys' various accounts; Rippy's works; Platt, *Latin America*; J. Brown, *Socioeconomic History*; and above, n. 26, 48, 92. Belaunde, *Bolívar*, p. 34, says 40,000 (!) copies of Bentham's *Principles of Morals and Legislation* were sold in Latin America before 1828. Torres Villar, *constitución*, p. 70, speaks of Bentham's popularity in Mexico and Central America; and see Hale, *Mexican Liberalism*, pp. 94, 154 ff.; and below, Ch. 10.

96. Cited in Robertson, *Rise*, p. 180.

97. See A. W. Bunkley, *The Life of Sarmiento* (Princeton: Princeton University Press, 1952).

98. Eugenio Pereira Salas, "Jeremías Robinson, agente norteamericano en Chile (1818–1823)," *Revista Chilena de Historia y Geografia* no. 82 (1937):201–36; Pine, "Role"; Chandler, *Inter-American Acquaintances*, pp. 116–28; Wilgus, "Some Activities," p. 201; William L. Neumann, "United States Aid to the Chilean Wars of Independence," *HAHR* 27 (1947):204–19; Dorothy B. Goebel, "British American Rivalry in the Chilean Trade, 1817–1820," *JEcH* 2 (1942):190–202; Tanner, "South American Ports," p. 75, cited a United States merchant complaining that in 1822 the Chilean legislature, while discussing raising tariffs, closed the custom house and then produced a new commercial code "so complicated and intricate" it was "almost an entire preventive to commerce." Tanner adds consistency came only in 1830. It was a complaint common to North Americans doing business in Latin America. And see Edward B. Billingsley, *In Defense of Neutral Rights: The United States Navy and the Wars of Independence in Chile and Peru* (Chapel Hill: University of North Carolina Press, 1967) for the years 1818–1824, who says, "In essence, the naval vessels became floating banks" (p. 166); and who cites Commodore Charles Stewart: "I believe it impossible for any commanding officer to be in the Pacific without giving offense to one side or the other" (p. 190).

99. Valencia Avaría, *pensamiento*, pp. 41–42; and Luis A. Valencia Avaría, "La declaración de independencia de Chile," *Boletín de Academia Chilena de Historia* 9 (1942):37–50, where he cites O'Higgins to Cruz, Jan. 22, 1818: "Brazil has just given us a noble example of *liberalismo*" (p. 44); and see Stephen Clissold, *Bernardo O'Higgins and the Independence of Chile* (New York: Praeger, 1969), pp. 236–38. In 1824, special tax concessions were offered foreigners as well as nationals establishing plants for finishing textiles and copper: Will, "Introduction"; pp. 6–8; Pereira Salas, "Robinson," p. 235.

100. Valcarcel, "Peru," pp. 409–18; Tanner, "South American Ports," 10 ff.; Billingsley, *Defense*, passim.

101. Parks, *Colombia*, pp. 113–15; Alfred Hasbrouck, *Foreign Legionaries in the Liberation of Spanish America* (1928; reprint ed., Octagon, 1969); David Bushnell, "El 'modelo' angloamericano en la prensa de la emancipación; una aproximación cuantitativa de su impacto," an unpublished study showing European mentions, understandably, outnumbering those of the United States; cf. David Bushnell, "The Development of the Press in Gran Colombia," *HAHR* 30 (1950):440–41, and Olson, "Early Americans," 137 ff.

102. Elías A. Pino Iturrieta, "Modernidad y utopia: el mensaje revolucionario del *Correo de Orinoco*," *Boletín Histórico* (Fundacion John Boulton, Caracas), no. 32 (1973):254 ff.; and see Bushnell, "Development."

103. Pino Iturrieta, "Modernidad," p. 259; and see pp. 265, 275.

104. Parks, *Colombia*, p. 131; David Bushnell, *The Santander Regime in Gran Colombia* (1954; reprint ed., Westport, Conn.: Greenwood, 1970), pp. 158, 164–65, 264. He says from 1822 growers in interior New Granada campaigned for exclusion of United States flour, in use on the coast, and that there was support from Bogotá for them, but liberal professional men representing Cundinamarca and Boyacá, although also wheat-growing areas, continued to support open trade in flour, so that it was allowed in although with a huge luxury import tax affixed, but was still cheaper than interior transport made the domestic product (p. 154). By 1826 Colombia had a stiff tariff on imports, had licensed monopolies, and was protecting planters of coffee, cacao, indigo and sugar (p. 139). And see García Samudio, *Independencia*, pp. 109–11; and Bierck, *Gual*.

105. *Gaceta de Caracas*, June 9, 1814. Lecuna and Bierck, *Selected Writings*, 1:79–80.

106. The earliest known text is in English; there is a facsimile edition by the Comisión Editora de los Escritos del Liberator, under the auspices of the President of the Republic of Venezuela (Caracas, 1972). Lecuna and Bierck have a rather stilted translation of another version. Of Spain, Bolívar asked: "Without manufactures, without its own production, without arts, sciences, or even a mercantile

policy, can it monopolize the trade of half the world?'' And see Onís, *United States*, 67 ff.; Shepherd, ''Bolívar''; and J. Fred Rippy, ''Bolívar as Viewed by Contemporary Diplomats of the United States,'' *HAHR* 15 (1935):287–97.

107. Bolívar to Gual from Puerto Prince, November 11, 1816; *Cartas*, 2d ed., 1:335. Gual did as instructed: Bierck, *Gual*, p. 136. And see J. León Helguera, ''Bolívar: una interpretación de su política económica en la teoría y la practica,'' *Bolétin Histórico* (Caracas), no. 17 (1968):107.

108. Cited in Ocampo, *proceso*, p. 472.

109. *Proclamas y discursos*, ed. Vicente Lecuna (Caracas: Lit. y Tip. del Comercio, 1939), pp. 210–11; and see Pine, ''Role,'' pp. 459–79.

110. *Cartas*, 2d ed., 2:342. Torres to Juan Germán Roscio, April 12, 1819, in Guillermo Hernández de Alba, ''Origen de la doctrina panamericana de la confederación,'' *RHA* 22 (1946):380 ff.

111. *Cartas*, 2d ed., 2:338.

112. *Cartas*, 1st ed., 12 vols. Vols. 1–10, ed. Vicente Lecuna (Caracas, 1929–30); Vol. 11, ed. Vicente Lecuna and Manuel Pérez Vila (New York, 1948); Vol. 12 ed. Lecuna and Pérez Vila (Caracas, 1959), 3:266.

113. Against inviting the United States and Haiti to the Panama Congress: he wrote to Santander on May 30, 1825 of both, ''for they are foreigners and different than us.'' Cited in ibid., p. 474; cf. Shepherd, ''Bolívar,'' p. 292; and see pp. 287–93; and *Cartas*, 1st ed., 5:14, 16, 155–56. Bierck, *Gual*, p. 448, and Onís, *United States*, pp. 69–70, think him not averse to the United States attending the Congress, only worried about British displeasure at extending the invitation.

114. Shepherd, ''Bolívar,'' p. 278. John Alderson, an English trader in Venezuela, whom Bolívar liked and respected, made the arrangements for Fernando's education in the United States, authorizing an associate, the Philadelphia merchant Thomas Spackman, to be trustee for young Bolívar, who in 1826 went on to the University of Virginia (Olson, ''Early Americans,'' pp. 285–86).

115. *Cartas*, 2d ed., 5:154–55.

116. Ibid.; and, for his admiration of Washington, also pp. 204, 367; Onís, *United States*, pp. 70–71; and García Samudio, *Independencia*, p. 208.

117. *Proclamas*, p. 342. Ocampo, *proceso*, p. 486, n. 96, adds that the speech was published in the *Gaceta de Colombia* of November 26, 1826. Shepherd, ''Bolivar,'' p. 292, cites Daniel F. O'Leary writing that Bolivar recommended ''an intimate and extremely close alliance with England and North America.''

118. Letter to General Antonio Gutiérrez de la Fuente, January 16, 1827, in *Cartas*, 2d ed., 5:347.

119. May 19, 1829, cited in Shepherd, ''Bolivar,'' p. 297.

120. Guayaquil, July 30, 1829; *Cartas*, 1st ed., 9:48.

121. August 5, 1829; *Cartas*, 2d ed., 7:260, cf. 9:68–69.

122. Letter of September 13, 1829, in Daniel F. O'Leary, *Ultimos años de la vida pública de Bolívar: Memorias del General O'Leary* (Madrid: Editorial América, 1916), p. 577; and Lecuna and Bierck, *Selected Writings*, 2:738.

123. See *Cartas*, 1st ed., 9:48, 60.

CHAPTER 10

1. *People of Plenty* (University of Chicago Press, 1954), p. 135.

2. Wallerstein, ''The Rise and Future Demise of the World Capitalist System; Concepts for Comparative Analysis,'' *CSSH* 16 (1974):387–415; and Immanuel Wallerstein, *The Modern World System II: Mercantilism and the Consolidation of the European World Economy, 1600–1750* (New York: Academic Press, 1980).

3. Chaunu, *L'Amerique et les Ameriques* (Paris, 1964); Chaunu, *Histoire*; Robinson and Gallagher, ''The Imperialism of Free Trade,'' *EcHR*, (2d ser.) 6 (1953):1–15; *Imperialism: The Robinson and Gallagher Controversy*, William Roger Louis, intro. (New York: New Viewpoints, 1976), pp. 217–21; Braudel, *Capitalism*; and see Mauro, *L'expansion*; and Semmel, *Rise*.

4. See D. A. Chalmers, "Developing on the Periphery: External Factors in Latin American Politics," in J. Rosenau, ed., *Linkage Politics* (New York: Free Press, 1969), pp. 67–93.

5. David Hume, *The Philosophical Works*, 3 vols. (London, 1882), 3:301–21.

6. Ellis, "Habits," p. 164.

7. See above, Ch. 7.

8. Gómez Hoyos, *revolución*, 1:334.

9. ˙Ibid., 2:64.

10. Ibid., 2:284.

11. John Roberts, *Revolution and Improvement: The Western World, 1775–1847* (Berkeley and Los Angeles: University of California Press, 1976), p. 18.

12. Michael Oakeshott, "The Political Economy of Freedom," in his *Rationalism in Politics* (New York: Basic Books, 1962), p. 37.

13. H. J. Habakkuk, in *New Cambridge Modern History* (Cambridge, 1957–79), vol. 8, *The American and French Revolutions, 1763–1973*, ed. G.A. Godwin (1965), p. 54; and see Gunnar Myrdal, *The Political Element in Economic Theory* (London: Routledge and Kegan Paul, 1953), p. 106, and passim. (My thanks to Jo Saxe for the latter reference.)

14. See Werner Krauss, " 'Patriote,' 'patriotique,' 'patriotismo,' à la fin de l'Ancien Regime," in *The Age of the Enlightenment: Studies Presented to Theodore Besterman*, W. H. Barber, et al. (Edinburgh and London; Oliver and Boyd, 1967), pp. 387–94; and Vilar, "nation."

15. Yohoshua Arieli, *Individualism and Nationalism in American Ideology* (Cambridge, Mass.: Harvard University Press, 1964); cf. Bailyn, *Ideological Origins*; Bercovitch, *Puritan*.

16. Espejo, *Primacías*, pp. 16, 41, 83–84; the *informe* of the Mexican consulado is in Florescano and Gil, *Descripciones*, 1:75.

17. Kenneth R. Minogue, *The Liberal Mind* (London: Methuen, 1963), p. 3; and see above, Ch. 9, n. 24.

18. Garry Wills, "Prolegomena to a Reading of the Declaration," in Lally Weymouth, ed., *Thomas Jefferson, the Man; His World, His Influence* (New York: Putnam's, 1973), p. 76.

19. Keith, "Independent America," p. 43.

20. David S. Landes, "The Nature of Economic Imperialism," *JEcH* 21 (1961):510.

21. Vicen Vives, *Economic History*, p. 552.

22. Ibid.; and see Juan M. Herrero, "Notas sobre la ideología del burgués español del siglo XVIII," *AEA* 9 (1952):306–8.

23. Llombert, "Mercantilismo," in Gil Novales, *Homenaje á Salamon*, p. 336.

24. Ortiz de la Tabla Ducasse, *Comercio*, p. 368.

25. Morgan, "American Revolution."

26. Phelan, *People*, pp. 34–35, makes this point.

27. Cf. Stoetzer, *Scholastic Roots*, who confuses dissenting tradition with continuity per se.

28. See Miller, "Covenant"; Bercovitch, *American Jeremiad*.

29. Cited in Pole, *Pursuit*, p. 49.

30. Méndez Plancarte, *Humanistas*, pp. 47–49.

31. R. R. Palmer, *The Age of the Democratic Revolution*, 2 vols. (Princeton: Princeton University Press, 1959), 1:214.

32. Guerra [Mier], *Historia*, passim.

33. Gómez Hoyos, *revolución*, 2:22–30.

34. Peggy K. Liss, "The United States Declaration of Independence and Latin America, 1776–1808," a paper read at the Fourth International Conference on the Enlightenment, Yale University, 1975.

35. Franklin L. Ford, "The Revolutionary-Napoleonic Era: How Much of a Watershed?" *AHR* 69 (1963):26.

36. Nash, *Urban Crucible*, p. 317; and for an illustration of a provincial tertulia: Villalobos, *Tradición*, opposite p. 160.

37. Brading, "Government"; Chance and Taylor, "Estate"; Phelan, *People*; Mörner, *Race Mixture*; and so on; and Duncan J. Macleod, *Slavery, Race, and the American Revolution* (Cambridge, 1974); and Gary Nash, "Red, White, and Black: The Origins of Racism in Colonial America," in

Nash, ed., *The Great Fear: Race in the Mind of America* (New York: Holt, Rinehart, and Winston, 1970), pp. 1–26.

38. The phrase is Halperín's in *Historia*, p. 116; Charles C. Griffin, "Aspectos económico-sociales de la época de la Emancipación Hispanoamericana," in Mesa Redona de la Comisión de Historia, IPAGH, 4 vols. (Caracas: Academia de Historia, 1961), 1:347–60; and see Trevor Colbourn, ed., *Fame and the Founding Fathers: Essays by Douglass Adair* (New York: Norton, 1974), p. 24: Adair concludes, "The love of fame, the ruling passion of the noblest minds...transmuted the leaden desire for self-aggrandizement and personal reward into a golden concern for public service and the promotion of the commonwealth as a means to gain glory." For examples of the influence of Napoleon: Levene, *mundo*, p. 159; *Despertador Americano*, p. 60: "The intrepid Allende, the favorite son of Mars, our invincible Captain in whose elevated and generous spirit shines all the military talents Europe admires in the Corsican, without the selfish ambition which obscures the virtues of that monster."

39. Thus Posada, pp. 156–57, cites the informe of Colonel Blas Lamota to the king, August 11, 1815, concerning the comuneros: "Their leaders were the fathers and relatives of those who had promoted and maintained [the revolution] of the year 1810." And see Maxwell, "Generation"; Gómez Hoyos, *revolución*; and above, passim.

40. In this section I follow, principally, Halperín-Donghi, *Historia*; Tulio Halperín-Donghi, *The Aftermath of Revolution in Latin America*, trans. Josephine de Bunsen (New York: Harper & Row, 1973); Griffin, "Economic and Social Aspects."

41. Henretta, *Evolution*; Lockridge, *Social Change*; and Nash, *Urban Crucible* for England and British North America; cf. García-Baquero, *Cádiz;* David R. Ringrose, "Perspective on the Economy of Eighteenth Century Spain," in Vilar et al., *Historia,* who discusses regional competition, and above, n. 40.

42. *Aftermath*, p. 38.

43. Morton J. Horowitz, *The Transformation of American Law, 1780–1860* (Cambridge, Mass.: Harvard University Press, 1977), especially pp. 624–28; M. J. Horowitz, "The Legacy of 1776: The Relationship between Legal Theory and Economic Policy," *Journal of Law and Economics* 19 (1976):621–32; Ralph Lerner, "Commerce and Character: The Anglo-American as New-Model Man," *WMQ* 36 (1979):3–26; Christopher Lasch, in "William Appleman Williams on American History," *Marxist Perspectives* 1 (1978):120, explains, in an important point, that Williams sees the Constitution as an economic doctrine "not because it reflected the personal interests of the framers but because it provided the legal basis for an integrated mercantilist economy and an independent national state"; and cf. McDonald, *We the People*.

44. *Federalist Paper* no. 11.

45. Cited in Karl Polanyi, *The Great Transformation* (Boston: Beacon Press, 1957), p. 137.

46. Charles Patrick Neill, "Daniel Raymond, an Early Chapter in the History of Economic Theory in the United States," *Johns Hopkins University Studies in History and Politcal Science*, ser XV:6 (1897):12–19, 46. Cf. Kenneth V. Lundberg, "Daniel Raymond, Early American Economist" (Ph.D diss., University of Wisconsin, 1953); and Paul K. Conkin, *Prophets of Prosperity: America's First Political Economists* (Bloomington: Indiana University Press, 1980), Ch. 4.

47. Basadre, "Historia," p. 661; and Valencia Avaría, "declaración," p. 4, cites an example.

48. Cited in Maravell, "Cabarrús," p. 297.

49. Dealy, "Prolegomena," p. 49. Russell Fitzgibbon, "The Process of Constitution Making in Latin America," *CSSH* 3 (1960):1. And see Torre Villar, *constitucion*, p. 78, for a list of those drawn; and Belaunde, *Bolívar*, 29 ff.

50. Halperín-Donghi, *Historia*, p. 89; Rafael Heliodoro Valle, *Cartas de Bentham a José del Valle* (Mexico: Editorial Cultura, 1942); Miriam Williford, *Jeremy Bentham on Spanish America* (Baton Rouge: Louisiana State University Press, 1980); Hale; R. S. Smith, "English Economic Thought," p. 310, states Bentham's advice was sought by liberals in the Spanish Cortes of 1820–23; and see above, Ch. 9, n. 95.

51. See above, Chs. 5, 9; particularly, in Ch. 5, n. 61, Shaler's Pan-American scheme of 1812, probably a forerunner of Clay's American system, and Arthur Whitaker's comment, in his *United States*, p. 585, concerning 1824: "The administration's Latin American policy and its policy of

commercial reciprocity were twin producers of the same rationale of emancipation, the emancipation of man and the emancipation of commerce.'' United States policy concerning Latin America continued to function on those two principles into the twentieth century.

52. Cited in Pereira Salas, *primeros contactos*, p. 313; and see Ch. 9, n. 57.

53. See above, Ch. 9, n. 28.

54. Hale, *Mexican Liberalism*, pp. 198 ff.; Brading, *nacionalismo*, pp. 143–46, 161 ff.; J. Rodríguez, pp. 127–28.

55. *Archivo de don Bernardo O'Higgins*, ed. Ricardo Donoso, et al. 25 vols. (Santiago de Chile: Nascimiento, 1946–48) 3:42–44; and Billingsley, *Defense*, p. 104. Cf. Humphreys' various accounts of British reports; Street, *Gran Bretaña*, and so on. Parra Pérez, *Historia*, 2:163, cites Vansittart, the British envoy in Venezuela, writing to Miranda, August 19, 1811, expressing an oft-repeated attitude toward the peninsula having bearing on feelings about Hispanic peoples as a whole: ''Spain continues being what it has been from the beginning; a scene of individual heroism and of collective imbecility.''

56. See Arthur P. Whitaker, *Nationalism in Latin America, Past and Present* (Gainesville: University of Florida Press, 1962); Arthur P. Whitaker and David C. Jordan, *Nationalism in Contemporary Latin America* (New York: Free Press, 1966).

57. *Escritos de Simón Rodríguez*, 2 vols., comp. by Pedro Grases (Caracas: Imprenta Nacional, 1954), 1:xxxiv.

58. Barbier, ''Trade,'' p. 20.

59. Wilkins, *The Emergence of Multinational Enterprise* (Cambridge, Mass.: Harvard University Press, 1970): see pp. 10–11, 17–18 in particular.

60. Wallerstein, ''Rise,'' p. 412. Cf. Ronald E. Müller and Richard J. Barnet, *Global Reach: The Power of the Multinational Corporations* (New York: Simon & Schuster, 1974).

INDEX

Listed herein are first citations of authors, and titles cited in text but not in Notes.

331

Free Port Act, British, 19, 20
Free Port Act, Spanish, 20
Free trade, 16, 22–23, 65, 81, 106, 108, 240; and enlightened self-interest, 222–24; Jefferson on, 45, 57; Jovellanos on, 70, 74; and liberty, 32, 43; and morality, 25; Spanish-American, 132, 144–45. *See also* Commerce, neutral; Free trade regulation of 1778; *Reglamento de comercio libre* of 1797
Free trade decree of 1765, 65, 81
Free trade regulation of 1778, 71, 112, 132, 133; effect of on Spanish Americans, 134–35, 136; extension of, to Vera Cruz and Lima, 148
French Revolution, vii, 149; appeal of, to Spaniards, 226; and constitutionalism in Spain, 149; as descendant of American Revolution, 226; influence in Bahia, 177; influence of, on Spanish America, 155–56, 162, 169–71, 226
Frontier policy, British, 21
Fry, Howard T., 254n99
Fulgencio López, Casto, 303n53

Gaceta de Buenos Aires, 204
Gaceta de Colombia, 218
Gaceta de Gobierno Imperial de México, 214
Gaceta de México, 89, 97, 154–55, 189, 190, 205
Gadsden, Christopher, 42
Galbis Díez, María del Carmen, 295n52, 305n2
Gallagher, John, 222; and Robinson, Ronald Edward, 222, 327n3
Gallatin, Albert, 188, 284n41, 286n53
Galpin, W. Freeman, 316n26
Gálvez, Bernardo de, 114–15, 128, 133, 137, 157, 162
Gálvez, José de, 65–66, 67, 82, 85, 92–95, 114, 128, 129, 130, 133, 134, 138, 141–42, 147, 150, 191, 229
Gamboa, Francisco Javier de, 95, 153
Gandia, Enrique de, 279n12, 291n27
Garcia, Genaro, 313n10
García-Baquero González, Antonio, 264n8, 292n37
García Chuecos, Hector, 303n53
García de Sena, Manuel, 200–201, 203, 205, 210, 238; *Articles of Confederation* translated by, 205; Constitution of 1787 translated by, 205; *Historia concisa de los Estados Unidos,* 201, 215; *La independencia de la Costa Firme, justificada por Tómas Paine treinta años ha,* 200, 205; and state constitutions, 200; U.S. as exemplar to, 201
García Icazbalceta, Joaquín, 299n16
García Melero, Luis Angel, 267n55
García Samudio, Nicolás, 295n56
Garcilaso de la Vega, el Inca, 99, 125, 165, 167
Gardner, Lloyd, LaFeber, Walter F., and McCormick, Thomas J., 278n2
Gardoqui, Diego de, 114, 120, 121, 127, 148, 149, 150, 162, 165; house of, 29–30

Gares, Albert J., 281n25
Garner, Richard L., 273n26
Gatell, Frank Otto, and Weinstein, Allen, 262n99
Gates, Eunice J., 289n9
Gay, Peter, 223, 247n33
Gazeta de Madrid, 147, 149, 172, 175
Geertz, Clifford, 169, 304n66
Gemery, Henry A., and Hogendorn, Jan S., 258n36
Genêt, Edmund, 121, 164
Geraldino, Don Tomás. *See also* FitzGerald, Sir Thomas
Gerbi, Antonello, 275–76n59
Gibbon, Edward, 25
Gibson, Charles, 273n26
Gilbert, Felix, 107, 108, 223, 250n54, 278n2
Gilbert, Geoffrey N., 257n18
Gil de Taboada, Francisco, 151, 184
Gilmore, Robert L., 315n21
Gil Munilla, Octavio, 252n81
Gil Novales, Alberto, 269n68
Giménez Fernández, Manuel, 269n66, 276n63
Gipson, Lawrence, 257n16, 265n35
Girard, Stephen, 116, 200, 205, 206
Glendenning, Nigel, 265n35
Glick, Thomas F., 321n62
Glover, Richard, 4
Godoy, Juan José, 166, 168
Godoy, Manuel, 149, 150, 165, 186, 310n46; *Memoirs* of, 186
Goebel, Dorothy B., 257n21, 311n64, 326n98
Goebel, Julius, 252n81
Goetzmann, William H., 278n2, 286n54
Gómez Hoyos, Rafael, 277n80
Góngora, Mario, 267n53
González, Ariosto D., 319n46
González Casanova, Pablo, 269n67, 309n38
González y González, Luis, 299n18
Gooch, Sir William, 32, 35
Good neighbor policy, early, 111
Gottschalk, Louis, 300n33
Goya, Francisco, 73
Gracie, Archibald, 117
Graham, Richard, 222
Grampp, William D., 279n7
Gran Colombia, British influence in, 217–18
Grantham, Lord, 20
Grases, Pedro, 289n16, 303n53; and Harkness, Alberto, 317n28
Gray, William H., 318n35
Great Awakening, 32, 34–38, 229
Greene, Jack P., 247n19, 254n107, 259n47; 261nn70, 71
Greenleaf, Richard E., 289–90n17, 299n21, 304n64
Gribbin, William, 287n64
Griffin, Charles C., 233, 281n27, 316–17n26, 318n34, 329n38
Grimaldi, 70

Robertson, William, *History of America*, 125, 129, 130
Robertson, William S., 279nn11, 12, 312n1, 323n78; 324nn82, 83, 325n87
Robinson, Jeremy, 216–17
Robinson, Ronald Edward, and Gallagher, John, 222, 327n3
Robinson, William Davis, 179, 202, 218, 318n34, 322n71
Rocafuerte, Vicente, 210, 325n91
Rocha, Ignacio de la, 274n49
Rocha Pita, Sebastiâo da, 274n45
Rochford, Lord, 20
Rodney, Caesar, 212
Rodríguez, Jaime E., 315–16n25
Rodríguez, José Honorío, 312–13n3
Rodríguez, Mario, 293n42, 316n25
Rodríguez, Simón, 168, 238, 330n57
Rodríguez Casado, Vicente, 267n58, and Calderón Quijano, José Antonio, 311n69
Rodríguez de Valle, Mariana, 306n16
Rodríguez Vicente, Encarnación, 272n15
Rodríguez Vicente, María E., 271n4
Rogelio Alvárez, José, 273n36
Rogers, Alan, 261n70
Rojas, José Antonio (of Chile), 130, 131, 135, 198
Rojas, José Antonio (of Mexico), 183, 186, 190, 309n38
Romanticism: vogue for, in U.S., 125–26, 210; and Latin American liberators, 233, 236
Romero, José Luis, 305n2
Romero, Tomás Antonio, 153, 161, 174
Romero del Valle, Emilia, 298n10
Ronan, Charles E., 275n56, 293n43
Rosenau, J., 328n4
Rousseau, Jean Jacques, 129; *Emile*, 139; *Social Contract*, 204
Rowe, J. H., 277n76
Royal Academy of History (Madrid), 138
Royal Society of Arts (London), 15, 64
Rubio Mañé, Ignacio J., 299n17, 322n65
Ruigómez de Hernández, Maria Pilar, 270n75
Ruiz, Ernesto, and Gonzáles de Linares, 267n56
Ruiz, Hipólito, 295n49
Rule Britannia, 4, 11, 288n1
Rush, Richard, 212
Russell, Nelson Vance, 253n87
Russell-Wood, A.J.R., 273n29, 324n83
Rutter, Frank R., 316n26
Rydjord, John, 254n99, 284n40, 302n48

Saavedra, Francisco de, 114, 128–29, 130, 131, 138, 150, 172, 296n62
Sachs, William S., 261n80; and Hoogenboom, Ari, 257n18
Saco, José Antonio, 248n45
Saeger, James S., 277n77
Saint Augustine (Florida), 30, 33, 77, 79

Saint Dominque (Haiti), 17, 114, 149, 152, 163; revolt in, 164, 176, 280n17, 302n46; effects of, on Spanish and Portuguese America, 160, 161, 163. *See also* Santo Domingo
Salas, Manuel de, 135, 162, 181; on Chile, 181–82, 207; on open trade, 181, 198
Saldarriaga, Roberto Botero, 304n62
Salem, as slaving port, 27
Salvucci, Richard J., 289–90n17
Sánchez Agesta, Luis, 265n19
Sánchez Navarro, José Melchor, 189
San Javier, Conde de, 88, 165–66
San Juan de Ulúa, 20
San Luis de Potosí, uprising in, 85
San Martín, José de, 209, 216, 217
San Miguel, Antonio de, 177, 230, 294n47
Santander, Francisco de Paula, 218, 221
Santiago de Chile, 9; *cabildo* of, 198; *consulado* of, 162, 174, 181
Santiago de Cuba, 9, 12, 33
Santo Domingo, 108, 112; influence of revolt in, 170, 171, 174, 176, 178, 179, 191. *See also* Saint Domingue
Santos, Juan, 98, 99
Sarrailh, Jean, 266n48
Savelle, Max, 245n3, 246–47n18, 255n2, 262n92
Scelle, George, 248n45
Schlesinger, Arthur M., Jr., 278n1
Schlesinger, Arthur M., Sr., 27, 230, 256n6, 261n71
School of Mines (Mexico), 190
Schurz, William L., 249n50, 293n45
Schutz, John A., 279n9
Schwartz, Stuart B., 273n32, 298n13
Seaburg, Carl, and Paterson, Stanley, 316n26
Seagrove, James, 116, 286n51
Sealove, Sandra, 284n41
Selva Alegre, Marqués de (Montúfar, Juan Pío), 159, 183, 198
Semanario de agricultura, industria, y comercio, 181
Semanario Político y Literario, 214
Semmel, Bernard, 246n12
Seneca, 158
Serrano y Sanz, Manuel, 285n47
Seven Years' War, 17–18, 21, 30, 46, 60
Sewall, Joseph, 260n66
Sewall, Samuel, 32, 118, 123
Shafer, Robert J., 267n56
Shaler, William, 118, 124, 174, 200, 201, 231, 285n43
Sharp, William F., 277n74
Shelburne, Lord, 20, 22, 23
Shepherd, James F., and Walton, Gary M., 258n34
Shepherd, William R., 285n47, 319n41
Sheridan, Richard B., 251n75, 253n92, 262n86, 302n46

Wilgus, A. Curtis, 280n15, 319n41, 322n70
Wilhite, John F., 275n54, 295n49, 300n31
Wilkins, Mira, 239, 330n59
Wilkinson, James, 118–19, 120, 214, 215, 280n15, 311n66, 314n13
Will, Robert M., 308n31
Williams, Eric, 252n75
Williams, Glyndwr, 250n62
Williams, Harold D., 282n32
Williams, Judith B., 249n45
Williams, Stanley T., 262n103
Williams, William A., 279nn1, 2
Williford, Miriam, 329n50
Willing, Captain James, 115
Willing, Thomas, 30, 116, 261n72
Willing and Morris, 31, 114, 117, 167, 283n37
Wills, Garry, 227–28, 328n18
Wilson, A. M., 257n16
Wilson, Charles, 246n8
Wilson, James, 42
Winch, Donald, 252n81
Winter, J. M., 250n55
Wolf, Eric, 289–90n17
Wolff, Inge, 309n43
Wood, Gordon S., 262n98

Wood, William, 248n40
Woodham, John E., 301n36
Workman, James, 126
Worthington, William G. D., 217
Wortman, Miles, 296n62, 301n37
Wright, Almon R., 270n78
Wright, Esmond, 262n97
Wright, J. Leitch, Jr., 258n35, 279n11, 283n35
Wright, Louis B., 259n49
Wrigley, E. A., 227, 252n76

Yela Utrilla, Juan F., 270n75
Yermo, Gabriel, 185
Yogev, Gedalia, 248n44
Young, Alfred F., 262n86
Young, Arthur, 253n92

Zahendra, Peter, 318n32
Zavala, Iris M., 298n9
Zavala, Silvio, *Homenaje a,* 301n38
Zea, Francisco, 168, 218, 321n62
Zerécero, Anastasio, 313n11
Zimmerman, A. F., 312n1
Zipaquirá, 157, 218; *Capitulaciones* of, 142, 291n34